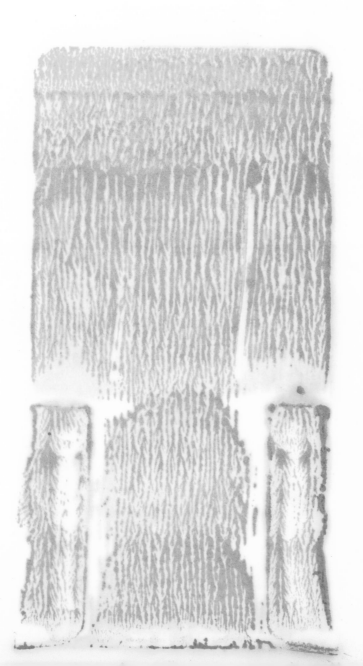

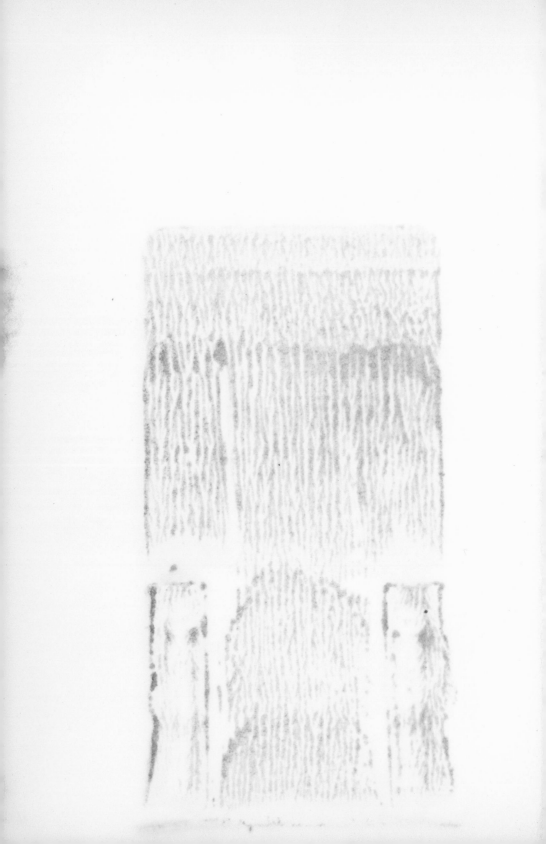

An Introduction
to Personality

Prentice-Hall Psychology Series
Richard S. Lazarus, Editor

Prentice-Hall International, Inc., *London*
Prentice-Hall of Australia, Pty. Ltd., *Sydney*
Prentice-Hall of Canada, Ltd., *Toronto*
Prentice-Hall of India (Private) Ltd., *New Delhi*
Prentice-Hall of Japan, Inc., *Tokyo*

An Introduction
to Personality

A Research Approach

DONN BYRNE
University of Texas

Prentice-Hall, Inc.   Englewood Cliffs, New Jersey

Library of Congress Catalog Card Number: 66–11186

PRINTED IN THE UNITED STATES OF AMERICA
C-49158

Preface

Psychological science proceeds in irregular paths at varying speeds; with a little help, students can witness, appreciate, and even participate in this process. Whether one eventually becomes a psychologist or never takes another course in the area, acquaintance with the workings of behavioral science is an integral part of education. And, with the intrinsic interest provided by human behavior, the field of personality is in some ways an ideal context in which to introduce undergraduates to behavioral science.

This text had its origin in the author's attempts over the past several years to introduce students to personality as a field of research. It is my conviction that the most important contribution to society which psychologists can presently make is an understanding of how the scientific method is utilized in studying behavior. In this book the field of personality is presented from the inside. The reader is shown where ideas originate, how these ideas are translated into research, and how theoretical speculations and research findings are interconnected. A given line of research is placed in its historical context, specific research is described in some detail, and the work of various investigators is integrated to form a structure of accumulating conceptual clarity. As frequently as possible, an investigator's research strategy, interpretation of a set of findings, or theoretical speculations are expressed in his own words.

The field of personality is defined here as that area of psychology which concentrates on the study of individual differences along various behavior dimensions, including personality measurement, development, structure, dynamics, and change. It is somewhat unusual to concentrate only on selected areas of current research interest in personality; however, at the present time, personality research appears to be focusing on the development of limited theories based on work with selected variables rather than on the traditional broad general theories of personality, a decided shift in emphasis over the past decade or two.

When the student has finished this text, he will *not* possess (1) a theory which provides understanding of all behavior (2) the key to optimal adjustment (3) a way to categorize each individual he meets with a complete personality description, or (4) information which is guaranteed to solve his major behavioral problems. What the student *will* have, however, is an introduction to the ideas, methods, and a portion of the findings of one of the most exciting and most challenging of activities—the scientific study of human behavior.

Among the many individuals whose comments and suggestions contributed to this book, I would like to give special thanks to Dr. Richard S. Lazarus. The comments and criticisms of David McClelland, Quinn McNemar, and Janet Taylor Spence were also extremely helpful. In addition, I would like gratefully to acknowledge the help of my wife and my parents who took on the unexciting though crucial chores of typing the manuscript, writing for permission to use copyrighted material, checking references, reading proofs, and holding the children at bay while Daddy finished one more chapter.

DONN BYRNE

Contents

Part One

BACKGROUND

CHAPTER 1

Science and the Study of Personality

To live in the latter half of the twentieth century is to live in an era in which science has become ascendant in influencing human activities. In the world's two most powerful nations, scientists are accorded an honored position in society, and scientific education is consistently encouraged and supported. A recent survey of occupations in the United States found that scientists are outranked in prestige only by supreme court justices and physicians. Occupations ranked below scientists include those of state governor, cabinet member, banker, factory owner, and artist [Abelson, 1964].

At the same time, there seems to be very little general understanding concerning what it is that scientists do or what it means to utilize the scientific method. For most people, "science" evokes images of test tubes or rockets and memories of biology labs in which the "experiments" never quite coincided with the workbooks. Whatever it is that scientists do is incomprehensible and somewhat frightening.

Given this context, students who enroll in an introductory course in psychology often learn with some degree of surprise and disbelief that psychologists describe their work as a scientific endeavor. Perhaps because of its relative youth and perhaps because of its potentially threatening power, the most general response of nonpsychologists to the "science of behavior" is either ridicule or open hostility. A sample of three items

3

from recent publications serves to provide a flavor of this negative reaction:

Nothing raises eyebrows faster than the idea that science can find "laws" of human behavior. Human differences are too vast for generalizations that apply with any exactitude to individuals [*Time* magazine, Feb. 14, 1964, p. 43].

Psychology, which is the study of things people with common sense know already, has discovered that kids are ornery.

The earnest gents and ladies in sensible shoes have been "understanding" the little disgusters for the last generation, with the result that our jails are full, the streets of our cities are unsafe after nightfall . . .

. . . it may make normal readers retch, but psychologists describe spanking as "some form of primary negative reinforcement."

Negative reinforcement is what bred the sturdy race that spanned this continent, and I'd like to see it return to fashion [Richard Starnes, columnist for the Scripps-Howard newspaper chain, quoted in the *American Psychologist*, 1963, p. 510].

This book is about brain-watching, the art, its practitioners, and its subjects, some 50,000,000 hapless Americans [Martin L. Gross in *The Brain Watchers* (New York: Random House, 1962)].

If these quotations constitute a representative sample of public opinion concerning psychology as a science, the typical beginning psychology student must experience some degree of dissonance as his instructor and his textbook dwell on the *science* of behavior. In time, however, some proportion of the students are able to rearrange their stereotypes to include experimental psychology in a cubbyhole labeled "science."

For those who pursue the study of psychology further, many find themselves in a course with the term "personality" in its title. Here, reason is assailed once more; again the subject matter is described as falling within the realm of science. In order to accept such an unlikely notion, the typical student must: (1) alter somewhat his conception of science, and (2) have some degree of contact with that research area in which personality variables are investigated. It is the goal of the author in the next several hundred pages to bring about both of these accomplishments.

Goals of a Science of Personality

MAKING SENSE OUT OF THE ENVIRONMENT

In a surprisingly short period of time, representatives of our species have moved haltingly from a precarious existence around the banks of various sources of fresh water to the complex life with which we are each familiar. The rate of change of both our physical and our conceptual tools is an increasingly rapid one. The time between the first use of fire and the invention of the wheel was considerably longer than the time between the invention of the wheel and the flight of the first airplane. Considering a more recent time span, at the beginning of this century the indoor toilet was just being installed in the homes of those with enough money and enough spirit of adventure to try out new gadgets. At the end of this century, rocket flights to various points in space will be commonplace.

Nevertheless, sheer survival on this planet has not been easy for a relatively frail physical organism such as man. Survival has been possible primarily because of man's ability to deal with environmental threats and problems at an abstract level and to pass on his conceptualizations to others. Dangers such as hunger, disease, cold weather, and attacks by those of his own and other species constantly recurred. Over a vast span of time, many different conceptual approaches were developed for meeting difficulties and making some sense out of a confusing and frightening environment. Included are supernatural dogmas, philosophical doctrines, and political ideologies. One of the many ways in which individuals have tried to bring meaning and predictability into their environment and to obtain some control over it is by means of an approach which has been given the name *science*. Within this approach, a series of assumptions and rules of procedure have emerged over the centuries; they suggest a way to go about acquiring and evaluating and extending knowledge.

Before discussing personality as a field of science, it may prove helpful to consider in a more general way the goals of all scientific endeavors. It is often said that the scientific method is utilized in order to gain understanding, prediction, and control of that which is being studied.

UNDERSTANDING: WHY? HOW?

Description and Naming as Understanding. Certainly each of us wants to know why things happen in the world or how it is that they come about. And, when an explanation is available, we seem to feel better; understanding has been achieved. It is frequently asserted [for example, Marx, 1951], that understanding is the basic goal of science. In one sense, however, understanding is the easiest thing in the world to attain. Skinner notes:

When we say that man eats *because* he is hungry, smokes a great deal *because* he has the tobacco habit, fights *because* of the instinct of pugnacity, behaves brilliantly *because* of his intelligence, or plays the piano well *because* of his musical ability, we seem to be referring to causes. But on analysis these phrases prove to be merely redundant descriptions [Skinner, 1953, p. 31].

Simply naming an event or process seems to be sufficient for providing an aura of understanding. Perhaps children first gain some degree of mastery over the world by learning to name various aspects of their environment. A frightening and inexplicable noise becomes "thunder," and an unexpected and blinding light becomes a "flashbulb." To have a word means that adults are familiar with such things and are not afraid of them. In addition, the word can be said over and over to oneself, permitting the fear to extinguish.

In later years, much the same word-magic still is effective in reducing uncertainty and providing understanding. A murderer was motivated by watching violence on TV programs. A war hero received his courage from one of his great-grandfathers who fought in the Civil War. The liberal philosophy expounded by various political leaders brought about crime in the streets and topless bathing suits. A housewife explains her headaches by saying that they are psychosomatic. A colleague of the author was once asked by a student in class, "Why did the Eskimos develop the custom of abandoning their old people in the snow to die?" Facetiously, the instructor replied, "Because they have long subsisted on a diet of whale blubber." Apparently satisfied with this "explanation," the 35 students carefully wrote the material in their notes.

Often, a somewhat more elaborate and sophisticated verbal explanation is developed. For example, a small boy is drowned, and his parents in their despair wonder *why* this terrible thing happened. What attempts might be made to give them understanding? The suggestion could be made that the event happened because the River God was hungry. It happened as part of God's mysterious plan. It happened because the boy had a strong need for independence which led him to venture away from his home into exciting activities. It happened because his father had spent an immoral youth, and this was divine punishment. It happened because the boy's death drive was stronger than his life drive. It happened because a neighborhood witch put a hex on him. It happened because the boy of his own free will chose to die. It happened because the boy had an unconscious need for self-punishment. Each of these explanations seems to offer understanding, but we have no basis on which to select among them.

After-the-Fact Explanations. A major difficulty in evaluating alternative explanations such as those cited above is that they are usually offered after the event has taken place. And man's flexibility and inventiveness are such that almost any notion can be twisted and revised in order to make an after-the-fact explanation of any event. This holds true whether the descriptive conceptualizations are provided by psychoanalysis, stimulus-response theory, theology, or the delusional system of a paranoid schizophrenic. Any ideas which depend entirely on their ability to offer understanding are not likely to be devastated by contradictory data. One is reminded of the patient who complained to a visitor that the psychiatrists were poisoning his soup. The visitor took a sip and said that it tasted all right to him. The patient nodded, "You see how clever they are?"

Since "why" questions are essential in building theoretical systems in science, understanding must be an important goal. What is needed is some sort of criterion to determine when it is that understanding has been achieved.

PREDICTION: WHEN? WHAT?

Predictive Accuracy as the Criterion of Understanding. The criterion of understanding adopted by scientists has been that of prediction. Thus, we may say that any attempts to increase understanding (naming, describing in different terms, or building complex verbal explanations) are of value only if the result is: (1) more accurate prediction of the original phenomena, or (2) accurate prediction of additional phenomena. For example, as will be discussed in Chapter 12, the observation of the behavior of clients in psychotherapy led to the proposition that individuals strive to maintain self-consistency. Once the elements of an individual's self-concept are determined, it should be possible to make specific predictions about his behavior in therapy—what topics will be talked about, what material will be distorted, what ideas will arouse defenses, and so forth. Further, predictions can be made about quite different kinds of situations in which self-congruent and self-incongruent elements are involved: situations including learning, perception, physiological responses, and the like. If these various types of predictions prove accurate, the concept of self-consistency is clearly a useful one.

Explanation at any level of complexity is useful if it increases predictive accuracy. There is no magic point at which "complete understanding" is achieved. In science, concepts and theories are valued to the extent that they allow scientists to make predictions that they would not otherwise have been able to make.

Subjective Feeling of Understanding vs. Predictive Accuracy. The differences between subjective understanding (*Verstehen*) as a goal of science and prediction as a goal have been well stated by Holt:

> In one sense, it is proper to say that we understand poliomyelitis when we have isolated the responsible viruses and have identified the conditions under which they attack and cripple a person, but this is not *Verstehen*. That conception is an empathic, intuitive *feeling* of knowing a phenomenon from the inside, as it were. To take a more congenial example, we do not understand why a particular boy becomes delinquent from knowing that he comes from a neighborhood that an ecological survey has determined to be economically deprived and socially disorganized; whereas after we have read Farrell's *Studs*

Lonigan and have seen such conditions and the embeddedness of delinquency in them portrayed with artistic power and vividness, then we understand (in the sense of *Verstehen*) the relation between these phenomena.

From this example, it should be clear that the feeling of understanding is a subjective effect aimed at by artists, not scientists. In science, when we say we understand something, we mean that we can predict and control it, but such aims are foreign to the romantic viewpoint. When Allport says (as of course Freud and many others have said also) that novelists and poets have been great intuitive psychologists, in some ways the greatest psychologists, the statement has two (not necessarily coexistent) meanings: that literary men have known many significant variables of and propositions about personality (e.g., the role of unconscious incestuous wishes in determining many kinds of behavior), or, that they have been able to create the most vivid, compelling portraits of people, which give us the sense of knowing and understanding them. The latter effect is achieved by judicious selection and artful distortion, not by exhaustive cataloguing and measurement of traits, motives, or structural relations. Indeed the idea of a catalogue is the very antithesis of art, just as a painful realism that tries to copy nature slavishly is the death of an artistic endeavor.

Here we see the issues drawn clearly. Is personology to be an art, devoted to word portraits that seek to evoke in the reader the thrill of recognition, the gratifying (if perhaps illusory) feeling of understanding unique individuals? Or is it to be a science, which enables us to study these same persons in all their uniqueness and to derive from such study general propositions about the structure, development, and other significant aspects of personality? If we elect for a science, we must abandon art whenever it takes us in a different direction than the one demanded by the scientific method, and we must recognize that the ideal of an idiographic science is a will-o'-the-wisp, an artistic and not a scientific goal. Science may be supplemented by art, but not combined with it [Holt, 1962, pp. 388–390].

Correctness of Explanations.   Whenever a prediction fails, then the conceptualization which led to that prediction must be altered to take account of the inaccuracy. Successive changes in the formulation are made in order to increase predictive accuracy. Of course, accurate prediction is no guarantee of the correctness of one's theoretical formulation.

For example, even when the earth was considered to be the center of the universe, astronomers were able to make relatively accurate predictions of the movements of the moon, sun, and planets. The planets offered the greatest difficulty, but the theories utilized complex epicycles as the planetary pathways "around the earth." The only thing wrong with this formulation was that it turned out to be inconsistent with later data. When the sun was conceptualized as being located at the center of the solar system, the new theory depicted all of the planets as traveling in smooth elliptical orbits around it. The new formulation still yielded the same accurate predictions provided by the old theory and in addition it enabled astronomers to account for previously inconsistent data.

Another sort of example is provided by the various ideas concerning the causes of yellow fever. At one point night air was thought to bring on the disease because some protection was afforded when windows were kept closed at night. The reason that this conceptualization led to accurate predictions concerning prevention, of course, was because the closed windows were preventing the entry of mosquitoes. Once the idea of mosquitoes as the causal agent was proposed, it could be tested by having volunteers expose themselves to mosquito bites. The test showed that yellow fever developed after such exposure; thus, the night air was irrelevant. At still another level, the mosquito is irrelevant, too, unless it is carrying the yellow fever virus.

Many such examples may be found in the field of personality as well. In Chapter 11 we will discuss the effects of aging on intellectual functioning. In the initial investigations, individuals at different age levels were tested, and it was found that 20-year-olds obtained higher scores than 40-year-olds, who did better than 60-year-olds, and so forth. A number of formulations were built describing the way in which abilities reach a peak and then begin a rapid decline. Such ideas fit the data well. When additional data became available involving the *retesting of the same individuals*, however, the predictions based on the theory of intellectual decline were wrong. Not only is there lack of support for the notion of intellectual deterioration with age, but individuals actually show a gain in IQ over their life span. The earlier studies simply involved differences among different generations, not differences to be expected within one generation as aging progressed.

The nature of the "real" world cannot be ascertained independently of the outcome of our predictions about it. Therefore, accurate predictions should be taken to mean that one's present conceptualization is provisionally correct, but that it may be supplanted by a better one at any time.

CONTROL: WHAT ARE THE PRACTICAL IMPLICATIONS?
OF WHAT USE IS IT?

In the laboratory the ability to control phenomena means that the scientist is able to manipulate certain independent variables and predict accurately the effect on certain dependent variables. When such control is attained, however, another type of utilization of the knowledge becomes possible: the control of some aspect of the world outside of the laboratory. What are some of the issues involved when the application of scientific knowledge is considered as a goal of science?

Seeking Knowledge for Its Own Sake. There is a venerable academic tradition which places a high value on the principle that knowledge should be sought not for practical reasons but for its intrinsic worth. Thus, support is gained for sciences which are unlikely to yield applied benefits (for example, archeology), for the humanities (history, for example), and for the arts.

In most of the sciences, however, a certain amount of conflict tends to exist between those individuals actively engaged in basic research and those who feel that the ultimate outcome of such work should be useful to society. The general culture, as expressed in Congressional support for research grants and popular articles describing scientific discoveries, is clearly oriented toward the application of laboratory findings for the benefit of mankind. Support for basic research can generally be obtained, however, by pointing out that basic research almost inevitably leads to findings, sometimes unexpected, with practical implications. For example, prior to the early 1940's, the work of nuclear physicists was seemingly far removed from application. Today, the applied aspects of this field are omnipresent. In addition, the history of science suggests strongly that work on immediate applied problems has not generally proven to be the most effective way to solve such problems. One need only think of alchemists attempting to transmute lead into gold or Indian medicine men in the Southwest attempting to control the weather by performing the appropriate dance.

Control Outside of the Laboratory: Value Judgments. One difficulty which arises with the application of scientific knowledge is the fact that value judgments must be made. Should large portions of a city's population be destroyed in order to hasten the end of a war? Is it right to fluoridate a town's water supply over the protests of a frightened minority in order to aid in the prevention of dental cavities? Is it right to pass a compulsory sterilization law in order to decrease the incidence of schizophrenia in the population? Is it right to use subliminal messages flashed on a movie screen in order to increase the sales of a particular product? Is it right to design neighborhoods in such a way that interpersonal contacts are increased and personal isolation is decreased? These decisions are different from those usually required of scientists; there are no generally accepted criteria for moral concepts such as "right."

Part of the problem, undoubtedly, is the fact that control activities which affect human behavior, even in minor ways, raise a considerable amount of anxiety. Farber has discussed this phenomenon:

It was stated earlier that, if the determinants of behavior were known, and if enough of them were susceptible to manipulation, then it would be possible to control behavior. It was also noted that this proposition arouses the most intense annoyance and anxiety in many people, including psychologists, who for good reasons, abhor the idea of a totalitarian technocracy [Bergmann, 1956]. In its superficial aspects, one can rather readily understand why the concepts of "control" and "despotism" are sometimes equated. If behavior can indeed be controlled by manipulating its determinants, then individuals with the requisite knowledge could and very possibly would exercise this control.

On the one hand, we must recognize that different societies and different individuals have different goals. What is desirable or reinforcing for one may be frustrating and punishing for another. We are only too liable to the delusion that our own goals are the only reasonable ones. Thus, when I try to change a person's behavior or attitudes, I am appealing to his better judgment; when you try to do so, you are using propaganda; and when "they" do so, they are brainwashing. To complicate matters further, this multiplicity of motives and goals extends to the intrapersonal sphere. The behavior that is instrumental to the satisfaction of one motive may frustrate the satisfaction of another.

On the other hand, our respect for the rights of others to their particular goals and the instrumental acts whereby they are achieved should not lead us to the romantic delusion that these are spontaneous products of unfettered choice. No one escapes control by the physical environment short of death; and no one escapes control by his social environment short of complete isolation. Almost the entire period of childhood is given over to the acquisition of new behaviors, goals, and motives, under the guidance of parents, family, and teachers. Be it wise or unwise, deliberate, impulsive, or unconscious, such guidance inevitably has its effects. It is difficult, in fact, to think of any kind of social interaction that has absolutely no effect on behavior. That the effects are unintentional or unwanted does not negate them [Farber, 1964, pp. 12–14].

Validity of the Application. One final question which arises in the application of scientific knowledge is that of validity. Does the procedure actually do what is claimed for it? Does it work? The question here is not one of deliberate falsehood or the activity of charlatans. Rather, the question deals with honest differences of opinion in evaluating the relevant evidence and with individual differences in the willingness to utilize imperfect techniques. It is here that some relatively basic conflicts may arise between those oriented toward prediction and those oriented toward control. Rodgers outlines some of the differences:

It seems to me that the fundamental difference between academic and professional psychology is the same difference that many areas of science have operationally recognized by forming engineering or professional schools for applied work and academic departments for basic work. Examples are chemical engineering versus chemistry and medicine versus physiology. Fundamentally, the role of basic research, which I shall equate with academic departments, including academic psychology, is *to ask prototypic questions and to seek generalizable answers that are completely accurate within the limitations of known data*. The academic answer must apply to any event within a definable class of events, and the particular one to which it is applied or from which it is generalized is incidental. Questions that are not prototypical of a class of events, i.e., that are of relevance to only a single case or single proposition, are considered trivial. Hair-splitting inaccuracies are considered adequate bases for disqualification of academic assertions and must be dealt with, according to the rules of the game, by either changing the answers to fit the questions with precise accuracy or reformulating the questions to fit the precise limitations of the answers as they apply to known data. Thus, precise accuracy and generality are the hallmarks of academic respectability. In contrast, the role of the engineer, applied scientist, or professional is *to provide usable answers to important questions about particular rather than general events.* The answers need not be prototypically correct if they are the most usable or satisfactory available, from a utilitarian point of view. Similarly, they need not apply to any event except the particular one that is the focus of the question. That is, the specific case need not be viewed in terms of its prototypical characteristics; and no other event, regardless of how similar in kind, can be substituted for the particular one about which the applied question is asked. An answer that does not apply adequately to a particular situation is disqualified, regardless of how precisely or comprehensively it deals with a class of events that does not include the immediate one. Thus, immediate utility and specificity are the hallmarks of professional respectability [Rodgers, 1964, pp. 675–676].

The applied field most closely related to personality psychology is that of clinical psychology. Here we find the application of assessment techniques and of procedures designed to bring about changes in personality. For many academic psychologists, clinical practice today is analogous to the medical practice of previous centuries. That is, the patient's distress clearly merits attention and the motivation of the professionally oriented psychologist to provide help is genuine, but the available techniques are no more effective than the leeches, lancets, and laudanum of a previous medical era. On the other hand, many clinicians criticize academic psychologists as too cautious or even socially irresponsible in focusing on artificial laboratory problems when there are real-life problems to be met. The professional man often feels that like the proverbial drunk: ". . . the academician spends his time looking under the lamppost, where the light is good, for the . . . quarter that was dropped in the gutter half a block away" [Rodgers, 1964, p. 677].

It is most securely within the scientific tradition for personality psychologists to adhere to prediction as the primary goal toward which they aim. Research in personality is directed toward the construction of theories which are powerful in terms of allowing accurate prediction of human behavior. Probably the goals of prediction and control are sufficiently different that they appeal to quite different individuals. Recognizable differences exist between a science and a profession, and psychology may someday follow the example of other disciplines and formally divide into two separate (but equal) groups engaged in these different types of activity.

We will now turn more specifically to the field of personality and the type of scientific activity which it entails.

General Experimental Psychology and Individual Differences

Not until the latter part of the last century was the notion of studying behavioral variables seriously pursued. Over time, the type of behavior investigated has widened from relatively simple processes, such as perceptual thresholds and reaction time, to include *any* behavior of *any degree of complexity*, ranging from light avoidance in amoebas to learning in the flatworm to mental illness in man to international hostility.

Within the field of psychology, there are many areas of research interest. No psychologist investigates all types of behavior. Thus, some psychologists work only with animal learning, some psychologists investigate only leadership behavior in small groups, and other psychologists deal only with man-machine systems. Where does the field of personality fall within all of this?

TWO DISCIPLINES OF SCIENTIFIC PSYCHOLOGY

Two major emphases in the study of behavior may be distinguished. On the one hand are the efforts to determine general behavioral regularities. That is to say, lawful relationships are found which hold true or are assumed to hold true for all individuals. One way to characterize the work of such psychologists is the search for lawful relationships between antecedents and consequents, between independent variables and dependent variables, or in a language comfortable to many psychologists, between stimuli and responses. Psychological research which best fits this definition is usually given the title general experimental psychology. As Underwood [1949, p. 1] states: *"Psychologists attempt to determine the relationships between responses of the organism and the events which prompt those responses."*

A problem arises, however, in dealing with general behavioral regularities. Whenever a stimulus or a series of stimuli is presented to several individual organisms (especially if they are human beings), they tend to differ in the response which they make. To some psychologists, it is precisely such differences among subjects that is of the greatest interest. This other emphasis—that of individual differences—has been called correlational psychology, and it is here that personality psychology has its roots. Cronbach states the case very well in contrasting experimental psychology with the other major type of emphasis—correlational psychology or individual differences:

Individual differences have been an annoyance rather than a challenge to the experimenter. His goal is to control behavior, and variation within treatments is proof that he has not succeeded. Individual variation is cast into that outer darkness known as "error variance." For reasons both statistical and philosophical, error variance is to be reduced by any possible device. You turn to animals of a cheap and short-lived species, so that you can use subjects with controlled heredity and controlled experience. You select human subjects from a narrow subculture. You decorticate your subject by cutting neurons or by giving him an environment so meaningless that his unique responses disappear. . . . You increase the number of cases to obtain stable averages, or you reduce N to 1, as Skinner does. But whatever your device, your goal in the experimental tradition is to get those embarrassing differential variables out of sight.

The correlational psychologist is in love with just those variables the experimenter left home to forget. He regards individual and group variations as important effects of biological and social causes. All organisms adapt to their environments, but not equally well. His question is: what present characteristics of the organism determine its mode and degree of adaptation?

Just as individual variation is a source of embarrassment to the experimenter, so treatment variation attenuates the results of the correlator. His goal is to predict variation within a treatment. His experimental designs demand uniform treatment for every case contributing to a correlation, and treatment variance means only error variance to him [Cronbach, 1957, p. 674].

Whereas the background of experimental psychology lies in the traditional laboratory approach to science in which independent variables are manipulated and the effect on dependent variables determined, the historical background of personality psychology is much closer to everyday life experiences. For thousands of years prior to the advent of modern psychology, there was a general awareness of and interest in individual differences. Essentially, the language of description developed in such a way that we tend to describe other individuals in terms of their standing along an indefinite number of *dimensions*. Whether we are characterizing a political candidate or a blind date or a character in a novel or a next-door neighbor, the same sorts of dimensions are utilized in each instance. For example, someone is described in terms of the extent to which he is intelligent-stupid, kind-cruel, dominant-submissive, liberal-conservative, anxious-calm, contented-unhappy, ambitious-lazy, crazy-sane, devious-straightforward, creative-commonplace, social-unsocial, crude-refined, impulsive-cautious, interesting-dull, outgoing-withdrawn, and so on and so on. In fact, if one were to take any such description of a given person and list all of the dimensions utilized and that person's position on each, the end product is what we mean by that individual's "personality."

In its earliest stages, the field of personality psychology did not actually go a great deal beyond that point. There was speculation about which dimensions should be included in personality descriptions, speculation about why people differ in various ways, and speculation about the factors responsible for changes in personality. In more recent times, as Cronbach indicated, this interest in dimensions of individual differences has grown in sophistication, and attempts are made to measure the dimensions of personality with some precision, to determine the extent to which relationships exist between and among these dimensions, and to provide personality descriptions in a more specific and more quantified fashion.

Perhaps the most distinctive emerging feature of the field of personality at the present time is the tendency to combine the experimental and correlational approaches.

PERSONALITY AS A FIELD OF RESEARCH

In this text, the *personality* of an individual will be defined as the combination of all of the relatively enduring dimensions of individual differences on which he can be measured. The *field of personality*, then, is defined as that branch of psychology which deals with dimensions of individual differences. These dimensions are defined as *personality variables*.

Primarily because it is helpful in describing the types of research activity going on in this field, the interests of personality psychologists may be divided into subcategories. The particular divisional system to be described here will be followed throughout the text.

Personality Measurement. If personality psychologists are concerned with individual differences, obviously one major task within the field is the construction of appropriate instruments to measure personality variables. The step of going from the cultural use of terms such as time or temperature or prejudice to the scientific measurement of them is a difficult and an essential one. In the field of personality, a considerable amount of research activity has been directed toward the construction of appropriate instruments to measure personality dimensions.

In this way relatively unspecific and sometimes vague concepts about people are transformed into specific, standard, quantified variables which are amenable to scientific investigation. An individual is no longer "sort of prejudiced toward Negroes"; rather, he has a specific score on a standardized measure of anti-Negro prejudice which places him a specific distance above the mean of the general population on this dimension.

Included under personality measurement are test construction and the evaluation of existing tests.

Personality Development. A second area of interest within the field is the study of the antecedent variables which are responsible for individual differences along personality dimensions. Personality psychologists are not only interested in measuring the current position of individuals along these dimensions, but also in determining the reason for the differences.

With a wide range of different attitudes concerning Negroes, for example, it is reasonable to search for the conditions which bring about a given degree of prejudice. For example, one might investigate the effects of parental prejudice on the prejudice of their offspring, the effects of different amounts and types of experiences with Negroes on prejudice, or the effects of different degrees of frustration on prejudice.

Included under personality development are studies of genetic influences, prenatal influences, and environmental influences on individual differences along personality dimensions.

Personality Structure. The way in which the various personality dimensions fit together to form the overall structure of personality is a third area of study within the field. Because of the pervasive effects of many specific genetic, prenatal, and environmental factors, many dimensions of individual differences are related to one another. In other words, the various dimensions which together make up the personality structure are not completely independent.

When an individual's score on a test of racial intolerance is known, one may make a better than chance prediction about his response on a measure of political-economic conservatism; these two variables are related. Similarly, scores on the measure of prejudice are related to such behavior as voting for or against legislation on civil rights. When several such dimensions or behavioral characteristics are interrelated with one another and are unrelated with other sets of dimensions (for example, intelligence or anxiety), we may speak of clusters or factors within the overall personality structure. As knowledge about personality dimensions grows, very probably a time will come when there is an agreed-upon way in which personality structure and the dimensions and clusters within it are described; but at present no uniformity exists with respect to which dimensions should be included or how they fit together.

Research on personality structure includes both correlational studies in which the relationship between two or more dimensions is determined and theoretical and mathematical studies which attempt to organize what is known about personality dimensions into a coherent, overall picture.

Personality Dynamics. The interest in the study of personality structure is in the interrelationships among all of the relatively stable, enduring characteristics of an individual—a cross-section of an individual at a given point in time. The interest in the study of personality dynamics is in the effect of personality variables on the individual's behavior in response to a changing stimulus world—the effect of the interaction between stimulus variables and personality variables on behavior.

An example of such research would be an experimental situation in which subjects were required to read several passages of prose material and later to recall as much as possible of what had been read. Half of the subjects are high in prejudice and half low in prejudice. Each subject reads passages in which the content is either (1) neutral, (2) negative to Negroes, or (3) positive to Negroes. We would predict that high- and low-prejudiced individuals would not differ in the first condition, that high-prejudiced subjects would remember more of the material in the anti-Negro condition, and that low-prejudiced subjects would remember more in the pro-Negro condition. Thus, a stimulus variable (content of the passages) and a personality variable (prejudice) would interact to determine the response (recall of the passages).

Research on personality dynamics consists primarily of experimental investigations in which there is a manipulation of stimulus variables and a division of the subjects in terms of one or more personality variables.

Personality Change. A final area of personality research is concerned with alteration of personality variables. Even though personality dimensions represent relatively stable and enduring characteristics, changes in such variables are possible at any age level.

With respect to anti-Negro prejudice, research examples would include experimental investigations such as those made to determine the effects of different types of persuasive communications on attitudes toward Negroes and field studies such as those made to determine the effect of school integration on prejudice.

PERSONALITY IN RELATION TO OTHER FIELDS OF PSYCHOLOGY

In many respects, psychologists whose interests place them in the field of personality (or personality–social psychology) occupy a middle ground within the field of psychology. The identification of broad areas of interest often divides psychologists roughly into experimental and clinical psychologists. The identity of the former rests on the historical base of psychology as a laboratory science, and the label "experimentalist" most often refers to a psychologist who engages in research in the areas of learning, perception, or psychophysiology. In its present form, clinical psychology is largely a post–World War II phenomenon, a rapidly growing field which now encompasses over one-half of the members of the American Psychological Association (APA). While research methodology has consistently been included as part of the graduate training of clinicians, their identifying characteristic is an interest in the application of diagnostic and therapeutic skills for the purpose of identifying and alleviating the emotional problems of maladjusted individuals.

Personality psychologists, on the other hand, are somewhat different from either experimentalists or clinicians. They share a research orientation and methodology with experimentalists, but the content of their research tends to be markedly different. Like clinicians, personality psychologists are interested in the complex variables involved in human behavior, but they are much more inclined to focus on normal rather than abnormal functioning and are rarely inclined to engage in service work in an applied setting.

Division 8 of the APA (Personality and Social Psychology) has recently been one of the fastest growing areas in the field. Between 1948 and 1960, the membership of Division 8 increased 297 per cent; by way of comparison, Division 3 (Experimental Psychology) increased 40 per cent, and Division 12 (Clinical and Abnormal Psychology) increased 189 per cent [Tryon, 1963]. Since about 1960, personality has emerged as a major field of specialization among doctoral candidates [Vance and MacPhail, 1964].

The Plan of This Book

This text is divided into four sections. The first section contains two introductory chapters which deal with some general issues pertinent to the study of personality. In the present chapter, an attempt has been made to introduce the general notion that personality psychology is an area of research interest within the general realm of science, to outline some of the general goals toward which scientific activity is directed, and to give a brief overview of personality psychology and its relationship to the rest of the field. The following chapter will consider some of the assumptions underlying personality research and will present a description of the way in which research progresses.

The second section of the book consists of five chapters which concentrate on the methodology and examples of research in the five subdivisions of the field: personality measurement, personality development, personality structure, personality dynamics, and personality change.

The third section consists of five chapters describing in some detail the work that has been carried out and summarizing what is known with respect to a representative sample of five personality dimensions: authoritarianism, need for achievement, manifest anxiety, intelligence, and self-concept. The number of dimensions which have been the object of investigation and which could have been included in this section is very large. These particular five dimensions were selected as examples because (1) there has been a considerable amount of research dealing with each, and (2) they represent quite varied kinds of personality dimensions. The five variables provide a sampling of research on individual differences in ideology, motivation, emotion, ability, and self-image.

Thus, the study of personality will be approached in a relatively broad way to provide a picture of the variety of methods and approaches characteristic of the field and in a relatively narrow way to provide a close-up in depth of a limited number of personality dimensions.

The emphasis throughout this text will be on an examination of research aimed at gaining knowledge about behavior rather than on attempts to describe and characterize particular individuals. Nevertheless, the final section will show that it is possible to take the personality variables which are usually studied one or two at a time in research and "put them back together again" with respect to a specific individual. The relatively molecular way in which science must proceed does not eliminate the possibility of learning something about the molar functioning of a whole person; rather, it makes such learning possible.

Summary

Though the latter half of the twentieth century is in many respects an age of science, general understanding of the scientific method is quite limited. A major goal of this book is to provide the student with an appreciation of the study of personality as one part of the ongoing work within behavioral science.

One of the many ways in which individuals have attempted to bring order and predictability into their environment is by means of an approach which has come to be known as science. The goals of science are often identified as understanding, prediction, and control. Without any further criterion, understanding is not a satisfactory goal in that it is relatively easy to achieve an illusion of understanding through simple naming, elaborate verbal descriptions, or after-the-fact explanations. Prediction may be considered as the goal of science or as the criterion of understanding. Explanation at any level of complexity is useful if it increases predictive accuracy. Accurate prediction is no guarantee of the correctness of a theoretical formulation; any conceptualization is only provisionally correct and may be supplanted by a better one. When laboratory control of phenomena is attained, it is also possible to control some aspect of the world outside of the laboratory. There is a long-standing academic tradition that knowledge should be sought for its own sake rather than for practical reasons. One difficulty for the scientist in applying his findings is that value judgments often must be made which have nothing to do with science. A final issue concerns the validity of the application. Individuals differ markedly in their willingness to utilize admittedly imperfect techniques in order to influence events in the outside world. For this and other reasons, many fields are divided into those individuals engaged in basic research and those engaged in professional application.

As psychology has developed, its two major research emphases have been general experimental psychology and correlational psychology. The background of experimental psychology lies in the traditional laboratory approach to science in which independent variables are manipulated and their effect on dependent variables determined. The historical background of personality psychology is in the centuries-old way of describing other individuals in terms of their standing along an indefinite number of dimensions. This description of individuals led to attempts to measure these personality dimensions and to investigate the relationships between and among them. Perhaps the most distinctive feature of the field of personality at the present time is the tendency to combine the experimental and correlational approaches. An individual's personality is defined as the combination of all the relatively enduring dimensions of individual differences. The field of personality is defined as that branch of psychology which deals with dimensions of individual differences. The field is further divided into personality measurement, personality development, personality structure, personality dynamics, and personality change. The field of personality is a rapidly growing one which shares a research orientation with experimental psychology and an interest in complex areas of human behavior with clinical psychology.

This text is divided into four sections. The first contains introductory material dealing with some general issues in the field. The second section concentrates on the methodology of the five areas of personality research. In the third section is a sample of the research which has been conducted on five personality dimensions: authoritarianism, need for achievement, manifest anxiety, intelligence, and self-concept. The final section discusses the problem of combining personality variables in order to provide a description of an individual.

CHAPTER 2

Conducting Research
on Human Behavior

Before an examination of the way in which personality is studied and of specific research findings with personality variables, the student may find it helpful to take a more general look at the assumptions underlying such research and at the way in which this research is conducted. In addition, as an example, a series of investigations dealing with relatively complex human behavior will be presented in some detail.

Two Assumptions Underlying Personality Research

ASSUMPTION I—BEHAVIOR IS LAWFUL

The lawfulness of behavior is the basic premise in psychology; animal organisms, including human beings, do not behave in a random or otherwise unpredictable manner. There is a lawful regularity of antecedent and consequent events for every aspect of behavior, regardless of its simplicity or complexity, regardless of its importance or unimportance in human affairs. This assumption is often designated as determinism.

Free Will. Though a deterministic assumption is obviously necessary for behavioral science, it tends to arouse opposition and arguments against it, even from many behavioral scientists. For the most part, the opposition may be attributable to the fact that our cultural heritage does not include the notion that behavior follows natural laws. In fact, our society tends to make quite different assumptions about the behavior of man. As Immergluck suggests:

The notion that *behavior*, as indeed all other events in nature, is lawfully related to antecedent and attendant events, and that such relationships may be quantitatively described, has been indispensable in at once liberating psychology from its metaphysical ancestry and bringing it into the fold of natural science. The road from ancient vitalism to modern determinism, however, has been neither smooth nor straight. Many curves, detours, and even backward turns have marked its course. In part, these delays in accepting a fully deterministic conception of behavior are probably due to an understandable reluctance to relinquish venerated and cherished philosophies of human nature. The notion that man is, in his barest essence, a free agent propelled by self-initiated inner forces that defy, by their very nature, prediction or scientifically ordered description customarily applied to inanimate events, is deeply engraved not only in the thoughts and values of Western civilization but, to some extent at least, in man's self-conceptualizations throughout the history of all human societies [Immergluck, 1964, p. 270].

Thus, the assumption of predictable behavior is incompatible with the theological and legal assumption of free will. Can psychologists assume that individuals ever choose to perform specific behaviors on the basis of an autonomous, unknowable force such as will? May one engage in behavior which is independent of the predictable regularities of natural laws? If Assumption I is accepted, the answer obviously is "No." Every behavior must necessarily be conceptualized as the result of lawful interactions between it and antecedent events. If Assumption I is not accepted, behavioral science is a waste of time, for there can be no science of behavior. There is no direct way to settle such controversy; the fruitfulness of the assumption that behavior is lawful can only be determined through the success or failure of those who are attempting to build a science of behavior.

One way in which one may accept the assumption of determinism and at the same time adjust to our cultural belief in free will is to separate one's research assumptions from one's everyday life assumptions. Boring describes this solution to the conflict:

In the antithesis between freedom and determinism we see what is perhaps the best known instance of cognitive dissonance that the scientist encounters. Determinism is a paradigm which science has long accepted. . . .

So in science the paradigm of determinism works well. It is a good policy for science. It is, however, dissonant with practical policies of living, and for 99 per cent of his life the scientist is a human being, not only outside the laboratory but in his conduct of experimentation and in all his relations with people. Any social occasion that implies his own duty or responsibility is founded upon the paradigm of freedom. All morality and altruism and affection, as well as hatred and opposition, imply freedom. Language is shot through and through with the implication that men are free to choose. If ever a policy was justified by almost universal use, it is the theory that man is free to choose. . . .

The scientist chooses the paradigm of determinism when he designs his experiment, when he theorizes, when he is thinking scientifically. As a practical man he needs to believe in his freedom and usually in the freedom of others, unless he is being a psychologist, when he may examine the behavior of a subject in respect to the conditions that determine it. It may be said that determinism is the broader and more positive paradigm, for its complement, freedom, is negative, consisting in a preference for ignorance [Boring, 1964, pp. 681–682].

Human Dignity. Still another group of psychologists, associated with the "humanistic" movement, actively object to the idea of a deterministic, mechanistic model of man's behavior as somehow degrading to mankind [for example, Bugental, 1963]. For this sort of criticism, Immergluck has a reply:

Does, however, determinism in fact corrode the concept of human dignity? Perhaps only if we have chosen, in an a priori manner, to equate dignity with free will. On the other hand, should a deterministic framework propel us to search ceaselessly for specific and general behavioral laws, we might, some day, understand not only the variables that lead to neurosis, feeble-mindedness, mental illness, and delinquency, but perhaps also the richness and complexity of the specific events and factors which lawfully shape intelligence, problem-solving skills, behavioral integration, and creativity. We might even be able to use such knowledge to advantage. And would this alone not constitute eloquent testimony to the dignity of man? [Immergluck, 1964, p. 280]

An additional point is made by Farber:

The notion of scientific laws as mandatory or coercive results from confusing scientific laws with judicial or legislative laws. If one does not obey a judicial law, one is punished; but if one does not obey a scientific law, the law is inaccurate and must be modified. Scientific laws do not make anything happen. They are merely statements of what does happen under certain conditions. Natural phenomena do not depend on scientific laws. Rather, the converse is true—the statement of the law depends on the nature of the observed phenomena [Farber, 1964, p. 7].

Limitations. Two other, somewhat minor, problems are raised by the assumption of lawfulness and predictability. A misunderstanding sometimes arises to the effect that psychologists are planning to compete with palmists and readers of tea leaves in predicting the future. A more precise statement of the proposition would be that behavior *in a given stimulus situation* is predictable. Therefore, any behavioral law must be quite specific with respect to the stimuli involved. The fact that Frustration A elicits hostile behavior does not necessarily mean that Frustration B will have the same effect. In the same way, the fact that Test A and Test B each were designed to measure introversion does not necessarily mean that scores on the two instruments will be related. We should also note that the fact that a lawful relationship is found in a controlled laboratory situation does not necessarily mean that the same relationship will be found in the uncontrolled stimulus situations outside of the laboratory. In physics, the effect of gravitational force on falling bodies is specified *in a vacuum*. When the falling speed of an object in "the real world" is under consideration, the effects of many additional variables (for example, wind speed and direction, resistance offered by the shape and size of the object) must be known. Not only must caution be used in generalizing from the laboratory to the nonlaboratory situation, but it is equally true that findings in one uncontrolled stimulus situation may not generalize to a different uncontrolled stimulus situation. For example, the effect of stress on intellectual performance in an academic setting may or may not be the same as the effect of stress in a military setting.

The second minor problem is the fact that organisms change over time; hence the predictions for a given organism with respect to the same stimulus situation on two different occasions might well be different. As an obvious example, the amount of fear aroused in response to an unexpected clap of thunder should differ from the amount of fear aroused when it thunders a second time. Similarly, a joke is not as funny after the first hearing. One's response to the words on a menu at a French restaurant is different before and after having learned the language. In short, organisms are affected by what has occurred previously, and this influences their response to subsequent stimuli. Perhaps, then, we should say that behavior in a given stimulus situation is predictable *if the relevant antecedent variables affecting the organism are known.*

ASSUMPTION II—SCIENTISTS CAN INVESTIGATE ONLY OPERATIONALLY
DEFINED VARIABLES

Operationism. The scientific method and the philosophy of science have evolved over the centuries as a set of procedures and concepts useful in advancing the acquisition of knowledge. If psychologists hope to attain the success achieved by their colleagues in the older and more advanced sciences, they are most likely to do so by utilizing that same method and philosophy. One of the more basic concepts is operationism. An operational definition of a term is simply a verbal statement which specifies the observable conditions or procedural rules under which the term is used in defining a concept or variable [Bechtoldt, 1959]. Stevens [1939, p. 222] summarizes the central theme of the philosophy of science in these terms: ". . . *science seeks to generate confirmable propositions by fitting a formal system of symbols (language, mathematics, logic) to empirical observations, and the propositions of science have empirical signifi-*

cance only when their truth can be demonstrated by a set of concrete operations." Stevens goes on to add that only propositions based upon operations which are public and repeatable are admitted to the body of science and that a term denotes something only when there are concrete criteria for its applicability.

When anyone uses a term such as anxiety or intelligence or creativity, he is often referring loosely to a variety of observable and unobservable aspects of behavior. When someone indicates that a given person is "anxious," he may convey to each person who hears it a very special kind of unverbalized meaning picked up from friends, relatives, books, movies, and other sources in the culture and from his own private, subjective, internal world of experience—these various unverbalized meanings are not observable. Such meanings may be highly idiosyncratic, inconsistent among various individuals, and even inconsistent over a period of time for the same individual. If, for example, an experimenter reported simply that he found male adolescents to be more anxious than female adolescents, he might have in mind any combination of various meanings of anxiety. In turn, the finding might convey 50 different meanings to 50 different readers.

In order to bring such a hodgepodge of vague elements into the realm of scientific inquiry, concepts must be defined in quite a different way, that is, operationally. A person may be defined as being anxious if he is one who says, "I feel nervous," has trembling hands, reports that he feels apprehensive about the future, complains of numerous vague physical ailments, goes about hurriedly, obtains a high score on a psychological test measuring anxiety—all of which are observable aspects of behavior. When the variables under investigation are observable and are defined in sufficient detail, other experimenters are able to utilize the same variables. An experimenter does not simply employ "an unpleasant stimulus" but rather an electric shock of a specified voltage attached to the right index finger of each subject. Subjects are not simply differentiated into "anxious and nonanxious" individuals, but are selected in terms of scoring above the eightieth percentile or below the twentieth percentile on the Manifest Anxiety Scale [Taylor, 1953]. The behavior under study is not simply "work efficiency" but the number of anagrams from a specific list correctly solved in a five-minute period. "Operationism" involves only the recognition that knowledge can best be gained and communicated through procedures which are observable, specific, and open to repetition by other investigators. Even so, the concept is of central importance in science and, strangely enough, is a matter of controversy for some individuals.

Science and the Unobservable. If scientists deal with that which is tangible, what about concepts which cannot be defined in that way? George Gaylord Simpson points out:

. . . the materials of science are literally material. The observations of science are of material, physically or objectively observable phenomena. Its relationships are material, natural relationships. This is not to say that science necessarily denies the existence of nonmaterial or supernatural relationships, but only that, whether or not they exist, they are not the business of science [Simpson, 1964, p. 91].

Thus, if one cannot define a concept in terms of observables (hell, for example), the concept is simply not open to scientific inquiry. Utilizing the scientific method, there is literally no way even to begin answering the question of whether there is a hell. To believe that theology and science could ever be in disagreement about such issues is to misunderstand science.

Pseudo-Problems.   One benefit of operationism is that scientists are extricated from pseudo-problems such as the ancient question of whether a tree falling in an uninhabited forest makes a noise. If "noise" is defined as dial readings on a machine that detects sound waves, then one can easily demonstrate that noise does occur even in an uninhabited forest. If, on the other hand, "noise" is defined as a verbal report about auditory stimulation, then noise cannot occur in such a forest. And, either definition is equally acceptable, providing that it is clear which one is being employed.

An equally false problem is the question of whether the operationally defined variable is *really* a measure of the concept. Does the Manifest Anxiety Scale *really* measure anxiety? Does the Stanford-Binet *really* measure intelligence? Does a thermometer *really* measure temperature? Such questions assume that some identifiable, pure, formless, nonoperational anxiety or intelligence or temperature exists somewhere in the abstract. It is meaningless to talk about the amount of correspondence between operational measures and the real variable, because there is no *real* variable. It is, however, meaningful to ask about the correspondence between one's abstract definition and the operational definition. In the following chapter, we will discuss this question in terms of what is called "face validity." However, even more important is to determine the relationship between the operationally defined variable and other operationally defined variables.

We should note that a given concept, such as anxiety, may be defined in terms of many different operations by different experimenters. One investigator may define anxiety in terms of scores on the Manifest Anxiety Scale, another in terms of amount of perspiration on the palm as measured under specified conditions, and still another in terms of behavior ratings by a clinical psychologist. Each definition is perfectly acceptable, though one may eventually prove to be a more useful variable in research than the others. As the field progresses one hopes: (1) that general agreement will be reached concerning the defining operation or operations for a given term, and (2) that unrelated operations will be given different names.

Criticisms of Operationism. Two sorts of negative reactions are often heard with respect to operationism, and usually from the same individuals who are critical of the assumption that behavior is lawful. The reasons for the negative reactions are somewhat puzzling, but they may have something to do with a generalized distrust of any scheme which proposes a deterministic, mechanistic, quantitative universe in which events occur in a lawful manner. There is a much longer history of schemas which propose a universe filled with free agents whose interaction is unpredictable and nonquantifiable. As various branches of science have progressed, the mysterious and unpredictable nature of many phenomena has disappeared. A hurricane is not attributed to the anger of the sea god. An eclipse of the sun is not seen as a warning to change our evil ways. An influenza epidemic is not interpreted as the handiwork of a witch doctor casting an evil spell. Human behavior, however, is perhaps the last stronghold for those who prefer to view the world as an abstract mystery. At any rate, what are the specific criticisms of operationism?

First, the critics say that an operational definition is too narrow and that the rich meaning of a term is lost when it is reduced to something as specific and circumscribed as a test score or an experimental procedure. It is difficult to imagine what an investigator would actually do or how he would report what he had done in an experimental study of anxiety in which the variables were defined only in abstract, nonspecific, unobservable, nonoperational terms. With respect to narrowness, we should point out that no one claims to encompass all of the rich cultural meaning of concepts such as anxiety, intelligence, or hunger into a single score or a specific condition. In order to formulate an operational definition which more closely matches the cultural meaning, one probably must employ a large number of discrete operations which together approximate the cultural meaning. Most definitions from the culture are probably too broad and too inclusive for meaningful scientific investigation. Often, scientists find that they are better off with more than one operational definition of a given concept if the different definitions represent unique variables which are at least partially independent of one another. As Zubin [1965] has pointed out, the temperature reading of a mercury thermometer does not encompass all that is meant by an individual when he expresses feelings of being hot or cold. The mercury readings plus the humidity level plus barometric pressure plus wind speed probably do account for most of the perceived temperature differences. Nevertheless, these entities are separate variables, operationalized in quite different ways, and each has its own antecedents and consequents.

A second type of negative reaction to operationism is of a somewhat different order. The necessity for defining variables in terms of specific observables in research is sometimes misinterpreted to mean that it is improper even to speculate in nonoperational terms. Stevens says that operationism:

. . . is not opposed to hypotheses, theories, or speculation. It seeks merely to discover criteria by which these things may be detected and labeled. It is not opposed to poetry, art, or religion. It wants only to know the difference between these things and science [Stevens, 1939, p. 230].

Furthermore, if any scientists felt compelled to stick so close to operations that they were afraid to engage in vague, ill-defined speculative thinking, it would almost certainly be detrimental to rapid advancement in science.

How Does Scientific Activity Proceed?

As for a general definition of science or a general set of rules by which knowledge is obtained in science, it is the author's observation that such definitions and rules tend to obscure rather than clarify. In a book intended to give laymen some understanding of what science is all about, James B. Conant indicated that he hoped to dodge the problem of definition, feeling that science could best be understood by reading about how individual scientists have actually proceeded in their work. The definition which he goes on to offer is a descriptive one:

As a first approximation, we may say that science emerges from the other progressive activities of man to the extent that new concepts arise from experiments and observations, and the new concepts in turn lead to further experiments and observations. The case histories drawn from the last three hundred years show examples of fruitful and fruitless concepts. The texture of modern science is the result of the interweaving of the fruitful concepts. The test of a new idea is therefore not only its success in correlating the then-known facts but much more its success or failure in stimulating further experimentation or observation which in turn is fruitful. This dynamic quality of science viewed not as a practical undertaking but as developments of conceptual schemes seems to me to be close to the heart of the best definition. It is this quality which can be demonstrated only by the historical approach, or else learned by direct professional experience [Conant, 1947, p. 37].

So, the essence of scientific activity lies not in the nature of that which is observed, not in technological apparatus, not in memorization of the facts which have been gathered. The specific phenomena which are observed simply define the branch of science. The technological apparatus is often forbidding to the uninitiated, but the use of most techniques, from a centrifuge to an electronic computer, can be learned by any normally functioning individual who has received the proper instruction. All of the accumulated facts do not have to be memorized by each investigator: having them available in written form is much more efficient. Science, instead, is a dynamic, often exciting, often frustrating process in which a reciprocal interaction takes place between observation and conceptualization.

Keeping in mind the general considerations regarding the assumptions of lawfulness and the necessity of dealing with observables in research, we will examine briefly the way in which scientific activity proceeds. The description of a complex activity almost always tends toward oversimplification. Furthermore, not every piece of research follows the pattern to be described; perhaps no piece of research has ever followed it exactly. Nevertheless, the following steps are to some degree characteristic of much that goes on in research fields such as personality.

UNCONTROLLED OBSERVATION

A science of behavior has many possible starting points, but all starting points must include observation of behavior somewhere in the initial stages. The observation may be of oneself, others in one's everyday environment, patients in psychotherapy, experimental subjects, or infrahuman animals.

When scientists engage in uncontrolled observations, what are the characteristics of this procedure? At the observational stage, there is no reason to be overly concerned about experimental rigor. One of the most exciting and important aspects of science can be seen in the attempt of an acute observer to make conceptual sense of some aspect of the world. For example, a therapist notes that a patient's paralyzed hand can be moved following the patient's expression of previously unrecognized hostility toward his father. A child psychologist hears a small girl attribute blame for an accident to an inanimate object. A professor observes that his students seem to joke and laugh uproariously just before an examination is administered. If an individual observes such events, wonders about them, and tries to make provisional sense of them, he has engaged in the initial activity necessary for the progress of behavioral science. The aim is to arrive at fruitful concepts which will then lead to more refined observations. Rogers makes a similar point:

It is my opinion that the type of understanding which we call science can begin anywhere, at any level of sophistication. To observe acutely, to think carefully and creatively—these activities, not the accumulation of laboratory instruments, are the beginnings of science. To observe that a given crop grows better on the rocky hill than in the lush bottom land and to think about this observation, is the start of science. To notice that most sailors get scurvy but not those who have stopped at islands to pick up fresh fruit is a similar start. To recognize that, when a person's views of himself change, his behavior changes accordingly, and to puzzle over this, is again the beginning of both theory and science. I voice this conviction in protest against the attitude which seems too common in American psychology, that science starts in the laboratory or at the calculating machine [Rogers, 1959, p. 189].

GENERALIZATION

As soon as the observations are expressed in symbols which go beyond the immediately observed stimulus, generalization to a class of events is taking place. This process constitutes the first step or the most primitive level of theory-building. Most people, of course, leave their generalizations at this level. Everyone builds up a series of concepts, often unverbalized and often incorrect, which influence their interpretations of behavior. Novelists have long been aware of these guiding speculations which people hold. Quite often a fictional character is made to express a generalization or series of generalizations about behavior. James Fenimore Cooper, for example, has Deerslayer speculate about heredity and environment as joint contributors to behavioral differences. Judith asks him:

"In what is a gift different from a nature? Is not nature itself a gift from God?"
"Sartain; that's quick-thoughted and creditable, Judith, though the main idee is wrong. A natur' is the creatur' itself; its wishes, wants, idees, and feelin's as all are born in him. This natur' never can be changed in the main, though it may undergo some increases or lessening. Now, gifts come of sarcumstances. Thus, if you put a man in a town, he gets town gifts; in a settlement, settlement gifts; in a forest, gifts of the woods. A soldier has soldierly gifts, and a missionary preaching gifts. All these increase and strengthen until they get to fortify natur' as it might be, and excuse a thousand acts and idees. Still the creatur' is the same at the bottom; just as a man who is clad in regimentals is the same as the man that is clad in skins. The garments make a change to the eye, and some change in the conduct perhaps; but none in the man. Herein lies the apology for gifts; seein' that you expect different conduct from one in silks and satins from one in homespun; though the Lord, who didn't make the dresses, but who made the creatur's themselves, looks only at his own work. This isn't ra'al missionary doctrine, but it's as near it as man of white color need be" [Cooper, 1841, pp. 404–405].

Not only novelists, but waitresses, kindergarten teachers, bus drivers, and used-car salesmen all observe human behavior and all develop general notions about it. "Fat people are jolly." "Mexican kids can't be trusted." "It's human nature to have wars and revolutions." "Any guy who walks like that must be queer." "Spare the rod and spoil the child." "Everybody's out to make a fast buck." The difficulty is that most people do not go beyond their original generalizations. Most important, they do not have adequate means by which to check their ideas in order to discard the incorrect ones and expand on those that are valid. In order to move from the generalizations of everyday life and the pages of novels, one must specify operations and engage in empirical research to test the validity of the generalizations.

VERIFICATION

Most nonscientists seem to rely primarily on congruent validation to "test" their generalizations. That is, any new observations which are congruent with one's generalizations are accepted as evidence for the correctness of one's ideas. Contrary observations are conveniently ignored. For example, a belief that Negroes are dirty may be confirmed by observing working-class Negroes at the end of the day. The fact that working-class whites are also dirty at the end of the day or that Negroes in other situations are not dirty can easily be ignored. An attempt to verify hypotheses by obtaining new data in a controlled and objective manner is uniquely scientific.

The second section of this book is concerned primarily with those verification procedures which are most used in the field of personality. As will be seen in connection with the process of verification, considerations such as experimental controls, reliability of measurement, and replicability of findings assume crucial importance. The primary concern is to carry out the verification procedure in such a way that one is not deceived into accepting that which is not so or rejecting that which is.

THEORY-BUILDING

The essence of theory-building is the attempt to formulate increasingly broader generalizations which take the established relationships beyond the particular events involved in a specific observation. By giving a more comprehensive explanation of the observations, theories make possible deductions, which in turn lead to the making of new observations. Previously unrelated empirical events are unified in a more comprehensive framework. Rogers gives an example:

I like to think of the discovery of radioactivity by the Curies. They had left some pitchblende ore, which they were using for some purpose or other, in a room where they stored photographic plates. They discovered that the plates had been spoiled. In other words, first there was the observation of a dynamic event. This event might have been due to a multitude of causes. It might have been a flaw in the manufacture of the plates. It might have been the humidity, the temperature, or any one of a dozen other things. But acute observation and creative thinking fastened on a hunch regarding the pitchblende, and this became a tentative hypothesis. Crude experiments began to confirm the hypothesis. Only slowly was it discovered that it was not the pitchblende, but a strange element in the pitchblende which was related to the observed effect. Meanwhile a theory had to be constructed to bring this strange phenomenon into orderly relationship with other knowledge. And although the theory in its most modest form had to do with the effect of radium on photographic plates, in its wider and more speculative reaches it was concerned with the nature of matter and composition of the universe [Rogers, 1959, p. 190].

In psychology, the types of theories constructed vary greatly. Are there any guiding principles which would be of help in constructing theories or in evaluating the theories of others? One approach has been to follow the example of an established science such as physics. Among others, Spence has consistently argued for such a model and has described theories in the following manner:

Empirical science, aiming as it does at general principles that will provide for the explanation and integration of particular events, has evolved comprehensive systems of terms (concepts) and sentences that may be arranged in a hierarchy. Highest in the hierarchy of the language of any science are the abstract terms and statements that provide for theories of wide scope and great precision. These theoretical concepts, if they are to serve this function, must be connected in one manner or another to the terms lower in the hierarchy, and ultimately to a class of elementary, undefined terms and sentences that have direct experiential reference [Spence, 1960, p. 73].

Professor Spence has also noted that theory-building in physics and in psychology are not at the same stage of development at the present time:

In some areas of knowledge, for example present day physics, theories serve primarily to bring into functional connection with one another empirical laws which prior to their formulation had been isolated realms of knowledge. The physicist is able to isolate, experimentally, elementary situations, i.e., situations in which there are a limited number of variables, and thus finds it possible to infer or discover descriptive, low-order laws. Theory comes into play for the physicist when he attempts to formulate more abstract principles which will bring these low-order laws into relationship with one another. Examples of such comprehensive theories are Newton's principle of gravitation and the kinetic theory of gases. The former provided a theoretical integration of such laws as Kepler's concerning planetary motions, Galileo's law of falling bodies, laws of the tides, and so on. The kinetic theory has served to integrate the various laws relating certain properties of gases to other experimental variables.

In the less highly developed areas of knowledge, such as the behavior and social sciences, theory plays a somewhat different role. In these more complex fields the simplest experimental situation that can be arranged usually involves such a large number of variables that it is extremely difficult, if not impossible, to discover directly the empirical laws relating them. Theories are brought into play in such circumstances as a device to aid in the formulation of the laws. They consist primarily in the introduction or postulation of hypothetical constructs which help to bridge gaps between the experimental variables. Examples of such theoretical constructs are legion in psychology, *e.g.*, Tolman's "demand," Hull's "excitatory potential," Lewin's "tension system" and a host of other mentalistic and neurophysiologically-sounding concepts [Spence, 1944, pp. 47–48].

Where does psychology, and more specifically the field of personality, stand with respect to theory? Much that we label as "personality theory" is not theory in the formal sense but rather a mixture of observations, generalizations, pre-theoretical speculation, and hypotheses. It is easier to extend the speculations than it is to carry out the data-gathering procedures necessary to confirm the deductions from the speculations and thus to extend the network of facts. Considerable agreement exists that our present theories are lacking in many respects and that the construction of better behavioral theories is badly needed:[1]

Until constructs are introduced in some such precise fashion as Hull employs, one really does not have a scientific theory, for it is only under such conditions that the possibility of verification or refutation exists. Unfortunately, much of what has passed for theory in psychology has been sadly lacking in this respect, a state of affairs which is largely responsible for many of the "theoretical" controversies, and for the low regard in which theory is held in some quarters in psychology. That theory construction has not always been intelligently pursued, however, is no reason for doing without theory. Without the generalizations which theories aim to provide we should never be in a position to predict behavior, for knowledge of particular events does not provide us with a basis for prediction when the situation differs in the least degree. The higher the level of abstraction that can be obtained the greater will be both the understanding and actual control achieved [Spence, 1944, p. 62].

Most personality theories are broad in scope and attempt to supply an explanatory framework covering essentially every aspect of human behavior. We may fairly state that existing personality theories tend to be far too ambitious in their aims and far too limited in their predictive power. Thus, when anyone attempts to explain war as the result of man's death drive, or the content of folk tales as the expression of the racial unconscious, or the acceptance of dictatorships as the result of man's fear of freedom, clearly the development of personality theory has a long way to go.

What, then, is our solution? Spence points out:

---

[1] This rather pessimistic view of the state of theory development in psychology by Spence in 1944 remains true as evidenced by the later writings of Spence (1957) and of others (for example, Bergmann, 1953; Farber, 1964; Feigl, 1951).

It should be noticed that such comprehensive physical theories . . . are formulated only after there is available a considerable body of empirical laws relating concepts of a fairly abstract nature, *i.e.*, highly generalized laws. It would hardly seem necessary to have to say that no such comprehensive, highly abstract theories exist today in psychology, for the simple reason that we do not even have a well developed body of very general laws in any area of our field [Spence, 1960, p. 82].

Thus, a potentially fruitful approach to theory-building in the science of personality would seem to be the establishment of behavioral laws and the construction of small theories dealing with specific and limited behavioral events rather than the development of a general theory of personality. These small "personality theories" would, initially, be limited in scope but predictively powerful. As such theories are built, the formulation of more general concepts will tie them together into increasingly inclusive overall theories. This, however, is an end-point rather than a starting point. First, we need to devise psychological laws analogous to those of the pendulum, of gases, of the lever, of the effect of gravity on momentum, and so forth. As satisfying and useful as it would be to have a complete theory of behavior immediately available, a more limited and more attainable goal is necessary at the present. In the following section, we will discuss a specific research example, following the progress from uncontrolled observations to a behavioral law.

An Example of Research on Relatively Complex Social Behavior

A LANGUAGE IN WHICH TO CONCEPTUALIZE RESEARCH IN PERSONALITY

Psychologists have not as yet agreed on the most useful way to represent behavior conceptually in order to investigate it. Solutions have included mental images, stimulus-response connections, perceived reality, and the total organized interrelationship between the organism and its environment. Which, if any, of these diverse approaches will prove to be the most fruitful will be known only on the basis of future developments. Spence points out:

The problem here is really one of the size of the "units of description" that the scientist is to employ, and this brings us back to the criterion of acceptability of a scientific term which we referred to as *significance*. By the *significance* of a scientific concept is here meant the extent to which a concept or variable aids or enters into the formulation of laws. Significant concepts in science are those which are discovered to have functional relations with other concepts. Unfortunately, there are few if any rules for deciding *a priori* which concepts will and which ones will not be significant. Whether elementaristic concepts or units of description which, like the Gestaltists, are nearer the "meaningful" common sense level, are to be chosen is entirely a pragmatic matter of which ones are most successful—*i.e.*, which ones lead to the discovery of laws. This can be ascertained only by trying them out [Spence, 1948, p. 71].

In describing research in this text, stimulus and response elements will serve as the units of description. One can conceptualize behavior in this particular way without at the same time committing oneself necessarily to any particular ready-built theory of behavior.

As we have noted, the assumption that it is the business of behavioral science to explicate the relations between objectively defined environmental and behavioral events is in itself no theory, but rather a metatheoretical or pretheoretical preference. Those who adopt this approach, especially if they have an interest in the phenomena of learning, are likely to use the terms "S" and "R" to refer, respectively, to the environmental and behavioral events, and the familiar formula "S-R" to indicate a relation between these two classes of variables.

. . . its adoption does not imply a single level or kind of conceptualization of either "stimulus" or "response" [Brown, 1961; Miller, 1959]. It does not imply that S-R laws are the only ones of importance in psychology [Spence, 1948]. It does not imply any particular stand with respect to the necessity or desirability of introducing hypothetical constructs in accounting for behavior. And it certainly does not imply any substantial agreement concerning either the specific observable variables or hypothetical variables of which particular responses or response classes are a function. In brief, "S-R" is simply a type of terminology employed by some empirically-minded psychologists, including some who are also theoretically inclined [Farber, 1964, pp. 32–33].

In spite of the neatness with which one can write S-R on a piece of paper or on a blackboard, we should recognize that S-R units are simply abstractions which, hopefully, will be useful in building a science of behavior. As Kendler and Kendler [1962] note, the use of S-R language does not mean that behavior *actually* consists of S-R connections. Rather, we represent behavior in that way. In a similar vein, Spence remarks:

One often hears criticisms to the effect that behavioristic concepts are too elementaristic, too atomistic, or that they fail to portray the real essence or true meaning of man's behavior. These latter critics often complain bitterly about the impoverishment of the mind, and of the lack of warmth and glowing particulars in the behaviorist's picture of psychological events. Some of these criticisms merely reflect, of course, a lack of appreciation on the part of some "psychologists" as to the difference between scientific knowledge of an event on the one hand and everyday knowledge, or the kind of knowledge the novelist or poet portrays, on the other. Either by reason of training or because of their basically nonscientific interests, these critics have never really understood the abstract character of the scientific account of any phenomenon. The only reply that can be made to such a critic is to point out that the scientist's interests are quite different from his. There are, of course, other legitimate interpretations of nature and man than the scientific one and each has its right to be pursued. The behavior scientist merely asks that he be given the same opportunity to develop a scientific account of his phenomena that his colleagues in the physical and biological fields have had. If there are aspects of human or animal behavior for which such an account cannot ever be developed, there are not, so far as I know, any means of finding this out without a try. Unfortunately, the attitudes of too many psychologists with regard to this matter are not such as are likely to lead them to the discovery of such knowledge. The difficulty, I fear, is that too many persons whose interests are non-scientific have become psychologists under the mistaken impression that psychology is one of the arts [Spence, 1948, pp. 70–71].

We will now turn to an illustrative study of human behavior.[2]

INFORMAL OBSERVATIONS

It is scarcely startling to observe that when two individuals express dissimilar views about a subject, the subsequent interaction grows more heated and perhaps even violent. Both in observing others and in terms of subjective experience, one can note that disagreements about religion, politics, moral values, and even matters of taste may lead to negative evaluations of the disagreeing individual, anger, and at times to overt hostility. Further, the stimulus individual need not be physically present or even aware of the existence of the one responding to him. Thus, the negative response may be toward a political candidate speaking on television, the author of a book, or a newspaper columnist. The converse observation of two individuals expressing similar views followed by a subsequently more friendly interaction, may also be made.

Long before the advent of behavioral scientists, similar observations were noted. Jonathan Swift satirized the effects of such disagreements in politics and religion by discussing one of the major sources of dispute in Lilliput:

Besides, our Histories of six Thousand Moons make no Mention of any other Regions, than the two great Empires of *Lilliput* and *Blefuscu*. Which two mighty Powers have, as I was going to tell you, been engaged in a most obstinate War for six and thirty Moons past. It began upon the following Occasion. It is allowed on all Hands, that the primitive Way of breaking Eggs

---

[2] For heuristic reasons, a few liberties have been taken with the research example utilized here. For one, the attraction variable was reported as two separate scores in the earlier articles, whereas here only the combined score is reported. Irrelevant portions of the design have not been described, for example, the findings about need for affiliation in the second experiment. Strict chronological order is not followed. Finally, the research is limited to that conducted by the author and his students in order to be able to present a consistent and interrelated series of investigations using the same variables, same population, and same rationale throughout.

before we eat them, was upon the larger End: But his present Majesty's Grand-father, while he was a Boy, going to eat an Egg, and breaking it according to the ancient Practice, happened to cut one of his Fingers. Whereupon the Em-peror his Father, published an Edict, commanding all his Subjects, upon great Penalties, to break the smaller End of their Eggs. The People so highly resented this Law that our Histories tell us, there have been six Rebellions raised on that Account; wherein one Emperor lost his Life, and another his Crown. These civil Commotions were constantly fomented by the Monarchs of Blefuscu; and when they were quelled, the Exiles always fled for Refuge to that Empire. It is computed, that eleven Thousand Persons have, at several Times, suffered Death, rather than submit to break their Eggs at the smaller End. Many hundred large Volumes have been published upon this Controversy: But the Books of the *Big-Endians* have been long forbidden, and the whole Party rendered incapable by Law of holding Employments [Swift, 1726, pp. 40–41].

Actually, one need not journey to an imaginary land to find an example of the effects of attitudinal or belief differences on behavior. For example, the Christians of the fourth century were divided by a multitude of doctri-nal disputes, including that between the Homoiousians and Homoousians. The former group believed that the essence or substance of the Son is similar to, but not the same with, that of the Father. The latter group be-lieved that the essence or substance of the Father and the Son is the same. This difference of opinion led to war, murder, rape, pillage, and torture. With respect to Constantius' edict to enforce the "correct" belief, Gibbon observed:

The execution of this unjust law, in the provinces of Thrace and Asia Minor, was committed to the zeal of Macedonius; the civil and military powers were directed to obey his commands; and the cruelties exercized by this Semi-Arian tyrant in the support of the *Homoiousian*, exceeded the commission, and disgraced the reign, of Constantius. The sacraments of the church were ad-ministered to the reluctant victims, who denied the vocation, and abhorred the principles, of Macedonius. The rites of baptism were conferred on women and children, who, for that purpose, had been torn from the arms of their friends and parents; the mouths of the communicants were held open, by a wooden engine, while the consecrated bread was forced down their throat; the breasts of tender virgins were either burnt with red-hot egg-shells or inhumanly compressed between sharp and heavy boards [Gibbon, 1776, pp. 630–631].

GENERALIZING FROM OBSERVATIONS

Can any generalization be offered that would serve to bring together these diverse observations? One might speculate that the expres-sion of similar attitudes, values, and opinions evokes a positive affective response while the expression of dissimilar attitudes, values, and opinions evokes a negative affective response. As Heider [1958, p. 184] suggests,

"That similar people tend to associate and to like each other is the point of many proverbs."

In addition to proverbial statements, generalizations concerning the effects of agreement and disagreement have been made by many individuals, including Samuel Johnson:

JOHNSON. '. . . being angry with one who controverts an opinion which you value, is a necessary consequence of the uneasiness which you feel. Every man who attacks my belief, diminishes in some degree my confidence in it, and therefore makes me uneasy. . . .' MURRAY. 'It seems to me that we are not angry at a man for controverting an opinion which we believe and value; we rather pity him.' JOHNSON. 'Why Sir, to be sure when you wish a man to have that belief which you think is of infinite advantage, you wish well to him; but your primary consideration is your own quiet. If a madman were to come into this room with a stick in his hand, no doubt we should pity the state of his mind; but our primary consideration would be to take care of ourselves. We should knock him down first, and pity him afterwards. No, Sir, every man will dispute with great good humour upon a subject in which he is not interested. I will dispute very calmly upon the probability of another man's son being hanged; but if a man zealously enforces the probability that my own son will be hanged, I shall certainly not be in a very good humour with him' [Boswell, 1791, pp. 266–267].

Before proceeding to the stage of verification, we will pause at the level of observation-generalization and consider a description of the sort of behavior which has been described in stimulus-response terms. As a first step, consider a specific observational example.

Two college students meet for the first time while waiting to see a faculty member. The subject of integration arises, and one of the students expresses his views on the subject. He indicates that he is strongly opposed to integration for a number of reasons. Integration violates the social mores of the culture, it involves a mixing of two groups of individuals who are at different levels of social evolution, the Bible is against it, diseases would be spread, and intermarriage would almost certainly lead to the mongrelization of the races. After hearing these remarks, the other student says that he disagrees on every point and then is asked to enter the professor's office. When asked to give his impression of the student to whom he had been talking, the student in the office indicates that he does not like the other person, that he would not care to work with him, that he appears to be somewhat below average in intelligence, that he must not keep informed about current events, that his values are immoral, and that he is not very well adjusted.

Beginning with the complex series of stimuli presented by the stranger outside the office and ending with the other student's evaluation of that stranger, the behavioral events may be described in terms of the sequence depicted in Figure 2–1.

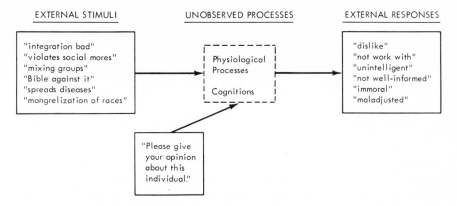

EXTERNAL STIMULI   UNOBSERVED PROCESSES   EXTERNAL RESPONSES

FIG. 2–1. *Sequence of stimulus and response events.*

Note that the term S in this S-R sequence refers to a series of stimuli which presumably have something in common. Both individually and as an integrated whole, these stimuli initiate a multitude of internal physiological and cognitive responses which, in turn, act as stimuli for other physiological and cognitive responses. At some point, overt responses are elicited, and various statements about the stranger are verbalized.

Though Figure 2–1 does provide a description of the specific observation in the example, it does not depict the more general relationship between similarity-dissimilarity of attitudes and attraction. That is, the Lilliputian dispute over eggs, the theological controversies about the essence of the Father and Son, Johnson's ideas about the effects of controverting someone's opinion, proverbs, and our observation of the two college students may be tied together by a general proposition: the greater the similarity of attitudes and beliefs expressed by another individual to one's own attitudes and beliefs, the more positive the affective response toward that individual. In Figure 2–2 the generalized sequence is depicted.

VERIFICATION OF GENERALIZATION THAT ATTRACTION IS A
FUNCTION OF ATTITUDE SIMILARITY-DISSIMILARITY

Proceeding from the level of anecdote and speculation, what steps are necessary to verify empirically the sort of generalization given above and diagrammed in Figure 2–2? Obviously, other anecdotes could be

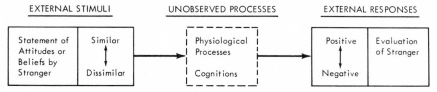

EXTERNAL STIMULI   UNOBSERVED PROCESSES   EXTERNAL RESPONSES

FIG. 2–2. *Generalized sequence of stimulus and response events.*

39

presented in which attitude similarity did not lead to attraction or attitude dissimilarity to dislike; other proverbs do exist ("opposites attract") which suggest a reverse proposition; quite different explanations might be offered to explain the cruelty of Macedonius and his troops; and Samuel Johnson's after-dinner assertions are insufficient grounds for a law of behavior.

Among other things, verification will require that we define the variables operationally so that any investigator anywhere could repeat our procedures. The somewhat arbitrary nature of devising or selecting appropriate operations should not be overlooked. General guidelines do exist to be followed in terms of standards of measurement, experimental design, and the like. There are no guidelines, however, for translating terms such as "attitudes and beliefs" or "evaluation of stranger" into specific operations.

An experiment was performed by the author [Byrne, 1961a] as one step in exploring the effect of attitude similarity-dissimilarity on attraction. In order to have a specific set of attitudes and beliefs about which subjects could agree or disagree, a list of 26 topics was obtained from a pilot group and built into a 26-item attitude scale which took the following form:

5.   Belief in God (check one)
          —— I strongly believe that there is a God.
          —— I believe that there is a God.
          —— I feel that perhaps there is a God.
          —— I feel that perhaps there is no God.
          —— I believe that there is no God.
          —— I strongly believe that there is no God.

23.   Political Parties (check one)
          —— I am a strong supporter of the Democratic party.
          —— I prefer the Democratic party.
          —— I have a slight preference for the Democratic party.
          —— I have a slight preference for the Republican party.
          —— I prefer the Republican party.
          —— I am a strong supporter of the Republican party.

The subjects who were selected for the experiment (34 college students) were given the 26-item attitude scale and simply asked to express their opinions on each issue. A few weeks later, each of these subjects was given another copy of this attitude scale, already filled out. They were told that students in another class had been given the same scale, and that they were being asked to examine each other's responses (name removed) in order to determine how much they could learn about one another from this information alone. The subjects actually received a scale that had been filled in by the experimenter. For 17 of the subjects, the "stranger" expressed opinions just like those of each subject on all 26 items; for each of the other 17 subjects, the stranger had opposite opinions on all 26 issues.

The response measure consisted of six seven-point rating scales dealing with their opinions about and evaluations of the stranger (shown in Figure 2–3). The last two items specifically ask about liking or attraction while the first four deal with various aspects of evaluation.

Fɪɢ. 2–3. *Interpersonal Judgment Scale*

Your Name: ————————

INTERPERSONAL JUDGMENT SCALE

1. Intelligence (check one)
    ———— I believe that this person is very much above average in intelligence.
    ———— I believe that this person is above average in intelligence.
    ———— I believe that this person is slightly above average in intelligence.
    ———— I believe that this person is average in intelligence.
    ———— I believe that this person is slightly below average in intelligence.
    ———— I believe that this person is below average in intelligence.
    ———— I believe that this person is very much below average in intelligence.

2. Knowledge of Current Events (check one)
    ———— I believe that this person is very much below average in his (her) knowledge of current events.
    ———— I believe that this person is below average in his (her) knowledge of current events.
    ———— I believe that this person is slightly below average in his (her) knowledge of current events.
    ———— I believe that this person is average in his (her) knowledge of current events.
    ———— I believe that this person is slightly above average in his (her) knowledge of current events.
    ———— I believe that this person is above average in his (her) knowledge of current events.
    ———— I believe that this person is very much above average in his (her) knowledge of current events.

3. Morality (check one)
    ———— This person impresses me as being extremely moral.
    ———— This person impresses me as being moral.
    ———— This person impresses me as being moral to a slight degree.

———— This person impresses me as being neither particularly moral nor particularly immoral.

———— This person impresses me as being immoral to a slight degree.

———— This person impresses me as being immoral.

———— This person impresses me as being extremely immoral.

4. Adjustment (check one)

———— I believe that this person is extremely maladjusted.

———— I believe that this person is maladjusted.

———— I believe that this person is maladjusted to a slight degree.

———— I believe that this person is neither particularly maladjusted nor particularly well adjusted.

———— I believe that this person is well adjusted to a slight degree.

———— I believe that this person is well adjusted.

———— I believe that this person is extremely well adjusted.

5. Personal Feelings (check one)

———— I feel that I would probably like this person very much.

———— I feel that I would probably like this person.

———— I feel that I would probably like this person to a slight degree.

———— I feel that I would probably neither particularly like nor particularly dislike this person.

———— I feel that I would probably dislike this person to a slight degree.

———— I feel that I would probably dislike this person.

———— I feel that I would probably dislike this person very much.

6. Working Together in an Experiment (check one)

———— I believe that I would very much dislike working with this person in an experiment.

———— I believe that I would dislike working with this person in an experiment.

———— I believe that I would dislike working with this person in an experiment to a slight degree.

———— I believe that I would neither particularly dislike nor particularly enjoy working with this person in an experiment.

———— I believe that I would enjoy working with this person in an experiment to a slight degree.

———— I believe that I would enjoy working with this person in an experiment.

———— I believe that I would very much enjoy working with this person in an experiment.

The mean responses of the two groups of subjects on each scale are shown in Table 2–1. For each rating, 7 indicates the most positive response (for example, very much above average in intelligence), 4 indicates a neutral

Table 2–1   EFFECT OF SIMILAR VERSUS DISSIMILAR ATTITUDES
ON ATTRACTION AND EVALUATION

Rating Scales	Stranger with Attitudes Similar to Those of Subject on 26 Issues	Stranger with Attitudes Dissimilar from Those of Subject on 26 Issues	df	t
Attraction	13.00	4.41	32	14.29*
Intelligence	5.65	3.06	32	9.37*
Knowledge of Current Events	4.65	2.65	32	5.51*
Morality	5.76	3.47	32	4.14*
Adjustment	6.00	2.71	32	9.36*

* $p < .001$

response (for example, average), and 1 indicates the most negative response (for example, very much below average). The two attraction ratings are added together to form one score with 14 indicating the most positive and 2 the most negative response. It may be seen that, as proposed in the generalization, the subjects responded more positively to a stranger with similar attitudes than to one who held attitudes dissimilar from their own. A similar stranger is better liked, and is evaluated as more intelligent, better informed, more moral, and better adjusted than a dissimilar one. Each difference was highly significant statistically. The generalization that attitude similarity leads to positive evaluations while attitude dissimilarity leads to negative evaluations is consistent with the experimental findings.

In some respects, we have not proceeded very far from the original observations. One might suggest that at this point we really do not know any more about the phenomenon than did Jonathan Swift or Samuel Johnson. We should note, however, that these new observations were carried out in a controlled situation and may be observed first-hand by anyone who cares to repeat the procedure. Further, with the variables operationalized and the behavior quantified, one may take some additional steps.

MORE PRECISE SPECIFICATION OF THE STIMULUS-RESPONSE
RELATIONSHIP

Where does an investigator proceed from this point? No printed sets of instructions or answers appear "in the back of the book" to inform experimenters which step should follow which, but there are a number of general modes of attack which make sense. One possibility is to obtain a more explicit notion of the relationship between the stimulus variable and the response variable.[3] In the experiment just described, two extreme points on a stimulus dimension were chosen: 26 out of 26 similar attitudes versus 26 out of 26 dissimilar attitudes. One might wonder whether such extreme differences in the stimulus are necessary to elicit differences in responses; certainly it would be unusual to encounter either type of stranger in real life. Further, with more points represented along the stimulus dimension, we should be able to plot corresponding points along the response dimension if a functional relationship really does exist.

To explore these possibilities, a new experiment was conducted [Byrne, 1962] in which only seven attitude items were used. With this small number of items, it was possible to present the subjects with all possible variations in proportions of similar and dissimilar attitudes expressed by a stranger. A total of 112 subjects filled out a seven-item attitude scale. As in the first study, the subjects later were presented with a copy of one of the scales purportedly filled out by a stranger. Subjects were randomly assigned to one of eight possible groups with respect to the relationship between the stranger's attitudes and their own. For one group, the stranger had similar attitudes on all seven topics, for a second group the stranger had similar attitudes on six topics and a dissimilar attitude on one, for a third group the stranger had similar attitudes on five topics and dissimilar attitudes on two, and so forth. In the eighth group the stranger held opinions opposite to those of the subject on all seven topics. Again, after reading through the "stranger's" scale, the subjects were asked to evaluate him on the six rating scales.

The results showed that a relationship does exist between the relative number of similar and dissimilar attitudes held by a stranger and attraction toward that stranger; complete similarity or dissimilarity is not necessary to obtain the effect. By means of analysis of variance (see Chapter 6), degree of similarity was found significantly to influence attraction ratings. With this information, we can say that *degree* of attitude similarity-dis-

---

[3] From this point on, we will confine our interest to the dependent variable of attraction as measured by the last two items on the Interpersonal Judgment Scale.

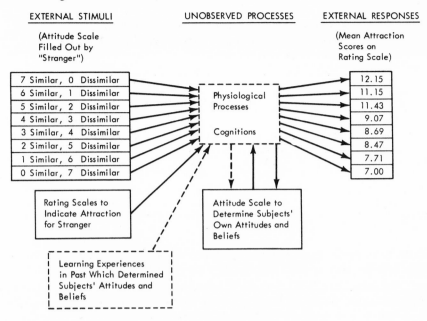

EXTERNAL STIMULI   UNOBSERVED PROCESSES   EXTERNAL RESPONSES

(Attitude Scale   (Mean Attraction
Filled Out by   Scores on
"Stranger")   Rating Scale)

7 Similar, 0 Dissimilar		12.15
6 Similar, 1 Dissimilar	Physiological	11.15
5 Similar, 2 Dissimilar	Processes	11.43
4 Similar, 3 Dissimilar		9.07
3 Similar, 4 Dissimilar	Cognitions	8.69
2 Similar, 5 Dissimilar		8.47
1 Similar, 6 Dissimilar		7.71
0 Similar, 7 Dissimilar		7.00

Rating Scales to
Indicate Attraction
for Stranger

Attitude Scale to
Determine Subjects'
Own Attitudes and
Beliefs

Learning Experiences
in Past Which Determined
Subjects' Attitudes and
Beliefs

FIG. 2–4. *Expanded behavior sequence.*

similarity significantly influences attraction—which takes us one small step beyond the original observations and generalizations. Our diagram of the behavior sequence now is expanded as shown in Figure 2–4.

The diagram depicts the behavior of various individuals under varying stimulus conditions. The response of any given individual can be predicted with better than chance accuracy simply on the basis of knowing: (1) his attitudes on the seven issues, and (2) the responses of a stranger on an attitude scale dealing with the same seven issues.

Given this indication of a lawful relationship between the attitude stimulus and the attraction response, being able to state the function in still more general terms should prove useful. One investigation [Byrne and Nelson, 1965] was conducted to determine whether the stimulus dimension consisted of *proportion* of similar attitudes, *number* of similar attitudes, or some *interactive function* of these two variables. Using 168 subjects and a series of attitude scales ranging in length from four items to 48 items, the same general procedures were followed as described in the two preceding investigations. The mean attraction scores for the various groups are shown in Table 2–2. Analysis of variance indicated that only the variable of proportion of similar attitudes exerted a significant effect on attraction. No effect was attributable to number of similar attitudes or the interaction between the two variables. Thus, one may identify the stimulus dimension

Table 2–2 MEAN ATTRACTION SCORES TOWARD STRANGERS
WITH VARYING NUMBERS AND VARYING PROPORTIONS
OF SIMILAR ATTITUDES*

Proportion of Similar Attitudes	Number of Similar Attitudes			Total (Proportion)
	4	8	16	
1.00	11.14	12.79	10.93	11.62
.67	10.79	9.36	9.50	9.88
.50	9.36	9.57	7.93	8.95
.33	8.14	6.64	6.57	7.12
Total (Number)	9.86	9.59	8.73	

* From Byrne and Nelson, 1965, p. 660.

in terms of proportion of similar attitudes and plot the functional relationship between this variable and the dependent variable of attraction.

Combining data from a series of attraction studies which had employed attitude scales of varying lengths with a total of 790 subjects, the investigators [Byrne and Nelson, 1965] plotted attraction scores as a function of proportion of similar attitudes as shown in Figure 2–5. A straight-line

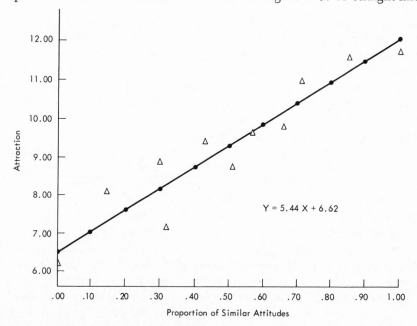

$$Y = 5.44 X + 6.62$$

FIG. 2–5. *Attraction toward a stranger as a linear function of proportion of similar attitudes. (Adapted from Byrne and Nelson, 1965, p. 661.)*

function was fitted to the data by the least-squares method. The solution yielded the formula $Y = 5.44X + 6.62$. That is, the attraction response (Y) of any subject toward a stranger can be predicted by multiplying 5.44 times the proportion (X) of attitudes expressed by the stranger which are similar to those of the subject and adding a constant of 6.62. At least within the limitations of the operations employed in these studies, we have progressed to a relatively precise statement of the relationship between a stimulus dimension and a response dimension, and this allows us to make behavioral predictions with greater than chance accuracy.

THEORY-BUILDING

Proceeding from informal observations through generalizations about these observations to a series of experimental investigations, we have arrived at an empirical law of behavior, the type of low-level law suggested earlier in the chapter. Such a law is quite specific in its description of a limited class of behavior and it provides predictive power. What is the next step? Obviously, being able to extend the generality of this S-R relationship would be advantageous. One possibility is to speculate as to "why" this particular stimulus has an effect on this particular response. One such line of speculation will be outlined.

Given data of the sort presented here, a number of investigators [for example, Byrne and Wong, 1962; Newcomb, 1956] have proposed that the most general explanatory concept to account for the effect of attitude similarity-dissimilarity on attraction is reward and punishment. That is, when one individual receives positive reinforcement from another, positive affect is elicited and directed toward the rewarding person. Negative reinforcement from another person engenders negative affect which is directed toward the punishing person. The relative proportion of rewards and punishments associated with a given individual is at least one important determinant of attraction toward him.

Why should the expression of similar and dissimilar attitudes have this effect? Attitudes in this instance are assumed to be a special case of reward and punishment. The motive involved is the learned drive to be logical and to interpret correctly one's stimulus world [Dollard and Miller, 1950; Festinger, 1950, 1952, 1954; Newcomb, 1953]. A child must learn the correct labels to apply to the stimulus events in his environment (for example, Mama, thirsty, little), the proper sequence of cause and effect relationships (for example, pulling down on the handle opens the refrigerator), and the distinction between reality and fantasy (last summer's vacation versus last night's dream). The learning which must take place is sometimes difficult, is spread over a long period of time, and continues throughout our lifetime. That is, we continually strive to make sense out of our physical and social world. Especially difficult is the social world of attitudes, beliefs, opinions, and values concerning politics, religion, race relations, and the like. About such topics there is simply no way to determine whether we are correct in making sense out of the stimulus data. When another person agrees with us and hence offers consensual validation concerning the correctness of our position, our "correctness" is supported. Frustration of this motive to be logical and correct takes place when others disagree with our views, when they offer consensual invalidation. Therefore, the finding that the expression of attitudes congruent with those of a subject elicits a positive response while discrepant attitudes elicit a negative response may be interpreted on a reward and punishment basis.

This particular line of speculative theorizing contains several distinct propositions, each of which could lead to the formulation of specific hypotheses which would be open to empirical verification. Speculative theorizing about the relationship of attitude similarity-dissimilarity to attraction suggests: (1) that interpersonal attraction is a function of the proportion of rewards and punishments received, (2) that there is a motive to be logical and accurate in interpreting the environment, and (3) that the expression of similar and dissimilar attitudes acts as positive and negative reinforcement with respect to that motive. We will examine briefly efforts to verify these three propositions and thereby attempt to extend the generality of the empirical law relating attitude similarity-dissimilarity to attraction.

VERIFICATION OF THEORETICAL PROPOSITIONS

1. Attraction Is a Function of Proportion of Rewards and Punishments. As a test of the first hypothesis, McDonald [1962] conducted an experiment, described in greater detail in Chapter 6, in which the drive was one of achievement or desire to do well in a task involving creativity and imagination. Subjects made up original stories in response to seven pictures, and each story was rated on a ten-point scale by another student (a confederate) who pushed a button that turned on one of ten lights to indicate the rating for each story. A proposition was made that variations in the proportion of rewards and punishments (high and low ratings) given by the stooge would exert a significant effect on the attraction ratings. Regardless of the merit of a given story, it was given a relatively high or relatively low rating according to a predetermined schedule. Each of the 192 subjects was assigned to one of eight groups. After the experimental session, each subject was asked to fill out the Interpersonal Judgment Scale with respect to the "other student." McDonald's findings were as predicted, as may be seen in Table 2–3.

Table 2–3   MEAN ATTRACTION SCORE TOWARD STRANGER
WHO RATED CREATIVITY OF STORIES

Creativity Ratings	Attraction
7 High, 0 Low	11.33
6 High, 1 Low	11.08
5 High, 2 Low	10.62
4 High, 3 Low	10.33
3 High, 4 Low	9.88
2 High, 5 Low	8.96
1 High, 6 Low	9.12
0 High, 7 Low	8.38

Taking McDonald's data and plotting them in terms of attraction as a function of proportion of high and low creativity ratings, Byrne and Nelson [1965] again found a linear relationship. The specific formula in this instance was $Y = 2.98X + 8.47$. Since the linearity of the relationship held across two quite different stimulus situations, the proposition is supported. A law of attraction was proposed as $A_x = m \, PR_x + k$ or attraction toward X is a positive linear function of the proportion of positive reinforcements received from X.

2. *There Is a Motive To Be Logical and Accurate in Interpreting the Environment.* The postulation of such a motive was based on an attempt to justify the suggestion that the effects of attitude similarity-dissimilarity are attributable to rewards and punishments. That is, this hypothesized motive is being positively and negatively reinforced by similar and dissimilar attitude statements. Empirical work seeking evidence for such a motive system is only in the beginning stages.

One research approach has been undertaken [Byrne and Clore, 1965] with the aim of devising a way to arouse such a motive and to measure the effects of this arousal. The assumption was made that this motive is activated in situations in which the meaning of stimuli is unclear, in which it is difficult to predict the sequence of events, and in which reality and fantasy are not clearly differentiated. Ideally, one would create a stimulus situation analogous to that faced by a very young child, or by a psychotic patient out of touch with reality, or by each of us in our dreams. Specifically, the stimulus actually used was an 8mm sound motion picture in color which was put together by the author and two undergraduate research fellows.[4] With three individuals independently taking random movie scenes and later splicing them together, the resulting 11-minute film is, at least, an unusual one. Scenes include ceramic figures of natives

---

[4] Daniel Stephaniak and Carole Hampton.

cooking a missionary, a chess game played with cosmetic bottles, a girl swimming, a confusing ride through the tops of trees, Mr. Ed, the talking horse, a car motor starting, seals, a battleship, and a great many other unrelated elements. The sound tract is predominantly the music of *Voodoo Suite*.

In attempting to get a measure of the drive, the experimenters asked subjects to give the one word which best described the movie, to write a paragraph discussing the meaning of the movie, and to fill out nine five-point rating scales dealing with how they felt while watching the movie. In addition to questions concerning how entertained, disgusted, anxious, and bored they felt, five scales were designed specifically to measure the hypothesized motive: feelings of unreality, similarity to feelings when dreaming, feeling of uneasiness, feeling of confusion, and desire to know what others thought.

In the experiment, 40 subjects were shown the experimental movie, and 40 were shown a control movie, *Life in Morocco*, which was a documentary sound color film of approximately the same length as the experimental movie. All subjects were told that the research dealt with movies as instructional materials, and that they would later be asked questions about the meaning of what they had seen.

On the rating scales the two groups responded quite differently, as is shown in Table 2–4. Analysis of variance indicated a highly significant

Table 2–4   REACTIONS TO EXPERIMENTAL VERSUS
              NEUTRAL MOVIE

	Experimental Group	Control Group
Feelings of Unreality	2.2	1.4
Similarity to Feelings When Dreaming	1.8	1.2
Uneasiness	2.3	1.4
Confusion	2.8	1.1
Desire to Know What Others Thought	3.3	2.0
Combined Score on the Five Scales	12.5	7.2

difference between the groups. In addition, the experimental subjects said that they felt less entertained, more disgusted, and more anxious during the movie than did the control group. In the open-ended responses, the words most commonly used to characterize reactions to the experimental movie were curiosity, interest, strangeness, bewilderment, confusion, insecurity, tension. Nevertheless, the subjects attempted to impose meaning on the movie by interpreting it as "showing the progress of time," "difference between savagery and civilization," "animal instincts of man," "life and death," and "thoughts of the man cooking in the pot."

Thus, some support has been gained for the existence of a motive to be logical and accurate and for some of the propositions concerning the effects of its arousal.

3. Similar and Dissimilar Attitude Statements Act as Positive and Negative Reinforcements. Golightly [1965] reasoned that if the reinforcement interpretation of attitude similarity-dissimilarity is correct, attitude statements could be used just like any other positive and negative reinforcers to alter behavior in a learning situation.

A 45-item attitude test was administered to a large group of introductory psychology students, and 60 students were selected to serve as subjects. The learning task consisted of a simple discrimination problem. The subjects sat in front of a wooden screen which contained a window for the presentation of stimulus cards. On each trial, a card appeared with a circle and a square on it. Each time, one was large and one small, one black and one white. Each of the eight possible combinations of shape, size, color, and position appeared in random order in each block of eight trials. Each subject was simply told that the experiment dealt with learning. A stimulus card appeared in the window, the subject chose one of the two figures and said it aloud, and immediately afterward a card was presented through a slit for the subject to read.

The discrimination to be learned was small-large. For half of the subjects the correct choice was "small," and for the other half the correct choice was "large." There were three groups of 20 subjects each. The crucial test was provided by the group in which attitude similarity-dissimilarity served as the reinforcing stimuli. For comparison, another group was to be given a more traditional type of reinforcement. The control group received no reinforcement. In the traditional reward-punishment group, the choice of the correct stimulus figure was followed by the presentation of a card with the word "RIGHT" on it; the choice of the incorrect figure was followed by the presentation of a card with the word "WRONG" on it. In the attitude similarity-dissimilarity group, the choice of the correct stimulus figure was followed by the presentation of a card containing a statement agreeing with the subject's viewpoint on one of the topics from the attitude scale; the choice of an incorrect figure was followed by the presentation of a card containing a statement disagreeing with the subject's viewpoint. For example, "There is definitely a God," or "There is no God." "The Democratic Party is best," or "The Republican Party is best." In the control group, regardless of the correctness of the subject's response, he received a card containing a neutral statement relevant to one of the attitude topics. For example: "Most modern religions are monotheistic." "Political conventions are held in large cities." Trials were continued until the subject made eight consecutive correct responses or until 96 trials were completed.

The findings are shown in Figure 2–6. Analysis of variance indicated that both the traditional reward-punishment group and the attitude similarity-dissimilarity group performed better than the neutral control group. Thus, in a learning task, performance was significantly influenced by attitude statements. This finding lends strong support to the interpretation of the effect of similar and dissimilar attitudes as reward and punishment.

Clearly, research involving creativity ratings of stories, response to a nonmeaningful movie, and discrimination learning has taken us rather far from the original observations of the effects of similar and dissimilar attitudes. Whatever the ultimate fruitfulness of the particular formulations

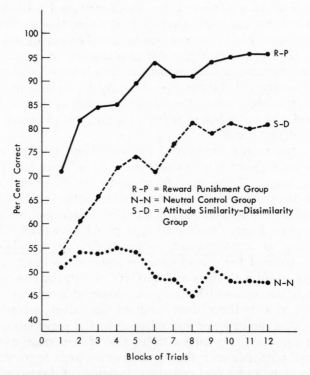

FIG. 2–6. *Learning curves for the three groups of subjects, showing percentage of correct responses over eight-trial blocks as a function of experimental conditions. (Adapted from Golightly and Byrne, 1964, p. 798.)*

presented here, hopefully this material is helpful in demonstrating the way in which research on human behavior may proceed.

With this brief overview of assumptions and procedure in studying behavior, we will now turn to a more detailed consideration of the five varieties of research which characterize the field of personality.

Summary

Among the assumptions underlying research in the field of personality is that concerning the lawfulness of behavior. This position runs counter to many of the thoughts and values characteristic of Western civilization; behavior predictability is incompatible with the doctrine of free will. Some individuals resolve the conflict by adhering to deterministic beliefs in the laboratory and a belief in free will in their everyday lives. Those in the humanistic movement reject a deterministic model of behavior as somehow degrading to mankind. Despite such objections, the assumption is made here that behavior in a given stimulus situation is predictable if the relevant antecedent variables affecting the person are known. A second assumption is that science can investigate only operationally defined variables. In order to achieve uniformity of meaning, to make clear which concepts are amenable to scientific inquiry, and to avoid pseudoproblems, variables must be reducible to concrete, observable operations or procedures. The meaning of an operationally defined concept is not necessarily identical to the cultural definition of the concept. Further, operationism does not imply a criticism of speculation or nonoperational thinking; it simply clarifies the difference between such activities and the formal propositions of science.

Science is a dynamic process in which a reciprocal interaction takes place between observation and conceptualization. Scientific activity begins with observation, often in informal, uncontrolled situations. As soon as the observations are expressed in symbols which go beyond the immediately observed stimulus, generalization to a class of events is taking place. Generalization constitutes the first step or the most primitive level of theory-building. Though everyone observes and generalizes about behavior, it is in the process of verification that science offers something unique. The primary concern of science is to carry out the verification procedure in such a way that one is not deceived into accepting that which is not so or rejecting that which is. The next step, theory-building, is the attempt to formulate increasingly broader generalizations which take the established relationships beyond the particular events involved in a specific observation. With theories, one may make deductions which lead to the making of new observations and to the unifying of previously unrelated empirical events in a more comprehensive framework. Many psychologists have used physics as a model to follow in building theories. At the present time, however, psychology is at the stage of establishing relatively low-level laws of behavior, while physics is at the stage of building theories which unify existing laws. Seemingly, a fruitful approach to theory-building in the field of personality is the establishment of behavioral laws and the construction of small theories dealing with specific and limited behavioral events rather than the development of a general theory of personality.

Among the many ways in which psychologists have conceptualized behavior is in terms of stimulus-response units. S-R units are simply abstractions which, hopefully, will be useful in building a science of behavior. As an example of research on complex social behavior, a sample of work on interpersonal attraction was presented. A common observation is that the expression of dissimilar views leads to negative interpersonal interaction and that the expression of similar views leads to positive interaction. Generalizations concerning the effects of agreement and disagreement on attraction have also been made. An attempt to describe this proposed relationship in stimulus-response terms was presented. Verification of the proposition that attraction is a function of attitude similarity-dissimilarity requires that the variables be specified operationally. An experiment was described in which the investigators found that response to a completely agreeing (26 out of 26 issues) stranger was more positive than response to a completely disagreeing (26 out of 26 issues) stranger. A second investigation used only seven attitude items and explored various combinations of partial agreement and disagreement. The findings showed that a relationship exists between degree of attitude similarity and attraction. Still another investigation determined that the crucial independent variable is proportion of similar attitudes rather than simply number of similar attitudes. With a large number of subjects, the relationship between proportion of similar attitudes and attraction was found to be a linear one, described by the formula: $Y = 5.44X + 6.62$. Theoretical speculation about such findings has included the suggestion that interpersonal attraction is a function of rewards and punishments received, that there is a motive to be logical and accurate which is satisfied by consensual validation and frustrated by consensual invalidation, and that the expression of similar and dissimilar attitudes acts as reward and punishment. Working from these speculations, one experimenter utilized high and low ratings of creative productions as rewards and punishments, and a linear relationship between the proportion of such rewards and attraction toward the stranger who administered them was found. In another experiment, an experimental movie was designed to arouse the motive to be logical and accurate; compared to a control movie, this film was found to arouse feelings of unreality, feelings similar to those of dreaming, uneasiness, confusion, and a desire to know what other subjects were thinking. In a third experiment, the proposition was made that if the reinforcement interpretation of attitude similarity-dissimilarity were correct, attitude statements could be used as positive and negative reinforcers in a learning situation. In a simple discrimination learning task, subjects were taught to make a small-large discrimination by the presentation of attitude statements similar to the subject's own views after correct responses and the presentation of dissimilar statements after incorrect responses.

Part Two

METHODOLOGY

CHAPTER 3

The Measurement of Behavior

Among the essential requirements of any science is the development of reliable and valid instruments with which to measure the variables under investigation. In examining the history of any given field of science, one of the progressive changes which may be observed is the steady improvement in measuring instruments through the years. Obviously, however, no advantage is gained in developing precise measuring tools in the absence of theoretical developments with respect to those variables being measured. At the same time, theoretical advances in the absence of adequate measuring devices are at best limited. Much of the history of science is made up of the reciprocal contribution of theory and technique.

As a relative youngster among the sciences, psychology suffers from immaturity in both its theoretical formulations and its measuring devices. Especially in investigations of human behavior, the problem of measuring response variables and of measuring personality variables has been a formidable one. In the present chapter, we will discuss some of the problems involved in such measurement and some of the solutions which have been developed to solve such problems. The reader should bear in mind that the measurement problems which face psychology are not in any way conceptually different from the measurement problems which have been faced by other disciplines. The major difference is the fact that analogous problems are being solved in different centuries.

Science and the Measurement of Variables

PHYSICAL SCIENCES AND BEHAVIORAL SCIENCES

An example of the parallels between the development of physical measures and of behavioral measures was given by Zubin at a symposium at Columbia:

The question is often raised about the lag between measurement in personality and in the physical sciences. We regard personality evaluation as still highly intuitive, subjective, and hence, unreliable and invalid. But all measurement begins in this fashion. The first measures of length, weight, time, temperature, touch, etc. were originally subjective, self-referred, and intuitively based. Let us look at the measurement of subjective warmth. Since there is no documentary evidence for man's initial attempts at gauging the cause and degree of subjective warmth, we shall resort to fantasy. Come with me to a cave in some prehistoric Ice Age, before fire was invented, and listen to a symposium on the origin of subjective warmth feelings. One savant declares that warmth depends on the number of skins covering the body. Another claims that it depends on duration of exposure to the sun. A third postulates swift running as the source of warmth and the distance covered as a measure. The medicine man in their midst raises a controversy because of his claim that his patients often report and feel warm without the benefit of any of the other factors mentioned. The sym-. posium ends without a resolution. But someone later invents fire and demonstrates that by adding faggots to the fire, subjective warmth is raised in all the inhabitants of the cave and by the same token removal of faggots reduces it. The first break-through has occurred. Man can manipulate an external agent to raise and lower the temperature at will. But this is still far from measurement. The first known historical break-through occurs in Egypt, where rating scales are developed for measuring warmth in four steps—with warmth likened at one extreme to the hottest day of summer, and at the other extreme to the coldest day of winter. Eventually, the expansion of mercury with increase of subjective warmth is noted, and the thermometer is born, and finally, humidity and air pressure are recognized as important factors, and the present day discomfort index emerges. What were the essential steps in the process? First, the discovery of a means of inducing a subjective experience by external control. Second, the development of an external criterion for measurement independent of the self-referred subjective experience. The same process, no doubt, held true of the other measures which have attained great objectivity. Pain is still a subjective phenomenon without an external criterion, and without measurable ways of inducing it, though recent efforts along these lines show considerable promise. Intelligence tests became objective when mental age scales were substituted for subjective impressions. Anxiety, depression, elation are still in the rating stage. In my fantasy, I sometimes imagine that we may find a life-bearing planet, somewhere in space, where anxiety has already been measured, but where warmth or length are still on the intuitive level [Zubin, 1965, pp. 194–195].

In Zubin's example, he depicts a gradual evolvement of temperature measurement from an original subjective period in which there were verbal labels for the concept and little else up to a stage in which there is relatively precise measurement with mercury level in a thermometer.

The major reason that the measurement of behavior appears to be a different sort of problem than the measurement of variables in the physical sciences is simply the difference in the ages of the different disciplines. The passage of time, for example, was an early measurement problem, and solutions included changes in the length of shadows, markings on a wax candle, amount of water passing through a small hole in a jug, passage of sand through a hole in an hourglass. By 1589, measurement was sufficiently precise to allow Galileo to investigate the speed of falling bodies. At the same time, measurement was too imprecise to allow him to confirm his belief that light had a finite velocity.

QUANTIFICATION OF MEASURES OF BEHAVIOR

What is there about a device such as a thermometer that makes it a measuring instrument? The primary characteristic of measurement is the ability to differentiate along a scale. The differentiation may be along a simple *ordinal scale*, which defines an order of events (hottest day in summer to coldest day in winter), or along a more precise scale with *equal intervals* (division marks on a centigrade thermometer). Quantification, the assigning of numbers to points on these scales, has been found to be of great utility in science because of the advantages inherent in mathematical handling of data. Generally, also, the finer the differentiation that can be made along a scale, the more useful is the measuring device. A two-point scale (hot-cold) is not as differentiated as the thermometer in your home, which in turn does not give as fine a differentiation as the usual instrument found in a research laboratory.

Various types of measurement differ in large part in terms of fineness of differentiation. As with variables in the physical sciences, the measurement of behavior can be approached via several measurement techniques. The measurement of intelligence will be used to illustrate these various approaches.

Ranking. One of the most simple approaches to behavior measurement is that of ranking individuals along a dimension. If an experimenter had no other measuring device available, he could ask a judge or group of judges to rank order a group of subjects from most bright to most stupid. This is a relatively primitive sort of measurement, and it brings with it a number of measurement difficulties to be discussed shortly. A special problem with ranking is that ordering becomes extremely difficult when the group gets relatively large. One can rank order three people in terms of brightness much more easily than one can rank order thirty people, and ranking 300 people is practically impossible. Another problem with ranking as a measurement technique is that it gives information only within a given group, and the information may not be applied across groups. The individual who is ranked number one in brightness in one group may be the brightest or least bright or somewhere in the middle in another group. It is advantageous when the measurement of a given variable moves beyond the stage of ranking.

Two-Point Rating Scales. A step in measurement which is about as simple as ranking is classification along a two-point scale: present-absent, hot-cold, small-large, long-short, true-false, anxious-nonanxious, sane-insane, smart-dumb. Whether the rating is done by the subjects themselves, an observer, or a group of observers, one can categorize each member of a group as falling into one of two classifications, bright or stupid. Here, the size of the group presents no particular problems, and generalization to other groups about the meaning of a classification is possible. Differentiation is extremely gross, however, and a finer measure is preferable.

Longer Rating Scales. Further differentiation and discrimination can be obtained with most behavior measures simply by extending the two-point scale into a longer ordinal scale. With intelligence, for example, the ratings can be made along a three-point, five-point, or nine-point scale. Instead of simply bright-stupid, a series of ordinally discriminable terms could be employed. For example:

> Extremely Bright_____
> Bright_____
> Average_____
> Stupid_____
> Extremely Stupid_____

When numbers are assigned to the above scale points, from 5 for extremely bright to 1 for extremely stupid, a measuring device is available which differentiates individuals along a five-point dimension. One difficulty with this approach is that meaningful differentiation beyond seven or nine points on a rating scale is very hard to obtain. Theoretically, the scale could be any number of points, but raters are ordinarily not able to respond that way.

Three difficulties are common to all three of the measurement techniques discussed thus far. First, close agreement between judges is difficult to obtain when judges are asked to rank or rate a group of subjects. Generally, agreement requires that the behavior in question be carefully and specifically defined, that the judges be well trained in making such decisions about subjects, and that they have spent an equal amount of time observing the subjects under the same or comparable conditions. A second difficulty is related to the first. The global nature of most rankings and ratings provides little or no information about the specific behavioral elements which entered into the decision to assign a given rank or rating to a particular subject. Third, there is a marked limit on the degree of differentiation which can be obtained with these measures; there are built-in restrictions on the fineness with which subjects can be ordered and discriminated. In order to obtain greater objectivity, a more specific identification of the behavior being measured, and finer differentiation, the development of other measuring techniques is necessary.

Utilizing Physical Dimensions. One familiar method of improving measurement in psychology is through the use of an existing scale from other sciences. For example, behavior can be measured in terms of *time,* and the objectivity and differentiation can be as great as in any other science because the measure is a well-developed one. Time has been used, for example, in measuring speed of rats in a straight-alley runway, time required by a group to complete the solution of a complex task, and length of time required to learn a series of nonsense syllables. One will note that the behaviors which are measured in this way must be defined in extremely specific terms. If an investigator's definition of intelligence included the ability to learn a complex task quickly, he could devise such a task and measure each subject's speed of learning with as much precision as existing timing devices permit. The quantification or dimensionalization of intelligence would consist of units of time with the smallest amount of time required to learn the task constituting the greatest intelligence.

Frequency. Still another way of dimensionalizing behavior is through the use of a frequency measure. A particular response (for example, lever pressing) can occur over and over. A behavior measure could be the total number of times the response occurred in a given situation or its frequency during a given interval of time. With intelligent behavior, as with many aspects of human behavior, the utilization of frequency measures brings with it special problems. For example, the number of times a subject could solve the complex task or define a word or supply a given bit of information would be meaningless. Human beings learn very quickly and grow tired of monotony very easily. Frequency of performing such tasks might be an indication of tolerance for repetitious tasks or compulsivity or lack of imagination rather than intelligence.

With studies of human behavior, most measuring devices have been built on a variation of the principle of frequency. Instead of determining the number of times a given response follows a given stimulus, frequency counts are made of the number of times a particular kind of response follows a variety of discrete stimuli which presumably have something in common. Frequency counts, then, are made across different behaviors which are presumably related. The subject is asked to solve a series of complex tasks, to define a number of different words, and to supply a number of different bits of information. The primary problem which arises in this technique is that of determining whether such a series of responses may meaningfully be added together to obtain a frequency count and hence to provide a dimensionalization of a given type of behavior. We will return to this problem in the following sections.

Reliability of Measurement

A variable is measured when one can order it along a dimension. The consistency with which this ordering is done is the reliability of measurement. Obviously, good measurement is consistent, and bad measurement is inconsistent. Inconsistency in measurement is labeled measurement error. In any field, instruments which are inconsistent provide data which are far from ideal to the scientist. A set of numbers obtained from an unreliable instrument is messy because such numbers in part reflect the variable under study and in part reflect random and inconsistent measurement errors. The lawful relationships which the scientist is seeking are often obscured partially or completely by the errors in the measuring device. Imagine the task of attempting to work with time measures if one's only instrument were a clock in which the minute hand moved around the dial in irregular stops and starts at varying speeds. One may note, however, that a considerable amount of psychological work utilizes measuring devices which are not much of an improvement over an irregular-interval clock. This fact should not be interpreted to mean that psychological measurement is doomed to unreliability by its very nature or that reliable measurement cannot be obtained. On the contrary, improvements in measurement methodology may be viewed as one of the great challenges and one of the accomplishments of current investigations.

STIMULUS CONSISTENCY

Identifying the Stimulus. Any measuring instrument utilized in psychological research may be conceptualized as consisting of a stimulus which evokes a response from the subject. The response is then quantified according to a particular scoring system. The term *reliability* has only recently come to be used in connection with stimulus consistency. Probably the major source of measurement error is the result of unintentional inconsistencies introduced by variations in the stimulus.

Never in psychological research can the investigator control or even specify all of the stimuli which are impinging on the receptors of an organism. When, for example, a test is administered to a subject, the test materials themselves are only a part of the stimulation to which the subject may be responding. In Figure 3–1 a typical situation is depicted in

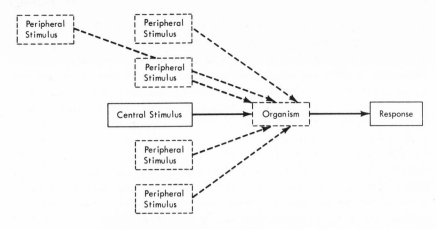

Fig. 3–1. *Central and peripheral stimuli.*

which the central stimulus could be a questionnaire test, a series of photographic slides, the verbalizations of a stooge, or numbers shown on an instrument panel. Even though such a central stimulus may be identified and so labeled by the experimenter, such an identification is to some degree arbitrary because the observed response may well be either entirely or partly a function of one or more of the peripheral stimuli which are also present.

Let us say, for example, that a psychologist is investigating responses to four cards of the Thematic Apperception Test (TAT); subjects are asked to construct stories for which each picture might be an illustration. The central stimulus in Figure 3–1, then, would consist of those cards and the accompanying instructions. Individual differences in responding to these cards might, if scored according to certain systems, prove to be a useful personality variable. Individual differences in response are not necessarily the result of differences along personality dimensions. For example, if the four pictures constituting the central stimulus were changed in some way for each subject, individual differences in the content of the stories might obviously be a function of differences in the pictures. While no experimenter would deliberately change the stimulus for each subject, the possibility of accidental changes is an ever-present hazard. Therefore, every investigator must describe the central stimulus in painstaking detail so that it may be reproduced as exactly as possible by any experimenter who wishes to study the same variable. Unless others are able to create the same stimulus on subsequent occasions, work with that stimulus cannot be of value in contributing to psychological knowledge. In this specific example, the four illustrations could be reproduced photographically, and the report of the investigation could specify such elements as the size of the photographic slides used, the type of slide projector, intensity of the light source, distance of the lens from the screen, distance of the subject from the screen, duration of the exposure of the slide, and the instructions given to the subjects during the testing session. Of course, distance from the screen or duration of exposure may have no influence on the content of the stories produced by subjects. Until research has demonstrated which variations in the central stimulus are important and which are unimportant, however, it is probably better to err on the side of caution.

An even greater problem in maintaining consistency of the stimulus variable is presented by the possibility of variations' in the peripheral stimuli which are not controlled, measured, or even identified by the experimenter. The room brightness may be indicated but room temperature ignored. Instructions may be reproduced verbatim, but the sex of the researcher or his tone of voice may not be identified. Subjects may respond differently if they are taking part in an experiment, a classroom demonstration, or a diagnostic testing session run by the counselling center. After the subjects assemble in the testing room, a joking remark by someone in the back row that this is a test of latent homosexuality may lead to different responses than when the test has been identified as a measure of verbal fluency. Voluntary subjects may respond differently from those who are forced to serve experimental hours. Differences in previous experiences with psychological tasks may lead to response differences. Even such variables as the time of day, month of the year, day of the week, previous events of the day for each subject, and barometric pressure may represent stimulus variables which contribute to response differences.

Even this partial list of possibilities shows clearly that a thorough specification of the stimulus is an almost impossible undertaking and one which has never been carried out in psychological research. The possible influence of any type of stimulus variation on any given response measure can only be determined by research. For example, it has been found that particular types of responses are influenced by the age of the experimenter [Mussen and Scodel, 1955], room decor [Maslow and Mintz, 1956], race of experimenter [Rankin and Campbell, 1955], the anxiety and hostility of the experimenter [Sanders and Cleveland, 1953], sex of the experimenter [Doris and Fierman, 1956], information about the purpose of the investigation [Henry and Rotter, 1956], and the presence of other subjects [Kimble, 1945].

The major point to keep in mind is that all such variations in both the central and peripheral stimuli potentially contribute to differences in the response among different subjects.

Equivalence of Different Stimuli. A related problem in stimulus consistency is that of combining stimuli which are known to be different in one or more ways but which are supposed to be equivalent with respect to evoking a given response dimension. For example, when several vocabulary items are administered in an intelligence test, these separate stimulus units are assumed to have something in common even though each vocabulary word is different from each other word. The only reason that it makes sense to combine responses to obtain a vocabulary score (number of correct definitions) is if the definitions of the words "orange" and "Mars" and "amanuensis" are in fact responses to an equivalent series of stimuli.

For a psychological test, items are judged to be equivalent if they elicit correlated responses. Thus, a test may be evaluated for this type of reliability by correlating each item with each other item or by correlating scores on half of the test with scores on the other half. Perhaps the commonest method is to correlate scores on the odd-numbered items with scores on the even-numbered items; the resulting coefficient is called the split-half reliability or the *coefficient of internal consistency*.[1] With the example of the four pictures, responses to slides number one and three should correlate with responses to slides number two and four. If this correlation is not a relatively high one (in the .80's or .90's), it may be preferable to study the four pictures as four separate "tests" rather than to combine nonequivalent stimuli and hence add nonequivalent responses.

The other situation in which equivalence of stimuli is essential is when two different stimuli or sets of stimuli are given the same name and are utilized as alternate, interchangeable measures of the same variable. A high correlation between the responses given to the two forms of the measure, known as the *coefficient of equivalence*, indicates that it is reasonable to utilize the two forms of the test as interchangeable measures. For example, if the four pictures in our example constituted a measure of hostility, an alternative form of the test, made up of four other pictures, might be useful. A necessary step, however, would be to determine whether the two sets of pictures actually elicit highly correlated responses.

RESPONSE CONSISTENCY

Identifying the Response. As with stimuli, an almost infinite series of responses are occurring at any one time as depicted in Figure 3–2. Again we may speak of central and peripheral responses, and to an even greater degree than with stimuli, the identification of the central response is in many respects arbitrary.

In the example of the TAT cards, certain aspects of the content of the material written by the subject are considered to be the central response, and all other responses are ignored. We may decide to focus attention only on phrases in the stories which deal with hostility and count the number of such phrases written by each subject. At the same time, we

---

[1] Since these two halves of the test are shorter than the actual test and since reliability is affected by test length, the correlation is multiplied by two and divided by one plus the correlation to obtain the corrected reliability coefficient. This correction is known as the Brown-Spearman formula.

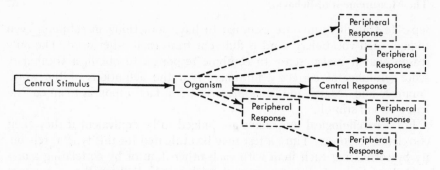

Fig. 3-2. *Central and peripheral responses.*

ignore the physiological responses of the subject, his writing speed, other overt muscular movements, the intensity with which the pencil was pressed, and so on. Even with respect to the stories themselves, all other verbal content is ignored, and the multitude of possible ways that the material could be scored (for example, number of words, noun/adjective ratio, size of handwriting, number of pleasant vs. number of unpleasant words) are not considered. Such peripheral responses may, of course, be related to the central response, and they may even form an integral part of what should be considered as the central response. Unless such facts are determined experimentally for a given stimulus-response combination, the experimenter must simply make the best possible decision about the identity of the response and ignore the rest.

Ideally, response measurement either does not affect the response being studied or the effects are known. If the subject knows that the response is being measured or if he can perceive the measurement process, the measuring technique becomes a part of the stimulus situation. Its effects on the response are usually unknown. Human behavior is quite likely to be influenced by the presence of a movie camera, a tape recorder, an observer who takes notes, or the knowledge that one's written material will pass into the hands of a psychological experimenter. So long as these conditions remain constant across experiments, behavior remains just as lawful as under any other conditions. However, one may tend to generalize too freely from situations in which the stimulus includes such elements to situations in which such elements are not present.

Finally, we should note that in identifying the central stimulus and measuring it, psychologists should obtain as complete a record as possible of other responses to store away for future consideration. If we find later that the central response occurs in close association with any of these supposedly peripheral responses or that one or more of them should actually be identified as the central response in this situation, predictive accuracy may suffer. For example, responses may be labeled as identical when they are in fact different had we also included certain peripheral stimuli in our definition. Hostile phrases written in response to a given picture accompanied by a rapidly tapping foot may prove to be quite different from the same description accompanied by a deep yawn. To consider the two sets of hostile phrases as identical may decrease our ability to predict either one. An analogous situation would be to examine only pie crust and assume that all pies are identical. The idea that pie crust plus filling forms a more meaningful unit to identify would constitute a methodological breakthrough in the study of pies. At psychology's stage of development, we can try to keep information about the pie filling on file until we find out whether we need it.

Equivalence of Different Responses. With respect to measurement consistency, the same central response must be identified each time a measurement is taken. Otherwise, inconsistency in the response measure may simply rest on the fact that different responses are being measured. Primarily this identification requires careful definition of the response and the way that it is to be quantified. In the example, "hostile phrases" should be described in some detail, preferably with examples of hostile and nonhostile material. The adequacy of such definitions and of the individuals who utilize them is indicated by the correlation between the scores of two different scorers who independently quantify the same material. Objective measurement requires that different individuals scoring the same response variable arrive at approximately the same numerical score. Without very high *interjudge consistency* (in the neighborhood of .90), reliable measurement is impossible. Careful training of scorers is helpful in improving this type of reliability. Ideally, response measurement is based on simple perceptual tasks (counting black marks on a true-false answer sheet, reading a number on a dial) which can be performed with almost perfect accuracy by clerical personnel.

A different type of problem with response consistency is that of stability over time. The *coefficient of stability* or test-retest reliability is the correlation between scores on two administrations of the same test over a period of time. Inconsistency in this respect could be the result of one or more of the other types of unreliability: changes in the peripheral stimuli, poorly defined response, unreliable scoring, and so forth. Possibly, variations in scores of otherwise reliable measuring instruments over time also reflect meaningful personality changes.

Validity of Measurement

Validity of measurement refers to the "truth" of the measure, the degree to which the test is capable of achieving certain aims, or, as is often stated, a test's validity is the extent to which it measures that which it purports to measure. As with reliability, different types of validity have been defined. The simplest form can be dismissed rather easily. Many texts dealing with testing refer to *face validity*. A measure has face validity to the extent that the elements which it contains are related logically or reasonably to the construct which the test is supposed to be measuring. For example, if someone constructed an intelligence test, the instrument would have face validity if it contained items such as vocabulary, arithmetic, reasoning, memory, and the like. An "intelligence" test which required the subject to exhibit strength, or inquired about his sexual habits, or tested his knowledge of Swahili would not be considered by most observers to be a likely intellectual measuring instrument unless there were a considerable amount of evidence to this effect. A more sophisticated derivative of face validity is that attribute which is labeled *content validity*. If a test is supposed to constitute a sample of a particular universe of items or situations or areas of knowledge, for example, evidence should be presented that it does in fact constitute such a sample. An algebra test, for example, should consist of items sampling this field. For most measuring instruments we do not have a definition of the universe of items, and hence there is no way to determine whether a specific test contains an adequate sample. Even if a test does have face validity and/or content validity, however, we still know nothing about the validity of the instrument in terms of the other three types. Two basic approaches to validity should be considered.

PREDICTION TO CRITERION IN APPLIED SETTINGS

The type of validity which is most often discussed in introductory psychology texts and in many measurement texts is really suited only to applied situations in which there is a specific criterion behavior which the test is designed to predict. Let us say that a manufacturer employed a number of workers on an assembly line who were engaged in the task of assembling radio parts. The employer would be interested in hiring individuals for this job who could perform the task quickly and accurately. If the training required to learn the task were relatively time consuming, it might be a fairly expensive undertaking to hire a new employee, train him for the job, and then find out that his performance was substandard. In such a situation, the development of an employee-selection device would be of great value. Each prospective employee could be given this test, and a prediction made about his future ability to assemble radio parts quickly and accurately. The decision to hire him could be based on his score on the test.

In constructing a test to predict a specific criterion such as this, the task would be to select items or behavior samples of whatever kind which required the type of ability needed for assembling radio parts. After following one of the test construction procedures to be discussed later in this chapter, the test constructor could determine the validity of his new instrument by giving it to a large number of prospective employees. After they had gone through the training period and were actually working on the job, samples of the criterion behavior would be obtained (for example, number of parts assembled correctly during five different 30-minute periods). The validity of the test would be the correlation between test scores and criterion scores. The higher the correlation, the more valid the test and the more accurately job performance could be predicted. If someone else developed another test to predict the same behavior and if it correlated more highly with the criterion than did the original test, the newer test would be more valid than the original one.

A great many tests of this sort have been developed. Thus, one could speak of the validity of a college entrance test for predicting grade-point average, the validity of a personnel selection device for predicting job performance, the validity of an audition for predicting performance in a play, and the validity of a physical examination for predicting illness.

A distinction is sometimes made between *predictive validity* and *concurrent validity*. The former refers to the correlation between test scores and criterion performance obtained at some subsequent time, as in the example given of assembling radio parts. Concurrent validity refers to the correlation between test scores and criterion performance obtained without an appreciable time interval occurring in between.

In spite of the reasonableness of the idea of face or content validity and in spite of the usefulness of the notion of predictive and concurrent validity in applied situations, none of these concepts is of particular use in evaluating most behavioral measures in psychological research. We must turn to another type of validity.

TO WHAT ARE SCORES ON THE INSTRUMENT RELATED?

Except for tests designed to predict behavior in specific situations, no one coefficient can sensibly be interpreted as describing the validity of a test. One can, however, talk about *construct validity*, which "is evaluated by investigating what qualities a test measures" [APA, in press].

Any other conceptualization of validity tends to create a certain amount of confusion when utilized to evaluate personality tests. The major point here is that no single criterion exists by which the test can be "validated." How, then, could one determine if a test of hostility or anxiety or achievement motivation was a valid one? Each of these personality variables refers to a multitude of behaviors. Tests which measure these attributes would be expected to predict behavior in a variety of situations.

Validity is determined by the investigation of as many relationships as possible. Scores on a test of hostility, for example, should be related to a variety of other test scores, to a number of other behaviors, and to responses in many kinds of experimental situations. It is not really reasonable to speak of such tests as valid or invalid. Rather, it is more realistic to indicate that a given instrument has been found to be related to such and such variables. The only meaningful validational question, then, is: "To what are scores on the instrument related?"

This approach to validity also gets us away from another sort of confusion concerning tests. Tests are often conceptualized as an artificial substitute for some other, real-life behavior in which the investigator is interested. The test to predict radio-assembling ability is an example. The test might well be composed of verbal and nonverbal material which involved behavior relevant to the radio assembly task. The test represents a short-cut or more simple way of measuring this behavior than actually placing the prospective employee on the job and seeing how he does. No one is interested in the test behavior except as a substitute for and predictor of actual performance on the job itself. Again, most personality tests must be conceptualized in a different way. A hostility test is not just a sample or artificial substitute for some other real behavior, any more than a thermometer is an artificial substitute for what we *really* mean by temperature. Rather, it is an instrument which measures a variable which should be related lawfully to other variables and which should be of interest in its own right.

One part of the validity question is that of the name of the instrument. Much of the research controversy concerning any given instrument centers around the seemingly minor problem of the instrument's name. Any test that is reliable is a measure of something in that it yields a consistent quantification of behavior. The name of that behavior and hence the name of that measuring instrument should be based primarily on the meaning of the behavior in terms of its relationships with other variables. If two tests have the same name, they should be related to the same variables and to each other. If two tests have different names, they should *not* be related to the same variables or to each other. Since such knowledge cannot be available to the test constructor the moment his test is put together, the name of an instrument should be thought of as a tentative label which is subject to change as new information becomes available. Perhaps one should always visualize a statement following the name of each test to the effect: "In view of the item content of this test and its relationships with other variables, at this time the instrument appears best to be conceptualized as a measure of hostility (or whatever)."

Constructing Reliable Measuring Instruments

Since most of the variables in which personality psychologists are interested are not yet well measured, a great deal of the work in the field of personality is concerned with the task of developing adequate measuring instruments for research and of improving existing instruments. Several approaches to test construction have been widely utilized by psychologists, and they will now be examined at some length.

INTUITIVE APPROACH

In any test construction procedure, the initial step is that of obtaining or originating a series of stimulus items which make logical sense as eliciting the sort of behavior in which the investigator is interested. There are no hard and fast rules to follow in this undertaking, and there is probably a liberal portion of both theory and art in devising any behavior measure. Once the items have been assembled, one of the other test construction techniques to be described may be applied in evaluating the items and hence in verifying the efficacy of the original selection process. In the intuitive approach to test construction, the initial selection itself is assumed to be sufficient for the investigator's purposes.

At first glance, it does not seem likely that simply assembling test items via the armchair approach would yield a reliable instrument. Throughout the research literature in personality, however, numerous examples exist of the usefulness of just this approach. As one example of the successful utilization of intuition in test construction, we will examine one of the many scoring systems devised for the Rorschach ink blots.

Hermann Rorschach, a Swiss psychiatrist, developed the ink-blot technique over a period of ten years, and he then published a monograph describing the test, *Psychodiagnostics*, in 1921. The general principles underlying all projective tests, of which the Rorschach is the prototype, is the notion that in perceiving and interpreting a relatively ambiguous and unstructured stimulus, the needs and emotions and thoughts of the perceiver are projected into his responses. This projection includes even unconscious material; hence, projective techniques were seen as a relatively disguised way of revealing to the tester or therapist those motives of which the patient was unaware. Various types of ambiguous stimulus material have been utilized in projective devices including cloud photographs, blots of ink, pictures, recordings of sound effects, and cut-out figures which the subject arranges in a stage setting. Rorschach worked primarily with ink blots, and after a considerable period of exploration, settled on five colored and five black-and-white blots.

Many techniques have been utilized in interpreting and scoring responses to these blots. Rorschach delineated a number of dimensions along which responses differed. They included such variables as form perception or the clearness and accuracy of perceptual processes, the percentage of animal content which was supposed to indicate the sterility of thought processes, responses to the white space which was interpreted as an indication of restlessness and hostility, and movement responses which Rorschach believed indicative of strongly felt wishes. Obviously, if this sort of test were in fact the royal road to the unconscious, it would be of extreme value in both application and research. In the United States, beginning in the post-World War II boom in clinical psychology, the Rorschach became the most popular testing instrument in clinical work and was utilized in literally hundreds of research investigations. The research yielded a great deal of negative data with respect to the reliability of many of the scoring categories, the accuracy of many of the assumptions about the meanings of the various types of response, and the utility of the test as a predictor of behavior. Nevertheless, many specific scoring schemes have proven to be useful behavior measures, and a sophisticated effort at constructing an improved ink-blot test has been carried out by Wayne Holtzman and his associates [Holtzman, Thorpe, Swartz, and Herron, 1961] at the University of Texas.

As an example of the intuitive approach to test construction, however, almost every scoring category devised by Rorschach and later investigators could serve. One such scheme which has proven useful is the Elizur hostility score. Elizur conceived of hostility as a general system of tension not tied to any definite object:

Hostility will denote feelings of resentment and enmity, which are often repressed in our culture but almost inevitably show up in the individual's distorted attitudes toward people, either being too antagonistic or too submissive [Elizur, 1949, p. 248].

His scoring system is based on the presence of elements of hostility in responses given to the Rorschach. A response in which hostility is expressed obviously and explicitly is scored H: "an angry face," "a type of face I hate," "two animals fighting," "a gun." Responses in which hostility is expressed to a lesser degree or in a symbolic manner receive half points and are scored h: "gossiping women," "the red represents struggle," "a primitive war mask," "teeth."

The reliability of this intuitively constructed measuring system was investigated in two ways. Eight graduate students at Columbia University independently scored the protocols of 30 volunteer students; the average intercorrelation coefficient among them was .82. The split-half reliability was .75. In addition, validational evidence was obtained in that this score was found to correlate significantly with indications of hostility in questionnaires, self-ratings, and interview material. In subsequent research a body of evidence has been obtained with respect to the relationships between the Elizur hostility score and other variables.

This scoring system and countless other possible examples demonstrate that the intuitive procedure can be quite useful as a first step in test construction. With care, a series of items can be selected which yield sufficiently reliable scores for exploratory research. It is assumed that, should the measure prove useful, greater precision could be obtained for future work if effort were expended on subsequent improvements in the instrument.

INTERNAL CONSISTENCY OR BOOTSTRAP APPROACH

Item selection can be improved beyond simple intuitive judgments about their meaning by determining the extent to which responses to a given item are in fact related to responses elicited by other items in the test. In a sense, the test is "lifted up by its own bootstraps."

The usual procedure is to begin with an instrument constructed by the intuitive approach. Rather than utilizing the instrument in correlational or experimental research, however, it is subjected to a series of test-construction analyses. Commonly, the instrument is administered to a relatively large number of subjects, and their responses are scored according to the intuitively based scoring system. Then, the relationship between the score on each item and the score on the total test is determined. A good item is one which is significantly related to total score in that it is measuring some portion of the same behavior dimension. A bad item is one which is unrelated to the dimension being measured by the majority of the items. In effect, this procedure provides an empirical check or verification of the investigator's skill in constructing test items and of his success in putting together a consistent measuring device.

As a second step in this approach, cross-validation is appropriate. Because some of the items which are found to correlate with the total score in the obtained sample are probably not actually related to the dimension in the total population, cross-validation provides a way to identify and eliminate these items. Generally, the entire procedure of administering the test, scoring it with the intuitive scoring system, and correlating each item with the total score is repeated on a new sample of subjects. Those items which are significantly related to the total score in both samples are considerably more likely to be consistent measures of the dimension rather than just chance relationships.

In the third section of this book, several examples of the successful use of the bootstrap approach will be given. The following illustration is drawn from an attempt to devise a true-false test to measure attitudes about food and eating.

From a number of different lines of interest, psychologists have theorized about and conducted experiments dealing with eating and attitudes about eating. For example, there has been a long-standing interest in child-rearing practices in relation to eating problems. Studies of parental behavior often include questions about parents' responses to difficulties associated with food and about the subsequent reactions of the child: weaning, eating a sufficient amount and variety of food, table manners. A typical finding is that of Sears, Maccoby, and Levin [1957] that the mothers of children with feeding problems tend to be relatively punitive, cold, and rejecting. In a somewhat broader way, various personality theorists have speculated about personality traits or types in which attitudes about food, oral needs, and various food-related behaviors play a prominent part. Examples are the oral-passive type of Freud and Abraham, the receptive orientation described by Fromm, Adler's pampered child, Horney's compliant character, and Sheldon's viscerotonic temperament. The behavior proposed by these theorists for such individuals includes a tendency to gain support from parents, friends, authorities, and God; a tendency to be optimistic, friendly, and loving when things go well and anxious and distraught when rebuffed; the seeking of consolation in eating and drinking because being fed is equated with being loved; conforming behavior; and a desire to please and succeed without effort.

In view of these considerations, it would seem of potential value to have a measuring instrument to identify those who fall at various points along a dimension of positive versus negative attitudes toward food and food related cues. The majority of the research in this area, however, has been confined to aversive reactions to specific foods.

The author and two of his colleagues [Byrne, Golightly, and Capaldi, 1963] felt that a much broader array of attitudes concerning food than simply aversions should constitute a personality dimension of possible interest and usefulness. To construct an instrument to measure this dimension, the bootstrap technique was employed. A true-false format was arbitrarily chosen. The first task was to write a pool of items which, it was hoped, would cover an array of eating experiences. A total of 221 items were written, and these were grouped into three categories. Examples of each are given below:

Past Attitudes and Habits

Discipline was usually enforced shortly before or after the evening meal.
My father enjoyed eating.
Less than an average amount of conversation occurred at mealtime in my family.
Business matters were often discussed at meals (chores, etc.).
Sometimes my mother would give me my favorite food when I was sick or unhappy.

Food Preferences

> I like apricots.
> I like chili.
> I like green salad.
> I like liver.
> I like sardines.

Present Attitudes and Habits

> In general, I prefer a slow leisurely meal to a quick, hurried one.
> I do not care much for desserts.
> A good wife must be a good cook.
> Watching people eat makes me hungry.
> I often buy refreshments at movies, ball games, and the like.

The investigators felt that neither theory nor past research offered a firm enough basis to permit reliance on the intuitive approach to test construction. On the other hand, there is no obviously acceptable external criterion of food attitudes. Therefore, the approach used was that of an internal-consistency item-analysis. An intuitive scoring system was devised on the basis of 50 items which the authors agreed were the best potential measures of food attitudes.

All 221 items were administered to 400 students (200 males, 200 females). The students were divided equally into two samples, the second for cross-validational purposes. All of the tests were scored according to the 50-item intuitive scoring system. For each sex, a frequency distribution was plotted. Kelley [1939] found that stable coefficients could be obtained by examining the responses of only the individuals in the upper 27 per cent and the lower 27 per cent of the distribution. For purposes of the item-analysis, the upper 27 per cent were assumed to be on the positive end of the food dimension and the lower 27 per cent were assumed to be on the negative end. Any item on which these "food likers" and "food dislikers" differed significantly would thus be related to the total dimension. For each of the items the information was tabulated as is shown in Table 3–1.

The numbers in the table represent actual data from the 100 males in Sample I for Item 9 ("Our family seemed to be in a better disposition at and shortly after meals than before"). Using a special table [Thorndike,

Table 3–1 ITEM ANALYSIS OF FOOD ATTITUDE SCALE

Response to Item	Lower 27% (Food Dislikers)	Upper 27% (Food Likers)
True	13	21
False	14	6

1949], we find that the response to this item correlates .33 with the total dimension. With 100 subjects, this correlation is significant at beyond the .01 level. The same procedure is followed for all 221 items.

To cross-validate, the entire process is repeated on the 100 males of Sample II. For Item 9, the responses were as shown in Table 3–2.

Table 3–2

Response to Item	Lower 27% (Food Dislikers)	Upper 27% (Food Likers)
True	13	19
False	14	8

The correlation in Sample II is .23, which is significant at beyond the .05 level. Since the decision had been made to retain only those items which were significant at the .05 level or better in *both* samples, Item 9 became part of the final scale and the scoring key is "true."

For the males, 62 items met the criterion of acceptability and were retained for the final scale. A repetition of the item analysis and the cross-validation for the two female samples yielded 65 items. With a new sample of 159 subjects, split-half reliability was found to be .73 for the male scoring system and .74 for the female scoring system. A total of 96 subjects took the Food Attitude Scale on two different occasions, separated by six weeks. Test-retest reliabilities were .86 for males, .82 for females.

A conceptually similar, but more elaborate, method of constructing tests via the internal-consistency approach is through the use of factor analysis. Instead of simply making up a scoring system and determining those items which are significantly related to it, factor analysis would allow us to determine the relationships and more specifically the patterns of relationships among *all* of the items. A series of items, such as the initial pool for the food-attitude scale described above, might be found to have not one dimension but two or more. These factors would presumably be composed of relatively homogeneous items which measure particular aspects of attitudes about food. The advantages of the factor analytic method is that the final result would be purer dimensions, each measuring independent components of the variables in question.

EXTERNAL CRITERION APPROACH: CORRELATIONAL

Whenever an external criterion exists for the variable being measured, it is possible and usually desirable to utilize it for the selection of items. Following the initial construction of an intuitively based test, items are evaluated in terms of their relationship with the criterion. When responses to a given item are found to be significantly related to the external criterion in both an original sample and in a cross-validational sample, that item is retained as part of the new testing instrument.

In the correlational method, responses to the proposed test items are compared with respect to groups differing on the criterion variables. The latter may consist of groups differing in scores on another test designed to measure the same variable, groups categorized as different on some basis (male-female, occupation, psychiatric diagnosis), or groups identified as behaving differently in some situation (success vs. failure in pilot training, high vs. low production on a job, successful vs. unsuccessful completion of psychotherapy). Those test items which do differentiate between such groups are assumed to measure some aspect of behavior which is different in the two groups; hence, test responses should be predictive of group membership and its related behaviors. This approach is a familiar one in test construction, and from many possible examples which could be drawn, the development of one of the scales of the Minnesota Multiphasic Personality Inventory (MMPI) will be described.

Until quite recent times, the care and treatment of individuals characterized by manifestations of abnormal behavior lay entirely in the domain of medicine. Thus, such terms as *mental illness, mental patients, therapy,* and *cure* are closely associated with behavior abnormalities. In addition, the names which are applied to the emotionally disturbed are based on a classification system developed by physicians. Emil Kraepelin, in Germany, noticed in his practice that certain behavioral symptoms tended to occur together in patients. With other illnesses, the classification of diseases according to symptoms was proving useful in that specific causes and specific treatments could be sought. Kraepelin regarded mental illness as organic in origin, and, in an 1883 psychiatric text, he described, classified, and labeled mental patients in a system that is basically the one followed by psychiatrists today.

Kraepelin's diagnostic categories have been modified and extended, and now they are used even by physicians and psychologists who do not adhere to the notion of organic mental diseases. One of the first steps in most institutions designed to treat mental illness is the diagnosis of incoming patients. Generally, psychiatric diagnosis is based on interview material, case history information, and observations of the patient's behavior. One difficulty with this procedure is that it is not as reliable as it should be. A reliable measuring instrument to supplement or even replace observational judgments would obviously be advantageous to diagnosticians.

At the University of Minnesota in the 1930's and 1940's, a psychologist named Starke R. Hathaway and a physician, J. Charnley McKinley, worked on the development of such an instrument. The external criterion procedure which they followed is best shown by describing the construction of one of their scales, Psychopathic Deviate. This diagnostic category is now known as Antisocial Reaction and refers to individuals who lack ethical and moral values, show impulsivity and irresponsibility, fail to profit from mistakes, seek immediate gratification rather than plan for future gains, put up a good front of external charm, have defective interpersonal relationships, reject authority, and lack insight into their own behavior.

The first step [Hathaway and McKinley, 1940] was to develop a pool of items. Originally, over 1,000 statements were compiled based on clinical experience, psychiatric examination direction forms, psychiatric textbooks, various instructions for obtaining case history material in medicine and neurology, and from earlier tests of personal and social attitudes. The final scale consists of 550 items to be answered true or false either on an IBM sheet or by sorting the questions (printed on cards).

Essentially, the procedure they followed was to administer the items to a normal group and to a group consisting of subjects fitting a particular diagnostic category. The answers of the two groups to each item were compared, and any item on which they differed was considered a measure of the behavior evidenced by the diagnostic group. For the Psychopathic Deviate (Pd) Scale, the criterion group consisted of patients diagnosed psychopathic personality, asocial and amoral type. They ranged in age from 17 to 22 years, and none were psychotic or neurotic. These patients had histories of stealing, lying, truancy, sexual promiscuity, alcoholic overindulgence, forgery, and other delinquent behaviors. The normal group, used in constructing several of the scales, was composed of 339 Minnesota residents and 265 high school graduates applying for admission to the University of Minnesota. The basis for labeling them "normal" was their statement that they were not under a doctor's care at the time of taking the test.

After item-by-item analysis of the two groups, an item was selected for inclusion in the Pd Scale if it showed a difference between groups of at least twice its standard error. After other comparisons and sifting of items, 50 were chosen for the final scale.

This scale has been found to have a test-retest reliability of from .71 [McKinley and Hathaway, 1944] to .80 [Cottle, 1950] with normal subjects. A great deal of validational evidence has been accumulated, including the McKinley and Hathaway [1944] finding that the scale differentiates normals from male prisoners diagnosed as psychopathic personalities at a federal reformatory and from patients with that diagnosis at the Psychopathic Unit of the University of Minnesota Hospital.

Similar test construction procedures were followed in developing the other MMPI clinical scales: Hypochondriasis, Depression, Hysteria, Masculinity-Femininity, Paranoia, Psychasthenia, Schizophrenia, and Hypomania.

EXTERNAL CRITERION APPROACH: EXPERIMENTAL

If one can manipulate experimentally the behavior to be measured, another possibility for test construction opens up. Rather than depend on correlations with other behaviors or on group differences, the investigator is able to bring about the condition he wishes to measure and then determine those items which measure it best. An experimental and a control group are used. Both groups receive the same prospective test material (for example, questionnaire items, projective test) but are treated differently with respect to some other stimulus condition. In a sense, the test constructor keeps the central stimulus the same for both groups and manipulates a portion of the peripheral stimuli in a particular way. For example, a page of incomplete sentences might be given to subjects in both groups, but the experimental group is insulted and frustrated just before the test is administered. Any differences between the two groups in responding to the incomplete sentences would presumably be a function of differences in the peripheral stimuli of insults and frustration. Item by item, those responses which differentiated the two conditions could be ascertained. After cross-validation on new experimental and control groups following the same procedure, a hostility scoring system for incomplete sentences would have been devised. When the test is then administered in further research to groups under neutral conditions, some subjects will be found to respond like the subjects in the experimental groups in which hostility had been aroused. Presumably, such subjects are responding to peripheral stimuli which are like those hostility-arousing conditions of the experimental groups. Thus, one could define such high scoring individuals as more hostile.

This approach to test construction has not been utilized as extensively as have the other approaches discussed. In part, this is a function of our inability to manipulate many of the variables we desire to measure. We have not, for example, been able to create experimental conditions to make subjects more intelligent, more prejudiced, or more hypochondriacal. Primarily, the experimental approach to test construction has been utilized with respect to motivational states which are manipulable: achievement, affiliation, sex, and the like. As an example of this approach, the measurement of need for affiliation by means of thematic apperception materials will be described.

Next to the Rorschach ink blots, undoubtedly the most widely used projective test in both research and clinical application has been the Thematic Apperception Test. The TAT consists of a series of 19 pictures (primarily drawings and paintings) and one blank card[2] for which subjects are instructed to make up stories. As with other projective tests, the TAT was developed as a way of getting past an individual's defenses to reveal unconscious material. The method was developed during the 1930's at the Harvard Psychological Clinic [Morgan and Murray, 1935; Morgan and Murray, 1938]. The work of Henry A. Murray will be discussed in greater detail in Chapter 9.

As with the ink blots, the TAT is not a test in the usual sense of the term. Rather, it consists of a standard stimulus which is administered in a relatively standard way. The responses which are obtained, however, are utilized in a wide variety of ways ranging from subjective interpretation of the whole protocol to intuitively based methods of scoring for certain variables to highly specific scoring systems based on careful test-construction procedures. One of the latter systems will serve as our example of an experimental criterion approach.

One of the needs described by Murray [1938] in his theory of personality was need for affiliation, often abbreviated as n Affiliation or n Aff. This concept refers to a general motive to establish, maintain, and restore positive affective relationships. Unsatisfied with existing subjective efforts to measure this need, Shipley and Veroff [1952] set out to devise a reliable and valid TAT method. Their subjects consisted of the members of two fraternities at the University of Pennsylvania. The two organizations were similar in social background of the members, status on the campus, and size; one was arbitrarily selected as the experimental group (37 subjects) and the other as the control group (45 subjects). Both groups were tested in their fraternity houses and both were given the same five thematic apperception pictures in a group by means of a slide projector.

Just prior to the administration of the test, the differential treatment was given. In the control group, the subjects simply took a food preference test because "the Navy was interested in the food likes and dislikes of young men." In the experimental group, an attempt was made to arouse affiliation need. These subjects were told that the Navy was interested in friendship patterns of groups. First, each man was asked to stand up one at a time while all the other subjects judged him on a rating sheet with respect to 15 characteristics (for example, conceited, entertaining, sincere). Second, they were asked to select the three individuals in the group whom they would choose as close personal friends. These sociometric tasks were intended to arouse the affiliative motive.

---

[2] Actually, there are 30 TAT cards plus a blank card, but only 20 are given to any one subject. Of the 30, 10 are given to all subjects, 8 only to males, 6 only to females, and one each to male adults only, female adults only, adults only, boys only, girls only, and boys and girls only.

In order to compare the two groups with respect to items in the TAT stories, an intuitive scoring system had to be devised. The investigators chose to score the material and compare the groups on eight categories of response:

Affiliation Imagery. Objective statement in the story that a person is separated from another and is concerned about it or concerned about possible separation.

Unrelated Imagery. No mention of an affiliative loss or separation.

Need. Statement of a desire for the recovery, maintenance, or attainment of a friendly or loving relationship.

Instrumental Activity. Someone in the story plans or acts to preserve or gain a friendly or loving relationship.

Goal Anticipation. Someone is anticipating the recovery, loss, or gain of a friendly or loving relationship.

Obstacle. Either personal shortcomings or environmental obstacles to preserving, obtaining, or recovering a relationship.

Affective Goal State. Statement of feeling or emotion about attaining, preserving, or losing a goal relationship.

Thema. When the main plot is concerned with gaining, preserving, or losing a friendly or loving relationship.

When the two groups were compared by means of t tests on each category, only Goal Anticipation and Affective Goal State failed to differentiate them. Thus, a scoring system based on the remaining categories could be utilized as a measure of n Affiliation. Shipley and Veroff cross-validated their findings using a correlational technique (men accepted and rejected for fraternity membership), and the experimental procedure was later repeated by Atkinson, Heyns, and Veroff [1954]. This scoring system was found to be quite reliable ($r = .93$) in terms of interscorer consistency, but later work on split-half and test-retest reliability [Byrne, McDonald, and Mikawa, 1963] suggests that further refinement is needed to increase the consistency of measurement. Validational data include the findings that, compared to low scorers, those high in n Aff are rated by their peers as more approval-seeking [Atkinson, Heyns, and Veroff, 1954], make more local telephone calls and write more letters [Lansing and Heyns, 1959], and are more perceptually sensitive to faces than to neutral stimuli [Atkinson and Walker, 1956].

GENERALIZATION OF TEST CONSTRUCTION METHODOLOGY

The foregoing discussion may sound as if the only type of measurement of interest in the field of personality is that of paper and pencil instruments. It may also sound as if the concepts of reliability, validity, and test construction apply only to such instruments. Neither point is true. Historically, much of the work on behavior measurement has dealt with paper and pencil tests, primarily because of their amenability to group administration and relative ease of scoring. As the field progresses, however, we undoubtedly will see an increasing number and variety of behavioral measures which are quite different in form from our present testing instruments. And, the concepts which have been discussed in this chapter apply equally well to any type of measurement. Let us take just one brief example of an observational measure to demonstrate what is meant.

If an investigator were interested in studying hostile mother-child interaction as a variable in his research, he would need to go through the same steps as if he were putting together a questionnaire. First he decides on a stimulus, in this instance an experimental room furnished like a living room except that it contains a one-way mirror for observation. Mothers and their children serve as subjects and are asked to "wait" in the room. Next he must make some decision about the responses to be scored. He might want to define hostile interaction as instances in which the mother punished the child physically, and he would need to define these responses so that observers could reliably identify them. He might want to categorize hostile behavior as physical or verbal and as directed from mother to child or from child to mother. Whatever decision he made as to responses, he would need to define them with care, to decide on the type of test-construction procedure to be followed, and to determine the various types of reliability of his scoring system.

With the intuitive approach, the investigator would simply define certain responses as hostile, determine the reliability of the scoring, and utilize this technique in his research. The bootstrap approach would require that a number of subjects be placed in the situation, their responses scored according to the intuitive scoring system, and the relationship between each type of response and total hostility score determined. Similarly, each type of response could be scored for the group and then a factor analysis performed. The correlational-external-criterion approach would require that some other behavior of the subjects be measured so that each response could be compared with these external evidences of hostility. Examples are paper and pencil hostility questionnaires, ratings by friends of the mother-child hostility in other situations, or judgments of hostility in the family by trained interviewers. The experimental-external-criterion approach would require that two groups of subjects be selected. The members of the control group would simply be asked to wait in the "sitting room" until the psychologist was free to see them. Those in the experimental group could be given insulting and frustrating instructions just prior to the waiting period. Differences between the groups would be assumed to be a function of the greater hostility in the latter group.

Summary

Among the essential requirements of any science is the development of reliable and valid instruments with which to measure the variables under investigation. Especially in the study of human behavior, the problem of measuring response variables and of measuring personality variables has been a formidable one.

The major reason that the measurement of behavior appears to be a different sort of problem than the measurement of variables in the physical sciences is simply the difference in the ages of the different disciplines. The primary characteristic of measurement is the ability to differentiate along a scale, and the most useful scales are those that involve quantification. Among the various possible approaches to the measurement of behavior are the ranking of individuals along a dimension, classification on a two-point rating scale, and rating on a longer ordinal scale. With all three of these techniques interjudge agreement is difficult to obtain, little information is provided about specific behavioral elements, and the degree of differentiation among subjects is limited. Techniques which in part overcome these difficulties are the utilization of physical dimensions and the construction of response-frequency measures.

The consistency with which a variable is ordered along a dimension is the reliability of measurement. Perhaps the major source of measurement error is in inconsistencies introduced by variations in the stimulus variable. When stimuli are combined as in a typical test, they must be equivalent in terms of eliciting highly correlated responses as determined by a coefficient of internal consistency. When two different stimuli or sets of stimuli are given the same name and utilized as interchangeable measures, they must also yield highly correlated responses as evaluated by the coefficient of equivalence. Response inconsistencies contribute to measurement unreliability, and difficulties arise in identifying the response and in determining the equivalence of different responses. Interjudge consistency in identifying the responses is necessary; the consistency of responses over time is determined by the coefficient of stability.

Validity of measurement is the extent to which a measuring instrument measures what it purports to measure. In addition to or even in the absence of face and content validity, one must evaluate instruments in terms of other types of validity. When the measure is designed to predict a specific criterion in an applied setting, its validity is the correlation between the test scores and the criterion. Depending on the time sequence of the test behavior and the criterion behavior, this type of validity is known as either concurrent or predictive validity. In personality research there is generally no specific criterion by which an instrument can be evaluated. Instead, construct validity is important, and the question is: "To what are scores on the instrument related?"

There are a number of approaches to the construction of reliable measuring instruments. In the intuitive approach, responses to some existing instrument or to a new set of stimuli are simply defined as the variable. Elizur's hostility scoring system for the Rorschach ink blots is an example of this approach. The internal consistency or bootstrap approach goes a step beyond the intuitive method in that the intuitively defined responses are evaluated by means of item-analysis techniques. The Food Attitude Scale was constructed by this method with the writing of items, item-analysis in which responses to each item were correlated with the total score, and a cross-validation in which the latter procedure was repeated. An external criterion may be used in test construction either with a correlational or an experimental approach. In the correlational method, responses to test items are compared with respect to groups differing in the criterion variable. The scales of the MMPI were built in this way. In the experimental method, the behavior to be measured is experimentally manipulated, and the response differences in the experimental and control groups constitute the criterion for item selection. The need-for-affiliation scoring system for the TAT was devised in this way. Test construction methodology is not confined to paper and pencil instruments but is applicable to the measurement of any behavior.

CHAPTER 4

Determining the Antecedents
of Individual Differences

In order to bring knowledge concerning personality variables into an antecedent-consequent framework, psychologists have had to devise methodologies designed to identify the antecedents of those personality variables for which measures exist. Thus, any time that a reliable measuring instrument becomes available for hostility or dependency or authoritarianism or whatever, one can then seek the antecedents of differences along such dimensions.

The antecedent-consequent model runs into certain difficulties, however, in the area of personality. Within an experimental situation one can manipulate the proper independent variables and influence temperature in a room, acidity in a beaker of liquid, or running speed of rats in a straight-alley runway, but a basic difference exists between this type of dependent variable and the typical personality variable. The difference lies in the relative complexity and generality and stability of the latter. Thus, the typical personality variable is likely to have developed as a function of a number of antecedents operating over a relatively long period of time, to be sufficiently broad as to be operative in a wide variety of situations, and to be of such stability that it is relatively unaffected by variations in the immediate stimuli.

Given these problems, the study of personality development has consistently been plagued with the difficulties involved in developing an adequate research methodology. In the present chapter, we will explore three broad classes of antecedent variables (genetic, prenatal, and experiential) and the types of research approaches which have been undertaken within each.

One further point should be mentioned. In spite of the difficulties presented, the study of personality development is potentially one of the most important areas of personality research. Knowledge of the antecedents of individual differences along personality dimensions is of theoretical importance because of the potential integrative power of developmental laws which involve the joint influences of heredity and learning on human differentiation. That is, such formulations should tie together a great many behavioral findings which are now independent.

With respect to importance in terms of the application of psychological knowledge, probably mankind stands to benefit more by altering developmental influences than through any other conceivable manipulation of variables. Seemingly the maximal possibility of developing intelligent, achieving, adjusted, creative, healthy, independent, adaptive adults is through a knowledgeable manipulation of the variables involved in conception, prenatal care, and child-rearing. Society's best chance of eliminating mental illness and crime or of increasing the incidence of intellectual genius and creative attainments will be through alterations in developmental influences rather than through efforts to alter the functioning of adults. With these laudable but distant goals in mind, we will turn to a consideration of present approaches to research in this area.

Genetic Determinants of Personality

Man has had some notions about the transmission of characteristics across generations for many thousands of years. The idea of breeding dogs, for example, in order to obtain a strain with desired anatomical or behavioral characteristics is at least 10,000 years old. It was inevitable that the concept would eventually be generalized to human beings. As a way of improving society, Plato in *The Republic* suggested:

It necessarily follows . . . from what has been acknowledged, that the best men should as often as possible form alliances with the best women, and the most depraved men, on the contrary, with the most depraved women; and the offspring of the former is to be educated, but not of the latter, if the flock is to be of the most perfect kind. . . . As for those youths, who distinguish themselves, either in war or other pursuits, they ought to have rewards and prizes given them, and the most ample liberty of lying with women, that so, under this pretext, the greatest number of children may spring from such parentage [Davis, 1849, p. 144].

Knowledge of the mechanisms involved in hereditary transmission was lacking until comparatively modern times, however. Progress was made by such individuals as Linnaeus who in 1735 described and categorized animals and plants into species and by Charles Darwin with *The Origin of Species by Means of Natural Selection* in 1859 which offered an explanation for the highly specialized behavioral and morphological aspects of species. We should note that Darwin's achievement with the theory of evolution was made in the absence of knowledge about the way in which inheritance worked. As he stated:

The laws governing inheritance are for the most part unknown. No one can say why the same peculiarity in different individuals of the same species, or in different species, is sometimes inherited and sometimes not so; why the child often reverts in certain characters to its grandfather or grandmother or more remote ancestor; why a peculiarity is often transmitted from one sex to both sexes, or to one sex alone, more commonly but not exclusively to the like sex [Darwin, 1859, p. 6].

MECHANISMS OF HEREDITY

The work of an Augustinian monk in a monastery in Brunn, Moravia constituted the first important step toward modern hereditary thought. Gregor Mendel investigated the crossing of different varieties of pea plants, and he traced the distribution of various characteristics through many generations. When plants of different varieties (for example, short and tall) were crossed, all of the first-generation offspring resembled one of the parents (for example, tall). He labeled such a characteristic as *dominant* and the characteristic which did not appear in the first generation as *recessive*. In further work, Mendel found that plants with recessive traits bred true, one-third of the plants with dominant traits also bred true, and that two-thirds of the plants with dominant traits had both types of offspring. To account for these findings, he proposed the operation of two elements in each individual (one from each parent) which determined a given trait. Any offspring of this individual would receive one or the other of these elements (on a chance basis) plus one of the other parent's pair. The possible combinations in an individual are AA (two dominant elements, dominant trait develops), aa (two recessive elements, recessive trait develops), and Aa (one dominant and one recessive element, dominant trait develops).

Though Mendel's work was first reported in 1865, not until its "rediscovery" in 1900 did it begin to influence other investigators. Mendel's elements, now called genes, were conceptualized as the basis for transmission. With advances in the technology of microscopes and in the use of dyes to study cell structure, cytologists found tiny bodies in cell nuclei which they called chromosomes. Each species had a characteristic number of chromosomes which were represented in every cell of each individual member of the species; the chromosomes were present in pairs which split in two when gametes were formed in sexual reproduction; and half of the individual's chromosomes were contributed by each parent. Genes were conceived to be extremely small structures which were located on the chromosomes.

As knowledge advanced, the laws governing heredity were found to be somewhat more complex than the principle of simple dominant and recessive characteristics. For example, some genes are only partially dominant, and an Aa offspring shows intermediate traits; genes located on the same chromosome yield a series of linked or correlated characteristics while genes on different chromosomes determine independent characteristics; genes on the chromosome determining sex will determine sex-linked characteristics; and an entire series of genes may contribute in varying degrees to a given characteristic. Genes seem to be made up of a complex chemical compound called DNA, and this compound may undergo changes, called mutations, which result in changes in the characteristics determined by the genes. Not all of the causes of mutations are known, but their rate is increased by such things as the application of certain chemicals, irradiation, and extremes of temperature. A further complication is that environmental variables can enhance or inhibit the development of a given characteristic, and this interaction of genetic and environmental determinants may operate differently at different points in the individual's developmental history.

With this very brief overview as an introduction, we will turn to the research which has been conducted on behavioral genetics at the human level.

FAMILY RESEMBLANCES

As is obvious, genetic determination of various anatomical characteristics is responsible for the physical resemblances which occur within a family. Similarities among siblings or between parents and their children are taken for granted with respect to such things as hair and eye color, height and weight, and a multitude of other aspects of physical appearance. The notion of behavioral traits as inherited and as constituting family characteristics is an old and widely accepted one. We will examine some of the ways in which families have been studied in order to gain information concerning genetics and behavior.

Determining Family Pedigrees: Social Adjustment. Among the earliest studies of family resemblance were those which traced a family through several generations and tallied the number of family members who were financially successful, received a higher education, committed crimes, and so forth. For example, Esterbrook traced the Jukes family over a 130-year period and 2,094 individuals. He found:

One half of the Jukes were and are feeble-minded, mentally incapable of responding normally to the expectations of society, brought up under faulty environmental conditions which they consider normal, satisfied with the fulfillment of natural passions and desires, and with no ambition or ideals in life [Esterbrook, 1916, p. 85].

A similar investigation was conducted by Goddard [1912] dealing with two branches of the family founded by Martin Kallikak. One branch descended from an affair with a feeble-minded girl Kallikak met in a tavern and consisted of 480 individuals who resembled the Jukes family in their poor societal adjustment. The branch that descended from his marriage were primarily normal and successful members of society.

Two major difficulties are built into the family-pedigree approach of which the Jukes and Kallikak studies are examples. First, criteria such as success or social adjustment, as judged on the basis of family records, newspaper entries, interviews, and the like, are somewhat tenuous and open to the possibility of considerable subjective judgment and inconsistency. Even with extremely objective criteria, however, an insoluble weakness remains. The family-pedigree approach necessarily confounds environmental and genetic influences. Common experiences as well as common genes are shared among family members. What is needed is a means of separating the two types of antecedents. With the development of objective behavioral measures and the use of statistical techniques, a different type of family-resemblance study became possible. As might be guessed, a great many studies focused on intelligence as a variable, but a discussion of the IQ data will be reserved for a later chapter.

Closeness of Family Relationship and Expectancy Indices: Schizophrenia. Besides the intelligence variable, the greatest amount of research interest has centered on psychopathology, especially schizophrenia.

Neither the older term, *dementia praecox* (mental deterioration at an early age), nor the newer term, schizophrenia (splitting of the personality), provides a very accurate description of the disorder. Though a good deal of popular writing has misinterpreted the "split-personality" label and mistakenly identified schizophrenia with multiple personality, the term actually refers to a very different sort of diagnostic group. The psychiatric label of schizophrenia includes a variety of kinds of reaction, types of symptom, and severity of disturbance. The common elements, however, include apathy or indifference to events in the surrounding environment, inappropriateness of emotional response, withdrawal from reality, and in fully developed cases, bizarre delusions and hallucinations. Since about one fourth of those admitted to mental hospitals for the first time are diagnosed schizophrenic, this type of behavior obviously represents a serious social problem. Knowledge of the antecedents of schizophrenic functioning is being sought by a great many investigators using a wide variety of techniques. One approach has been to seek evidence for genetic factors which predispose an individual to respond to stress with the characteristic symptoms of the schizophrenic.

The work of Franz J. Kallmann, a psychiatrist, is illustrative of one type of family-resemblance study. Over a number of years Kallmann [for example, 1946] has obtained data on the incidence of schizophrenia in members of the same family who differ in degree of genetic relationship. On the basis of such data, one can state the probability of schizophrenia developing in individuals related, in differing degrees, to a schizophrenic individual. If hereditary factors contribute to schizophrenia, such probability figures would be found to differ as a function of degree of relationship. As may be seen in Table 4–1, a summary of some of Kallmann's find-

Table 4–1   PROBABILITY OF THE INCIDENCE OF SCHIZOPHRENIA
AMONG INDIVIDUALS WITH DIFFERENT DEGREES OF
RELATIONSHIP TO A SCHIZOPHRENIC PATIENT

Relationship	Probability of Schizophrenia
Unrelated Person	.008
Step-Sibling	.018
Half-Sibling	.070
Full Sibling	.143
Fraternal Twin	.147
Offspring	.164
Identical Twin	.858

ings do support the notion of the contribution of hereditary factors. If an unrelated person living down the street develops schizophrenia, the probability of individual A developing the disorder is .008 or less than one in a hundred. If one of A's brothers or sisters becomes schizophrenic, the odds are slightly over 14 out of 100 that A will follow suit. If A is one of a pair of identical twins and the other twin is diagnosed schizophrenic, the probability is very great (.858) that A will join his twin in the mental hospital. Such data have led a number of workers in this area to accept the notion that to some extent the development of schizophrenia depends on the presence of specific genes.[1] As Book indicates:

The most likely explanation of present data would be that the schizophrenic psychoses are basically caused by major gene differences which express them-

---

[1] We should note that a great many criticisms have been made of Kallman's methodology and conclusions, and that many investigators question the evidence of a strong genetic component in schizophrenia [for example, Jackson, 1960].

selves regularly in homozygotes (i.e., in a recessive manner) and occasionally in heterozygotes (i.e., in a dominant manner).

As in other genetical diseases, it is obvious that schizophrenic psychoses are not thought to be caused exclusively by major gene differences, but that the effect of these genes is modified by other genes and, of course, by thus far unspecified environmental factors. The important conclusion that I think is fully justified is that major gene differences are the basic prerequisite for the initiation of a chain of events which may result in a psychosis. Unless this specific genetical prerequisite exists, the illness will not occur, provided we are not dealing with a supposedly rare nongenetical schizophrenic syndrome [Book, 1960, pp. 29, 31].

Comparison of Fraternal and Identical Twins: Personality Variables. In the data on incidence of schizophrenia just discussed, perhaps the most convincing comparison was that between siblings born at the same time (fraternal twins) and siblings born at the same time who also share the same genetic properties (identical twins). In his doctoral research at the University of Minnesota, Gottesman based his investigation of the heritability of personality variables on just such comparisons. In outlining the twin method, he pointed out:

Bacteria, fruit flies, and mice have contributed greatly to the body of genetic knowledge, but the application of this knowledge to the causes of variation in human behavior raises difficulties. Moreover, relatively few direct methods are available to the researcher in human behavior genetics because of such problems as those introduced by uncontrolled mating, small numbers of offspring, heterogeneous environments, and the uniqueness of one individual's heredity. Of the available methods, the twin method approaches the ideal experimental design. Galton [1875] first called attention to the possible usefulness of twins for casting light on the nature-nurture problem. The underlying principle is simple and sound: since MZ twins have identical genotypes, any dissimilarity between pairs must be due to the action of agents in the environment, either postnatally or intrauterine; DZ twins, while differing genetically, have certain environmental similarities in common such as birth rank and maternal age, thereby providing a measure of environmental control not otherwise possible. When both types of twins are studied, a method of evaluating either the effect of different environments on the same genotype or the expression of different genotypes under the same environment is provided. This means, with respect to any given genetically determined trait, that there should be a greater similarity between MZ than between DZ twins [Gottesman, 1963, pp. 7–8].

Gottesman compared 34 pairs of identical twins and 34 pairs of same-sexed fraternal twins (aged 14 to 18) on 17 MMPI scales and the 14 factors of the High School Personality Questionnaire (HSPQ) [Cattell, Beloff, and Coan, 1958]. Gottesman very carefully selected his subjects to insure a random sampling of the twin population of the high schools in Minneapolis, Robbinsdale, and Saint Paul. Further, he matched the two types of twins with respect to age, sex, intelligence, and socioeconomic factors in order to control as many factors as possible which could conceivably influence scores on the personality tests. Table 4–2 shows those scales on

Table 4–2 COMPARISON OF IDENTICAL AND FRATERNAL TWINS ON THE MMPI AND HSPQ SCALES

Scales	Correlation Between Pairs of Identical Twins	Correlation Between Pairs of Fraternal Twins	Proportion of Total Trait Variance Associated with Genetic Factors
	r	r	H
MMPI			
Depression	.47*	.07	.45
Psychopathic Deviate	.57**	.18	.50
Psychasthenia	.55**	.20	.37
Schizophrenia	.59**	.19	.42
Social Introversion	.55**	.08	.71
Welsh Anxiety	.45*	.04	.21
HSPQ			
Sober and Serious vs. Enthusiastic	.47*	.12	.56
Group Dependency vs. Self-Sufficiency	.60**	.15	.56

* $p < .01$
** $p < .001$

which there was a significantly higher correlation between the test scores of identical twins than between the scores of fraternal twins. These data represent further evidence that personality variables related to psycho-pathological behavior such as schizoid functioning and feelings of depression are in part the result of hereditary factors. In addition, behavior related to introversion-extraversion are in part genetically determined. How are such complex individual differences influenced by genes? Gottesman suggests:

Among the key constructs from genetics, *reaction range and polygenic inheritance* are central to the methodology used and interpretation of results. Heredity fixes a reaction range; within this framework a genotype determines an indefinite but circumscribed assortment of phenotypes, each of which corresponds to one of the possible environments to which the genotype may be exposed. The classical Mendelian model of dominant and recessive gene inheritance will not handle the data on continuous variation, the kind observed with human behavior. Polygenic systems are posited to account for quantitative inheritance, the phenotypic effects being simply a function of the number of genes present [Gottesman, 1963, p. 19].

EXPERIMENTS OF NATURE

When variables are not amenable to experimental manipulation, one may often utilize a naturally occurring situation as if it were a laboratory experiment. That is, real life variations in stimulus conditions are treated in an experimental design just as though they had been manipulated by the experimenter. This approach lacks the degree of control possible in a laboratory situation, but certain types of information can be obtained in no other way.

Comparison of Foster Children with Natural and Foster Parents. A rather obvious way to investigate the effects of genetic determinants on behavior would be to separate children from their natural parents at birth and place them in a different family. In this way, behavioral variables which are dependent on hereditary factors should be similar for children and their natural parents while resemblances between children and their foster parents would be expected for behavior dependent on learning. For humanitarian reasons, such experiments cannot, of course, be undertaken. Nevertheless, precisely the same situation is provided through natural causes when infants are adopted or placed in foster homes.

A number of research difficulties are presented by this approach. For one, an investigator cannot place particular children in specific foster homes in order to test a given hypothesis. The subjects must be utilized as they are. Second, obtaining subjects can be extremely difficult because placement agencies often do not wish to provide the names of children or of either set of parents, foster parents often do not wish to take part in a research project centered on the special status of their child (for example, some do not inform the child that he is adopted), and the natural mothers are frequently not eager to serve as subjects, especially in the instances where the child is illegitimate. The natural fathers are usually even more difficult to obtain as research subjects.

Despite such obstacles to research, a number of investigators have utilized foster children comparisons as a way of studying human genetics. Almost all of these investigations have been concerned with intelligence and will be discussed in Chapter 11.

Comparison of Identical Twins Reared Together with Identical Twins Reared Apart: Emotional Instability. Several ways in which twin data are used in research have already been discussed in the family resemblance studies. There is, however, still another possibility. In the relatively rare instances in which identical twins have been separated in infancy and reared separately in different families, a unique opportunity is provided to determine the extent to which behavioral variables are independent of environmental determinants. Any similarities between identical twins reared together are very likely to be a joint function of identical genes and nearly identical environments. Similarities between identical twins reared in different families are presumably almost entirely the result of genetic influences. If the foster home placements have not been chosen systematically on the basis of similarity, any resemblance between the separated twins is probably a function of hereditary factors. Further, if the degree of similarity is no different for twins reared under the two types of conditions, it is further suggested that environmental variables within a fairly wide range do not affect that behavior.

Again, intelligence has been of primary interest to investigators of twins reared separately. However, Newman, Freeman, and Holzinger [1937] included other variables in their classic twin study. One of these variables was emotional instability as measured by the Woodworth-Mathews Personal Data Sheet. The total investigation used as subjects 50 pairs of identical and 50 pairs of fraternal twins in Chicago and the surrounding suburbs. Each pair was reared together from birth. There were also 19 pairs of identical twins who had been separated in infancy and reared apart. These latter subjects were brought to Chicago for testing. Over a two-day testing period, all subjects were given a series of intelligence tests, a few other personality scales, and a physical examination.

In comparing the similarity between identical twins who were reared together with the similarity of those who were reared apart, the investigators employed a number of approaches. For one, they obtained the difference between the scores of the two members of each pair and then compared the two groups in terms of the relative magnitudes of these differences. On the emotional instability variable, no significant difference was found between the difference scores for the two groups: in fact, the twins reared together had slightly greater differences.

In addition, correlations were computed for the pairs comprising each group of twins for each variable. Table 4–3 shows the results for the emotional instability variable along with comparative data on a few physical measures. Obviously, any similarities in these six variables attributable to hereditary factors operate whether the twins grow up in the same or in different environments. Even though the correlations between identical twins in emotional instability are not as great as for the physical variables, we should note that in each instance the *degree* of similarity is the same irrespective of environmental similarities.

Another consideration, however, is the likelihood that the homes of the separated twins might by chance be very similar or very dissimilar.

Table 4–3   COMPARISON OF IDENTICAL TWINS REARED
TOGETHER AND APART

	Reared Together r	Reared Apart r
Standing Height	.98	.97
Sitting Height	.96	.96
Weight	.97	.89
Head Length	.91	.92
Head Width	.91	.88
Emotional Instability	.56	.58

The independence of emotional instability from environmental influence is further shown by taking this possibility into account. Five judges rated the two homes for each pair of separated twins in terms of how different they were with respect to educational, social, and physical and health variables. If environmental variables influenced emotional instability, the differences between separated twins should be greatest in those homes that were the most different. Twin differences for the 19 pairs correlated .04 with amount of educational difference between the homes, —.08 for amount of social difference, and —.29 for amount of physical and health difference. None of the three coefficients is significantly different from zero. The largest of the relationships (physical and health differences) is actually in the unexpected direction; the greater the difference between the homes, the less the difference between the twins.

SELECTIVE BREEDING

The technique of choice in studying the genetics of behavior is that of selective breeding. The built-in difficulties of the alternate approaches which we have been discussing may be highlighted by an analogy. If Mendel had been unable to control the mating patterns of his plants, the possibility of his deriving the concept of dominant and recessive characteristics seems remote. The observation of plants in a natural setting with uncontrolled cross-fertilization, extreme variations in soil and moisture conditions, and so forth, would make the laws of genetics difficult if not impossible to formulate.

Research on behavior genetics at the human level necessarily must be limited by such restrictions. As an alternative possibility, selective breeding may be employed in the study of other species. One of the possible outcomes of this research is the generalization of the laws to human behavior.

A number of controls should be observed in work on selective breeding as Hall [1951] has indicated. For example, the procedures for raising, handling, and testing the animals must not be allowed to vary because of the very great possibility that the behavior in question will be influenced by experiential variables. Similarly, uniformity across generations and across experimenters must be maintained for room temperature, feeding schedules, type of living cages, and the age at which the animals are tested; the animals should all be healthy and fertile. Any accidental cross-breeding should, of course, be made impossible. With environmental differences controlled, the effects of genetic differences may be investigated in relative isolation from extraneous influences.

Breeding to Obtain Differences in a Behavioral Character-istic: Emotionality. In a great many rat studies, emotionality is opera-tionally defined by the amount of defecation and urination in a strange situation. Hall [1938] placed one animal at a time in a brightly lighted circular enclosure (known as an open-field test) for two minutes a day for 12 days and recorded whether any defecation or urination occurred. Scores could range from 0 (no defecation or urination on any of the 12 days) to 12 (defecation or urination on each day). Hall began with a group of 145 rats and obtained their emotionality scores. The mean was 3.86. Then the rats with the highest scores were allowed to breed with one an-other, and those with the lowest scores were also interbred.

Through 12 generations, this procedure was repeated. Emotionality scores were determined, and then highest scoring and lowest scoring rats were selected for breeding with mates like themselves. The mean emo-tionality scores for the inbred groups for each generation are shown in Table 4–4. The emotional group shows a relatively systematic increase over

Table 4–4   MEAN EMOTIONALITY SCORES FOR THE TWO GROUPS
OF RATS ACROSS TWELVE GENERATIONS[*]

Generation	Emotional Group Mean	Nonemotional Group Mean
First	3.07	.46
Second	4.72	1.94
Third	3.92	1.02
Fourth	4.69	1.40
Fifth	4.96	.41
Sixth	6.87	.51
Seventh	7.82	.17
Eighth	8.37	1.07
Ninth	10.31	1.68
Tenth	10.41	1.45
Eleventh	10.11	1.05
Twelfth	10.40	1.65

[*] Adapted from Hall, 1951, p. 308.

the generations until they level off at the ninth generation. In a relatively short period of time, the two groups are clearly producing offspring which differ markedly in this behavior.

After pure strains are obtained with respect to a given behavior, pairs differing in the characteristic are allowed to breed much as Mendel crossed pure tall and pure short varieties of garden peas. For the last three generations shown in Table 4–4, Hall also mated pairs of emotional and nonemotional rats. As shown in Table 4–5, the offspring in each instance were much like the original group of 145 with which the research began. The amount of variability in the offspring indicates that pure emotional

Table 4–5   EMOTIONALITY OF OFFSPRING OF CROSSES
BETWEEN EMOTIONAL AND NONEMOTIONAL GROUPS*

Parent Generation	Emotionality Score of Offspring	
	Mean	Standard Deviation
Tenth	4.53	3.84
Eleventh	2.81	2.15
Twelfth	3.00	2.55

* Adapted from Hall, 1951, p. 324.

and nonemotional strains had not yet been obtained. We can conclude, though, that nonemotionality is dominant over emotionality because the emotional strain was slower in showing the effect in subsequent generations, and the offspring of the cross-bred rats resembled the nonemotional group more than the emotional group.

Prenatal Determinants

One of the most persistent and widespread beliefs concerning human development over the past centuries has been the idea that the experiences of a pregnant woman determine various characteristics in her offspring. A suggestion has been made that a frightening experience will leave its mark on an unborn child; for example, a mother who experienced fright at the sight of a gorilla would be likely to bear an ape-like child. A great many individuals believed that one could influence an unborn child's interests and attitudes through the activities of the pregnant mother; women would attend concerts and read the classics for the sake of the child's later cultural tastes. With increasing sophistication in the last several decades, these colorful beliefs are rapidly disappearing.

Probably in part as a reaction to these earlier propositions, it was taught for many years that the fetus is well insulated in the womb and hence is more or less unaffected by events occurring outside of the womb [Montagu, 1959]. Even though the mother's exposure to Beethoven may not have a notable effect on the musical tastes of the fetus, it has been equally fallacious to assume that the nature of all events which take place during the nine months of gestation are irrelevant. Probably the crucial factor is that the developing child is bathed in a chemical environment and is wholly dependent on the mother for the intake of nourishment and the elimination of wastes. These circumstances lead to the probability that the mother's physiological functioning should be of great importance in determining various aspects of the development of the fetus. We will examine a portion of the research in this area.

MISCELLANEOUS INFLUENCES ON INFANT HEALTH

Most of the research to date on prenatal influences has been in the field of medicine and has centered on such variables as premature births, infant diseases, and mortality rates. Though not directly related to personality, the impressive number of maternal variables which have been found to influence the health of the fetus suggests that increased behavioral research would be of great potential value.

If we combine such categories as miscarriages, stillbirths, defective development, infant diseases, and infant mortality under the term abnormalities of birth, a great many factors have been found to increase the likelihood of such abnormalities. The incidence of these problems is greater for women who are very young or very old, and for those who have high blood pressure, diabetes, or hyperthyroidism. Hypothyroidism in the mother brings about goiter and cretinism in the infant. When the mother and father are incompatible with respect to the Rh factor in the blood, the probability of stillbirths or infant deaths increases considerably. There are a number of infectious diseases that may be transmitted to the fetus with undesirable consequences; included are smallpox, chicken pox, measles, mumps, scarlet fever, cancer, malaria, tuberculosis, and some forms of influenza. When the mother contracts German measles during the first 12 weeks of pregnancy, the probability of having a defective child increases markedly. The bacteria which cause syphilis can lead to the death of the fetus, or if the infant is born, it may be blind, deaf, or suffer from a heart defect.

In addition to diseases, other factors have been found to have damaging effects. Simpson [1957] with a sample of 7,499 mothers found that as the number of cigarettes smoked per day increases, the percentage of premature babies increases. Massive doses of X rays early in pregnancy lead to various abnormalities of birth. The nutrition of mothers during gestation has been found to have an effect on the rate of miscarriages, stillbirths, premature births, infant deaths, diseases during the first six months of life, birth weight, and even IQ of the child, as will be discussed in Chapter 11.

MATERNAL AGE AND MONGOLOIDISM

From the age of 35 on, women who bear children are increasingly likely to produce a mentally defective child classified as mongoloid (half of the cases are born to mothers 35 and over). The name was given to the disorder because there is some physical resemblance between these children and members of the Mongoloid race such as an epicanthic fold over the eye and a relatively flat nose. These children tend to have low IQ's (15 to 25), to be cheerful and friendly, to imitate various things they see and hear, and to die in early childhood.

Research suggests that hormonal changes associated with aging are responsible for the improper development of the fetus. Presumably, it will eventually be possible to supply the proper hormones to the pregnant woman, thus changing the prenatal environment and thereby preventing developmental anomolies such as mongoloidism [Montagu, 1959].

EMOTIONAL STRESS AND CLEFT PALATE

Severe emotional stress during the first ten weeks of pregnancy may be responsible for the development of a cleft palate in the fetus. In addition to clinical evidence with human subjects, animal research provides some impressive support. One of the concomitants of stress is the secretion of hydrocortisone. When this hormone is injected into pregnant mice or rats at the period when the palate is being formed in the embryo, almost 90 per cent of the offspring are born with cleft palates [Montagu, 1959].

EMOTIONAL STRESS OF MOTHER AND EMOTIONALITY
IN THE OFFSPRING

As with the cleft palate research, experimental investigations of prenatal influences tend to be limited to subjects below the human level. Much research interest has centered on maternal anxiety or stress, utilizing rats as subjects.

Ader and Belfer [1962] conditioned 20 female rats to press a lever when a light and buzzer were presented in order to avoid receiving an electric shock. After learning, the animals were mated with randomly selected males. When the females became pregnant, they were randomly assigned to either the experimental or control group. The experimental females were returned to the conditioning apparatus twice a day, the light and buzzer were presented once each time, but no more electric shock was administered. The rats in the control group did not undergo this experience.

When the litters were born, a portion of the offspring in each group was reared by their natural mothers and a portion was reared by mothers in the other group in order to control for postnatal influences on behavior. When the offspring were between 30 and 40 days old, they were tested for emotionality in an open-field situation in one one-minute trial. Both amount of defecation and amount of movement in the open field were recorded. Defecation increases and movement decreases with emotionality. After the animals were 135 days old, the test was repeated.

In the open-field test, the offspring of the experimental mothers were significantly less active than the offspring of the control mothers, regardless of whether they were reared by their own mothers or mothers from the other group. The differences were no longer present by the time of the second test. There were no significant differences in defecation. Thus, there is some evidence that maternal stress experienced during pregnancy has an effect on the early behavior of the offspring.

POSITIVE EMOTIONAL EXPERIENCES OF MOTHER AND
EMOTIONALITY IN THE OFFSPRING

Perhaps the opposite of subjecting the pregnant mother to stress is not simply a nonstress control experience but some sort of positive experience. One such manipulation that has been utilized in rat research is that of "handling" at regular intervals by the experimenter.

Ader and Conklin [1963] randomly assigned pregnant rats to either an experimental or control group. Those in the experimental group were handled for 10 minutes at a time three times a day (morning, afternoon, and evening) throughout pregnancy. Each time, the animal was picked up and held loosely in one hand. The mothers in the control group were not handled.

Again, at birth a portion of the "pups" was given to foster mothers either in the other group or in the same group. Approximately half of the animals were tested for emotionality in the open field test at 45 days and half were tested at 120 days. Both movement and defecation were measured.

In this experiment, movement in the open field was unrelated to whether the mother had been handled or not. Both at 45 days and at 100 days, however, significantly more of the offspring of the control group mothers defecated than did the offspring of the handled mothers. Presumably, the handling experienced by the mothers during pregnancy decreased the amount of emotionality in the offspring, and this effect still held after the offspring were 100 days old.

Experiential Determinants of Personality

By far the greatest amount of research on the antecedents of personality has been concerned with experience. Studies of child-rearing attitudes and practices, of childhood learning, and of cultural influences on development all fit within this general framework.

Once again, we should note the existence of a number of general obstacles to research of this type. Naturalistic observation of the interaction of parents and their children is almost impossible to conduct. In the instances in which an investigator has visited within the home setting or families have been brought to an observation room, obviously the behavior is likely to be a seriously distorted version of that which normally occurs. The use of hidden microphones and cameras placed in homes without the knowledge of the occupants would overcome the artificiality problem but would create much more serious ethical and legal difficulties.

A second and more practical approach is to ask individuals about their child-rearing attitudes or experiences. As with observations, distortion by the subjects obviously occurs because of faulty memory, conscious or unconscious tendencies to present themselves in a favorable light to the experimenter, and even misperception of motives, attitudes, and responses. Even with the best of intentions, one has difficulty remembering accurately various aspects of past interactions in the family. Robbins [1963] compared the child-rearing information given by parents of three-year-olds with reports they previously gave in a series of interviews beginning with the birth of the child. The questions included such things as the child's birth weight, age of weaning, age at which bladder training was begun, whether he sucked his thumb, and how well he slept at six months. The parents were quite inaccurate in remembering such details, especially items such as weaning and toilet training and thumbsucking, and the inaccuracies tended to be in the direction of the recommendations of child-rearing experts. Yarrow points out:

> Stripped of all elaborations, mothers' interview responses represent self-descriptions by extremely ego-involved reporters. In addition, for the much-studied middle and upper-middle class mothers, these are self-reports in an area in which prescriptions and taboos have been dinned into the culture through *Ladies Home Journal* as well as Spock or Gesell or Children's Bureau. How well then can we expect the mother to report interactions of which she is a part and on which the culture has placed distinct values? [Yarrow, 1963, p. 217]

Other investigators attempt to eliminate these problems by utilizing experiments of nature and by conducting laboratory experiments with children and with infrahuman animals.

We should note that the difficulties and obstacles to research noted here do not in any way devalue the research which has been done. There is certainly no reason to suppose that lawful relationships cannot be established with respect to behavior elicited in artificial observational settings, in verbal questionnaires about child rearing, or in animal research on the effects of early experience. The only cautions to be noted are that the *direct study* of family interactions cannot be attempted and that the *immediate application* of the findings of other types of investigations to actual child-rearing practices is very likely to be a mistake. Information for parents which informs them that X behavior on their part will lead to Y behavior on the part of their offspring is still an unattained goal and not an immediate product of current research on experiential antecedents.

CORRELATES OF CHILD-REARING ATTITUDES AND PRACTICES

In addition to the investigation of the effects of parental behavior on the behavior of their offspring, some research interest has centered on the question of the determinants of the differences in child-rearing practices. The variables studied have included socioeconomic class, personality differences, and the type of child-rearing advice to which parents are exposed.

Socioeconomic Class. The child-rearing attitudes and practices of parents have been found to be in part a function of the socioeconomic class to which the parents belong. Class membership means many things, of course. Different class levels involve differences in income, in occupation, and in education for example. Any findings concerning the effects of class must eventually be explained in terms of more basic variables such as differences in attitudes developed by a high school vs. a college graduate.

Bayley and Schaefer [1960] sought to find relationships between socioeconomic variables and observational ratings of maternal behavior. The subjects were part of the Berkeley Growth Study [Jones and Bayley, 1941]. A group of 56 mothers were observed and rated on nine characteristics at testing periods during the first three years of their child's life. A subsample of 34 of these mothers was interviewed several years later, and the same variables were rated in this interview situation. The judges who made the ratings were unaware of the socioeconomic status of the subjects. The socioeconomic variables which were used were number of years of education of each parent, father's occupational level, family income, social rating of the home and neighborhood, and a total socioeconomic scale consisting of all of the indices combined. In general, these variables correlate highly with one another, averaging about .60. An additional variable, sociocultural level, was obtained from ratings made by an interviewer who visited the home. The findings regarding the relationship between socioeconomic level and child-rearing behavior may be summarized fairly briefly:

Socioeconomic Level	Socioeconomic Level
Correlates Positively with:	Correlates Negatively with:
Granting Autonomy	Excessive Contact
Cooperation	Punitiveness
Equalitarian Treatment	Intrusiveness
Expressing Affection	Irritability
	Ignoring of Child

Bayley and Schaefer comment:

Although the relationships are very moderate, these findings are in the direction of agreement with other studies that indicate warmer, more accepting, and permissive attitudes among the higher S-E status mothers, and more dominating and punitive attitudes among the lower status mothers [Bayley and Schaefer, 1960, p. 69].

To the extent that differences in the mother's behavior along these dimensions lead to consistent behavioral differences in their children, the variables associated with the family's socioeconomic status must be included in formulations of personality antecedents.

Needs. The Parental Attitude Research Inventory or PARI was developed by Schaefer and Bell [1958] to measure 23 different parental attitudes. A subsequent factor-analysis by Zuckerman, Barrett-Ribback, and Monashkin [1958] indicated that the PARI scales actually measure three attitudinal dimensions: Authoritarian-Control (authoritarian, suppressive, punitive, and restricting attitudes), Hostility-Rejection (hostility towards children and husband and rejection of the maternal role), and Democratic Attitude (equalitarian beliefs and values). Presumably, these three dimensions would be related to other personality variables in the parents as well as to their children's behavior.

A portion of an investigation by Zuckerman and Oltean [1959] dealt with the relationship between child-rearing attitudes as measured by the PARI and certain of the motivational variables measured by the Edwards Personal Preference Schedule or EPPS [Edwards, 1954] in a group of 24 mothers of college students. The relationship between the two types of variables is shown in Table 4–6. As the table shows, the mother who tends to be hostile and rejecting also tends to have a high need for achievement, a low need for nurturance, a high need for aggression, and a low need for affiliation. A very similar pattern holds for the Authoritarian-Control attitudes.

We should point out that this type of investigation strongly suggests that child-rearing attitudes and practices are not isolated behavioral acts.

Table 4–6   CORRELATIONS BETWEEN PARI CHILD-REARING
             FACTORS AND EPPS NEEDS

| | PARI | | |
EPPS	Authoritarian-Control	Hostility-Rejection	Democratic Attitudes
Need for Achievement	.40	.48*	−.16
Need for Nurturance	−.40	−.59**	.23
Need for Aggression	.27	.41*	−.13
Need for Affiliation	−.43*	−.67**	−.04
Need for Deference	.23	.27	.00
Need for Hetero-sexuality	−.20	−.02	.05

* $p < .05$
** $p < .01$

Rather, they are integrally related to other personality variables. Child-rearing behavior should be predictable from knowledge of other characteristics of the parents and vice versa. Also implied is that any relationship found between child-rearing variables and subsequent behavior of the child is probably a function of a great many interrelated parental tendencies. For example, a mother who is hostile and rejecting toward her child also stresses achievement and success and tends not to place a high value on affiliative and nurturant activities. Whatever effect her hostile behavior exerts on her offspring is almost necessarily in part a function of the other behaviors, too.

   Authoritative Information. Even though research on the effects of child-rearing practices is in a relatively primitive stage, almost inevitably various individuals and agencies attempt to supply advice and guidance to meet parental demands for information. Such advice varies widely from decade to decade; probably the basis depends more on whatever middle-class fads are current than on research evidence [Orlansky, 1949]. Nevertheless, at any given time the advice is given by pamphlets, by magazines, and by pediatricians, and one may reasonably expect that child-rearing practices will be to some degree affected by this material.

   One investigation of the influence of this sort of information was carried out in Salt Lake City by Cole, Shaw, Steneck, and Taboroff [1957]. Just prior to the study, child-rearing information had been distributed for a five-year period. The city was divided into eight geographic areas, and 25 families in each area were interviewed, with 87.5 per cent cooperating. The respondents were asked about nursing, bed wetting, sexual education, emotional disturbances, and adolescent withdrawal.

   The results suggested that the available information did influence the responses of the subjects to the interview. The greatest assimilation of current concepts of child-rearing was by those in the younger age groups which was interpreted to mean that the knowledge is most influential for those individuals who are actively engaged in rearing children.

CHILD-REARING BEHAVIOR AND PARENTAL REPORTS OF CHILD'S BEHAVIOR

One of the most common approaches to the study of child-rearing antecedents of behavior has been through interviews with parents, usually with the mother. Both the parental measures and the child behavior measures are obtained from this one source. As an example of this type of research, a portion of a large-scale study by Sears, Maccoby, and Levin [1957] will be described.

Procedure. A group of 379 mothers was selected for individual interviews concerning their child-rearing practices and the behavior of their children. These subjects all lived in two suburbs of a large metropolitan area of New England. Each mother had a child enrolled in public kindergarten at the time of the interview. In each family, both parents were American-born, were living together, and were the natural parents of the kindergarten child. None of the children was a twin or possessed a handicap. In addition to these restrictions, the investigators also wanted to have a fairly equal representation of mothers of children who were only, first, middle, and youngest children in the family and of mothers who represented different social classes. With respect to occupations, the husbands ranged from unskilled laborers to professional and managerial men.

The interview was a semi-structured one in which a series of open questions was presented and then the replies were explored further whenever appropriate. The interviews were conducted by ten female research assistants who recorded the entire two-hour conversation with each mother. Verbatim, typed transcripts of the recordings were prepared, and the ten judges used this material to rate the behavioral dimensions for both mother and child.

Effects of Breast-Feeding vs. Bottle-Feeding. After birth, the first major interactions between parent and child are those having to do with feeding. Decisions must be made concerning breast vs. bottle, schedule vs. self-demand, and age of weaning. Even after infancy, the eating process is one of the recurrent activities in which parent-child interactions take place, often with problems arising such as what to eat, how much to eat, table manners, and so forth. Maternal differences in handling each of these situations were expected to be important in determining various aspects of the child's behavior. A good many of the interview questions of Sears, *et al.*, dealt with feeding.

One question had to do with breast-feeding vs. bottle-feeding. The authors note:

In spite of the ready-made biology of the mother-child relationship, the first question a mother has to ask, in Western society, is whether or not to breast-feed her child. This is no new issue. Among the artifacts of early Egyptian civilization are a variety of devices for artificial feeding. They range from objects that look like syringe bulbs to miniature teapots with a spout. Evidently even that long ago mothers were already seeking substitutes for themselves, but for what reason we do not know. Today, in the United States, breast-feeding is so far from automatic that a quite fashionable pro-breast-feeding cult has been formed, as if to resurrect a lost art [Sears, *et al.*, 1957, p. 67].

In the group of mothers sampled, 39 per cent breast-fed their child at least for a while, though the majority of women did not utilize this technique at all. The investigators divided the group into those who used a bottle exclusively, those who breast-fed the infant less than three months, and those who used breast-feeding for three months or more. Then, these three groups were compared with respect to several aspects of the behavior of their children, including behavior related to food such as "feeding problems" and behavior in other areas such as "bed-wetting at age 5." On *none* of the behaviors was there a consistent relationship between type of feeding and later behavior. Obviously, the behaviors in question do have antecedents, and very likely maternal differences in feeding the child have lasting effects on the child. Nevertheless, the simple choice of breast vs. bottle is not a determinant of the sort of behaviors which were investigated here.

Effect of Punishment and Permissiveness on Aggressive Behavior. Aggression and hostility are inevitable childhood behaviors with which parents must deal. If frustration of goal-directed activity leads to aggression, then the process of socialization—training children to become members of even a simple society—must involve a considerable amount of frustration. The child cannot eat immediately when he is hungry, cannot defecate or urinate whenever or wherever the urge arises, cannot do as he pleases with the property of others. The resulting aggression also must be socialized to some extent, but the way that this is done and the limits of allowable aggression differ greatly across families.

When mothers were asked about the amount of aggression shown by the child in the home, the replies ranged from none (4 per cent) to highly aggressive (17 per cent). Presumably the amount of aggression shown was in part a function of the way in which the parents responded to aggressive behavior. Two variables were studied. First, mothers differed considerably in their permissiveness for three types of aggression (toward parents, toward siblings, toward other children). Those who were not at all permissive believed that the behavior should not be allowed to occur under any circumstances and that it should be stopped immediately. At the other end of this dimension were mothers who were entirely permissive (child has a right to hit parents or shout angrily at them; children should fight it out if they quarrel because it is a natural part of growing up). The second parental behavior was that of the severity of punishment for aggression toward parents. At some point, even the most permissive parent stops the aggression in some way (no one allows his child to maim or kill others, for example). Again, vast differences occur among parents in what they do. Aggression toward parents was treated by some (9 per cent) with only very mild punishment and disapproval. Parents at the other extreme (4 per cent) responded with anger, hostility, beatings, and severe deprivation of privileges. What effects do these differences in permissiveness and punishment have on the aggressiveness of the children?

The parents of the highly aggressive children were compared with respect to permissiveness and type of punishment. The greatest percentage of highly aggressive children (41.7 per cent of the aggressive boys and 38.1 per cent of the aggressive girls) had mothers who were highly permissive about aggression and who also punished it severely. The smallest percentage of highly aggressive children (3.7 per cent of the boys and 13.3 per cent of the girls) had mothers with the opposite pattern: nonpermissive about aggression and mild punishment. Mothers with mixed patterns of permissiveness and punishment contributed a medium number of the highly aggressive children. In interpreting these results, Sears, *et al.*, point out:

Our findings suggest that the way for parents to produce a nonaggressive child is to make it abundantly clear that aggression is frowned upon, and to stop aggression when it occurs, but to avoid punishing the child for his aggression. Punishment seems to have complex effects. While undoubtedly it often stops a particular form of aggression, at least momentarily, it appears to generate more hostility in the child and lead to further aggressive outbursts at some other time or place. Furthermore, when the parents punish—particularly when they employ physical punishment—they are providing a living example of the use of aggression at the very moment they are trying to teach the child not to be aggressive. The child, who copies his parents in many ways, is likely to learn as much from this example of successful aggression on his parents' part as he is from the pain of punishment. Thus, the most peaceful home is one in which the mother believes aggression is not desirable and under no circumstances is ever to be expressed toward her, but who relies mainly on nonpunitive forms of control. The homes where the children show angry, aggressive outbursts frequently are likely to be homes in which the mother has a relatively tolerant (or careless!) attitude toward such behavior, or where she administers severe punishment for it, or both [Sears, *et al.*, 1957, p. 266].

Effect of Maternal Warmth and Punishment Techniques on the Development of Conscience.   Sears, Maccoby, and Levin define three ways in which the activities of the child may be controlled. The first control which is applied is that of parents who play the role of policeman with do and don't, yes and no, in response to each behavior. As the child grows, a second type of control develops, self-control based on fear of punishment and hope of reward. Behavior is a function of what the child has learned and of the availability of the control agent to administer rewards and punishments. A third type of control is the most effective of the three and is independent of any type of external control; the child genuinely accepts the parents' rules and standards as his own. When the rules are broken, the punishment is not from the outside but from within in the form of guilt, shame, and anxiety. An investigation of the antecedents of the latter type of control, or conscience, was included in the Sears study.

Ratings of the offspring in terms of conscience development again revealed marked differences. Children ranged from no conscience (13 per cent), in which the child was reported to hide, deny, or show no signs of unhappiness when naughty, to considerable evidence of conscience (20 per cent), in which the child feels unhappy when naughty, confesses his wrongdoings, and wants to be forgiven.

As with aggression, two maternal variables were found to be of importance. *Maternal warmth* involves love, acceptance, enthusiasm, and outgoing affection toward the child. Ratings of the interview material were based on a variety of statements. For example, a mother rated high in warmth said:

Well, as soon as my work is done, if she's around, I'll call her and say, "Come on, let's have some fun"; and we'll sit down and she'll sit on my lap, and sometimes I rock her back and forth, and kiss her. She likes to be kissed, she loves it, and I'll cuddle her, and she loves to be cuddled. Or I'll play a game with her [Sears, *et al.*, 1957, p. 53].

A mother rated low in warmth said such things as:

I, as a child, never kissed my parents, but I'll kiss him goodnight, or kiss him good-bye, something like that, hug him, that's about all. We're not over —not overdo it [Sears, *et al.*, 1957, p. 55].

Punishment techniques used in training the child constituted the second variable. One type of punishment technique which has proven to be of great importance in developmental research is that called *withdrawal of love*. While parents are unlikely to verbalize their behavior in those terms, they do behave toward the child in ways which may be defined as withdrawing love. The mother may look coldly at the child, turn her back, refuse to listen to him, keep him out of the family circle, threaten to go away and leave him unless he is good, or tell him that he is making her sad. The essence is that parental warmth and affection are dependent on the child's good behavior. Among the mothers in the research sample, 26 per cent never used this technique or used it only slightly, and 10 per cent used it to a considerable degree.

The greatest percentage (42 per cent) of children rated high on conscience development were found to be those whose mothers were rated high on emotional warmth and who often used withdrawal of love as a punishment technique. The authors suggest that conscience development is dependent upon identification with the parents and that identification is fostered by warmth and by punishment involving withdrawal of love.

OFFSPRING'S BEHAVIOR AND OFFSPRING'S REPORT OF ANTECEDENTS

Attempts to isolate personality antecedents through the study of only one generation have also approached the problem via the offspring. In this type of study, the offspring's behavior is measured and then the antecedent variables determined on the basis of the responses of these same subjects.

Aggressive Behavior and Perception of Parents in Fantasy. Aggressiveness in children was found by Sears, *et al.*, to be a function of maternal permissiveness and the severity of punishment. Kagan [1958] approached the same problem from the vantage point of aggressive children. He hypothesized that aggression would be most likely to be expressed by children who perceive their parents as hostile and nonnurturant and who do not feel dependent on parental support in time of need.

The subjects were boys (first through third graders) in a public school in Columbus, Ohio. Their perception of their parents was determined by asking them to make up stories in response to a series of 13 pictures (for example, a crying boy sitting on the floor and a woman standing behind the boy, looking down at him). The stories were then scored by two judges for dependency, parental anger toward a child, and so forth. Aggression was measured by teachers' ratings of 118 boys on a five-point scale on two behaviors: "tendency to start fights at the slightest provocation," and "tendency to hold in anger and not to express it overtly." On the basis of these ratings, 21 extremely aggressive and 21 extremely nonaggressive subjects were selected.

Stories involving dependency on adults were more frequent among the nonaggressive boys while stories involving anger between parent and child were more frequent for aggressive boys. Kagan suggests:

If the fantasy can be regarded as representative of reality, these results may be interpreted as partial validation for the hypothesis that prohibitions on aggressive behavior are more likely to be learned and practiced when the child is dependent on his parents and perceives them as nurturing and gratifying. Under these conditions the child should be anxious over possible loss of parental gratifications if he fails to adopt the parental prohibitions on aggressive behavior [Kagan, 1958, p. 316].

Occupational Aspiration and Perception of Relationships within the Family. In much of Western civilization the motive to achieve, to succeed, to move upward socially has been stressed in a wide variety of ways over a fairly long period of time. However, individuals differ in their tendencies either to strive for upward social mobility or to remain content with their current status and expectations. A good deal of the psychoanalytic literature has interpreted a success orientation as a neurotic striving for power and recognition. The basis is insecurity which in turn stems from unsatisfactory interpersonal relationships in early childhood.

Dynes, Clarke, and Dinitz [1956] attempted to test this proposition by obtaining the level of occupational aspiration and also information about their early family life from a group of 350 college students. Aspiration was measured by a scale developed by Reissman [1953]. The questions ask about the willingness of the subject to forego certain satisfactions in order to achieve occupational advancement (for example, moving about the country, keeping quiet about political views). The subjects' evaluations of their family life were measured by a second questionnaire which dealt with such variables as degree of attachment to parents, amount of conflict, feelings of rejection, and childhood happiness.

Responses to the level of aspiration scale were used to divide the subjects into high aspirers and low aspirers. It was found that these two groups gave quite different responses concerning their family life. Compared to individuals with low aspirations, the subjects with a high level of aspiration were significantly more likely to indicate that they felt unwanted by one or both parents, to feel that their parents showed favoritism to some child in the family, to indicate feelings of less attachment to both parents, to believe that their childhood was not extremely happy, to say they confided less frequently in their fathers than in their mothers, and to say that they feared punishment from their fathers.

Dynes, *et al.*, suggest:

Unsatisfactory interpersonal relationships in the family of orientation were significantly related to high aspirational levels and satisfactory relationships were related to lower aspirational levels.

Since increasing attention is being given to the development of "happy" and socially well-adjusted persons by some of our institutions and social agencies, the question arises whether modifications will occur in the future to the success orientation of American society. It may well be that the increasing emphasis on personal happiness, rather than on personal achievement, will serve to augment the growing quest for security [Dynes, *et al.*, 1956, p. 214].

PARENTAL BEHAVIOR AND BEHAVIOR OF THEIR OFFSPRING

The difficulty with investigating only the parent or only the child is that the hypothesized antecedent and consequent are not independent of one another. Whether we are asking the mother about signs of conscience development in her child or asking a college student about whether his parents rejected him, the comparison of these responses with other behaviors of the same subjects severely limits our interpretation of the resulting findings. Are we dealing with accurate representations of the other person in the parent-child interaction or with possibly distorted perceptions of that person? When independent measures of both parent and child can be obtained, that particular difficulty is bypassed.

Maternal Response to Aggression and Anti-Semitism in the Offspring. A number of theorists have stressed the role of displaced aggression in ethnic prejudice. A minority group becomes the scapegoat for aggression engendered by frustration experienced in other situations, such as parent-child interactions. Weatherley [1963] hypothesized that harsh, restrictive parental response to childhood aggression leads to resentment toward authority and also fear of expressing this resentment; therefore, the child learns to displace aggression onto safer targets, such as members of a minority group.

The subjects were 39 non-Jewish undergraduate females and their mothers. Minority group prejudice was measured by scores on the Anti-Semitism Scale (discussed in more detail in Chapter 8) and a test which involves evaluation of Jewish proper names vs. non-Jewish names. Each mother was contacted by mail and asked to complete a questionnaire dealing with the way she responded to her daughter's childhood aggression.

The more punitive and stern was the mother in responding to childhood aggression, the more prejudiced was the offspring on both measures of anti-Semitism. We should note that maternal punitiveness was unrelated to the daughter's evaluation of non-Jewish names, which suggests that the displaced aggression is specifically directed toward minority group members rather than toward people in general.

Parental Child-Rearing Attitudes and Social Deviancy in Their Offspring. It is relatively difficult and hence relatively rare in the literature to obtain data on both parents as well as on their offspring. In attempting to find the parental attitudes related to socially deviant behavior in preadolescent boys, Winder and Rau [1962] were able to obtain data on such family constellations.

Social deviance was measured by the Peer Nomination Inventory (PNI) in which classmates rate one another on aggression, dependency, withdrawal, depression, and likeability. The children were drawn from a group of 710 boys (fourth, fifth, and sixth graders) in Palo Alto schools to whom the PNI was given. The final sample consisted of 118 mothers, 108 fathers, and their children. The Stanford Parent Attitude Questionnaire was given to the parents who came to the school to take part in the research. This test measures 27 variables for mothers and 28 for fathers.

The children were divided into high, medium, and low groups on each variable of the PNI, and then the parents of the three groups were compared on their scores on the scales of the parent questionnaire. Considering deviancy across the first four PNI scales, boys who were considered by their peers as aggressive, dependent, withdrawn, and/or depressed tended to have parents who were ambivalent (rejection *and* demonstration of affection) and punitive, and mothers who had low self-esteem. Winder and Rau say:

> If we assume that the parent attitudes being measured by this inventory are in fact antecedent to the development of deviant behavior in the children, then we might interpret these findings as indicating that children who experience relatively intense frustration in their interactions with their parents will come to exhibit with considerable intensity a diverse set of maladaptive behaviors. These maladaptive behaviors will ordinarily include aspects of hostile aggression, overdemanding and inappropriate bids for attention, withdrawal from friendly interaction with peers, and such manifestations of sadness and distress as frequent crying [Winder and Rau, 1962, p. 422].

The fifth variable, likeability, also yielded parental differences. The boys most popular with their classmates tended to have parents who are not aggressive or punitive and who have low demands for aggression from their child; the mothers are satisfied with themselves and with relationships within the family; the fathers have a high regard for their sons and evaluate them as competent.

CROSS-CULTURAL COMPARISONS

An increasingly popular approach to experiential antecedents of individual differences has been that of cross-cultural comparisons. Within the typical American community, one can obtain parental differences in child-rearing attitudes, punishment techniques, methods of socializing the child, and the like, and one can attempt to relate these variables to the behavior of the offspring. When such antecedent variables are viewed in the context of the range of variation practiced by those in other cultures around the world, the American samples appear to be relatively homogeneous. Thus, we are dealing with a somewhat restricted range with our antecedent variables. The gain of a wider range of child-rearing practices is in part offset by a weakness of the cross-cultural approach. If Society A and Society B differ in child-rearing practices and in some other behavior, the child-rearing practices may well have been the antecedents of the behavior. Since the societies are also likely to differ in countless ways in addition to the way they raise children, it is not really possible to isolate the variables with any certainty. When there is congruence between such findings and those from other types of investigation, one is on much surer ground.

Socialization Anxiety and Guilt.   As was noted in the Sears, *et al.* [1957] investigation, the development of conscience and the tendency to feel anxious and guilty over one's wrongdoing is of considerable theoretical and practical interest. In their large-scale cross-cultural study of child training and personality, Whiting and Child [1953] also included this variable. Their approach has set a pattern for much subsequent work.

The basic data were contained in extracts from ethnographic reports concerning 75 primitive societies. Typical behavior patterns of each group were determined with respect to a series of child-rearing variables and a series of adult behaviors which presumably were the consequents. Judgments about each society on specific variables were made by research assistants. One of the child-rearing variables studied was *socialization anxiety,* which is defined as the amount of anxiety aroused in the child by the process of imposing inhibitions on oral, anal, sexual, dependent, and aggressive behavior. Societies were assumed to arouse more anxiety in the children the shorter the time of transition from indulgence to inhibition, the more severe the punishment technique employed, the more frequently punishment was used, and the more emotional conflict actually reported in the children. An example will serve to illustrate the range of differences across cultures.

Severity of training concerning aggression ranged from active encouragement of aggressive behavior to severe discouragement. Very high socialization anxiety in this area is represented by the Harney Valley Paiute:

If siblings fight among themselves, the older ones are whipped. If a child strikes his parents, they hit him back. Children are told that a big owl or a wildcat will take them off if they do not mind. They are told that if they get angry when they eat they will swell up. Over and over again they are told that they should love their parents and their siblings and should not be angry with them nor fight with them. They are severely punished for destroying birds' eggs or hurting any bird or animal.

Probably more important than this direct punishment is the fear of aggression which they acquire by observing their parents and hearing them discuss sorcery and fighting. If there is a fight in the community, mothers gather up their children and take them away. They are frightened that sorcery will be "thrown around" and will accidentally or purposefully hit the children. Children see their parents reacting with anxiety to the danger of sorcery. They observe that their parents are afraid to express aggression overtly for fear of being accused of sorcery. They are admonished never to laugh or make fun of other people lest they be attacked. They are warned always to be polite, to speak to people and to speak pleasantly. They hear much gossip about sorcerers and how dangerous such individuals are.

The result is that a child is afraid to express aggression for fear of punishment from his family directly, or because of fear of punishment by others. He shares his family's anxiety about expressing aggression. Furthermore, because of certain beliefs connected with sorcery and the acquisition of bad power, he develops a fear that he will express his aggression unconsciously [Whiting, 1950, pp. 68–69].

Encouragement of aggression and low socialization anxiety about it are represented by the Siriono:

Within play groups aggression is freely expressed. When boys are playing with their bows and arrows (boys' arrows always have blunt ends, and their bows shoot with little force), accidents sometimes occur, and occasionally one child shoots another intentionally, even though boys are admonished not to point their weapons at any human target. When such accidents or shootings occur (children are seldom wounded as a result of them), a fight usually breaks out, and the child who has been hit often strikes back at the boy who shot him. Adults generally take no part in these fights (they usually laugh at them), but the loser almost always runs crying to his parents for protection. . . . Considerable teasing and torturing—such things as pinching the genitals, poking fingers in the eyes and scratching—of young children by older children takes place. A young child most often protects himself from such attacks with a brand of fire or a digging stick, and if he catches off guard the older child who molested him, he may burn him rather severely or give him a sharp rap on the head. Older girls, too, sometimes tease young children by pretending to suck from their mothers' breasts, and this invariably arouses aggression in the latter, who sometimes strike their tormenters with considerable force. Under such circumstances, older children are not allowed to express counter aggression [Holmberg, 1946, pp. 227, 230–234].

For their consequent variables, Whiting and Child concentrated on beliefs and activities concerning illness. With respect to guilt, the variable was the extent to which the patient blames himself for having gotten sick. There were 35 societies on which information was available so that the judges could rate them as to whether illness was blamed on the patient, on others, or on no one.

The hypothesis to be tested was that guilt feelings grow out of early fears in the socialization process. Thus, the greater the socialization anxiety in a group, the greater should be the feelings of guilt. For the 35 societies, the two variables correlate .29, which is statistically significant and in the predicted direction. When the five areas of socialization are considered separately (see Table 4–7), guilt is found to be significantly related only to socialization anxiety concerning aggression. The relationship to oral socialization anxiety is almost significant.

The small magnitude of the obtained relationships induced the investigators to seek further the antecedents of guilt. They hypothesized that the earlier the socialization training was begun, the greater would be the development of conscience and guilt. This hypothesis was tested by correlating guilt over illness scores with age of onset of the socialization of various

Table 4–7   RELATION BETWEEN PATIENT RESPONSIBILITY FOR
ILLNESS AND SOCIALIZATION ANXIETY IN EACH
OF FIVE SYSTEMS OF BEHAVIOR[**]

System of Behavior	r with Patient Responsibility
Oral	.25
Anal	.06
Sexual	.02
Dependence	.18
Aggression	.28[*]

[*] $p < .05$
[**] Adapted from Whiting and Child, 1953, p. 236.

aspects of behavior. Significant negative correlations were obtained for heterosexuality ($r = -.74$), modesty training ($r = -.50$), weaning ($r = -.42$), and independence training ($r = -.34$). As predicted, the older the child when the training is started, the less guilt. Whiting and Child comment:

> Our hypothesis and findings about the age of socialization, lastly, are relevant to our general interpretation because they have to do with whether threats of loss of parental love occur at a time when the child greatly needs parental love, or whether they instead occur at a time when the child has attained a degree of independent mastery of his world which makes it easier for him simply to abandon pursuit of parental love or of an internal substitute for it [Whiting and Child, 1953, p. 262].

EXPERIMENTAL STUDIES OF CHILDREN

In each of the approaches to the study of experiential antecedents discussed so far, the investigators simply take individuals as they are and seek relationships between variables. While one cannot bring about major changes in family configurations or child-rearing practices in order to determine the effects on the child's behavior, one can utilize children as experimental subjects.

Two somewhat different lines of research interest may be distinguished. Some experimental child psychologists approach the problem with established concepts and findings from general experimental psychology, such as stimulus generalization or reinforcement schedules or the effect of drive level on performance, and then investigate their applicability to children. Other investigators begin with a more traditional developmental problem, such as dependency or identification or delay of gratification, and then devise experimental situations in which such variables may be studied in the laboratory. Obviously, these two approaches sometimes overlap.

Extinction of Smiling Response as a Function of Reinforcement Schedule. Laboratory studies of partial reinforcement of simple responses in a variety of species generally find that extinction is more rapid for responses which were learned on a schedule of regular reinforcement than for responses learned on an irregular schedule. Brackbill [1958] sought to extend this finding concerning operant conditioning to the smiling response of human infants.

Her subjects were eight normal infants between the ages of three and one-half and four and one-half months. Four were assigned to the regular reinforcement group, four to the intermittent reinforcement group. The procedure for each subject involved three experimental periods. First, during an operant period the baby was observed for eight five-minute intervals to ascertain the operant (or existing) rate of smiling. In the conditioning period, reinforcement (experimenter smiled, spoke softly to the subject, and picked it up for 30 seconds) was given after each smile for the regular reinforcement group and after only a portion of the smiles for the intermittent reinforcement group (regular, then on a 2:1 ratio, then a 3:1 ratio, and then a 4:1 ratio). In the final or extinction period, no further reinforcements were given and the number of smiling responses were observed for 13 five-minute intervals.

Infants in both groups increased the rate at which they smiled in the conditioning period compared to the operant period. As hypothesized, there was significantly faster extinction of the smiling response in the group which had received regular reinforcement than in the group which had received intermittent reinforcement. In addition the investigators found that protest responses (crying and fussing) were negatively related to smiling responses. That is, as smiling increased during conditioning, protests decreased; the reverse took place during extinction. Thus, the frequency with which a given response is made by an infant was concluded to be a function of the schedule of reinforcement for that response and of the strength of existing competing responses.

Aggression as a Function of Frustration and Imitation of Real and Fantasy Models. A good deal of concern has been expressed from many sources with respect to the possible effects of fantasy models on the behavior of children. Vociferous criticism has been made of the content of movies, comic books, and television programs. With aggressive behavior, it has been hypothesized that the portrayal of aggression in fantasy form may determine the way in which aggression is expressed but will not itself arouse the motive. Bandura, Ross, and Ross [1963] utilized three levels of reality (real life, film, and cartoon) in depicting an aggressive model in order to determine the effects of this model on the subsequent behavior of children.

The subjects were 96 nursery school children ranging from approximately three to five years of age. They were divided into three experimental groups and one control group with 24 subjects in each. One group observed an adult acting aggressively, one group observed the same individual in a film, and a third group watched a movie depicting an aggressive cartoon character. Half of the subjects were exposed to a model of the same sex as themselves, half to a model of the opposite sex. The control group had no exposure to an aggressive model.

The aggressive behavior of the model involved hostility toward a five-foot inflated Bobo doll: sitting on it, punching it, hitting it with a mallet, tossing it in the air, and kicking it, all accompanied by appropriate verbal expressions. Subjects were tested for aggressive behavior in a different experimental room after a mild frustration (removing highly attractive toys with which the child was playing) to arouse aggression. Among the available toys remaining was a Bobo doll; the subjects were observed and their behavior recorded for 20 minutes.

Subjects in all three experimental groups were found to be more aggressive in the test situation than were subjects in the control group. Further, specifically imitative aggression (like that of the model) was greater for those who saw an aggressive model than for those in the control group. There was not much difference among the three experimental conditions in influencing aggressive behavior, but in general exposure to the filmed human models was the most effective in eliciting and shaping aggressive behavior. Boys were found to behave more aggressively than girls. Bandura, *et al.*, conclude:

The results of the present study provide strong evidence that exposure to filmed aggression heightens aggressive reactions in children. Subjects who viewed the aggressive human and cartoon models on film exhibited nearly twice as much aggression than did subjects in the control group who were not exposed to the aggressive film content [Bandura, *et al.*, 1963, p. 9].

EXPERIMENTAL STUDIES OF ANIMALS

          Still another approach to the study of behavior antecedents is the utilization of nonhuman subjects in experiments. One of the most obvious reasons for employing animals is that much of the theorizing about the effects of early experience centers around traumatic and disruptive events to which human subjects could not be purposefully exposed. We will look at two such studies, one using mice and the other monkeys.

          The Influence of Infantile Trauma and Genetic Factors on Emotionality. Many personality theorists have proposed that exposure to extreme stress early in life has deleterious effects on later emotional stability. Earlier in this chapter, some of the evidence concerning the genetic determination of differences in emotionality was discussed. These two types of antecedents probably interact in determining adult behavior. For example, a stress situation of given magnitude should have a greater effect on individuals genetically predisposed to emotionality than to those with relatively nonemotional constitutions.

Lindzey, Lykken, and Winston [1960] utilized four different inbred strains of mice. Animals within each strain were assigned to either the experimental or control group at birth; a total of 259 mice were used. Each litter was raised with its mother for 24 days, and then the animals were weaned and taken from the mother. The only difference in treatment of experimental and control animals was that the former were placed in a tub for six minutes on four successive days and exposed to a loud, shrill, auditory stimulus for two minutes, beginning when they were four days old. The control subjects were also placed in the tub at the same age but without the accompanying loud noise.

Subsequent emotionality was determined on ten successive days using the tub (without the auditory stimulus) as an open-field test beginning at 30 days of age. Defecation and/or urination were determined for each trial. This test was repeated when the mice were 100 days old.

The results of the 30-day test clearly showed the effects of both genetic and experiential differences in the subjects. As shown in Table 4–8, the

Table 4–8   MEAN PERCENTAGE OF ANIMALS DEFECATING OVER THE
TEN DAYS IN THE 30-DAY OPEN-FIELD TEST*

Strain	Control Group	Experimental Group
1	34.3	40.4
2	67.0	74.3
3	77.1	90.5
4	84.5	90.3

* Adapted from Lindzey, et al., 1960, p. 9.

four strains were different from one another, and the experimental subjects showed more emotionality than the control subjects within each strain. We might note that fewer experimental animals in the least emotional strain showed signs of stress than did control animals in the most emotional strain. Again on the open-field test conducted when the animals were 100 days old, emotionality was found to be influenced significantly by differences in the strains and by the treatment in infancy.

The investigators suggested that this evidence implies that attempts to determine the effects of early experience on adult human behavior should allow for the contribution of genetic variables. As Lindzey, *et al.*, point out:

. . . we may expect that a variety of different empirical findings might be observed in similar studies as a consequence of investigators dealing with Ss of various genetic backgrounds, rather than as a result of faulty experimental technique. In general, this is a finding that makes life more complex for both investigator and theorist, and in an area where there has never been any shortage of complexity [Lindzey, *et al.*, 1960, p. 13].

The Effect of Infantile Isolation on Heterosexual Behavior. A great deal of stress has been placed on the mother-child relationship by personality theorists. Evidence for this emphasis in personality research is shown by the number of investigations cited in this chapter which have dealt with that relationship. When an infant is deprived of this relationship by the death of its mother, hospitalization of either mother or child, placement in an institution, and so forth, a number of observational reports indicate that there are devastating effects on the infant's health and behavior. As part of the ongoing work at the primate laboratory at the University of Wisconsin, Harlow [1962] has reported a number of studies dealing with the effects of early experience on the adult behavior of monkeys.

At one point, the investigators were in the process of creating unfriendly and inconsistent surrogate mothers in order to study the development of neuroses in infant monkeys. Though the early efforts were not successful, 47 infant monkeys were separated from their mothers at birth and raised in cages, some with substitute mothers and some without, where they had no physical contact with peers though they could see and hear other infants. After these subjects were five to seven years old and sexually mature, it became obvious that they were not normal. Harlow says:

We have seen them sitting in their cages strangely mute, staring fixedly into space, relatively indifferent to people and other monkeys. Some clutch their heads in both hands and rock back and forth—the autistic behavior pattern that we have seen in babies raised on wire surrogates. Others, when approached or even left alone, go into violent frenzies of rage, grasping and tearing at their legs with such fury that they sometimes require medical care.

Eventually we realized that we had a laboratory full of neurotic monkeys. We had failed to produce neurotic monkeys by thoughtful planning and creative research, but we had succeeded in producing neurotic monkeys through misadventure. To err is human [Harlow, 1962, p. 6].

In addition to these behaviors, the monkeys who had experienced such an unusual childhood showed no interest in normal sex behavior. When male and female pairs were placed together in the same cage, they did not mate. Next, an attempt was made to mate these animals with normal animals of the opposite sex, again without success. Harlow describes this:

At this point we took the 17 oldest of our cage-raised animals, females showing consistent estrous cycles and males obviously mature, and engaged in an intensive re-education program, pairing the females with our most experienced, patient, and gentle males, and the males with our most eager, amiable, and successful breeding females. When the laboratory-bred females were smaller than the sophisticated males, the girls would back away and sit down facing the males, looking appealingly at these would-be consorts. Their hearts were in the right place, but nothing else was. When the females were larger than the males, we can only hope that they misunderstood the males' intentions, for after a brief period of courtship, they would attack and maul the ill-fated male. Females show no respect for a male they can dominate.

The training program for the males was equally unsatisfactory. They approached the females with a blind enthusiasm, but it was a misdirected enthusiasm. Frequently the males would grasp the females by the side of the body and thrust laterally, leaving them working at cross purposes with reality. Even the most persistent attempts by these females to set the boys straight came to naught. Finally, these females either stared at the males with complete contempt or attacked them in utter frustration. It became obvious that they, like their human counterpart, prefer maturer men. We realized then that we had established, not a program of breeding, but a program of brooding [Harlow, 1962, p. 7].

Since other laboratory-raised monkeys show normal heterosexual behavior, the deviancy of these subjects was apparently the result of the early isolation experience. Further work was undertaken in which infant monkeys were separated from their real mothers, raised by an artificial mother (cloth-covered wire frame) but given the opportunity to play with other monkeys in infancy and childhood. In these subjects, normal sexual responses developed. A great deal of experimental work is obviously needed to determine the precise nature of the stimulus conditions under which normal versus abnormal heterosexual behavior is determined.

Summary

In spite of a number of obstacles to data collection in this area, the study of personality development is potentially one of the most important aspects of personality research with respect to both theory and application.

Speculations dealing with the heritability of behavioral characteristics are of ancient origin, but knowledge of the laws of heredity began in 1865 with Mendel's work with pea plants. His findings led eventually to the discovery of chromosomes, genes, and DNA. The study of the influence of hereditary factors on human behavior has been hampered by the impossibility of experimental manipulation of the variables. The family resemblances method includes the study of family pedigrees, similarity of behavior as a function of the closeness of family relationships, and the comparison of fraternal and identical twins. Even though laboratory experiments are not possible in work on human genetics, one can utilize experiments of nature. Included here are studies of the similarity between adopted children and their natural and foster parents and studies of the similarity of identical twins reared together compared with those reared separately. Finally, the laboratory method of selective breeding is used with nonhuman subjects.

A second major area of developmental research is that concerned with the prenatal period. Most of the research has centered on medical concerns and has dealt with miscarriages, stillbirths, defective development, infant diseases, and infant mortality. These conditions have been found to be a function of such factors as age of the mother, various disease entities, and the number of cigarettes smoked per day by the mother. Other investigations have found that mongoloidism is more likely when the mother is 35 or older and that cleft palate can be the result of severe emotional stress during the first ten weeks of pregnancy. In animal research, the amount of stress experienced by the mother during pregnancy has been found to have a lasting effect on the emotionality of the offspring.

The greatest amount of research on personality development has been with the effects of early experience on behavior. Obstacles to research include the impossibility of naturalistic observation of parent-child interactions, distortions in verbal reports of child-rearing attitudes and practices, and the practical difficulties involved in experimental investigations in this area. The determination of the correlates of child-rearing behavior has involved research on socioeconomic class, personality variables such as needs, and exposure to authoritative information. Many investigators have simply studied the behavior of parents (primarily mothers) and then obtained their reports of their child's behavior. Others have used the offspring as subjects and then obtained their reports of their parents' behavior. An approach superior to either of these is the investigation of the behavior of both parents and their children. Because of the relative homogeneity of child-rearing practices within the American culture, some research workers have turned to cross-cultural comparisons. In this method, the typical child-rearing behavior of a group of societies is determined and correlated with some other typical behavior which is hypothesized to be a consequent of child-rearing practices. Experimental studies of children have involved the application of the concepts and methodology of general experimental psychology to child subjects and the study of more traditional developmental variables in a laboratory setting. Finally, the effects of early experiences such as infantile trauma and isolation on later behavior are investigated in laboratory experiments with animals.

CHAPTER 5

Personality Structure

Personality structure may be conceptualized as a static representation of the organized interrelationship of personality variables. At any given point in time one can describe an individual in terms of his standing on all known personality dimensions. In effect, we present a psychological picture of all of his characteristics and the way in which they fit together. A major obstacle to presenting such a picture of personality is the fact that personality psychologists have not as yet agreed upon the best way to represent the interrelationships of personality dimensions in forming an organized whole.

The major attempt to reduce the masses of correlational data concerning individual differences into a model which depicts the structure of personality has been through the use of factor analysis [Guilford, 1961]. With personality structure conceptualized as the interrelationship of an unknown number of behavior dimensions, factor analysis is a mathematical procedure which can be used to determine the least number of dimensions that can best describe personality. If, for example, it were found through factor analysis that there were only three basic dimensions of individual differences, the complete range of personality structure could be described by a model such as that in Figure 5–1. Any specific individual is represented by a point within the sphere which indicates the person's relative position on each dimension. Since there are a great many more dimensions than three, personality structure must be represented as a series of intersecting lines in n-dimensional space with a given individual represented as a point within this space.

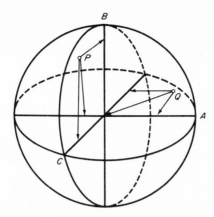

FIG. 5–1. *A dimensional model of personality structure involving three personality variables* (A, B, *and* C) *and the representation of two individuals* (P *and* Q) *with respect to the three variables.* (*Adapted from Guilford, 1961, p. 3.*)

Whether or not factor analysis and *n*-dimensional space prove to be the most fruitful approaches to personality structure, most of the actual research at the present time is several steps removed from the problem of the overall organization of personality. In this chapter, we will be concerned primarily with the investigation of simple relationships between personality dimensions. The integration of such findings into a single structure is yet to be accomplished.

Correlation Between Two Different Responses Made by an Individual

When an investigator determines the relationship between two different responses made by an individual, neither of these responses is conceived as causing the other. Rather, the establishment of such a relationship indicates only that there is a link between the two responses, and that link must be sought in one of several ways in subsequent research. Without further research, one cannot ascertain from the correlation itself any information about the reason for the relationship.

The situation may be conceptualized as in Figure 5–2. Whenever a

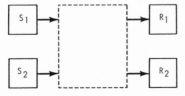

FIG. 5–2. *Correlation between two responses.*

lawful relationship is found between R_1 and R_2, it suggests that an unobserved variable within the organism is common to both S-R systems. Something has rendered the stimuli and hence the responses at least partially equivalent. Thus, there may be physiological attributes or the traces of past learning experiences which intervene between stimulus and response in each instance. Such a finding can be of theoretical importance when effort is made to seek the common factor or of practical importance when one response is utilized to predict the other.

Whenever abilities or skills are involved in the responses yielding a relationship, the probability is raised that there is a common constitutional factor in each stimulus-response element. For example, Seashore and Seashore [1941] obtained reaction time to a sound stimulus for 50 college men. A total of 50 trials was given with each hand and each foot, and averages were obtained. They found that the reaction time of the two hands correlated .92, of the two feet .93, and reaction time for hands correlated .81 with reaction time for feet. These relatively high relationships are probably the result of the fact that each of the behaviors requires approximately the same sensory, neural, and muscular functioning which is differentially efficient for different individuals.

With the other types of response, the same guess might be made but with somewhat less certainty. We will take a look at two of the tasks which make up an intelligence test for children, the WISC [Wechsler, 1949]. The vocabulary portion of the test consists of asking the subject to answer the question, "What is a ———?" or "What does ——— mean?" The easiest words include bicycle, knife, and hat. The tester keeps going through the list until five consecutive failures occur. In the middle range are words such as nitroglycerine, microscope, and shilling, while at the hardest extreme are dilatory, flout, and traduce. At any given age, individuals differ widely in the number of words which can be defined correctly and in the quality of the responses. These differences clearly reflect such experiential factors as the vocabulary of the parents, the contact the child has had with reading material, and the amount and kind of schooling. However, children very similar in these respects may nevertheless be quite different in vocabulary level.

One of the other subtests is called Block Design. Both the stimulus and the response are quite different from that involved in the vocabulary test. A group of small blocks of the type shown in Figure 5–3 are given

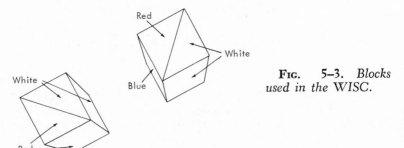

Fig.   **5–3.** *Blocks used in the WISC.*

to the subject, and he is asked to use the blocks to make a design like the one the examiner shows him. As with the vocabulary words, the series of designs ranges from relatively simple ones to relatively difficult ones. In addition, the subject is timed in his performance. Extra points are given for very rapid completion of a design, and no credit at all is given after a specific limit has been reached. Again, a considerable range of individual differences is found in the number of designs which can be completed and in the speed with which they are done.

With block design skill, the effects of parents, reading, or school would seem to be of considerably less importance than in the case of vocabulary. Nevertheless, a significant relationship exists between how well children do on one task and how well they do on the other. With 200 children at each of three age levels, Wechsler [1949] found correlations of .33 for 7½-year-olds, .54 for 10½-year-olds and .42 for 13½-year-olds. Thus, these two abilities are related, and scores on the two tasks are combined as part of the operational definition of intelligence. We may reasonably suggest that both constitutional and learning variables account for the relationship between the two behaviors.

Still other response-response relationships seem to be entirely attributable to learning. The author administered an attitude scale to 160 undergraduates who indicated their opinions concerning seven topics on six-point rating scales. Two of these items dealt with smoking and drinking, and responses ranged from very much in favor to very much against each of these activities. Responses to the two items correlated .58. One would guess that in these students' families they experienced either a relatively permissive or a relatively restrictive orientation toward nicotine and alcohol, and this consistency is reflected in the correlation coefficient.

The Correlation Coefficient

While much of personality research utilizes correlational statistics to some extent, the determination of the structure of personality depends almost entirely upon the correlational method and sophisticated derivatives of it. Before discussing examples of research on personality structure, it may be helpful to provide some background with respect to the correlation coefficient. Those students who are already familiar with such material may wish to skip the present section.

CORRELATION

If a relationship between two variables has been found to be a linear one, its direction and its magnitude can be expressed by a single statistic: the correlation coefficient or r. "Direction" refers to whether high scores on one variable are associated with high or with low scores on a second variable. A positive correlation indicates that those who obtain high scores on variable X tend to obtain high scores on variable Y, and that low scores on X tend to go with low scores on Y. For example, a positive correlation is usually found between IQ scores and grades in school; students with high IQ's tend to get higher grades than students with low IQ's. A negative correlation indicates that those who obtain high scores on variable X tend to obtain low scores on variable Y, and vice versa. For example, a negative correlation has been found between test anxiety and grades in school; students high in test anxiety tend to get lower grades than students low in test anxiety.

The "magnitude" of a relationship indicates the *degree* to which two variables are related. A perfect positive correlation is indicated by a coefficient of 1.00 while a perfect negative correlation is −1.00. When there is absolutely no relationship between two variables, the correlation is 0.00. In order to be able to interpret the meaning of correlation coefficients which fall at other points between plus and minus 1.00, we must know several additional facts about this statistic.

A correlation describes the relationship between two sets of variables. The most usual situations are ones in which each individual has been measured on two different variables (or on the same variable on two different occasions) or situations in which meaningful pairs of individuals (parent-child, husband-wife, twins, pairs of friends, and the like) have been measured on the same or different variables. In any event, the data sheet is made up of a list of pairs of numbers. An example of the computation of the correlation between the two variables shown in Table 5–1 is given at the end of this chapter. It is found that $r = .89$.

Table 5–1   SCORES OBTAINED BY SUBJECTS ON TWO VARIABLES

	Variable X	Variable Y
Subject 1	10	12
Subject 2	30	28
Subject 3	41	38
Subject 4	6	22
Subject 5	19	20
Subject 6	8	15

Since 1.00 is a perfect relationship, obviously .89 indicates a very high relationship. Two questions need to be answered, however. How likely is the relationship to be found in another sample? How can an *r* of .89 be interpreted? We now turn to these problems.

STATISTICAL SIGNIFICANCE

The inferences that psychologists make about their experimental findings with relatively small samples of the population are expressed in terms of *levels of significance*. If an investigator reports that he performed an experiment to test problem-solving ability and found that in his sample of 80 subjects the mean score of boys was higher than the mean score of girls at the 5 per cent level of significance, he is indicating that the chances are only 5 out of 100 (probability of .05) that this same difference would not hold true in the total population, and the chances are 95 out of 100 (probability of .95) that they would hold true. Such a statement is possible by virtue of the application of probability theory to samples of data. We will not go into the details of the mathematical theory or the statistical manipulations by which one arrives at such statements. Suffice it to say that with a sample of a given size, a difference of a given magnitude between groups, and variations of a given amount within each group, one can apply formulas and utilize tables and arrive at a significance level. In the example, there is no way to know with absolute certainty whether boys and girls *really* differ in problem-solving ability or whether this particular sample yielded a chance finding which is not true for the total population. If in the total population boys and girls really do not differ in this ability and if 100 experimenters with 100 different samples of subjects had conducted the same experiment, five of them would be expected to find sex differences significant at the .05 level. Obviously, repetition of an experiment in which essentially the same findings are shown increases the probability of their validity tremendously. Whatever the probability figure, the best a scientist can ever do is make an estimate or bet. At the 5 per cent (.05) level of significance, the odds are 95 to 5 (or 19 to 1) that the finding is a real one. If the finding reaches the 1 per cent (.01) level of significance, the odds reach 99 to 1. At the .1 per cent (.001) level, the odds are 999 to 1 that the finding is a true one, one that would be found again if the study were repeated on a new sample, and one that holds true for the entire population and was not just a fluke of this particular sample. Obviously, the higher the significance level, the more certain we can feel about the results. Scientific facts are never a *complete* certainty unless the total population is available for study, which of course is highly unlikely. As experiments are repeated, however, and findings replicated, the probability of their being a function of chance shrinks to a negligible quantity.

With correlation coefficients, the same sort of inferences must be made with respect to betting on the repeatability of finding the relationship in subsequent samples. The significance level of a particular correlation coefficient depends entirely on how large it is found to be in a given sample (its magnitude) and the number of subjects who make up the sample. The larger the correlation and the bigger the sample, the greater the probability of the relationship holding true for the total population.

In order to obtain an idea of the relationships between size of sample, size of correlation coefficient, and level of significance,[1] a portion of a significance table is presented in Table 5–2.

Table 5–2   CORRELATION AND SIGNIFICANCE

Size of Sample	r at .05 level	r at .01 level
3	.997	.999
4	.95	.99
5	.88	.96
6	.81	.92
7	.75	.87
8	.71	.83
9	.67	.80
10	.63	.77
20	.44	.56
30	.36	.46
40	.31	.40
50	.28	.36
60	.25	.33
70	.24	.31
80	.22	.29
90	.21	.27
100	.20	.26
500	.09	.12
1,000	.06	.08

As the table makes obvious, a correlation may be of a very small magnitude and yet indicate a true relationship. With 1,000 subjects, for example, a correlation of only .08 is still significant at the .01 level. A correlation

---

[1] To compute the significance level of a coefficient obtained with a sample of a given size, one must obtain an $\frac{x}{\sigma}$ to enter in a normal probability table. If N is greater than 30, the formula is:

$$\frac{x}{\sigma} = \frac{r}{\frac{1}{\sqrt{N-1}}}$$

If the quantity obtained in this formula reaches 1.96, the coefficient is significant at the .05 level. If it reaches 2.58, it is significant at the .01 level. If N is less than 30, the the formula is:

$$t = \frac{r}{\sqrt{\frac{1-r^2}{n-2}}}$$

With $N-2$ degrees of freedom, the size of t necessary to reach the .05 and .01 levels of significance can be obtained in a t table.

coefficient that small is not very useful for predictive purposes, but the best bet is that there is a real relationship between the variables. This brings us to the second question about correlations: What interpretation may be placed on a correlation of a given magnitude?

INTERPRETATION OF A CORRELATION COEFFICIENT:
PREDICTIVE ACCURACY

When the correlation between two variables is a real one, we can predict a score on one variable from knowledge of the score on the other with greater than chance accuracy. The higher the correlation (the closer to + or − 1.00), the more accurate the prediction. The prediction of one variable from another involves the use of a regression equation. The accuracy or precision of this prediction is determined by the standard error of estimate. We will take an example of a significant relationship which has been reported by several investigators and follow through in some detail the implications of the notion that one variable can be predicted from another when the two are correlated.

A number of investigators have found [Anastasi, 1958] that the IQ score of either parent (variable X) correlates approximately .50 with the IQ score of their óffspring of either sex (variable Y). Since this is a relatively stable finding across a number of samples, we can use this information to predict a child's IQ on the basis of knowledge about the IQ of either of his parents. To make such a prediction, we must know the correlation between the two variables, the mean of the population on each variable, and the standard deviation of the population on each variable. As was indicated, parent-child IQ's correlate .50. If we use the Wechsler Adult Intelligence Scale or WAIS [Wechsler, 1958] for the parents and the Wechsler Intelligence Scale for Children or WISC [Wechsler, 1949] for the offspring, the population means are approximately 100 and the standard deviations approximately 15 on each variable. So: $r = .50$, $M_x = 100$, $M_y = 100$, $SD_x = 15$, and $SD_y = 15$. The general formula for predicting Y (the IQ of a child) from X (the IQ of a parent) is:

$$Y' = r \frac{SD_y}{SD_x} X + (M_y - r \frac{SD_y}{SD_x} M_x)$$

In the formula, X is the IQ score of any specific parent, and Y' is the predicted IQ score of that parent's offspring.

As an example, let us assume that a father has an IQ of 150, and you wish to predict the eventual IQ of his newly born son. To gain some understanding of the meaning of a correlation, we will take three different levels of possible relationships of parent-child IQ's. First, we will look at the prediction which would be made if the correlation between X and Y were zero. Then, we will examine the differences in prediction when there is some relationship, in this case the actual one of .50. Finally, we will look at the perfect prediction situation, a correlation between X and Y of 1.00.

$r = 0.00$. A correlation of zero between the two variables would mean that the IQ of parents gave you absolutely no information which would help in predicting the IQ of their offspring. In the regression equation, had the correlation been zero, the father with an IQ of 150 would be predicted to have a son with the following IQ:

$$Y' = 0 \frac{15}{15} 150 + (100 - 0 \frac{15}{15} 100)$$
$$Y' = 100$$

This means that with no relationship between X and Y, the best prediction of Y is the population mean on the Y variable no matter what score is obtained on the X variable. Whether the father has an IQ of 150 or 82, the best prediction would be that the child would have an IQ of 100.

The accuracy with which you can predict one variable from another is shown by a statistic which utilizes the correlation coefficient, the standard error of estimate. $SD_{y.x}$ is the standard error of the Y' scores as predicted from the X scores and the formula is:

$$SD_{y.x} = SD_y \sqrt{1 - r^2}$$

The larger the correlation coefficient, the smaller the standard error of estimate and hence the greater the accuracy of prediction. In our example, had the correlation been zero, $SD_{y.x}$ would equal $15\sqrt{1 - 0.00^2}$ which equals 15. Thus, where there is no relationship between variables, the standard error of estimate of the predicted Y scores is simply the standard deviation of Y in the population.

The standard error of estimate allows you to state the precision of your prediction in terms of probability within certain limits. In this instance, the prediction is that all sons will have an IQ of 100 with $SD_{y.x}$ equal to 15. This means that with a father of 150 IQ (or a father with any IQ), about two-thirds of the time that such a prediction is made the son's actual IQ will fall between 100 ± 15 or between 85 and 115. About 95 per cent of the time the actual IQ will be between 100 and $\pm(2)(15)$ or between 70 and 130. Almost always, the actual IQ will be between $100 \pm (3)(15)$ or between 55 and 145. The student will recognize that predictions are simply being made in terms of multiples of the standard error, utilizing a normal curve table which may be found in any introductory text on statistics.

One way to conceptualize such predictions is in terms of the percentage of the variance in the predicted variable which can be accounted for on the basis of knowledge of the other variable. The square of the correlation coefficient indicates how much of the variance of Y can be accounted for by X in making predictions with the regression equation. With a correlation of 0.00, you can account for 0 per cent of the variance in Y by a knowledge of X. As has been indicated, it does not help to know anything about X, the prediction is the same regardless. With respect to predictive accuracy, none exists, except that errors can be minimized by utilizing population statistics and betting that everyone will have a mean score. Betting on the mean is the best guess that can be made in such situations since the prediction is the least wrong the greatest number of times. If the mean is the predicted score each time, the standard error of estimate indicates how often the prediction is wrong by how much. With a zero correlation the standard error of estimate is the same as the standard deviation of Y, so the variance accounted for by a knowledge of X is zero.

$r = .50$.   It was reported that the actual correlation between parental IQ and that of their offspring is .50. What does this knowledge do for us? What does a correlation of this magnitude mean? How does it affect our predictive accuracy?

Looking at the regression equation, if a father had an IQ of 150, what could you predict about the eventual IQ of his new-born son? Substituting in the formula:

$$Y' = .50 \; \frac{15}{15} \, 150 + (100 - .50 \, \frac{15}{15} \, 100)$$
$$Y' = 125$$

Now we have a prediction which is specific for this son and this father, one which actually utilizes the known relationship between the variables. The IQ of any father (or mother) could be put into the formula and the specific IQ of his son (or daughter) could be predicted. With fathers of varying IQ's, the prediction of the sons' IQ's would also vary.

How accurate is this prediction? The standard error of estimate is $SD_{y.x} = 15\sqrt{1 - .50^2}$ or 13. In terms of accuracy, this means that about two-thirds of the time we make such a prediction about the sons of fathers with 150 IQ, the son's actual IQ will fall between 125 ± 13 or between 112 and 138. About 95 per cent of the time the actual IQ of the son will be between $125 \pm (2)(13)$ or between 99 and 151. Almost always, the actual IQ will be between $125 \pm (3)(13)$ or between 86 and 164.

With these data, obviously our prediction is a more specific one, and also a more accurate one. We have narrowed the range of predictive accuracy. We have gone from predicting that everyone will fall on the population mean to predicting a very specific number, and the range of inaccuracy around this prediction is more narrow. The narrowness or precision of this range is a function of the magnitude of the relationship between X and Y. We have gone from a situation in which our predictive powers account for zero per cent of the variance (0.00^2) to one in which our prediction accounts for 25 per cent of the variance $(.50^2)$.[2] This also informs us that 75 per cent of the variance is as yet not accounted for and is as yet unpredicted.

$r = 1.00$.   If the correlation had been 1.00, prediction would be perfect. The IQ of a parent would tell you exactly the IQ of his off-spring. For the 150 IQ father, the regression equation would be

$$Y' = 1.00 \frac{15}{15} 150 + (100 - 1.00 \frac{15}{15} 100)$$
$$Y' = 150$$

How accurate is this prediction? The standard error of estimate is $SD_{y.x} = 15 \sqrt{1 - 1.00^2}$ which equals zero. This means that every time we make a prediction about the IQ of an offspring of 150 IQ fathers, the offspring's actual IQ will be 150. When the correlation coefficient is squared, it tells us that 100 per cent of the variance is accounted for. All variations in Y are predicted.

The three examples which have been discussed are shown in Table 5–3. As the magnitude of the relationship increases, the prediction of Y' changes, the standard error of estimate becomes smaller, the percentage of variance in the predicted variable which can be accounted for becomes greater, and the range of error becomes narrower. With this discussion as a background, the student should be better able to evaluate correlation coefficients of various sizes.

OTHER MEASURES OF RELATIONSHIP

Before leaving the subject of correlational statistics, other common measures of relationship should be mentioned. In the preceding discussion, the impression may have been given that the correlation co-efficient as an indicator of predictive accuracy only applies to the two-variable situation. Not only can we have a relationship between X and Y and hence predict Y from X, but Y can also be related to any number of other variables which may be combined to predict Y. The statistic which

---

[2] The variance of a distribution of scores is the mean of squared deviations of each individual score from the mean of the distribution. The variance may be determined by squaring the standard deviation. Thus, the variance of the WISC scores is 15^2 or 225. If we knew everything there was to know about the antecedents of intelligence, our predictor variables would account for all of that 225; each individual's IQ would be predicted without error. With a parent-child correlation of .50, we would say that 25 per cent of the variance can now be accounted for (or predicted) on the basis of parental intelligence and 75 per cent will be unaccounted for or unpredicted. These figures can be obtained by squaring the standard error of estimate: $13^2 = 169$. This figure is the variance which is not predicted from X. And, 169 is 75 per cent of 225; the amount of the variance which *is* predicted is the difference between 169 and 225 or 56, which is 25 per cent of 225.

Table 5–3   PREDICTING WITH CORRELATIONS OF
DIFFERENT MAGNITUDES

Magnitude of r	0.00	.50	1.00
Prediction of Son's IQ when Father's IQ is 150	100	125	150
Standard Error of Estimate	15	13	0
Percentage of Variance in Y Accounted for by X	0%	25%	100%
Actual IQ of Offspring Will Fall Within the Following Ranges:			
68.27% of the time	85–115	112–138	150–150
95.45% of the time	70–130	99–151	150–150
99.73% of the time	55–145	86–164	150–150

describes such a situation is the *multiple correlation coefficient*. The interpretation of a multiple r in terms of utilization in a regression equation, standard error of estimate, percentage of the variance accounted for, and the like, is like that of the ordinary correlation coefficient. Returning briefly to the IQ example, would prediction of a child's IQ be any better if we knew the IQ of each of his parents? The only additional bit of information needed for the formula is the fact that the IQ's of husbands and wives have been found to correlate .50. If r_{12} is the correlation between offspring and father, r_{13} the correlation between offspring and mother, and r_{23} the correlation between mother and father, the multiple correlation is:

$$r_{1.23} = \sqrt{r_{12}\left(\frac{r_{12} - r_{13}\,r_{23}}{1 - r^2_{23}}\right) + r_{13}\left(\frac{r_{13} - r_{12}\,r_{23}}{1 - r^2_{23}}\right)}$$

$$r_{1.23} = .57$$

Thus, knowledge about the IQ's of both parents provides slightly greater power in predicting the IQ of their offspring; 32 per cent of the variance can be accounted for. The standard error of estimate is computed as before: $SD_{1.23} = SD_y \sqrt{1 - r^2_{1.23}}$ which equals 12.33. To continue the example further, a regression equation can be written in which information about both parents contributes to the prediction of the child's IQ. If the father with an IQ of 150 had a wife who also had an IQ of 150, their son's (or daughter's) IQ could be predicted as follows (X_2 is the father's IQ and X_3 the mother's IQ):

$$Y' = \left(\frac{r_{12} - r_{13}\,r_{23}}{1 - r^2_{23}}\right)\left(\frac{SD_y}{SD_{x2}}\right)(X_2) + \left(\frac{r_{13} - r_{12}\,r_{23}}{1 - r^2_{23}}\right)\left(\frac{SD_y}{SD_{x3}}\right)(X_3) +$$

$$\left[M_y - \left(\frac{r_{12} - r_{13}r_{23}}{1 - r^2_{23}}\right)\left(\frac{SD_y}{SD_{x2}}\right)(M_{x2}) - \left(\frac{r_{13} - r_{12}r_{23}}{1 - r^2_{23}}\right)\left(\frac{SD_y}{SD_{x3}}\right)(M_{x3})\right]$$

$$Y' = 133$$

Note that the predicted IQ is different from that which was based on knowledge about only the father, and the prediction is a slightly more accurate one. Though the computation becomes more difficult, more variables may be added to the multiple correlation coefficient and to the regression equation so long as they contribute to the accuracy of prediction.

The use of the correlation coefficient is appropriate for any situation in which the two variables represent continuous measures and in which the relationship is a linear one. Other types of situations frequently arise, however, and the student should refer to an introductory statistics text for further information about the use of other types of coefficients, their computation, and their interpretation.

Correlates of Dimensions of Personality

Historically, the most characteristic type of research conducted in the field of personality has been the determination of the correlation between a given personality variable and some other behavior. There are two major forms which this research can take. First, the relationship between any pair of personality dimensions may be determined by obtaining a group of subjects, administering the two measuring instruments, and computing the correlation between the two sets of scores. Second, the personality dimension may be hypothesized to be associated with some behavior which does not constitute another personality dimension. Studies of this type most often involve administering the personality measure, obtaining the other response measure (for example, political preference, church attendance, school major), and then determining whether the two are associated.

We will examine a representative sample of correlational studies with variables consisting of attitudinal, motivational, emotional, ability, and adjustment measures.

ANTI-NEGRO PREJUDICE: THE DESEGREGATION SCALE

One of the most characteristic of human behaviors is the tendency to group other human beings on some discriminable basis and then to respond as if all members of that group were similar. An almost limitless variety of bases for categorization exists, including religious beliefs, political affiliation, nationality, area of residence within a country, sex, race, age, type of disease contracted, college attended, occupation, and the fact that one rides a motorcycle. The generalized attitudes, beliefs, and opinions concerning those fitting within a given group are called stereotypes. Even when the elements of a stereotype are partially accurate (for example, Japanese tend to be shorter than Americans), the predictions based on stereotypes are likely to be inaccurate for many and in some instances almost all members of the group.

In the United States, the members of the Negro race, though constituting one-tenth of our population, have perhaps been the object of prejudice more consistently and over a longer span of time than any other group of individuals. In a study by Katz and Braly [1933], a group of 100 undergraduates indicated the traits most associated with 10 different national and racial groups. For Negroes, the five most commonly mentioned traits were superstitious, lazy, happy-go-lucky, ignorant, and musical. In 1963, Fishbein found that the most frequently given behavioral characteristics were musical, athletic, friendly, uneducated, and unintelligent. Even though a given set of attitudes and beliefs concerning a group may be widely held in a given society, individual differences in the strength of such attitudes are apt to be great. And, differences along attitudinal dimensions may be conceptualized as a personality variable just as may any other relatively stable dimension of individual differences.

One of the measures of anti-Negro prejudice which has been constructed for research use is the Desegregation Scale [Kelly, Ferson, and Holtzman, 1958]. Beginning with a pool of 200 statements reflecting attitudes toward the Negro, the investigators selected the best 76 of these for further refinement. Using the Thurstone [Thurstone and Chave, 1929] scaling method, 102 college students rated the items in terms of favorableness toward the Negro as expressed by each item. The final form of the scale consists of the 26 items with the least variance in terms of favorableness ratings. The selected items also represent approximately equal points along the 11-point scale of favorableness. Below are samples of the items and their scale value, 11 representing the least favorable end of the scale:

10.4 The Negro will remain ignorant and superstitious despite equal educational opportunities.

8.9 Negroes living in white neighborhoods lower the standards of cleanliness.

7.7 Admitting Negroes to white schools would not work because most Negroes do not have the necessary background to keep up with white students.

4.3 The Negro race will eventually reach the cultural and intellectual level of white people.

3.4 I would not object to participating in school athletics with Negroes.

2.1 I would not object to dancing with a good Negro dancer.

1.1 The best way to solve the race problem is to encourage intermarriage so that there will eventually be only one race [Kelly, *et al.*, 1958, p. 307].

All 26 items were placed in a questionnaire to which subjects are asked to respond with degrees of agreement. Each item is scored from 0 to 4 with high scores representing negative attitudes toward Negroes. Total scores range from 0 to 104.

             Relationship between Anti-Negro Prejudice and Anti-Semitic Prejudice.   One question which might be asked concerning any attitudinal dimension is its generality. If individual differences in attitudes toward the Negro are a function of specific experiences with representatives of that race or a function of specific knowledge about the characteristics of Negroes, anti-Negro prejudice should constitute a relatively specific and isolated trait. On the other hand, if anti-Negro attitudes are a function of such variables as displaced hostility or general ethnocentrism, various types of prejudice should be interrelated. In the latter instance, people who have a relatively negative attitude toward Negroes should also be negative toward other minority group members, toward foreigners, toward those who disagree with them politically, and so forth.

Kelly, *et al.* [1958] obtained data relevant to this question with respect to the Desegregation Scale and a special six-item Anti-Semitism (AS) Scale. Items from the AS Scale include:

1. One trouble with Jewish businessmen is that they stick together and prevent other people from having a fair chance in competition.
2. I can hardly imagine myself marrying a Jew.
3. There may be a few exceptions, but in general Jews are pretty much alike.
4. The trouble with letting Jews into a nice neighborhood is that they gradually give it a typical Jewish atmosphere.
5. To end prejudice against Jews, the first step is for the Jews to try sincerely to get rid of their harmful and irritating habits.
6. There is something different and strange about Jews; it's hard to tell what they are thinking and planning, and what makes them tick [Adorno, Frenkel-Brunswik, Levinson, and Sanford, 1950, p. 142].

The subjects were 547 undergraduates at the University of Texas who filled out a questionnaire containing both measures of prejudice.

The investigators found a statistically significant correlation of .49 between attitudes toward Negroes and attitudes toward Jews. As has been found in other studies of prejudice, attitudes of prejudice tend not to be isolated dimensions of personality but an integral part of a more general pattern of behavior. Thus, about 24 per cent of the variance in anti-Semitism scores can be accounted for on the basis of anti-Negro attitudes and vice versa. An overlap may occur between these two dimensions in terms of the antecedents of ethnic prejudice and of absence of ethnic prejudice. If an individual's score on the Desegregation Scale is known, his score on the Anti-Semitism Scale can be predicted with better than chance accuracy, and the prediction of attitudes toward Negroes is possible from knowing an individual's attitudes toward Jews.

Relationship between Anti-Negro Prejudice and Field of Study in College.   A more complex type of response is represented by the courses, major, and occupations selected by an individual in college. Such choices are in part a function of abilities; most people are not bright enough to become nuclear physicists. In part, the choices are determined by family pressures, the amount of contact an individual has had in the past with representatives of the field, and the degree to which an instructor in an introductory course manages to light a spark of interest. In addition to such variables, however, personality determinants are also likely to be operative. A given set of interests or values or aspirations would not be expected to be independent of individual differences along quite different dimensions. Thus, those who have strong nurturant needs might be expected to find social service fields of great appeal. And, those who have well-developed habits of compulsivity might respond positively to any area of specialization involving precision and detail and negatively to any area characterized by complexity and ambiguity.

What predictions might be made with respect to a personality variable such as anti-Negro prejudice? For reasons discussed in some detail in Chapter 8, those high in prejudice should respond well to areas stressing practical and concrete and conservative matters as opposed to areas stressing humanistic and abstract and liberal content. Also most people do not care to be exposed to viewpoints directly opposed to their own or to information which contradicts what they believe. Since areas such as sociology and anthropology and psychology are quite apt to present material inconsistent with anti-Negro attitudes, they are not likely to be chosen as majors by these individuals.

In the Kelly, *et al.* [1958] study of anti-Negro attitudes among Texas undergraduates, the subjects who took the Desegregation Scale were also asked to indicate their major field of study at the University. It was found that prejudice scores were significantly different across majors. As shown in Table 5–4, the most prejudiced students are found in the field of business and the least prejudiced in the social sciences.

We should note also that the findings may be explained in other ways than the possibility that personality variables influenced choice of major. Certain aspects of the course content may influence attitudes toward Negroes or possibly both choice of a field of study and prejudice were determined by some unknown third factor.

Table 5–4   RELATIONSHIP BETWEEN MAJOR FIELD OF STUDY
             AND ANTI-NEGRO PREJUDICE*

Field	Mean Score on Desegregation Scale
Business	53.3
Pharmacy	48.9
Education	46.7
Engineering	45.2
Humanities	44.9
Fine Arts	42.5
Natural Sciences	41.4
Social Sciences	39.6

* Adapted from Kelly, *et al.*, 1958, p. 312.

NEED FOR HETEROSEXUALITY: EDWARDS PERSONAL
PREFERENCE SCHEDULE

When motivational systems are classified or catalogued, the usual practice is to dichotomize needs into those which have a physiological basis and those which are learned. This sort of breakdown will not stand very close scrutiny in that almost all physiological needs are modified by learning and all learned needs obviously involve physiological structures and functions.

The sexual drive is one which presents special difficulty to those who classify. Its physiological components include hormonal secretions and concomitant bodily activities (for example, the production of eggs and sperm). At the same time, the satisfaction of sexual needs is not essential to the life of the organism as is the case with other physiological needs. Further, almost every aspect of sexual activity from characteristic drive strength to type of goal behavior is subject to modification by experiential variables. Thus, the prediction of sexual behavior can probably proceed as well with an emphasis on the learned aspects of sexual motivation as with an emphasis on its physiological base.

Chapters 3 and 9 discuss the work of Henry A. Murray in the area of motivation. Among the needs he outlined is the need for sex. Murray's definition of this need was incorporated by Edwards as the manifest need for heterosexuality:

To go out with members of the opposite sex, to engage in social activities with the opposite sex, to be in love with someone of the opposite sex, to kiss those of the opposite sex, to be regarded as physically attractive by those of the opposite sex, to participate in discussions about sex, to read books and plays involving sex, to listen to or to tell jokes involving sex, to become sexually excited [Edwards, 1959, p. 11].[3]

A somewhat unusual approach to the development of a measuring instrument to assess this need was made by Allen Edwards at the University of Washington. In 1953 Edwards published an article in which he reported a substantial correlation between the social desirability of the behavior described by a test item and the percentage of individuals who indicate agreement with the item. Subsequent work [Edwards, 1957; 1959] suggested that a great many personality tests were confounding the variable which they purported to measure with social desirability, as will be discussed in greater detail in Chapter 10. In building a test to measure 15 of the manifest needs outlined by Murray, Edwards [1959] attempted to control for the social desirability of item content. Instead of asking a subject to agree or disagree with a given item, the Edwards Personal Preference Schedule (EPPS) requires the subject to choose between two statements in terms of which is *more* characteristic of what he likes. On the basis of preliminary item-scaling, each pair of items is matched for social desirability. Presumably, the response to such items will be influenced by item-content rather than by social desirability.

The final version of the EPPS measures 15 manifest needs, including heterosexuality. Edwards [1959] found that the heterosexuality scale has the highest split-half reliability (.87) of the 15 EPPS scales, and it has a test-retest reliability of .85 over a one-week period.

Relationship between Need for Heterosexuality and Conformity. Sexual motives and sexual behavior tend to occupy a special position in human affairs. Over the world man has taken the primitive drive for sexual release and molded it into an astonishing variety of forms which include such diverse institutions as temple prostitutes, celibate priesthoods, tribal incest taboos, polygamy and polyandry, veiled women, burlesque shows, censorship boards, high school sex clubs, pornography laws, and magazines for homosexuals.

At the present time in this country, the mores regarding sex remain confused. On the one hand, a glorification of sexual activity is manifested in ways ranging from publicity for Hollywood "love goddesses" to the culture-wide encouragement of youthful dating. At the same time, restrictions on sexual expression are prevalent both in legal statutes and in social practice. Not surprisingly, surveys find enormous differences among individuals in the frequency and manner of sexual expression or in the amount of conflict and anxiety felt in response to sexual stimuli. For example, sexual passages from several current novels were found to make some col-

---

[3] Reprinted by permission. Copyright 1954, © 1959, The Psychological Corporation, New York, New York. All rights reserved.

lege males feel anxious while others felt angry and disgusted [Byrne and Sheffield, 1965].

A variable which might be expected to be related to the strength of the need for heterosexuality is the general tendency to conform to the demands of those in positions of authority. The verbalized and codified values regarding sexuality are rather clear. Moderate and standard sexual activity within marriage is good. Any other type of sexual activity or even undue interest in sexual matters is bad. We might hypothesize that those who tend in general to conform to authority figures would also conform in the area of sexuality.

In building the California Psychological Inventory (CPI), Gough [1957] included the variable *achievement via conformance* which he defined as "those factors of interest and motivation which facilitate achievement in any setting where conformance is a positive behavior." Subjects were rated by their acquaintances on this dimension and divided into high and low conformance subgroups. Those items which were answered differently by the two groups were incorporated as achievement-via-conformance items in the CPI.

The relationship between the dimensions of need for heterosexuality and achievement via conformance was reported as part of an investigation by Dunnette, Kerchner and De Gidio [1958]. A group of 102 engineers, product supervisors, salesmen, and sales managers were given both the EPPS and the CPI.

Among the significant relationships reported, need for heterosexuality correlated —.20 with achievement via conformance. Thus, there is a small though significant tendency for those who score high on the sexual dimension to score low on the conformance dimension and vice versa. Only four per cent of the variance in n sex is accounted for by conformity, however.

Relationship between Fiancés in Need for Heterosexuality. Courting behavior is perhaps one of the more peculiar aspects of modern life. There are relatively ritualistic ways in which sexually mature, unmarried individuals are expected to form a series of transitory pairings, to take part in a number of entertainment-centered activities together, and eventually to decide by mutual consent to make one of the pairings permanent. Since about one-third of American marriages end in divorce and an unknown proportion of the remainder involve dissatisfactions in varying degrees, the courting process and the selection procedures are far from perfect in their functioning. Behavioral science is able to offer very little help at this time to improve the process. We can, however, study premarital and marital behavior in order to begin the acquisition of knowledge about this aspect of interpersonal behavior.

On a number of grounds, one would predict that the need systems of two individuals would be an important consideration in determining attraction betwen two prospective partners. Since a major portion of an individual's need gratification is either directly or indirectly a function of the behavior of a spouse, incompatibility in need strengths could lead to considerable dissatisfaction. Note that needs would not necessarily have to be similar. In some instances (for example, motives to dominate others or to submit to others), it might be preferable for the two partners to be as different as possible. With regard to need for heterosexuality, similarity would be expected to be more rewarding than dissimilarity. To the extent that dating behavior provides information concerning needs, one would hypothesize that couples who like one another well enough to plan marriage would not be randomly paired with respect to their motivational patterns. Banta and Hetherington [1963] obtained 29 pairs of engaged couples as subjects. Each was given the EPPS and the need scores of the engaged pairs were correlated. The results are shown in Table 5–5.

Table 5–5 CORRELATIONS BETWEEN NEEDS OF ENGAGED COUPLES

Significant at .05 Level or Better		Not Significant at .05 Level	
Need for	r	Need for	r
Heterosexuality	.79	Succorance	.36
Deference	.52	Change	.29
Endurance	.51	Dominance	.25
Orderliness	.48	Affiliation	.24
Abasement	.44	Aggression	.16
Autonomy	.39	Nurturance	.16
Exhibitionism	.39	Achievement	−.01
Intraception	.38		

Of interest is the finding that couples are most similar in their sexual drive, which suggests the possibility that this aspect of the relationship between males and females receives the greatest stress in our culture. Different antecedents could easily have led to similar needs, and the latter similarity acted to attract the partners to one another. Another, less likely, possibility is that the couples were attracted on the basis of other variables, and their interactions somehow brought about need similarity through alteration of one or both partners.

TOLERANCE FOR POSTPONED NEED GRATIFICATION: PREFERENCE
FOR DELAYED REINFORCEMENT

In many theories of personality, an important place is assigned to the development of tolerance for postponing immediate gratification in order to obtain more valued rewards at some future time. In individual terms, greater maturity is shown by those who, when an impulse is aroused, are able to pause, compare the present reward with a future one, and then delay the gratification of that impulse at least temporarily.

Civilization is built on a foundation of impulse control in which drives of hunger, sex, elimination, and so forth, are satisfied in particular ways at particular times in specific contexts. Primitive people, small children, and psychopaths are unable to function properly in such an environment. One of the greatest tasks facing children and their parents is the inculcation of behavior which involves delay and postponement of drive satisfaction. And, the teaching varies in its success. Obviously, a complex series of variables are responsible for the vast differences among individuals in willingness to delay gratification. For example, consider the student who attends college and goes through graduate school in order to obtain advanced scientific or professional training. The entire process revolves around delay and at least partial nonsatisfaction of primary and secondary drives in the expectation of greater future rewards. By way of comparison, consider the person who drops out of school, commits minor burglaries to obtain money, and participates with a gang in a sexual assault on a young woman. Is there any way to measure such differences in impulse control and to study this dimension as a personality variable?

Most investigations of this behavior have utilized some variation of a technique in which subjects must choose between a small immediate reward and a larger reward which is available after a time delay. Among others, Mischel and Gilligan [1964] have utilized a measure of gratification delay in which children are given 17 choices and in each instance the decision involves a small immediate reward vs. a large delayed reward. For example, they must choose between a small notebook now and a larger one in a week, a small magnifying glass now or a larger one a week later, and 15 cents now or 30 cents in three weeks.

Relationship between Delay of Gratification and Cheating. Mischel and Gilligan [1964] hypothesized that those who are unable to postpone gratification in order to receive a larger reward would be likely to succumb to temptation and cheat in situations in which success or some sort of victory was of importance to them. Their subjects were 49 sixth-grade boys in Boston who were given the 17 choices between immediate and delayed reward. The situation used to provide an opportunity to cheat was a shooting gallery or ray gun game in which each boy shot a ray gun at a moving rocket target. Points were given for hitting the target, and brightly colored sportsman badges were given for those getting a sufficient number of points. Actually, the game was arranged so that the subject could not get enough points to win a badge unless he falsified his score. To make the latter possible, the experimenter left the room during each game and asked the subject to write down his own scores and add them up. If they wrote down their actual score of 17, no prizes would be given. With a score of 20, they would win a badge, with 25 points a better badge, and with 28 points the best badge. So, one measure of cheating was the number of points over 17 which a subject reported. A second measure of cheating for those who cheated at all was the number of trials which went by before cheating began.

For each measure of cheating, a significant correlation with immediate vs. delayed reward preferences was found. Preference for immediate reward correlated .31 with amount of cheating in the game and (for those who did cheat) —.38 with the number of trials which elapsed before they began to cheat. The authors conclude:

> The obtained findings also increase confidence that the willingness or ability to delay gratification, as measured in simple, direct behavior choices, does indeed predict behavior in a realistic situation requiring the deferral and inhibitions usually subsumed under "ego strength" or "impulse control" constructs [Mischel and Gilligan, 1964, p. 417].

Relationship between Delay of Gratification and Age. As was pointed out earlier, children must learn to delay the gratification of impulses to some extent in order to function in any culture. Since this tolerance for postponement is almost certainly learned over a relatively long period of time rather than all at once, we would expect differences in this behavior across age levels. That is, with increasing age a higher and higher proportion of children should be able to delay the gratification of their impulses.

As part of a cross-cultural investigation in Trinidad, Mischel [1958] obtained data on 53 male and female children aged 7, 8, and 9. The subjects consisted of 35 Negroes and 18 East Indians. In a preliminary study with other subjects, the investigator found that two reinforcements, a one-cent and a ten-cent piece of candy, were clearly perceived as different and that all of the children preferred the ten-cent candy. In the main investigation, the children filled out a research questionnaire and then the experimenter was introduced to the children. The experimenter proceeded as follows:

He displayed the two kinds of reinforcements and said: "I would like to give each of you a piece of candy, but I don't have enough of these (indicating the larger, more preferred reinforcement) with me today. So you can either get this one (indicating the smaller, less preferred reinforcement) right now, today, or, if you want to, you can wait for this one (indicating) which I will bring back next Wednesday (one week delay interval)." To insure clarity these instructions were repeated in rephrased form and both reinforcements were carefully displayed. The fact that getting the (smaller) candy today precluded getting the (larger) one next week, and vice versa, was stressed. Ss were asked to indicate their choice by writing "today" (T) or "next week" (W) on their questionnaires. The response made here was the measure of choice of a larger (or more preferred) delayed reinforcement or a smaller (less preferred) immediate reinforcement. Ss were seated sufficiently far apart from each other to insure reasonably that their choices were made independently in this group setting [Mischel, 1958, p. 59].

Though Mischel was interested in testing several hypotheses, we will be concerned here only with the data regarding age. The children were divided into the 28 who preferred the immediate reinforcement and the 25 who preferred the delayed reinforcement. When they were further divided into separate age groups, as shown in Table 5–6, the proportion of subjects who preferred the larger delayed reinforcement to the smaller immediate reinforcement increased as age increased.

Table 5–6   RELATIONSHIP BETWEEN AGE AND PREFERENCE
FOR IMMEDIATE VS. DELAYED REINFORCEMENT

	Age		
	7	8	9
Proportion Choosing Delayed Reinforcement	.19	.52	.80
Proportion Choosing Immediate Reinforcement	.81	.48	.20

Using a chi-square analysis, Mischel found the relationship to be a significant one. He concludes:

This relationship between Ss' age and preference for delayed reinforcement is in accord with nonexperimental discussions of such a relationship to the effect that with increasing maturity comes the increasing ability to delay gratification. This finding is not inconsistent with an interpretation of preference for delayed reinforcement as a learned behavior which is, in part, a function of the expectancy that the promised reinforcement will issue from the social agent in spite of time delay. With increasing age the potentiality for developing a strong expectancy of this kind increases *if* the individual continues to gain reinforcing experiences within this area, thus building up the relevant expectancies, but not as a function of growing older or biological maturation per se [Mischel, 1958, p. 60].

CREATIVE ABILITY: RATINGS, DIFFERENTIAL REACTION
SCHEDULE, AND COMPOSITE ORIGINALITY SCORE

The study of creativity presents a research challenge. A knowledge of the antecedents and correlates of originality and a knowledge of the types of behavior influenced by this ability would be of great importance to the field of personality. One of the most difficult challenges, however, is that of measurement. By definition, we are dealing with behavior which involves new and different responses to stimuli and the tendency to perceive hitherto unforeseen relationships or implications in a situation. The usual approach of ability tests quickly runs into absurdity (for example, a multiple choice question with instructions to choose the most original alternative). To date, attempts to measure creativity have been of three major types. All three will be discussed briefly in examples drawn from the work at the Institute of Personality Assessment and Research (IPAR) at the University of California at Berkeley.

Ratings. One approach selects those who are recognized as creative in a given field of endeavor. In this way, their success in their chosen work as judged by experts serves as the measure of creative ability. MacKinnon [1962] defined creativity as a process extended in time and characterized by originality, adaptiveness, and realization. He chose the field of architecture to seek creative individuals. First, five professors of architecture each nominated the 40 most creative architects in the United States; a total of 86 different men were named. Of these, 64 were invited to come to Berkeley to participate in a research project, and 40 accepted. All 64 who were invited were rated as to creativity by 11 editors of architectural journals and by the 40 research subjects. The latter two sets of ratings correlated .88, which suggests fairly good agreement concerning what is meant by creativity in this field. As comparison subjects, two additional samples of architects who matched the creative group in age and area of residence were obtained. One group consisted of architects who had worked in association with one or more of the 64 most creative; the other group was made up of architects who had not worked with any of them. New creativity ratings were made of those in all three groups on a seven-point scale by architectural experts. The mean ratings of 5.46 for the creative ones, 4.25 for those associated with them, and 3.54 for the third group were significantly different from one another. MacKinnon carried out a number of investigations comparing these three groups, and one of these will be described shortly.

Questionnaire. A paper and pencil questionnaire with the true-false response format has been devised by Gough [1957b] as a measure of the factors underlying originality. The resulting test, the Differential Reaction Schedule, measures five factors. Each is made up of 20 items which correlate with that factor and not with the other four. Gough's definitions of the factors and a sample item from each are given below:

1. *Intellectual competence.* The capacity to think, to reason, to comprehend, and to know.

   I don't like to work on a problem unless there is the possibility of coming out with a clear-cut and unambiguous answer.   F

2. *Inquiringness as a habit of mind.* An unending curiosity about things, about people, and about nature; an inner spur toward resolution and discernment.

> I get sort of annoyed with writers who go out of their way to use strange and unusual words.   F

3. *Cognitive flexibility.* The ability to shift and to adapt, and to deal with the new, the unexpected, and the unforeseen.

> For most questions there is just one right answer, once a person is able to get all the facts.   F

4. *Esthetic sensitivity.* A deep-seated preference for and appreciation of elegance of form and of thought, of harmony wrought from complexity, and of style as a medium of expression.

> I would like to hear a great singer in an opera.   T

5. *Sense of destiny.* This includes something of resoluteness and (naturally) of egotism, but over and above these a belief in the foregone certainty of the worth and validity of one's own future and attainment.

> Barring emergencies, I have a pretty good idea what I'll be doing for the next ten years.   T   [Gough, 1957b, p. 9.]

Original Responses. A third approach to the measurement of originality is that of Barron [1957] who used a series of different measures to obtain a composite originality score. Three tests were devised by Guilford, Wilson, and Christensen [1952] at the University of Southern California. Unusual uses requires the subject to list six uses to which each of several common objects can be put; infrequently named uses are scored for originality. Consequences B asks the subject what would happen if certain changes were suddenly to occur; clever and remote consequences are scored. In Plot Title B, two story plots are given, and the subject provides titles which are scored for cleverness. Barron also gave the Rorschach ink blots and a special ink blot test [Barron, 1955] which were scored for the number of original or unusual responses given. Stories told in response to the Thematic Apperception Test cards were rated for originality by two judges. Subjects were asked to make as many words as possible out of the letters in the word "generation," and the number of infrequent but correct solutions scored. Finally, the subjects were asked to write a story using all of a list of 50 randomly selected words; the story was then rated for originality. A subject's composite originality score consisted of the sum of the standard scores on all eight tests.

With each of these approaches to the measurement of creative talent, a vast number of correlational studies have been conducted which provide a great deal of information about the position of this dimension in the structure of personality. From this wide array, we will select only two examples.

Relationship between Creativity and Perception by Others. In Barron's [1957] work with the composite originality score, the social stimulus value of creative individuals was investigated. A persistent cultural stereotype equates creativity with odd behavior, lack of social skills, and a generally deviant orientation. The insanity of Jonathan Swift, the homosexuality of Oscar Wilde, and the drug addiction of Edgar Allan Poe make more colorful reading than the relatively normal lives of Thomas Hardy, Nathaniel Hawthorne, and James Fenimore Cooper. Whether greater than chance relationship exists between creative ability and inadequate social adjustment is another question.

Barron selected a group of 100 Air Force officers with a mean age of 33. Most were married, had at least two children, and were combat veterans. In groups of ten, the subjects spent a full three days at IPAR taking the creativity battery as well as other paper and pencil tests and situational tests, being interviewed, and participating in group discussions, charades, and the like. Observations of the subjects by the staff were made, and the assessments summarized by means of a Q-sort of 76 statements and an adjective checklist. These assessments were made without knowledge of the subject's performance on the creativity battery.

For the 25 subjects with the highest and 25 with the lowest composite originality scores, comparisons were made of the way they were described by the staff judges. A number of statements from the Q-sort yielded significant differences between the most and least creative subjects. The most creative were described as:

1. Verbally fluent, conversationally facile
2. High degree of intellect
3. Communicates ideas clearly and effectively
4. Highly cathects intellectual activity
5. An effective leader
6. Persuasive; wins others over to his point of view
7. Concerned with philosophical problems and the meaning of life
8. Taking an ascendant role in his relations with others [Barron, 1957, p. 733].

The least creative were described as:

1. Conforming; tending to do the things that are prescribed
2. Stereotyped and unoriginal in his approach to problems
3. Having a narrow range of interests
4. Tending not to become involved in things
5. Lacking social poise and presence
6. Unaware of his own social stimulus value
7. Slow personal tempo

8. With respect to authority, submissive, compliant, and overly accepting
9. Lacking confidence in self
10. Rigid, inflexible
11. Lacking insight into own motives
12. Suggestible
13. Unable to make decisions without vacillation, hesitation, and delay [Barron, 1957, p. 734].

On the adjective checklist, similar differences were found. Significantly more often the most creative subjects had the following words checked in describing them; interests wide, clever, imaginative, planful, poised, determined, talkative, logical, rational, shrewd, civilized, loyal, mature, versatile, efficient, initiative, resourceful, reflective, quick, enterprising, energetic, organized, and fairminded. The least creative were significantly more often described as dull, commonplace, simple, slow, apathetic, rigid, unassuming, and conventional. Obviously, creative and noncreative individuals are perceived differently by others, but these differences do not fit the cultural stereotype very well.

Relationship between Creativity and Femininity of Interests. Within almost every culture, men and women are assigned different roles and come to behave differently with respect to attitudes, interests, values, and the like. The differences across cultures are sufficiently great as to suggest that learning plays a more important part in this differentiation than does the fact of biological difference in reproductive mechanisms. One of the most extensive studies of personality differences of males and females in our culture was carried out by Terman and Miles in 1936. The summary of their findings would seem to hold as well today as it did three decades ago:

From whatever angle we have examined them the males included in the standardization groups evinced a distinctive interest in exploit and adventure, in outdoor and physically strenuous occupations, in machinery and tools, in science, physical phenomena, and inventions; and, from rather occasional evidence, in business and commerce. On the other hand, the females of our groups have evinced a distinctive interest in domestic affairs and in aesthetic objects and occupations; they have distinctly preferred more sedentary and indoor occupations, and occupations more directly ministrative, particularly to the young, the helpless, the distressed. Supporting and supplementing these are the more subjective differences—those in emotional disposition and direction. The males directly or indirectly manifest the greater self-assertion and aggressiveness; they express more hardihood and fearlessness, and more roughness of manners, language, and sentiments. The females express themselves as more compassionate and sympathetic, more timid, more fastidious, and aesthetically sensitive, more emotional in general (or at least more expressive of the four emotions considered), severer moralists, yet admit in themselves weaknesses in emotional control and (less noticeably) in physique [Terman and Miles, 1936, pp. 447–448].

Though there are measurable differences between the sexes in many personality characteristics, a great many individuals share the interests of the opposite sex. Many males have quite "feminine" values and interests, and many females have an extremely "masculine" outlook. Such differences by no means imply homosexuality. A rather consistent finding has been that the most creative males tend to have feminine interests.

All three of the creativity measures we have discussed have been utilized in research which included the variable of masculinity-femininity as measured by the Mf scale of the MMPI. This is a 60-item scale composed of items which are answered differently by males and females.

In the MacKinnon [1962] study of creative architects, the MMPI was administered to all three groups. He found that the "most striking aspect of the MMPI profiles" of the creative subjects was the extremely high peak on the Mf scale. In Barron's [1957] investigation of the 100 Air Force officers, the composite originality scores on the eight tests correlated .33 ($p < .01$) with Mf scores. And, Gough's [1957c] findings with the Differential Reaction Schedule administered to 70 medical school applicants are shown in Table 5–7. Gough's data suggest that some aspects of creativity are much more closely associated with femininity than others.

Table 5–7   CORRELATION BETWEEN THE DIFFERENTIAL REACTION SCHEDULE AND THE Mf SCALE OF THE MMPI

	r
Total Originality	.33*
Intellectual Competence	−.06
Inquiringness as a Habit of Mind	.22
Cognitive Flexibility	.20
Esthetic Sensitivity	.48*
Sense of Destiny	.02

* $p < .01$

Why should femininity of interests be related to creativity and originality at all? Two somewhat different hypotheses have been proposed. MacKinnon suggests that the relationship indicates greater self-insight and freedom of expression among creative individuals:

The evidence is clear: The more creative a person is the more he reveals an openness to his own feelings and emotions, a sensitive intellect and understanding self-awareness, and wide-ranging interests including many which in the American culture are thought of as feminine. In the realm of sexual identification and interests, our creative subjects appear to give more expression to the feminine side of their nature than do less creative persons [MacKinnon, 1962, p. 488].

Barron provides another possible interpretation, tolerance for complexity:

In a sense, the recognition by men of impulses or interests which are considered more appropriate in women, or at least more characteristic of women than of men in this culture, may be seen as one aspect of the more basic disposition to allow more complexity and contradictions into consciousness; this assumes, of course, an initial biological bisexual disposition in both men and women. Thus the more original men would permit themselves to be more aware of tabooed interests and impulses, and would seek to integrate these superficially discordant phenomena into a more complex whole [Barron, 1957, p. 737].

INTROVERSION-EXTRAVERSION: THE Si SCALE

Among the contributions of the late Swiss psychiatrist, Carl G. Jung, to personality theory was the concept of introversion-extraversion. In Jung's system one of the basic attitudinal divisions into which man could be categorized was defined by the direction taken by the libido in relation to the outside world. These inborn temperamental differences led either to subjective (introverted) functioning in which the self is uppermost or to objective (extraverted) functioning in which the outside world is uppermost in importance. Jung describes these attitudes as follows:

The first, if normal, is revealed by a hesitating, reflective, reticent disposition, that does not easily give itself away, that shrinks from objects, always assuming the defensive, and preferring to make its cautious observations as from a hiding place. The second type, if normal, is characterized by an accommodating, and apparently open and ready disposition, at ease in any given situation. This type forms attachments quickly, and ventures, unconcerned and confident, into unknown situations, rejecting thoughts of possible contingencies. In the former case, manifestly the subject, in the latter the object, is the decisive factor [Jung, 1928, p. 41].

This dichotomy was adopted by many theorists and has led to a considerable amount of research. We should note that several of Jung's assumptions about introversion-extraversion are quite often ignored by those who have adopted the terms: the genetic basis of the types, the unconscious development of the type opposite from the overt one, and the danger of neurosis or psychosis resulting from overdevelopment of either attitude type.

Many attempts have been made to measure this dimension of personality, but we will select just one as an example. Drake [1946] conceptualized introversion-extraversion as being made up of three subvarieties: thinking, social, and emotional. His plan was to build an empirically derived MMPI scale to measure the social component. As a criterion measure, he utilized an earlier measure of this dimension, the Minnesota T-S-E Inventory, which was scored for social introversion-extraversion. He selected 50 students who scored above the 65th percentile on this test and 50 who scored below the 35th percentile. The responses of these two groups were then compared for each item on the MMPI; those 70 items which were answered significantly differently by the two groups were selected for the *Si* key. New subjects were then selected and given the MMPI, which was scored with the new *Si* key, and the Minnesota T-S-E Inventory, which was scored for social introversion-extraversion. For 87 female students the two scores correlated .72 and for 81 male students, .71. The test-retest reliability of the *Si* scale in a group of 100 normals over a one-day to four-month period has been found to be .93 [Hathaway and McKinley, 1951].

   Relationship between Social Introversion-Extraversion and Perception of Human Movement on the Rorschach. Among the many determinants for which responses to the Rorschach ink blots are scored is that of human movement. When a subject's interpretation of the meaning of a blot includes movement, the response is either scored for human, animal, or inanimate movement. Examples of human movement would be "two clowns clapping hands," "two ballet dancers whirling around," "hand with index finger pointing," and "two natives beating on drums." In the Rorschach Prognostic Rating Scale (RPRS), Klopfer, Ainsworth, Klopfer, and Holt [1954] have further refined the scoring of human movement by giving greater credit for these responses if they involve more expansive activity, if they are given spontaneously rather than after questioning by the tester, and if they concern real people in our own culture. Thus, a weighted human movement or Weighted M score is obtained.

   Among the hypotheses advanced as an interpretation of this response is that it is indicative of empathy:

> The capacity for seeing human figures in the Rorschach blot materials is related to the capacity for good empathetic relationships with other human beings [Klopfer, *et al.*, 1954, p. 264].

On the basis of the empathy hypothesis alone, a relationship between Weighted M responses and social introversion-extraversion could be predicted. On a more prosaic basis, one could hypothesize that those individuals who have had the most contact with people in social situations would be more likely to perceive people in an ambiguous situation than would socially isolated individuals. Such concepts as familiarity could be invoked to predict differences in the probability of a given type of response being evoked by the blots. Whatever the explanation, a relationship between Si scores and Weighted M scores would be expected.

In an attempt to validate the RPRS by comparing ink blot responses to MMPI responses, Adams, Cooper, and Carrera [1963] administered both tests to 36 male neuropsychiatric patients in a general medical and surgical hospital for veterans. Interjudge reliability of the RPRS was determined for each of the six component scores and for the total score; correlations between the two judges ranged from .93 to 1.00.

All of the MMPI scales were correlated with the total RPRS scores and each component score. Our interest here is in the relationship between Si scores and the human movement responses. Adams, et al., say:

> Klopfer has mentioned a large number of personality functions which are positively associated with M. These include inner stability, the capacity for self-realization, self-acceptance, the capacity for empathy and identification with others, the ability to utilize creative inner resources, tolerance for frustration, creative potentials, and the capacity for self-commitment in relationships with others. These descriptions imply that Weighted M mirrors the extent to which the subject adopts a self-confident, active, effective role in interpersonal relationships. The correlations . . . generally support such an interpretation. All ten clinical scales of the MMPI are negatively correlated with Weighted M, as expected in a measure of generalized effectiveness.
>
> The highest single correlation ($r = -.57$, $p < .001$) was with the Si scale, the items of which express social uneasiness, special sensitivities, insecurities, and worries . . . [Adams, et al., 1963, p. 29].

Relationship between Social Introversion-Extraversion and Participation in Extracurricular Activities. A rather direct and obvious relationship which should hold is that between social introversion-extraversion and social behavior. Individuals on the extraverted end of the dimension should seek out social contacts, interact with others, and participate in group-centered activities, while those on the introverted end of the dimension should prefer more solitary pursuits.

Drake and Thiede [1948] obtained Si scores from the MMPI protocols of 594 females who applied to the University of Wisconsin Student Counselling Center for assistance. In addition to the MMPI, each subject filled out an information blank which requested information about her high school extracurricular activities in terms of her participation in literary pursuits, dramatics, debating, music and art, athletics, and student government. They were scored for the number of different types of activities in which they took part; therefore, scores ranged from zero to six.

A subsidiary finding was that the size of the community in which the high school was located was related to amount of participation. Therefore, the subjects were subdivided according to community size. Table 5–8 shows a comparison of mean Si scores for the least and most active stu-

Table 5–8   COMPARISON OF *Si* SCORES AND PARTICIPATION
IN HIGH SCHOOL EXTRACURRICULAR ACTIVITIES

Population of Home Community	Least Active Students (0–2 activities) Mean Si Score	Most Active Students (3–6 activities) Mean Si Score
Farm–2,499	57.85	49.71
2,500–9,999	54.73	48.53
10,000–99,999	55.94	45.72
100,000–over	52.09	47.67

dents. For every size community, the most active students have significantly ($p < .0005$) lower *Si* scores (less socially introverted) than the least active students.

A further comparison was made for college activities for the 283 non-freshmen in the sample. The students who took part in no college activities had a mean *Si* score of 53.15, while those who took part in two or more college activities had a mean of 48.17. This difference is also significant at $p < .0005$.

At both the high school and college level, then, there is a greater than chance relationship between social introversion-extraversion as measured by the *Si* scale and amount of participation in nonacademic school activities.

From the diverse sample of correlational studies presented in this chapter, we see that the task of integrating such data into a coherent structural model is going to be an extremely difficult accomplishment. In future personality texts, it should be possible to describe the structure of personality rather than a series of discrete correlational findings.

Summary

Personality structure may be conceptualized as a static representation of the organized interrelationship of personality variables. Personality structure can be represented as a series of intersecting lines in n-dimensional space. At the present time, most studies involve simply the relationship between personality dimensions.

The establishment of a relationship between two sets of responses indicates that a link exists between them, and that link may be sought in subsequent research. A common constitutional factor may account for the relationship between two stimulus-response units, as when reaction time for the hands is found to correlate with reaction time for the feet. With other responses, such as those on intelligence test subscales, very likely both constitution and learning contribute to the correlation. Still other responses such as attitudes probably owe their relationship entirely to the effects of learning.

While much of personality research utilizes correlational statistics to some extent, the study of structure rests almost entirely upon the correlational method. The direction and magnitude of a linear relationship can be expressed by a single statistic: the correlation coefficient. Direction refers to whether high scores on one variable are associated with high or low scores on a second variable. The magnitude of a relationship indicates the degree to which two variables are related.

Statistical significance refers to the probability that a given result with a specific sample holds for the total population or is just a chance finding. The significance level of a correlation coefficient depends on its magnitude and on the number of subjects included in the sample. A correlation between two variables indicates that one can predict scores on one from scores on the other with greater than chance accuracy; the higher the correlation the more accurate the prediction. The prediction of one variable from another involves the use of a regression equation. The accuracy or precision of this prediction is determined by the standard error of estimate. With a correlation of zero, the predicted Y score is always the population mean, the standard error of estimate is always the population standard deviation, and the amount of variance in Y which can be accounted for by X is zero. With a correlation of 1.00, the prediction of Y from X is perfect, the standard error of estimate is zero, and 100 per cent of the Y variance can be accounted for by X. When more than one variable is used to predict Y, a multiple correlation coefficient may be utilized.

Studies of personality structure consist of the determination of the correlation between two personality variables or between a personality variable and some other type of response. Several examples were given. Anti-Negro prejudice as measured by the Desegregation Scale has been found to be related to anti-Semitic prejudice and to choice of college major. Need for heterosexuality on the Edwards Personal Preference Schedule has been found to be related to a measure of conformity, and pairs of fiancés were found to be more similar in this need than in any other need measured by the EPPS. Preference for delayed as opposed to immediate gratification is negatively related to cheating behavior and positively related to age. Three approaches to the measurement of creativity were described: ratings, the Differential Reaction Schedule, and a composite originality score based on eight measures of response infrequency. Creative individuals are perceived as more intelligent, clever, socially effective, personally dominant, and verbally fluent, and less conforming, rigid, apathetic, and dull than noncreative individuals. Femininity of interests is consistently found to be characteristic of those high in creativity. The Si scale of the MMPI measures social introversion-extraversion and has been found to be positively related to the tendency to perceive human movement on the Rorschach and to the amount of participation in extracurricular activities in both high school and college.

COMPUTATIONAL EXAMPLE: CORRELATION COEFFICIENT

Computation of the Pearson product-moment correlation coefficient (named in honor of Professor Karl Pearson who developed this statistic) may be undertaken in any one of several ways. The defining formula is:

$$r = \frac{\Sigma xy}{NSD_xSD_y}$$

The x represents the difference between each X score and the mean of the X scores, and y is the difference between each Y score and the mean of the Y scores. The sum of the products of these difference scores is divided by the product of the number of pairs of scores times the standard deviation of the X scores times the standard deviation of the Y scores. An easier method of calculation is through the use of a scatter diagram as described in most beginning statistics texts. Still easier, if a desk calculator is available, is the use of the gross score formula:

$$r = \frac{N\Sigma XY - \Sigma X\Sigma Y}{\sqrt{N\Sigma X^2 - (\Sigma X)^2} \quad \sqrt{N\Sigma Y^2 - (\Sigma Y)^2}}$$

As an illustration of the latter method, we will return to the imaginary data for the six subjects in Table 5-1. The necessary quantities are shown in Table 5-9.

Table 5-9   QUANTITIES FOR GROSS SCORE FORMULA COMPUTATION

Subjects	X	Y	X²	Y²	XY
1	10	12	100	144	120
2	30	28	900	784	840
3	41	38	1681	1444	1558
4	6	22	36	484	132
5	19	20	361	400	380
6	8	15	64	225	120
N = 6	ΣX = 114	ΣY = 135	ΣX² = 3142	ΣY² = 3481	ΣXY = 3150

When these figures are substituted in the formula:

$$r = \frac{(6)(3150) - (114)(135)}{\sqrt{(6)(3142) - (114)^2} \; \sqrt{(6)(3481) - (135)^2}} = .89$$

CHAPTER 6

Personality Dynamics

The study of personality dynamics is often described as research which "emphasizes drives, motives and interplay of forces involved in relatively momentary relations with the environment" [Jenness, 1962, p. 479]. Personality structure is the static, organized interrelationship of personality variables; dynamics involves the joint effect of structure and of external stimuli on behavior. In this text, then, the *study of personality dynamics* is defined as any research which involves response as a function of both a stimulus variable and at least one personality variable. Thus, in this type of research the approaches of general experimental psychology and of differential psychology begin to merge.

The Integration of Experimental and
Differential Psychology

Science is concerned with establishing and describing lawful relationships between and among variables. In psychology, two types of relationships may be distinguished: stimulus-response and response-response. Examples of the former are the effect of consistency of reinforcement on resistance to extinction, the effect of nonlove-oriented disciplinary techniques on conscience development, and the effect of emotionally arousing propaganda on opinion change. Response-response relationships have been the focus of attention in the previous chapter on personality structure and include such relationships as that between scores on an anxiety questionnaire and galvanic skin response, between intelligence

158

and grades in school, and between political ideology and rigidity. Traditionally, S-R relationships have been characteristic of general experimental psychology while R-R relationships have been more commonly found in the field of personality. More than in any other type of research, work on personality dynamics has brought together the two approaches. Experimental psychologists are becoming more inclined to utilize individual-differences variables as part of their research designs while personality psychologists are increasingly engaged in the running of controlled experiments in which stimulus variables are manipulated.

A RESEARCH EXAMPLE

A typical investigation in this area corresponds to some extent to the following hypothetical example. Let us say that an experimenter is interested in determining the effect of varying amounts of frustration on aggressive behavior. Subjects are brought into a research cubicle and presented with a task. They are given a box full of marbles and told that their manual dexterity will be determined by their ability to carry out a simple job. They must take each marble singly, insert it in a small tube leading to a receptical, and continue this process as rapidly as possible until all of the marbles are transferred. The subjects are informed that there is a time limit; if they fail to complete the task quickly enough, a loud buzzer will sound and the work must stop.

Actually, all of the subjects in the experimental conditions are made to fail by sounding the buzzer when they have transferred three-fourths of the marbles. Frustration is manipulated by varying the amount of reward which they are told they will receive if the task is completed: $5.00, $10.00, $20.00, and $40.00. Aggression is measured by a rating scale (which they fill out after the experiment) evaluating the experimenter and the research itself.

As shown in Figure 6-1, the stimulus S_1 (magnitude of the reward which is not obtained) is varied, and the effect on R_1 (aggression ratings) is determined. We will say that such an investigation finds that hostility scores on the rating scales increase significantly as a function of the amount of reward which is available but not attained. Given sufficient data of this kind, we can write a formula specifying the relationship between S_1 and R_1.

At this point we have an experimental investigation which does not involve personality variables. That is, individual differences are ignored. Such research may move into the area of personality dynamics for a number of reasons. Perhaps the experimenter notes a considerable amount of response variance within each condition. For example, some subjects in the $20.00 condition express more hostility than is average for the $40.00 condition, while others express less hostility than is average in the

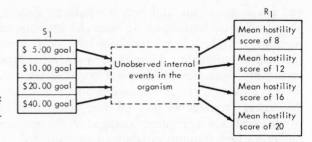

FIG. 6–1. *Effect of frustration on aggression.*

$10.00 condition. Obviously, other antecedents are influencing the response besides S_1. If these other antecedents are at least in part represented by a personality variable, we could subdivide the groups further on the basis of their standing on such a variable, and hence predict their responses more accurately.

On the other hand, the impetus for this sort of research may just as easily originate in an interest in a particular personality variable. Let us say that a personality psychologist is interested in the dimension of aggression anxiety. Probably as the result of early experiences involving aggressive acts and the response of parents to them, individuals come to differ in characteristic ways with respect to their attitudes concerning aggression. Some can freely verbalize hostility when it is appropriate in a given situation, while others are inhibited or blocked because of anxiety about expressing such feelings.

After some preliminary work, the researcher is able to build a measuring instrument, an Aggression Anxiety Scale, which is an adequately reliable test. He finds that it is related in the hypothesized way to the child-rearing attitudes of parents, to responses to other personality tests dealing with hostility, and to ratings by peers of aggressivity. Thus, there is a measuring device for the dimension and some knowledge concerning its antecedents and its structural properties.

The investigator now becomes interested in the effects of this aspect of personality on responses in situations in which aggression is aroused. Rather than an interest in characteristic responses across a variety of stimulus situations, the interest here shifts to the effect of this characteristic trait on responses to a specific stimulus situation. It might be predicted that the greater the frustration which is administered the greater the aggression ($S_1 \longrightarrow R_1$), but also that the greater the aggression anxiety the less the aggression ($R_2 \longrightarrow R_1$). Since both types of variables would be operative in the situation, both would influence the response ($S_1 + R_2 \longrightarrow R_1$), but in opposite directions.

The research now would involve some additional steps. The Aggression Anxiety Scale could be administered prior to the experiment and subjects divided into three groups (high, medium, and low aggression anxiety) on the basis of their test scores. Some of each aggression-anxiety group would be assigned to each of the frustration conditions. Our design now would involve four levels of frustrating stimuli and three levels on the personality dimension. Assuming that both stimulus variable and the personality variable were found to have an effect on the response, the imaginary experiment could be diagrammed as in Figure 6–2.

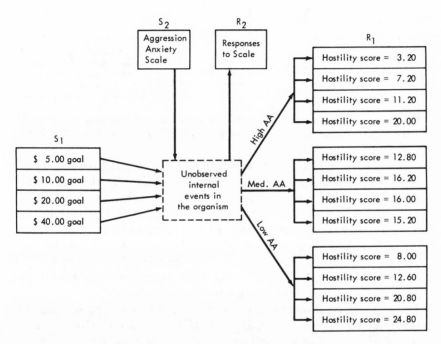

Fig. 6–2. *Effect of frustration and aggression anxiety on aggression.*

From the point of view of the traditional differential psychologist, we now have additional information about the dimension of aggression anxiety. From the framework of research on personality dynamics, we may add that a particular aspect of behavior is more predictable. Prediction is more accurate because the investigator has included two different types of antecedents in his research, the immediate stimulus situation and organismic differences indicated by the personality variable. These two types of antecedents *interact* in determining the response.

RATIONALE

The drawing in Figure 6–3 depicts the general case of an experiment involving personality dynamics. Though a lawful relationship

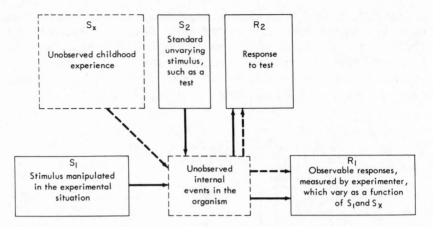

FIG. 6–3. *An experiment in which a stimulus variable and a personality variable jointly influence a response variable. (Adapted from Byrne, 1964, p. 41.)*

may exist between S_1 and R_1, the fact that there are variations among subjects in R_1 suggests that there are other antecedents to this response in addition to S_1. To the extent that these other antecedents are uncontrolled stimuli in the experimental situation, they may later be identified and controlled, hence decreasing the variations among subjects in R_1. If, however, the antecedents are unobserved internal processes in the subjects and if the antecedents of these processes are unobserved events in the past history of the subject (S_x), no amount of increased experimental rigor will increase the accuracy with which R_1 can be predicted.

The solution to this dilemma lies in the use of the type of measuring device represented by a personality test. If we can assume that the effects of S_x on the organism will influence a variety of responses, we can construct a standard stimulus $(S_2,$ a test) and obtain responses to it $(R_2,$ test scores) which presumably vary as a function of S_x. By means of this approach, we are able to use individual differences in R_2 to increase the accuracy with which we can predict the S_1-R_1 relationship. Since we cannot observe or control S_x or its effects, only through the use of R_2 as a substitute can we ever achieve predictive accuracy in the experimental situation.

Data Analysis in Research on Personality Dynamics

The two most common approaches to data analysis in research on personality dynamics are the correlation coefficient and analysis of variance. The student who is well-versed in statistical analysis may wish to skip the following section.

CORRELATION BETWEEN STIMULUS AND RESPONSE

When cause and effect relationships are found in psychology, we are dealing with a correlation between a stimulus variable and a response variable. Bergmann and Spence [1944] describe these laws as $R = f(S)$, or response is a function of a stimulus. Here, too, the magnitude of the relationship, the standard error of estimate, the amount of predictable and unpredictable variance, and the like are as important in evaluating experimental findings as in evaluating relationships between responses.

Perhaps a word of caution with respect to "cause and effect" should be interjected. The concept of a causal relationship can create as many problems as does the goal of understanding discussed in Chapter 1. Does stimulus X *cause* response Y? In terms of ultimate causation or a total explanation for the response, the answer must be "no." The response could not have occurred had not the organism inherited certain characteristics, had not its receptors and neurones and effectors been functioning properly, and so forth. One might even consider that the response could not have occurred if the subject's great-grandparents had not emigrated to this country from Europe or if the planet Earth had been located a few thousand miles closer to the sun in its orbit. To extricate ourselves from such fruitless wanderings, again we turn to the concept of prediction. Event X can be loosely conceived as the cause of Y if the occurrence of Y can be predicted from the presence of X. A more usual terminology is to say that Y is elicited by or evoked by X.

Note here that the term "correlational approach" is usually defined as nonexperimental research. Therefore, an investigation involving a correlation between a stimulus and response is "correlational" only in the sense that a particular statistic is utilized.

An example of the use of correlational analysis in an experimental situation will demonstrate the utility of this method. The hypothetical experiment which involved the effect of four levels of frustration on hostility ratings could be analyzed in terms of the correlation between stimulus and response. The hypothetical data are given in Table 6–7 (see the computational example at the end of this chapter). If we take the numbers representing degree of frustration ($5.00, $10.00, $20.00, and $40.00) as the X variable and the hostility scores as the Y variable, a Pearson product-moment r may be computed as described in the previous chapter. For the 120 subjects, the correlation is .69, which is significant at beyond the .01 level. Thus, about 48 per cent of the variance in hostility scores can be predicted on the basis of the stimulus condition to which the subjects were exposed, while about 52 per cent of the variance remains unpredicted.

When a personality variable is also included in the investigation, one means of analysis is to recompute the stimulus-response correlation separately for each of the subgroups of subjects divided on the basis of the personality variable. Using the data in Table 6–7, the frustration-hostility correlations were determined for the 40 subjects in each of the three aggression-anxiety groups. In our example, significant S-R relationships are found only for the high and low groups ($r = .95$ and $.90$) while the same relationship for those with medium aggression-anxiety scores is only $.20$, which is not significantly different from zero. Obviously, we can make better predictions of the hostility responses on the basis of stimulus conditions plus scores on the personality test than on the basis of only one of them.

ANALYSIS OF VARIANCE TO DETERMINE EFFECTS OF
STIMULUS VARIABLES AND PERSONALITY VARIABLES ON RESPONSES

The variance of a set of scores is the sum of the squares of the difference between each score and the mean score, divided by the total number of scores or $S^2 = \dfrac{\Sigma x^2}{N}$. The square root of the variance is the standard deviation. The concept of variance was introduced briefly in the preceding chapter in terms of the amount of variance of the Y variable which could be predicted on the basis of the X variable, using a regression equation. Our interest there was in determining the proportion of Y variance which could and could not be predicted from a knowledge of X. This same general concept is utilized in another type of analysis of research data. The question answered by the analysis of variance technique is whether a given variable is or is not contributing to the total variance of the dependent variable to a statistically significant degree.

Simple Analysis of Variance. We will again use the frustration experiment as an example. Each subject was assigned to one of the experimental conditions and the mean hostility score for each group determined. At present, the personality variable will not be considered.

We can compute the total variance of the hostility scores, and then the question to be answered is whether the stimulus variable (degree of frustration) contributed to this total variance. The general rationale is to conceptualize each subject's score in terms of two sources of variation: the deviation of the score from the group mean and the deviation of the group mean from the overall mean. Thus, the difference between each score and the overall mean is the sum of these two difference scores. In the same way, the total variance of the scores is the sum of these two types of variance, the variance owing to individual differences within each group and the variance owing to differences between groups.

Let us look first at the variance within each group. Why should there be any at all? Subjects within each group were exposed to the same frustration level, so why did not every subject give exactly the same hostility response? Presumably, a vast number of unknown and/or uncontrolled determinants are operating. Subjects are of different sexes, different ages, and different religions. They inherited different genes. They have spent a great many years undergoing vastly different experiences in their families, in school, and so forth. Any number of everyday-life frustration conditions (for example, hunger, sex, sleep) probably contribute to hostility and affect the subjects differently in unknown ways. Any number of conceivably relevant personality dimensions exist on which subjects undoubtedly differ but about which we know nothing. Finally, any unreliability in either the stimulus dimension or in the response measure adds to these differences. All of these factors together, operating beyond the control or knowledge of the experimenter, make for differences within each group. This range of scores may be conceptualized in terms of variance, and we speak of it as within group variance or error variance. We do not know its antecedents and, at least for this experiment, have no way to seek its antecedents.

The second source of variance involves the differences between the group means and the overall mean. Why should differences exist here? There are two possibilities. First, if the stimulus conditions had no effect on the response variable, we would still expect differences among groups for the same reasons we would expect differences among individuals. All of the unknown antecedents which make for variations within groups act in the same uncontrolled and unmeasured way to affect the groups. If the frustration did not have any influence on the hostility response, the differences among group means should be of the same general magnitude as the differences among individual scores within the groups. The second possibility to be considered is that the stimulus conditions do have an effect on the hostility responses. If degree of frustration influences hostility, group means will differ from the overall mean over and above the reasons just discussed. Variance between groups will be a function of uncontrolled antecedents *and* of the systematic differences in the stimulus manipulated by the experimenter.

Analysis of variance simply allows us to ascertain whether between-group variance is sufficiently larger than within-group variance to allow us to conclude that the stimulus variable contributed significantly to the total variance. It would take us too far afield to go into the background leading to the computation of an analysis of variance. Suffice it to say that the computation involves obtaining estimates of the population variance based on the between-group variance and on the within-group variance. The between-group variance estimate (s^2_b) is divided by the within-group variance estimate (s^2_w) to yield an F ratio. If the between-group variance is simply due to the same factors as the within-group variance, s^2_b and s^2_w will be of about the same magnitude, and hence F will be about 1. How much larger than 1 an F must be in order for us to conclude that there was a difference between groups depends on the number of subjects in each group and the number of groups. Tables are available in most introductory statistics texts which indicate the magnitude of F necessary to reach acceptable levels of significance with various numbers of subjects and various numbers of groups.

Complex Analysis of Variance. When the type of experimental situation which we have been discussing includes a personality variable, the analysis of variance design may easily be extended to include this new information. In our example, there were the four frustration conditions and the three levels of aggression anxiety; each subject thus falls into one of 12 groups or cells, with 10 subjects per cell. With respect to both the stimulus variable and the personality variable, we are asking whether either or both of them contribute to the total variance of the dependent variable to a statistically significant degree. Each subject's score may be conceptualized in terms of its deviation from the mean of the cell and the deviation of the particular stimulus condition mean from the overall mean and the deviation of the mean of the particular level on the personality variable from the overall mean. There is, in addition, one further source of variance: the interaction. The latter concept involves the question of whether the effect of the stimulus variable on the response variable is different for different levels of the personality variable or vice versa. For example, possibly frustration affects hostility only for individuals high or low in aggression-anxiety but does not affect those with medium aggression-anxiety scores. One way to conceptualize the interaction is as that variance which is left over when the other three sources of variance are subtracted from the total variance.

The general question becomes a series of questions in a complex analysis of variance. Is the variance estimate based on between-experimental conditions significantly larger than the within-cell variance estimate? Is the variance estimate based on between-levels on the personality variable larger than the within-cell variance estimate? Is the variance estimate based on the interaction larger than the within-cell variance estimate? The computational example at the end of the chapter will show that all three sources of variance (stimulus variable, personality variable, and the interaction between them) are statistically significant.

The meaning of the interaction can best be understood by examining Figure 6-4. It indicates that the low and high aggression-anxiety groups were affected similarly by the experimental manipulation with the low groups simply responding at a higher level of hostility at each point. The group with medium aggression-anxiety scores responded at approximately the same level of hostility irrespective of the frustration condition to which it was exposed.

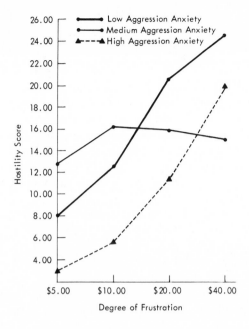

FIG. 6–4. *Interaction of frustration and aggression anxiety.*

We may note that the effect of including the personality variable was to reduce the variance within cells. In a sense, from among the multitude of possible antecedents of the individual differences or error variance within cells, we have selected one antecedent and divided subjects into more homogeneous subgroups. Presumably, we could continue dividing subjects on the basis of other personality and stimulus variables (if their effects were known) until there was no longer any within-cell variance. As with a correlation of 1.00, perfect prediction would be achieved when all subjects in each cell gave the same response on the dependent variable, resulting in zero error variance.

Though we will not go into examples here, the student should note that analysis of variance can be extended to more than two dimensions with any number of stimulus and personality variables considered at one time. As the design becomes more complex, both computation and interpretation become correspondingly more difficult.

Selected Examples of Research on Personality Dynamics

Perhaps the best means of demonstrating the way in which experimental and differential psychology tend to come together in work on personality dynamics is to examine a sample of such research.

ATTRACTION AS A FUNCTION OF REWARD-PUNISHMENT
AND AFFILIATION NEED

As was discussed briefly in Chapter 2, a good deal of the research on interpersonal attraction has been based on the notion of reinforcement. That is, individuals are attracted to one another, form friendships, marry, and the like, to the extent that the relationship offers reward value or positive reinforcements to the two participants. According to the theory, the greater the proportion of positive reinforcements received by individual A from individual B, the greater is A's attraction toward B. Most of the research in this area has utilized attitude similarity as positive reinforcement and attitude dissimilarity as negative reinforcement. A great many studies have reported a greater than chance relationship in attitudes between friends, engaged couples, and marital partners [Bonney, 1946; Byrne and Blaylock, 1963; Newcomb and Svehla, 1937; Precker, 1952; Schooley, 1936]. Experimental studies of the type outlined in Chapter 2 have provided relatively substantial evidence that the expression of similar attitudes by another person evokes positive responses toward him while the expression of dissimilar attitudes evokes negative responses.

The interpretation of attitude similarity-dissimilarity as positive and negative reinforcement has been strengthened by several types of supporting evidence. In the investigation by McDonald [1962] mentioned earlier, the reasoning went as follows: Other investigators have found a positive relationship between the proportion of similar attitudes expressed by a stranger and attraction toward him. If attitude similarity acts as a positive reinforcement, then a different type of positive reinforcement should have the same influence on attraction. McDonald chose an achievement-related task in which the subjects were rated by another student (a stranger to them) with respect to how well they did. Since the stranger was in fact a confederate of the experimenter, the ratings could be deliberately assigned in specific proportions of high and low in order to provide appropriate proportions of positive and negative reinforcements. Since the subject knew nothing about the stranger and interacted with him only in the experimental situation, the hypothesis was that attraction toward the stranger would be a function of the proportion of positive reinforcements. The total situation is best described by the instructions which were given to the subjects. Just prior to hearing this material, a prearranged drawing was held in which the subject found that he would be the "speaker" and the stooge would be the "listener."

Creativity and imagination are vague and ambiguous terms. Yet, it is known that these abilities are highly important in determining one's success in his vocation, in school, and in establishing good interpersonal relationships with others. What we are investigating in this experiment are the factors that lead one person to attribute creative ability to another person. In other words, we are trying to discover some of the cues that individual A utilizes in appraising the creativity of individual B.

Here is how we will do this. The person who drew the lot of the "speaker" will demonstrate his capacity for creativity which, in turn, will be evaluated by the person who drew the lot of the "listener." The speaker will demonstrate his creative potential by telling the listener a series of seven brief stories. After hearing each story, the listener will evaluate it and give the story a score. It is important that the person playing the role of the speaker introduce into each of his stories as much imagination, cleverness, and ingenuity as he can. The speaker will be provided with a set of seven pictures to use in making up his stories, and he must tell a story about each picture. The listener's only task is to listen and to appraise each story by giving it a score.

To insure that the listener's judgments of the speaker's stories will be made solely upon the basis of the stories and nothing else, the speaker and listener will not be permitted to see each other during the performance of this task. The speaker will sit in a room and, with the aid of a microphone, tell his stories to the listener, who will be in an adjoining room provided with a loud-speaker.

Here is how the listener will transmit his scores of the stories to the speaker. On the table in the speaker's room is a panel containing a horizontal row of lamps numbered 10 through 1. In the listener's room is a panel of corresponding switches numbered 10 through 1. If the listener feels the story is a good one, he should push switch number 10, 9, 8, 7, or 6. Lamp number 10 indicates the maximum positive score. If the listener feels the story is a poor one, he should push switch 5, 4, 3, 2, or 1, with number 1 indicating the most negative score. Hence, after the completion of each story, the speaker will receive feedback by way of the score lamps as to how the listener evaluated the quality of that story.

Each of the 192 subjects was assigned to one of eight experimental conditions in which a predetermined number of high ratings (lights 7–10) and low ratings (lights 1–4) were given, regardless of the quality of the story told. One group of subjects received seven high ratings and no low ones, the next group received six high ratings and one low one, and so on to the eighth group which received no high ratings and seven low ones. Immediately after the story-telling session, the subjects were told the following:

Your partner, the listener, has been asked to write a personality sketch of you based upon what he thinks he has learned about you as you performed this task. Of course, even though you have been doing all of the talking during the past 15 or 20 minutes, you may have gotten some ideas about the person to whom you have spoken. Remember that you have been engaged in a two-man communication situation, and that even though the listener has not spoken to you, he has been communicating and reacting to you by scoring or evaluating your potential for creativity and originality. There is evidence from other research which shows that an accurate impression of a person can be gained from sources other than his verbal behavior. What we are interested in at this point in the experiment is whether you, the speaker, have learned anything about and formed any impression of the person who has been reacting to you. With this purpose in mind, fill out the accompanying Interpersonal Judgment Scale.

As was described in Chapter 2, this scale has two seven-point ratings which measure attraction. The first asks how much the subject thinks he would like or dislike the other person, and the second asks how much he would enjoy working with him. The two scales added together are defined as the dependent variable of attraction.

One way of testing the significance of this stimulus-response relationship and of describing it is by means of a correlation coefficient. The correlation between proportion of high ratings received from the stranger and attraction toward him was found to be .45, which with 192 subjects is highly significant. This linear relationship between stimulus and response is shown in Figure 6-5. The triangles indicate the mean attraction scores of the subjects in each of McDonald's eight groups. In McDonald's study, the affiliation-need variable was included in the design, and hence the study was one of personality dynamics. The development of a TAT scoring system for n Aff and some of the research which has been conducted with this variable were described in Chapter 3. It was hypothesized, on the basis of previous findings, that when subjects were divided into high, medium, and low need-affiliation subgroups, the effect of the proportion of positive reinforcements on attraction would be in part a function of n Aff.

McDonald measured n Aff by having another experimenter administer four thematic apperception slides to groups of subjects several weeks before

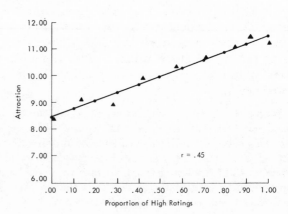

FIG. 6–5. Correlation between stimulus and response.

the experiment. The protocols were then scored for n Affiliation according to the Heyns, Veroff, and Atkinson [1958] manual. On the basis of these scores, subjects were classified as low (scores of 0–2), medium (scores of 3–4), or high (scores of 5 and above) on the affiliation dimension. These three groups of subjects were divided evenly across the eight experimental conditions.

One possibility for correlational analysis, and the one McDonald selected, is to obtain the stimulus-response correlation separately for the three groups of subjects (high, medium, and low need-affiliators) and thus determine whether scores on the n Aff variable had any influence on responses to the stimulus variable in the experimental situation. Another possibility would be to obtain the correlation between the personality variable and the response variable and then utilize this coefficient plus the stimulus-response correlation to obtain a multiple correlation. In either instance, it would be determined whether prediction of attraction was enhanced by a knowledge of both the reinforcement conditions and n Aff scores.

The stimulus-response relationships as determined separately for the three n Aff groups is shown in Table 6–1. We see that for each group there is a significant positive relationship between stimulus and response, with the high n Aff individuals yielding the greatest relationship and the medium n Aff individuals the lowest. The question remains, however, as to whether these differences are sufficiently large to indicate a significant effect of the personality variable on the S-R relationship. It was found that even the largest difference (.53 vs. .33) was not great enough to be statistically significant.

Table 6–1   RELATIONSHIP BETWEEN PROPORTION OF HIGH RATINGS
AND ATTRACTION FOR SUBJECTS
HIGH, MEDIUM, AND LOW IN n AFFILIATION

	N	r
High n Aff	64	.53*
Medium n Aff	64	.33*
Low n Aff	64	.48*

* $p < .01$

The use of a multiple correlation analysis would be justified only if the personality variable were related to the response variable. When experimental conditions are ignored and n Aff scores correlated with attraction scores for all 192 subjects, the resulting coefficient of —.05 indicates no relationship between the two variables. Thus, in this situation, attraction toward a stranger is a function of the proportion of positive reinforcements received, and no additional influence is attributable to affiliation need.

DEPRECIATION OF A STRANGER AS A FUNCTION OF
AGREEMENT-DISAGREEMENT AND SELF-IDEAL DISCREPANCY

Worchel and McCormick [1963] devised a situation in which subjects were given a psychological problem about which they and another subject were to state an opinion. The subject stated his or her opinion first; the second "subject" was actually a tape recording. Half of the subjects heard the voice of a stranger who shared their opinion and half heard a disagreeing stranger.

The personality variable was the amount of discrepancy between each subject's self-concept and his ideal self. This behavior dimension will be discussed in greater detail in Chapter 12. Worchel and McCormick described individuals with very high self-ideal discrepancy as self-depreciating, anxious, and insecure and those with very low discrepancy as having a facade of adjustment maintained by repressive defenses. Presumably, the best-adjusted individuals obtain medium self-ideal discrepancy scores. The hypothesis was that an interaction would occur between the agreement-disagreement conditions and the personality variable in that the low-discrepancy individuals would respond to a disapproving stranger with greater hostility than would high- and medium-discrepancy subjects. The medium-discrepancy individuals were expected to tolerate the disagreement while the high-discrepancy individuals would alter their own judgments.

Subjects took part in the experiment individually. There was a total of 60 students, 20 at each discrepancy level as measured by the Self-Activity Inventory (SAI) [Worchel, 1957]. Half of each group was randomly assigned to either the agreement or disagreement condition. The experiment was presented as a measure of psychological ability. The subjects were to read a problem and make a decision about the best solution. The problem was:

Sammy Gardner is a college junior at a large Southwestern college. His college existence has been somewhat isolated as he lived alone for his first two years. He always seems somewhat withdrawn and apart from the other boys he associates with. When he started his junior year, he moved into a dormitory. It was not long before his roommate discovered that he seemed to be filled with great animosity toward others. At times he was brutal. On two different occasions he was known to have chased a boy with a pair of scissors and irrationally cut off his hair. Another incident started when a boy in the dormitory failed to comply with orders Sammy gave in a very authoritative manner. When the boy rejected his wishes, Sammy threatened to kill him.

It is known that Sammy's home life is somewhat unstable and that he seldom, if ever, goes home to see his parents. He seems happier living with his brutality and imposing his will upon others.

You are Sammy's roommate. Which of the following solutions would you pursue in attempting to solve this problem?

(A) Try to help Sammy by casually questioning him and getting him to talk about his problems. Try to find out what things in his home life may be bothering him.

(B) Talk with the Dean of Student Life. Describe Sammy's behavior and ask the Dean's advice as to what should be done [Worchel and McCormick, 1963, p. 592].

Then, a second subject (the tape recording) was asked to give his solution. The voice over the loudspeaker gave one of the following statements, depending on the subject's own response and on the condition to which he was assigned:

A. I would choose solution A because Sammy seems to be reacting against authority as we noticed in the case where he didn't want to go home on the holidays and visit his folks. They probably make him feel insecure against the type of authority that they seem to be. And being his roommate and one of his own age and experience, I would probably be the closest person to him so possibly I could help him by his coming to trust me and try to show him where I thought he was going wrong.

B. I would choose solution B because I feel that I don't know enough about psychology to be of any help to Sammy and his problem. And I think that the Dean is more qualified in that line of work than I am and that would put the responsibility more on the superior shoulders. He would be the person to have this responsibility placed on him, and the one that would know what to do and how to help Sammy out of his problems [Worchel and McCormick, 1963, p. 593].

After hearing this, each subject was asked to rate "the other student" on a positive-negative scale as to independence, tolerance, broadmindedness, flexibility, agreeability, voice, psychological insight, and intelligence. These ratings were added together to yield a depreciation score. The mean depreciation scores are given in Table 6–2. The most negative response

Table 6–2 MEAN DEPRECIATION SCORES OF SUBJECTS WITH HIGH, MEDIUM, AND LOW SELF-IDEAL DISCREPANCY TOWARD AN AGREEING OR DISAGREEING STRANGER

Subject's Self-Ideal Discrepancy	Stranger	
	Agreeing	Disagreeing
High	2.4	2.5
Medium	2.4	2.6
Low	2.4	3.0

to the disagreeing stranger was, as predicted, by the subjects with the least self-ideal discrepancy.

The significance of the effects of experimental conditions, personality differences, and the interaction was determined by analysis of variance. As shown in Table 6–3, the ratings of the disagreeing stranger were significantly more negative than those of the agreeing stranger, and there was a significant interaction between experimental conditions and self-ideal discrepancy. Thus, the hypothesis was confirmed.

Table 6–3 VARIANCE TABLE FOR DEPRECIATION SCORES

Source	Sum of Squares	df	Variance Estimate	F
Between Rows (Self-Ideal)	42.4	2	21.2	2.4
Between Columns (Agree-Disagree)	50.4	1	50.4	5.7*
Interaction	56.0	2	28.0	3.2*
Within	475.2	54	8.8	

* $p < .05$

LEARNING AS A FUNCTION OF NOVEL STIMULI AND CREATIVITY

Learning theorists usually employ such relatively well-established reinforcing stimuli in their investigations of both human and infrahuman subjects as food, water, money, praise, and the like. Learning research is frequently concerned with the effects of positive and negative reinforcements and of varying schedules of reinforcement and nonreinforcement on behavior. When an investigator is primarily interested in determining whether a new stimulus acts as a reinforcer, the emphasis shifts somewhat. An established experimental situation is employed, and the new stimulus is utilized as the reinforcing agent. If learning is obtained, evidence is thereby provided that reinforcement is involved. If it is hypothesized that a given stimulus acts as reinforcement only for given individuals, a personality dynamics design may be employed.

Houston and Mednick [1963] proposed that creative individuals have a "need for novelty"; therefore, novel stimuli should be need-satisfying and hence reinforcing for them. Creative people should not find familiar stimuli reinforcing, nor should noncreative people find novel stimuli reinforcing.

The measure of creativity bears some relation to the instruments used by Barron [1957] and described in the previous chapter. Rather than waiting for subjects spontaneously to give remote or unusual responses, a task is presented in which correct responses are possible only if the subject is able to make remote associations. The Remote Associates Test (RAT) consists of 30 items which require the subject to find the associative link between three words. Examples are:

1. surprise line Democratic

2. rat blue cottage

The correct answers are "party" and "cheese." The test was given to a large number of undergraduates at the University of Michigan; 30 high-creative (scores of 22–29) and 30 low-creative (scores of 4–19) subjects were selected for the experiment.

The task was a verbal conditioning situation in which nouns and non-nouns were presented in pairs; subjects were asked to select one of the words and were reinforced for choosing the nouns in the experimental group. The instructions were as follows:

I am going to show you some cards, one at a time. On each card there are two words. I want you to look at both words and say aloud the one you like best. In response to each word you say aloud I will say a word, or give you an association. For example, if I show you a card with the words "pencil" and "telephone" on it and you choose "pencil" I might say "paper." If you said "telephone" I might say "call." So, for each card you will choose one of the two words and say it out loud and I will give you a response word. Pay attention to the words and associations because I shall ask you to do something else later on. Any questions? [Houston and Mednick, 1963, p. 138]

A series of 160 index cards was used with a pair of words (noun and non-noun) typed one above the other in the center of each card.[1] The two words were matched for frequency of occurrence in the language as measured by a count of words occurring in printed material [Thorndike and Lorge, 1944]. The response of the experimenter to each choice by the subject was either a novel stimulus or a familiar stimulus. Novel stimuli were defined as associations infrequently or never given to the words in a normative group, and familiar stimuli were the most commonly given associations to the words. For example, if the words were FATHER and WHITE, a choice of father would be followed by either "mother" (familiar) or "eggbeater" (novel).

Subjects were assigned to either an experimental or a control group. All subjects were given an operant period consisting of the first 40 items;

---

[1] In addition, another 20 cards were interspersed after every 8 cards as fillers. On these cards were two non-nouns, and the purpose of using them was to prevent the subjects from perceiving the purpose of the experiment.

the experimenter responded with the most common associate regardless
of which word was chosen. For the remaining 120 items, the experimental
subjects were given a *novel* association each time a noun was chosen and
a *common* association each time a non-noun was chosen. In the control
group, common associations were given for either choice.

In an interview following the testing session, no subjects were able
to verbalize the purpose of the experiment. The data were divided into
blocks of 40 items and the number of nouns given per block determined.
The data depicted in Figure 6–6 suggest that learning occurred only for
the high-creative subjects in the experimental group, as hypothesized. Anal-

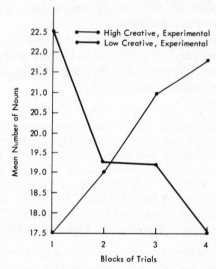

FIG. 6–6. *Effect of
novel stimuli on re-
sponses of high- and
low-creative individuals.*
(*Adapted from Hous-
ton and Mednick, 1963,
p. 139.*)

ysis of variance was used to test the significance of these differences. The
interaction between creativity and trials in the experimental group was
significant at beyond the .001 level. In addition to supporting the hypothesis that novel stimuli would be reinforcing to creative individuals,
the data indicate that the opposite is true for noncreative individuals.
Houston and Mednick remark:

Of considerable interest is the behavior of the low creative experimental
group which shows a marked and significant tendency to avoid the improbable
associations and/or approach the highly probable associations. Here again some
further analytical research is needed to separate out the effect of these two
variables. However, if we can for the moment argue in a mildly tautological
fashion it is clear why low creative individuals become that way. The individual
who eschews unusual ideas and/or prefers the highly probable is not likely to
develop highly creative solutions to problems [Houston and Mednick, 1963,
pp. 140–141].

PHYSIOLOGICAL RESPONSES AS A FUNCTION OF THREATENING STIMULI AND DEFENSE MECHANISMS

Psychologists have long been interested in the effects of stress or threat on physiological processes. Dependent variables have included heart rate, blood pressure, secretion of adrenaline, and amount of perspiration present on the skin. Research to date has not provided very impressive evidence of clear-cut functional relationships between stressful stimuli and physiological responses. One problem, as with any area of research, has been that of measurement. Only in recent years with the development of sophisticated polygraphs, multichannel amplifiers, and sensitive electrical recorders could certain types of research even be undertaken. A second difficulty lies in the complexity of the physiological processes and their interaction:

Emotion is characterized by many combinations of bodily change. There are overt manifestations that are readily observable, and there are organic and physiological changes that are revealed only by special procedures and recording devices. All bodily changes during emotion are dependent on complex underlying processes that become integrated by the autonomic nervous system, the cerebrospinal system, and the endocrine glands. The complexity of these interactions makes it clear that the measurement of bodily change in emotion can never be definitive or exhaustive. We can only hope, by judicious choice, to make our procedures reasonably representative of the activity of the organism as a whole [Lindsley, 1951, pp. 473–474].

A third source of research difficulty for the experimental psychologist in this area involves the effects of individual differences in response to threat:

However, it is not profitable on the basis of present experimental evidence to attempt to account for all the varieties of emotional expression. These explanations will have to await further research. Many of the nuances of behavior undoubtedly depend upon learning and habituation, which, reinstated through memory and ideation and operating through the complex network of intracortical connections, make possible emotional responses that represent varying gradations between maximal excitement and its opposite—relaxation and sleep [Lindsley, 1951, p. 509].

A number of investigators use an approach which attempts to overcome these difficulties. A standard emotion-arousing stimulus and a limited number of well-measured physiological response variables are utilized along with personality variables in a systematic exploration of their interrelationships. At the University of California at Berkeley, Richard S. Lazarus and his associates undertook such a project. As a stressful stimulus, they selected a highly disturbing 17-minute motion picture entitled *Subincision*. As Lazarus, Speisman, Mordkoff, and Davison describe it:

The movie was taken by an anthropologist, G. Roheim, working with an aboriginal Australian tribe known as the Arunta, and was originally obtained from the American Museum of Natural History by social psychologist V. Nowlis. It depicts one of the important ceremonials of this tribe and very vividly presents a sequence of crude operations performed with a piece of flint on the penis and scrotum of several adolescent boys [Lazarus, Speisman, Mordkoff, and Davison, 1962, pp. 3–4].

In one of the initial investigations in the series Lazarus, et al. [1962] utilized 35 male and 35 female undergraduates to compare the effects of the *Subincision* film with that of a control film, *Corn Farming in Iowa*. Each subject saw both films. Measures were made of skin conductance (amount of perspiration on the skin), heart rate, and adrenaline in the urine. In addition, the Adjective Checklist of Mood [Nowlis and Nowlis, 1956], some open-ended interview questions, and a tension self-rating scale were administered. The stressor movie was found to cause significant changes in skin conductance, heart rate, mood on the adjective checklist, responses to the interview questions, and in tension ratings.

Subsequent research has involved a number of questions, including the effects of different instructions and/or sound tracks on responses to the movie, the effect of repeated exposure to the film, and the investigation of personality variables which influence response to stress. Many of the personality variables used in this research program involved defense mechanisms, one of which is described as follows:

Anxiety-reducing activities which are unconsciously motivated are given the label of defense mechanisms. Various descriptions of these mechanisms, originating almost exclusively in psychoanalytic theory, have been proposed over the years. A unidimensional categorization which encompasses many diverse mechanisms grew out of the research of the new look in perception in the 1940's: repression-sensitization. At one end of this continuum of defensive behaviors are those responses which involve avoidance of the anxiety-arousing stimulus and its consequences. Included here are repression, denial, and many types of rationalization. At the sensitizing extreme of the continuum are behaviors which involve an attempt to reduce anxiety by approaching or controlling the stimulus and its consequences. The latter mechanisms include intellectualization, obsessive behaviors, and ruminative worrying [Byrne, 1964, pp. 169–170].

One of the measures of repression-sensitization that has proven useful in stress research is the 127-item Repression-Sensitization (R-S) Scale [Altrocchi, Parsons, and Dickoff, 1960; Byrne, 1961; Byrne, Barry, and Nelson, 1963] which utilizes MMPI items. The test is scored for sensitization; so high scores indicate sensitizing defenses and low scores repressing defenses.

The R-S Scale was first employed in the Berkeley stress studies by Lazarus and Alfert who found that those with low scores on the R-S

Scale indicated less anxiety and depression on the Nowlis Mood Scale than did those with high scores, while the reverse pattern was found for skin conductance. They concluded:

Judging from these Nowlis patterns, verbally derived measures of stress response in the form of dysphoric affect interacts with personality variables in a direction opposite from what is found with autonomic indicators. High deniers refuse to admit disturbance verbally but reveal it autonomically, while low deniers are apt to say they are more disturbed while showing less autonomic reactivity [Lazarus and Alfert, 1964, p. 202].

Following this work, Davison [1963], in his doctoral research at Berkeley, was interested in a variety of factors influencing adaptation to a threatening stimulus. A group of 48 male undergraduates viewed *Subincision* three different times with a week separating each viewing; several physiological

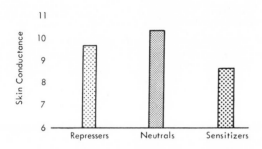

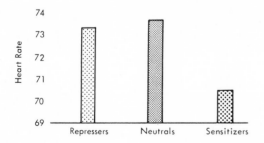

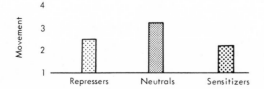

Fig. 6–7. *Physiological response to stress as a function of defenses.*

and psychological responses were measured each time. Davison administered a number of personality scales to his subjects, including the R-S Scale.

When subjects were divided into repressers, sensitizers, and neutrals (those with medium scores), it was found that defense mechanisms significantly influenced reaction to the movie in terms of skin conductance, heart rate, and general bodily movement. The findings are shown in Figure 6–7. The figure shows that the neutral subjects show the greatest physiological response to threat, closely followed by repressers; the sensitizers show the least physiological disturbance. A possible interpretation of the findings is that the development of a consistent defensive pattern protects an individual against physiological stress and that sensitization is a better protection than repression.

Response to Hostile Wit as a Function of Stress and Self-Ideal Discrepancy

From the time of Freud's [1905] formulations concerning the function of wit and humor in personality dynamics, a considerable degree of interest has existed in the study of response to humorous material. Freud and others have differentiated humor into several categories, and presumably response to each category has its own antecedents. For example, a positive response to nonsense humor, such as puns and word play, should not be determined by the same variables as response to sexual humor. The latter type of material is called wit, and this material was hypothesized by Freud to serve as a substitute means for the expression of disguised or latent motives, most usually sex or hostility.

In addition to internal determinants, such as motives and defenses, there is also reason to believe that amusement is affected by situational factors. As has long been noted [for example, Darwin, 1897], individuals in situations of danger or stress will laugh heartily at the smallest joke. In a number of investigations, situational variables have been manipulated in an attempt to influence humor responses, including frustration [Strickland, 1959; Sears, Hovland, and Miller, 1940], sexual stimulation [Strickland, 1959], and anxiety [Byrne, 1958].

One such study that utilized both situational and personality variables is that of O'Connell [1960]. He employed several types of humor, but we will describe only one of these: hostile wit. A pool of 65 jokes was assembled, and each joke was typed on a filing card. These were classified by 11 judges as to humor category. Among the 30 used in the experiment were 10 unanimously judged to be hostile wit. One was:

While Emperor Augustus was traveling through his domains, he noticed a man in the crowds who bore a striking resemblance to himself. He beckoned to him to come over and asked:

"Was your mother ever employed in my home?"

"No, sire," replied the man, "but my father was" [O'Connell, 1960, p. 265].

O'Connell hypothesized that hostile wit would seem funnier in stressful situations where hostile impulses are aroused but not directly expressed. The wit would serve as a way of expressing such impulses. As in the Worchel and McCormick [1963] study described earlier, O'Connell further hypothesized that in the stressful situation the low self-ideal discrepancy individuals would respond more positively to the hostile wit than would the high-discrepancy individuals.

The 136 subjects were given the SAI as a measure of self-ideal discrepancy at one class meeting and exposed to the experimental manipulation at another. A total of 68 subjects was assigned to the nonstress condition and 68 to the stress condition. The stress condition was created as follows:

. . . a faculty member accompanied the E on the second day and became the instigator of both failure-stress and insult techniques. He introduced himself as a professor of clinical psychology who was shocked and appalled at the attitude of the class in taking the SAI the previous class period. The results of the test, he said, pointed out that the members were either lying about themselves or were grossly maladjusted. He also stated that since the tests reflected a marked lack of adjustment, the majority of the class should give serious consideration either to leaving college or to changing their majors. After reiterating the insults and threats a few times, the instigator informed the students that they would be given one more test, and that they should display some maturity in taking it, rather than performing like high school freshmen. They were also admonished against communicating with their neighbors in any way [O'Connell, 1960, p. 265].

Immediately afterward, the humor test was administered. Subjects responded to each joke on a five-point scale from 0 (dislike very much) to 4 (like very much).

A three-way analysis of variance was employed to determine the effects of stress vs. nonstress conditions, low vs. high self-ideal discrepancy, and sex of the subject on response to hostile wit. As may be seen in Table 6–4, none of the three main effects significantly influenced liking for hostile wit, but several of the interaction effects were significant. The self-ideal times stress interaction indicated that, as hypothesized, the low-discrepancy group liked hostile wit better under stress while the high-discrepancy group preferred it under nonstress conditions. The interactions involving sex differences are a little more complicated. They indicate that only the male subjects conformed to the hypothesis. Among the females, the low-

Table 6–4   VARIANCE TABLE FOR HOSTILE WIT SCORES*

Source	Sum of Squares	df	Variance Estimate	F
Between Rows (Self-Ideal)	31.0	1	31.0	1.01
Between Columns (Stress-Nonstress)	3.01	1	3.01	.98
Between Blocks (Male-Female)	45.8	1	45.8	1.50
S-I times Stress Interaction	190.5	1	190.5	6.23**
S-I times Sex Interaction	291.0	1	291.0	9.51***
Stress times Sex Interaction	48.2	1	48.2	1.58
S-I times Stress times Sex, triple Interaction	285.4	1	285.4	9.33***
Within	3,916.8	128	30.6	

* Adapted from O'Connell, 1960, p. 266.
** $p < .05$
*** $p < .01$

discrepancy subjects preferred hostile wit under both conditions. As O'Connell says:

Females seem to be an exception to the predictions of present theories. In the present experiment, it was the well adjusted girls who were able to take advantage of Hostile Wit under both stress and nonstress conditions. Perhaps if our culture frowns upon hostile wit for women, only certain types of women rely upon this mechanism for tension reduction [O'Connell, 1960, p. 268].

WORD ASSOCIATION FAULTS AS A FUNCTION OF WORD
CHARACTERISTICS AND SUBJECT CHARACTERISTICS

As our last example of work in personality dynamics, we will turn to an area which brings together such diverse research interests as clinical diagnosis, language and verbal learning, and personality dimensions involving cognitive styles.

One of the oldest procedures in personality testing is that of the word-association technique. A series of words are presented to the subject one at a time and his responses recorded. Various aspects of the response can be scored, including such variables as time between stimulus and response, content of the response, and formal characteristics of the stimulus-response pair. In the nineteenth century, Galton in England and later Wundt in Germany utilized this approach to investigate the nature of associative processes. Soon the interest shifted to the use of word association as a technique for studying abnormal thought processes (Kraepelin in Germany), detecting guilt and revealing hidden thoughts (Munsterberg in Germany), and for revealing complexes or areas of emotional disturbance (Jung in Switzerland).

One of the most commonly studied variables is that of reaction-time faults. A fault is scored if the subject blocks completely in trying to give a response to a particular word or if a relatively long period elapses before a response is given. In the clinical use of the word-association test, such faults are generally considered as indicative of anxiety and unconscious conflicts in a particular area. In more recent years, however, a good deal of experimental attention has been focused on the effect of the stimulus words themselves on the responses. If stimulus words differ systematically in the number of faults which they elicit, diagnostic interpretation of the faults may often be in error. For example, Laffal [1955] reasoned that words for which there are a large number of possible responses would be more likely to elicit blocking or long reaction times than words for which only a few different responses could reasonably be given. A subject might block on one of the former types of words not because of unconscious conflicts but, like most other subjects, because many competing responses were available. Laffal administered a 100-item list to 80 students at the State University of Iowa. He found that to some stimulus words as many as 48 or 49 different response words were given by different individuals: threat, tease, tempt, insult. At the other extreme, 10 or fewer different response words were given by subjects to other stimulus words: thirst, melody, stumble, shove, garage, rip. When he scored the subjects for number of reaction-time faults (2.6 seconds or more to respond) on each word, this variable was found to correlate .78 with the number of different responses available for the word. In other words, 61 per cent of the variance in length of reaction time was found to be predictable on the basis of the characteristics of the stimulus words themselves. He concludes:

Response faults in word association, it is seen, are largely a function of the nature of the associational response hierarchy of the stimulus word. Response faults are most likely to occur where there are many competing responses in the response hierarchy, and less likely to occur where there are strongly dominant responses in the hierarchy. Such an analysis does not completely rule out the role of emotional factors in the production of response disturbances. It would seem, however, that emotional factors might be most reasonably adduced to explain response faults only in words with strongly dominant responses. In such cases the fault might reflect S's need to avoid the dominant response . . . [Laffal, 1955, p. 268].

Still another sort of variable has recently been found to influence response to the word-association test. Moran, Mefferd, and Kimble [1964] have isolated three personality variables which they label as *idiodynamic sets*.

They note that in the free word-association task, the instructions are, "Tell me the first word you think of." Whether this word is a synonym or a contrast or a definition or whatever is entirely up to the subject. Over the years, a number of investigators have noted that individuals often respond to this task in a characteristic way, as if they had a set to respond with a particular class of words. If such associative or idiodynamic sets constitute measurable dimensions of personality, response to word-association items could conceivably be predicted in part on the basis of these variables.

The identification of three such dimensions by Moran, *et al.* [1964] was accomplished through factor analysis of the responses of 79 normal and 79 matched acutely psychotic schizophrenic patients to 125 words administered over four successive days. The 15 variables which were factor analyzed included synonym responses (for example, blossom . . . flower), contrast responses (for example, dark . . . light), logical coordinate responses (for example, blue . . . yellow), superordinate responses (for example, cabbage . . . vegetable), functional responses (for example, needle . . . thread), and reaction time. For both samples of subjects, the variables were intercorrelated and a factor analysis carried out.

The same three factors were obtained for normals and schizophrenics, and the investigators interpreted them as representing idiodynamic sets. The three sets are: object-referent (functional responses), concept-referent (synonym and superordinate responses), and speed (contrast and coordinate responses). These sets have been found to be relatively stable over time, to hold equally well for both sexes, and even to hold in a different culture with the words and associations given in Spanish (university students in Mexico City). The sets may be conceptualized as personality variables involving differences in cognitive styles.

Moran, *et al.* [1964] found that some words evoke functional responses more easily (bark . . . dog; nail . . . hammer; thirsty . . . water), some evoke synonym and superordinate responses (crow . . . bird; tug . . . boat; strangle . . . choke), and some evoke contrast and coordinate responses more easily (boy . . . girl; bitter . . . sweet; long . . . short). Since Laffal found that association faults in response to words are a function of the number of different responses evoked by the words, subjects with different idiodynamic sets might be found to have different numbers of responses available depending on the interaction between a given word and their set. Therefore, association faults would be expected to be in part a function of the interaction between the kind of responses evoked by the word and the kind of responses given by individuals with a particular set.

From their group of normal subjects, Moran, *et al.* [1964] selected 12 individuals representing each idiodynamic set and 20 words which elicited primarily one kind of response. They then plotted the number of associative faults (delayed reaction time, distant responses, reproduction faults) for

Table 6–5   WORD ASSOCIATION FAULTS IN RELATION TO TYPE
              OF STIMULUS WORD AND IDIODYNAMIC SET OF
              SUBJECTS—NORMAL GROUP*

| | Stimulus Words | | |
Subject Set	Functional	Synonym-Superordinate	Contrast-Coordinate
Functional	5.7	9.6	8.3
Synonym-Superordinate	11.0	11.0	12.5
Contrast-Coordinate	9.0	11.0	7.2

*Adapted from Moran, et al., 1964, p. 8.

each group as shown in Table 6–5. Note that subjects with a given set tend
to have the least number of association faults in responding to words
which elicit responses congruent with their set.

Even though psychotics give a greater number of faults, the schizophrenic subjects showed the same response pattern as the normals. Table
6–6 shows that, once again, faults are the least when the word evokes
responses corresponding with the subject's set.

Table 6–6   WORD ASSOCIATION FAULTS IN RELATION TO TYPE
              OF STIMULUS WORD AND IDIODYNAMIC SET OF
              SUBJECTS—SCHIZOPHRENIC GROUP*

| | Stimulus Words | | |
Subject Set	Functional	Synonym-Superordinate	Contrast-Coordinate
Functional	12.3	16.2	16.4
Synonym-Superordinate	19.8	18.7	19.9
Contrast-Coordinate	13.5	15.4	10.8

*Adapted from Moran, et al., 1964, p. 15.

Seemingly, Laffal's warning, quoted earlier, concerning the interpretation of associative faults in terms of emotional factors should be extended
even further. We might hypothesize, for example, that a long reaction time
to a functional word by an individual with a functional set is of more
diagnostic significance than a long reaction time to a contrast-coordinate
word by the same individual.

We have seen, then, in this sample of investigations involving personality dynamics that it can be of great value to study stimulus variables
and personality variables simultaneously. The findings emerging from
such work could not have been obtained either in traditional experiments
or in traditional correlational studies; thus, this approach represents a
unique contribution of the field of personality.

Summary

Personality dynamics may be defined as any research which involves response as a function of both a stimulus variable and a personality variable.

More than any other type of research, work on personality dynamics tends to bring together the S-R approach of experimental psychology and the R-R approach of differential psychology. A hypothetical example of research in personality dynamics was given in which hostility was found to be a function of frustration as manipulated by the experimenter and aggression anxiety as measured by a personality test. The rationale for utilizing personality variables in experimental investigations has to do with the lasting effects of past events on present behavior. If the past events were unobserved or unobservable and if their effects on the organism influence responses to current stimuli, accuracy in predicting responses will be increased through using personality variables as measures of the lasting effects.

The two most common approaches to data analysis in research on dynamics are the correlation coefficient and analysis of variance. The relationship between a stimulus variable and a response variable may be specified in terms of the correlation between the two. In research on personality dynamics, stimulus-response correlations may be computed separately for different levels on the personality variable. The variance of a set of scores is the sum of the squares of the difference between each score and the mean score, divided by the total number of scores. Analysis of variance allows us to determine whether stimulus variables and/or personality variables are contributing to the total variance of the response variable. In a simple analysis of variance, the effect of a single variable is determined. The total variance is the sum of the variance owing to individual differences within groups and the variance owing to differences between groups. Estimates of the population variance are made on the basis of the within-group variance and on the basis of the between-group variance. When the latter is divided by the former, the resulting F ratio indicates whether the between-groups variance estimate is sufficiently larger than the within-group variance estimate to indicate a significant effect. In a complex analysis of variance, the effects of two or more variables (for example, a stimulus variable and a personality variable) on a response variable are determined. Here, estimates of the population variance are made on the basis of within-group variance, between-rows variance, between-columns variance, and the variance attributable to the interaction between rows and columns. Interaction is present, for example, if the effect of a stimulus variable on a response variable is different for different levels of a personality variable.

Several examples of personality dynamics research were presented. Attraction toward a stranger was found to be a linear function of the proportion of positive reinforcements given by the stranger, regardless of the subject's affiliation need. In another investigation, agreement-disagreement by a stranger and the discrepancy between the subject's self and ideal self were found to interact in influencing depreciation of the stranger; depreciation of a disagreeing stranger was greatest for subjects with low self-ideal discrepancy. The effect of novel versus familiar stimuli on learning a simple verbal response was found to be a function of the subject's creativity; novel stimuli acted as positive reinforcers for creative individuals and negative reinforcers for noncreative individuals. With a movie of a primitive operation as the stressful stimulus, physiological responses as measured by skin conductance, heart rate, and general bodily movement were found to be in part a function of characteristic defense mechanisms. Neutrals show the greatest physiological responsivity, repressers less, and sensitizers the least. Response to hostile wit was found to be an interactive function of stressful conditions, self-ideal discrepancy, and the sex of the subject. Among males, those with low self-ideal discrepancy respond more positively to hostile wit under stressful conditions and less positively under neutral conditions than those with high discrepancy; among females, those with low self-ideal discrepancy prefer hostile wit under both conditions. Though response faults on the word-association test are often interpreted as indicative of anxiety or conflict, they have been found to be in large part predictable on the basis of both stimulus and personality variables. Response faults are most likely to occur when the stimulus word elicits many competing associations rather than a few and when the associations elicited by the stimulus word are not consistent with the subject's idiodynamic set.

COMPUTATIONAL EXAMPLE: SIMPLE ANALYSIS OF VARIANCE

As an exercise, a computational example will be presented. The student who has never been involved in working with an analysis of variance problem should find it helpful to work through the problem as presented. In each instance, the reader should note that a variance estimate is being determined by using a gross score formula to obtain sums of squares and then dividing this figure by degrees of freedom to obtain a variance estimate. The degrees of freedom in the estimate of a population variance depend on how many of the deviation scores are free to vary. Since the sum of the deviation scores must equal zero, as soon as all of the scores but one are known, there is only one value which that last score could be. Similarly with the deviation of group means from the overall mean: when all but one are known, the last one is not free to vary. For analysis of variance, the degrees of freedom for within is the number of subjects per group minus 1, summed for all the groups. The degrees of freedom for between is the number of groups minus 1.

Table 6–7   COMPUTING A SIMPLE ANALYSIS OF VARIANCE:
THE EFFECT OF FRUSTRATION ON HOSTILITY GROUPS

	$5.00 goal	$10.00 goal	$20.00 goal	$40.00 goal
	0	4	8	12
	0	4	8	12
	2	6	10	14
	2	6	10	14
	4	8	12	16
	4	8	12	16
	4	8	12	16
	4	8	12	16
	6	10	14	18
	6	10	14	18
	6	10	14	18
	6	10	14	18
	8	12	16	20
	8	12	16	20
	8	12	16	20
	8	12	16	20
	8	12	16	20
	8	12	16	20
	10	14	18	22
	10	14	18	22
	10	14	18	22
	10	14	18	22
	12	16	20	24
	12	16	20	24
	12	16	20	24
	12	16	20	24
	14	18	22	26
	14	18	22	26
	16	20	24	28
	16	20	24	28

Number of
Subjects $m =$ 30   +   30   +   30   +   30 = N = 120

Sum of
Scores $\Sigma X =$ 240   +   360   +   480   +   600 $= \Sigma\Sigma X$ = 1,680

Sum of
Squared
Scores $\Sigma X^2 =$ 2,480   +   4,880   +   8,240   +   12,560 $=$ $\Sigma\Sigma X^2$ = 28,160

Sum of
Scores,
Squared $(\Sigma X)^2 =$ 57,600   + 129,600   + 230,400   + 360,000 $= \Sigma(\Sigma X)^2$ = 777,600

Mean $M =$ 8.00   12.00   16.00   20.00   Overall Mean = 14.00

Total Variance:

$$\text{Total Sum of Squares} = \frac{1}{N}\,[N\Sigma\Sigma X^2 - (\Sigma\Sigma X)^2] =$$

Table 6–7   COMPUTING A SIMPLE ANALYSIS OF VARIANCE: THE
EFFECT OF FRUSTRATION ON HOSTILITY GROUPS (Cont.)

$$\frac{1}{120} [(120)(28,160) - (1,680)^2] = 4,640$$

$N = 120$

$$\text{Variance} = \frac{4,640}{120} = 38.67$$

Estimate of Population Variance Based on Within-Variance:

$$\text{Within Sum of Squares} = \frac{1}{m} [m\Sigma\Sigma X^2 - \Sigma(\Sigma X)^2] =$$

$$\frac{1}{30} [(30)(28,160) - 777,600] = 2,240$$

Degrees of Freedom $= 116$

$$\text{Variance Estimate: Within} = \frac{2,240}{116} = 19.31$$

Estimate of Population Variance Based on Between-Variance:

$$\text{Between Sum of Squares} = \frac{1}{N} [C\Sigma(\Sigma X)^2 - (\Sigma\Sigma X)^2] =$$

$$\frac{1}{120} [(4)(777,600) - (1,680)^2] = 2,400$$

Degrees of Freedom $= 3$

$$\text{Variance Estimate: Between} = \frac{2,400}{3} = 800$$

Given the variance estimates in Table 6–7, the F ratio may be determined. In most research articles, the results of an analysis of variance are summarized as shown in Table 6–8. In our example, the variance attributable to differences between groups was highly significant. As could be concluded from the correlational analysis of these same data earlier, the stimulus variable had a significant effect on the response variable.

Table 6–8   VARIANCE TABLE

Source	Sum of Squares	df	Variance Estimate	F
Between Groups (Frustration)	2,400	3	800.00	41.43*
Within	2,240	116	19.31	

* $p < .001$

The data based on both the stimulus conditions and the personality variable from our mythical experiment are presented in Table 6–9 as a sample of the computational steps taken in a complex analysis of variance design. The only new element is the interaction. Degrees of freedom for the interaction equal the degrees of freedom for between rows multiplied by the degrees of freedom for between columns.

Table 6–9 COMPUTING A COMPLEX ANALYSIS OF VARIANCE: THE EFFECT OF FRUSTRATION AND AGGRESSION-ANXIETY ON HOSTILITY

Aggression-Anxiety Groups	Frustration Groups							
	$5.00 goal		$10.00 goal		$20.00 goal		$40.00 goal	
Low	10	8	20	12	18	20	22	24
	10	8	14	12	18	22	22	26
	8	8	12	12	20	22	24	26
	8	6	12	10	20	24	24	28
	8	6	12	10	20	24	24	28
Medium	16	12	14	16	14	16	12	16
	16	12	14	16	14	16	12	16
	14	12	14	18	16	16	14	16
	14	10	16	18	16	18	14	18
	12	10	16	20	16	18	16	18
High	6	4	10	8	14	12	18	20
	6	2	10	6	14	10	18	20
	4	2	8	6	12	10	20	20
	4	0	8	4	12	8	20	22
	4	0	8	4	12	8	20	22

	$5	$10	$20	$40	Total
Low	$\Sigma X = 80$	$\Sigma X = 126$	$\Sigma X = 208$	$\Sigma X = 248$	$\Sigma X_1 = 662$
	$\Sigma X^2 = 656$	$\Sigma X^2 = 1,660$	$\Sigma X^2 = 4,368$	$\Sigma X^2 = 6,192$	$\Sigma X_1^2 = 12,87\bullet$
	$M = 8.00$	$M = 12.60$	$M = 20.80$	$M = 24.80$	$M_1 = 16.55$
	$m = 10$	$m = 10$	$m = 10$	$m = 10$	$N_1 = 40$
Med.	$\Sigma X = 128$	$\Sigma X = 162$	$\Sigma X = 160$	$\Sigma X = 152$	$\Sigma X_m = 602$
	$\Sigma X^2 = 1,680$	$\Sigma X^2 = 2,660$	$\Sigma X^2 = 2,576$	$\Sigma X^2 = 2,352$	$\Sigma X_m^2 = 9,268$
	$M = 12.80$	$M = 16.20$	$M = 16.00$	$M = 15.20$	$M_m = 15.05$
	$m = 10$	$m = 10$	$m = 10$	$m = 10$	$N_m = 40$
High	$\Sigma X = 32$	$\Sigma X = 72$	$\Sigma X = 112$	$\Sigma X = 200$	$\Sigma X_h = 416$
	$\Sigma X^2 = 144$	$\Sigma X^2 = 560$	$\Sigma X^2 = 1,296$	$\Sigma X^2 = 4,016$	$\Sigma X_h^2 = 6,016\bullet$
	$M = 3.20$	$M = 7.20$	$M = 11.20$	$M = 20.00$	$M_h = 10.40$
	$m = 10$	$m = 10$	$m = 10$	$m = 10$	$N_h = 40$
Total	$\Sigma X_5 = 240$	$\Sigma X_{10} = 360$	$\Sigma X_{20} = 480$	$\Sigma X_{40} = 600$	$\Sigma\Sigma X = 1680$
	$\Sigma X_5^2 = 2,480$	$\Sigma X_{10}^2 = 4,880$	$\Sigma X_{20}^2 = 8,240$	$\Sigma X_{40}^2 = 12,560$	$\Sigma\Sigma X^2 = 28,16\bullet$
	$M_5 = 8.00$	$M_{10} = 12.00$	$M_{20} = 16.00$	$M_{40} = 20.00$	
	$N_5 = 30$	$N_{10} = 30$	$N_{20} = 30$	$N_{40} = 30$	

Overall Mean $= 14.00\bullet$
$N = 120$

Table 6–9 COMPUTING A COMPLEX ANALYSIS OF VARIANCE: THE EFFECT OF FRUSTRATION AND AGGRESSION-ANXIETY ON HOSTILITY (Cont.)

Total Variance:

$$\text{Total Sum of Squares} = \frac{1}{N} [N\Sigma\Sigma X^2 - (\Sigma\Sigma X)^2] =$$

$$\frac{1}{120} [(120)(28,160) - (1680)^2] = 4,640$$

$$N = 120$$

$$\text{Variance} = \frac{4,640}{120} = 38.67$$

Estimate of Population Variance Based on Within Variance:

$$\text{Within Sum of Squares} = \frac{1}{m} [m\Sigma\Sigma X^2 - \Sigma(\Sigma X)^2] =$$

$$\frac{1}{10} [(10)(28,160) - (80^2 + 126^2 + 208^2 +$$

$$248^2 + 128^2 + 162^2 + 160^2 + 152^2 + 32^2 +$$

$$72^2 + 112^2 + 200^2)] = 447.20$$

Degrees of Freedom $= 108$

$$\text{Variance Estimate: Within} = \frac{447.20}{108} = 4.14$$

Estimate of Population Variance Based on Between-Columns Variance:

$$\text{Between-Columns Sum of Squares} = \frac{1}{N} [C\Sigma_c (\Sigma X)^2 - (\Sigma\Sigma X)^2] =$$

$$\frac{1}{120} [4(240^2 + 360^2 + 480^2 + 600^2) - (1680)^2] = 2,400$$

Degrees of Freedom $= 3$

$$\text{Variance Estimate: Between Columns} = \frac{2,400}{3} = \underline{800}$$

Estimate of Population Variance Based on Between-Rows Variance:

$$\text{Between-Rows Sum of Squares} = \frac{1}{N} [R\Sigma_r (\Sigma X)^2 - (\Sigma\Sigma X)^2] =$$

$$\frac{1}{120} [3(662^2 + 602^2 + 416^2) - (1680)^2] = 822.60$$

Degrees of Freedom $= 2$

Table 6–9   COMPUTING A COMPLEX ANALYSIS OF VARIANCE: THE EFFECT OF FRUSTRATION AND AGGRESSION-ANXIETY ON HOSTILITY (Cont.)

$$\text{Variance Estimate: Between Rows} = \frac{822.60}{2} = 411.30$$

Estimate of Population Variance Based on Interaction Variance:
Interaction Sum of Squares = Total Sum of Squares —
(Sums of Squares for Columns, Rows, and Within) =
4,640 — (447.20 + 2,400 + 822.60) = 970.20

Degrees of Freedom = 6

$$\text{Variance Estimate: Interaction} = \frac{970.20}{6} = 161.70$$

As may be seen in Table 6–10, the complex analysis of variance indicates significant effects for the stimulus variable, the personality variable, and the interaction between them.

Table 6–10   VARIANCE- TABLE

Source	Sum of Squares	df	Variance Estimate	F
Between Rows (Aggression-Anxiety)	822.60	2	411.30	99.35*
Between Columns (Frustration)	2,400.00	3	800.00	193.24*
Interaction	970.20	6	161.70	39.06*
Within	447.20	108	4.14	

$* \, p < .001$

CHAPTER 7

Personality Change

By definition, the major focus of interest in the field of personality is on the consistent, stable, unchanging aspects of behavior. At the same time, there is a considerable degree of both theoretical and applied concern with the possibility of bringing about changes in behavior. From the learning theorist working in an animal laboratory to the clinical psychologist interacting with a therapy patient, knowledge of the laws governing behavioral change is of paramount importance.

When we go beyond the everyday domain of psychologists and consider current issues in society, such as political indoctrination or brainwashing, the rehabilitation of criminals, the effectiveness of advertising, or the effects of integration on interracial attitudes, it is obvious that the practical implications of work on personality change are enormous. We will examine some general theoretical considerations in relation to change, look at the methodological problems involved in measuring change and in analyzing data dealing with change, and then sample some of the research which has involved both deliberate attempts to change personality and also behavioral change which has resulted as a by-product of ongoing events.

Theoretical Considerations

A great many theories have been constructed with behavioral change as a central or even exclusive consideration. Rather than attempt to present brief and necessarily inadequate synopses of such theories, a few of the general aspects of change theories will be discussed. The student should keep in mind that each theorist was directly concerned with a specific body of observed data which was congruent with his formulations, and that no existing theory provides the basis for accurate prediction of all of the data.

Unpleasant Consequents of Behavior. What are the necessary conditions which lead to alterations in otherwise stable behavioral patterns? There seems to be agreement among a great many theorists, ranging historically from Sigmund Freud to Clark Hull, that behavior does not change unless it is in some way unsatisfactory to the organism in its present form. So long as a given behavior acts to satisfy an individual's needs, it is not discarded in favor of a new behavior. From the viewpoint of an outside observer, the behavior in question may appear totally unsatisfactory, morally reprehensible, or even contrary to the long-term best interests of the individual. It would be argued, nevertheless, that unless the behavior brought positive reinforcement, it would not be maintained by the individual.

In psychoanalysis, an attempt is often made to increase the frustration level and anxiety of the patient in order to motivate him to work at the process of change. For example, Freud [1919] suggested that sexual abstinence played a role in facilitating change. Similarly, phobic patients were encouraged to engage in the feared behavior with the rationale that the resulting discomfort would further the therapeutic effort.

In describing the necessary conditions for successful psychotherapy, Dollard and Miller indicate that changes in behavior are considerably more likely if the present behavior causes difficulty:

> Motivation is important for learning. Because psychotherapy must overcome conflict, and this inevitably arouses fear, it requires strong motivation. From this point of view, the prognosis is good if the patient is extremely miserable because his misery will motivate therapy, and it is bad if he is self-satisfied. . . .
> Other things equal, the more disadvantageous the symptoms are, the stronger the motivation for therapy should be. Some symptoms, such as perversions and drug addictions, are exceedingly effective in reducing drives. Thus the patient has less motivation for therapy and the treatment of such symptoms is exceedingly difficult. The prognosis is improved, however, the more pressure the patient's environment puts on him to abandon these symptoms and the more trouble they cause him [Dollard and Miller, 1950, p. 234].

With respect to established personality characteristics, one can assume that they represent a stable and at least partially satisfying adjustment to the stimulus world. It follows from this that changes in behavior are more likely to occur when there are stimulus changes either within the organism or in his external environment. In an experiment, patterns of reinforcement are altered so that an established behavior leads to nonreinforcement while a new behavior is now rewarded. A psychotherapist creates a new environmental setting in which old rationalizations and perceptions are not accepted while different verbalizations are warmly reinforced. A propagandist or an educator provides a new set of information or beliefs or skills, the adoption of which is rewarded. In a political prison, the environment is drastically changed and the only satisfactory behavior is that acceptable to the interrogators. In a new culture, the old language, customs, and values are largely a handicap while the development of new response patterns can bring a variety of rewards. With increasing age, there are internal physiological changes and external changes in the demands and the expectancies of others which necessarily lead to new adjustments.

Self-Actualization. Some theorists argue with the basic premises assumed in such a depiction of the antecedents of change. Rather than conceptualizing man as an organism responding to stimuli and behaving in whatever way brings about the greatest drive satisfaction, some psychologists (for example, Carl Rogers, Robert W. White, Abraham Maslow) characterize man as a striving organism with built-in mechanisms for growth and change. Thus, Rogers proposes:

The organism has one basic tendency and striving—to actualize, maintain, and enhance the experiencing organism.

. . . The words used are an attempt to describe the observed directional force in organic life—a force which has been regarded as basic by many scientists, but which has not been too well described in testable or operational terms.

We are talking here about the tendency of the organism to maintain itself—to assimilate food, to behave defensively in the face of threat, to achieve the goal of self-maintenance even when the usual pathway to that goal is blocked. We are speaking of the tendency of the organism to move in the direction of maturation, as maturation is defined for each species. This involves self-actualization, though it should be understood that this too is a directional term. . . . It moves in the direction of greater independence or self-responsibility. Its movement, as Angyal [1941, pp. 32–50] has pointed out, is in the direction of an increasing self-government, self-regulation, and autonomy, and away from heteronymous control, or control by external forces [Rogers, 1951, pp. 487–488].

Even from the viewpoint of the self-theorists, however, external stimulus changes are important and often essential in bringing about behavior changes. It is through maladaptive interactions with others that an individual develops a self-concept which requires distortion or denial of certain experiences. It is primarily through quite different types of interaction (for example, nonthreatening relationship with a therapist) that the natural processes of growth and self-expansion and accurate perception of the stimulus world can once again operate.

Thus, we see that quite diverse theorists would agree that in both laboratory and everyday-life situations, changes in stimuli seem to result in changes in responses. The possibility of altering an individual's stimulus world sets the stage for the alteration of at least a portion of his characteristic behavior. To proceed from that general notion to the specifics of what stimulus changes will lead to precisely what response changes is another matter.

SELECTING THE NEW BEHAVIOR

For personality to change, the elimination of old responses is not sufficient. In addition, new behavior must occur. The problem here is two-fold. On theoretical grounds we may inquire on what basis new responses are most likely to be elicited. On practical grounds the relative efficiency of different assumptions governing behavior selection must be determined.

When a given behavior is eliminated, new behavior could occur on an essentially random or trial-and-error basis, on the basis of specific predisposing factors (inherited or learned), as the result of external determinants, on the basis of a cognitive appraisal of the most effective way to reach a goal, on the basis of complex internal dynamics, or on the basis of a general predisposing factor common to all individuals. Most of the basic notions concerning behavior change originate, as one might expect, in the field of learning. A very brief overview of a few of these different positions will provide some idea of the varied emphases.

Trial-and-Error. The trial-and-error notion was propounded by early learning theorists [for example, Thorndike, 1913]. Among relatively modern theorists, the late Edwin R. Guthrie came closer to the notion of trial-and-error learning than anyone else. His basic law of learning was one of simple association: "A combination of stimuli which has accompanied a movement will on its recurrence tend to be followed by that movement" [Guthrie, 1935, p. 26]. In an experiment by Guthrie and Horton [1946], a specially designed box was used in which a cat, if it in any way touched a small pole, was permitted to escape into a room in which it had been fed salmon. They found that whatever accidental behavior led to touching the pole was then performed by the cat on subsequent trials. If the first escape came through biting the pole, the cat bit the pole each time. Another cat, if he had backed into the pole the first time, backed into it each successive time. Thus, behavior occurs on a trial-and-error basis; any stimulus can accidentally become associated with any response, and behavior tends to be repeated in a stimulus situation in a stereotyped fashion. To bring about a deliberate change in behavior, one simply arranges the situation so that the undesired behavior cannot occur when the cues are present and so that the desired behavior will occur [Guthrie, 1942].

Habit-Family Hierarchy. Hull [1937] proposed the habit-family hierarchy as a derived principle of behavior. In some instances based on innate factors but in more instances based on learning, sets of habits of different strengths are available to the organism. If a given response is blocked, the next strongest habit in the hierarchy will be given. Hull's definition was:

A *habit-family hierarchy* consists of a number of habitual behavior sequences having in common the initial stimulus situation and the final reinforcing state of affairs [Hull, 1937, p. 16].

As he described it:

. . . the introduction of a barrier will cause the organism to shift from one behavior sequence *directed* to a reinforcing state of affairs to another *directed to the same* reinforcing state of affairs [Hull, 1937, p. 27].

When reinforcement is given following one of the responses down the hierarchy, that response will move up the hierarchy in terms of the probability of its occurring in the presence of the stimulus. Presumably, behavior can be altered by failing to reinforce undesirable behavior and then reinforcing more desirable responses which are farther down in the series.

Reinforcement of Operant Responses. The purely external determinants of new responses are probably given the greatest stress by Skinner. He distinguishes responses which are elicited by known stimuli (respondents) and those not a function of known stimuli (operants). Operant responses are characteristic of most human behavior. Such responses can come to have a relationship with stimuli through reinforcement. The stimulus does not elicit the response as with a respondent behavior such as a reflex; rather, the stimulus becomes an occasion for the operant behavior to occur. Behavior change takes place because operant responses become associated with new reinforcing stimuli. A specific response can be taught by shaping a desired behavior through successive approximations. Thus, a new behavior can be gradually taught and connected to a specific stimulus. Skinner gives an example:

Animal trainers are well versed in this method. As a sort of *tour de force* I have trained a rat to execute an elaborate series of responses suggested by recent work on anthropoid apes. The behavior consists of pulling a string to obtain a marble from a rack, picking the marble up with the fore-paws, carrying it to a tube projecting two inches above the floor of the cage, and dropping it inside. Every step in the process had to be worked out through a series of approximations, since the component responses were not in the original repertoire of the rat [Skinner, 1938, pp. 339–340].

Cognitive Expectancies. Edward C. Tolman's learning theory laid stress on cognitive elements; organisms were proposed to alter their behavior through the learning of sign-significate relations rather than responses. Thus, a rat learns the pattern of a maze (forms a cognitive map of the situation) rather than a series of muscle responses or S-R links. Organisms form hypotheses or expectancies about ways to attain goals, act on the basis of these expectancies, and alter their behavior whenever the hypotheses prove incorrect. For example, Tolman said:

Consider a chimpanzee or a nursery-school child. The little animal (partly by accident and partly as a result of innate propensity) chances, let us say, to embark upon dominance behavior. He engages in a few fights and establishes a high dominance-status in his group. He therewith discovers (*that is, learns*) the instrumental fact that this establishing of high dominance-status is a *means* to obtaining practically all of a limited food supply, or to obtaining an especially prized toy, if he be the nursery-school child. He discovers that his basic biological drives of hunger or of play become thereby better satisfied. On the other hand, in some other quite different situation he may learn the instrumental value of using collective techniques instead. . . . Learning is thus a "reasonable" activity which tends to keep the individual well-adjusted to the actual environmental realities [Tolman, 1942, pp. 59–60].

Increased Consciousness and Analytic Interpretations. Sigmund Freud was concerned primarily with neurotic individuals and with specific ways to bring about changes in patients through psychoanalysis. He was also working within a framework which was not bounded by operational definitions, testable hypotheses, or the criterion of prediction. From this quite different background and quite different body of operations, Freud [1920] suggested that the neurotic is unable to find enjoyment or to achieve. Enjoyment is impossible because the libido is attached to fantasied objects rather than to real ones. Energy is expended by the ego in repression of the libido, and hence the individual does not have enough energy remaining to be able to achieve. In psychoanalysis, through interpretations made by the analyst, the ego becomes wider and accepts more unconscious material into consciousness. As a result, the libido's attachment to fantasied objects and to symptoms is broken and new outlets are found for the libido. Through interpretations, the ego grows in strength and is better able to coordinate the demands of reality, the id, and the superego. One might guess, then, that new behavior (the channeling of the libido) is selected on the basis of the analyst's interpreting the behavior as reality-oriented, biologically satisfying, and morally acceptable.

Natural Development of Good Adjustment. Primarily among self-theorists in the field of personality, such as Rogers, the new behavior is viewed as proceeding naturally from the organism. Describing a client in therapy, Rogers indicates:

> Gradually he comes to experience the fact that he is making value judgments, in a way that is new to him, and yet a way that was also known to him in his infancy. Just as the infant places an assured value upon an experience, relying on the evidence of his own senses . . . so too the client finds that it is his own organism which supplies the evidence upon which value judgments may be made. He discovers that his own senses, his own physiological equipment, can provide the data for making value judgments and for continuously revising them. No one needs to tell him that it is good to act in a freer and more spontaneous fashion, rather than in the rigid way to which he has been accustomed. He senses, he feels that it is satisfying and enhancing [Rogers, 1951, pp. 522–523].

Rather than trial-and-error, a hierarchy of habits, shaping of operant behavior, or insight, Rogers proposes that the organism will behave in a natural and well-adjusted fashion if he is provided with a safe and accepting environment.

Given this variety of theoretical notions, it is not surprising that descriptions of behavioral change and techniques for bringing about change are equally varied. To take just one example, among psychotherapists there are those who rely on extinction of undersirable responses and reinforcement of desired ones, those who attempt to shape specific operant behavior in an experimental-like setting, those who stress insight and cognitive restructuring, those who interpret libidinal attachments in terms of unconscious strivings, and those who attempt to create an atmosphere of acceptance assuming that the impetus for change is within the patient.

RETENTION OF THE NEW BEHAVIOR

Once a change in behavior occurs, such that a new response or series of responses are made by the organism, under what conditions will the new responses become characteristic of the organism? An individual may become fearful on a roller coaster ride or angry while viewing a political candidate without fearfulness or hostility becoming his usual modes of behavior. Similarly, a patient in psychotherapy may become less neurotic or a prisoner of war may profess his allegiance to the ideology of his captors without these new behaviors becoming permanent aspects of his response system. What variables influence this temporary versus permanent aspect of the new behavior?

Simple Association. In outlining the different theoretical positions concerning the selection of new behavior, this issue was touched upon. The simplest possibility is that once a response is associated with a stimulus, the two always remain connected unless new stimulus-response associations are formed. Guthrie [1942, p. 30] proposed: "A stimulus pattern gains its full associative strength on the occasion of its first pairing with a response."

Reinforcement. Most learning theorists, however, have stressed the importance of reinforcement in strengthening the S-R relationship. In Hull's system, responses are learned only if they are rewarded. Reward consists of the reduction of either primary or secondary drives. Thus, Hull [1943] postulated that when a response and a stimulus occur in close temporal contiguity along with a need-reduction (or with a stimulus that has in the past been associated with need-reduction), the tendency of that stimulus to evoke that response is increased. Learning is a positive function of the magnitude of need reduction and a negative function of the delay between response and reinforcement. Further, successive reinforcements are additive, so habit strength is also a positive function of the number of reinforcements received.

Skinner, too, stresses the role of reinforcement in strengthening responses, but there are a number of differences between his formulations and those of Hull. Reinforcement of a response leads to increases in the reflex reserve and hence determines the total number of operant responses that will be emitted. However, the size of the reserve is not a simple function of number of reinforcements. Periodic or intermittent reinforcement is more efficient in building a reserve than is regular or consistent reinforcement [Skinner, 1938]. Rather than specifying need-reduction, positive reinforcement is simply ". . . those stimuli which strengthen responses when presented (e.g., food strengthens bar-pressing behavior)" [Keller and Schoenfeld, 1950, p. 61]. Negative reinforcement consists of those stimuli which strengthen behavior when they are removed. By observing the effect of a given stimulus on a response, one can determine whether it is a positive reinforcer, a negative reinforcer, or neither.

Understanding and Insight. The role of reinforcement in learning was rejected by Tolman. Rather than habits strengthened by reinforcement, expectancies are learned and then the performance of a response is in part a function of expectancies. The major effects of reward and punishment are with respect to performance, not with respect to the learning of expectancies. Learning is influenced primarily by variables which lead to the formation of a Gestalt of the whole (togetherness, belongingness, and so forth) and by variables which favor association (frequency, recency, emphasis, and the like). All such variables are important only because they foster understanding or insight concerning the situation.

Since Freud did not focus on specific behaviors, speaking meaningfully of the retention of new behavior is difficult. Psychoanalysis is not conceived as a process by which behavior A is eliminated and behavior B instituted in its place. Rather, certain functions and processes are changed, and this new functioning may lead to any number of different future behaviors. Any change which took place was presumed to influence a variety of other changes at all levels of consciousness. It also follows that a great deal of change may take place without removing *all* symptoms of maladjustment. The types of changes that occur are: (1) greater ability to make compromises among the demands of reality, id, and superego, (2) increased capacity for enjoyment, (3) increased capacity for achievement, (4) increased availability of unconscious material to consciousness, and (5) increased capacity to regress in the service of the ego [Luborsky and Schimek, 1964].

Types of Social Interactions. Rogers has not been as concerned with the retention of new behavior as with the origin of maladjusted behavior and techniques for bringing about better adjustment. Presumably, however, detrimental post-therapy changes can occur. Since the structure of the self is formed through interaction with others and since interaction in therapy leads to beneficial changes in self-structure, deleterious interactions after therapy could lead to still more changes. In speaking of childhood experiences, Rogers indicates:

Social experiences, social evaluations by others, become a part of his phenomenal field along with experiences not involving others—for example, that radiators are hot, stairs are dangerous, and candy tastes good.
It is at this stage of development, it would seem, that there takes place a type of distorted symbolization of experience, and a denial of experience to awareness, which has much significance for the later development of psychological maladjustment [Rogers, 1951, p. 499].

The specific details of the variables determining the development of self-structure and later alterations in it are seen by Rogers as problems which learning theorists will hopefully be able to solve.

Interpersonal Context. In addition to the general principles mentioned here, a number of other variables influencing the retention of new behavior have been identified. For example, most investigators dealing directly with the problem of personality change place strong emphasis on the importance of the interpersonal context. Therapists stress the quality of the therapeutic relationship. Social psychologists point to the pervasive importance of the response of others to an individual's behavior, including the audience in role-playing experiments, peer groups, and reference groups. In forcible indoctrination, considerable attention is paid to establishing a dependent relationship with the interrogator and also to utilizing the influence of other prisoners. Quite likely, other human beings are among the most powerful sources of reinforcement available.

Dissonance Reduction. In work on the theory of cognitive dissonance, Festinger [1961] has presented evidence that learning is more effective when rewards are small than when they are large. Engaging in behavior for which the reward is insufficient leads to inconsistent or conflicting or dissonant cognitions. Since dissonance motivates behavior which is dissonance-reducing, one possibility is to value the behavior more highly. The individual comes to perceive the behavior as desirable in its own right rather than as a way to obtain a reward. Festinger concludes:

> It seems clear that the inclination to engage in behavior after extrinsic rewards are removed is not so much a function of past rewards themselves. Rather, and paradoxically, such persistence in behavior is increased by a history of nonrewards or inadequate rewards. I sometimes like to summarize all this by saying that rats and people come to love things for which they have suffered [Festinger, 1961, p. 11].

In a similar way, Aronson and Carlsmith [1963] have shown that mild negative reinforcement is more effective than strong negative reinforcement in changing behavior. They suggest that refraining from a desired behavior in response to a mild threat is dissonance-producing, and dissonance reduction is achieved by devaluing the behavior. A further extension of these ideas even argues against the kind of insight or understanding which Tolman stressed. Festinger and Freedman speculate:

> This would seem to suggest that the child who has sufficient reasons for not cheating—whether it is in terms of desire to receive a reward, avoid a punishment, or avoid social consequences—would feel less dissonance as a result of not cheating than a child who has less good reasons. Since the child has sufficient reasons and feels little dissonance, he may not develop a moral value or restriction against cheating. He may not cheat because he is convinced it is a bad idea, but, on the other hand, he may not think that cheating is bad per se. In some sense he will be freer in that he does not blindly follow a moral code, but he is also freer in that under appropriate circumstances he may feel free to cheat in much the same way that a child who refrains only from fear is free when the fear is removed. In other words, the child who is given good reasons for not cheating may not develop as strong a moral code as a child who is given less good reasons and told merely that it is wrong [Festinger and Freedman, 1964, pp. 234–235].

       Situational Constancy. As a final point, we should note that on a good many bases, it would be hypothesized that the new behavior is more likely to be retained if the situation which brought it about remains the same. If there is a blocking of old responses and the development of new ones (whether through simple association, reinforcement, insight, or whatever), the new behavior is more likely to continue if the post-learning conditions are similar to the learning conditions. This is quite possibly the reason that therapists are beginning to stress the importance of what happens to the patient outside of the therapy hour [Murray, 1964], that "brainwashing" is quite ineffective in achieving lasting conversion in attitudes and beliefs [Holt, 1964], that even powerful psychopharmacological agents seem to have only temporary effects on personality [Zubin and Katz, 1964], and that the behavioral effects of isolation experiences, as in the sensory deprivation experiments, are short-lived. It seems that there must be continued stimulus support for the new behavior.

Measuring Personality Change

Two special problems arise in research on personality change which do not occur in the other types of personality research already discussed. First is the problem of devising adequate measuring instruments for assessing the same variable in the same subjects on more than one occasion. Second is the problem of selecting the appropriate experimental design and statistical analysis for investigating behavioral change.

MEASURING BEHAVIOR ON MORE THAN ONE OCCASION

In a great many scientific endeavors, one must measure variables repeatedly over a period of time. With most physical variables, repeated measurement causes little or no difficulty. Length and weight and temperature, for example, may be assessed hourly or daily without causing any measurement problems. Similarly, many variables used in psychological research can be measured over and over: frequency of lever pressing, speed in a runway, galvanic skin response. In these various instances, there is no need to have more than one scale or thermometer or lever or clock or polygraph; the same instrument serves equally well on each occasion.

Personality variables, as they are most often measured with existing techniques, create difficulties if they are used in this same way. If an intelligence test, an ink blot test, a series of thematic apperception slides, or a questionnaire is given to a subject repeatedly, something different is involved than in ascertaining his weight repeatedly. The subject may remember his previous responses, may become bored by the repetition of content, may deliberately strive to be consistent (or inconsistent) over trials, may discuss his answers with others if the time interval between measurements is long enough and modify his subsequent responses as a result, may become more proficient as a function of repeated practice in instances where ability is involved, and so on and so forth. One solution to these sorts of problems is the development of a series of equivalent measures of each personality variable. The specific content is different across forms, but the responses elicited by Form A are equivalent to those elicited by Form B, Form C, and so forth. Further, it does not matter in which order the forms are administered. Changes in test scores from form to form represent genuine changes along the personality dimension and not artificial changes resulting from inadequate measuring instruments.

Unfortunately, for most personality variables any investigation of change would have to be preceded by a long and difficult period of test construction in which the goal was a series of parallel assessment devices. With few exceptions [for example, Holtzman, Thorpe, Swartz, and Herron, 1961; Moran, Kimble, and Mefferd, 1960; Scheier and Cattell, 1960; Terman and Merrill, 1937], alternate forms are not available for measuring personality variables on more than one occasion. Until such instruments become available, the most usual practice will probably continue to be the readministration of the same test. Whether with equivalent forms or with the same tests readministered, the approach to data analysis remains the same. We will now turn to the statistical analysis of personality change.

COMPARING REPEATED MEASURES OF ONE GROUP OF INDIVIDUALS

Changes in Frequencies, Proportions, and Means. Though the major portion of this section will be devoted to analysis of variance, we should note that several other statistical techniques may be applied to simple situations of assessing change between time 1 and time 2. For example, one might have a situation in which subjects are given a test and divided into high versus low on a given dimension, exposed to the change agent, and then retested. On the second set of scores, the subjects are divided into high and low on the same basis as in the original testing. The situation is depicted in Table 7-3, which is presented with the computational example at the end of this chapter. The problem may also be approached in terms of frequencies or proportions. Another approach is to test for the significance of the difference between means. Computational details are provided at the end of this chapter.

For small samples (arbitrarily defined as N less than 30), one must use a t test in determining the significance of the change in means from time 1 to time 2. Since the t test yields the same results as the F ratio, we will not go into computational details.

Analysis of Variance. For the sake of clarity, we will again take a hypothetical experimental situation. Assume that an experimenter was interested in determining the effects of psychotherapy on depression. He has available three parallel forms of a Depression Scale which yield equal means, equal standard deviations, and which correlate with one another in the high .90's. Each form of the scale asks questions about the subject's worries, moodiness, unhappiness, feelings of worthlessness, and the like, but no specific question appears more than once on the three scales.

The situation chosen for study is a student health center at a university.

Among the students referred for psychotherapy, a large number are classified as having predominant symptoms of depression. If psychotherapy is effective in ameliorating undesirable behavior, one would hypothesize that depression would be less after exposure to therapy. In addition, the reduction in depression should not represent a temporary change but a lasting one. As subjects, 15 therapy referrals showing depressive symptoms are selected. Each is given Form I of the Depression Scale, and then assigned to a therapist for several months of treatment. At the termination of therapy, each subject takes Form II of the Depression Scale, and six months after that is recalled and given Form III of the test.

With respect to personality change, the question is whether the psychotherapy experience had an effect on depression. Our statistical analysis must compare the three sets of test scores to determine whether there is a change over time. Using the hypothetical data shown in Table 7–4, we find that the mean depression scores at the three time samplings are 30.00, 20.00, and 24.00. To determine if the three means are significantly different from one another, we may utilize an analysis of variance. There is a difference between this type of situation and the one-way analysis of variance discussed in the previous chapter. The difference lies in the fact that instead of three independent groups of subjects, we have one group of subjects measured three different times. This fact leads to a different approach in analysis.

When the data are arranged as in Table 7–4, we may obtain the means of the scores for both rows and columns. The former are the mean scores of individuals across the three testings, and the latter are the means of the group of individuals on each occasion. From the earlier discussion, we will see that the total variance is a function of the deviation of each row mean from the overall mean (individual differences) and the deviation of each column mean from the overall mean (effect of psychotherapy). Because each of the cells contains only one score, there is no variation within cells to contribute to the total variance; this also means that the population variance cannot be estimated from the within variance and used for comparison with the other estimates. There is, nevertheless, another source of variance and one which can be used to estimate the population variance and hence used as error variance to determine the significance of the other effects. An interaction occurs between rows and columns which may be thought of as the deviation of each score from what would be predicted on the basis of row and column means. This interaction or "leftover" variance is used as the error term in this type of analysis of variance. As was pointed out in discussing the other analysis of variance designs, we are interested in determining whether the variance is simply the result of unknown antecedents (as represented by the interaction or error variance) or the result of the experimental manipulation (in this instance, psychotherapy). We can also determine if differences across individuals contribute significantly to the total variance, but this effect is almost always significant and of little or no interest to the investigator. The population variance is estimated from the error variance, from the individual differences or between-row variance, and from the treatment effect or between-column variance. F ratios are computed to determine if either of the latter two estimates of variance are significantly larger than the estimate based on error variance.

Table 7–5 gives a computational example in which sums of squares are obtained and then divided by degrees of freedom to obtain variance estimates which are used in computing the F ratios. The outcome of this hypothetical experiment is shown in Table 7–6 which indicates significant row and column effects. Of concern to the experimenter are the column effects; the experimental manipulation had a significant effect on the dependent variable of depression.

COMPARING REPEATED MEASURES OF MORE THAN
ONE GROUP OF INDIVIDUALS

The type of personality-change experiment just described is a common one, and it provides a reasonable beginning for exploratory research in a problem area. As with any experimental investigation, however, the problem of a control group must be raised. The argument can be made that with personality dimensions as the dependent variable, a control group is superfluous. That is, if the personality test has been found to have high test-retest reliability (with approximately equal means) over a period of time comparable to that used in the experiment, these reliability data are equivalent to a control group.

A major difficulty with this argument is the fact that the conditions under which subjects are tested in an experimental investigation are almost never comparable to those in the standardization or reliability procedures. For example, in the study just described, possibly psychotherapy had no effect on depression. Conceivably, the initially high scores were a function of being referred for psychological help ("they must think I'm crazy"), the post-therapy low scores a function of having gotten used to the idea of receiving treatment in a clinic ("lots of people come here and besides it's fun to talk about myself"), and the slight rise in scores six months later a function of worry about the tester's intention ("maybe they found out something they aren't telling me"). In order to avoid this type of alternative explanation of results, it is obviously advantageous in research on personality change to utilize a control group.

In our example, the experimenter could add a second group of 15 subjects who do not receive psychotherapy during the course of the experiment. They, too, would be chosen from the referrals to the counselling center who evidenced depressive behavior. They would be tested and then placed on a "waiting list" for psychotherapy. On two more occasions (at the times the experimental group was tested), they would be given the other two forms of the Depression Scale. The results for the imaginary control group are shown in Table 7–7 in which their Depression Scale means on the three occasions are 30.00, 28.00, and 30.00. The comparison between the two groups gives us much more convincing evidence concerning the effects of psychotherapy than did an examination of the experimental group alone. We might note that the experimental design to be described may be extended to include still other groups; for example, one might want to compare a control group, a group receiving client-centered psychotherapy, and a group undergoing psychoanalysis.

The type of analysis of variance used to determine the significance of such data represents a combination of the type just described and the type described in the previous chapter. In determining the difference between the experimental and control groups, the comparison is like that utilized in the work on personality dynamics. The population variance is estimated on the basis of the differences between the two groups and on the basis of individual differences within each group. If the former is significantly larger than the latter, we conclude that the subjects in the two experimental conditions (psychotherapy vs. waiting in a control group) responded differently on the dependent variable (depression). In determining the effect of the testing periods, the interaction between the testing periods and conditions, and the individual differences, estimates of the population variance based on these three sources of variance are compared with (that is, divided by) the error variance estimate based on a combination of the two row-by-column interactions.

A computational example is again provided. Table 7–8 gives the computational steps for obtaining the variance estimates. The analysis of variance (Table 7–9) indicates that there was a significant difference between the experimental and control groups (lower depression scores in the psychotherapy group), a significant difference over time which is further clarified by the significant interaction between times and conditions (depression scores went down over time in psychotherapy but remained approximately constant in the control condition), and the usual significant individual differences.

With this brief introduction to some of the problems of measurement and data analysis, we will turn to a few examples of research on personality change.

Selected Examples of Research on Personality Change

In part because of methodological difficulties, research on personality change has been relatively limited. Even in connection with an active applied technique such as psychotherapy, research to determine its effectiveness in altering specific dimensions of personality has not been of great quantity. Most of the research on change has been of two types. On the one hand, those interested in client-centered therapy have been concerned with changes in self-concept and self-ideal discrepancy; this work will be discussed in Chapter 12. In contrast, most experimental work on change has dealt with opinion or attitude variables, presumably because these dimensions appear to be easier to change than needs, abilities, traits, and the like. In spite of the somewhat limited range in the variables studied, the following examples serve to demonstrate the possibilities for research on personality change.

PSYCHOTHERAPY: CHANGES IN ADJUSTMENT

Is Psychotherapy an Effective Change Agent? When we move from the research example using psychotherapy to the actual practice of psychotherapy, we immediately find that the area is not characterized by an orderly accumulation of data showing that psychotherapy is effective in altering this or that behavior to a specific degree. Rather, therapy research is characterized by controversy and disagreements concerning whether this procedure has *any* effect on *any* behavior. Part of the difficulty lies in methodology—lack of appropriate measuring instruments, the practical and ethical considerations in establishing appropriate control groups, and the time involved in carrying out the necessary longitudinal studies. Beyond these problems, however, lie theoretical confusions (for example, nonoperational definitions of goals) and inter- and intra-professional disputes which range from the definition of therapy as treatment performed exclusively by physicians to the conviction that the practice of clinical psychology has no place in a scientific discipline. Given this combination of problems, the task of the researcher in this area is a difficult one.

Even when data are available, they seem to create more controversy rather than greater clarity. One of the most eminent critics of psychotherapy is Hans Eysenck at the University of London. In 1952, Eysenck obtained data which allowed him to compare improvement rates for severe neurotics receiving only custodial care in state hospitals with the rates for similar patients undergoing psychotherapy. The latter were based on data available in the literature dealing with a total of 7,293 patients. His conclusions were as follows:

In general, certain conclusions are possible from these data. They fail to prove that psychotherapy, Freudian or otherwise, facilitates the recovery of neurotic patients. They show that roughly two-thirds of a group of neurotic patients will recover or improve to a marked extent within about two years of the onset of their illness, whether they are treated by means of psychotherapy or not. This figure appears to be remarkably stable from one investigation to another, regardless of type of patient treated, standard of recovery employed, or method of therapy used. From the point of view of the neurotic, these figures are encouraging; from the point of view of the psychotherapist, they can hardly be called very favorable to his claims.

The figures quoted do not necessarily disprove the possibility of therapeutic effectiveness. There are obvious shortcomings in any actuarial comparison and these shortcomings are particularly serious when there is so little agreement among psychiatrists relating even to the most fundamental concepts and definitions. Definite proof would require a special investigation, carefully planned and methodologically more adequate that these *ad hoc* comparisons. But even the much more modest conclusion, that the figures fail to show any favorable effects of psychotherapy, should give pause to those who would wish to give an important part in the training of clinical psychologists to a skill the existence and effectiveness of which is still unsupported by any scientifically acceptable evidence [Eysenck, 1952, pp. 322–323].

A number of individuals responded to Eysenck's article critically. Among these was Rosenzweig [1954] who suggested that Eysenck's generalizations were far too broad and sweeping on the basis of relatively poor data. Specifically, he criticized the weaknesses in diagnosis (perhaps those who did not receive treatment were less ill), in defining the control group (perhaps there were therapeutic elements in the "custodial care"), and in the criteria of improvement (perhaps different criteria were used in evaluating treated and nontreated patients). Rosenzweig goes beyond those specific criticisms to present his viewpoint:

What good is psychotherapy? As good as man's faith in his humanity. Men have always believed in their ability to change for the better and to help each other so to change—through mutual assistance, love, religion, and art. Conceived in the broadest terms psychotherapy derives from the same faith and, employing of necessity some of the same means, attempts to formulate them more precisely. The question is not, then, whether psychotherapy does any good—one might as reasonably ask, "Is life worth living?"; the question is *how* does therapy accomplish its ends in those fortunate instances where, despite the adverse odds, it manages to succeed. It is to the process, not the superficially appraised end result—to the disorganization or organization of forces which may spell illness and partial death or health and growth—that attention should be directed if we are to learn anything about psychotherapy [Rosenzweig, 1954, p. 303].

Faith in man's humanity is an admirable sentiment, but data are more satisfying to the behavioral scientist.

Individual Psychotherapy vs. Group Psychotherapy vs. No Treatment. Both sides in the continuing controversy over psychotherapy agree that more and better research is badly needed. One of the better investigations is that of Barron and Leary [1955] using 150 psychoneurotic patients. All of the patients had applied for psychotherapy at the out-patient clinic of the Kaiser Foundation Hospital in Oakland, California. Of these, 85 were given group psychotherapy, 42 received individual psychotherapy, and 23 were placed on a waiting list for approximately six months before receiving any treatment. The therapy subjects each were in treatment on a weekly schedule for at least three months. The psychotherapists consisted of experienced psychiatrists, social workers, and psychologists. The MMPI was administered to all subjects when they applied for therapy and then a second time after either the psychotherapy or the waiting period. The average age of the patients was 32, the average educational level was one year of college, and the group contained 97 women and 53 men. The treatment and control groups did not differ significantly in age, education, sex, or diagnosis. There was also no difference across groups in mean scores on any of the subscales of the first MMPI.

Scores at time 1 were compared with scores at time 2 for each group. In both therapy groups, there was a significant decrease in depression, hysteria, hypochondriasis, and lie scores and a significant increase in ego strength. In group psychotherapy, there was also a significant decrease in paranoia and psychasthenia. If these had been the only two groups employed, it might have been concluded that both types of treatment were effective in bringing about behavioral changes, with group psychotherapy being somewhat more effective than individual psychotherapy. The patients at the end of treatment gave evidence of being in a more positive mood, having fewer physical symptoms, and being more realistic about themselves.

When the control group is also considered, however, the optimistic picture becomes somewhat clouded. The nontreated subjects had a pattern of change very similar to the treated ones. The investigators compared the amount of change for each therapy group with the amount of change in the nontreatment group. On only one of the MMPI scales was there significantly more change in the treatment group than in the control group, and this difference was true only for the individual psychotherapy patients. On the K scale, the control group became slightly less defensive over time and the individual therapy group became significantly more defensive over time. Barron and Leary [1955, p. 245] conclude: "For the most part, however, the changes tended to be in the same direction for treatment and nontreatment groups, and of almost equal magnitude."

ROLE PLAYING: CHANGES IN OPINION

General Principles of Role Playing. A number of theorists in personality and social psychology have found it useful to conceptualize a great deal of interpersonal behavior in terms of roles. Within any culture individuals may play a great many roles in the course of a lifetime. There are roles within a family (for example, son, brother, father), roles in school (for example, pupil, teacher, class cut-up), roles in interpersonal interactions (for example, customer, salesman), occupational roles (for example, bus driver, physician, real estate agent), and countless others. With each role goes a place in the status hierarchy and a series of expected behaviors. Those who play the roles tend to incorporate the role characteristics as integral aspects of themselves. The new teacher or new mother or new senator may feel somewhat awkward and artificial in adjusting to the new role, but the new behavior soon seems natural.

Sarbin [1964b] has outlined some of the general considerations by which the playing of a role leads to behavioral changes. He defines role enactment as: ". . . the performance of patterned behaviors where the antecedent conditions include assignment to a position in the social structure" [Sarbin, 1964b, p. 177].

If the playing of roles in everyday life brings behavioral changes, what is the effect of assignment to a role in a controlled laboratory situation? In a variety of investigations, role playing has been found to influence somatic processes (for example, gastric secretions), performance (for example, behavior of foremen in an industrial organization), attention (for example, decreasing ambiguity in a social situation), and dispositional characteristics (for example, beliefs, values, attitudes).

Sarbin has also outlined some of the essential elements in role theory. First, the role must be enacted effectively by the individual. Effectiveness must be judged by observers. In order to perform effectively, an individual must have role expectations which correspond with those of the observers. The individual must perceive the role and its demands accurately in terms of his social group. Individuals differ in the effectiveness of role playing as a way of changing their behavior. The greater the subject's role-taking aptitude and the more similarity there is between present self and role, the more effective the role playing will be. Finally, reinforcement will influence the effect of role playing on subsequent behavior.

Influence of Role Playing on Opinion Change. Janis and King [1954] were interested in determining the conditions under which role playing leads to actual changes in personal opinions. Their first step was to determine whether role playing in a laboratory situation actually brought about opinion change or as they phrased it, whether "saying is believing."

As a measure of initial opinion, a questionnaire was administered to a large group of college students. They were asked their opinions concerning the number of movie theaters that would still be in business in three years, the total supply of meat that would be available for the civilian population of the U.S. in 1953, and the number of years that would elapse before the discovery of a completely effective cure for the common cold. Approximately four weeks later the subjects were asked to give a talk based on an outline prepared by the experimenter. The arguments were highly biased and the evidence was interpreted as supporting only one viewpoint. All of the viewpoints were different from the individual opinions of the subjects. The active participant subjects were asked to play the role of a sincere advocate of a given point of view. Two other subjects (passive controls) read the same outline and were present when the talk was presented. Each subject delivered a talk on one of the topics and listened to talks on the other two. Immediately after the last of the three talks, they were asked to rate each speaker on a number of variables, but the crucial questions concerned their present opinion on each topic.

The active participants and passive controls did not differ in their initial opinions on any of the topics. On two of the topics, the active participants were significantly more influenced than the passive controls. A portion of these data is presented in Table 7-1. While the two groups did not differ with respect to the third topic, the active participants were significantly more confident of their post-experimental opinions than were the passive controls.

Table 7-1   OPINION CHANGE IN ACTIVE PARTICIPANTS
              IN ROLE PLAY VERSUS PASSIVE CONTROLS

	Topic					
	Movie Theaters		Meat Shortage		Cold Cure	
	Active	Passive	Active	Passive	Active	Passive
Percentage Showing Sizable Change	45%	21%	41.5%	17%	40%	45%
p	.01		.01		N.S.	

In discussing possible mechanisms underlying the opinion changes, Janis and King propose:

During the experimental sessions there were no apparent sources of external social rewards from the environment. Since the others present remained silent, the active participant had no opportunity to know how they were reacting to his talk, except possibly by subtle signs from their facial expressions or from their bodily movements. But even in the absence of any external cues to social approval, it seems probable that *anticipations* concerning such approval would occur if the individual felt that he was performing well, as expressed in his self-ratings. Thus, expectations of favorable audience reactions may have occurred less frequently among Ss who were required to perform the relatively difficult task of presenting the unfamiliar technical material in Communication C than among those who were required to perform the less difficult task of presenting Communication A or B. The increase in opinion change produced by role playing might be mediated by the individual's sense of achievement or his elated feelings about the adequacy of his oral performance. One hypothesis that would follow from this assumption is that when a person conforms outwardly to social demands by playing a role which requires him to advocate a given opinion, he will begin to believe what he is saying if he is made to feel that he says it well [Janis and King, 1954, p. 217].

REINFORCEMENT: CHANGES IN ATTITUDE

The same learning principles which account for changes in behavior in T-mazes, Skinner boxes, and in paired-associate learning of nonsense syllables will eventually permit the prediction and control of changes in more complex behaviors as represented by personality dimensions. While direct generalization from the learning laboratory to other situations may be premature at the present time, there are many promising research attempts to extend learning concepts to other areas.

Doob [1947] conceptualized attitudes as implicit anticipatory responses which mediate overt behaviors and which develop on the basis of reinforcement; that is, attitudes are habits. Thus, attitudes are held because they have been reinforced, they should extinguish if they are not reinforced, and alternate attitudes should be acquired if they result in reinforcement.

Proceeding from Doob's formulations, Scott [1957] investigated the effects of reward and punishment on expressed attitudes. Students in a series of 29 psychology discussion sections were asked to indicate their attitudes concerning universal military training, night hours for women students, and de-emphasis of football. Each class was assigned one of the three issues to debate, and four subjects were chosen from each class (two favorable and two unfavorable with respect to the issue). The subjects were given the task of debating the issue in front of the class, but each was required to argue for the position opposite to that which they themselves held.

The debates were held two weeks after the original attitude questions were given. Each pair of debators spoke for three minutes while the opponents were out of the room and later for another two minutes of rebuttal, also with the opponents absent. Then, all four debators came into the room together, and the class voted on which team did the better job. The instructor pretended to count the ballots while a student tallied results on the board, but the experimenter had actually determined ahead of time who would be announced as winner and loser. At that point, all class members including the debators were asked to indicate their present attitude concerning the issue that had been debated. A control group was formed by selecting a group of students from the same classes who did not debate. We should note that this experiment could be conceptualized in terms of role playing with differential success experimentally manipulated.

Those subjects who debated and were told that they were found to have won changed their attitudes away from their original position significantly more than either the control group or the debaters who lost. The amount of change in the latter two groups was not significantly different. Scott summarized:

> The experiment was designed to give both winners and losers equivalent contact with arguments for the opposite side, and to give both the experience of verbalizing these arguments as if they were their own. What distinguished the two groups was the brief experience of either group approval or group disapproval for their performances. These performances involved principally the oral presentation of arguments—verbal behavior to which they were unaccustomed. The vote of "win" is presumed to have reinforced the verbal behavior and with it the accompanying implicit responses—attitudes and cognitive support for them. The vote of "lose" presumably weakened whatever response tendencies had been established by the overt behavior or by cognitive contact with the opposite side, so that Ss reverted to their pre-existing attitudes.
>
> If the opinion post-tests be regarded as valid reflections of Ss attitudes following the experimental stimulus, then one may conclude that social reward for expressing a new opinion tends to reinforce the concomitant attitudes, whereas social disapproval of the new behavior tends to lead to nonreinforcement of the accompanying attitudes. It appears that, in the present experiment, the brief experience of reward or punishment was a significant factor in accounting for attitude change, rather than the more prolonged experience of cognitive contact with opposing arguments [Scott, 1957, p. 74].

We should also note that the author suggested that the new opinions were quite likely only transitory. Given a change in their social environments which would permit continued reinforcement of the new behavior, such attitude change might be expected to endure.

DISSONANCE REDUCTION: CHANGES IN VALUES

Festinger [1957] has proposed a theory of cognitive dissonance which is relevant to a great many aspects of behavior, including personality change. He proposed that when an individual holds two inconsistent cognitions, dissonance is produced. Since dissonance is unpleasant to the individual experiencing it; his subsequent behavior is directed toward the reduction of dissonance. Reduction can take place in many ways, but the alteration of cognitions and the addition of new cognitions are among the most common. When one of the elements in the dissonant situation is part of a personality dimension, a change in this dimension represents one of the possible dissonance-reducing alternatives. In such a situation, personality change can presumably be initiated through the creation of dissonance.

In his doctoral dissertation at Stanford, Mills [1958] investigated changes in moral values as a function of dissonance reduction. He proposed that whenever an individual is presented with a temptation to violate moral standards and then makes the decision not to do so, dissonance is created. That is, the violation would be rewarding, and that fact is dissonant with the decision not to engage in the behavior. The greater the motivation to violate the moral standards, the greater the dissonance. There are also facts consonant with choosing the moral behavior—chances of getting caught, type of punishment that would be inflicted, and beliefs that the behavior is wrong. The fewer the number of these restraints, the greater the dissonance that is created when the individual decides not to engage in the behavior. With a strong temptation and weak restraints, the person who does not violate moral standards should have a great deal of dissonance. If he can increase his belief in the wrongness of the behavior, this change should help in reducing dissonance.

For the person who decides to violate moral standards, the reverse would hold. With a weak temptation and strong restraints, engaging in the behavior should be quite dissonant. Dissonance can be reduced here by weakening the restraints, for example by decreasing his belief in the wrongness of the behavior.

The procedure used by Mills was described as follows:

A questionnaire concerning attitudes toward cheating was given to sixth grade students in their school classrooms. The following day a contest was administered, also in the school classrooms. The contest was designed so that cheating could be detected, although this was not apparent. It was run under three different conditions: High Motivation-Low Restraint (a large prize was offered for winning and it was made to seem easy to cheat without being detected); Low Motivation-Low Restraint (a small prize was offered for winning and it was made to seem easy to cheat without being detected); High Motivation-High Restraint (a large prize was offered for winning and it was made to seem quite difficult to cheat without being detected). One day after the contest the attitude questionnaire was readministered. A control group did not receive the contest but was given the questionnaire twice, with the same two day interval [Mills, 1958, p. 519].

Mills found that those who did not cheat in the contests became more negative in their attitudes concerning cheating and those who did cheat became more positive concerning cheating. The control group did not have these changes. Analysis of variance revealed that the difference between cheaters and noncheaters was a significant one $(p < .01)$. Mills further found that with high motivation and low restraint, there was a greater effect than with low motivation and low restraint. With high motivation and high restraint, the results were somewhat ambiguous.

The general hypothesis, then, was confirmed. Moral values seem to be subject to at least temporary changes on the basis of the individual's conforming to or departing from those values. And, the greater the temptation to engage in the prohibited behavior, the greater is the change in values that takes place afterward.

PERSUASION: CHANGES IN BELIEFS, PRACTICES, AND ATTITUDES

Interest is widespread in the possibility of changing the beliefs and practices of large numbers of people simultaneously through the use of various techniques of persuasion. In advertising, a vast amount of money is spent in the attempt to convince consumers to behave in a way beneficial to the advertiser. With information or propaganda (the term depending on whether it is the good guys or the bad guys), most governments are continually engaged in an effort to present their nation, their policies, and their ideology in the most favorable light possible. In this country, each political candidate must persuade a sufficient number of voters that he should be elected to office, and the persuasive techniques range from televised speeches to "documentary" movies to scantily clad girls passing out campaign buttons. In addition, a great many governmental and nongovernmental agencies institute projects to convince the public to wear safety belts, build fall-out shelters, get polio shots, extinguish their camp fires, make charity donations, refrain from driving while drunk, and so forth.

Though there is a considerable body of psychological research concerned with the comparative effectiveness of various persuasive techniques, most of the efforts expended on persuasion are based on tradition, intuition, and common sense. At Yale University under the direction of the late Carl I. Hovland, a systematic program of research on attitude and opinion change was instituted with the support of the Rockefeller Foundation. With a sufficient amount of such research, eventually persuasive efforts should be based on known effects of specific techniques.

One frequently used technique in persuasive communication is the arousal of fear or anxiety by indicating to the audience the danger involved in failure to adhere to the communicator's message. Janis and Feshbach [1953], as part of the Yale studies, conducted an investigation of the effects of fear arousal. They selected communications dealing with dental hygiene to be presented to groups of high school students. Each group was given a 15-minute lecture containing the same series of recommendations concerning oral hygiene practices. The recorded lectures differed only in the amount of fear appeal involved. Group I was given a strong fear appeal in which the material emphasized the painful consequences of tooth decay and diseased gums in that infections can spread throughout the body and cause arthritic paralysis, kidney damage, or total blindness. Group II received a moderate appeal in which the dangers were described in a milder and more factual manner. In Group III, a minimal appeal was given in which little mention was made of the consequences of tooth neglect. The slides accompanying the lectures were appropriate to the three conditions. Group I saw vividly portrayed photographs of tooth decay and mouth infections, milder examples were shown to Group II, and Group III received X-ray pictures, diagrams, and photographs of healthy teeth. A control group received a lecture on a completely different topic, the structure and functioning of the human eye.

The subjects were all freshmen in a Connecticut high school. One week before the communications, a questionnaire was administered containing items dealing with dental hygiene. Immediately after the lectures, another questionnaire was administered to determine reactions to the presentations. One week later, a third questionnaire was given to ascertain the lasting effects of the communications on dental beliefs, practices, and attitudes.

First of all, it was found that the three communication groups differed in the amount of worry and anxiety evoked by the lectures; the strong appeal group indicated the greatest disturbance. The groups were also compared in terms of what they had learned of the factual information contained in all three dental lectures. The three groups were not different in the amount of information gained, and all three had higher dental information scores than the control group which received the lecture on the eye.

The questionnaire given one week after the experiment was compared with the one given one week before the experiment to determine the relative effects of the communications on dental hygiene behavior. The results are shown in Table 7–2. The most effective communication was that using the minimal appeal, and the least effective was that with the strong fear-arousing elements. The follow-up also included some "counter-propaganda" material concerning refutation of some of the lecture material on toothbrushes. The control group was most influenced by this material, followed by the group receiving the strong appeal, and then the moderate appeal group; the minimal appeal group was least affected by the counter-propaganda. The authors conclude:

> The outcome of the present experiment by no means precludes the possibility that, under certain conditions, fear appeals may prove to be highly successful. For instance, the Strong appeal was found to be maximally effective in arousing interest and in eliciting a high degree of emotional tension. The evocation of such reactions might augment the effectiveness of mass communications

Table 7–2   EFFECT OF THE COMMUNICATIONS
             ON DENTAL HYGIENE BEHAVIOR

Type of Change in Behavior from Precommunication to Postcommunication	Control Group	Strong Appeal to Fear	Moderate Appeal to Fear	Minimal Appeal to Fear
More Like Recommendations	22%	28%	44%	50%
Less Like Recommendations	22%	20%	22%	14%
No Change	56%	52%	34%	36%
Net Change in Direction of Recommendations	0%	8%	22%	36%

which are designed to instigate prompt audience action, such as donating money or volunteering to perform a group task. But if the communication is intended to create more sustained preferences or attitudes, the achievement of positive effects probably depends upon a number of different factors. Our experimental results suggest that in the latter case, a relatively low degree of fear arousal is likely to be the optimal level, that an appeal which is too strong will tend to evoke some form of interference which reduces the effectiveness of the communication. The findings definitely contradict the assumption that as the dosage of fear-arousing stimuli (in a mass communication) is increased, the audience will become more highly motivated to accept the reassuring recommendations contained in the communication [Janis and Feshbach, 1953, pp. 87–88].

NEGRO-WHITE INTERACTION: CHANGES IN PREJUDICE

A great many individuals on both sides of the civil rights controversy have expressed the belief that legal measures cannot be effective in changing interracial feelings and attitudes. The notion has been expressed that a change must occur in the hearts and minds of men before racial integration can be effectively instituted. One of the first responses to the Supreme Court ruling concerning desegregation of schools was a plea for time in order to bring about changes in attitudes before integration was thrust upon people. The "stairstep" plan of integrating one grade per year was instituted by many Southern school districts based, at least in part, on this sort of reasoning.

A counterargument rests on the basic assumption that ethnic prejudice thrives best in an atmosphere of ignorance about the target group. Rather than individual human beings with diversified good and bad qualities like one's companions in the in-group, the out-group members form a relatively indistinguishable mass sharing the stereotyped characteristics; even their physical appearance is uniform in that they all look alike. To maintain this in-group out-group difference, it is very helpful to segregate the outgroup in every way possible. Thus, those who are targets of prejudice are found in ghettoes, in Harlems, in Chinatowns, in Little Mexicos, on reservations, and so forth. What contact there is between the majority and minority group tends to be in master-servant interactions which only serve to strengthen the notion of superiority-inferiority. After a century of post-slavery separate-but-equal Negro and white relations in the South, the perpetuation of racial prejudice is really not at all surprising.

What happens, however, when an outside force is applied to bring the groups together? A growing body of data suggests that interaction leads to more positive interracial attitudes. Such findings have been reported with respect to housewives dwelling in integrated federal housing projects [Deutsch and Collins, 1951; Wilner, Walkley, and Cook, 1952], students participating in a special university seminar involving interracial contacts [Smith, 1943], graduate students in integrated leaderless discussion groups [Mann, 1959], officers and enlisted men in desegregated infantry platoons [United States War Department, 1947], merchant seamen in integrated crews [Brophy, 1956], and workers in various interracial settings [Gundlach, 1956; Palmore, 1955].

Studies of the effects of school desegregation on attitudes have been relatively few in number. For one thing, the tension and potential tension involved in this matter have not made it particularly easy for the behavioral scientist to intrude with the administration of prejudice scales before and after the event. One series of studies that has been conducted utilized repeated samplings of University of Texas students through the years of desegregation [Kelly, Ferson, and Holtzman, 1958; Young, Benson, and Holtzman, 1960; Young, Clore, and Holtzman, 1966]. We should note that the research design employed here relies on a cross-sectional approach to personality change. That is, change in a given population is measured, but different individuals serve as subjects in the various time samplings.

The first of these investigations [Kelly, et al., 1958] was conducted in 1955, a few months after the 1954 Supreme Court decision on segregated schools. The measure of prejudice was the 26-item Desegregation Scale which was discussed in Chapter 5. A stratified random sample of 547 undergraduates was selected and their attitudes toward Negroes obtained. In the years following this study, the course of integration moved steadily on. An increasing number of Negro students enrolled at the University of Texas. Nationally, events such as the 1957 crisis at Central High School in Little Rock transpired. In 1958 the second investigation [Young, et al., 1960] was carried out, again sampling the Texas student body with the same proportion of males and females, members of various religious groups, and so forth. A total of 497 students was given the prejudice measure. In the following six years, even greater changes occurred with respect to integration. Nationally, there was both violent and peaceful activity. At the University of Texas and in the local community, dramatic changes took place. Theaters and restaurants gradually were integrated. All University facilities from intercollegiate athletics to dormitory room assignments were opened to all students. In the spring of 1964 the third sample was obtained with a total of 576 students [Young, *et al.*, 1966].

The results are shown in Figure 7–1. The mean Desegregation Scale scores were 46.2 in 1955, 45.3 in 1958, and 39.7 in 1964. Thus, the first three years yielded little change but the decrease in prejudice by 1964 was a significant one. Not only total scores, but responses to individual items also revealed significant shifts in opinion between 1958 and 1964. Analysis of variance revealed significantly more positive responses toward Negroes for the following items:

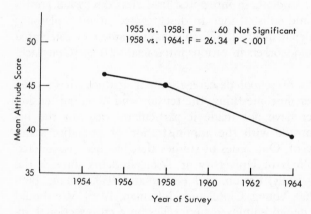

1955 vs. 1958: F = .60 Not Significant
1958 vs. 1964: F = 26.34 P < .001

FIG. 7–1. *Mean anti-Negro attitude scores for the three University of Texas surveys.*

The prospect of intermarriage between Negro and White is repulsive to me.

The best way to solve the race problem is to encourage intermarriage so that there will eventually be only one race.

I would consider dating a Negro, providing he or she met all of my other standards.

I would not hesitate to join a fraternity or sorority which admitted Negroes.

I would not object to dancing with a good Negro dancer.

The effect of interracial contact on changes in prejudice is by no means the only possible interpretation of these findings. Possibly, for example, extremely prejudiced families no longer send their offspring to this integrated university. Possibly prejudice has decreased, but as the result of other variables rather than integration. A further bit of indirect evidence suggests that the greater the amount of time spent in the University the lower the prejudice score. The mean in 1964 for first-year students is 42.31, for second-year students 40.61, for third-year students 39.65, for fourth-year students 37.16, and for fifth-year students 33.88. Whatever the ultimate explanation, however, clearly different attitudes are held by Texas undergraduates in 1964 than in 1958 and 1955.

Additional supporting data concerning the influence of desegregation should also be mentioned. Hyman and Sheatsley report similar changes throughout the country:

"Do you think white students and Negro students should go to the same schools or to separate schools?" In 1942 fewer than a third of all whites favored the integration of schools. The attitudes of Southern whites at that time were about as close to unanimity as one ever comes in surveys of the U.S. public: only 2 percent expressed support for integration. Among Northerners in that period integration also represented a minority view, endorsed by only 40 percent of white adults.

By 1956, two years after the Supreme Court decision against racial segregation in public schools, national approval of integrated schools had risen to approximately half of the total white population; in the North it had become the majority view, endorsed by three out of five white adults. Even the South was far from immune to the changing situation. Earlier only one person in 50 had favored school integration; in 1956 the proportion was one in seven. The most recent figures now show not only that the long-term trend has continued but also that in the South it has accelerated. Today a substantial majority of all white Americans endorse school integration. In the North the figure has continued its steady climb and now stands at approximately three out of every four adults. But whereas in the 14 years from 1942 to 1956 the proportion of Southern whites who accepted this principle rose only from 2 percent to 14 percent, the proportion has now risen to 30 percent in just seven years since that time [Hyman and Sheatsley, 1964, p. 17].

They further conclude:

Close analysis of the current findings, compared with those of the 1956 surveys, leads us to the conclusion that in those parts of the South where some measure of school integration has taken place, official action has preceded public sentiment, and public sentiment has then attempted to accommodate itself to the new situation [Hyman and Sheatsley, 1964, p. 20].

AGING: CHANGES IN RIGIDITY-FLEXIBILITY

With a steadily lengthening life span, interest is greater than ever before in the study of the effects of aging on various aspects of behavior. One area of interest is in personality changes which accompany the aging process. As Kuhlen outlines the problem:

> . . . it is almost self-evident that age in itself is not a particularly meaningful psychological variable. Age is *time* in which other things of importance happen. Among these important "other things" are: biological changes; changes in cognitive abilities; changes in habit strengths (flexibilities, rigidities); changes in patterns of reward, threat, punishment, opportunity, deprivation, training schedules, the latter tending to be culturally age-graded; and changes in motivation. Most research thus far has been aimed at determining the degree to which variables such as these are age-related. Few studies have been designed to examine the significance of these variables as *independent* variables producing age-relatedness in other characteristics [Kuhlen, 1964, p. 554].

Seemingly, research in this field must be directed first toward establishing the specific personality characteristics which do reveal changes and then toward seeking the specific antecedent conditions which bring about the changes.

In his doctoral research at the University of Washington, Schaie [1958] investigated differences in rigidity-flexibility across the age span 20 to 70. As in the prejudice research, a cross-sectional design was used. Rigidity was defined as ". . . a tendency to perseverate and resist conceptual change, to resist the acquisition of new patterns of behavior, and to refuse to relinquish old and established behavior patterns" [Schaie, 1958, p. 3]. On a number of bases, it would be predicted that individuals become increasingly rigid and less flexible as they grow older.

Rigidity was measured by a series of tests. The Capitals Test requires subjects to copy a paragraph (for example, The Duke DREW his sword) and then copy it reversing capitals and lower-case letters (for example, tHE dUKE drew HIS SWORD). The subject is given two and a half minutes and rigidity is measured by comparing correct responses in the two paragraphs. In the Opposites Test there are three series of 40 stimulus words each. On the first list, the subject is supposed to respond with opposites, on the second list with synonyms, and on the third list with synonyms to words in capitals and with opposites to words in lower-case letters. The Scale of Rigidity is a 22-item scale constructed by Gough. The Rigidity Index is a 9-item questionnaire with items such as, "Do you feel strongly inclined to finish whatever you are doing to spite of being tired of doing it?"

The subjects were members of a prepaid medical plan. The final sample consisted of 500 subjects, divided into 25 men and 25 women in each five-year age interval from 20 to 70.

On the basis of previous factor-analytic research, three types of rigidity as well as a composite rigidity score were identified. The relationship be-

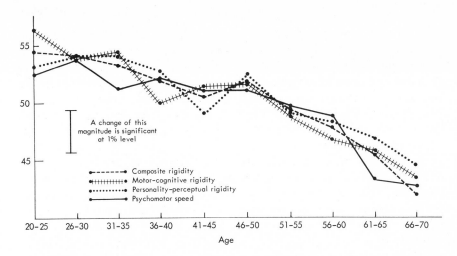

Fig. 7–2. *Age changes in several measures of rigid behavior. (Adapted from Schaie, 1958, p. 11.)*

tween test scores and age is shown in Figure 7–2. Analysis of variance indicated a significant relationship between each of the rigidity measures and age. As age increased, flexibility decreased. Schaie concludes:

From these data it would appear that loss of flexibility would become noticeable in the forties and fifties, and that by the fifties an average loss of approximately one population SD has occurred. In terms of the dimensions tested it appears then that, whether by maturational change or environmental effect, there is a progressive and significant decrement with age in the ability of the average adult to react to environmental change [Schaie, 1958, p. 12].

From this brief sample of investigations of personality change, we may see that research possibilities are just beginning to be explored. The application of the theoretical principles and the methodology of the field of learning to the alteration of significant human behavior has barely begun. Rather than a reliance on traditional techniques to bring about change (for example, psychotherapy, information giving, the arousal of fear), future research seems much more likely to be influenced by such potentially important change agents as role playing, reinforcement variables, dissonance reduction, persuasion, and environmental manipulation.

Summary

Though the major focus of interest in the field of personality is on the consistent, stable, unchanging aspects of behavior, there is also a concern with the possibility of bringing about changes in behavior.
A great many theorists have proposed that behavior does not change

unless it is in some way unsatisfactory to the organism in its present form. A few theorists have laid greater stress on man as a striving organism with built-in mechanisms for growth and change. The selection of the new behavior has been formulated in a number of different ways. Thorndike and later Guthrie stressed a trial-and-error process of behavior selection. Hull proposed the habit-family hierarchy; when a given response is blocked, the next strongest habit in the hierarchy is given. In Skinner's system, behavior change is proposed to occur whenever operant responses become associated with new reinforcing stimuli. Tolman's theory is a cognitive one in which behavior is assumed to alter on the basis of hypotheses or expectancies about the best way to attain goals. In psychoanalytic treatment, Freud proposed that the interpretations made by the analyst led to the patient adopting new behavior. For Rogers, the new behavior proceeds naturally from the organism. The new behavior is retained on the basis of simple association (Guthrie), need-reduction (Hull), reinforcement (Skinner), understanding or insight (Tolman), increased conscious functioning (Freud), or through the nature of subsequent interpersonal interactions (Rogers). Other aspects of change which have been stressed are the importance of other human beings as sources of reinforcement, the effectiveness of small rewards and punishments as opposed to large ones, and the necessity of having the stimuli after learning remain similar to those present during learning.

The measurement of personality change presents problems in that a series of equivalent instruments must be constructed for repeated assessments. Ideally, the instruments are each highly reliable and valid, and have equal means, variances, and covariances. When a group is measured on two occasions with respect to a personality dimension, the change may be evaluated in terms of frequencies, proportions, or mean differences. When analysis of variance is used to evaluate a group's change, each score is conceptualized in terms of variance attributable to row differences (individual differences), column differences (changes over time), and the interaction between the two (error). Estimates of the population variance based on the first two are divided by an estimate based on error variance to obtain F ratios. It is preferable, of course, to add a control group, and then the analysis of variance involves a combination of two different approaches. For comparing the experimental and control groups, an estimate of the population variance based on between-group differences is divided by an estimate based on individual differences. For determining the effects of the time intervals, of the interaction between groups and the time interval, and of individual differences, estimates of the population variances based on these three effects are each divided by an estimate based on error variance (row-by-column interaction).

Most of the research on personality change has concentrated on self-changes in psychotherapy and on changes in opinion and attitude variables.

Considerable controversy exists over whether psychotherapy has any effect on personality change, and changes in adjustment as measured by the MMPI have been found to be no greater for therapy patients than for nontreated control patients. Role playing refers to the performance of patterned behaviors in which the role has an agreed-upon position in the social structure. Simply playing the role of a sincere advocate of an opinion was found to bring about opinion changes in the direction of that portrayed in the role. It has further been found that reinforcement for verbalizing an attitude different from one's current attitude leads to changes in that dimension. Dissonance theory proposes that two inconsistent cognitions are dissonant, and that the existence of dissonance motivates behavior to bring about dissonance reduction. On the basis of this theory, it was hypothesized and found that individuals who cheated became more lenient in their values concerning cheating and those who did not cheat became more negative in their views toward cheating. Persuasion involves the use of many specific techniques; strong fear and anxiety arousal were found to be much less effective in changing beliefs and practices than mild, nonfear-arousing approaches. While it is often proposed that attitudes of prejudice should change before racial integration can be effective, it has been found in a number of contexts that racial integration leads to more positive in-terracial attitudes. The internal and external changes that accompany aging lead to many behavioral changes. For example, flexibility shows a steady and regular decline with age from the 20's to the 70's.

COMPUTATIONAL EXAMPLE: FREQUENCY CHANGES, CHANGES IN
PROPORTIONS, AND CHANGES IN MEANS

In Table 7-3, for frequencies, the letters represent the number of individuals in each cell (A = number of subjects high at time 1 and low at time 2, and so forth). Given the information as shown in the table, a chi square (X^2) may be computed from the formula:

$$X^2 = \frac{(A - D)^2}{A + D}$$

If X^2 reaches 3.84, the change is a significant one at the .05 level; if X^2 is 6.64, it is significant at the .01 level. For proportions, each letter in

Table 7-3 DETERMINING CHANGES IN FREQUENCIES AND PROPORTIONS

		Frequencies				Proportions	
		Time 2				Time 2	
		Low	High			Low	High
Time 1	High	A	B	Time 1	High	a	b
	Low	C	D		Low	c	d

the table represents the proportion of the total number (a = proportion high at time 1 and low at time 2, and so forth). The significance of the change may be determined by the formula:

$$z = \frac{d-a}{\sqrt{(a+d)\ N}}$$

If z reaches 1.96, the change is significant at the .05 level; if z reaches 2.58, the significance level is .01.

Another approach is to test for the significance of the difference between means. One must compute the two means (time 1 and time 2), the two standard deviations, and the correlation between the two sets of scores. One must also determine the standard error of each mean:

$$S_M = \frac{SD}{\sqrt{N}}.$$

Given those quantities, the significance of the difference is determined as follows:

$$z = \frac{M_1 - M_2}{\sqrt{S_{M_1}^2 + S_{M_2}^2 - 2r_{12}\,S_{M_1}\,S_{M_2}}}$$

Again, z must equal 1.96 to reach the .05 level, and 2.58 for the .01 level.

COMPUTATIONAL EXAMPLE: ANALYSIS OF VARIANCE
OF REPEATED MEASURES

Table 7-4   SCORES OF 15 PSYCHOTHERAPY PATIENTS ON DEPRESSION
SCALE TAKEN BEFORE, IMMEDIATELY AFTER,
AND SIX MONTHS AFTER TREATMENT

Subject	Before	Immediately After	Six Months After	ΣX	Mean
1	30	20	22	72	24.00
2	32	24	28	84	28.00
3	28	16	22	66	22.00
4	34	24	26	84	28.00
5	30	22	26	78	26.00
6	36	24	30	90	30.00
7	28	18	20	66	22.00
8	26	18	22	66	22.00
9	30	18	24	72	24.00
10	32	22	24	78	26.00
11	30	22	26	78	26.00
12	24	12	18	54	18.00
13	30	20	22	72	24.00
14	32	24	28	84	28.00
15	28	16	22	66	22.00
ΣX	450	300	360	$\Sigma\Sigma X = 1110$	
Mean	30.00	20.00	24.00		Overall Mean = 24.67

Table 7–5   COMPUTATION OF SUMS OF SQUARES AND VARIANCE
ESTIMATES FOR DEPRESSION SCALE SCORES OBTAINED
BEFORE, IMMEDIATELY AFTER, AND SIX MONTHS
AFTER PSYCHOTHERAPY

Subject	Before	Immediately After	Six Months After	ΣX	ΣX^2
1	30	20	22	72	1,784
2	32	24	28	84	2,384
3	28	16	22	66	1,524
4	34	24	26	84	2,408
5	30	22	26	78	2,060
6	36	24	30	90	2,772
7	28	18	20	66	1,508
8	26	18	22	66	1,484
9	30	18	24	72	1,800
10	32	22	24	78	2,084
11	30	22	26	78	2,060
12	24	12	18	54	1,044
13	30	20	22	72	1,784
14	32	24	28	84	2,384
15	28	16	22	66	1,524
ΣX	450	300	360	$\Sigma\Sigma X = 1110$	
ΣX^2	13,628	6,184	8,792	$\Sigma\Sigma X^2 = 28,604$	

Total Variance:

Total Sum of Squares =

$$\frac{1}{N} [N\Sigma\Sigma X^2 - (\Sigma\Sigma X)^2]$$

$$= \frac{1}{45} [(45)(28,604) - (1110)^2]$$

$$= 1,224.00$$

$N = 45$

Variance $= \dfrac{1,224}{45} = 27.20$

Variance Estimate: Between Rows

Between-Rows Sum of Squares =

$$\frac{1}{N} [R\Sigma_R (\Sigma X)^2 - (\Sigma\Sigma X)^2]$$

$$= \frac{1}{45} [15 (72^2 + 84^2 + 66^2 + 84^2 + 78^2 + 90^2 + 66^2 + 66^2 \\ + 72^2 + 78^2 + 78^2 + 54^2 + 72^2 + 84^2 + 66^2) - 1110^2]$$

$$= 424$$

Degrees of Freedom $= 14$

Variance Estimate: Between Rows $= \dfrac{424}{14} = 30.28$

Variance Estimate: Between Columns

Between-Columns Sum of Squares $=$

$$\frac{1}{N} [C\Sigma_c (\Sigma X)^2 - (\Sigma\Sigma X)^2]$$

$$= \frac{1}{45} [3 (450^2 + 300^2 + 360^2) - (1110)^2]$$

$$= 760$$

Degrees of Freedom $= 2$

Variance Estimate: Between Columns $= \dfrac{760}{2} = 380.00$

Variance Estimate: Error

Error Sum of Squares $=$ Total Sum of Squares $-$

Sums of Squares for Columns and Rows

$$= 1,224 - (424 + 760)$$

$$= 40$$

Degrees of Freedom $= 28$

Variance Estimate: Error $= \dfrac{40}{28} = 1.43$

Table 7–6   VARIANCE TABLE

Source	Sum of Squares	df	Variance Estimate	F
Between Rows (Individual Differences)	424	14	30.28	21.17*
Between Columns (Psychotherapy Effects)	760	2	380.00	265.73*
Error: Row by Column Interaction (Subjects by Times)	40	28	1.43	

$*\ p < .001$

COMPUTATIONAL EXAMPLE: ANALYSIS OF VARIANCE OF REPEATED
MEASURES FOR TWO DIFFERENT GROUPS

Table 7–7   SCORES OF 15 CONTROL GROUP SUBJECTS ON DEPRESSION
SCALE TAKEN ON THREE OCCASIONS
CORRESPONDING TO THE EXPERIMENTAL GROUP

Subject	Time 1	Time 2	Time 3	ΣX	Mean
1	28	26	30	84	28.00
2	32	26	26	84	28.00
3	30	32	34	96	32.00
4	26	24	28	78	26.00
5	28	22	22	72	24.00
6	30	32	34	96	32.00
7	34	32	36	102	34.00
8	36	30	30	96	32.00
9	30	32	34	96	32.00
10	24	22	26	72	24.00
11	32	26	26	84	28.00
12	34	36	38	108	36.00
13	26	24	28	78	26.00
14	30	24	24	78	26.00
15	30	32	34	96	32.00
ΣX	450	420	450	$\Sigma\Sigma X = 1{,}320$	
Mean	30.00	28.00	30.00	Overall Mean = 29.33	

Table 7–8   COMPUTATION OF SUMS OF SQUARES AND VARIANCE
ESTIMATES FOR DEPRESSION SCALE SCORES OBTAINED AT
THREE TIME PERIODS FOR EXPERIMENTAL AND
CONTROL GROUPS

Condition	Subjects	Time Periods 1	2	3	ΣX	ΣX^2
	1	30	20	22	72	1,784
	2	32	24	28	84	2,384
	3	28	16	22	66	1,524
	4	34	24	26	84	2,408
	5	30	22	26	78	2,060
Experimental	6	36	24	30	90	2,772
	7	28	18	20	66	1,508
	8	26	18	22	66	1,484
	9	30	18	24	72	1,800
	10	32	22	24	78	2,084
	11	30	22	26	78	2,060
	12	24	12	18	54	1,044
	13	30	20	22	72	1,784
	14	32	24	28	84	2,384
	15	28	16	22	66	1,524
	ΣX	450	300	360	$\Sigma\Sigma X = 1110$	
	ΣX^2	13,628	6,184	8,792		$\Sigma\Sigma X^2 = 28{,}604$

Table 7–8   COMPUTATION OF SUMS OF SQUARES AND VARIANCE
              ESTIMATES FOR DEPRESSION SCALE SCORES OBTAINED AT
              THREE TIME PERIODS FOR EXPERIMENTAL AND
              CONTROL GROUPS (Cont.)

	1	28	26	30	84	2,360
	2	32	26	26	84	2,376
	3	30	32	34	96	3,080
	4	26	24	28	78	2,036
	5	28	22	22	72	1,752
Control	6	30	32	34	96	3,080
	7	34	32	36	102	3,476
	8	36	30	30	96	3,096
	9	30	32	34	96	3,080
	10	24	22	26	72	1,736
	11	32	26	26	84	2,376
	12	34	36	38	108	3,896
	13	26	24	28	78	2,036
	14	30	24	24	78	2,052
	15	30	32	34	96	3,080

ΣX	450	420	450	$\Sigma\Sigma X = 1,320$
ΣX^2	13,652	12,040	13,820	$\Sigma\Sigma X^2 = 39,512$
$\Sigma\Sigma X$	900	720	810	$\Sigma\Sigma\Sigma X = 2,430$
$\Sigma\Sigma X^2$	27,280	18,224	22,612	$\Sigma\Sigma\Sigma X^2 = 68,116$

Total Variance:

Total Sum of Squares =

$$\frac{1}{N} [N\Sigma\Sigma\Sigma X^2 - (\Sigma\Sigma\Sigma X)^2]$$

$$= \frac{1}{90} [(90)(68,116) - (2,430)^2]$$

$$= 2506$$

$N = 90$

$$\text{Variance} = \frac{2506}{90} = 27.84$$

Variance Estimate: Between Blocks (Experimental Conditions)

Between-Blocks Sum of Squares =

$$\frac{1}{N} [B\Sigma_B (\Sigma X)^2 - (\Sigma\Sigma\Sigma X)^2]$$

$$= \frac{1}{90} [2(1110^2 + 1320^2) - (2,430)^2]$$

$$= 490$$

Degrees of Freedom $= 1$

Variance Estimate: Between Blocks $= \dfrac{490}{1} = 490$

Variance Estimate: Between Rows in Each Condition (Within)

Combined Between-Rows Sum of Squares $=$

$$\frac{1}{N} [R\Sigma_R (\Sigma X)^2 - (\Sigma\Sigma X)^2] + \frac{1}{N} [R\Sigma_R (\Sigma X)^2 - (\Sigma\Sigma X)^2]$$

$$= \frac{1}{45} [15 \ (72^2 + 84^2 + 66^2 + 84^2 + 78^2 +$$
$$90^2 + 66^2 + 66^2 + 72^2 + 78^2 +$$
$$78^2 + 54^2 + 72^2 + 84^2 + 66^2) - (1110)^2]$$
$$+ \frac{1}{45} [15 \ (84^2 + 84^2 + 96^2 + 78^2 + 72^2 +$$
$$96^2 + 102^2 + 96^2 + 96^2 + 72^2 +$$
$$84^2 + 108^2 + 78^2 + 78^2 + 96^2) - (1320)^2]$$

$$= 424 + 592$$

$$= 1016$$

Degrees of Freedom $= 28$

Variance Estimate: Between Rows in Each Condition $= \dfrac{1016}{28} = 36.28$

Variance Estimate: Between Rows (Individual Differences)

Between-Rows Sum of Squares $=$

$$\frac{1}{N} [R\Sigma_R (\Sigma X)^2 - (\Sigma\Sigma\Sigma X)^2]$$

$$= \frac{1}{90} [30(72^2 + 84^2 + 66^2 + 84^2 + 78^2 +$$
$$90^2 + 66^2 + 66^2 + 72^2 + 78^2 +$$
$$78^2 + 54^2 + 72^2 + 84^2 + 66^2 +$$
$$84^2 + 84^2 + 96^2 + 78^2 + 72^2 +$$
$$96^2 + 102^2 + 96^2 + 96^2 + 72^2 +$$
$$84^2 + 108^2 + 78^2 + 78^2 + 96^2) - (2,430)^2]$$

$$= 1,506$$

Degrees of Freedom $= 28$

Variance Estimate: Between Rows $= \dfrac{1506}{28} = 53.78$

Variance Estimate: Between Columns

Between-Columns Sum of Squares $=$

$$\frac{1}{N} [C\Sigma_C (\Sigma X)^2 - (\Sigma\Sigma\Sigma X)^2]$$

$$= \frac{1}{90} [3 (900^2 + 720^2 + 810^2) - (2{,}430)^2]$$

$$= 540$$

Degrees of Freedom $= 2$

Variance Estimate: Between Columns $= \dfrac{540}{2} = 270.00$

Variance Estimate: Columns by Blocks Interaction

Columns by Blocks Interaction Sum of Squares $=$

Block by Column Subtotal Sum of Squares — Sums of Squares
for Columns and Blocks

$$= \frac{1}{N} [BC\Sigma\Sigma(\Sigma X)^2 - (\Sigma\Sigma\Sigma X)^2] - (540 + 490)$$

$$= \frac{1}{90} [(6) \underset{-\ 1030}{(450^2 + 300^2 + 360^2 + 450^2 + 420^2 + 450^2)} - (2{,}430)^2]$$

$$= 260$$

Degrees of Freedom $= 2$

Variance Estimate: Columns by Blocks Interaction $= \dfrac{260}{2} = 130$

Variance Estimate: Error

Error Sum of Squares $=$ Total Sum of Squares —
Sums of Squares for Rows, Columns,
and Column by Block Interaction

$$= 2506 - (540 + 1506 + 260)$$

$$= 200$$

Degrees of Freedom $= 56$

Variance Estimate: Error $= \dfrac{200}{56} = 3.57$

Table 7–9   VARIANCE TABLE

Source	Sum of Squares	df	Variance Estimate	F
Between Blocks				
(Exp. Conditions)	490	1	490.00	13.51*
Within (Subjects in Same Block)	1016	28	36.28	
Between Rows (Individual				
Differences)	1506	28	53.78	15.06*
Between Columns (Times)	540	2	270.00	75.63*
Interaction: Columns by Blocks				
(Times by Exp. Conditions)	260	2	130.00	36.41*
Error: Pooled Row by Column				
Interaction				
(Subjects by Times)	200	56	3.57	

* $p < .001$

Part Three

SELECTED EXAMPLES

OF PERSONALITY

RESEARCH

CHAPTER 8

Authoritarianism

Authoritarianism refers to an attitudinal system which consists of a number of interrelated antidemocratic sentiments including ethnic prejudice, political conservatism, and a moralistic rejection of the unconventional. An attitude is a predisposition to respond either positively or negatively toward an object or a class of objects. Each of us holds a large number of relatively enduring beliefs, opinions, values, and judgments which involve attitudinal components. Subjectively, such elements appear relatively independent of one another and seem to be based, at least in one's own case, on an objective evaluation of factual evidence. Our own particular feelings concerning the Catholic Church, liberal political philosophy, communism, Negroes, modern novels, labor unions, nuclear testing, television programming, big business, sports cars, and everything else are those which would be held by any sensible person who knew the facts. The possibility that our attitudes toward such stimulus objects are the inevitable consequents of past experiences, that many such components are lawfully interrelated in ideological clusters, and that these characteristics form an integral part of our personality structure is somewhat less readily acceptable. One of the best examples of personality research directed toward an attitudinal variable is provided by work on authoritarianism.

The concept of authoritarianism owes a debt, of sorts, to Adolf Hitler. When the Nazi party seized political power in Germany in 1933, the world witnessed the beginning of one of the most thoroughgoing authoritarian regimes to control a major nation in modern times. Authoritarian ideology and its associated behaviors pervaded every aspect of German life. Prompted in large part by the horrors of Hitler's anti-Semitism, the American Jewish Committee established a Department of Scientific Research for the purpose of initiating fundamental studies of prejudice and of stimulating such studies by others. This group was interested in learning the characteristics of those who establish authoritarian societies and of those who readily accept this ideology. Specifically, they hoped to be able to identify and describe the *potentially* fascistic individual and to seek the determinants of this pattern of behavior.

Among the products of the research directed toward such problems was a monumental work entitled *The Authoritarian Personality* by T. W. Adorno of the Institute of Social Research, Else Frenkel-Brunswik of the University of California, Daniel J. Levinson of the Harvard Medical School, and R. Nevitt Sanford of the University of California. The work of this group and their colleagues was carried out throughout the late 1940's and was published in 1950. Their interests ranged over ethnocentrism, anti-Semitism, antidemocratic ideology, and political and religious beliefs. Their methods included a unique and fruitful blend of clinical and research approaches.

As an overriding goal, the conviction of the investigators was that:

. . . the object of knowing what are the psychological determinants of ideology is that men can become more reasonable. It is not supposed, of course, that this will eliminate differences of opinion. The world is sufficiently complex and difficult to know, men have enough real interests that are in conflict with the real interests of other men, there are enough ego-accepted differences in personality to insure that arguments about politics, economics, and religion will never grow dull. Knowledge of the psychological determinants of ideology cannot tell us what is the *truest* ideology; it can only remove some of the barriers in the way of its pursuit [Adorno, *et al.*, 1950, p. 11].

The impact of this project on subsequent research and theory in psychology has been of considerable magnitude. In the present chapter, the focus will be on the authoritarianism variable, both as defined in the original study and as studied subsequently in the succeeding decade and a half.

Theoretical Background

The underlying theory of the nature of the authoritarian personality had its origin in diverse sources—previous research, psychoanalytic theory, observations of actual behavior, and attempts to make theoretical sense out of the seeming diversity of specific behaviors which are manifested by extreme authoritarians. The variables which were postulated as characterizing central trends in the authoritarian individual are presented below. The plan of the investigators was to form a tentative definition of authoritarian characteristics and then to construct test items to attempt to measure these characteristics.

CONVENTIONALISM

Rigid Adherence to Conventional, Middle-Class Values. The proposal that conventionalism constituted a factor in the authoritarian make-up was based on the observations that: (1) susceptibility to fascism characteristically develops in conventional middle-class environments, and (2) unconventional individuals tend to be free of prejudice. The fact that a great many conventional individuals are democratic, tolerant, and equalitarian in outlook raised some problems. It was, therefore, proposed that when conventional values are based on a fully developed individual conscience, such values should not be related to antidemocratic trends. When the values are external in origin, however, a different situation exists. An individual whose ideas of right and wrong are a function of contemporary, external social pressure would be expected to be receptive to antidemocratic ideology. While this distinction between two different types of conventional behavior makes sense, it is a difficult distinction to make operationally and one which would be expected to create difficulties in the writing of test items. That is, subjects would have to indicate the basis of their conventionalism, not just their beliefs and behavior.

AUTHORITARIAN SUBMISSION

Submissive, Uncritical Attitude toward Idealized Moral Authorities of the Ingroup. Because the Nazi creed stressed submission to authority, desire for a strong leader, and subservience of the individual to the state, this type of submission was included among the probable characteristics of authoritarians. In writing the items, the guess was made that authoritarian submission would characterize relationships to all authority figures—parents, older people, leaders, supernatural beings, and the like. Complete submissiveness was hypothesized to occur because of a deficiency in conscience development. In addition, fear of any negative or hostile feelings toward authority could lead to an exaggerated over-emphasis on the reverse, the submission to such authority.

AUTHORITARIAN AGGRESSION

Tendency to Be on the Lookout for, and to Condemn, Reject, and Punish People Who Violate Conventional Values. From a number of theoretical positions, it would be hypothesized that individuals who are forced to adhere completely to a conventional mold and to submit to authority without complaint would experience feelings of hostility. The expression of such hostility would seem most justifiable (and most safe) to these individuals if it could be directed toward those who violate conventional mores. "I don't hate my father; it's the beatniks who make my blood boil." Thus, hostility is displaced from the appropriate targets in the ingroup onto inappropriate targets in the outgroup. The latter, depending on the particular environmental circumstances, can consist of Jews or communists or sexual offenders or any other identifiable group. Not only is the authoritarian able to give vent to his hostility, but he does so for "good" reasons based primarily on distortions of religious morality and patriotism.

DESTRUCTION AND CYNICISM

Generalized Hostility, Vilification of the Human. In addition to displacing hostility onto outgroups, another outlet for authoritarians is a generalized hostility which includes "justifiable" expression of aggression toward mankind, contempt for human nature, and cynicism concerning the motives of others. Among other things, one's own hostility is more acceptable if "everybody" acts that way or if it is simply "natural."

POWER AND "TOUGHNESS"

Preoccupation with the Dominance-Submission, Strong-Weak, Leader-Follower Dimension; Identification with Power Figures; Overemphasis upon the Conventionalized Attributes of the Ego; Exaggerated Assertion of Strength and Toughness. Because of internal weaknesses and fears, the authoritarian is hypothesized to react with an overemphasis on strength and power—his own and that of his group. Especially important is to have a leader who provides power and to be identified as a member of a group with such attributes: strongest nation on earth, master race, world-wide communist movement, and so forth. The authoritarians would be expected to submit completely to the orders of such power sources and, in turn, to be ruthless in exercising power when the situation arises. An example would be an SS trouper who obeyed his superiors without question and displayed his own tyranny over his subordinates and victims.

SUPERSTITION AND STEREOTYPY

The Belief in Mystical Determinants of the Individual's Fate, the Disposition to Think in Rigid Categories. Among the mechanisms which may account for belief in mystical and fantastic forces is the tendency to avoid personal responsibility for various feelings and acts and consequences by locating the blame on forces external to oneself, including unknowable external forces. By stereotypy, or the disposition to think in rigid categories, is meant the tendency to resort to primitive, oversimplified, black-and-white explanations of human affairs. Successful authoritarian leaders capitalize on these tendencies by providing a simple rationale for past difficulties and future achievements. Such complex events as war, depression, crime, and a utopian society emerge as straightforward problems with straightforward solutions promised by slogans and catch phrases. In addition, these leaders do well when they attach elements of the mysterious to themselves and their regime. Such leaders often provide themselves with supernatural ancestors, as did Roman and Japanese emperors, they appear in public rarely and then only with pomp and ceremony, as with Nazi torchlight parades, their destiny is mystically intertwined with that of the nation, they are free from illness, and they have divine protection from assassins.

ANTI-INTRACEPTION

Opposition to the Subjective, the Imaginative, the Tender-Minded. It was hypothesized that authoritarians tend to respond to concrete, clearly observable, tangible facts and to oppose reliance on feelings, fantasies, speculations, and imagination. The underlying dynamics are suggested as fear of "wrong" thoughts, of feelings and emotions which might get out of hand. Not surprising is that the sort of "prying" characteristic of psychological testing and psychotherapy is viewed with great suspicion and concern. Totalitarian nations and authoritarian political groups tend to reject these activities along with any artistic endeavor which tends to arouse frightening or dangerous thoughts and feelings. Thus, censorship of art, including books, movies, and plays, seems necessary and right to the authoritarian.

PROJECTIVITY

The Disposition to Believe that Wild and Dangerous Things Go on in the World, the Projection Outwards of Unconscious Emotional Impulses. One of the most pervasive characteristics of authoritarians, as postulated by the Adorno group, is the ability to transfer internal problems to the external world—taboo impulses, weaknesses, fears, responsibilities. Thus, the authoritarian sees the most unacceptable aspects of himself in the world around him. Especially prominant are the projections of sexual and aggressive impulses. He is surrounded by depraved individuals engaging in sexual excesses—outgroup members, foreigners, people in high places, college students, neighbors. Equally rampant in the world around him is hostility—crime waves, subversion, plots in the government, threats from abroad. Such projection shades rather easily into paranoid delusions, and the beliefs of authoritarians sometime assume a rather bizarre form. For example, stories were widely circulated in 1963 that the government was secretly training cannibals in Georgia and that millions of Red Chinese troops were massed just over the Mexican border.

SEX

Exaggerated Concern with Sexual "Goings-on." The authors of the authoritarian scale felt that sexual concerns were sufficiently basic to give this characteristic a prominent position in their description. As has been discussed, a tendency exists to punish those who violate sexual mores, to censor sexual material, and to project sexual excesses onto others. It is suggested that for these individuals, sexual impulses must be strongly attached to anxiety cues. The anxiety is reduced by means of projection of the impulses onto others and an expression of hostility toward those who express such impulses. "I would never even think of engaging in sexual intercourse before marriage, but half of the high school kids belong to sex clubs."

Construction of the California F Scale

BUILDING THE SCALE

Following the formulation of the theoretical description outlined above, questionnaire items were written which attempted to tap the various characteristics of authoritarians. An effort was made to write items which were indirect and which were neither too wildly irrational nor too objectively factual. Each item was written in the form of a declaratory sentence, and the subject was asked to respond by indicating the appropriate degree of agreement on a scale ranging as follows:

Response	Score
Strong support, agreement	7
Moderate support, agreement	6
Slight support, agreement	5
Slight opposition, disagreement	3
Moderate opposition, disagreement	2
Strong opposition, disagreement	1
(omitted items receive a score of 4)	

In the first scale which was assembled, a total of 38 items were written, mixed with other items in a questionnaire, and administered to four groups consisting of a total of 295 subjects. The split-half reliability of the F Scale ranged from .56 to .88 in the four groups, with a mean reliability of .74. In order to improve the scale and attempt to achieve adequate internal consistency, the responses of this group of subjects were utilized for item-analysis procedures. The discriminatory power technique was employed. A frequency distribution of authoritarian scores was plotted, and those subjects falling in the highest and lowest quartiles identified. Then, the mean item score of the low quartile group was subtracted from the mean item score of the high quartile group *for each item*. The larger the difference, or the extent to which the item distinguished between those in the highest and lowest quartiles on the entire test, the better the discriminatory power (DP) of the item.[1] A DP of zero would mean that the item was not measuring that which the rest of the scale was measuring. Of the original items, the best were:

> Obedience and respect for authority are the most important virtues children should learn. (DP = 3.09)

> Sex crimes, such as rape and attacks on children, deserve more than mere imprisonment; such criminals ought to be publicly whipped. (DP = 2.81)

Among the worst items, subsequently discarded as measures of authoritarianism, were:

> Reports of atrocities in Europe have been greatly exaggerated for propaganda purposes. (DP = .43)

> The modern church, with its many rules and hypocrisies, does not appeal to the deeply religious person; it appeals mainly to the childish, the insecure, and the uncritical. (DP = .19)

In an effort to improve the measuring instrument, the Berkeley group constructed a second version of the F Scale. They retained the 19 best items of the first scale, rewrote four of the worst items, and devised 11 new ones. This second form of the F Scale was administered to five groups consisting of a total of 286 subjects. The item-analysis and subsequent revision were well worth the effort in that split-half reliabilities were found to vary from .81 to .91 with a mean of .87. Once again, the DP of each item was obtained in order to provide a basis for an improved third version of the scale.

Even though the second scale was adequate, the authors hoped to build an even better measuring instrument. For one thing, two of their most discriminating items had become outdated:

> After we finish off the Germans and Japs, we ought to concentrate on other enemies of the human race such as rats, snakes, and germs.

---

[1] The authors also considered each item's discriminatory power with respect to the Anti-Semitism Scale, but for reasons of clarity the present discussion will omit that material.

It is more than just chance that Japan had an earthquake on
Pearl Harbor Day, December 7, 1944.

For the third scale, those two items plus five others were discarded, and
three new ones[2] were added. This final F Scale was administered to 14
groups with a total of 1,518 subjects. Reliabilities ranged from .81 to .97
with a mean of .90. Thus, the test was found to be sufficiently reliable to
measure authoritarianism with enough consistency to warrant its utilization in research. The items in this final scale and the facet or facets of authoritarianism which they were designed to measure are shown in Table
8–1 in the order of their DP's. The first item shown in the table is the best
measure of authoritarian ideology, the second item the second best, and
so forth.

Table 8–1   THE CALIFORNIA F SCALE

Rank	DP	Item
1	4.00	Sex crimes, such as rape and attacks on children, deserve more than mere imprisonment; such criminals ought to be publicly whipped, or worse. (AA, S)
2	3.82	What the youth needs most is strict discipline, rugged determination, and the will to work and fight for family and country. (AA, PT)
3	3.71	There is hardly anything lower than a person who does not feel a great love, gratitude, and respect for his parents. (AA)
4	3.56	Every person should have complete faith in some supernatural power whose decisions he obeys without question. (AS, SS)
5	3.38	Young people sometimes get rebellious ideas, but as they grow up they ought to get over them and settle down. (AS)
6.5	3.31	Obedience and respect for authority are the most important virtues children should learn. (C, AS)
6.5	3.31	Homosexuals are hardly better than criminals and ought to be severely punished. (AA, S)
8.5	3.17	Nowadays when so many different kinds of people move around and mix together so much, a person has to protect himself especially carefully against catching an infection or disease from them. (P)
8.5	3.17	People can be divided into two distinct classes: the weak and the strong. (SS, PT)
10	3.16	No sane, normal, decent person could ever think of hurting a close friend or relative. (AS)
11	3.06	Some day it will probably be shown that astrology can explain a lot of things. (SS)
12	3.00	Nowadays more and more people are prying into matters that should remain personal and private. (AI, P)
13	2.97	If people would talk less and work more, everybody would be better off. (C, AA, AI)

[2] One of these three was later discarded.

Table 8–1   THE CALIFORNIA F SCALE (Cont.)

14	2.93	An insult to our honor should always be punished. (AA, PT)
15	2.88	Most of our social problems would be solved if we could somehow get rid of the immoral, crooked, and feeble-minded people. (AA)
16	2.83	When a person has a problem or worry, it is best for him not to think about it, but to keep busy with more cheerful things. (AI)
17	2.72	Science has its place, but there are many important things that can never possibly be understood by the human mind. (AS, SS)
18	2.71	The wild sex life of the old Greeks and Romans was tame compared to some of the goings-on in this country, even in places where people might least expect it. (P, S)
19	2.65	Human nature being what it is, there will always be war and conflict. (DS)
20	2.64	The true American way of life is disappearing so fast that force may be necessary to preserve it. (DC)
21	2.60	What this country needs most, more than laws and political programs, is a few courageous, tireless, devoted leaders in whom the people can put their faith. (AS, PT)
22	2.58	No weakness or difficulty can hold us back if we have enough will power. (PT)
23	2.55	Familiarity breeds contempt. (DC)
24	2.51	Some people are born with an urge to jump from high places. (SS)
25	2.26	Most people don't realize how much our lives are controlled by plots hatched in secret places. (PT, P)
26	2.19	A person who has bad manners, habits, and breeding can hardly expect to get along with decent people. (C, AA)
27	2.00	Nobody ever learned anything really important except through suffering. (AS)
28	1.98	Wars and social troubles may someday be ended by an earthquake or flood that will destroy the whole world. (SS, P)
29	1.73	The business man and the manufacturer are much more important to society than the artist and the professor.(C, AI)

Key: C = Conventionalism; AS = Authoritarian Submission; AA = Authoritarian Aggression; DC = Destructiveness and Cynicism; PT = Power and "Toughness"; SS = Superstition and Stereotypy; AI = Anti-intraception; P = Projectivity; S = Sex.

ACQUIESCENT RESPONSE SET

A considerable body of methodological criticism has been leveled at the F Scale because of the fact that each item is worded in such a way that agreement with the content of the item indicates authoritarianism. Thus, the scores obtained on this instrument potentially involve a confounding of authoritarian tendencies with another personality variable: acquiescent response set. Acquiescence refers to the tendency of some individuals to indicate agreement with almost any sweeping generalization that is stated as a test item. Among others, Jackson and Messick [1958] and Chapman and Campbell [1957] have argued for the desirability of building tests such as the F Scale with response style controlled. For example, half of the items could be worded in such a way that disagreement with the item content indicates the personality trait being measured. Acquiescence is a potentially interesting personality variable in its own right, and special tests have been constructed to measure it [for example, Couch and Keniston, 1960]. One difficulty with having the F Scale and various other tests confounded with acquiescent response set is that correlations between such tests may be a function of an actual relationship between authoritarianism and some other variable or possibly only an artifact caused by the common element of acquiescence.

With respect to building an F Scale which is independent of acquiescent tendencies, various efforts to date have met with only limited success. The typical procedure is to write a series of items in which the content of the original items is stated in a reverse way. Then, subjects are given both the original F Scale and a new scale made up of the reversed items. As Christie, Havel, and Seidenberg [1958] point out, consistent ideology among subjects would result in correlations between the two scales approaching 1.00. Instead, most such studies report relatively low positive relationships, zero relationships, and even negative relationships [Bass, 1955; Chapman and Campbell, 1957; Christie, et al., 1958; Couch and Keniston, 1960; Jackson and Pacine, 1961; Leavitt, Hax, and Roche, 1955].

A necessary step in building a successful balanced scale is to identify a number of reversed items which are significantly correlated with the original scale. One such attempt was reported by Byrne and Bounds [1964]. A 54-item F Scale was constructed in which half of the items were from the original test (positively worded with respect to authoritarian content) and half were reversed in content. This test was administered to 186 Texas undergraduates. Of the 27 reversed items, only five were found to correlate significantly with the original F Scale. The other 22 items do not appear to be measuring authoritarianism. The successful reversals, all from Christie, et al. [1958], were:

The findings of science may some day show that many of our most cherished beliefs are wrong.

It is highly unlikely that astrology will ever be able to explain anything.

People ought to pay more attention to new ideas, even if they seem to go against the American way of life.

Insults to our honor are not always important enough to bother about.

> It's all right for people to raise questions about even the most
> sacred matters.

If a sufficient number of such items can be built, obviously a revised F Scale can be constructed in which acquiescent response set is controlled.

Antecedents of Authoritarianism

THEORETICAL CONSIDERATIONS

The most obvious origins of a system of attitudes and beliefs such as authoritarianism would seem to lie in the experiences of an individual with parents and others relatively early in his development. Presumably, these influences would be of two major varieties. Probably of greatest importance are those forces which bring about the development of the underlying characteristics which make antidemocratic beliefs accepted: repression, denial of aggressive and sexual impulses, externally oriented problem-solving techniques, such as projection and displacement. Second, there must be contact with the specific ideas and beliefs that form the content of authoritarian ideology.

In the original Berkeley studies, a number of clinical investigations (utilizing interviews, case histories, and projective tests) were carried out in order to provide information about the highest and lowest scoring subjects. In addition, these somewhat loose and uncontrolled observations led to a multitude of hypotheses amenable to verification in future research.

Of course, when subjects talk about their parents or their childhood experiences, these recollections may or may not be accurate representations of what actually happened. The position taken by the Berkeley group, however, was that all such material was of potential importance in understanding differences between those high and low in prejudice, ethnocentrism, and authoritarianism. On the basis of the material that was collected, the following conclusions were tentatively drawn with respect to differing family experiences of those scoring on different extremes of such scales:

Prejudiced subjects tend to report a relatively harsh and more threatening type of home discipline which was experienced as arbitrary by the child. Related to this is a tendency apparent in families of prejudiced subjects to base interrelationships on rather clearly defined roles of dominance and submission in contradistinction to equalitarian policies. In consequence, the images of the parents seem to acquire for the child a forbidding or at least a distant quality. Family relationships are characterized by fearful subservience to the demands of the parents and by an early suppression of impulses not acceptable to them.

The goals which such parents have in mind in rearing and training their children tend to be highly conventional. The status-anxiety so often found in families of prejudiced subjects is reflected in the adoption of a rigid and externalized set of values: what is socially accepted and what is helpful in climbing the social ladder is considered "good," and what deviates, what is different, and what is socially inferior is considered "bad." With this narrow path in mind, the parents are likely to be intolerant of any manifestation of impulses on the part of the child which seems to distract from, or to oppose, the desired goal. The more urgent the "social needs" of the parents, the more they are apt to view the child's behavior in terms of their own instead of the child's needs.

Since the values of the parents are outside the child's scope, yet are rigorously imposed upon him, conduct not in conformity with the behavior, or with the behavioral facade, required by the parents has to be rendered ego-alien and "split-off" from the rest of the personality with a resultant loss of integration. Much of the submission to parental authority in the prejudiced subject seems to be induced by the impatience on the part of parents and by the child's fear of displeasing them.

It is in the area of social and political attitudes that the suppressed yet unmodified impulses find one of their distorted outlets and emerge with particular intensity. In particular, moral indignation first experienced in the attitude of one's parents toward oneself is being redirected against weaker outgroups.

The lack of an internalized and individualized approach to the child, on the part of the parents, as well as a tendency to transmit mainly a set of conventional rules and customs, may be considered as interfering with the development of a clear-cut personal identity in the growing child. Instead, we find surface conformity without integration, expressing itself in a stereotyped approach devoid of genuine affect in almost all areas of life. . . . Even in the purely cognitive domain, ready-made clichés tend to take the place of spontaneous reactions. Whatever the topic may be, statements made by the prejudiced as contrasted with the unprejudiced are apt to stand out by their comparative lack of imagination, of spontaneity, and of originality and by a certain constrictive character.

Faithful execution of prescribed roles and the exchange of duties and obligations is, in the families of the prejudiced, often given preference over the exchange of free-flowing affection. We are led to assume that an authoritarian home regime, which induces a relative lack of mutuality in the area of emotion and shifts emphasis onto the exchange of "goods" and of material benefits without adequate development of underlying self-reliance, forms the basis for the opportunistic type of dependence of children on their parents. . . .

This kind of dependence on the parents, the wish to be taken care of by them, coupled with the fear ensuing from the same general pattern, seems firmly to establish the self-negating submission to parents just described. There are, however, certain cues which seem to indicate the presence, at the same time, of underlying resentment against, and feelings of victimization by, the parents. . . .

Resentment, be it open or disguised, may readily be understood in view of the strong parental pressures to enforce "good" behavior together with the meagerness of the rewards offered. As a reaction against the underlying hostility, there is often rigid glorification and idealization of the parents. The artificiality of this attitude may be recognized from the description of the parents in exaggerated, superlative (and at the same time stereotyped and externalized) terms.

Usually it is only this admiration which is admitted and ego-accepted. The resentment, rendered ego-alien, is the more active through the operation of mechanisms of displacement. . . .

The orientation toward power and the contempt for the allegedly inferior and weak, found in our typical prejudiced subjects, must likewise be considered as having been taken over from the parents' attitude toward the child. The fact that his helplessness as a child was exploited by the parents and that he was forced into submission must have reinforced any existing antiweakness attitude. Prejudiced individuals thus tend to display "negative identification" with the weak along with their positive though superficial identification with the strong.

This orientation toward the strong is often expressed in conscious identification with the more powerful parent. Above all, the men among our prejudiced subjects tend to report having a "stern and distant" father who seems to have been domineering within the family. It is this type of father who elicits in his son tendencies toward passive submission, as well as the ideal of aggressive and rugged masculinity and a compensatory striving for independence. Furthermore, the son's inadequate relation to his mother prevents him from adopting some of the "softer" values.

In line with the fact that the families of the prejudiced, especially those of our male subjects, tend to be father-dominated, there is a tendency in such families toward a dichotomous conception of the sex roles and a relative separation of the sexes within the family [Adorno, *et al.*, 1950, pp. 385–387].

With respect to the equalitarian individuals on the opposite end of the prejudice-ethnocentrism-authoritarianism continuum, family characteristics are described more or less as the reverse of that outlined above. That is, less obedience is expected of the children, parents are less status-ridden, less anxious about conformity, and less intolerant of socially unacceptable behavior. Equalitarian individuals have more affection within the family, and their emotional life is characterized by greater freedom.

TRADITIONAL FAMILY IDEOLOGY

Among the many hypotheses which emerge from the foregoing material, an important one is concerned with differences in family structure and functioning in the background of authoritarians and equalitarians. Levinson and Huffman [1955] selected an autocratic-democratic dimension to investigate. They termed the general beliefs of the autocratic extreme as "Traditional Family Ideology" and predicted that the democratic-autocratic dimension of family structure would be found to be associated with the equalitarian-authoritarian dimension of personality.

Their first step was the construction of a scale to measure attitudes about family organization: the Traditional Family Ideology (TFI) Scale. This instrument was conceptualized as an extension or application of the material from the clinical interviews discussed above. Five major characteristics of autocratic families were included in the scale:

Conventionalism. There should be a rigid and unyielding emphasis on conformity, cleanliness, practicality, upward status mobility, and the like, and a punitive attitude toward those who fail to follow this pattern. Democratic families should be more flexible and more tolerant of deviations.

Authoritarian Submission. The family is a hierarchical structure in which wife obeys husband, children obey mother, younger siblings obey older ones, and so forth. In the equalitarian home, the family is a more democratically organized group (or "committee") in which decisions are reached by a sharing of opinions.

Exaggerated Masculinity and Femininity. To the autocratic parent, men are men and women are women with little overlap of traits or functions. Children must be taught the appropriate sex roles early and not deviate from them in interests, values, clothing, toys, activities, and so forth. Democratic parents, too, recognize differences in appropriate sex roles in our culture, but they do not hold to rigid dichotomies. Males and females are more likely to share certain interests and duties and emotional experiences.

Extreme Emphasis on Discipline. To the autocrat, rules are of paramount importance, and rule violations must not be permitted. As a result, discipline is strict. Also, this orientation allows the power-figure an acceptable outlet for aggression in that he can administer punishment (often involving physical pain) for a "good" reason. The democratic homes place a greater emphasis on the child understanding the reasons for rules and less emphasis on rigid conformity to them, and they utilize love-oriented punishment techniques.

Moralistic Rejection of Impulse Life. With the pressures of the autocratic home, the child is required to inhibit and deny a large part of his feelings and desires. For example, it would be taboo to have impulses appropriate to the opposite sex, feelings of hostility toward either parent, sexual wishes, or intense emotions of any kind. In democratic families, considerably more tolerance and acceptance of such impulses should be found.

The original TFI Scale consisted of 40 items to which subjects responded on an agree-disagree basis as with the F Scale. The original test was found to have a split-half reliability of .84, but a later investigation with a refined version reported a split-half coefficient of .92 and a test-retest figure of .93 over a six-week interval. With 109 subjects, Levinson and Huffman performed an item-analysis, using the Discriminatory Power technique. Five of the items failed to discriminate high and low scorers and were discarded. Of the remaining 35 items, the seven most discriminating were:

A child should not be allowed to talk back to his parents, or else he will lose respect for them. (DP = 3.5)

The family is a sacred institution, divinely ordained. (DP = 3.3)

Women who want to remove the word obey from the marriage service don't understand what it means to be a wife. (DP = 3.2)

There is a lot of evidence such as the Kinsey Report which shows we have to crack down harder on young people to save our moral standards. (DP = 3.1)

A man can scarcely maintain respect for his fiancée if they have sexual relations before they are married. (DP = 3.1)

Some equality in marriage is a good thing, but by and large the husband ought to have the main say-so in family matters. (DP = 3.0)

It goes against nature to place women in positions of authority over men. (DP = 3.0)

In the initial investigation with this instrument, the TFI and the California F Scale were administered to 109 subjects enrolled in adult evening psychology classes at Cleveland College. The age range was 20 to 40. For this group, the predicted positive relationship between TFI and authoritarianism was found: the two scales correlated .73. Authoritarianism appears to be associated with adherence to traditional family ideology. This finding was later replicated in five groups totaling 507 subjects in the Boston area; an average correlation of about .70 was found.

Levinson and Huffman rightly indicated that this correlational finding should be considered an initial step in a series of investigations of the antecedents of authoritarian characteristics. One is tempted, however, to speculate briefly on the possible explanation for the obtained relationship. The correlation between the two tests suggests the possibility that authoritarians are raised in autocratic homes, equalitarians in democratic homes. In fact, the nature of these homes and the interpersonal interactions in them may account in large part for such personality differences.

DISCIPLINARY TECHNIQUES

In the TFI study, a general family orientation was described, and adherence to this orientation was found to have a substantial relationship with authoritarianism. Contained within the description of the autocratic family, however, were a number of specific elements. Each of these could well be the object of a series of investigations. In his doctoral dissertation at Duke, Hart [1957] focused on disciplinary techniques.

The way in which parents attempt to control child behavior in the socialization situation has been hypothesized as one of the consequents of authoritarianism-equalitarianism and also as one of the antecedents of that personality dimension. Hart selected the Whiting and Child [1953] breakdown of punishment techniques as varying from love-oriented to nonlove-oriented. The former serve to maintain the child's striving for parental love and include denial of love, threats of denial of reward, and threats of ostracism. Nonlove-oriented techniques, on the other hand, tend to focus on the importance of obeying rules, the violation of which leads to punishment. The latter techniques include physical punishment, threats of physical punishment, and ridicule. On the basis of earlier speculations by Adorno, *et al.* and by Levinson and Huffman, Hart hypothesized that authoritarian parents would select nonlove-oriented techniques in disciplining their children.

A group of 126 mothers was selected for study; each had at least one child between the ages of two and one-half and five and one-half. Individual interviews were scheduled, and each mother was asked a series of questions about her most probable response to her child's behavior in a series of situations. The mothers were asked about their own behavior in 38 situations covering aspects of the following:

1. *Feeding and oral activities,* such as "he insists on eating with his fingers" and "he seldom finishes meals."
2. *Cleanliness–toilet training,* such as "he frequently has toilet accidents because he won't interrupt his play."
3. *Sex,* including sexual curiosity, sexual and obscene remarks, handling genitals, body exposure.
4. *Aggression,* including insolence and impudence, hitting and pushing, temper tantrums, explicit disobedience, and willful property damage.
5. *Dependence,* including lack of self-reliance and attempting to gain parental support, such as "he whines or begs for help unnecessarily."
6. *Independence,* including situations that suggest that the child is showing initiative, curiosity, and assertiveness, such as "he insists on his own way with other children" and "he wanders away from home."

The mothers were also asked a number of other questions and were given the F Scale. Three judges decided which disciplinary category the mothers' responses indicated. Two out of three judges had to agree for the scoring to be made.

To test the hypothesis concerning the relationship between disciplinary techniques and authoritarianism, each mother's F Scale score was correlated with the number of situations (out of the 38) in which she indicated that she would respond with a nonlove-oriented technique. The correlation was .63, thus confirming the hypothesis.

Evidence from other studies is supportive of the reported findings. Lyle and Levitt [1955] measured authoritarianism in fifth-grade children by means of the Children's Antidemocratic Scale. To ascertain the childrens' perception of the punitiveness of their parents, a 20-item sentence completion test was constructed. Items were of the sort, "When I disobey my parents, they. . . ." A small but significant relationship was found between authoritarianism and amount of parental punitiveness expressed on the incomplete sentences test; the correlation was .32.

PERMISSIVENESS-RESTRICTIVENESS

Still other support comes from an investigation of the Parental Attitude Research Inventory by Zuckerman and Oltean [1959]. As was described in Chapter 4, this instrument has been found to contain three factors: authoritarian-control, hostility-rejection, and democratic attitude. The F Scale was found to correlate only with the first of these factors. The relationship was a substantial .51 in a group of 32 female psychiatric patients and .61 in a group of 88 student nurses.

Block [1955] at the Institute of Personality Assessment and Research at the University of California administered a group of items dealing with "restrictiveness" versus "permissiveness" in child-rearing attitudes to 100 military officers. Restrictive statements included:

When adults are entertaining, a child should "be seen but not heard."

Firm and strict discipline makes for strong character in later life.

Children need some of the natural meanness taken out of them.

Permissive statements included:

A child should be permitted to have secrets from his parents.

Jealousy among brothers and sisters is a very common thing.

Children have a right to make a mess just for the fun of it.

On the basis of responses to the items, the 20 most restrictive and 20 least restrictive fathers were selected for additional study. After a three-day assessment period, eight psychologists who had observed the subjects evaluated each by means of a Q-sort description. A great many of the specific Q-sort items differentiated permissive and restrictive fathers. In summary:

The men expressing restrictive attitudes toward child-rearing are perceived by competent observers as more submissive, suggestible, conforming, indecisive, ineffectual and over-controlled. The men expressing permissive attitudes toward child-rearing are evaluated as more self-reliant, ascendant, rebellious toward authority figures, persuasive, counter-active and sarcastic [Block, 1955, pp. 44–45].

The restrictive group was found to score significantly higher on the F
Scale than the permissive group.

On the basis of the correlational findings that have been reported, we
may reasonably speculate that a circular pattern of cause and effect may
be operating with respect to child-rearing practices and authoritarianism.
The relationships are shown schematically in Figure 8–1. The authori-

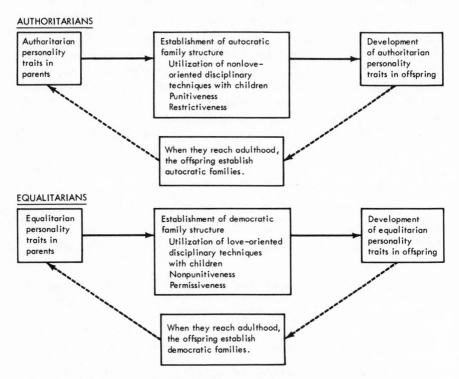

FIG. 8–1. *Possible antecedents and consequents of authoritarianism.*

tarian or equalitarian characteristics of parents lead them to structure
their families and raise their children in quite different ways. The consequences for the children include the development of personality characteristics like those of the parents. On reaching adulthood, these individuals
repeat the pattern, and so it continues from generation to generation.

AUTHORITARIANISM AND TRADITIONAL FAMILY IDEOLOGY
ACROSS GENERATIONS

In order to confirm the sort of proposition depicted in Figure 8–1, a great deal of additional research must be undertaken. The
major flaw in the data thus far presented is the reliance on intra-individual
approaches in which scores on the F Scale are found to be related to some

other behavior within a group of subjects. Two untested assumptions are built into the generalizations about the child-rearing antecedents of authoritarianism. Husbands and wives are tacitly assumed to be similar to one another in both authoritarianism and in child-rearing practices. Even more strongly, parental authoritarianism and child-rearing techniques are assumed to be positively related to these characteristics in their offspring. Without studying husband-wife and parent-child relationships, assessing the probable accuracy of these formulations is difficult.

In a recent investigation [Byrne, 1965], 108 college students plus the mothers and fathers of each were given the F Scale and the TFI Scale of Levinson and Huffman [1955]. As in the studies reported earlier, the correlation between the two tests was substantial ($r = .62$ for students, $r = .61$ for fathers, $r = .61$ for mothers). Across generations, however, the relationships are considerably smaller. For the 49 male students, their F Scale scores correlated .33 ($p < .01$) with the TFI scores of their fathers and .14 (not significant) with the TFI scores of their mothers. For the 59 female students, the corresponding coefficients were .10 and .14, neither of which is statistically significant. The most useful information for predicting authoritarianism in the offspring was found to be the F Scale scores of each parent. If the authoritarianism of both parents is considered, a multiple r of .40 for male offspring and .33 for female offspring is found. Obviously a great deal of the variance in authoritarianism must be accounted for on the basis of variables other than parental authoritarianism and traditional family ideology.

One possible clue lies in differences between the parents. Similarity between husbands and wives was significantly greater than zero for each scale ($r = .30$ for the F Scale and $r = .26$ for the TFI Scale), but the relationships are not of great magnitude. When the parents were divided into high, medium, and low thirds on the basis of their authoritarian scores, all possible patterns of husband-wife combinations were found. It was suggested that the influence of parental authoritarianism and its correlates on the ideology of their offspring could quite possibly be affected by such husband-wife differences. For example, a family with an authoritarian father and equalitarian mother might have a different effect on children than a family with the reverse pattern; similarly, such husband-wife differences could affect sons and daughters differently.

With just the knowledge of mother-father differences in the 108 families, an exploration of possible pattern effects was undertaken. Authoritarian offspring were found to be most likely to develop in families in which neither parent is low F and the same-sexed parent is high F. Conversely, equalitarian offspring are most likely to be found in families in which at least one parent is low F and the same-sexed parent is *not* high F.

At the very least we may conclude that the rather simple picture that has been drawn to contrast authoritarian and equalitarian home atmospheres and their effects on offspring will need to be replaced by a somewhat more complicated conceptualization of the antecedents of authoritarianism.

The Place of Authoritarianism in the Structure of Personality

A great many of the investigations of the California F Scale have consisted of establishing correlational relationships with other personality dimensions and with behavior in various types of situations. A sample of these correlational findings are discussed in the present section.

PREJUDICE

One of the initial reasons for developing the F Scale was the desire by Adorno, *et al.*, to construct a scale that would measure prejudice in a relatively indirect way without mentioning any minority group by name. Authoritarianism was conceptualized as a general trait, while prejudice toward any specific group simply represented one manifestation of the trait. Two of the other scales which the Berkeley group developed dealt with prejudice more directly; therefore, the F Scale was expected to correlate with these measures.

The group's starting point in the study of prejudice was an investigation of anti-Semitism, partly because of the recency of the grotesque horror of prejudice carried to its logical extreme by the Nazis and partly because of the long and unenviable history of the Jewish people as the objects of bigotry and persecution. The suggestion was made that organized anti-Semitism presents a major threat to democracy because it serves as a rallying-cry for antidemocratic political movements. In addition, attitudes toward Jews were thought to constitute an important personality variable per se. As Levinson puts it:

The irrational quality in anti-Semitism stands out even in casual everyday discussions. The fact that people make general statements about "the Jew," when the Jews are actually so heterogeneous—belong to every socioeconomic class and represent every degree of assimilation—is vivid evidence of this irrationality. This striking contrast between the Jews' actual complexity and their supposed homogeneity has suggested the hypothesis that what people say against Jews depends more upon their own psychology than upon the actual characteristics of Jews [Adorno, *et al.*, 1950, p. 57].

The approach to the construction of the Anti-Semitism (A-S) Scale was similar to that of the F Scale. A sample of the items was given in Chapter 5.

In some of the original investigations of the Anti-Semitism and F

Scales, four groups with a total of 295 individuals took both tests. Correlations ranged from .49 to .57 with an average of .53. Thus, as was hypothesized, authoritarianism is positively related to espousal of anti-Jewish attitudes.

Still another part of the original series of authoritarian studies dealt with ethnocentrism. Ethnocentrism refers to cultural narrowness, the tendency to be ethnically centered and rigidly to accept one's own culture while rigidly rejecting anything different from it. The Ethnocentrism (E) Scale which was constructed included items from the A-S Scale along with such additional items as:

> Negroes have their rights, but it is best to keep them in their own districts and schools and to prevent too much contact with whites.

> The worst danger to real Americanism during the last 50 years has come from foreign ideas and agitators.

> Filipinos are all right in their place, but they carry it too far when they dress lavishly and go around with white girls.

> It is only natural and right for each person to think that his family is better than any other.

With a relatively large number of groups totaling over 2000 subjects, the E Scale was found to correlate with the F Scale from .56 to .87 with a mean of .73. Thus, a strong tendency exists for authoritarianism to be associated with ethnocentrism.

In the United States, perhaps the central object of prejudice is the Negro race. Because of the number of individuals involved and the complex historical and legal elements intermixed, psychological and sociological studies of anti-Negro prejudice have tended to predominate in investigations of bigotry. Probably in part because of other factors (for example, regional differences) which serve to confound the relationships, authoritarianism is generally found not to be as highly correlated with attitudes toward Negroes as might be expected from the anti-Semitism and ethnocentrism findings. As described in Chapter 5, Kelly, Ferson, and Holtzman [1958] devised a Desegregation Scale to measure negative attitudes toward Negroes and reported that scores on this instrument correlated .33 with the F Scale. With another group of 73 University of Texas undergraduates, Wong [1961] found a .28 correlation between the two tests. In a third investigation, Klein [1963] reported a correlation of .17 between the F Scale and a Negro Attitude Scale in a group of almost 1,000 undergraduates. In each instance, the relationship between authoritarianism and anti-Negro prejudice is a significant one, but of relatively low magnitude. Hites and Kellogg [1964] administered two specific questions concerning integration of public schools and integration of churches along with the F Scale to 141 college students in the Deep South. Authoritarianism was found to correlate significantly ($r = .55$ $p < .01$) with anti-Negro prejudice as measured by these items.

HOSTILITY

One of the basic characteristics originally ascribed to the high authoritarian individual is that of hostility. This hostility is hypothesized to be a generalized drive but it is directed primarily toward outgroups and toward those who violate cultural mores. Many of the items on the F Scale were designed to reflect this hostile component. In addition to the prejudice studies, other empirical evidence is also available which supports the hostility hypothesis.

In his doctoral dissertation at Western Reserve University, Meer [1955] investigated the hostility of authoritarians as revealed in their verbal reports of their dreams. From a group of 116 undergraduates, 38 high-authoritarian and 33 low-authoritarian subjects were selected. Dream reports had been collected during the semester by the students' instructors. The mean number of dreams per subject was 9.6; high and low authoritarians did not differ in this respect. Each dream was scored by a judge (who had no knowledge of the F Scale scores) for aggressive and friendly encounters with various characters appearing in the dreams. Characters were divided into members of the ingroup (family members, friends, and acquaintances) and of the outgroup (strangers). The intensity of the aggression was scored on an eight-point scale ranging from "feeling hostile but no outward expression" to "intentional killing." Interjudge reliability was relatively high. Those high in authoritarianism reported significantly more aggression toward outgroup characters than toward ingroup characters; those low in authoritarianism did not report dreams containing this difference. With respect to friendly acts, authoritarians reported significantly more such acts with ingroup than with outgroup members; again, equalitarians did not make the differentiation. These findings suggested the following interpretation:

Intense aggression is likely to arise between parents and children, between husband and wife, between siblings and between close friends and relatives. The expression of such aggression tends to be anxiety producing so that indirect means of expressing this impulse are employed in order to keep anxiety at a minimum. One of the characteristics of dreams, according to Freud, is that they allow forbidden impulses to be expressed without the dreamer's being aware of it. . . . If these ideas are applied to the problem of the meaning of strangers in dreams, the hypothesis may be advanced that the greater intensity of aggression with strangers than with family, friends, and acquaintances is due to the indirect expression of aggression with highly cathected objects [Meer, 1955, p. 77].

A more generalized type of hostility in authoritarians was the object of a study by Siegel [1956]. A Manifest Hostility Scale (MHS) was built utilizing MMPI items primarily. Siegel selected 114 items that appeared to reflect hostility and submitted these to five judges for independent evaluation. They obtained 80 per cent or better agreement on 53 of the 114 items; three of these were later eliminated. The remaining 50 items were found to have a split-half reliability of .84. They consist of such statements as:

> I have very few quarrels with members of my family. (False)

> I like to poke fun at people. (True)

> I sometimes tease animals. (True)

> I never have "temper tantrums." (False)

Both the F Scale and the MHS were given to 60 male students at the University of Buffalo and to 60 male veterans applying for treatment at a Mental Hygiene Clinic. Each group was divided into high, medium, and low thirds on the basis of F Scale scores. In both the college and the veteran samples a significant positive relationship existed between authoritarianism and hostility. The means are shown in Table 8–2.

Table 8–2   AUTHORITARIANISM AND MANIFEST HOSTILITY

F Scale	Mean Manifest Hostility Score
University	
High	17.2
Medium	12.6
Low	12.6
Veterans	
High	20.8
Medium	16.8
Low	14.0

In each of these investigations of hostility, an association was found between F Scale scores and a *verbal report* of hostile feelings, behaviors, or perceptions. Whether those high and low on the authoritarian dimension differ in the frequency or the intensity or the direction of their overt aggressive acts is another question and one not answered by these studies. In a simulated war game situation in which hostile behavior was defined in terms of pushing a switch to launch missiles against a possible enemy, scores on the F Scale were found to be unrelated to readiness to start a "war" under either neutral or hostility-arousing conditions unless the subjects also held anti-Russian attitudes [Bounds, 1964]. A further investigation, utilizing the same experimental situation, found that under certain experimental conditions authoritarianism was related to aggressing against the "enemy" [Abrams, 1964]. Specifically, when the instructions indicated a high value (saving the homeland) and low personal cost (no one will be hurt and the missile will destroy itself over the North Pole if the information about the enemy was a false alarm), those high in authoritarianism launched missiles more readily than did equalitarians.

POLITICAL AND ECONOMIC BELIEFS

One of the basic dimensions of political ideology is that complex combination of beliefs and values concerning man and his relation to the state and to the existing social order: liberalism versus conservatism. Because such beliefs cover broad aspects of life and because no definitive way exists to test their respective assumptions experimentally, it is not surprising to find that adherence to one or another position is related to a number of personality variables. That is, individuals seem to respond on the basis of internal needs and values as much as to external arguments and "facts."

In their original series of investigations, Adorno, *et al.* [1950] suggested that adherence to right-wing or conservative politics should be related to antidemocratic beliefs because fascism is the most extreme right-wing political and economic structure and ideology. A Politico-Economic Conservatism Scale was built in an attempt to measure such trends as support of the American status quo, resistance to social change, and support of conservative values. It includes items of the form:

America may not be perfect, but the American Way has brought us about as close as human beings can get to a perfect society.

In general, full economic security is bad; most men wouldn't work if they didn't need the money for eating and living.

With over 2,000 subjects in a wide variety of groups, correlations were found between the PEC Scale and the F Scale ranging from .22 to .72 with an average of .52. Various other investigators in subsequent studies have confirmed this relationship between authoritarianism and conservatism.

Since a number of quite specific issues are involved in liberal-conservative differences, it is not surprising to find the F Scale related to the position which individuals take on many seemingly diverse topics. As his doctoral dissertation at Stanford, Mahler [1953] built a Socialized Medicine Attitude Scale; examples of items are:

> The quality of medical care under the system of private practice is superior to that under a system of compulsory health insurance. (Disagree)

> A compulsory health program would be a realization of one of the true aims of a democracy. (Agree)

> Any system of compulsory health insurance would invade the privacy of the individual. (Disagree)

With a group of 106 Stanford students, Mahler found that his scale correlated —.30 with the F Scale. That is, the more positive the attitude toward socialized medicine the less authoritarian the individual tends to be.

Authoritarianism is correlated with and hence predictive of other types of political behavior besides that of marking responses on an attitude scale. Before the nomination of candidates and presentation of party platforms in the 1960 presidential campaign, Wrightsman, Radloff, Horton, and Mecherikoff [1961] obtained the presidential choices and F Scale scores of 1,142 college students in nine colleges and universities in four sections of the country. They found that authoritarian scores of those who supported different candidates were significantly different. Table 8–3 shows the eight

Table 8–3   MEAN F SCALE SCORES OF SUPPORTERS
             OF DIFFERENT PRESIDENTIAL CANDIDATES*

Candidate	Mean F Scale Score
Orville Faubus	32.5
Lyndon B. Johnson	32.2
John F. Kennedy	29.8
Richard M. Nixon	29.3
Nelson Rockefeller	29.0
Hubert Humphrey	27.8
Stuart Symington	26.5
Adlai E. Stevenson	26.0

* Adapted from Wrightsman, et al., 1961, p. 44.

candidates and the mean F scores of those who gave each candidate as his first choice. Because of the wide spectrum of beliefs which characterize each party, there are greater F Scale differences within each party than between parties. Among these students, Democrats had a mean of 29.1 and Republicans a mean of 29.4. Independents, with a mean of 27.7, were significantly less authoritarian than members of either major party.

The importance of the candidate's political ideology in determining his relative appeal to authoritarians and equalitarians was shown by Leventhal, Jacobs, and Kudirka [1964] in two investigations. The first was conducted just before the 1960 presidential election. The hypothesis was made that Kennedy's advocation of the New Frontier would appeal to those low in authoritarianism, while Nixon's preference for the status quo would appeal to those high on this dimension. In the period one to two weeks before the election, 76 undergraduates at Yale indicated their preference with respect to the two candidates and also took the F Scale. A significant relationship was found between F Scale scores and political choice, with authoritarians preferring Nixon. In addition, on a series of issues of national and international importance, subjects assumed that the candidate they had chosen was more similar in opinion to themselves than was the candidate they had rejected.

In an attempt to extend these findings, Leventhal, *et al.* [1964] then employed an experimental situation in which a candidate's ideology could be manipulated. At the time of the 1962 congressional elections, pairs of candidates were described to three different samples of students. One group was presented with a conservative Republican versus a liberal Democrat, one with a liberal Republican versus a conservative Democrat, and the third group was given two candidates who had the same ideology. The subjects were 189 male undergraduates at Yale. The ideology of the candidates was given in terms of their opinions about federal aid to urban redevelopment, increased social security benefits, increased minimum wages, greater unemployment benefits, federal aid to education, and stricter antitrust legislation. Those with high scores on the F Scale voted for the conservative candidate, and those with low scores voted for the liberal candidate, regardless of party label. When the two candidates had the same ideology, authoritarianism was not related to choice. The authors point out that authoritarianism would be expected to affect choice of candidates only in the relatively small and well-educated segment of the population where a definable ideology is present, only if the candidates are reasonably consistent in espousing liberal or conservative ideology, and only if such ideological positions are more salient than other characteristics of the candidates.

For the 1964 presidential election, Milton and Waite [1964] utilized the TFI Scale of Levinson and Huffman [1955] rather than the F Scale. In the summer of 1964, the TFI Scale was administered to 401 students at the Universities of Tennessee and Georgia. The students were then asked which of the following three men they preferred as President of the United States: Goldwater, Johnson, Wallace. Analysis of variance yielded a highly significant F ratio; as hypothesized, the highest TFI Scale scores were attained by those preferring Wallace and the lowest scores by those preferring Johnson.

Still other types of politically relevant behavior have been found related to authoritarianism. Beginning in 1949, the University of California at Berkeley was shaken by what became known as the "loyalty oath controversy." The Regents of the University, in the summer of that year, sent out a special noncommunist oath with the academic contracts for 1949–1950. A great many individuals refused to sign this oath on the grounds that: (1) there were no Communists on the faculty, and (2) the oath constituted a violation of tenure. In the succeeding furor, 18 nonsigning faculty members took their case to court while a number of nontenure employees (mostly graduate students) lost their positions. Handlon and Squier [1955] located 23 of the 29 nonsigners in the latter group and selected a random sample of 21 nontenured individuals who did sign the oath. Each subject was interviewed and given (among other things) the F Scale. Though there were many similarities between these two groups, one of the findings was that those who refused to sign were significantly less authoritarian than those who did sign the oath.

Still another investigation dealt with the proposition that those who ascribe to authoritarian ideology would respond positively to a society in which authoritarian values were the accepted mode. One approach to the investigation of this possibility is to find a group within our culture which is structured along authoritarian lines. In many respects the ideology of military life is authoritarian. For example, conventionalism, submission to and enforcement of authority, toughness, and hard-headedness would seem to be common characteristics. French and Ernest [1955] at Lackland Air Force Base built a Military Ideology Scale (MIS) to measure acceptance of the military. Items included:

> An airman who salutes smartly and proudly can be counted on to perform his duties in the same fashion. (Agree)

> Reveille formation is an unnecessary waste of time and sleep. (Disagree)

Subjects were a total of 186 airmen in basic training. The MIS was found to correlate between .35 and .54 with the F Scale in different subgroups. Even though authoritarianism is positively related to acceptance of military ideology, it was not found to be related to the decision to make the service a career.

MALADJUSTMENT

In the theoretical description of authoritarians and equalitarians, a number of characteristics of the former suggest less than optimal psychological functioning. Thus, authoritarians were described as rigid, conforming, repressing, denying, projecting, and displacing. Equalitarians, on the other hand, were indicated to be more flexible, more free, more aware of their impulses, and less likely to utilize unconsciously determined defense mechanisms. In a 1954 article, Masling suggested that the primary reason for these differences in characterization stemmed from a lack of objectivity in the social scientists who were investigating authoritarianism. His general point is a good one: "There seems to be a tendency to use the term 'authoritarian' as a mild profanity which one could use to describe other people (never oneself)" [Masling, 1954, p. 318]. Masling also indicated that at that time only four studies had investigated the relationship between authoritarianism and mental health and that not one of them found any relationship. Actually, only one of the four utilized the California F Scale. In that particular investigation, no relationship was found between authoritarian scores and responses to the Rotter Incomplete Sentences Test. Obviously, considerably more evidence would be needed to be able to state with any degree of confidence that authoritarians are or are not more maladjusted than equalitarians.

One small bit of support for Masling's general proposition came from Freedman, Webster, and Sanford [1956] who administered the F Scale and the MMPI to two large samples of freshman women ($N = 441$, and $N = 225$). Of the 12 scales of the latter test, three were found to be *negatively* correlated with authoritarianism to a significant degree in both samples. Authoritarians were less defensive, less hysterical, and less paranoid than equalitarians.

Since anxiety is a prominent component of most forms of behavior pathology, the notion that authoritarians were maladjusted would lead to the prediction of a relationship between the F Scale and a measure of anxiety. Singer and Feshbach [1959] used the Taylor Manifest Anxiety Scale (see Chapter 10) as an anxiety measure. With 147 male undergraduates as subjects, a correlation of .34 was found between the two tests. Davids [1955], using 20 male undergraduates, reported a correlation of .69 between the F Scale and the MAS. However, Davids and Eriksen [1957] with 48 Naval enlisted men found the two scales unrelated. Possibly, population differences (undergraduates versus sailors) account for these discrepant findings.

Criminal behavior represents a particular type of maladjustment. Among the 14 groups who were given the final version of the F Scale by Adorno, *et al.*, 110 San Quentin prisoners obtained the highest score (item mean = 4.73). Aumack [1956], in an investigation of 85 murderers at San Quentin, reported that their mean authoritarian scores were the highest yet reported in any investigation. The item mean was 4.77 compared with 3.90 for the general population and 3.30 for University of California students.

Still another approach to the relationship between authoritarianism and maladjustment has centered on the possible effects of authoritarian parents on maladjustment in their offspring. Kates and Diab [1955] studied the relationship between authoritarianism and attitudes about parent-child relationships as measured by the U.S.C. Parent Attitude Survey. This instrument contains three scales: Dominant, Possessive, Ignoring. The Dominant Scale contains items indicating a parent's desire to keep the child subordinate and conforming. The Possessive Scale has items dealing with keeping the child dependent. Ignoring refers to the parent's disregard of the child as an individual. The test was standardized and validated in terms of differences in responses of mothers of problem children and mothers of nonproblem children. In the Kates and Diab study, subjects were 172 students at the University of Oklahoma. The F Scale correlated .34 with Dominant and .28 with Possessive for female subjects and .29 with Ignoring for male subjects. Thus, authoritarian beliefs were positively associated with attitudes similar to those held by parents of problem children.

In studies of the etiology of schizophrenia, a number of investigators have focused on disturbances in the relationship between mother and child. A number of clinical observers have described mothers of schizophrenics as being demanding, dominating, domineering, and dependency-fostering. Dworin and Wyant [1957] administered the F Scale to 43 hospitalized schizophrenics, the mothers of 19 schizophrenic patients, and a control group of 21 volunteer women. The latter were of about the same age, educational level, ethnic, socioeconomic, and geographic background as the group of mothers. Both the patients and mothers of patients were found to have significantly higher mean F scores than the group of volunteers. In addition, an item-analysis was performed in order to determine specifically which items differentiated the schizophrenics and mothers of schizophrenics from the control group. The eleven differentiating items tended to emphasize obedience, discipline, gratitude, respect for parents, and avoidance of rebellious ideas. Not only do the mothers indicate a desire for obedience and the like, but they also expect strength, achievement, working, fighting, will-power, and force. Possibly the conflict between these two opposing demands contributes to the development of schizophrenia in the offspring of such mothers.

INTOLERANCE OF AMBIGUITY

Authoritarians have been described by Else Frenkel-Brunswik [1949; 1950] and others as more intolerant of ambiguous situations than equalitarians. The authoritarian is said to have no place in his cognitive structure for ambivalence or ambiguity; he sticks with simple, firm, often preconceived categories. Because of the widely diversified operations that have been used to define ambiguity tolerance, the data with respect to this hypothesis are not as clear-cut as they might be.

Intolerance of ambiguity has been defined as "the tendency to perceive (i.e., interpret) ambiguous situations as sources of threat" and *tolerance of ambiguity* as "the tendency to perceive ambiguous situations as desirable" [Budner, 1962, p. 29]. Budner developed a 16-item scale to measure tolerance-intolerance of ambiguity.

Sample items are:

> What we are used to is always preferable to what is unfamiliar. (Agree)

> A good teacher is one who makes you wonder about your way of looking at things. (Disagree)

This test and the F Scale were administered to nine groups of subjects. In each instance the correlations (.17 to .55) were positive; in six of the groups, the coefficients were significant.

To 282 freshmen at a Negro state college in Baltimore, Kelman and Barclay [1963] administered the F Scale and Walk's A Scale [O'Connor, 1952], which is another measure of intolerance of ambiguity. The latter scale consists of such items as:

> Nobody can have feelings of love and hate toward the same person.

> It is always better to have a definite course of action than to be vacillating among several possibilities.

> There is more than one right way to do anything.

In order to control for acquiescent response set, five of the A Scale items were worded to express the intolerant end of the continuum and three to express the tolerant end. The correlation between authoritarianism and this measure of intolerance of ambiguity was .43 ($p < .001$). An earlier investigation [Kenny and Ginsberg, 1958] had reported a correlation of .57 ($p < .01$) between the A Scale and a special F Scale measure of authoritarian submission in a sample of 76 female adults.

Millon [1957], using 69 introductory psychology students, studied intolerance of ambiguity with respect to responses to the autokinetic phenomenon. In a darkened room, a single, stationary light is visible; subjects generally report that this stimulus appears to be moving. After a number of trials, subjects tend to settle upon a norm for themselves in that the light seems to move in one particular direction for a very short distance. Millon took the number of trials to form such a norm as a measure of intolerance of ambiguity. Those high in authoritarianism formed norms significantly faster than those low in authoritarianism.

Finally, some negative evidence has been reported with respect to another sort of ambiguity measure. In three investigations [Davids, 1955; Davids, 1956; Davids and Eriksen, 1957] no relationship was found between the F Scale and response to ambiguous auditory stimuli in which confusing and contradictory ideas were presented and then rated by the subjects. The most plausible reason for these contradictory findings is that the various measures which have been proposed for intolerance of ambiguity have been found not to be interrelated:

. . . the nature of the task is a crucial element in the discrepant results of studies in this area. If no common factor of intolerance of ambiguity runs through all the tests employed in its name, then the discordant results are not too surprising [Kenny and Ginsberg, 1958, p. 304].

INTELLIGENCE AND EDUCATIONAL ATTAINMENT

In the original California studies, in groups ranging in size from 104 to 342, scores on the F Scale were found to correlate negatively with performance on various tests of intellectual ability: —.20 with the

Table 8–4   AUTHORITARIANISM AND INTELLECTUAL ABILITY

Investigators	Sample	Measure	Correlation with F Scale
Hollander [1954]	268 Naval Cadets	American Council on Education College Test	—.21
Jacobson and Rettig [1959]	354 Purdue Undergraduates	ACE Psychological Examination	—.39
		Quantitative Subscale	—.22
		Linguistic Subscale	—.26
		Purdue Placement Test in English	—.18
		Purdue Physical Science Test	—.53
Davids and Eriksen [1957]	48 Naval Enlisted Men	Naval General Classification Test	—.24
Davids [1955]	20 Male Undergraduates	Grade Point Average	—.40
Davids [1956]	22 Male Undergraduates	Grade Point Average	—.60
Lindgren [1962]	69 Female Laundromat Customers	Years of Education	—.29
	81 Male Laundromat Customers	Years of Education	—.31

Army General Classification Test, —.13 with Mechanical Comprehension, —.20 with Reading Comprehension, —.16 with Arithmetical Comprehension, and —.48 with the Otis Intelligence Test. Subsequent research has tended to confirm these relationships, as shown in Table 8–4. The reasons for these findings are somewhat more difficult to ascertain. Possibly, adherence to authoritarian beliefs requires relatively low intellectual ability while equalitarian ideology demands brightness. Such an explanation is probably too simple. For one thing, intelligence is related to educational attainment and to socioeconomic class. Both of the latter variables involve a number of behavioral influences such as differences in child-rearing practices. Whatever the ultimate findings concerning the mechanisms underlying the correlations, that a greater-than-chance negative relationship exists between authoritarianism and intellectual ability seems well established.

RELIGIOUS AFFILIATION AND RELIGIOUS ACTIVITY

Various aspects of religious behavior have been found to be related to authoritarianism and ethnocentrism. Jones [1958] examined the relationship between scores on the F Scale and responses to a 50-item background information form. He used two samples of Naval Aviation Cadets; one contained 389 subjects, the other had 397. The six religious items on the background form were examined in relation to authoritarianism. Two of the six items were significantly related to F Scale scores in both samples. The questions and the mean F scores of subjects giving each response are shown in Table 8–5.

Table 8–5   AUTHORITARIANISM AND RELIGION

Are you affiliated with a religious group:

	No	Yes, Protestant	Yes, Jewish	Yes, Roman Catholic
Sample 1	105.0	114.8	89.1	114.3
Sample 2	108.6	118.6	102.4	122.3

Did you prior to coming into the Navy attend church regularly?

	Yes	No
Sample 1	117.5	106.4
Sample 2	119.7	114.9

Thus we see that, compared to equalitarians, those high in authoritarianism: (1) are more likely to be Protestant or Roman Catholic than to be Jewish or unaffiliated with any church, and (2) are more likely to attend church regularly.

Data obtained by David Dustin and Robert K. Young on over 500 college undergraduates are consistent with these findings. In terms of religious preference, those students who indicated that they were Baptists, Episcopalians, or Catholics obtained the highest mean scores, while those with no religious affiliation were the least authoritarian. In between were students who were Jewish, Methodist, Presbyterian, or members of miscellaneous Protestant groups. Similarly, those who attended church more regularly (weekly or twice a month) were significantly more authoritarian than those who never or almost never attended church. The latter finding is not simply a reflection of nonaffiliated students. Even among those with religious affiliations, individuals who attend church regularly are significantly more authoritarian than those who stay away from church.

Similar findings with respect to the Ethnocentrism Scale led Adorno, et al., to suggest:

Belonging to or identifying oneself with a religious body in America today certainly does not mean that one thereby takes over the traditional Christian values of tolerance, brotherhood, and equality. On the contrary, it appears that these values are more firmly held by people who do not affiliate with any religious group. It may be that religious affiliation or church attendance is of little importance one way or the other in determining social attitudes, that the great majority of middle-class Americans identify themselves with some religious denomination as a matter of course, without thinking much about it [Adorno, et al., 1950, p. 219].

Dynamics of Authoritarianism

REPRESSION AND PROJECTION

One of the basic characteristics of authoritarian individuals in the original theoretical description was that of the tendency to repress. One of the best-designed investigations testing this hypothesis was an experiment by Kogan [1956]. The general notion was that if the repression hypothesis were accurate, authoritarians would find it more difficult to recognize threatening aggressive and sexual material than would equalitarians. He selected 42 sentences to be recorded on tape, partially masked by white noise in order to make recognition difficult. After three neutral practice sentences, subjects were given 14 neutral, 14 aggressive, and 14 sexual sentences in random order. Samples of the three types of sentences are:

Neutral
    You like to go swimming during the summer season.
    The thought of a good meal increases your appetite.

Aggressive
    Only your death would be a just punishment for you.
    Your mother is to blame for your worst faults.

Sexual

You have been unable to break your ugly sex habits.

You would have loved to share your father's sex life.

The subjects were 37 male undergraduates. In a group presentation, each sentence was played, the tape stopped, and the subjects were asked to write down what they had heard before the next sentence was played. Because of the white noise, accurate perception of the sentences was difficult. Each sentence the subjects wrote down was given a score ranging from 4 (perfect recognition) to zero (blank or a completely irrelevant guess). Then, each subject's recognition score for each of the three types of sentences was determined. Since the subjects would undoubtedly differ in auditory ability, differences in hearing were controlled by computing a sex/neutral and an aggressive/neutral ratio for each subject. Thus, recognition of the threatening material was measured in relation to recognition of neutral material; differences, then, should be a function of aggressive and sexual content rather than simply auditory differences. It was found that as authoritarian scores increased, ability to perceive the threatening material decreased. Scores on the F Scale correlated $-.39$ with the sex/neutral ratio and $-.38$ with the aggressive/neutral ratio.

We should note that repression of sexuality in authoritarians is not simply an avoidance or denial of everything sexual. Rather, what is repressed is their own unacceptable sexual feelings. Several of the F Scale items deal with an overconcern with sexuality and a projection of improper sexual impulses and behavior onto others. One experimental investigation [Rothstein, 1960] dealt with this latter tendency. From a group of 120 University of Massachusetts male undergraduates, 32 authoritarians and 32 equalitarians were selected. They were asked to watch a silent motion picture containing two five-minute scenes. An attractive female in her middle twenties played in both scenes. In one a sexy female was portrayed while in the other she was kind, affectionate, and understanding; half of the subjects saw the sexy scene first, half the kindly scene. Afterwards, they were asked a number of questions about the star of the film. The authoritarians rated the star as significantly more sexual than did equalitarians, and the authoritarians rated her as more sexual than kindly. Rothstein concludes:

Basic to the evolution of the personality structure of the authoritarian is the unacceptability of id impulses. Sexual strivings remain for the most part suppressed and isolated. However, since they are not integrated with the rest of personality, these impulses find projected and other displaced outlets, as in a heightened concern and moral indignation of sexual expression in others. One can then view the high authoritarian's essentially sexual perception of the star in terms of his projecting unacceptable sensual impulses onto her [Rothstein, 1960, p. 333].

Similarly, authoritarians have been found to be more likely to evaluate stimuli with sexual content as being pornographic than are equalitarians. Eliasberg and Stuart [1961] chose 13 35-mm. color slides of works of art showing nudes from the Metropolitan Museum of Art, the Museum of Modern Art, and Blaue Bucher. Examples are Modigliani's *Reclining Nude, 1918,* Gauguin's *Woman with Mangoes,* and Chabas' *September Morn.* The subjects were 219 male and female students. Each slide was projected on a screen for one minute, and subjects were asked to judge each as pornographic or not pornographic. The correlation between the number of pictures judged to be pornographic and F Scale scores was .46.

CONFORMITY AND OTHER GROUP BEHAVIOR

          The characteristics of conventionalism and authoritarian submission within the authoritarian syndrome have led a number of investigators to hypothesize that those scoring high on the F Scale should be conformists. In the widely used conformity procedure devised by Asch [1956], subjects are given a task such as judging the length of lines or matching the size of a standard object with an adjustable one. Presumably, the subject is one of a group of subjects carrying out the task. Actually, each subject is mixed in with a group of stooges who are instructed to give unanimously incorrect responses on a specified number of the trials. Conformity is defined as the number of trials on which the subject goes along with the group on the incorrect decisions. Barron [1953] has constructed a test which discriminates those who are independent and those who conform in the Asch situation. With San Francisco laundromat customers as subjects, Lindgren [1962] found that authoritarianism correlated —.29 with independence for 81 men and —.59 for 69 women.

In his doctoral dissertation at Western Reserve, Nadler [1959] utilized an Asch length-of-line judging task. Subjects were 70 college students. Nadler found a correlation of .48 between F Scale scores and frequency of yielding to incorrect group judgments about the line lengths.

At the Institute of Personality Assessment and Research at the University of California, a three-day assessment of 90 men was reported by Crutchfield [1955]. One of the procedures for 50 of the subjects dealt with conformity in groups of five men each (the other 40 served as controls). Slides were projected on a wall directly in front of the subjects, and each slide presented a question calling for a judgment by the subject. Some were perceptual judgments such as length of lines; some were matters of opinion. Each subject responded in order by pressing a button to indicate his choice among a series of alternative answers. Whenever the subject was in the fifth position, the "other members of the group" responded incorrectly. Actually, the information about the choices of the other four was faked; the experimenter actually presented the information to them. In this investigation, 21 of these critical conformity trials were mixed in with neutral trials. The conformity score was the number of these 21 trials on which the subject responded as he believed the group had done. The range was from one to 17 with a mean of eight. Scores on the F Scale were found to correlate .39 with this measure of conformity.

Wells, Weinert, and Rubel [1956] studied conformity in terms of response to the drawing shown in Figure 8–2. In the control group, 62 college

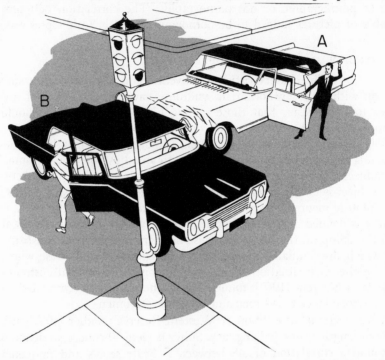

Fig. 8–2. *Which driver was at fault? (In the original drawing, the lower light was colored green and the upper light was colored red. Drawing by Nancy Secol.) (Adapted from Wells, et al., 1956, p. 134.)*

students were shown the picture and asked which driver was at fault in the accident. Only two blamed Driver B; the remaining 60 blamed Driver A. In the experimental group, another 62 students were shown the picture in a conformity situation. Each subject sat in a circle with four other students who appeared to be fellow subjects. Actually, they were stooges who said that Driver B was at fault; the real subjects responded last. In this situation, 21 subjects blamed B and 41 blamed A. The mean F Scale score of those who yielded to conformity pressure was significantly higher than for those who did not yield.

In spite of the number of investigations reporting a positive relationship between authoritarianism and conformity, we should note that for reasons which are as yet not determined, negative evidence is sometimes reported. For example, with two groups of Canadian undergraduates in two different conformity tasks, Gorfein [1961] found no relationship between scores on the F Scale and the tendency to conform.

In addition to conformity, other types of behavior in group situations have been investigated as relevant to authoritarianism. In two small group experiments [Haythorn, Couch, Haefner, Langham, and Carter, 1956; Haythorn, Haefner, Langham, Couch, and Carter, 1956], various combinations of authoritarians and equalitarians were formed into four-man groups. They were given the task of discussing, composing, role playing and recording a script for a movie scene involving a human relations problem. The entire task required about two and a half hours, and the interaction was observed through a one-way vision mirror. A great many differences were found in the rated behavior of High F vs. Low F leaders and followers. For example, authoritarian leaders were more likely to tell someone else to do something and to be autocratic, and they were less sensitive to others. Among other findings, equalitarian leaders were more likely to be sensitive, to show satisfaction, to ask for the expression of opinion, and to utilize effective intelligence. In general, the conclusion was that the equalitarian subjects were more effective in dealing with the task than were the authoritarians.

In a correlational study that has relevance for further experimental work on group behavior, Hollander [1954] predicted that authoritarians would be chosen by their peers as leaders in a military situation. A total of 268 cadets at the Naval School of Pre-Flight served as subjects. After three months of training, each subject was asked to nominate the three cadets whom they considered as best qualified and the three they considered least qualified for the position of student commander. As it turned out, leadership scores and authoritarianism were found to be *negatively* correlated $(r = -.43)$. The higher the F Scale score the less likely was the individual to be nominated as a leader, irrespective of the authoritarianism of the individual who made the nomination.

RIGIDITY AND RESISTANCE TO CHANGE

An hypothesis which has been made frequently is that authoritarians are more rigid in their behavior and are more resistant to change both externally and internally than are equalitarians.

In a number of experiments, rigidity has been defined as the inability to change set in order to solve the Einstellung water jar problems. In this task, a set is established by a series of arithmetical problems in which the requirement is to withdraw certain amounts of water from a large jar in order to obtain a specified quantity. A set is established by presenting a series of problems with a long solution such as jar B minus jar A minus jar C twice. Then a series of problems follows which may be solved by that same long method or more simply by jar A minus C. Those who continue using the long solution on the latter problems are defined as more rigid. Brown [1953] found that F Scale scores and Einstellung scores were related in ego-involved conditions (tests are "measures of intelligence and motivation"; the results are of "great importance") but not in relaxed conditions. Jackson, Messick, and Solley [1957] aroused achievement need in 54 Purdue undergraduates for whom F Scale scores were available and then administered the Einstellung task. The mean F Scale score of the 32 students who continued using the long solution was significantly higher than that of the 22 who switched to the short solution. On the other hand, French [1955] found no relationship between the F Scale and the Einstellung task under *either* relaxed or ego-involved conditions with a group of basic airmen at Lackland Air Force Base; she also reported no relationship between the F Scale and six other measures of rigidity. Once again, population differences may account for the inconsistent findings.

Resistance to changing one's opinion on the basis of new evidence was investigated by Mischel and Schopler [1959] who took advantage of a current newsworthy event to test an hypothesis. Shortly after Russia launched Sputnik I in 1957, students in two psychology classes were asked a number of questions including: "Which of the two countries (U.S. or U.S.S.R.) do you think is most likely to get to the moon first?" About three-fourths of the students chose the U.S.; choice was *not* related to authoritarianism. Within a month, Sputnik II carrying a live dog was launched; the U.S. had not yet had a successful satellite launching. At this point, when the questions were readministered, only about one-fourth of the students still chose the U.S.; the others changed their minds. It was suggested that those who still thought that the U.S. would reach the moon first were rigidly holding to their original position in the face of contradictory evidence. In each of the two classes, those who changed their predictions had significantly lower F Scale scores than those who maintained their original position.

A finding by Steiner and Johnson [1963] could be interpreted as further evidence of the resistance of authoritarians to change on the basis of new information. The subjects were 24 male students at the University of Illinois. After arriving at the laboratory, each was introduced to two other "subjects" who were actually working for the experimenter. After taking the F Scale, the subjects were informed that the research dealt with impression formation. In response to questions, Accomplice I indicated that he was a premedical student, a junior, and had a grade-point average better than B. Accomplice II reported that he was a physics major, a junior, and also had a grade-point average higher than B. The real subject answered similar questions about himself, and then each subject was asked to rate the other two students on 14 rating scales dealing with personality characteristics, knowledge, and skill. As a source of new information, a 32-item oral test of factual material was administered by the experimenter to each individual. Accomplice I gave unusual and incorrect answers to about one-third of the items while Accomplice II gave usual answers to all items. Presumably, this behavior provided mildly derogatory information concerning the knowledge or ability of Accomplice I. Following this procedure, each subject judged the others on the 14 rating scales a second time. In comparing the two sets of ratings, Steiner and Johnson found that the high F Scale subjects resisted the mildly derogatory information and rated the two partners equally favorably, just as they had done in the original rating. The low F Scale subjects lowered their evaluation of Accomplice I after seeing him perform less well on the oral test. While this finding is consistent with the other evidence concerning resistance to new information, the authors' interpretation is in terms of intolerance of trait inconsistency on the part of authoritarians. Perhaps these subjects found it hard to believe that "good people" possess both good and bad qualities.

Resistance of authoritarians to change on the basis of new evidence does not mean that they tend to maintain the same opinions under all conditions. It has been found, for example, that when an authority figure (an instructor) indicates a strong disapproval of the opinions given by students, the higher the score on the F Scale the greater the tendency of the students to change their opinions [Wright and Harvey, 1965].

Changes in Authoritarianism

Authoritarian characteristics are generally assumed to be relatively stable and enduring aspects of the individual. As with any personality variable, however, authoritarianism should be subject to alteration under suitable conditions. A few studies have been undertaken which constitute a beginning of the task of specifying those conditions under which authoritarian tendencies are likely to increase and those under which a change away from authoritarian beliefs occurs.

INCREASED AUTHORITARIANISM

With most psychological tests, changes in test scores are relatively easy to achieve by means of special instructions (for example, to respond in a particular uncharacteristic way) or by means of specially created conditions (for example, anxiety arousal). With the F Scale, Hollander [1954] administered the test to Naval Aviation Cadets under ordinary instructions and with instructions to respond to the scale *as though* it were "a test of military leadership potential" on which they wished to make a "good score." The authoritarian scores were significantly higher under the second conditions.

Perhaps more relevant to what is generally meant by change is an investigation by Kahn, Pollack, and Fink [1960] of the effects of convulsive therapy on authoritarianism in a group of 69 patients at Hillside Hospital in New York City. The F Scale was administered during the week before treatment began, on the day following the 12th treatment, and two weeks after treatment was terminated. The patients were divided into an experimental group of 59 subjects who received grand-mal convulsive therapy and a control group of 10 subjects who received subconvulsive electro-stimulation. All patients were treated three times a week for at least four weeks. Only in the experimental group did F Scale scores increase significantly during treatment. In addition, it was found that the greater the amount of brain dysfunction (measured by EEG recordings) induced by the treatment, the greater the increase in authoritarianism. Seven members of the control group were later placed in treatment; at that time they too revealed a significant increase in F Scale scores. Following treatment, the scores returned to their original level. Kahn, *et al.*, conclude:

The change in score with altered brain function is consistent with previous observations on the behavioral effects of convulsive therapy. In accord with our conceptual framework, greater agreement with F Scale items during treatment is related to increased stereotypy and difficulty in discrimination, as well as to increased acquiescence. This is part of a general process which has been noted in linguistic, perceptual and clinical behavioral measures [Kahn, *et al.*, 1960, p. 190].

Finally, a brief report is available of what appears to be a situation which might be expected to bring about a more lasting increase in authoritarianism. One would predict that interpersonal rewards in an authoritarian context should lead to ideological shifts in the direction of greater acceptance of authoritarian beliefs. Christie [1952] administered the F Scale to 182 white inductees in an Army basic-training center before and after completion of six weeks of infantry training. The group as a whole made no significant shift in authoritarianism. However, sociometric data were available concerning the degree to which each individual was accepted or rejected by other recruits and by the noncommissioned training personnel. The 55 recruits who were more accepted than rejected by *both* peers and superiors became significantly more authoritarian over the six-week period. Their mean score was not significantly different from that of the other 127 recruits on the original administration of the F Scale.

DECREASED AUTHORITARIANISM

One investigation which found a decrease in scores is some-what difficult to interpret. Aumack [1956] studied three groups of murderers at San Quentin prison who had been imprisoned for varying periods of time from less than a year to six years. He found a significant *negative* correlation of —.32 between authoritarianism and length of time in the prison.

An investigation with a firmer theoretical base was carried out by Singer [1960] as his doctoral dissertation at the University of Pennsylvania. Singer attempted to alter responses to the F Scale by means of verbal reinforcement of democratic statements made by the subjects. The F Scale and the E Scale were administered to 250 subjects. Of these, 48 females were chosen with pairs (matched on the basis of scores on both tests) serving in either the experimental or the control group. In the experiment, items of the F Scale were read to each subject who was asked to indicate agreement or disagreement with each. In the experimental group, each pro-democratic response was reinforced by the statement "good" or "right" from the experimenter. In the control group, no reinforcement was given. Singer found that in the experimental group, subjects gave more pro-democratic responses than they had previously. Generalization beyond the experimental situation is another matter, of course. Singer attempted to test this possibility with respect to responses to the E Scale. All subjects were readministered the E Scale immediately after the experimental situation. For half of each group, the experimenter remained in the room; for half, the experimenter was out of the room. Generalization of pro-democratic attitudes to the E Scale took place only in the condition where the experimenter remained in the room with the subject. When subjects were left alone, no change in ethnocentrism occurred. The results were interpreted in terms of social influence rather than as change in authoritarian beliefs.

A final investigation of change involves less experimental control than the Singer study but has a great deal of social significance if it proves to be a consistent finding. Levitt [1955] reported an investigation dealing with the influence of teachers' behavior on authoritarianism in grade-school children. The teachers in three grade-school classes (fourth, fifth, sixth) took part in a "causal" training program for a one-year period. The goal of this type of training program is indicated by the following definition:

Theoretically, a "causal" teacher is one who is pupil-centered rather than class-centered, who recognizes the dynamic complexity of human motivation in dealing with classroom problems, and whose reactions to classroom situations are based to a maximum possible extent on the motivations for pupil behavior rather than on that behavior itself. Concomitant with this general orientation are various attempts to assess pupil motivation, rather than to assign stereotyped causes to behavior [Levitt, 1955, p. 449].

Shortly after the teachers had finished the training program, the three experimental classes and six control-group classes (two fourth, two fifth, and two sixth grades) were administered the Children's Antidemocratic Tendency Scale. With differences in intelligence controlled statistically, the students in the experimental classes were found to be significantly less authoritarian than the students in the control classes at each grade level.

Current Status of Authoritarianism as a Personality Variable

The preceding overview of research dealing with the California F Scale shows clearly that authoritarianism has proven to be a useful concept as a dimension of personality. What issues seem to be most important in influencing future research on this variable?

RESPONSE SET

As suggested early in the chapter, the problem of acquiescent response set has plagued many users of the F Scale. To date, no satisfactory scale has been built which measures authoritarianism while controlling for any possible response set bias. Among others, Rorer [1965] has proposed that the entire issue has the crucial importance of a teapot tempest. After reviewing the evidence concerning set, Rorer says:

It seems safe to conclude that even if these studies are interpreted unequivocally as showing the effects of acquiescence, they show that effect to be small. Unfortunately, the long list of studies which have "demonstrated" the existence of acquiescence on the basis of dubious interpretations of statistically significant correlations of negligible practical value has created the illusion that acquiescence is widespread and of great importance, especially in the California F Scale [Rorer, 1965, p. 138].

Nevertheless, it would seem desirable to devise a sufficient number of test items with reversed content to permit the measurement of authoritarianism unconfounded, even in a minor way, by acquiescence.

FACTORS OF AUTHORITARIANISM

As is true with most widely used measuring instruments which were not constructed according to factor-analytic procedures, the F Scale has subsequently been factor analyzed by a number of investigators. When tests are found to contain more than one independent factor, one can argue that it would be advantageous to divide the test into a number of subscales so that independent dimensions of personality would not be combined inappropriately into one total score. With respect to the F Scale, Krug gives an example:

> If there exists a class of persons for whom *aggressive* is descriptive, but *conventional* is not, then a scale which treats the aggressive-but-not-conventional person as equivalent to the conventional-but-not-aggressive one, will necessarily obscure any relationships which exist for but one of these groups [Krug, 1961, p. 285].

Krug obtained a sample of 501 men and 203 women at Carnegie Tech and administered the F Scale in the standard way. Each item was correlated with each other item, and then six main factors were extracted from the resulting correlation matrix. The factors were labeled conventionalism (8 items), cynicism (6 items), sex and aggression (3 items), superstition and stereotypy (3 items), projectivity (6 items), and good versus bad people (3 items).

Krug suggested that each factor could serve as the starting point for scale construction or that factor subscores could be obtained from the present F Scale. Presumably, either approach could lead to higher relationships with other variables and hence better predictive power than is presently the case. In an investigation using the factor subscores rather than the overall F Scale score, Krug and Moyer [1961] correlated these "authoritarian subscales" with the various scales of the EPPS and the Guilford-Zimmerman Temperament Survey; a group of 684 college freshmen served as subjects. As hypothesized, the factor scores were differentially related to the other personality variables. For example, conventionalism was positively related to such variables as order, deference, endurance, restraint, and abasement and negatively related to autonomy and heterosexuality. Projectivity, on the other hand, was negatively related to objectivity, stability, friendliness, personal relations, and masculinity and positively related to succorance and aggression. These authors suggest that these findings provide evidence that new, factorially pure measures of the components of authoritarianism would lead to greater precision of measurement and greater theoretical clarity. Despite a number of factor-analytic studies of the original F Scale [for example, Bendig, 1959b; Bendig, 1960; Camilleri, 1959; Fructer, Rokeach, and Novak, 1958; O'Neil and Levinson, 1954], a new multi-factor approach to measurement has not as yet materialized.

DOGMATISM

Almost from its inception, the work on authoritarianism has been criticized as being influenced by the liberal biases of those conducting research in this area. The objectivity of the data is not questioned, but the types of behavior selected for study and the interpretations of research findings are characterized as having an anti-authoritarian basis. To the extent that this state of affairs represents the equalitarian, democratic, liberal values of many behavioral scientists, perhaps it is inevitable. If these values or biases lead investigators to overlook certain problems, greater objectivity would obviously be advantageous.

One possible example of such a tendency is the equating of certain general characteristics, such as rigidity, conventionalism, intolerance of ambiguity, and the like, with conservative or right-wing political philosophy. Quite likely, many of these same characteristics hold equally true for those with an extreme left-wing political orientation. A major research effort to investigate this possibility has been undertaken by Milton Rokeach at Michigan State University. The interest here was in the structure rather than the content of beliefs. "A person may adhere to communism, existentialism, Freudianism, or the 'new conservatism' in a relatively open or in a relatively closed manner" [Rokeach, 1960, p. 6].

To measure this more general characteristic of open- and closed-mindedness, Rokeach devised the Dogmatism Scale which contains such items as "In a heated discussion I generally become so absorbed in what I am going to say that I forget to listen to what the others are saying," and "A group which tolerates too much difference of opinion among its own members cannot exist for long." Research with the instrument has demonstrated that left-of-center groups (for example, communists) and right-of-center groups (for example, Catholics) both score high on the Dogmatism Scale. Only the right-of-center groups score high on the F Scale. In one study of English political groups, the communist party members scored lowest of all groups on the F Scale and E Scale and highest of all groups on the Dogmatism Scale.

Though more research data will help to clarify these relationships, probably many of the characteristics which have been ascribed to right-wing authoritarians are, in fact, characteristic of the dogmatic, closed-minded individual of whatever political persuasion. Future research should be able to investigate such variables independently.

EXPERIMENTAL INVESTIGATIONS

Finally, we should note that experimental investigations of antecedents, dynamics, and the conditions of change with respect to authoritarianism have been relatively neglected when compared to the number of correlational studies. Much is yet to be learned about the authoritarian personality, and the experimental method is likely to provide much of the needed information.

Summary

Authoritarianism refers to an attitudinal system which consists of a number of interrelated, antidemocratic sentiments. An attitude is a predisposition to respond either positively or negatively toward an object or a class of objects. Attitudes tend to be grouped into ideological clusters which are a part of the structure of personality. Research on authoritarianism as such a cluster of attitudes was pioneered by Adorno, Frenkel-Brunswik, Levinson, and Sanford just after World War II.

The underlying theory of the nature of authoritarianism had its origin in diverse sources. Authoritarians were described as characterized by conventionalism, authoritarian submission, authoritarian aggression, destruction and cynicism, power and "toughness," superstition and stereotypy, antiintraception, projectivity, and an exaggerated concern with sex.

Questionnaire items were written by Adorno, *et al.*, in an attempt to tap the various aspects of authoritarianism. A preliminary scale was subjected to an item-analysis, using the Discriminatory Power technique. The best items were retained, some items were rewritten, and some new ones added. This second form of the scale was again item-analyzed. A third and final scale retained the best of those items plus three new ones. The average split-half reliability was found to be .90. All of the items are worded in such a way that agreement is scored in the authoritarian direction. This raised the possibility that scores on the F Scale are in part a function of authoritarianism and in part a function of acquiescent response set. Ideally, a balanced scale will be built in which set is controlled by having half of the items worded so that disagreement indicates authoritarianism.

All of the research on the antecedents of this dimension has dealt with child-rearing attitudes and practices. On the basis of early observational data, it was hypothesized that authoritarian-producing families are characterized by expectations of obedience from the children, parents who are status-ridden, parental anxiety about conformity, and intolerance of socially unacceptable behavior. Subsequent research has found positive relationships between F Scale scores and traditional family ideology among adults, the use of nonlove-oriented disciplinary techniques among mothers, perception of parents as punitive among fifth-graders, authoritarian-control parental attitudes among female adults, and restrictiveness rather than permissiveness in child-rearing attitudes among military officers. One investigation utilized families consisting of mother, father, and offspring. Rather than traditional family ideology, the best predictor of offspring authoritarianism was parental authoritarianism.

Research on personality structure has demonstrated correlations between F Scale scores and a number of other behaviors. Authoritarianism is positively related to prejudice as defined by anti-Semitism, ethnocentrism, and anti-Negro attitudes. Hostility is also characteristic of authoritarians in that, compared with equalitarians, they indicate more aggression toward outgroup characters and more friendly acts with ingroup characters in their dreams and obtain higher scores on the Manifest Hostility Scale. In terms of overt aggressive behavior, a war game situation evoked greater aggression from authoritarians only under very specific conditions. With respect to political and economic beliefs, authoritarians are found to be conservative, to be against socialized medicine, to prefer conservative rather than liberal political candidates regardless of party label, to sign a controversial loyalty oath, and to be accepting of military ideology. While authoritarians are often described as maladjusted, evidence on this point is somewhat contradictory. Compared with equalitarians, those high on the F Scale respond no differently to an incomplete sentences test and are *less* defensive, hysterical, and paranoid on the MMPI. Scores of prisoners are higher than those of the general population. Authoritarian mothers respond to a parent-attitude scale as do mothers of problem children, while both schizophrenics and mothers of schizophrenics are high in authoritarianism. When intolerance of ambiguity is defined by responses to paper and pencil tests of this characteristic or by speed in adopting a norm in the autokinetic situation, F Scale scores are positively related to ambiguity intolerance. A great many findings indicate a negative relationship between authoritarianism and both intelligence and educational attainment. Compared to equalitarians, those high on the F Scale are more likely to be Protestant or Roman Catholic than to be Jewish or unaffiliated with any church and are more likely to attend church regularly.

Research on the dynamics of authoritarianism has been of several types. In a perceptual defense situation, authoritarians have relatively more difficulty perceiving sexual and aggressive auditory stimuli. Responding to two movies in which a female star appears, authoritarians rated her as significantly more sexual than did equalitarians and as more sexual than kindly; similarly they evaluate art work having sexual content as more pornographic. In a wide variety of conformity experiments, authoritarians have been found more responsive to group pressure than equalitarians. Other investigations find authoritarians less effective in dealing with a group task than equalitarians and less likely to be perceived as good leaders. Rigidity as measured by the Einstellung water jar problem is generally found to be characteristic of authoritarians, as is resistance to changing their opinions on the basis of new evidence. Authoritarians are more likely to change their opinions than are equalitarians in response to demands from an authority figure.

A handful of investigations have been concerned with changes in authoritarianism. Increases in F Scale scores have been found when subjects are told that the scale is a test of military leadership potential on which they should try to obtain a good score, during the course of convulsive electroshock therapy, and among recruits accepted by both peers and superiors during infantry training. Decreases in F Scale scores have been found to be a function of length of time murderers had served in prison, of reinforcement of pro-democratic responses by an experimenter, and among children whose teacher had taken part in a "causal" training program.

Among the issues which may influence future research in this area are attempts to control for acquiescent response set, attempts to build factorially pure subscales to differentiate various aspects of authoritarianism, attempts to separate the structure of beliefs (for example, dogmatism) from the content of beliefs (for example, liberal vs. conservative), and a greater stress on experimental rather than correlational investigations.

CHAPTER 9

Need for Achievement

Achievement need is a learned motive to compete and to strive for success. Because almost any activity from gardening to managing an industrial organization can be viewed in terms of competition and success versus failure, the need to achieve influences behavior in a large number of quite diverse situations. And because it is a *learned* motive, there are wide differences among individuals in their past experiences and hence in their motivation with respect to achievement.

Traditionally, motivational concepts have been of great importance in theories of personality, and often they play a crucial role [Hall and Lindzey, 1957]. Most accounts of behavior include some sort of moving or driving or energizing force which propels the organism. Brown [1961, p. 24] notes: "The ubiquity of the concept of motivation, in one guise or another, is nevertheless surprising when we consider that its meaning is often scandalously vague." Before discussing the research which has dealt with the achievement motive, we shall take a brief look at the general concept of motivation.

As was noted in Chapter 1, such motivational propositions as "man eats *because* he is hungry" are not explanations at all but circular descriptions. If, however, we define hunger in terms of independent conditions, such as hours of food deprivation, the proposition becomes predictively meaningful. That is, "man eats when he has been deprived of food for X period of time." Since the latter sort of statement refers to observable variables, what purpose is served by throwing in a concept such as hunger drive? Actually, a drive is simply a higher-order generalization which permits us to conceptualize a wide variety of different behaviors or different

S-R sequences within a single framework. Thus, eating hamburgers, driving to a grocery store, opening a can of soup, ordering a meal in a restaurant, placing a dime in a candy machine, turning right in a T-maze, and pressing a lever in a Skinner box all have a common conceptual component if we use a motivational term such as hunger. What else is involved in the use of motivational concepts? (1) The organism's state under specific conditions may be described in terms of *drive level.* As hours of deprivation increase, hunger drive increases. (2) The fact that the organism responds differently to different motivational conditions (for example, food deprivation, water deprivation, pain) leads to the concept of *drive stimulus,* a hypothetical internal cue which leads the organism to make the appropriate external response. For example, rats can learn to make one response to obtain food and a different response to obtain water; under conditions of food deprivation or water deprivation, the appropriate response is made. Finally, (3) there is the almost limitless variety of *instrumental responses* which may be learned as ways of obtaining (4) a given *goal* which reduces or satisfies the drive, as was suggested above. Not only are there many alternate instrumental responses, but many different goals may satisfy the same drive.

A distinction is usually made between *physiological* or *primary drives,* such as hunger and thirst and sex, and *learned* or *secondary drives,* such as fear [Miller, 1948] and affiliation [Shipley and Veroff, 1952] and need for achievement [McClelland, *et al.,* 1953]. Learned drives develop as a function of the specific experiences of the organism and could be defined simply as learned responses, but the concept of "drive" is useful here for the same reasons that the concept of primary drive is useful. That is, a learned drive is a higher-order generalization which allows us to tie together a variety of stimuli and responses. Achievement need, for example, should be a useful concept (1) if we can specify the stimulus conditions under which drive level is increased or decreased, (2) if subjects distinguish between this drive and other motivational conditions in terms of making differential responses, (3) if instrumental responses can be learned as ways of obtaining (4) identifiable goals which satisfy the drive. For example, we might attempt to arouse the achievement motive by telling subjects engaged in a group task that their individual performance on the task is a predictor of future success and that they should try to do better than their fellow group members. These instructions should lead to different behavior than instructions involving other motivations, such as stressing the importance of getting along well with and being liked by the other group members. The subjects who succeed in outperforming their competitors after achievement arousal should be better satisfied than subjects who fail. Finally, such specific goal-directed responses as increased effort, persistence, and the like should be observed under achievement-arousal.

Since our interest here is in achievement need as a personality variable, the major emphasis will be on the determination of individual differences in the strength of the motive. Presumably, the stimulus conditions which increase the level of this drive do not affect all individuals in the same way because of differences in past learning experiences. Since we cannot deal directly with these past experiences, the measurement of individual differences in motives follows the same pattern as the measurement of any other personality variable. A standard stimulus (a test) is presented to the subjects, and their responses are utilized as the measure of the variable in question.

Given this background, we will now trace some of the initial work which led to the current research on achievement need as a personality variable.

Theoretical Background of the Concept of Achievement Need

MURRAY, n ACH, AND THE THEMATIC APPERCEPTION TEST

Historical Background. Henry A. Murray (1893–   ) is a physician, chemist, psychoanalyst, and psychologist who has described his primary motivation as ". . . a stout affection for human beings coupled with a consuming interest in their emotions and evaluations, their imaginations and beliefs, their purposes and plans, their endeavors, failures, and achievements" [Murray, 1959, p. 9]. Murray was born in New York City, was graduated from Harvard University in 1915 as a history major, and then entered medical school at Columbia. After receiving the M.D. degree in 1919, he spent two years as an intern in surgery and then five years working in research in the areas of physiology and the chemistry of embryology. This work culminated in a Ph.D. degree in physiological chemistry at Cambridge University.

This background is obviously a nonpsychological one, and the change in Murray's career plans took place as the result of a number of factors. He has indicated that one determinant was his greater interest in the motives and thoughts of human beings than in the physiological aspects of their bodies. In addition, he had come to believe that human personality was the major problem of our time and ". . . not very far from proving itself an evolutionary failure . . ." [Murray, 1959, p. 11], that psychoanalysis was making great progress in the study of mental processes, and that he was personally best suited in terms of temperament to work in an area on the unknown frontiers of science. His early contacts with the academic psychology of the day had left him disappointed, however, and he turned instead to the medical practitioners of psychotherapy as a source of knowledge. A major influence was his first contact with Carl Jung in 1925:

. . . I had no scales to weigh out Dr. Jung, the first full-blooded, spherical—
and Goethian, I should say—intelligence I had ever met, the man whom the
judicious Prinzhorn called "the ripest fruit on the tree of psycho-analytical
knowledge." We talked for hours, sailing down the lake and smoking before
the hearth of his Faustian retreat. "The great floodgates of the wonder-world
swung open," and I saw things that my philosophy had never dreamt of.
Within a month a score of bi-horned problems were resolved, and I went
off decided on depth psychology. I had experienced the unconscious, something
not to be drawn out of books [Murray, 1940, p. 153].

Even though lacking formal training in academic psychology, Murray
became an Instructor in psychology at Harvard in 1927 and the following
year became an Assistant Professor and director of the Psychological Clinic
there. His training in psychoanalysis under Franz Alexander and Hans
Sachs was completed in 1937. There at the Harvard Psychological Clinic
in the 1930's he and his students and colleagues from a variety of fields
undertook a large-scale investigation of human personality. A portion of
this work led to the present approach to achievement need and will be described shortly.

In 1943, Murray joined the Army Medical Corps. He established and
directed a project designed to screen and assess candidates for the Office
of Strategic Services. His work in this connection brought him the Legion
of Merit in 1946. After his return to Harvard in 1947 and until his retire-
ment in 1962, his teaching and research interests continued to encompass
the fields of personality and clinical psychology.

Explorations in Personality. The multi-faceted work of
Murray's group at Harvard culminated in a book, *Explorations in Personality* [Murray, 1938], which was to have considerable impact on the
field of personality. The particular approach adopted in studying personality had a number of antecedents. Murray's unusual background, for example, was reflected in several ways. He has indicated that the practice
of medicine taught him that in order to arrive at a valid diagnosis, one
must inquire about the patient's memories of interior sensations and emotions. He says, ". . . I have never ceased to elicit direct expressions and
reports of interior experiences—somatic, emotional, and intellectual—not
only as sources of indications of overt actions to be executed in the future,
but as indications of occurrences that are intrinsically important" [Murray,
1959, p. 10]. Medical practice also left him with the conviction that a
group of trained collaborators using a wide variety of assessment techniques
on a single subject could arrive at a more accurate appraisal than could a
single investigator with a limited methodological range.

In studying "personology," the unit with which the Murray group chose
to work was the life history of a single individual (or as much of it as could
be sampled). The study of the responses of a great many individuals to a

specific stimulus was rejected in favor of the study of the behavior of a few individuals in as many situations as possible. Beginning with existing personality theories, the goal was to test hypotheses, develop new methodologies, discover empirical relationships, and in the process develop a new personality theory. The philosophical basis of Murray's approach to a science of personality is suggested by the following:

Now, at every stage in the growth of a science there is, it seems, an appropriate balance between broad speculation and detailed measurement. For instance, in the infancy of a very complex science—and surely psychology is young and complicated—a few mastering generalizations can be more effective in advancing knowledge than a mass of carefully compiled data. For in the wake of intuition comes investigation directed at crucial problems rather than mere unenlightened fact-collecting. Here we may point to the undeniable enrichment of our understanding and the impetus to further studies which has come from psychoanalytic theory. In its present stage personology seems to call for men who can view things in the broad; that is, who can apperceive occurrences in terms of the interplay of general forces. A man who has been trained in the exact sciences will find himself somewhat at a loss, if not at a disadvantage. He will find it difficult to fall in with the loose flow of psychologic thought. He will find nothing that is hard and sharp. And so if he continues to hold rigidly to the scientific ideal, to cling to the hope that the results of his researches will approach in accuracy and elegance the formulations of the exact disciplines, he is doomed to failure. He will end his days in the congregation of futile men, of whom the greater number, contractedly withdrawn from critical issues, measure trifles with sanctimonious precision [Murray, 1938, pp. 21–22].

The specific project described in *Explorations in Personality* involved small groups of about 13 subjects at a time who came to the Clinic three or four hours a week over a period of several months. The subjects were examined individually on as many as two dozen different tests and in experimental situations by as many as 24 experimenters. Subjects wrote autobiographies, filled out questionnaires, took ability tests, were given an hypnotic test and a level of aspiration test, responded to projective devices such as the Rorschach and the TAT, were placed in an emotional conditioning situation with measures of galvanic skin response and tremor, and took part in experiments involving such things as cheating, frustration, and memory for success versus failure. The observations and measurements of each subject's behavior in these and other situations were then put together by a five-man Diagnostic Council, and the end-product was a psychograph or reconstruction of the subject's personality from birth up to the present time.

The personality theory which emerged from this project is in many respects an eclectic one, borrowing terms and concepts from many theorists and combining them with original notions. The most influential portion of Murray's theory has been his approach to needs. As Hall and Lindzey indicate:

It is in the representation of man's striving, seeking, desiring, wishing, and willing that Murray's contributions to psychological theory have been most distinctive. One might fairly say that his position is primarily a motivational psychology. This focusing upon the motivational process is perfectly congruent with Murray's conviction that the study of man's directional tendencies holds the key to understanding human behavior [Hall and Lindzey, 1957, p. 171].

n *Ach.* One sort of influence on Murray's work from his medical and biological days not yet mentioned was his conviction that an early step in any discipline should be a classification of the entities and processes with which one is dealing. His taxonomy of human needs is one example of this concern. He distinguished and defined 28 needs, each designated by abbreviations such as *n* Aff (affiliation need), *n* Dom (dominance need), *n* Sex (sexual need), and the one which will be the focus of this chapter, *n* Ach or achievement need. This motive, *n* Ach, was defined as ". . . the desire or tendency to do things as rapidly and/or as well as possible" [Murray, 1938, p. 164]. Further, this need was described in a number of ways. For example:

Desires and Effects: To accomplish something difficult. To master, manipulate or organize physical objects, human beings, or ideas. To do this as rapidly, and as independently as possible. To overcome obstacles and attain a high standard. To excel one's self. To rival and surpass others. To increase self-regard by the successful exercise of talent. . . .

Actions: To make intense, prolonged and repeated efforts to accomplish something difficult. To work with singleness of purpose towards a high and distant goal. To have the determination to win. To try to do everything well. To be stimulated to excel by the presence of others, to enjoy competition. To exert will power; to overcome boredom and fatigue . . .

Fusions and Subsidiations: The *n* Ach fuses readily and naturally with every other need. Indeed, it is considered by some that the *n* Achievement—often called the "will-to-power"—is the dominant psychogenic need. Perhaps in most cases it is subsidiary to an inhibited need for Recognition. . . .

Social Forms: Every recognized profession or occupation may be regarded as a channel for the *n* Achievement [Murray, 1938, pp. 164–165].

In the questionnaire which was given to the subjects, the items designed to measure this need were:

1. I am driven to ever greater efforts by an unslaked ambition.

2. I feel that nothing else which life can offer is a substitute for great achievement.

3. I feel that my future peace and self-respect depend upon my accomplishing some notable piece of work.

4. I set difficult goals for myself which I attempt to reach.

5. I work with energy at the job that lies before me instead of dreaming about the future.

6. When my own interests are at stake, I become entirely concentrated upon my job and forget my obligations to others.

7. I enjoy relaxation wholeheartedly only when it follows the successful completion of a substantial piece of work.

8. I feel the spirit of competition in most of my activities.

9. I work like a slave at everything I undertake until I am satisfied with the result.

10. I enjoy work as much as play.

Thematic Apperception Test. One of the assessment procedures developed in the Harvard Clinic, the TAT, was a projective device which was to become a standard instrument in the practice of clinical psychology and which also became the object of intensive research interest. Morgan and Murray describe it:

The purpose of this procedure is to stimulate literary creativity and thereby evoke fantasies that reveal covert and unconscious complexes.

The test is based upon the well-recognized fact that when a person interprets an ambiguous social situation he is apt to expose his own personality as much as the phenomenon to which he is attending. Absorbed in his attempt to explain the objective occurrence, he becomes naively unconscious of himself and of the scrutiny of others and, therefore, defensively less vigilant. To one with double hearing, however, he is disclosing certain inner tendencies and cathexes: wishes, fears, and traces of past experiences. Another fact which was relied upon in devising the present method is this: that a great deal of written fiction is the conscious or unconscious expression of the author's experiences or fantasies.

The original plan was to present subjects with a series of pictures each of which depicted a dramatic event of some sort with instructions to interpret the action in each picture and make a plausible guess as to the preceding events and the final outcome. It was anticipated that in the performance of this task a subject would necessarily be forced to project some of his own fantasies into the material and thus reveal his more prevailing thematic tendencies. As the subjects who took this test were asked to interpret each picture—that is, to apperceive the plot or dramatic structure exhibited by each picture—we named it the "Thematic Apperception Test." Only by experience did we discover that much more of the personality is revealed if the S is asked to create a dramatic fiction rather than to guess the probable facts [Morgan and Murray, 1938, pp. 530–531].

The investigators settled upon a set of pictures which were administered as a test of "creative imagination." Subjects were instructed to make up a plot or story for which each picture could be used as an illustration. As one of the multiple procedures used in the Harvard project, the TAT was interpreted in terms of many variables, including the expression of needs. The authors suggested: "One of the chief virtues is that the subject reveals some of his innermost fantasies without being aware that he is doing so" [Morgan and Murray, 1938, p. 545].

For Murray's group, then, the TAT was only one assessment procedure among many, and achievement need only one personality variable among many. More specific attempts to use fantasy material to measure n Ach were not made until the late 1940's with the development of a quantified n Ach scoring system for thematic apperception stories.

Construction of the n Ach Scoring System

THE WESLEYAN PROJECT

Taking as a starting point the work of Murray, David C. McClelland (1917–   ) initiated a research project at Wesleyan University in 1947 which resulted in an extremely fruitful approach to the study of the need to achieve. Wesleyan was also the institution at which McClelland did his undergraduate work. He received the A.B. degree in 1938, the year in which *Explorations in Personality* was published. He went to Missouri for an M.A. in 1939, and then entered the graduate school at Yale. After the Ph.D. degree was awarded him in 1941, McClelland spent a year as an Instructor at the Connecticut College for Women before returning to Wesleyan for a very productive 14 years during which time his initial work on n Ach was carried out. In 1956, he moved to Harvard as chairman of the Center for Research in Personality and then as chairman of the Department of Social Relations.

From 1947 to 1952 the achievement motive was the central concern of the Wesleyan group working on a project sponsored by the Office of Naval Research. This work was summarized in book form in 1953 by McClelland, John W. Atkinson, Russell A. Clark, and Edgar L. Lowell. Interestingly enough, though they utilized Murray's concept of n Ach and Murray's TAT as a measurement technique, their approach to the study of personality was in dramatic contrast to Murray's:

. . . We have discovered–that concentration on a limited research problem is not necessarily narrowing; it may lead ultimately into the whole of psychology. In personality theory there is inevitably a certain impatience—a desire to solve every problem at once so as to get the "whole" personality in focus. We have proceeded the other way. By concentrating on one problem, on *one motive*, we have found in the course of our study that we have learned not only a lot about the achievement motive but other areas of personality as well. So we feel that this book can be used as one basis for evaluating the degree to which a "piecemeal" approach to personality is profitable, an approach which proceeds to build up the total picture out of many small experiments by a slow process of going from fact to hypothesis and back to fact again [McClelland, *et al.*, 1953, p. vi].

At Wesleyan, undergraduates are expected to become directly involved in research during much of their college careers. Thus, most of the data in the original *n* Ach project was collected by college seniors working on Honors theses or by first-year graduate students. In addition, the various individuals involved in the project were given a considerable degree of autonomy in conducting research on problems each thought to be significant, so long as *n* Ach was involved.

One source of impetus for research on *n* Ach was the belief that experimental work on secondary or acquired drives at the human level had been relatively neglected by psychologists. The TAT was chosen as a measuring device because fantasy, which is analogous to Freud's use of dreams, appeared to be a good place to look for the effects of motivation. Second, a long period of experimental work with animals suggested the usefulness of being able to manipulate motives experimentally. Thus, the original plan was to devise a way experimentally to manipulate a secondary drive and to determine the effect of this manipulation on fantasy material produced by the subject. Following this procedure, the researchers would be able to determine the specific aspects of fantasy which were indicators of the aroused motive rather than simply to rely on guesses about the meaning of such material.

As a first step, Atkinson and McClelland [1948] started with a primary motive about which a good deal is known (hunger) and ascertained the effects of food-deprivation on thematic apperception stories. A group of 81 male Naval personnel at a submarine training school was divided into groups that had been without food for one hour, four hours, and 16 hours. Seven thematic apperception pictures were projected on a screen, and the subjects wrote stories in response to each. Significant relationships were found between hours of deprivation and such content categories as an increase in the presence of deprivation themes in the stories and of activity successful in overcoming food deprivation, and a decrease in the amount of eating in the stories and in invitations to eating.

Given this success in measuring *n* Food with fantasy material, the experimenters moved on to the construction of an *n* Ach scoring system.

NEED FOR ACHIEVEMENT

First reported in 1949 by McClelland, Clark, Roby, and Atkinson, the test construction procedure followed the general plan of having groups under achievement-arousing conditions and groups under nonarousing conditions each write thematic apperception stories, of scoring these stories for a number of achievement-related categories, and of determining statistically which categories were reliable indicators of aroused n Ach. For a number of reasons, only male students were used in the group of over 200 subjects.[1]

The four pictures which were employed are described as follows in the order in which they were presented to the subjects:

1. Two men ("inventors") in a shop working at a machine.
2. Boy in checked shirt at a desk, an open book in front of him.
3. "Father-son." Card 7BM from the Murray Thematic Apperception Test.
4. Boy with vague operation scene in background. Card 8BM from the Murray Thematic Apperception Test [McClelland, *et al.*, 1953, p. 375].

The subjects were told:

This is a test of your creative imagination. A number of pictures will be projected on the screen before you. You will have twenty seconds to look at the picture and then about four minutes to make up a story about it. Notice that there is one page for each picture. The same four questions are asked. They will guide your thinking and enable you to cover all the elements of a plot in the time allotted. Plan to spend about a minute on each question. I will keep time and tell you when it is about time to go on to the next question for each story. You will have a little time to finish your story before the next picture is shown.

Obviously there are no right or wrong answers, so you may feel free to make up any kind of a story about the pictures that you choose. Try to make them vivid and dramatic, for this is a test of *creative* imagination. Do not merely describe the picture you see. Tell a story about it. Work as fast as you can in order to finish in time. Make them interesting. Are there any questions? If you need more space for any question, use the reverse side [McClelland, *et al.*, 1953, p. 98].

Each story was written on a piece of paper containing these four questions:

1. What is happening? Who are the persons?

2. What has led up to this situation? That is, what has happened in the past?

---

[1] The achievement motive in females apparently has different characteristics than in males, and almost all of the work described in this chapter is confined to male subjects. The problem of female n Ach is discussed at the end of this chapter.

3. What is being thought? What is wanted? By whom?

4. What will happen? What will be done?

A number of different procedures were employed in an attempt to find a way successfully to arouse the achievement motive: giving the subjects a success experience, a failure experience, a combination of the two, and so forth. In the relaxed condition, the experimenter was introduced as a graduate student gathering data on some paper and pencil tests; he acted as if he were not taking the situation seriously but only trying out some ideas. The tests included anagram tasks, a scrambled words task, motor-perseveration tests, and a task that involved writing backwards and forwards. The neutral condition was like the relaxed condition except that the experimenter presented the tests as a serious and meaningful project. The achievement-oriented condition involved instructions that a 12-minute anagrams task was a measure of intelligence used for evaluating officer candidates in World War II. In the success, failure, and success-failure conditions, the achievement-oriented instructions were used. In addition, subjects took the same tests used in the relaxed condition. After getting the test results, the subjects were given fake norms which led them to believe that they had done very well, very poorly, or very well on the first half and very poorly on the second half. All groups were given the TAT cards immediately afterward.

A number of categories of story content were scored by judges, and then the frequency of each content category occurring in the various experimental conditions was compared by means of analysis of variance. In the major analysis, the relaxed, neutral, and achievement-oriented conditions were compared. Each scoring category which yielded significant differences across groups was then defined as a fantasy response indicative of n Ach. The scoring system went through later refinements, and only the final version will be described here. A total of 11 categories is scored $+1$ each if they appear in a story, and one category is scored -1 if it appears. Thus, on the four stories, one can receive a total score as low as -4 and as high as 44.

The 12 categories which were found to vary across experimental conditions will be described. After each category, an example of the kind of material yielding this score will be given:

-1. Unrelated Imagery (UI) is scored for stories in which there is no reference to an achievement goal.

    Example: A young fellow is sitting in a plaid shirt and resting his head on one hand. He appears to be thinking of something. His eyes appear a little sad. He may have been involved in something that he is very sorry for. The boy is thinking over what he has done. By the look in his eyes we can tell that he is very sad about it. I believe that the boy will break down any minute if he continues in the manner in which he is now going.

+1. Achievement Imagery (AI) is scored for stories in which an achievement goal (success in competition with some standard of excellence) is included.

Example: A group of medical students are watching their instructor perform a simple operation on a cadaver. A few of the students are very sure they will be called on to assist Dr. Hugo. In the last few months they have worked and studied. The skillful hands of the surgeon perform their work. The instructor tells his class *they must be able to work with speed and cannot make many mistakes.* When the operation is over, a smile comes over the group. Soon they will be leading men and women in the field.

+1. Need (N) is scored if someone in the story states the desire to reach an achievement goal.

Example: A man is experimenting with a new alloy of iron, while his assistant looks on. Many years of research have led up to this situation. The two men have experimented and failed many times over but have stuck to their job. *Both men are hoping that at last they have succeeded* in making the strongest steel possible. They will test their alloy and find that it meets with their expectations. It will then be refined in great quantities for use the world over.

+1. Instrumental Activity (I) is scored if the activity of at least one of the characters in the story indicates that something is being done to attain an achievement goal, whether successfully or unsuccessfully.

Example: James Watt and his assistant are working on the assembly of the first steam engine. They are working out the hole for a slide valve of the first successful steam engine . . . All previous experiments have failed. Successful use of steam has not been accomplished. If the slide valve works, the first compound steam engine will be harnessed. *James Watt is pulling the pinion in place for the slide valve.* His assistant is watching. The purpose is to make a pinion to hold the yoke in place which will operate the slide valve. If the slide valve works satisfactorily, they will perfect it for use in factories and for use on the railway. *It will work.*

+1. Positive Anticipatory Goal State (Ga+) is scored if someone in the story anticipates goal attainment.

Example: The older man is advising the younger one on the choice of occupation. The older man is a doctor and *he sees prospects in the young man to* become a great surgeon. The younger man has just returned from the Army, and he is disappointed with the attitudes of the civilians and has given up hope of being a surgeon. The young man is thinking that it is useless to become a great healer if people are going to fight wars which amount to nothing more than mass murder. The older man will convince him that the world is not as bad as he believes, and he will return to medical school.

+1. Negative Anticipatory Goal State (Ga−) is scored if someone in the story anticipates frustration or failure with respect to the goal.

Example: A father is telling his son not to worry while in college because his health is more important, but to become a professional man and carry on in his father's footsteps. The son has flunked a few exams and feels very bad about it. His father has noticed his unusual behavior and thinks he should talk with his son. *The boy thinks he just can't make it through college,* but he really wants to. His father wants him to continue and become a professional man. The boy will go back to college full of resolution for better studying, and he won't let the work get the best of him, for "it is not life that matters, but the courage you bring to it."

+1. Personal Obstacle or Block (Bp) is scored when the story mentions that the progress of goal-directed activity is blocked by something for which the individual himself is responsible.

Example: A boy is daydreaming. He is a student who knows he has to study. *In the past he has had poor marks.* Now he realizes he must study harder or else his schoolwork will just be a waste of time. He thinks of the last mark and what will happen if he doesn't improve. This man will really study and prove to himself he is not a failure but will make good.

+1. Environmental Obstacle or Block (Bw) is scored when the story mentions that the goal-directed activity is blocked by something in the environment.

Example: Lawyer and client in conversation. The younger man came in for advice. He had a going business and was prospering, but a *new industry is driving his product off the market.* "Shall I be forced to give up?" "Shall I sue?" "What are my chances of success?" The lawyer explains that competition is legitimate and can't be sued. The man will go out and instead of selling, will convert his industry to a specialty along the same line only one which is not jeopardized. He will try to sell out.

+1. Positive Affective State (G+) is scored if someone in the story is described as feeling positively about goal attainment.

Example: A father is talking to his son. *He is telling him that he is proud of him because he is doing so well in school.* He wants his son to stay on the ball and keep getting good marks. He just knows his son will be a very successful businessman. The son has just come home from college after pulling honors all through the year. He never goes out and is always in his room studying. He never partakes in sports. They are both dreaming of what the son will be in the future, a successful businessman. The son can just see himself as the president of the biggest baby rattle company in the U.S. The boy will become meagerly and puny because of his studying. He will never have any fun out of life. He will always be a mope. Is it worth it?

+1. Negative Affective State (G−) is scored if someone in the story experiences an unpleasant feeling associated with failure to attain an achievement goal.

Example: This is the night before the big economics exam, and Johnny Jones is worried. He's got to get an A. He has been taking it easy all year and now wants to bring his average up with a good grade. He is *thinking what a damn fool he has been*, and why didn't he study the months before. He must get an A or he will have to take the course over. If he has to take the course over, he knows his father will give him the devil for not working hard the first part of the year.

+1. Nurturant Press (Nup) is scored when there are personal forces in the story which aid the character in his on-going achievement-related activity.

Example: The young boy is dreaming of what he hopes to do for the future. He is thinking of a great surgeon who saved his father's life and wishes to become such a man. His father needed an emergency operation. He watched the surgeon save his father's life. He is thinking he must work hard to reach his goal. But he is sure that is what he wants to do in life. He will see the surgeon again and *will be encouraged in his ambitions by the great man.*

+1. Achievement Thema (Ach Th) is scored when the achievement imagery is so elaborated that it becomes the central plot or theme of the story.

Example: A young boy is daydreaming about the past wars in which doctors have participated. He is not sure of the course to follow. He cannot decide whether or not to become a doctor. He is thinking about John Drake, the great surgeon of World War I, and his great feats in it. He was certainly a remarkable man. The boy will finally become a famous surgeon himself and in turn will be an incentive to the future doctors of the world to work hard and be interested only in the welfare of mankind [McClelland, *et al.*, 1953, pp. 110–138].

In the test construction procedure, an experimental manipulation was made of the achievement motive to identify and to validate those aspects of fantasy material which are affected by motive arousal. In most of the subsequent research in which n Ach is conceptualized as a personality variable, the thematic apperception pictures are given and the subjects' stories written in a neutral situation. The assumption is made, then, that differences in achievement fantasy in a neutral situation reflect differences in the characteristic level of this motive for each individual. Those who obtain very high n Ach scores in a neutral situation, for example, are assumed to function normally at a level attained by the experimental subjects only after an arousal experience manipulated by the experimenter. One can see that n Ach varies as a dependent variable in response to stimulus changes, but that in a standard neutral situation individual differences occur in the strength of n Ach. The latter sort of variation will be of most concern to us here.

RELIABILITY

Interjudge Consistency. When relatively complex subjective judgments must be made by those scoring a set of responses, as with the n Ach scoring system, considerable care is needed to be able to obtain adequate interjudge consistency in scoring. With *n* Ach, categories are defined in some detail, actual examples of scorable and nonscorable instances of each category are provided, and practice protocols are available for those learning the system. With about a week of preparation, one can learn the system well enough to attain an interjudge consistency of over .90 [McClelland, *et al.*, 1953]. In the original article describing *n* Ach [McClelland, *et al.*, 1949], a coefficient of .95 was reported. These coefficients are based on the scores of two judges scoring the same material independently and by one judge scoring the same material on two widely separated occasions.

> *Internal Consistency.* Attempts to build internally consistent sets of pictures have met with some difficulties. Atkinson [reported in McClelland, *et al.*, 1953] utilized an eight-picture set by combining the four original ones with four others in various orders of presentation. Scores on the two sets correlated .48, which becomes .65 when corrected by the Brown-Spearman formula. In addition, an "item-analysis" indicated that one of the eight pictures did not yield *n* Ach scores which correlated with the total *n* Ach score, so it was dropped from the set. The split-half reliability of the remaining pictures was found to be .78, corrected by the Brown-Spearman formula.

> *Consistency over Time.* Lowell [1950] administered two equivalent forms of the test to 40 male students with a one-week interval between testings. Test-retest reliability was found to be .22, which is not statistically significant. A later finding by Krumboltz and Farquhar [1957] with 169 students over a three-month period is consistent with this: test-retest reliability was .26. Birney [1959] utilized several different time intervals and obtained coefficients ranging from .03 (one-and-a-half years) to .56 (six months); situational influences appeared to be of greater importance than the time interval between testings, however. The best evidence for modest stability of the score over time has been provided by Morgan [1953] who obtained coefficients ranging from .56 to .64 over a five-week period. Using a three-week time period, Haber and Alpert [1958] found test-retest coefficients of .36 for cards which elicit few *n* Ach stories and .59 for cards which elicit a relatively large number of *n* Ach stories. Presumably one could construct a set of cards which would provide a very high coefficient of stability, but that has not yet been done.

> *Other Measures of* n *Ach.* We should note that other tests have been constructed in an attempt to measure *n* Ach, but none of these should be considered as alternate forms of the TAT system. For example, in the French Insight Test [French, 1958] verbal material is used to describe a situation, the subject writes a story in response to this, and the stories are scored using the McClelland system.

Among the variables measured by Edwards' Personal Preference Schedule, which was described earlier, is n Ach.

In various studies using the TAT system, the French Insight Test, and the EPPS, n Ach as measured by each is found to correlate zero with n Ach as measured by the others [Atkinson and Litwin, 1960; Himelstein, Eschenbach, and Carp, 1958; Marlowe, 1959; Melikian, 1958]. At the end of the chapter, this problem will be discussed in greater detail.

Antecedents of Need for Achievement

THEORETICAL BACKGROUND

The antecedents of individual differences in the achievement motive have been of considerable interest to those working with the n Ach variable. McClelland, et al. [1953] hypothesized that motives are learned on the basis of the type of affective experiences which are associated with specific kinds of behavior. With respect to n Ach, the relevant behavior should be that which occurs in situations involving standards of excellence and competition among individuals to attain these standards. When a child is raised in such a way that competition is stressed, the child is expected to perform well on various tasks by himself, and positive reinforcement is provided for doing well and negative reinforcement provided for failure, the strength of the child's motive to achieve should be relatively high. On the other hand, if competition is not stressed, if little encouragement is given to compete for standards of excellence, and if parents are equally accepting of success and failure, a strong achievement motive would not be expected to develop.

We would assume on general grounds that there are marked differences among cultures in their stress on achievement and success and marked differences among families within a culture. McClelland, et al., suggest:

The research problem then boils down to an attempt to discover whether individuals with high and low n Achievement scores have in fact been treated differently by their families as they were growing up. Our hypothesis is that individuals with high achievement motivation will have been forced to master problems on their own more often and earlier than individuals with low achievement motivation [McClelland, et al., 1953, p. 276].

One final point might be noted. With respect to a great many personality variables (for example, intelligence, anxiety, self-esteem, and perhaps even authoritarianism), value judgments about the desirable versus the undesirable end of the continuum are relatively clear. For most individuals in our culture, there would be a preference for raising bright, nonanxious, democratic children with realistically high self-esteem. There should be much less agreement, however, about the relative merits of competitive, achievement-oriented individuals who strive for success versus the noncompetitive individual who is satisfied with an average level of performance and is not overly concerned about spectacular success or the possibility of failure. Research dealing with the antecedents of n Ach, then, should be less clouded by problems of value judgments or parental concern with having made "mistakes" in child-rearing than is true of other areas of research on personality development.

CHILD-REARING PRACTICES ATTRIBUTED TO PARENTS

Severity. In the Wesleyan project, McClelland, *et al.,* [1953] obtained data dealing with life history and family background by means of a two-hour psychiatric interview with each of 30 subjects for whom n Ach scores were available. The psychiatrist and each subject were asked to rate each subject's parents with respect to democratic versus autocratic behavior, acceptance versus rejection of the offspring, indulgence of the child in terms of protectiveness and solicitousness, and casualness versus consistency with respect to parental policies about the child's upbringing.

When the four ratings were combined and considered as one dimension, severity, the correlation between the n Ach scores of the subjects and this measure of perceived parental behavior was .40 $(p < .05)$ for both the subject's own ratings and those made by the psychiatrist. The higher the n Ach score of the sons, the more the parents tended to be seen as autocratic, rejecting, nonindulgent, and tending toward neglect and rigidity. Among the individual scales, the highest single correlation (.49) was between n Ach and perceived rejection by the father. The more the sons felt loved and accepted by their fathers, the lower their achievement need.

Duties and Responsibilities. Two independent samples ($N = 135$ and 108) of 10–11-year-old boys were given the TAT and a scale asking for their description of their parents' behavior [Cox, 1962]. In both samples, a significant relationship $(p < .01)$ existed between achievement themes in the stories and the number of household duties and responsibilities in which the child said he participated. It was suggested that this measure reflects parental demands and expectations concerning distribution of duties and responsibilities in the home and perhaps also their more general demands and expectations.

MEASURES OF PARENTAL BEHAVIOR AND n ACH OF OFFSPRING

Independence Training. Children in all cultures have many skills and accomplishments which must be mastered at some point in the developmental process. They must learn to walk, to talk, to feed themselves, to urinate and defecate in specific places under specific circumstances, to dress themselves, and so on and so forth. Wide variations occur among cultures and among families within any one culture with respect to how early the child is expected to master a given behavior. It would seem reasonable to propose that parental insistence on early mastery would lead to higher achievement need and greater independence.

Winterbottom [1958] obtained n Ach scores on 29 boys in the eight-to-ten age group. In addition, the mothers of the boys were interviewed in order to obtain their attitudes concerning independence training. For example, the mothers were asked to indicate the age by which she demanded her son to learn each of a series of behaviors, including "to know his way around his part of the city so he can play where he wants without getting lost," "to take part in his parents' interests and conversations," "to be able to undress and go to bed by himself," and "to earn his own spending money."

The subjects were divided in terms of high n Ach and low n Ach scores, and the responses of their mothers compared. In terms of total number of demands, the groups did not differ. However, the mothers whose sons were high in n Ach expected the independence demands to be met at a significantly younger age than the mothers of low n Ach sons. For example, the mothers of high n Ach sons expected 60 per cent of the behaviors to be learned by age seven, whereas the mothers of those with low scores expected only 33 per cent of the behaviors to be learned by that age.

The greatest differences in demands were with respect to knowing his way around the city, trying new things for himself, doing well in competition, and making his own friends. McClelland, *et al.* propose:

The mother of the son with high n Achievement is interested in her son's developing away from her, in urging him to master things on his own, whereas the mother of the son with low n Achievement is willing to let such things slide and let him remain somewhat more dependent on her. Our initial hypothesis seems amply justified: *Achievement motivation in boys is associated with stress on independence training by their mothers* [McClelland, *et al.*, 1953, pp. 303–304].

Winterbottom also asked the mothers how they responded when the child was learning to do the various things. The n Ach scores of the sons of those mothers who reported responding with physical affection (kissing or hugging) was significantly higher than the n Ach scores of those whose mothers did not respond with physical affection. Thus, not only do the mothers of high need achievers expect and demand independent behavior at an early age, they supply physical rewards when the achievement demands are met.

Achievement Training. Rosen and D'Andrade [1959] suggested that achievement training (doing things well) should be differentiated from independence training (doing things by himself). Their subjects were 40 family groups each composed of a father, mother, and their son (age 9–11). The first step was the administration of four TAT cards individually to 140 boys, and then the selection of 20 high and 20 low *n* Ach scorers, matched for age, race, IQ, and social class. Half of each group were middle class and half were lower class. After making arrangements to visit the families, two experimenters (one male and one female) visited the home. The parents and their son sat at a table, and the experimenters explained that the boy would be asked to perform certain tasks as part of a project investigating factors related to success in school and later success in a career.

The goal was to create a situation in which to observe the behavior of parents while the son engaged in achievement-related behavior. The experimenters were interested in parental behavior with respect to the demands they placed on their sons, the type of sanctions employed to enforce the demands, and the amount of independence the child revealed in interacting with his parents. The tasks were designed in such a way that the boys would be somewhat dependent on their parents for aid. The five tasks involved building towers with irregularly shaped blocks with one hand while blindfolded, solving anagrams, making patterns out of blocks, tossing rings at a peg, and constructing a hat rack using two sticks and a C-clamp. The behavior ratings were made by both experimenters.

A number of comparisons were made between parents of high and low need achievers, and a few of these will be summarized. When asked how well their sons would do in stacking blocks, the parents of the high *n* Ach boys gave higher estimates than the parents of low *n* Ach boys. In the ring toss, parents were asked to decide how far away from the peg their son should stand; those with High *n* Ach sons selected a longer distance away than those with low *n* Ach sons.

The performance of the two groups of boys was also different. Those with high *n* Ach built higher block towers, constructed patterns faster, and made more anagram words than those with low *n* Ach. Boys high in achievement motive asked for less aid, were more likely to reject offers of help from their parents, and showed less negative and more positive affect than those low in achievement motive.

The experimenters rated the behavior of the parents along a number of dimensions, and these ratings yielded three major categories of behavior. These were warmth or amount of positive affect displayed by the parents while the boy was working, rejection or amount of negative affect displayed, and pushing or pressure placed on the boy to meet their expectations about his performance. A great many group differences were found.

For example, the mothers of high n Ach boys scored higher on warmth than the mothers of those with low scores. Rather than present the detailed findings, however, the conclusions of Rosen and D'Andrade will perhaps better serve the purpose:

> To begin with, the observers' subjective impressions are that the parents of high n Achievement boys tend to be more competitive, show more involvement, and seem to take more pleasure in the problem-solving experiments. They appear to be more interested and concerned with their son's performance; they tend to give him more things to manipulate than fewer; on the average they put out more affective acts. More objective data show that the parents of a boy with high n Achievement tend to have higher aspirations for him to do well at any given task, and they seem to have a higher regard for his competence at problem solving. They set up standards of excellence for the boy even when none is given, or if a standard is given will expect him to do "better than average." As he progresses they tend to react to his performance with warmth and approval, or, in the case of the mothers especially, with disapproval if he performs poorly.
>
> It seems clear that achievement training contributes more to the development of n Achievement than does independence training [Rosen and D'Andrade, 1959, p. 215].

As a footnote to these findings, we might note that there are social class differences in achievement motivation. Since independence training and achievement training by parents have an effect on the achievement needs of their offspring and since there are social-class differences in such child-rearing practices, it is perhaps not surprising to find that middle-class adolescents are higher in n Ach than are lower-class adolescents [Rosen, 1956].

CROSS-CULTURAL INVESTIGATION

In Chapter 4 the study of different cultures as a means of getting at antecedents of individual differences was discussed. This approach has been utilized with n Ach.

Achievement Imagery in Folk Tales. McClelland, et al., [1953] studied the relation between independence training and n Ach in cross-cultural research and in interview studies of American mothers. As a measure of modal n Ach for an entire culture, folk tales of eight North American Indian groups were selected and scored for achievement need in much the same way as if the stories had been produced by experimental subjects responding to TAT cards in a laboratory. As an honors thesis, G. A. Friedman selected eight Indian stories involving the same character, Coyote, a trickster hero common to several tribes. Achievement need scores were highest for the Navaho, followed in descending order by the Ciricahua Apache, Hopi, Comanche, Sanpoil, Western Apache, Paiute, and Flatheads. The scoring of the folk tales was done independently of any knowledge about the child-rearing practices of the different groups.

The ratings of independence training as practiced in the eight tribes were obtained from the Human Relations Area Files by Whiting and Child [1953] as part of their study discussed in Chapter 4. Independence training was defined in terms of initial indulgence, age at which independence training starts, and severity of training for independence. Differences among the groups in all three child-rearing variables were significantly related to tribal differences in *n* Ach scores. Achievement need was higher the less the initial indulgence, the earlier independence training was begun, and the more severe the training was. In interpreting these findings, McClelland, *et al.*, propose:

. . . there are two ways of conceiving what the amount of achievement imagery in folk tales means. On the one hand, it may reflect the modal achievement motivation of the many individuals who have told and retold the stories. If so, we might argue that the stress on independence training produces higher achievement motivation which is reflected in the stories told in the culture. On the other hand, a more likely and not completely incompatible hypothesis is that the cultural *n* Achievement score reflects a general emphasis on achievement in the culture which affects *both* child training and the kind of stories which are told in the culture, particularly since the stories may often be told to educate the young [McClelland, *et al.*, 1953, pp. 296–297].

Father Dominance. Bradburn [1963], on the basis of previous investigations, suggested that boys with high *n* Ach had dominant mothers while boys with low *n* Ach had dominant fathers who tended to interfere with their sons' attempts to achieve. Since families in Turkey reflect the traditional Islamic emphasis on male dominance, he hypothesized that Turkish men should be lower in achievement need than American men. He notes:

Almost universally, the Turks interviewed described their fathers as stern, forbidding, remote, domineering, and autocratic. Few of them had ever argued with their fathers, and those who had had done so at the price of an open break. . . .
. . . One man reported that even after he was married and had his own family, he did not dare smoke or even sit with his legs crossed in his father's presence or in any way contradict him [Bradburn, 1963, pp. 464–465].

To obtain comparable groups from the two cultures, 49 junior executives from Turkey were compared with 46 junior executives in the United States. The groups were alike in age and educational background. Achievement need was measured by means of a six-picture TAT. The Turkish stories were translated into English by professional translators.

The median *n* Ach score of the Americans was 11 while that of the Turks was 6.5. The difference is significant at the .001 level.

SEPARATION FROM FAMILY

Working within the Turkish culture, Bradburn [1963] hypothesized that since father dominance is associated with low n Ach, Turkish males who were separated from their fathers at a relatively early age would be higher in n Ach than those who remained under their fathers' influence.

His subjects were 47 teachers in a pedagogy program at the Gazi Institute, a teacher-training college in Ankara. Approximately half of them had lived apart from their parents since the age of 14 in Village Institutes. Life in the Institutes is free of the repressive family influence which would be expected to stifle the development of the need for achievement.

The hypothesis was confirmed. For those who had lived away from their parents by the age of 14, 16 were high in n Ach and 8 were low. For those who had remained with their parents, 8 were high and 15 were low in n Ach.

Thus we see that a relatively consistent picture of the child-rearing antecedents of the achievement motive is growing out of current research. Males high in the need to achieve perceive their parents as autocratic, rejecting, nonindulgent, and neglecting. These perceptions, however, do not appear to be very accurate representations of actual parental behavior. The mothers of those high in n Ach expect independent behavior to occur at an early age, and they reward such behavior with physical affection. In addition, parents of those high in n Ach expect a high level of performance and set relatively difficult standards, they display warmth and positive affect in response to achieving behavior, are involved in and pleased by their son's accomplishments, expect him to do better than average and respond with negative affect if he does not. The general pattern is one of firm and consistent stress on independence from parents as early as possible and a continuing expectation that the son should and will do better than his competitors, whatever the task. For those low in n Ach, the reverse pattern involves indulgence, encouragement of dependence on the parents as long as possible, dominance by the father, and a tendency to protect the child against failure.

The Place of Need for Achievement in the Structure of Personality

ACADEMIC PERFORMANCE

The importance of "motivation" among the factors influencing academic performance is clearly accepted at the anecdotal level, but efforts to obtain relevant empirical evidence run into some difficulty. For one thing, obviously a great many variables affect academic performance, including a great many different motive systems. Nevertheless, one of the variables should be n Achievement.

One of the first investigations [McClelland, *et al.*, 1953] involved 30 male students at Wesleyan. The correlation between n Ach and average grades for the three most recent semesters was .51 ($p < .01$). In addition, n Ach was significantly related to scores on the Scholastic Aptitude Test ($r = .42$).

In research with British children, Robinson [1961] found a significant positive correlation between n Ach and IQ ($r = .40$). In addition, when matched for intelligence, those children selected for academic excellence were significantly higher in n Ach than those not selected.

Cox [1962] obtained a sample of 96 10–11 year-old boys from five different schools and rated their academic proficiency on the basis of grades in arithmetic, composition, grammar, reading, and spelling. Achievement need was measured with the TAT. A significant positive relationship was found between achievement scores and school grades ($p < .02$). For those with the highest n Ach scores, 20 were above the median in grades and 10 below. For those with zero n Ach scores, 6 were above the median in grades and 15 below.

With 110 male students at the University of Pittsburgh, Bendig [1958] gave the n Achievement pictures and obtained each student's grade-point average for all preceding semesters at the university. The two measures correlated .22 ($p < .05$).

Five different groups ($n = 39$ to 62) of male high school juniors were given a 12-picture set of thematic apperception cards by Morgan [1953]. For most of the subjects, the Otis Quick-Scoring Mental Ability Test had been given in their freshman year, so IQ's were available as well as sophomore and junior grade-point averages. Achievement need scores correlated positively with grades in most of the groups, with .47 being the highest relationship found. There also was a positive relationship between IQ and n Ach in most of the samples, with .73 being the highest correlation.

A somewhat different sort of academic performance was investigated by Littig and Yeracaris [1963]. For 190 adult men in a community-wide survey, interviews were conducted which included questions concerning the amount of schooling the subjects had had; six n Achievement pictures were also administered. Academic achievement was divided into four levels: less than high school graduation, high school graduation, some college, and college graduation and beyond. A significant relationship ($p < .02$) between n Ach and academic level was found. For those low in achievement need, 52 per cent had not graduated from high school, and only 14 per cent had graduated from college. For those with high n Ach scores, the corresponding figures were 36 per cent and 33 per cent.

In spite of this series of findings, other investigations have not found a positive relationship between n Ach and academic performance [Cole, Jacobs, Zubok, Fagot, and Hunter, 1962; McClelland, *et al.*, 1953; Parrish and Rethlingshafer, 1954]. Besides the usual problems of possible sample differences, restricted range of ability in some groups, and differences in grading criteria across schools, there are other possible explanations for the inconsistencies. McClelland, *et al.*, discuss some of the problems:

Lowell had another group of 21 subjects who were administered one form of the measure of n Achievement under Neutral conditions and another form under Achievement-oriented conditions. He found that the correlation between past grades and n Achievement scores obtained under Achievement-orientation was .33. But most startling of all, the correlation with the difference between Neutral and Achievement-oriented n Achievement scores was .53 ($p < .05$). Those subjects whose scores increased most as a result of Achievement-orientation had higher college grades. This finding opens up a whole new area for speculation and experimental exploration. Thus, for instance, it could be argued that if you were trying to predict excellence of performance when achievement cues are present (i.e., under pressure), then the difference in n Achievement scores between Neutral and Achievement-oriented conditions might be the best measure of sensitivity to the demands of the situation. If, on the other hand, you wanted to predict who would be most apt to work hard when the cues did not demand it, then the n Achievement score obtained under Neutral conditions might be best. It is even possible that educational institutions differ in the amount of "pressure" or emphasis that is put on academic achievement. Consequently, the n Achievement score one would use for predicting grades in a particular institution would be a function of whether it was a "low pressure" or "high pressure" institution, since it is reasonable to expect that different people would get good grades in the two places [McClelland, *et al.*, 1953, pp. 239–240].

OCCUPATIONAL GOALS

An important expected correlate of the achievement motive would be any behavior related to striving for success. Perhaps occupation more than any other factor is associated with our culturally defined criteria of success, prestige, and status. If n Ach is measuring the sort of motive which involves striving for such goals, occupational plans should be a function of n Ach.

Minor and Neel [1958, p. 39] suggest: ". . . when an occupation is chosen, the person is in a position to perceive whether the job allows him to play the role he wants to play and whether the required role is in accord with his self concept." As subjects, they selected 50 male veterans of the Korean War. The n Ach cards were administered to each subject, and a counsellor determined the primary occupational preference of the individual at the beginning of counselling. A total of 20 occupations was ranked by each of a separate group of 50 judges. In the upper end of the prestige rankings were mechanical engineer, retail sales manager, high school teacher, and news reporter. At the lower end were barber, order filler, longshoreman, and guard. When the subjects were divided into high and low n Ach groups, they were found to be significantly different in terms of the prestige of their occupational choice. For the high n Ach group, 21 preferred high-status occupations and only 3 preferred low-status jobs. For the low n Ach group, 14 preferred low-status and 12 preferred high-status occupations. The data were also analyzed by correlating n Ach scores with the rank of the preferred occupation; the two variables correlated .74 ($p < .01$).

CONTROL OF TIME AND SPACE

A number of different correlates of the achievement motive may be conceptualized as sharing a common element involving control of the environment. The individual high in n Ach is described as one who manipulates his environment, is concerned with utilizing his time efficiently, plans ahead, is on the move, and so forth. Several of the investigations of the achievement motive have dealt with such factors.

Delay of Gratification. In Chapter 5, some of the work of Walter Mischel and others on delay of gratification was discussed. If high need achievers are planful, forward-looking, and desirous of maximizing success, they would be expected to be able to delay gratification in order to obtain greater rewards. Mischel [1961, p. 544] suggests: "Achievement fantasies may be thought of in part as reflecting as well as sustaining and mediating the individual's strivings for future rewards and attainments of excellence." For one thing, those high in n Ach have presumably learned to like work and hence to tolerate the waiting period between a given effort and extrinsic rewards.

The subjects were 112 Negro children aged 11–14 in Trinidad. One measure of delay preference, described earlier, involved a choice between a small 10¢ candy bar available now and a much larger 25¢ candy bar which would be available in a week. Two verbal items were also used to determine preference.

1. I would rather get ten dollars right now than have to wait a whole month and get thirty dollars then.

2. I would rather wait to get a much larger gift much later rather than get a smaller one now.

Need for achievement was measured by scoring the responses to five TAT-type cards.

Those children who chose delayed reward on the behavioral measure and on both verbal measures ($N = 37$) were significantly higher in n Ach than those who chose immediate reward on all three ($N = 30$). In terms of a correlation, the relationship between preference for delayed reward and n Ach was .27 ($p < .005$).

Time Imagery. Knapp and Garbutt [1958] assumed that high achievement need leads to a desire to manipulate the environment, an acute awareness of time and its value, and hence the perception that time moves rapidly. Four standard TAT pictures were administered to 73 male undergraduates along with a Time Metaphor Test. The latter instrument consists of 25 metaphors representing time. The subjects were asked to rate each phrase in terms of its appropriateness in evoking a satisfactory image of time. Correlations were computed between n Ach scores and the ratings given to each metaphor. Findings showed that high need achievers find metaphors involving speed and directness most appropriate for describing time, while low need achievers feel that slow or static metaphors are most descriptive. Table 9–1 gives the six metaphors which correlate most

Table 9–1 CORRELATION OF RATINGS OF APPROPRIATENESS OF TIME METAPHORS WITH n ACHIEVEMENT SCORES

Positive Relationship		Negative Relationship	
Metaphor	r	Metaphor	r
A dashing waterfall	.41	A devouring monster	−.49
A galloping horseman	.32	A quiet, motionless ocean	−.41
A bird in flight	.30	A stairway leading upward	−.37
A winding spool	.26	A string of beads	−.31
A speeding train	.23	A vast expanse of sky	−.31
A fleeing thief	.22	A large revolving wheel	−.23

positively and the six which correlate most negatively with n Achievement scores. The metaphors thought most appropriate by those high in n Ach were suggested by the authors to be related to:

. . . that body of thought and ideology which has been described under the term "Protestant ethic" [Weber, 1930]. In a sense, it reflects a Newtonian sense of time, one defined in terms of an absolute, impersonal, constant, and directional rate of change in the universe [Knapp and Garbutt, 1958, p. 433].

Other investigations have also dealt with n Ach and various aspects of time perception. Ricks and Epley [1960] scored the TAT stories of a group of 138 business executives in terms of the time span covered in each story. Those high in n Ach wrote stories which encompassed a longer period of time than those low in *n* Ach. Similarly, Heckhausen [quoted in McClelland, 1961] with a group of German university students found that *n* Ach correlated .46 (*p* < .01) with length of future time perspective in the stories.

McClelland [1961] reports a simple behavioral test of attitudes about time conducted by Cortes. The experimenter first checked his watch carefully and then announced to a class of senior high school boys: "It is now *exactly* X o'clock. Please raise your hand if your watch is fast by any amount. Now please raise your hand if your watch is slow." Significantly more of those high in achievement need (87 per cent) reported that their watches were fast, versus 44 per cent of those low in achievement need. McClelland [1961, p. 327] remarks, "For the individual with high *n* Achievement time is almost literally moving faster."

Aesthetic Preferences. With the general notion that aesthetic preferences should be related to personality variables, Knapp [1958] investigated reactions to Scottish Tartans as a function of *n* Ach. He obtained color photographs of 30 tartans selected from an original group of 200 on the basis of variety and the fact that judges varied in rating them for attractiveness. The subjects were 68 Wesleyan undergraduates for whom *n* Ach scores were available. They were asked to examine the photographs and to indicate their liking for each along an eight-point scale. A correlation was computed between ratings of each tartan and *n* Ach, and a few of these are shown in Table 9–2. In comparing the 10 tartans most liked and the 10 least liked by high need achievers, a number of differences were found. Those liked were almost uniformly somber, while those not liked were almost uniformly bright. The former were predomi-

Table 9–2   RELATIONSHIP BETWEEN *n* ACH AND RATINGS OF
ATTRACTIVENESS OF SCOTTISH TARTANS

Positive Relationship		*Negative Relationship*	
Tartan	*r*	Tartan	*r*
Campbell of Broadalbane Subdued blue-green with fine small yellow lines, open design	.18	Drummond Predominantly bright red tartan, moderately fine-textured, green secondary color.	−.20
Elliot Predominantly deep blue with dark open figure, very fine brown line.	.18	Hay Generally similar to Drummond save dominant red less saturated.	−.20
Anderson Complex, fine-textured asymmetrical colors but predominantly light blue.	.17	Sinclair Predominantly red, monotonously symmetrical with open design and secondary green.	−.16

nantly blue and the latter predominantly red. Knapp's interpretation of this finding is in terms of n Ach and an individual's relationship with the environment; those high in n Ach want a soft, passive environment, while those low in n Ach want a hard, active environment:

We venture, as a general hypothesis, that individuals and cultures fostering high achievement motivations will dislike strong and assertive stimuli generally in their fashions, dress, and ornament. They will regard with distaste and aversion bright colors, strong contrasts, and prefer subdued, even monotonous, decor. Now it has been demonstrated that n Achievement is *ceteris paribus*, higher among middle class children than among lower class children, and it has also been frequently observed that middle class propriety and conservatism in matters of dress distinguish them from the more colorful taste of lower socioeconomic classes. The "man in the grey flannel suit" expresses the quintessence of the middle class subdued taste [Knapp, 1958, p. 372].

Graphic Expression. One final investigation in this series involved an attempt by Aronson [1958] to determine differences in graphic expression between individuals high and low in the achievement motive. For 26 male college students, n Achievement scores were obtained. Following this, the subjects were asked to look at an abstract design projected on a screen for 1.8 seconds, and then to draw what they had seen. A content analysis procedure was carried out to compare the drawings of high and low scorers on the n Ach measure.

Those high in n Ach, compared to those with low scores, drew single, unattached, discrete lines rather than overlaid and fuzzy lines, left a smaller margin at the bottom of the page, drew more diagonal configurations, produced more S-shaped lines, and drew fewer multicurve lines. Examples are shown in Figure 9–1. Among the outcomes of this research was the development of an n Ach scoring system for graphic material which has been utilized in some of the cross-cultural work described in the following section. With subsequent groups of subjects, the relationship between n Ach scores and the graphic variables of discreteness versus fuzziness, amount of space in the margin, and so forth, were cross-validated.

The graphic scoring system for n Ach was undertaken without preliminary hypotheses concerning what sort of differences might be found, but McClelland suggests an interpretation:

Looked at as a whole, they do appear to define a "dynamic" approach to movement. That is, the "highs" seem to avoid repetition (fewer overlaid lines and multiple waves), and to fill up more of the space available with discrete and *different* lines, which more often than among the "lows" take the form of diagonals which physiognomically appear to be "going somewhere." They move or doodle restlessly, seeking variety rather than sameness in what they draw [McClelland, 1961, p. 304].

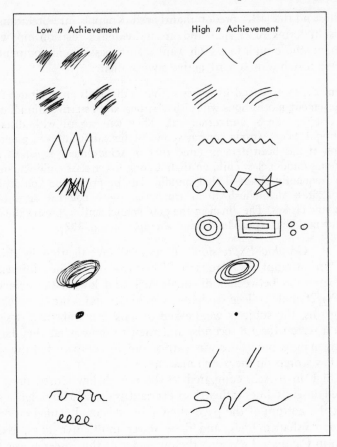

FIG. 9–1. *Differences in graphic expression as a function of* n *Achievement.*

THE ACHIEVING SOCIETY

One of the most unusual aspects of the *n* Ach scoring system in contrast to other personality measures is the fact that any prose material can be scored in the same way that the imaginative material given in response to thematic apperception cards is scored. Thus, unlike IQ tests or the California F Scale or almost any other widely used measure, *n* Ach scores may be obtained for individuals no longer alive or even for a cross-section of entire groups of individuals, including groups living centuries in the past. We have seen one example of this procedure in the scoring of the Indian folk tales. The possibility of utilizing the *n* Ach scoring system in this unusual way has led to an ambitious project by McClelland and his colleagues, an unusual type of research for psychologists in that it invades the domain of history, economics, and sociology. The general background for this research is given by McClelland in *The Achieving Society:*

From the top of the *campanile,* or Giotto's bell tower, in Florence, one can look out over the city in all directions, past the stone banking houses where the rich Medici lived, past the art galleries they patronized, past the magnificent cathedral and churches their money helped to build, and on to the Tuscan vineyards where the *contadino* works the soil as hard and efficiently as he probably ever did. The city below is busy with life. The university halls, the shops, the restaurants are crowded. The sound of *Vespas,* the "wasps" of the machine age, fills the air, but Florence is not today what it once was, the center in the 15th century of a great civilization, one of the most extraordinary the world has ever known. Why? What produced the Renaissance in Italy, of which Florence was the center? How did it happen that such a small population base could produce, in the short span of a few generations, great historical figures first in commerce and literature, then in architecture, sculpture and painting, and finally in science and music? Why subsequently did Northern Italy decline in importance both commercially and artistically until at the present time it is not particularly distinguished as compared with many other regions of the world? Certainly the people appear to be working as hard and energetically as ever. Was it just luck or a peculiar combination of circumstances? Historians have been fascinated by such questions ever since they began writing history, because the rise and fall of Florence or the whole of Northern Italy is by no means an isolated phenomenon [McClelland, 1961, p. 1].

The research which was undertaken in this project was an attempt to make sense of the economic growth and decline of cultures on the basis of the achievement motive. The general scheme formulated by McClelland and his colleagues as connecting links between *n* Ach and the achievements of a society is outlined in Figure 9–2.

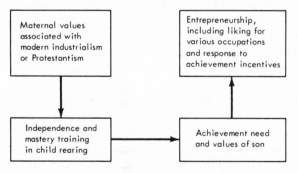

FIG. 9–2. *Proposed relationships among mothers' attitudes, sons' values, n Ach, and entrepreneurial behavior. (Adapted from McClelland, 1961, p. 58.)*

The Protestant Reformation and n Achievement. McClelland points out that the German sociologist Max Weber presented a description of the new character type brought about by the Protestant Reformation—a shift toward self-reliance and the new capitalistic spirit in Western Europe. In other words, the Protestant Reformation brought about the development of high need achievers.

If this general idea has any validity, a number of specific predictions may be tested. For example, drawing on the investigations of child-rearing antecedents of n Ach discussed earlier, Protestant parents should stress earlier independence training than Catholic parents. McClelland, Rindlisbacher, and de Charms [1955] obtained samples of Protestant, Irish-Catholic, and Italian-Catholic parents, matched for socioeconomic level, and administered Winterbottom's scale dealing with expectancies and demands concerning independent behavior. The differences between the groups were significant and in the predicted direction, with the Protestant parents expecting independence earlier.

Another prediction was that among male children, higher n Ach would be found for Protestants than for Catholics. With a group of German boys preparing for a university education, the mean n Ach of Protestants was 3.42 and of Catholics 1.77, a difference significant at the .05 level.

A still more general prediction would be that Protestant countries should be more economically advanced than Catholic countries. As a measure of economic development, McClelland [1955] used consumption of electricity as measured by kilowatt-hours per capita as of 1950. Since advanced economies tend to be primarily in the temperate zone, and since a number of Catholic countries are in Central America and the northern part of South America, nations lying in the tropics were omitted in order to make the test more fair. The Protestant countries (Norway, Canada, Sweden, United States, Switzerland, New Zealand, Australia, United Kingdom, Finland, Union of South Africa, and Denmark) were found to have an average of 1,983 kwh/cap in 1950. A significantly lower average of 474 kwh/cap was found for the Catholic countries (Belgium, Austria, France, Czechoslovakia, Italy, Chile, Poland, Hungary, Ireland, Argentina, Spain, Uruguay, and Portugal). Even when a correction is made for differences in natural resources, the Protestant countries do better than expected and the Catholic countries do worse than expected.

Though these findings are promising, the general formulations extended beyond differences between Protestants and Catholics. A sample of this further research will be described.

n Ach and Economic Growth. To assess a nation's mean n Ach, the decision was made to select children's readers used in the second to fourth grades and to score the stories in these books according to the n Ach scoring system. Such readers are relatively standardized within a country, are read by nearly all school children of a given age, and represent the popular culture. By going back in time one generation and obtaining n Ach scores, McClelland [1961] hoped to be able to predict the subsequent economic growth of various countries. Stories from 23 countries were collected from the time period 1920–1929 and scored for n Ach. Subsequent economic growth was measured as changes in kwh/cap between 1929 and 1950 in terms of deviation from expected growth. McClelland found that achievement need expressed in the children's stories correlated .53 ($p < .01$) with this index of economic growth. Children's stories for 1950 were also scored for n Ach, and no correlation was found between achievement scores and *previous* economic growth. McClelland concludes:

It is difficult to argue from these data that material advance came first and created a higher need for achievement. Rather the reverse appears to be true— high n Achievement levels are associated with subsequently more rapid economic development [McClelland, 1961, p. 93].

If this proposition is correct, however, the n Ach estimates for 1950 should be related to economic growth *after* 1950. McClelland [1961] used the six-year period 1952–1958 to measure rate of growth, again in terms of electrical output. The correlation between n Ach in the 1950 children's stories and deviation from expected economic growth between 1952 and 1958 was .43 ($p < .01$) for the 39 countries for which data were available.

A possible explanation for this group of findings is that n Ach in children's readers instills achievement need in the children who grow up to attain economic success. Among other considerations, the last finding argues against this in that the readers of the 1950 books were not yet adults during the 1952–1958 economic growth period. A more likely explanation is that the readers reflect ". . . the motivational level of the adults at the time they are published, perhaps particularly of the adults responsible for the education of children. . . ." [McClelland, 1961, p. 102.]

n *Ach and Changes within a Society.* An investigation by de Charms and Moeller [1962] sampled children's readers in the United States from 1800 to 1950. At least four books from each 20-year period were obtained and scored for the achievement motive. As an index of achievement in the society, the investigators secured the number of patents issued by the U.S. Patent Office for each 20-year period, divided by the population at the middle of each period. The index was patents issued per one million population. They found that achievement imagery in the readers rose rapidly from 1800 to 1890, and then declined steadily after that period. As shown in Figure 9–3, achievement imagery and the patent index show remarkably similar patterns. The two measures correlate .79 ($p < .003$). Affiliation imagery in the stories was also scored, and this motive revealed a steady increase over the same time period. These two trends led the authors to suggest:

These findings appear to be in accord with Riesman's analysis of the child rearing practices which lead to the inner- and other-directed character types. The parent rearing a child in the period of transition to inner-direction must equip him with a "gyroscope" which will fit him to remain on course in a society where it is impossible to foretell, due to increasing social mobility, what role he will be called upon to play. He must be equipped to be self-reliant and in-

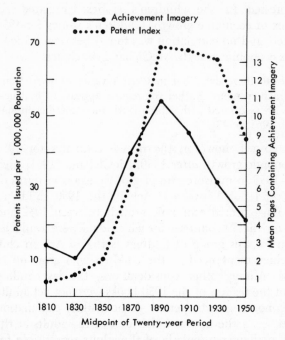

FIG. 9-3. *Achievement imagery and patent index in the U.S., 1800–1950. (Adapted from de Charms and Moeller, 1962, p. 139.)*

dependent. These are the aspects which Riesman sees in nineteenth century child rearing. The antecedents of achievement motivation seem clear.

On the other hand, with increasing urbanization and population density which result from technological advance, the child is no longer pushed to be independent, but learns the importance of other individuals in the environment. He must be taught to win approval. Although Riesman's argument is more complicated than this, the child rearing practices which he sees in contemporary United States culture seem to be ones which might lead to affiliation motivation [de Charms and Moeller, 1962, pp. 141–142].

In further research, the McClelland [1961] group also investigated the relationship between *n* Ach as estimated from various types of written material and graphic productions and economic growth in a variety of countries in the past. Space does not permit a full description of these studies, but a sampling of the findings will provide a general picture of this work.

For ancient Greece, *n* Ach was highest in the early period of growth (900 B.C. to 475 B.C.), began to decline during the climax of Greek civilization (475 B.C. to 362 B.C.), and reached a low point as the nation went into economic decline (362 B.C. to 100 B.C.) [Berlew, 1956]. Exactly the same pattern was found for Spain in the late Middle Ages for periods of economic growth (1200 to 1492), climax (1492 to 1610), and decline (1610 to 1730) [Cortes, 1960].

For England, from the time of the Tudors to the Industrial Revolution,

Bradburn and Berlew [quoted in McClelland, 1961] compared n Ach in English literature with rates of gain in coal imports at London 50 years later.

The correspondence of n Ach and economic activity in these three cultures is shown graphically in Figure 9–4.

n Ach and Interest in Business. Still another link in the general proposal concerning the achieving society concerns individual differences in n Ach and individual differences in attraction to and success in the field of business.

The Strong Vocational Interest Blank (SVIB) yields scores which compare an individual's response to the test items with the responses of individuals who are successful in various occupations. Among a group of college freshmen, the responses to the SVIB of the 20 per cent highest in n Ach were compared with the responses of the 20 per cent lowest in n Ach. The only occupational scales on which the two groups differed significantly were stockbroker, real estate salesman, advertiser, buyer of merchandise, and factory manager. In each instance, the occupation is in the field of business, and in each instance those high in n Ach were more like those in the field than were those low in n Ach.

An entrepreneurial job was defined by Meyer, Walker, and Litwin [1961] as one involving responsibility for initiating decisions, individual responsibility for the consequences of the decisions, objective feedback of the success of one's decisions, and risk. The investigators selected 31 managers in manufacturing plants as holding positions of this type. A group of 31 nonentrepreneurial specialists was also chosen, and the two groups matched for salary or status, age, years of education, and length of time with the company. All subjects wrote stories in response to six thematic apperception pictures. The mean n Achievement score of the managers (6.74) was found to be significantly higher than that of the specialists (4.77).

Within the business community, those involved in sales and marketing tend to have the highest level of n Ach [McClelland, 1961]. A relationship between n Ach and engagement in entrepreneurial occupations does not necessarily indicate that n Ach is responsible for occupational choice. Among other possibilities, the demands of such jobs could well have an influence on the test scores. The latter interpretation is not supported by a longitudinal study conducted by McClelland [1965a]. For 55 Wesleyan graduates who had taken the n Ach measure while in college, a 14-year follow-up was made to determine the type of occupations into which they had entered. It was found that 83 per cent of those in entrepreneurial occupations had received high n Ach scores while in college; only 21 per cent of those in nonentrepreneurial occupations had received high scores. A cross-validation study confirmed this relationship between achievement need in adolescence and later occupational choice.

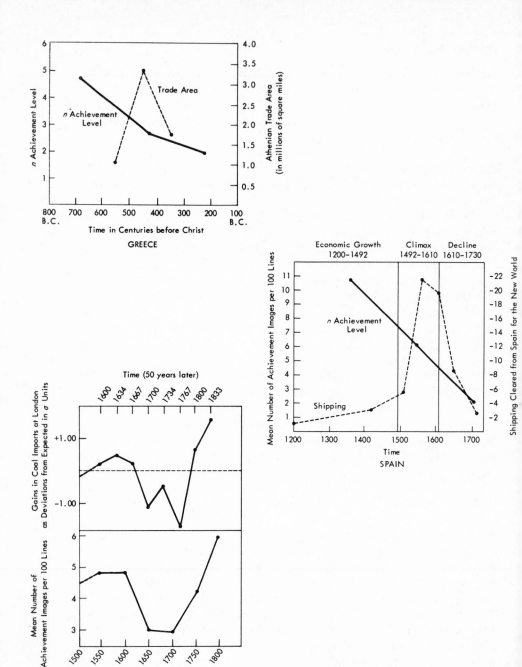

Fig. 9-4. n *Achievement and economic activity in Greece, Spain, and England. (Adapted from McClelland, 1961, pp. 120, 132, and 139. Courtesy of D. Van Nostrand Company, Inc.)*

Summarizing a number of business interest findings, McClelland suggests the following pattern:

In countries like the United States . . . there appears to have been a recruitment pattern that in ideal form ran somewhat as follows. The father moved from the country to the city and established himself perhaps as a skilled or semiskilled worker. The son was one of the 67 per cent of such people who not only wanted to but succeeded in establishing a small business, possibly because he had high *n* Achievement. He reached the lower middle class. The grandson, if he too had high *n* Achievement, expanded the business and eventually moved up into the business elite. . . . But *his* son, the great-grandson, is now part of what we have been calling the student elite. He goes to an Ivy League college and if he has high *n* Achievement, he aspires to one of the professions. If not, or if his school work is not good enough, or if he is made to go into the family firm, he goes into business and *takes with him a much more conservative ideology* than his upwardly mobile father or grandfather had. The reasons for having a conservative ideology are strong, much stronger than in his father's case, for he must maintain the family position, the capital, the business that his father established. He is also more often than not less suited for the business role than his father because he has less of the entrepreneurial spirit—that is, lower *n* Achievement. Certainly it is a widely accepted belief that sons who inherit their businesses have in general less "drive" than those who created them, though we do not as yet have factual evidence on differences in their *n* Achievement scores [McClelland, 1961, pp. 255–256].

We will return briefly to the studies of the achieving society when discussing changes in the achievement need and in discussing possible criticisms of this work.

Dynamics of the Need for Achievement

RESISTANCE TO CONFORMITY PRESSURES

Those high in achievement need are described as independent, furnished with an internal "gyroscope" of values, and oriented toward performing tasks well rather than toward pleasing others through conformity. On these bases, McClelland, *et al.* [1953] hypothesized that high *n* Ach should be associated with independent, nonconforming behavior as in the Asch conformity situation (described in the preceding chapter). They obtained TAT protocols from Professor Asch for 15 subjects who had yielded to an incorrect majority and for 15 who had given the correct responses and remained independent of the group in their perceptual judgments. A highly significant relationship between *n* Ach and conformity was found. For the 15 subjects above the *n* Ach median, 13 were independents; for the 15 subjects below the *n* Ach median, 13 were yielders. McClelland, *et al.*, [1953, p. 287] conclude: "They are independent in action as well as thought; their independence appears almost to be a consistent 'way of life.' . . ."

Krebs [1958] used a different conformity task. Subjects were briefly shown two slides, each containing a large number of objects. Subsequently, for a series of objects, they were asked whether each had been on slide A or slide B. Then the experimenter presented the subject with a list purportedly filled out by another student but which was actually a bogus scale designed to disagree with the subject's responses by a standard amount. As in McClelland's study, those subjects high in n Ach were significantly less likely to change their opinion to conform to the responses of the other student.

PERCEPTION, MEMORY, AND MOTIVE STRENGTH

Perceptual Recognition Thresholds. For a number of reasons, we would predict that individuals high in achievement need would be perceptually sensitive to achievement-related stimuli. McClelland and Liberman [1949] employed 30 stimulus words: 10 neutral, 10 related to achievement, and 10 related to security. The achievement words were further divided into positive (for example, success) and negative (for example, failure) words. Each word was exposed for .01 second at successively increasing illumination until the word was correctly recognized. In terms of n Achievement and perceptual thresholds, the only significant relationship was between n Ach scores and recognition of the positive achievement words. The higher the achievement need, the faster the recognition of positive achievement words.

Probably the most reasonable interpretation of this finding is in terms of familiarity. Numerous investigations [for example, Solomon and Postman, 1952] have found that perceptual accuracy increases as a function of an individual's familiarity with the stimulus. Individuals with high n Achievement would be expected to have greater familiarity with positive achievement words than would individuals with low n Achievement.

Recall of Interrupted Tasks. Ability to recall interrupted tasks in a Zeigarnik experiment is usually interpreted as an indicator of persistent striving to complete the tasks. If the tasks were defined as achievement-related, n Ach should be related to such striving and differences in ability to recall interrupted tasks should be a function of differences in the strength of the achievement motive.

Atkinson [1953] utilized three different experimental conditions in an attempt to vary the degree to which performance on a task was defined as evidence of the subject's ability. Those in the *relaxed condition* were told that the tasks were just being tried out, and the experimenter had no idea what they measured. In the *task-oriented condition* the subjects were told simply that the tasks were to be performed, but no mention was made of what they measured. In the *achievement-oriented condition,* the tasks were said to be measures of important abilities, and the subjects were told to do their best. Each subject had 20 tasks to be performed in one minute and fifteen seconds each; about half could be finished in that time limit and half could not. The latter, then, served as the interrupted tasks. After an interpolated activity, the subjects were asked to recall the 20 tasks.

Subjects high and low in *n* Achievement did not differ in their recall of the completed tasks under any of the experimental conditions. For the recall of interrupted tasks, however, an interaction occurred between *n* Ach and the conditions. The high *n* Ach subjects were superior to low *n* Ach subjects in recall in the achievement-oriented condition, the two groups did not differ in the task-oriented condition, and the low *n* Ach group had the higher recall score in the relaxed condition. Thus, there were differences in recall, and presumably differences in striving to complete the tasks, only when the instructions indicated a strong relationship or no relationship between performance and competence.

Resumption of Incomplete Tasks. Another measure of motivation on incomplete tasks is if the individual resumes the task following an interruption. If such tasks involve achievement motivation and if a success goal were attained during the interruption, there should be little motivation to resume the task. Weiner [1965] hypothesized that only for high need achievers would the interpolation of a success experience (the substitute goal) result in a decreased tendency to resume the interrupted task. For low need achievers, the success experience should not serve as a goal and should not have this effect. The probable effects of an interpolated failure experience are less clear, but the high *n* Ach group should still be strongly motivated to resume the incomplete task in order to attain the goal, while failure should simply increase the avoidance motivation of the low *n* Ach group with respect to the entire situation.

The subjects were male undergraduates at the University of Michigan. The task to be interrupted was one involving 20 different puzzles presented in booklet form. After the interruption, subjects were given a task involving the continuous tracing of geometrical designs. Half of the subjects were given a success experience (10 soluble designs), and half were given a failure experience (three soluble and seven insoluble designs). Afterward, during a "waiting period," the subjects were allowed five minutes to determine whether they would spontaneously resume the original tasks that had been interrupted.

The high *n* Ach subjects were significantly less likely to resume the interrupted task after success than after failure, while the reverse was significantly more likely for the low *n* Ach subjects. Thus, the notion that success in an achievement-oriented situation represents an appropriate goal for those with strong achievement motivation was supported.

PERFORMANCE IN ACHIEVEMENT-RELATED TASKS

A number of experimental situations have been devised which present the subject with a task to perform involving productivity, competition, or risk-taking. Since such stimulus situations are hypothesized to be of greatest relevance for individuals with strong motivation to achieve, the investigation of the dynamics of n Ach includes many studies dealing with this type of situation.

Interaction between Motive and Performance. Atkinson [1954] has formulated a theoretical statement of the expected relationship between motivation as measured by the TAT, environmental cues as manipulated by the experimenter, and performance. Characteristic motive strength is assessed by means of fantasy productions, and the experimenter's instructions serve to indicate an association or lack of association between the outcome of the performance and the specific motivation. "When the subject is both motivated and has the expectancy that a particular performance is instrumental to attainment of the goal, then the motive is engaged and manifested in overt striving" [Atkinson, 1954, pp. 79–80]. A diagram of this schema is shown in Figure 9–5.

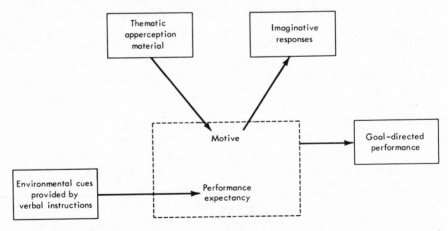

Fig. 9–5. *Joint determinants of goal-directed performance by motive and performance expectancy.* (*Adapted from Atkinson, 1954, p. 80.*)

One of the early studies by Lowell [1952] investigated the relationship between n Achievement scores and performance on simple tasks. Groups of 19 high n Ach and 21 low n Ach subjects were given a series of simple addition problems to solve during a 10-minute period. Throughout the time period, those high in n Ach solved more of the problems than did those low in n Ach. In contrast to this task which involved performance of a simple, well-learned behavior, Lowell also presented the subjects with a more difficult and more novel task. They were given scrambled words during a 20-minute time period: for example, WTSE could be unscrambled as WEST. High and low n Ach subjects performed at the same rate at first, but the high need achievers showed significant improvement over the experiment while those with low n Ach scores performed at the same rate from beginning to end.

Another sort of performance measure was used by Zatzkis [1949] who hypothesized that word output would be positively related to n Ach. A month after obtaining n Achievement scores from a group of 28 subjects, the experimenter asked them to write an essay on "What I would ideally like to get out of an elementary course in psychology." They were told that the essays would be read and graded in terms of "quality of thinking." Subjects low in n Ach produced essays with a mean number of 491.5 words, while those high in n Ach produced a mean of 543.3 words. Thus, word productivity in an achievement-oriented situation was significantly related to n Ach scores as predicted.

A somewhat different sort of prediction which would follow from Atkinson's general conceptualization is that the arousal of other motives in addition to the arousal of n Ach would eliminate performance differences in high and low need achievers. That is, if the instructions were designed to arouse just n Achievement, individuals high on this motive would perform better. If the instructions were designed to arouse n Ach plus additional motives, those individuals high in achievement need would not necessarily perform better than those low in achievement need. Atkinson and Reitman [1956] compared performance in an achievement-oriented condition versus a multi-incentive condition. One of the tasks was a series of arithmetic problems in a 14-page book. Both experimental groups received achievement-oriented instructions in which the experimenter emphasized the importance of doing well on the tasks which were said to be measures of important abilities. In the multi-incentive condition, the subjects were also promised $5.00 for the person who did best. In addition, the two experimenters walked around the room during the tests, casting disapproving glances at those not working hard, in an attempt to arouse the affiliation motive or desire to please the examiner. It was found that in the achievement-oriented condition, those high in n Ach did significantly better on the arithmetic problems than did those low in n Ach. In the multi-incentive condition, high and low need achievers did not differ. Thus, relationship between the achievement motive and task performance was eliminated when additional motives were aroused.

Not only is achievement need related to performance on a task, it should also be related to an individual's expectations about how well he could perform the task, especially if the task were a somewhat difficult one. On an anagrams task described to the subjects as "moderately difficult," there was a significant positive relationship between n Ach and the subjects' estimates of the likelihood that they would solve all of the anagrams [Feather, 1965]. This relationship did not hold when the same task was described to other subjects as a comparatively easy one. Feather hypothesized that the estimates made by the subjects were based on their past experiences of success and failure. Presumably, high need achievers have been more successful than low need achievers in performing somewhat difficult tasks.

RISK-TAKING BEHAVIOR

Theoretical Background. In extending the formulation of the interaction between motives and instructions in influencing performance, Atkinson [1957] proposed three variables as determinants of behavior. (1) A *motive* such as n Ach consists of a disposition to strive for certain kinds of satisfaction. There are avoidant as well as approach motives. Avoidant motives refer to individual differences in the painfulness of specific negative consequences of behavior. In achievement-related situations, one may assume that both the motive to achieve success (M_s) and the motive to avoid failure (M_f) are aroused. (2) An *expectancy* is an anticipation, usually aroused by situational cues, that a given behavior will lead to a specific consequence. (3) In addition, there is an *incentive* variable, which is the relative attractiveness of a specific goal or the relative unattractiveness of the consequences of a given goal-directed behavior. Atkinson proposed that the strength of the motivation to perform an act is a multiplicative function of the strength of the motive, the expectancy or subjective probability that the act will lead to attaining an incentive, and the value of the incentive.

In attempting to quantify each of these variables, Atkinson suggested that expectancy can be represented in terms of subjective probability of success ranging from 0.00 to 1.00. The difficulty of the task for the subject can be inferred from the subject's subjective probability of success (P_s); the harder the task, the lower a subject's P_s. Atkinson assumes that the incentive value of success (I_s) is a positive linear function of difficulty. So, $I_s = 1 - P_s$; the easier the task and the greater the probability of success, the less incentive value. The incentive value of failure (I_f) is defined as $-P_s$. For a very easy task (for example, $P_s = .90$), failure is humiliating ($I_f = -.90$); for a difficult task (for example, $P_s = .10$), little embarrassment over failure ($I_f = -.10$) occurs.

These formulations lead to a number of specific predictions, as outlined in Table 9–3. For example, in Section I of the table, if the motive to achieve success equals the motive to avoid failure, the resultant motivation is zero.

Table 9–3   MOTIVATION AS A FUNCTION
OF MOTIVE, EXPECTANCY, AND INCENTIVE[*]

	M_s	$\times P_s$	$\times I_s$ = Approach	M_f	$\times P_f \times I_f$ = Avoidance	Resultant Motivation (Approach − Avoidance)
I. Achievement Motive and Fear of Failure of Equal Strength						
Task A	1	.10	.90 = .09	1	.90 −.10 = −.09	0
Task B	1	.20	.80 = .16	1	.80 −.20 = −.16	0
Task C	1	.30	.70 = .21	1	.70 −.30 = −.21	0
Task D	1	.40	.60 = .24	1	.60 −.40 = −.24	0
Task E	1	.50	.50 = .25	1	.50 −.50 = −.25	0
Task F	1	.60	.40 = .24	1	.40 −.60 = −.24	0
Task G	1	.70	.30 = .21	1	.30 −.70 = −.21	0
Task H	1	.80	.20 = .16	1	.20 −.80 = −.16	0
Task I	1	.90	.10 = .09	1	.10 −.90 = −.09	0
II. Achievement Motive Stronger than Fear of Failure						
Task A	2	.10	.90 = .18	1	.90 −.10 = −.09	.09
Task B	2	.20	.80 = .32	1	.80 −.20 = −.16	.16
Task C	2	.30	.70 = .42	1	.70 −.30 = −.21	.21
Task D	2	.40	.60 = .48	1	.60 −.40 = −.24	.24
Task E	2	.50	.50 = .50	1	.50 −.50 = −.25	.25
Task F	2	.60	.40 = .48	1	.40 −.60 = −.24	.24
Task G	2	.70	.30 = .42	1	.30 −.70 = −.21	.21
Task H	2	.80	.20 = .32	1	.20 −.80 = −.16	.16
Task I	2	.90	.10 = .18	1	.10 −.90 = −.09	.09
III. Fear of Failure Stronger than Achievement Motive						
Task A	1	.10	.90 = .09	2	.90 −.10 = −.18	−.09
Task B	1	.20	.80 = .16	2	.80 −.20 = −.32	−.16
Task C	1	.30	.70 = .21	2	.70 −.30 = −.42	−.21
Task D	1	.40	.60 = .24	2	.60 −.40 = −.48	−.24
Task E	1	.50	.50 = .25	2	.50 −.50 = −.50	−.25
Task F	1	.60	.40 = .24	2	.40 −.60 = −.48	−.24
Task G	1	.70	.30 = .21	2	.30 −.70 = −.42	−.21
Task H	1	.80	.20 = .16	2	.20 −.80 = −.32	−.16
Task I	1	.90	.10 = .09	2	.10 −.90 = −.18	−.09

[*] Adapted from Atkinson, 1957, p. 362.

If the achievement motive is stronger than the fear of failure motive (Section II of the table), the resultant motivation would be positive, with the specific strength of the approach motivation a function of the magnitude of the various determinants. If the motive to avoid failure is stronger than the achievement motive (Section III of the table), the resulting motivation is avoidance. We will examine some of the investigations bearing on the predictive accuracy of this system.

Preference for Different Levels of Task Difficulty. The table shows that both approach and avoidance achievement motivation are greatest when uncertainty regarding the outcome is greatest, when $P_s = .50$. Given a free choice among a series of tasks, an individual high in n Ach should choose one such as Task E, which is of intermediate difficulty. The individual with relatively high fear of failure should want to avoid all of the tasks, but if he were forced to choose he should select either the most difficult ($P_s = .10$) or the easiest ($P_s = .90$) and avoid the tasks of intermediate difficulty.

McClelland [1958] reported findings supporting these hypotheses with a group of kindergarten children engaged in a ringtoss game. Those high in n Ach selected an intermediate range of difficulty; that is, they chose a moderate distance from which to throw the ring at the peg. Those low in n Ach selected an extreme in terms of difficulty, either right on top of the peg or so far away that success was almost impossible.

Another sort of situation was utilized by Clark, Teevan, and Ricciuti [1956] who asked college students to estimate their final exam grade (highest and lowest it could possibly be) and also to indicate what grade they would be willing to settle for if they could skip taking the final. Those who settled for an intermediate grade were significantly higher in n Ach than those who settled for either a grade near their maximum or minimum estimate.

In the Meyer, *et al.* [1961] study of managers and specialists discussed earlier, a Risk Preference Questionnaire was administered to the subjects. This instrument consisted of a list of pairs of betting choices, and the subjects were asked to choose the preferred alternative on each. Extremes of risk and nonrisk were defined as choosing $\frac{1}{6}$ or $\frac{5}{6}$ chance of winning. Intermediate risk was defined as choices of $\frac{2}{6}$, $\frac{3}{6}$, or $\frac{4}{6}$ chance of winning. The managers (who were found to be higher in n Ach) significantly more often selected the intermediate odds than did the specialists.

Persistence at Easy versus Difficult Tasks. If an individual is presented with a task of a given difficulty level, Atkinson's theory would allow us to predict the persistence with which the task would be pursued on the basis of approach and avoidance motives. Feather [1961] used the TAT measure of n Ach as an index of M_s and the Mandler-Sarason Test Anxiety Questionnaire as an index of M_f. The subjects were male undergraduates at Michigan. For those in the upper half of the n Ach distribution and lower half of the test anxiety distribution, M_s was assumed to be higher than M_f. For those with the reverse pattern, M_f was assumed to be higher than M_s.

The subjects were presented with a "Perceptual Reasoning" test of a line diagram on a card which the subject was supposed to trace with a red pencil without lifting the pencil or retracing a line. If, within 40 seconds, the task could not be done, the subject was free to start over with the same design on a second card (again with a 40-second deadline), then with a third card, and so on. If the subject gave up, he could go on to a second different design. Actually, the first design was an impossible task. Probability of success for tracing the design correctly was manipulated by means of instructions to the effect that a certain percentage of college students of the subject's age level are able to solve the problem. For item one, half of the subjects were told it was easy ($P_s = .70$), and half were told it was very difficult ($P_s = .05$). All subjects were told that the second task was of intermediate difficulty ($P_s = .50$).

Persistence was defined as the number of trials the subject attempted on the first design before giving up and going on to the second design. Predictions concerning differences in persistence can be made, using the schema in Table 9–3. For the group in which M_s is greater than M_f, the P_s of .05 yields a motivation score of .0475, and a P_s of .70 yields a motivation score of .21. Thus, these subjects should persist longer on the easy task than on the hard one. For the other group ($M_f > M_s$), the P_s of .05 yields a motivation score of $-.0475$ and a P_s of .70 yields a motivation score of $-.21$. Thus, these subjects should persist longer on the hard task than on the easy one. These differences in avoidance motivation may be conceptualized in terms of inhibitory tendencies of varying strength [Atkinson, 1964].

The same predictions may also be made on a second basis. After giving up on design one, the subjects must go on to design two with a P_s of .50. For the $M_s > M_f$ individuals, the motivation for design two is .25; subjects with the difficult task would be switching from a task eliciting .0475 motivation to one eliciting .25 motivation, while those with the easy task would be switching from a task eliciting .21 motivation to one yielding .25 motivation. Again, there is more reason for those with the difficult task to make the switch than there is for those with the easy task. In contrast, the $M_f > M_s$ individuals would have a $-.25$ motivation for design two. Here, subjects with the difficult task would be switching from a task eliciting $-.0475$ motivation to one eliciting $-.25$ motivation; those with the easy task would be switching from a task eliciting $-.21$ motivation to one eliciting $-.25$ motivation. For these individuals, those with the difficult task should most avoid switching.

Feather found, as predicted, that persistence on the easy task was greater than persistence on the difficult task for subjects high in achievement need and low in text anxiety. Persistence on the difficult task was greater than persistence on the easy task for subjects low in achievement need and high in test anxiety.

Clearly, the achievement motive is related to a number of different aspects of behavior in achievement-related situations, and Atkinson's theoretical model shows considerable promise for accurately predicting such behavior.

Changes in Need for Achievement

To date, relatively little work has been done on the problem of the variables influencing alterations in the characteristic level of the achievement motive. Two approaches have been considered, however, and both are of considerable theoretical and applied interest.

ALTERATIONS IN FAMILY STRUCTURE OR IN CHILD-REARING PRACTICES

In considering changes in the economic growth of a society as a function of changes in *n* Achievement, McClelland [1961] in *The Achieving Society* also sought an explanation for the society-wide changes in achievement need. The two major possibilities which were suggested involved prolonged absence of the father from the home and the rearing of children by low *n* Ach individuals employed by the parents.

Father Absence. Drawing on some of the developmental studies discussed earlier, McClelland [1961, p. 404] suggested that if dominant fathers are responsible for low *n* Ach, their absence would have the reverse effect; for example, "Wars may well have a marked and sudden effect on *n* Achievement by removing authoritarian fathers from the scene." He notes that *n* Ach showed a significant increase in both France and Germany between 1925 and 1950. Further data, obtained under more controlled conditions, are obviously needed. Nevertheless, it is intriguing to note the marked economic growth and seemingly high level of *n* Achievement since World War II in those countries most involved (for example, most of Western Europe, Russia, the U.S., Japan, China) compared to countries relatively isolated from the war (for example, Latin America, Africa, Ireland, Spain, Portugal, Turkey).

Another cause of widespread father absence in a culture is the kind of occupation in which he is engaged. If a job is such that the father is away from the home for extended periods of time, the *n* Ach of the offspring should be affected in a positive direction. McClelland [1961] points out that, historically, a high incidence of sea-faring nations showed abrupt increases in economic growth. He notes as examples the Greeks, early Etruscans, British, Japanese, Scandinavians, and Genoese, and one might add the New Englanders in this country. Thus, conceivably when large numbers of dominant fathers go down to the sea in ships, the achievement need of subsequent generations shows an increase. As still another speculation, one might wonder about the effect on future generations of the commuter culture in which the father leaves for work in early morning and returns home at the children's bed time. Functionally, these fathers are often as removed from their children's lives as if they had gone off to sea.

Child-Rearing by Slaves and Servants. Throughout history, as nations became economically and militarily powerful, slavery was instituted, and one of the major tasks assigned to slaves was the rearing of the master's children. McClelland [1961] hypothesized that the slave and the slave's children should be oriented toward dependence on the master, obedience, and compliance—precisely the kind of atmosphere to foster low achievement motivation. He points out that in this country, the Negro slaves would be expected to develop child-rearing practices emphasizing nonachievement factors. Their descendants, even though free, should still show these effects; he found that lower-class Negroes have the lowest average *n* Ach scores of any minority group tested. The exceptional Negroes who have moved into the middle and upper classes, on the contrary, are conspicuously high in *n* Ach.

If these general propositions about slavery are accurate, it follows that the slaveholders should also tend to develop low *n* Achievement over the generations because the slaves raise their children. In addition to their regular child-rearing practices with their own children, the slave would be expected to respond to the master's child by indulging his every whim, ingratiating him- or herself through spoiling the children. McClelland points out that those who founded the Southern plantations were probably high in *n* Ach, but the subsequent generations showed quite different patterns. Business enterprise in the U.S. has been associated with the North and even with the nonslaveholding portions of the South such as North Carolina. McClelland goes on:

What is most fascinating about such a possibility is that it suggests a rather simple, if ironic, account of the rise and fall of many great civilizations in the past. The argument runs as follows: a people with higher level of *n* Achievement tend to pursue business enterprise more rigorously and ultimately to become more wealthy. Nearly always in the past such wealth has been used to support slaves. Certainly this was the case in Ancient Greece. Beginning around 525 B.C. when a much larger proportion of Athenian families were wealthy enough to support slaves, each child of good family was ordinarily assigned two

slaves—a nurse and a pedagogue to go to school with him [Glotz, 1925]. Furthermore, in our sample of preliterate cultures, 45 percent of twenty cultures with
high n Achievement versus only 19 percent of 21 low in n Achievement had
slaves (chi square $= 3.29$ $p < .10$). In short, high n Achievement leads to increased wealth, which leads to more household slaves. But in Greece the more
general use of such slaves preceded by a generation or two the marked drop in
n Achievement. . . . Is it unreasonable to infer that the slaves undermined
the achievement training of their masters' children, although probably not
consciously? So, ironically, the masters were undone by the very instrument that
demonstrated, they thought, their mastery—namely, their enslavement of those
they had conquered. The irony lies in the fact that what happened was certainly
not *intentional* on either side. Explanations of the decline of civilizations in
terms of the "decay of moral fibre," although vague and *ad hoc*, do have at least
this kernel of truth in them: the institution of slavery in all probability undermined achievement training, which in turn lowered general n Achievement
level and made civilizations less enterprising in business and more vulnerable to
economic decline and ultimately attack and destruction from without [Mc-
Clelland, 1961, pp. 377–378].

An analogous effect could be proposed in modern societies when low n
Ach servants drawn from lower socioeconomic levels are assigned major
child-rearing responsibilities by the families who can afford this luxury.
As with the slave cultures, the pattern could involve enterprising activity
leading to wealth and the employment of servants, leading in turn to lower
n Ach and less business enterprise in succeeding generations.

ALTERATION IN FANTASY LIFE

A somewhat unusual approach to bringing about a change in
n Achievement has been undertaken by Burris [1958]. A group of college
students enrolled in a self-improvement course wrote thematic apperception
stories which were scored for achievement need. Then, in a series of eight
weekly sessions lasting 40 minutes each, they met to discuss the type of
achievement imagery in their stories. In effect, they were directed to engage
in fantasy activity centering on achievement and activity directed toward
achievement goals. One matched control group of students in the same
course met for counselling on how to study, while a second control group
did not meet for any special sessions.

After the end of the eight weeks, the test was readministered and scored
for achievement need. As predicted, the subjects in the experimental group
who had discussed achievement showed a significant increase in n Ach. This
finding alone would not be very impressive, but would suggest a simple
change in story content as a result of the discussions rather than a change
in motivation level. Burris went further, however, and compared the grade-
point averages the following semester of those who had shown an increase

in n Ach versus those who were in the control groups. He found a significantly greater increase in grade-point average for those students who had undergone the experimental treatment than for the controls.

While a greater amount of evidence is badly needed, this finding does suggest that a direct alteration of fantasy can lead to motivational changes. McClelland [1961] feels that this research indicates that what people daydream about affects what they do. He proposes research to test the hypothesis that courses oriented toward goals or fantasies may be more effective in changing behavior than courses oriented toward techniques.

In part influenced by the success of Burris' approach, McClelland [1965b] has instituted a large-scale project designed to increase n Achievement in business executives. Groups of individuals are brought together for one to three weeks of interaction centered on the acquisition of a high achievement motive. The general procedure includes training and practice in the production of achievement fantasy, group activities involving goal-setting and risk-taking with achievement-related tasks, role-playing activities, such as portraying a democratic father with high n Ach standards for his son, and an interpretation of cultural demands, values, and folklore in terms of relationship to n Ach. Such executive training sessions have been carried out in the United States, Mexico, and India. Among the data so far available concerning the effectiveness of these procedures is the finding that among Indian subjects who had participated in this project a significant increase occurred in "*unusual* entrepreneurial activity." Specifically, there was an increased incidence of unusual promotions, salary raises, and engaging in new business ventures in the two years following the course compared to the two years prior to the course. In a group of control subjects this change was not observed. McClelland noted that the training procedure doubles the normal rate of entrepreneurial activity "—no mean achievement in the light of the current pessimism among psychologists as to their ability to induce lasting personality change among adults" [McClelland, 1965b, p. 332].

At a more speculative level, McClelland concludes:

What, then, did happen to great civilizations like the Renaissance in Florence? The Florentines lost interest in achievement. Their dreams changed. They became more concerned with love and friendship, with art, with power struggles. The dominant Medici family illustrates the shift in motivation from Giovanni, the great merchant banker whose achievement drive led him into all corners of Europe, through Cosimo, *pater patriae*, who consolidated his father's gains, through Lorenzo, *Il Magnifico*, great patron of the arts, to his successors caught in a bloody struggle for pleasure, power and wealth for their own sake. What each generation wanted above all, it got. What saves such a statement from banality is the new fact that the psychologist has now developed tools for finding out what a generation wants, better than it knows itself, and *before* it has had a chance of showing by its actions what it was after. With such knowledge man may be in a better position to shape his destiny [McClelland, 1961, p. 437].

Current Status of Need for Achievement as a Personality Variable

OBJECTIVE MEASUREMENT

Given the relative difficulty involved in administering sets of TAT pictures, the subjectivity and consequent loss of reliability in the scoring system, and the amount of scoring time required per subject, it would be extremely helpful to have available a simple, objective measure of *n* Ach. In spite of the benefits to be gained by such an approach, one of the more puzzling aspects of the *n* Ach literature is the fact that the measurement of individual differences in this motive with the TAT approach yields scores unrelated to other measures of *n* Ach.

After reviewing many of the studies seeking relationships between the TAT measure and alternate objective measures, McClelland [1958, p. 38] stated: *"The conclusion seems inescapable that if the n Achievement score is measuring anything, that same thing is not likely to be measured by any simple set of choice-type items."* Further, he suggested that a fantasy measure of motivation is "purer" than a questionnaire measure such as the EPPS or the *n* Ach questions devised by Murray. In a questionnaire, the subject is asked in one way or another to describe himself, and numerous extraneous factors influence such responses. Undoubtedly, as many and perhaps more "extraneous factors" influence fantasy production as influence questionnaire responses. McClelland argues further that the self-descriptive approach to motivation appraisal has shown itself historically to be inadequate and that reliance on such measures has actually retarded the development of the psychology of motivation. This statement, too, is open to argument.

In any event, there is a measurement approach which could be undertaken in the future—the empirical method as described in connection with the MMPI and CPI. Since the TAT *n* Ach measure has identified an important personality dimension, it could be used now as a starting point or criterion for the construction of an objectively scored instrument. Rather than starting with a preconceived notion of what sort of objective items ought to measure *n* Ach, one could start with a large pool of miscellaneous items and administer them to subjects who had been identified as high or low in *n* Ach by means of the TAT. Given the relational fertility of the *n* Ach variable, it is difficult to believe that at least *some* of the questionnaire items would not be answered differently by the high and low achievement need groups. If so, one could build a measure of n Ach which was not dependent on the production of fantasy.

CAUSE AND EFFECT INTERPRETATIONS OF CORRELATIONAL FINDINGS

In some respects, the cross-cultural studies of n Achievement and the attempts to account for the achievement of nations on the basis of a personality variable are among the most exciting yet undertaken by personality psychologists. For a field still groping to develop even low-level behavioral laws, it is somewhat surprising to be in the position of predicting economic progress for nations and to be able to explain the rise and fall of empires.

The major danger in dealing with such data is the obvious one that a correlation between two variables does not necessarily mean that a causal relationship exists. McClelland is quite aware of this problem, of course, and in *The Achieving Society* he discusses a number of alternative explanations of his findings. There are two counterarguments which support McClelland's position, however.

First is the cumulative effect of a large body of consistent data. In reviewing the work on achieving societies, Mausner [1963] indicated great initial skepticism. He notes, for example, the fallacies of the correlational approach and the problems involved in measuring the modal needs of an entire nation on the basis of material such as the contents of fourth-grade readers. Nevertheless, he concludes: "This reviewer is won by the argument. The way in which the many pieces of the puzzle fit together is uncanny; the book has the feeling of a most successful detective story" [Mausner, 1963, p. 292].

The second sort of support comes from evidence aimed at making clear the connecting links between variables involved in the correlations. For example, differences between Catholic and Protestant countries in economic productivity could be explained in hundreds of ways besides that of differences in n Ach. When, however, parents belonging to the two religious groups are found to have different child-rearing practices and their offspring are found to differ in n Ach, the McClelland argument is strengthened considerably. More such links are needed. For example, James Morgan [1963], an economist, suggested that it would be convincing to see a study in which individuals whose behavior was directly contributing to a developing nation's economic growth (for example, working hard, accepting new ways of producing and consuming, taking appropriate risks) were shown to be higher in n Ach than individuals whose behavior was not contributing to economic growth. Positive evidence from a variety of such investigations would make the n Achievement thesis hard to refute.

ACHIEVEMENT NEED IN WOMEN

One of the more intriguing unresolved issues with the n Ach variable is the difference between males and females in achievement motivation. The general problem first became obvious in the original investigations of n Ach [McClelland, *et al.*, 1953]. Among other findings reported was that the achievement arousal conditions used in the construction of the test had no influence on the TAT stories of female subjects, and that some of the parent-child relationships which hold for male offspring are absent or even reversed for female offspring. One response to this state of affairs has been a tendency to direct most of the research interest to male subjects and ignore the problem of female achievement motivation. However, a few attempts have been made to explicate the reasons for the sex difference.

One of the first suggestions [Veroff, 1950] was that the thematic apperception pictures used to measure n Ach contain only male figures and hence were inappropriate for eliciting female achievement fantasy. With 46 female high school students, responses to three male pictures and three female pictures were compared under neutral versus achievement-arousing conditions. He found that the experimental conditions had no effect on story content but that the female subjects obtained significantly higher n Ach scores on the *male* pictures than on the female pictures. Similar results have been reported by Veroff, Wilcox, and Atkinson [1953] and by Lesser, Krawitz, and Packard [1963]. As McClelland, *et al.* [1953, p. 173] noted: ". . . *even girls project achievement striving primarily into the activities of men.*" As this statement suggests, there is apparently more to the problem than the sex of the figures in the TAT cards.

One line of reasoning suggests that males and females in our culture are, in fact, basically different with respect to achievement motivation. There are a number of differences in the roles of the two sexes with respect to achievement. For males, achievement means success in terms of intelligence, leadership, occupational prestige, and income—all of which depend in part on the individual's own ability and hard work. For females, achievement has two meanings. First, there is personal achievement which tends to involve social acceptance or popularity with peers of both sexes, and eventually it also means ability to run a home well as a mate, cook, housekeeper, and mother. Second, a female can achieve vicariously through the success of her husband or her sons. If these propositions have any merit, the type of conditions which would arouse n Ach and the type of behavior influenced by n Ach might well be different for females than for males.

The notion that the arousal conditions which are effective for males (for example, subjects told that intelligence or leadership or future success is being evaluated) are inappropriate for females was tested by Field [1951]. He compared the usual male-oriented arousal conditions with conditions involving social acceptability. The subjects were told that social acceptance by others was a predictor of future social acceptance; they were then given bogus evaluations indicating that they were socially acceptable or socially unacceptable to others. At this point the TAT cards were administered. Females receiving both types of acceptability ratings had a significantly higher n Ach score than those in the control group. For male subjects, the social acceptability conditions had no effect on their n Ach scores. Thus, n Ach is aroused in males by instructions stressing leadership and intelligence and in females by instructions stressing social acceptability.

The expression of female n Ach by means of the success of their husbands is supported by the findings of Littig and Yeracaris [1965]. A total of 179 married females in an upstate New York community were interviewed and given a six-card TAT measure. The interest here was in the occupational mobility of their husbands. Mobility was defined in terms of father's occupation (blue collar or white collar) and husband's occupation. If both father and husband were white collar workers or both were blue collar workers, there was no mobility. If father was blue collar and husband white collar, upward mobility was indicated. If father was white collar and husband blue collar, there was downward occupational mobility. Mobility was found to be significantly related to n Ach. Upward mobility was more characteristic of high n Ach females and downward mobility of low n Ach females. (For 177 male subjects, the same trends were found, but they were not statistically significant.) This study raises the question of whether the females' achievement need was influenced by their husbands' occupational status or whether their choice of a husband was influenced by their n Ach in relation to the males' occupational potential or whether their n Ach led them to exert influence on their husbands in terms of his occupational choice.

Future research on the achievement motive is most likely to include a much greater interest in the motivation of females and the effects of this motivation on behavior.

Summary

Among motivational variables of interest to personality psychologists over the last decade and a half, one which has been the focus of considerable research activity is the need to achieve.

Achievement need is a learned motive to compete and to strive for success. A motive or drive is a higher-order generalization and involves the concepts of drive level, drive stimulus, instrumental responses, and goal.

Henry A. Murray is a physician, chemist, psychoanalyst, and psychologist whose personality research at the Harvard Psychological Clinic in the 1930's included the formulation of the n Achievement concept and the development of the Thematic Apperception Test. Murray's research approach was one involving the use of multiple investigators and multiple techniques with a small group of subjects. The life history of a single individual was the unit with which he chose to work. The achievement motive was defined as the desire or tendency to do things as rapidly and/or as well as possible. The TAT is a projective test in which the subject responds to a series of pictures by making up a story for each.

Current research with the n Ach variable was begun at Wesleyan University in the late 1940's and early 1950's by David McClelland and his associates. Unlike Murray, the approach of these investigators was to focus on one motive using many subjects in a large number of experiments. After the effect of hunger arousal on TAT stories was determined, a similar method was utilized with the achievement motive. Different groups received different experimental instructions designed to elicit different levels of n Achievement, four TAT slides served as the stimuli for brief stories, and the story content was compared across groups. The content categories on which the experimental and control groups differed led to the scoring system for n Ach. The assumption is made that differences in achievement fantasy in neutral situations reflect individual differences in the characteristic strength of this motive. The n Ach variable can be scored with high interjudge consistency, but its split-half and test-retest reliabilities are only of moderate magnitude.

The antecedents of the achievement motive are hypothesized as parental differences in stressing the importance of competition, excellence of performance, and independence plus differences in the extent to which positive reinforcement is provided for doing well and negative reinforcement provided for failure. High n Ach males have been found to perceive their parents as autocratic, rejecting, nonindulgent, and neglecting. Mothers with high n Ach sons expect independence behavior at an earlier age than do mothers with low n Ach sons, and they reward such behavior with physical affection. Parents who produce high n Achievement offspring expect a high level of performance, set difficult standards, display positive affect for achievement and negative affect for failure. The general pattern is one of firm and consistent stress on independence from parents as early as possible and a continuing expectation that the son should and will do better than his competitors at any task.

Among the correlates of n Ach which have been investigated is academic performance. Achievement scores have been found to be positively related to college grades, measures of scholastic aptitude, IQ, grammar school achievement measures, high school grades, and for adults, number of years of education. Probably because of differences in populations, grading criteria, and amount of pressure for achievement, other investigators have not found a significant relationship between n Ach and academic performance. N Ach has been found to be related to the prestige of the occupation which is the individual's goal. A number of correlates of the achievement motive may be conceptualized as sharing a common element involving control of the environment. In comparison with low need achievers, high need achievers have been found to be better able to delay gratification in order to obtain greater rewards, to find metaphors involving speed and directness more appropriate for describing time than slow or static metaphors, to cover a longer time span and longer future time perspective in their stories, to have watches running fast rather than slow, and to prefer blue and somber colors rather than red and bright colors. In drawings, those high in n Ach draw single discrete lines rather than overlaid fuzzy lines, leave a smaller margin at the bottom of the page, draw more diagonal lines, draw more S-shaped lines, and draw fewer multicurve lines. One of the unusual aspects of the n Ach scoring system is that material may be scored for individuals no longer alive or for a cross-section of an entire group or nation. In *The Achieving Society,* McClelland attempted to make sense of the economic growth and decline of cultures on the basis of the achievement motive. If the Protestant Reformation was responsible for a shift toward self-reliance and the capitalistic spirit, a number of links between n Ach and religious beliefs would be hypothesized. Protestant parents have been found to stress earlier independence training than do Catholic parents, Protestant boys are higher in n Ach than Catholic boys, and Protestant countries are more economically advanced than Catholic countries. Using children's readers to assess a nation's n Ach, substantial correlations were found between n Achievement and subsequent economic growth for two different time periods. In the United States between 1800 and 1950, children's readers showed a steady increase in n Ach up to 1890 and then declined steadily; a corresponding pattern was shown by the number of patents issued per capita. For Ancient Greece, Spain in the Middle Ages, and England from the Tudors to the Industrial Revolution, a correspondence was found between n Ach and economic growth and decline. The SVIB has also been used to show that high need achievers are more like those successfully employed in various business occupations than are low need achievers. Entrepreneurial managers are higher in n Ach than are nonentrepreneurial specialists; individuals involved in sales and marketing have the highest n Ach scores in the business community. Further, n Ach scores obtained in college are predictive of later entrepreneurial activity.

In conformity experiments, those who yield to the incorrect majority are found to be lower in n Ach than are those who remain independent. In a perceptual task, the higher the achievement need, the lower the recognition threshold for positive achievement words—possibly as a function of differential familiarity. Memory for interrupted tasks is better for high need achievers under achievement-oriented conditions and better for low need achievers under relaxed conditions. When task interruption is followed by a success experience, high n Ach subjects are less likely to resume the task than are low n Ach subjects. N Ach is also positively related to performance on simple tasks, to word output on an essay, and to expectation of success. Under achievement arousal, those high in n Ach perform better than those low in n Ach, but when other motives are aroused in addition, the two groups do not differ. Atkinson has formulated a theory which proposes motivation as a multiplicative function of motive strength, the subjective probability that the act will lead to the attainment of the incentive, and the value of the incentive. When both motive to achieve success and motive to avoid failure are taken into consideration, a number of behavioral predictions may be made on the basis of Atkinson's schema. For example, individuals high in n Ach prefer tasks of intermediate difficulty while those low in n Ach prefer either very easy or very difficult tasks. Also, when M_s is greater than M_f, there is longer persistence on easy than on hard tasks; with M_f greater than M_s, there is greater persistence on difficult than on easy tasks.

So far, little work has concentrated on alteration in n Ach. McClelland has suggested that changes might be brought about through events which remove the dominant father from the home; examples are war or any occupation involving prolonged absence. A second source of change hypothesized is when the children of successful high n Ach parents are reared by low n Ach slaves or servants. One experimental study of change in n Ach consisted of a series of sessions in which low achievers were directed to engage in fantasy activity centering on achievement and the attainment of achievement goals. Compared to control groups, these individuals not only showed a significant increase in n Ach scores but also a significant increase in college grade-point average. More elaborate studies are now under way which attempt to increase the achievement motivation of business executives.

For a number of reasons a simple, objective measure of n Ach would be advantageous, but all such tests so far developed are unrelated to the TAT measure. One possibility for the future is an empirically developed objective measure. Much of the work on n Ach can be criticized in terms of a tendency for investigators to utilize cause and effect interpretations of correlational findings. Nevertheless, the sheer volume of consistent data with respect to such concepts as the achieving society and the increasing number of "linking" studies are supportive of the present formulations. Finally, n Achievement in women seems to be aroused by different conditions than is true for men in that acceptance or popularity are more relevant to female achievement than are leadership, intelligence, or success. Also, female n Ach can be expressed in terms of influence on a husband or on male offspring.

CHAPTER 10

Manifest Anxiety

Anxiety is often defined as an emotional state in which there is a vague, generalized feeling of fear. In a number of formulations [for example, Horney, 1945], three primary emotional responses are defined— pleasure, fear or anxiety, and anger. More often, however, psychologists eliminate the concept of emotion and deal with such phenomena simply in terms of motivation.

As a motive, anxiety has been of considerable interest to a wide variety of individuals involved in the study of behavior, from psychoanalysts to learning theorists. Therefore, one realizes with some difficulty that the word "anxiety" was hardly used in standard medical and psychological textbooks until the late 1930's after Freud had emphasized the importance of the concept [Sarbin, 1964a]. Freud's work on anxiety will be described in the following section of this chapter.

For psychologists, the focus on anxiety has been of several different kinds; we will examine these briefly. First, anxiety has been studied in terms of those stimuli which evoke it and the responses which define it. For example, individuals can be made fearful or anxious by means of pain or the threat of pain, by unexpected stimulus events such as a loud noise, and by that which is unusual or unknown. The effects of such stimulus events on behavior have been investigated by means of simple rating scales or verbal statements indicating increased anxiousness, but a primary research interest has been the investigation of physiological responses. For example, Ax [1953] has attempted to differentiate the physiological effects of fear and anger. Fear involves increased heart rate, respiration rate, muscle tension, and skin moisture. An increase in the amount of adrenalin in the blood also occurs. As will be seen later in this chapter, these known effects of frightening stimuli have led to many attempts to find relationships between verbal and physiological indices of anxiety.

Second, the fact that certain stimuli evoke fear or anxiety has led to research in which subjects learn to respond with fear to previously neutral stimuli through simple conditioning. One of the best known early demonstrations of learned fear was carried out by Watson and Raynor [1920]. A small boy who had no fear of rats was suddenly exposed to a loud, unexpected noise while playing with a white rat. Following this experience, he was not only afraid of the rat but also of a number of things which were in some way similar to the rat in appearance. A more extensive investigation of fear as a learned motive was conducted by Miller [1948a]. With rats as subjects, electric shock was used to elicit fear in a white compartment; on subsequent nonshock trials, fear was shown by the rats whenever they were placed in that compartment (that is, tenseness, crouching, urination, defecation). Apparently any stimulus can be paired with a fear-inducing stimulus and come to evoke fear itself. The parallel between such learned fear in the laboratory setting and the phobias, fears, and anxieties found in everyday life is a compelling one. For example, therapists are often confronted by patients for whom sexual cues evoke fear and anxiety. Why? A reasonable guess can be made on the basis of studies such as that of Hayward [1957]. Baby male rats were given electric shock whenever they were placed near female rats in heat; at maturity they tended to avoid female rats in heat significantly more than did the male rats in a control group.

A third sort of interest in fear and anxiety involves their drive properties. Because it is unpleasant to be fearful or anxious, any behavior which brings about drive reduction is reinforcing. The simplest drive-reducing response is physical avoidance of the stimulus. If escape is not easily accomplished, other responses which lead to the same goal may be learned. For example, in Miller's [1948a] experiment, once the rats had been taught to fear the white compartment, they were given the opportunity to escape into a black compartment if they turned a wheel which opened a door between the two compartments. Just as organisms can learn to perform a multitude of instrumental responses in order to obtain food or water or sexual satisfaction, Miller's rats learned to turn the wheel to escape the white compartment and obtain fear reduction. In psychoanalytic theory, the explanation for most defense mechanisms and more severe symptoms is that such behavior serves to reduce anxiety. Experimental evidence concerning the drive properties of anxiety demonstrates that Freud was probably correct in conceptualizing many behavior aberrations in terms of learning. In a book attempting to translate psychoanalytic theory into a scientific theory, Dollard and Miller note:

Throughout this book we emphasize the role of fear, or anxiety. This is partly because of its indubitable importance. It is also possible that it is overemphasized because the way it is learned and the effects that it produces are clear-cut and experimentally documented [Dollard and Miller, 1950, pp. 190–191].

Fourth, not only is anxiety unpleasant and hence motivational in terms of anxiety-reduction, but it has another type of motivational effect which it shares with all other motives—the facilitation of whatever reaction is being made by the organism. Hull [1943] proposed that the energizing effect of drive on behavior was independent of the specific antecedents which defined drive arousal. Thus, any given S-R sequence is facilitated equally by hunger, thirst, anxiety, or any other drive. As will be discussed shortly, research on the energizing effect of drive has very frequently utilized anxiety.

Finally, a fifth aspect of interest in anxiety is one which cuts across the other four: individual differences. In personality research, there has been interest in differences among individuals (1) in physiological responses to anxiety-evoking stimuli, (2) in the stimuli which they have learned to fear, (3) in the instrumental responses they have learned as means to reduce anxiety, and (4) in general drive level or emotional responsiveness. For example, the same stressful stimulus situation is found to evoke outwardly directed anger in some individuals, while in others it evokes inwardly directed anger and anxiety; the accompanying physiological responses are quite different [Funkenstein, King, and Drolette, 1957]. A number of attempts have been made to assess individual differences in their anxiety concerning classes of stimuli such as fear of examinations; test anxiety is determined by responses to such items as, "When the teacher says that she is going to find out how much you have learned, do you get a funny feeling in your stomach?" [Sarason, Davidson, Lighthall, Waite, and Ruebush, 1960]. Individual differences in instrumental responses which reduce anxiety have been studied with respect to many aspects of behavior, including the use of alcohol [Ullman, 1958], psychotic symptoms [Murray, 1962], and defense mechanisms [Byrne, 1964b].

In the present chapter the emphasis will be on the study of individual differences in generalized anxiety. This research involves to some degree all of the aspects of anxiety which have just been described. As an introduction to current anxiety research, the influence of two quite different theoretical movements will be described briefly: Freud's psychoanalytic theory and Hull-Spence learning theory.

Theoretical Background of the Concept of Anxiety

FREUD AND *Angst*

Historical Background. Sigmund Freud (1856–1939) was an Austrian physician whose early interests included neurology and the treatment of nervous disorders. Shortly after receiving the M.D. degree in

1881, he joined the Institute of Cerebral Anatomy to engage in research work. Leaving the Institute for the greater financial rewards of private practice, he grew increasingly interested in a number of nonphysiological approaches to the treatment of emotional problems, including hypnosis as practiced by Jean Charcot in treating hysterics and a novel procedure devised by Joseph Breuer which involved the patient's talking about symptoms and problems. After disagreeing with Breuer concerning the role of sexual conflicts in the development of hysterical symptoms, Freud went his own way in developing both psychoanalytic theory and the therapeutic techniques which constitute psychoanalysis. Hall and Lindzey contrast Freud's interests with those of his contemporaries in the psychological laboratories in Germany and the United States who dealt only with conscious processes:

> He [Freud] likened the mind to an iceberg in which the smaller part showing above the surface of the water represents the region of consciousness while the much larger mass below the water level represents the region of unconsciousness. In this vast domain of the unconscious are to be found the urges, the passions, the repressed ideas and feelings—a great underworld of vital, unseen forces which exercise an imperious control over the conscious thoughts and deeds of man. From this point of view, a psychology which limits itself to the analysis of consciousness is wholly inadequate for understanding the underlying motives of man's behavior.
> For over forty years, Freud explored the unconscious by the method of free association and developed what is generally regarded as the first comprehensive theory of personality. He mapped the contours of its topography, penetrated to the headwaters of its stream of energy, and charted the lawful course of its growth. By performing these incredible feats, he became one of the most controversial and influential figures in modern times [Hall and Lindzey, 1957, p. 30].

In Chapter 2, a process was described in which science moves from observation to generalization to verification to theory-building. In the third of these four phases we noted that such elements as operational definitions, controlled observational techniques (for example, experimental manipulation of independent variables), and the quantification of variables differentiated the procedures of scientists from those of the man in the street and from those of early philosophers attempting to explain behavior. The deliberate attempt to formulate a body of generalizations in the form of empirical laws tied together in a theoretical framework is characteristic of scientific endeavor. In Freud's work, we have an excellent example of a procedure in which the verification step is omitted, or more precisely where verification consists of additional uncontrolled observations. The "theory" which emerges consists of a heterogeneous combination of behavioral observations, nonoperational constructs, relationships between and among operational and nonoperational constructs, speculations, hypotheses, and analogies—all expressed nonquantitatively.

We should note that Freud's observational skills and brilliance were such that the resulting product, while less than a set of empirical laws or an acceptable theory, is considerably more than a literary exercise. The implications of many of his generalizations and hypotheses have had and will continue to have a strong influence on research dealing with human behavior. A psychoanalytic description of anxiety will serve as a sample of Freud's approach and as an introduction to current work on anxiety.

Freud's Conceptualization of Anxiety. Among the earliest detailed observations and speculations concerning anxiety were those reported by Freud [1926] in his monograph, *Inhibitions, Symptoms, and Anxiety*. Freud's writings on most topics tend to be organized without differentiation of observations, generalizations, and speculations. A somewhat different order from the original presentation will be followed here, in an attempt to present the basic points of his monograph.

1. *Descriptive Definitions of Anxiety*. Freud defined anxiety in terms of subjective feeling:

Anxiety, then, is in the first place something that is felt. We call it an affective state, although we are also ignorant of what an affect is. As a feeling, anxiety has a very marked character of unpleasure [Freud, 1926, p. 132].

In addition to "unpleasure," further qualifications were added in that this particular emotion was described as one which involved expectation, a quality of indefiniteness and lack of a specific object, and a generalized feeling of helplessness. Still other characteristics were the physical sensations accompanying the emotional experience, especially those involving the respiratory organs and the heart.

Though Freud himself was content to leave the concept at this relatively abstract level, obviously one could rather easily translate his observations into operational terms.

2. *Speculations Concerning the Antecedents of Anxiety*. Freud saw clearly that there were marked individual differences with respect to characteristic anxiety level, but he confessed his inability to specify how these differences came to be. In more general terms, he suggested that the psychical and physiological components of anxiety have their origin in the responses evoked by the process of birth:

In man and the higher animals it would seem that the act of birth, as the individual's first experience of anxiety, has given the affect of anxiety certain characteristic forms of expression.

. . . We are therefore inclined to regard anxiety-states as a reproduction of the trauma of birth [Freud, 1926, pp. 93, 133].

Specifically, Freud believed that the crucial element in the birth trauma which associated later stimulus conditions with it was a particular type of danger:

The situation of non-satisfaction in which the amounts of stimulation rise to an unpleasurable height without its being possible for them to be mastered psychically or discharged must for the infant be analogous to the experience of being born—must be a repetition of the situation of danger [Freud, 1926, p. 137].

The difficulty with such formulations, of course, is that this rather color-ful comparison of adult subjective feelings with those of the neonate does not lead to fruitful extensions. The hypothesis is untestable in its literal form because it concerns the unobservable elements of subjective experi-ences. While we might be able to utilize the subjective reports of adults as a convenient substitute, there is no conceivable way to translate the in-ternal perceptions of the emerging infant into terms amenable to scientific inquiry.

Even from a purely external viewpoint, little is to be gained from this proposition. Everyone is born and everyone experiences anxiety, so predic-tion from the theory is meaningless. Freud recognized much of this and indicated that Otto Rank had a more useful notion in suggesting that variations in the initial amount of anxiety (for example, quick vs. pro-tracted birth, births which lead to asphyxia in the infant) produce varia-tions in adult anxiety and hence neurosis. Rank's formulation accounts for individual differences and is open to empirical verification, but Freud [1926, p. 152] rejected it because it was too simple and because ". . . it floats in the air instead of being based upon ascertained observations."

3. *Speculations Concerning Stimuli which Evoke Anxiety.* In earlier writings, Freud [1895] speculated that anxiety was evoked whenever "excitation" (for example, sexual energy) accumulated because of some interference with its discharge. By 1926, he had quite different ideas about the process.

Freud hypothesized the occurrence of certain traumatic situations which lay bare the helplessness of the ego and thereby elicit automatic anxiety. Depending on the developmental stage which the individual has reached, these situations are birth, loss of mother, loss of penis, loss of the love of a loved object, and loss of the love of one's own superego. The response of anxiety is inexpedient, but the organism is simply built that way.

Other stimuli which arouse anxiety are those which indicate a threat that a traumatic situation will occur. Here, anxiety acts as a signal which is useful to the organism in that the organism is alerted to prevent situations of danger from occurring. In Freud's [1926, p. 134] words: ". . . anxiety arose originally as a reaction to a state of *danger* and it is reproduced whenever a state of that kind recurs."

4. *Speculations Concerning the Consequents .of Anxiety.* Perhaps Freud's greatest influence on subsequent research and theorizing about anxiety was with respect to its motivating properties. Anxiety is sufficiently unpleasant that it acts as an instigation to other behavior, the goal of which is anxiety reduction. Because of the specific type of behavior with which his work brought him in contact, he was primarily concerned with neurotic forms of anxiety reduction:

Anxiety is a reaction to a situation of danger. It is obviated by the ego's doing something to avoid that situation or to withdraw from it. It might be said that symptoms are created so as to avoid the generating of anxiety. But this does not go deep enough. It would be truer to say that symptoms are created so as to avoid a *danger-situation* whose presence has been signalled by the generation of anxiety [Freud, 1926, pp. 128–129].

In more specific instances, Freud suggested that anxiety produces repression in hysteria and that anxiety concerning the disapproval of the superego is responsible for obsessional neurosis. With respect to phobias, the real source of threat is unavoidable but if some other object can be substituted for the original one, anxiety can be avoided by staying away from the substitute. For example:

. . . as soon as the ego recognizes the danger of castration it gives the signal of anxiety and inhibits through the pleasure-unpleasure agency (in a way which we cannot as yet understand) the impending cathectic process in the id. At the same time the phobia is formed. And now the castration anxiety is directed to a different object and expressed in a distorted form, so that the patient is afraid, not of being castrated by his father, but of being bitten by a horse or devoured by a wolf [Freud, 1926, p. 125].

Given operations for measuring anxiety, one can see that these general ideas lead to a number of possible empirical tests. That is, specific cues are hypothesized to evoke anxiety, which, in turn, is hypothesized to evoke a wide variety of possible behaviors which should serve to bring about anxiety-reduction. Further, interference with the performance of those behaviors should re-evoke anxiety.

5. *Speculations Concerning Techniques to Reduce Anxiety.* As in much of Freud's description of therapeutic activity, a major goal was to render unconscious material conscious. In the simplest terms, neurotic symptoms are retained because the individual is unaware of the stimulus which evoked the anxiety which led to the symptoms. The ability to verbalize accurately concerning the danger cues was seen as the only way in which the individual could regain control of the situation:

Real danger is a danger that is known, and realistic anxiety is anxiety about a known danger of this sort. Neurotic anxiety is anxiety about an unknown danger. Neurotic danger is thus a danger that has still to be discovered. Analysis has shown that it is an instinctual danger. By bringing this danger which is not known to the ego into consciousness, the analyst makes neurotic anxiety no different from realistic anxiety, so that it can be dealt with in the same way [Freud, 1926, p. 165].

Given this overview of Freud's contributions to the study of anxiety, we will now turn to a very different and more recent approach.

HULL-SPENCE LEARNING THEORY AND R_A

Background. The life and career of Clark L. Hull (1884–1952) overlapped with that of Freud, but the background, training, and approach to a theory of behavior of the two men were widely dissimilar. Hull was born on a farm near Akron, New York; a few years later the family moved to another farm in Michigan. His early schooling was in a one-room rural school, with attendance in the spring and autumn often interrupted by farm work. At 17 he passed a teachers' examination and then taught for a year before entering high school. His first experience with higher education was at Alma College where he took courses in mathematics, physics, and chemistry, all of which led to the study of mining engineering. He was working as an engineer in Minnesota when he contracted poliomyelitis, which left him a partial invalid for a year. At this point he decided that he must change his occupational plans; after considering the ministry (the Unitarian Church because it seemed to be a "free, godless religion"), he decided on psychology.

Following another two years of teaching, he and his wife had saved enough money to enter the University of Michigan. After receiving a bachelor's degree in psychology, Hull taught for a year at a normal school in Kentucky for $75 a month. During that time, he applied for a graduate fellowship at Cornell and at Yale but was rejected by both. Finally, he was given a teaching assistantship at the University of Wisconsin and entered graduate school there. After receiving the Ph.D. degree in 1918, he remained at Wisconsin until 1929 at which time he accepted a position at Yale. His original research interests were varied and included an investigation of the effects of tobacco on mental efficiency, work on aptitude testing which led to a book on the subject, a dissertation dealing with concept formation, and a series of experimental studies of hypnosis which resulted in another book.

At Yale, hypnotic experiments met with medical opposition, and Hull was forced to terminate this line of inquiry. For a long period, he had been quite interested in the behaviorist approach of John B. Watson and especially in Watson's utilization of Pavlov's work on conditioning. In time, Hull's research interests were concentrated in the field of learning. Hull describes the theoretical position to which he came:

As the result of the considerations of these behavioral problems over a number of years, probably influenced considerably by my early training in the physical sciences, I came to the definite conclusion around 1930 that psychology is a true natural science; that its primary laws are expressible quantitatively by means of a moderate number of ordinary equations; that all the complex behavior of single individuals will utimately be derivable as secondary laws from (1) these primary laws together with (2) the conditions under which behavior occurs; and that all the behavior of groups as a whole, i.e., strictly social behavior as such, may similarly be derived as quantitative laws from the same primary equations. With these and similar views as a background, the task of psychologists obviously is that of laying bare these laws as quickly and ac-curately as possible, particularly the primary laws. This belief was deepened by the influence of my seminar students, notably Kenneth W. Spence and Neal E. Miller. It has determined most of my scientific activities ever since, and the longer I live the more convinced I am of its general soundness [Hull, 1952, p. 155].

Hull's experimental and theoretical contributions in the 1930's and 1940's had a profound and lasting effect on the field of psychology. As Boring has summarized it:

. . . We find him in the late 1930s, with the constant support of his in-dustrious students, formulating a logically rigorous scientific system for those facts of learning with which he was dealing. He counselled adherence to the *hypothetico-deductive method* in scientific work. That method consists in the setting up of postulates, in deducing from them experimentally testable conclu-sions, in performing the tests, and then, if the tests fail, in revising the postu-lates, or, if they succeed, in adding the postulates, for the time-being at least, to the body of science. That program ultimately took him into the abstractions of mathematical logic, and with five other colleagues he published in 1940 *Mathe-matico-Deductive Theory of Rote Learning: A Study in Scientific Methodology.* For most psychologists it is a difficult and forbidding book, but it shows what can be done with rigorous logic in a scientific context and helps to make most of psychology's postulates, none too well established, seem even more insecure than ever. In 1943 Hull published a simpler book which ordinary psychologists can read, *Principles of Behavior* [Boring, 1950, p. 652].

At the Institute of Human Relations at Yale, a group of behavioral scientists from various fields were brought together with the aim of making an integrated scientific contribution. In 1936, Hull, Miller, John Dollard, and O. H. Mowrer began a seminar which was concerned with seeking ". . . the essential identities lying in conditioned reflexes and behavior laws generally on the one hand, and, on the other, in the phenomena considered by Freud and his psychoanalytic associates" [Hull, 1952, p. 156]. Among the fruits of this endeavor were work on frustration and aggression by Dollard, Doob, Miller, and Sears [1939], the experimental analysis of social learning and imitation by Miller and Dollard [1941], Sears' [1944] experimental analysis of psychoanalytic phenomena, Miller's [1948b] analysis of the relationship between the analytic concept of displacement and the learning concept of generalization, the exposition of personality and psychotherapy by Dollard and Miller [1950], and Mowrer's [1953] application of the principles of learning theory to problems such as mental illness and psychotherapy. Hull himself had planned to include in his series of theoretical volumes one which dealt with deductions of the more elementary forms of social behavior, but his work was slowed down by poor health, and he wrote, ". . . as time passes I realize that I cannot possibly write this book, much as I desire to do so" [Hull, 1952, p. 162]. He died in the year that statement of regret was published.

One of Hull's early associates at Yale was Kenneth W. Spence (1907–   ), who entered Yale in 1930 after receiving his undergraduate education and a master's degree at McGill University. After being awarded the Ph.D. degree in 1933 under Yerkes, Spence remained on the faculty at Yale until 1937 and then spent a year at the University of Virginia. At that point, he began a long, productive, and extremely influential career at the State University of Iowa. Hull [1952, p. 159] notes: "He gave me detailed suggestions and criticisms regarding the text of *Principles of Behavior*, and after he became Chairman of the psychology department at the University of Iowa he directed many able empirical studies which contributed materially to the later development of the system." In terms of his experimental work, his major contributions to learning (or behavior) theory, his expositions of the philosophy of science, and his life-long influence on an outstanding array of students, Spence holds a very special place in behavioral science. He is one of the few psychologists who have been elected to membership in the National Academy of Science. Since 1964 he has been at the University of Texas.

Individual Differences in Emotional Responsiveness. In order to provide a sample of the Hull-Spence type of theory as a contrast to psychoanalytic formulations and to indicate the specific theoretical impetus for the development of the Manifest Anxiety Scale (MAS), one type of learning situation (classical conditioning) will be described. An *unconditioned stimulus* is one which regularly evokes an observable response (called an unconditioned response) such as the electric shock which evoked fear responses in Miller's rats. A *conditioned stimulus* is a stimulus which does not evoke that response until after it has been paired with or associated with the unconditioned stimulus; the white compartment was the conditioned stimulus to the overt fear responses in Miller's experiment.

Once conditioning or simple learning has taken place, the conditioned stimulus comes to evoke the response which is then labeled the *conditioned response*; after being subjected to shock in the white compartment, the rats exhibited fear whenever they were placed in it again.

Even in such a seemingly simple situation, a great many variables have been found to influence the relationship between the conditioned stimulus (S_c) and the conditioned response (R_p). For example, the probability of S_c evoking R_p has been found to be influenced by the number of trials (N) in which the conditioned stimulus and unconditioned stimulus were presented together; the more such pairings, the greater the probability that the response will follow the presentation of the stimulus. Another influence is the strength of the unconditioned stimulus (S_u); an intense stimulus (such as a strong electric shock) has a greater effect on performance than a weak one. Further, the more often the unconditioned stimulus has been presented (ΣS_u) with or without the conditioned stimulus the greater the response probability. There are individual differences in emotional responsiveness (R_A), and such responsiveness has a facilitating effect on simple conditioning. There are also a number of variables which have been found to have an adverse or inhibiting effect on performance—the number of successive responses (N_R) which the organism has made, the time between trials (T_R), and the amount of work involved in the response (W_R).

Now, we can easily catalogue these variables and indicate that they have such and such an effect on performance. Any theoretical scheme which would enable us to conceptualize the variables in a meaningful way, which would generalize to different situations, and which would lead to predictions about quite different kinds of behavior would obviously be advantageous. Hull [1943] proposed such a system, and his approach involved the postulation of hypothetical variables which were each ultimately defined in terms of observable variables such as those just described. Figure 10-1 shows a representation of the interrelationships among the various empirical and hypothetical variables in the conditioning situation.

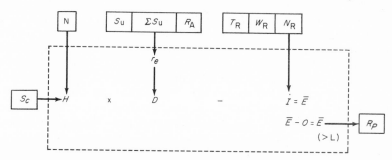

Fig. 10-1. *Representation of theoretical scheme in classical conditioning situation.*

The relationship between S_c and R_p is indicated to be a function of a series of different kinds of variables. The effects of several of the independent variables are conceptualized as influencing the strength of whatever habits (H) are activated in a given stimulus situation, while other independent variables are conceptualized as influencing the strength of a hypothetical emotional response (r_e), which in turn influences the strength of the total generalized drive state (D). In Hull's system, the strength of a response is determined by the effective excitatory potential (E). The magnitude of E is a multiplicative function of habit strength times drive $(H \times D)$. Those variables which have a negative effect on the strength of the response are conceptualized as a single inhibitory factor $(\dot{I})$. Thus, $E = f(H \times D - \dot{I})$. Still another hypothetical intervening variable, an oscillating inhibitory factor (O) is assumed to vary from moment to moment and hence to add an element of unpredicted response variance. The range of variation for a particular situation can be determined, however. In any event, O is subtracted from E to yield the momentary effective excitatory potential $(\bar{E})$. When this value is large enough to exceed the necessary threshold value (L), the observable response (R_p) occurs.

This type of theoretical system utilizes only constructs which may be defined in terms of observable operations, and relatively precise relationships between and among variables are specified. Where does the concept of anxiety fit into such a system?

With respect to the measurement of individual differences in emotional responsiveness (R_A), a personality variable came to be of interest to learning theorists working within this framework. Spence describes the rationale of the resulting measuring instrument:

> The third implication of our theoretical mechanism was based on the well-known fact or observation that individuals differ in the magnitude of their reflex responses to a given intensity of stimulation. By analogy, again, we were led to assume that individuals would differ characteristically in the magnitude of this response, r_e, to the same intensity of stressful stimulation. If now there were available some means of assessing differences in this emotional responsiveness of individuals, our theoretical schema would lead to the prediction that highly emotional subjects, as assessed by the measuring device, would exhibit a higher level of performance in aversive forms of conditioning than subjects who scored low on the device.
>
> The problem thus became one of attempting to develop a test for identifying individuals in the responsiveness of this hypothetical emotional mechanism. Such a test, of course, would have to be defined independently of the measures that were to be employed in testing the theoretical network, i.e., the measures of performance in conditioning and other learning situations. It was in connection with this portion of our theory that the Manifest Anxiety or A-scale was developed. The idea of using a self-inventory test that would differentiate subjects in terms of the degree to which they admitted to possessing overt or

manifest symptoms of emotionality was suggested by Taylor [1951] in a doctoral dissertation [Spence, 1958, pp. 132–133].

The development of this test and a portion of the considerable amount of research carried out with it will be described in subsequent sections of this chapter. Though the original interest was in obtaining a psychometric measure which was related to drive level, work on the MAS has not been confined to the learning laboratory. In fact, much of the work is closer in content to the types of problems which Freud discussed even though the methodology was developed in the context of Hull-Spence learning theory.

Construction of the Manifest Anxiety Scale

INITIAL ITEM SELECTION

The development of the MAS by one of Spence's doctoral students, Janet Taylor (later, Janet Taylor Spence), was first reported in an article describing one of the conditioning experiments [Taylor, 1951], but the test itself was later described in somewhat greater detail along with relevant psychometric data [Taylor, 1953].

As an item pool, approximately 200 items from the MMPI were given to five clinical psychologists with instructions to identify which of the items indicated manifest anxiety. They were also given a definition of this variable, which followed Cameron's description of chronic anxiety reaction:

The chronic anxiety reaction is characterized by the presence of persistently heightened skeletal and visceral tensions, which disturb a person's habitual rhythms of living and predispose him generally to give exaggerated and inappropriate responses on relatively slight provocation. In well-developed cases the patient's complaints and the examiner's findings together give a consistent clinical picture that is not difficult to recognize. The patient usually complains of tightness, aching or pain in his head, neck, shoulders, back and limbs which indicates increased muscular strain, particularly but by no means exclusively in the main postural groups. The generally increased reactivity of skeletal muscles can as a rule be clinically demonstrated in the brisk phasic stretch reflexes, the initial resistance to passive flexion and extension, and the fine to moderate tremors in fingers, tongue and sometimes lips and eyelids. The patient usually looks or acts strained in walk and posture, in facial expression, verbal reaction, gestures and other movements, and especially in response to intense or unexpected stimulation.

The common visceral complaints are those which we would expect from our knowledge of the visceral components of ordinary anxiety reactions. Thus, the patient tells us of loss of appetite or continual hunger, of difficulty in getting food down, nausea and regurgitation, abdominal discomfort, spastic constipation or chronic mild diarrhea, of urinary frequency and urgency, cardiac irregularities, breathing difficulties, secretory changes and cold, clammy extremities, of menstrual disorders or changes in sex pace, of dyspareunia or relative impotence.

The chronically anxious patient usually states that he cannot think clearly, concentrate or remember as he once could, and that he cannot seem to stick to any one task for long. Although these claims are seldom corroborated objectively by ordinary test procedures, one is not justified in concluding that therefore they are unfounded. Most test situations call for a relatively brief period of application to a task set by someone else, who also provides special social motivation. The patient's difficulty is in setting his own tasks and providing sufficient motivation himself to keep at them until they are completed. He is usually irritable, fatigued, worried and discouraged. In his thoughts he may return repeatedly to problems facing him or ruminate in a mildly compulsive manner over his possible errors of omission and commission. Many of his choices and decisions are made actually in response to his tensions rather than to factors in the objective situation.

It is obvious to an observer that the patient cannot let go and relax. His tensions contribute to his restlessness and interfere with adequate satisfaction in anything, and his restlessness and frustration contribute further to his tension. He falls asleep with great difficulty and only after a long period of tossing in bed; he awakens easily and once awake finds trouble in getting to sleep again. His sleep is often disturbed by anxiety dreams, sometimes of awesome or horrible predicaments, sometimes of his daytime fantasies and conflicts, which he carries over into the sleeping phases of his life in more or less recognizable forms. With this general background of unrelieved tension and strain, the patient is prone to develop anxiety attacks now and then, occasionally in response to stress which he can identify at the time, but more often not [Cameron, 1947, pp. 249–250].

On 65 of the items, agreement was 80 per cent or better among the clinicians that manifest anxiety was being tapped. Several investigations then employed this measure, which consisted of the 65 anxiety items mixed with 135 nonanxiety buffer items, in a booklet titled, "Biographical Inventory." The success of this research led Bechtoldt [1953] to attempt to improve the measuring instrument by carrying out an internal consistency item-analysis. The result was a 50-item scale made up of those items which had the highest correlations with the total score. The items and the scoring key for anxiety are given in Figure 10–2.

FIG. 10–2. *Manifest anxiety scale.*

---

1. I do not tire quickly.   (F)
2. I am troubled by attacks of nausea.   (T)
3. I believe I am no more nervous than most others.   (F)
4. I have very few headaches.   (F)
5. I work under a great deal of tension.   (T)
6. I cannot keep my mind on one thing.   (T)

Fɪɢ. 10–2. *Manifest anxiety scale* (*Cont.*)

---

7. I worry over money and business.   (T)
8. I frequently notice my hand shakes when I try to do something.   (T)
9. I blush no more often than others.   (F)
10. I have diarrhea once a month or more.   (T)
11. I worry quite a bit over possible misfortunes.   (T)
12. I practically never blush.   (F)
13. I am often afraid that I am going to blush.   (T)
14. I have nightmares every few nights.   (T)
15. My hands and feet are usually warm enough.   (F)
16. I sweat very easily even on cool days.   (T)
17. Sometimes when embarrassed, I break out in a sweat which annoys me greatly.   (T)
18. I hardly ever notice my heart pounding and 1 am seldom short of breath.   (F)
19. I feel hungry almost all the time.   (T)
20. I am very seldom troubled by constipation.   (F)
21. I have a great deal of stomach trouble.   (T)
22. I have had periods in which I lost sleep over worry.   (T)
23. My sleep is fitful and disturbed.   (T)
24. I dream frequently about things that are best kept to myself.   (T)
25. I am easily embarrassed.   (T)
26. I am more sensitive than most other people.   (T)
27. I frequently find myself worrying about something.   (T)
28. I wish I could be as happy as others seem to be.   (T)
29. I am usually calm and not easily upset.   (F)
30. I cry easily.   (T)
31. I feel anxiety about something or someone almost all the time.   (T)
32. I am happy most of the time.   (F)
33. It makes me nervous to have to wait.   (T)
34. I have periods of such great restlessness that I cannot sit long in a chair.   (T)
35. Sometimes I become so excited that I find it hard to get to sleep.   (T)
36. I have sometimes felt that difficulties were piling up so high that I could not overcome them.   (T)
37. I must admit that I have at times been worried beyond reason over something that really did not matter.   (T)
38. I have very few fears compared to my friends.   (F)
39. I have been afraid of things or people that I know could not hurt me.   (T)
40. I certainly feel useless at times.   (T)
41. I find it hard to keep my mind on a task or job.   (T)
42. I am usually self-conscious.   (T)
43. I am inclined to take things hard.   (T)
44. I am a high-strung person.   (T)
45. Life is a strain for me much of the time.   (T)
46. At times I think I am no good at all.   (T)
47. I am certainly lacking in self-confidence.   (T)
48. I sometimes feel that I am about to go to pieces.   (T)
49. I shrink from facing a crisis or difficulty.   (T)
50. I am entirely self-confident.   (F)

RELIABILITY AND NORMS

The internal consistency of the test was found to be relatively high, even before the item-analysis was carried out. Hilgard, Jones, and Kaplan [1951] reported a split-half reliability coefficient of .92 for the original 65-item test.

Stability of the test scores over time is also adequate for research. The MAS has been found to have a test-retest reliability of .89 over a three-week period, .82 over a five-month period, and .81 over nine to seventeen months [Taylor, 1953]. The means also remained relatively constant over time, so one is justified in conceptualizing manifest anxiety as an enduring personality characteristic.

With 1,971 introductory psychology students at the State University of Iowa, the mean MAS score was found to be 14.56 [Taylor, 1953]. Though the female students had a slightly higher mean score than the males, the difference between the sexes in manifest anxiety was not significant.

SOCIAL DESIRABILITY AND THE MAS

In discussing the California F Scale in Chapter 8, the measurement problem raised by acquiescent response set was indicated. With the MAS, some degree of balance exists with respect to acquiescence (39 items keyed TRUE, 11 items keyed FALSE), so one would not anticipate that the measurement of anxiety would be found to be greatly contaminated by this particular response set. To test this proposition, Chapman and Campbell [1959] reversed the wording of each MAS item in order to have a positive form (T = anxious response) and a negative form (F = anxious response) of the test. With a sample of 184 subjects, the two forms correlated .84. Thus, acquiescent response set does not appear to influence the MAS. However, another type of response set has been discovered.

Edwards [1953] published the first article in a series which raised the question of the effect of the social desirability of the content of test items on response to the items. He obtained judges' ratings of the social desirability of a series of questionnaire items. The correlation between the social-desirability value of an item as assigned by the judges and the proportion of subjects agreeing with the item content was found to be .87. This substantial relationship has been confirmed in other studies.

A related, but somewhat different concept, is Edwards' [1957] social-desirability hypothesis. He suggests that individuals differ in the tendency to give socially desirable responses to questionnaire items. He has built a 39-item Social Desirability (SD) Scale to measure this tendency. The higher an individual's score on the SD Scale, the more likely he will be to give socially desirable responses to test items which fall along this dimension. When scores on the SD Scale are found to correlate highly with scores on a given test, one interpretation is that the test is confounding social-desirability response set with whatever it is purporting to measure. SD Scale scores have been found to correlate highly with many personality tests, such as most of the MMPI scales [Edwards, 1959], including a correlation of —.84 with the MAS [Edwards, 1957]. One caution suggested by such findings is that correlations between the MAS and other tests loaded on the social-desirability variable may simply reflect the fact that both instruments measure (at least in part) the social-desirability set.

Can something be done to eliminate this problem? With a relationship of —.84, it would be extremely difficult to attempt to measure anxiety in the way Taylor has chosen and at the same time "control for" social desirability of item content. Conceivably, items could be found which are unrelated to social desirability but which are highly related to manifest anxiety. Perhaps more reasonable is to inquire whether the MAS and the SD Scale should be conceptualized as measuring the same dimension and then to determine the most appropriate name for it. Farber discusses this problem with respect to the MAS:

What, then, does the test measure?

In one sense, this is a trivial question, and requires but a trivial answer, though, unfortunately, one that constructors and users of tests sometimes fail to see, namely, that giving tests different names does not guarantee that they reflect different characteristics, and giving them the same names does not necessarily mean they reflect the same determinants. If all these highly inter-related measures are related to all other kinds of behaviors in the same way, they measure the same thing, regardless of their labels.

Occasionally, however, this confusion among the characteristics inferred from behavior is not merely nominal. For instance, height and weight are highly correlated in the general population, yet no one supposes they are merely different names for the same thing. What if defensiveness and desire to make a favorable impression are independent, but nevertheless empirically related in a given population? How, then, could we decide whether they reflect different organismic states or processes? Or better, if the one measure is related to some other mode of behavior, which hypothetical variable is responsible for the relation?

These are not trivial questions, and their answers are not easily come by. One kind of answer is simply the observation that there is never any guarantee in science against the inaccurate identification of determinants [Farber, 1964, p. 30].

To date, research findings suggest that the SD Scale and the MAS are measuring the same dimension of behavior. If so, the only problem is that of eventually deciding on the most appropriate name, as discussed in

Chapter 3. If, however, the two instruments are found to be measuring two different but highly related dimensions (like height and weight in Farber's example), the theoretical formulations of their respective antecedents, correlates, and consequents will of necessity diverge. In either event, to consider social desirability as a "response set" which simply constitutes a methodological weakness contaminating the MAS as a measuring device does not seem fruitful. The tendency to give socially desirable responses is either another name for manifest anxiety, or it is a personality variable worth studying in its own right.

Antecedents of Manifest Anxiety

Surprisingly little research has been directed toward the problem of determining the antecedents of individual differences in characteristic anxiety level.

One variable which has been investigated is the discrepancy between parental expectancies with regard to the behavior of their offspring and the actual behavior of the offspring. Presumably, a failure to live up to parental goals would be a continuing source of anxiety cues. Such a situation could arise because parental ideals were unreasonably high, because the offspring's behavior was actually inadequate, or from a combination of these two determinants.

A group of adolescent boys enrolled in a Summer Demonstration School at the University of California and their mothers were each given a series of 76 items as a Q-sort device [Stewart, 1958]. The boys were asked to describe themselves in three separate ways—as they perceived themselves, as they would like to be, and as they thought their mothers would like them to be. In addition, they were given the MAS. The mothers sorted the cards twice—to describe their sons as they are, and as they would like them to be. The items on the Q-sort involved inner strength and drive, self-control, social attitude, relationships with the opposite sex, intellectual abilities, home and family, physical characteristics, special talents, religion, and school relationships.

Stewart found that the greater the discrepancy between the son's self-description and his mother's description of her ideal for him, the more anxious the son. The MAS scores of the boys correlated .49 ($p < .01$) with the discrepancy between the boy's self and the mother's ideal son. Similarly, anxiety was positively related to the discrepancy between the son's self-description and his perception of his mother's ideal for him ($r = .25$, $p < .05$). Stewart [1958, p. 384] concluded that boys with low manifest anxiety ". . . were satisfied with themselves, met their perception of their mother's ideal for them, and perceived themselves as being the kind of person their mother actually wanted them to be."

The Place of Manifest Anxiety in the Structure of Personality

OTHER VERBAL MEASURES OF ANXIETY

A number of investigations with the MAS have been of a semivalidational nature. That is, the MAS and one or more other verbal tests purporting to measure anxiety are administered to a sample of subjects and intercorrelated. These studies fall into several categories.

Separation Anxiety. A special questionnaire (Lack of Protection Scale) was built by Sarason [1958] to measure anxiety as defined by Freud: separation anxiety. An example is, "When I was a child, I often wondered how much my father loved me." If the MAS is measuring the sort of anxiety discussed by Freud, the two measures should be related. Sarason [1961] found the two tests to correlate .30 in a group of 75 males and .65 in a group of 77 females; both coefficients are significant.

Symptoms. The Saslow Screening Test is a brief, self-administered test which contains questions about situations provocative of anxiety or discouragement, whether the subject bottles up his feelings under such circumstances, whether he feels sick or miserable if he does so, and whether he has any of a group of 24 symptoms as a result. An anxiety-proneness score is derived from the frequency and number of symptoms the subject ascribes to himself. Gleser and Ulett [1952] administered this instrument and the MAS to 151 normal males and 40 neuropsychiatric patients. They found that the two instruments correlated significantly in both groups, .56 for the normals and .68 for the patients. Another investigation, with 162 patients as subjects, reported a correlation between the two instruments of .63 [Matarazzo, Matarazzo, and Saslow, 1961].

Test Anxiety. One rather specific type of anxiety which has been measured by means of questionnaires is that involved in test-taking situations. Mandler and Sarason [1952] developed such a test (Test Anxiety Questionnaire or TAQ) which asks subjects about their subjective experiences in a testing situation, including uneasiness, accelerated heart-beat, perspiration, emotional interference, and worry before and during a test. Since the MAS was designed as a general measure of anxiety across various situations, a positive relationship would be expected between it and test anxiety scores. The MAS and TAQ have been found to correlate .53 among 25 male students at Michigan [Raphelson, 1957], .59 among 35 Harvard-Radcliffe undergraduates [Mandler and Cowen, 1958], .44 with a group of 340 Wisconsin students [Martin and McGowan, 1955], .43 in a group of community college students [Sinick, 1956], and .32

among 40 Stanford male undergraduates [Alpert and Haber, 1960]. A slightly different form of the TAQ was found to correlate with the MAS .46 with 75 males and .53 with 77 females at the University of Washington [Sarason, 1961]. Manifest anxiety and test anxiety are obviously related dimensions.

Rorschach Indicators. Various scoring determinants and combinations of determinants on the Rorschach have been utilized as anxiety indicators. In Chapter 3, Elizur's [1949] hostility scoring system for the Rorschach was described. At the same time that score was developed, Elizur devised a scoring system for anxiety content. Responses with relatively overt anxiety content ("a frightening giant") are given two points, while less overt content ("an unpleasant animal") receives a score of one. Goodstein [1954] obtained a correlation of .38 ($p < .01$) between MAS scores and Elizur's anxiety score for a group of 57 Iowa undergraduates. In another investigation, Goodstein and Goldberger [1955] sought the relationship between a number of Rorschach anxiety indicators and MAS scores. From a group of 139 psychiatric patients, the 16 with highest and 16 with lowest MAS scores were selected. The investigators found that the high-anxious patients gave significantly fewer responses utilizing the whole blot and significantly more responses utilizing surface shading, had significantly longer reaction times in responding to the blots, and (as in the previous study) had significantly higher anxiety scores than the low-anxious patients.

Thus, we find that a fairly diverse array of verbal anxiety measures ranging from other questionnaires to Rorschach responses are related to the MAS.

NONVERBAL MEASURES OF ANXIETY

Observations of Behavior. When a clinical psychologist or a psychiatrist makes judgments concerning a patient's anxiety level, he is probably utilizing a wide variety of verbal and nonverbal cues including gestures, voice pitch, and bodily movements. If such judgments have any degree of consistency and accuracy and if the self-report approach of the MAS is measuring the same behavioral dimension as that determined by observations of anxious behavior, test scores and judges' ratings should correspond.

With a college student population, Hoyt and Magoon [1954] asked eight experienced counsellors to rate the degree of manifest anxiety of some of their clients over the past six months. Manifest anxiety was defined in terms of behavior that leads to a client's classification as:

(a) Nervous (i.e., mannerisms such as nail biting, knuckle-cracking, chain smoking, profuse perspiration, etc.); (b) Tense (i.e., unable to relax, continually working under pressure, hand trembling, tics, etc.); (c) Easily embarrassed (i.e., readily blushes, stammers, etc.); (d) Worried (i.e., apprehensive over what will happen from day to day, doubts self continually, etc.) [Hoyt and Magoon, 1954, pp. 357–358].

The 289 clients were designated as high, medium, or low in anxiety. The correlation between counsellor ratings and MAS scores was .47. Buss [1955] repeated the Hoyt and Magoon study using the ratings of four clinical psychologists concerning 64 neuropsychiatric patients. Pooled ratings by these judges correlated .60 with manifest anxiety scores.

Lauterbach [1958] had three psychologists and one psychiatrist independently rate 44 patients referred for psychiatric consultation in a military hospital with respect to anxiety. The psychologists had relatively good interjudge agreement ($r = .78$ to .80), but their ratings were unrelated to those of the psychiatrist. The pooled psychologist ratings correlated .44 ($p < .01$) with the patients' scores on the MAS; the psychiatrist's ratings were not related to MAS scores. Using 151 male subjects, Gleser and Ulett [1952] found that a psychiatrist's ratings of anxiety after a one-hour interview correlated .61 with scores on the MAS. Apparently, individual differences exist among judges in defining anxiety and/or in ability to make accurate observations.

Buss, Wiener, Durkee, and Baer [1955] attempted to define anxiety in sufficient detail so that independent observers could agree with one another at a relatively high degree of consistency. A standard interview was conducted with 64 patients in the presence of four psychologists. Immediately after the interview, each psychologist independently rated the patient with respect to nine categories—observations of distractibility, restlessness, and physiological concomitants; patient's report of subjective feelings of tenseness, worry, somatic complaints, physiological concomitants, and muscular tension; and an overall rating of anxiety. The investigators found relatively high interjudge reliability on the ratings and a correlation of .60 between the overall anxiety rating and the MAS scores. Table 10–1 shows that the various categories of anxiety differed markedly in degree of relationship with the test scores. These findings were replicated by Siegman [1956].

Skin Conductance. The galvanic skin response (GSR) is a physiological index of anxiety in which changes in electrical resistance of the skin are determined by means of a galvanometer. Raphelson [1957] obtained continuous skin conductance records during an experiment involving competition in a complex perceptual-motor task. For the 25 male subjects, MAS scores were unrelated either to initial conductance level or to changes in skin conductance in the experimental situation. Silverman [1957] recorded skin conductance levels on 66 male undergraduates at NYU in a resting condition and while they were performing a task. During the task, a portion of the subjects received a shock threat while

Table 10–1   ANXIETY RATINGS AND MAS SCORES*

Category	Correlation with MAS
Observed:	
1. Distractibility	.16
2. Restlessness	.37
3. Physiological Concomitants	.22
Reported:	
4. Subjective Feeling of Tenseness	.52
5. Worry	.50
6. Somatic Complaints	.40
7. Physiological Concomitants	.68
8. Muscular Tension	.54
Clinical Integration:	
9. Overall Rating of Anxiety	.60

* From Buss, et al., 1955, p. 127.

others did not. Scores on the MAS did not correlate with the conductance readings in any of the conditions ($r = -.17$ to $.07$). Other attempts have been made to find a relationship between the MAS and physiological indices of anxiety.

Palmar Sweating. In addition to GSR measures, changes in the moisture of the skin may be measured by placing the index finger in an anhydrous ferrous chloride solution for one minute, letting the finger dry, and then placing it on a specially treated piece of paper. An electrical device is used to measure the amount of ferrous chloride deposited on the paper, which indicates the amount of sweat present on the finger [Mowrer, Light, Luria, and Zeleny, 1953]. Jackson and Bloomberg [1958] found *no* relationship between this physiological measure and MAS scores among 37 male neuro-psychiatric patients ($r = -.15$).

Blink Rate. A good deal of empirical evidence suggests that the rate of eye blinking increases in stressful situations [Meyer, 1953]. Jackson and Bloomberg [1958] obtained two one-minute observations of blink rate in a standard situation for 37 male patients. Scores on the MAS were unrelated to blink rate ($r = -.11$).

Serum Cholesterol. A growing body of evidence indicates that stress is one of the factors which brings about an elevation in the level of serum cholesterol [for example, Mann and White, 1953]. Golding and Harvey [1964] investigated the relationship between manifest anxiety and serum cholesterol using undergraduate males. From a group of 332 students, blood samples were collected for the 23 subjects with extremely high or low test scores. The two groups were found not to differ in mean cholesterol level. The correlation between the two variables was not significantly different from zero.

Muscle Action Potential. Sensitive electronic recording devices make it possible to record changes in electrical potential associated with muscle movements too faint to be observed visually. Recordings of muscle action potential have been interpreted as a measure of energy level or motivation. Rossi [1959] in his doctoral dissertation at Utah obtained MAS scores for a group of male and female students. In a reaction time experiment, muscle action potential recordings were made. Subjects with high MAS scores had higher muscle action potential scores than did low MAS subjects across four experimental conditions.

Conclusions. Apparently, then, judgments about anxiety made by experienced clinical workers are positively related to anxiety as measured by the MAS. The few negative findings can probably be attributed to differences among judges in defining anxiety and/or in competence with respect to this task. With respect to a variety of physiological indicators of anxiety, however, the findings are primarily negative. Several possibilities have been suggested to account for this lack of relationship including the possibility that anxiety as measured physiologically and as measured by a questionnaire are simply unrelated sets of responses.

Another possibility may account for the negative findings. Based on the notion of response specificity, Lacey and Lacey [1958] have proposed that the best index of physiological activity is obtained by measuring an individual on a series of physiological variables and then using each subject's highest score, regardless of what the variable is. For one individual, it might be GSR, for another heart rate, and so forth. As part of a larger investigation, Mandler, Mandler, Kremen, and Sholiton [1961] determined the relationship between MAS scores and this highest specific response index. With a six-channel polygraph, eleven measures of physiological activity were obtained, including heart rate, galvanic skin response, peripheral blood flow, and finger temperature. With a group of Harvard undergraduates as subjects, the typical nonsignificant correlations were obtained between scores on the MAS and individual measures of physiological activity (for example, MAS and GSR correlated .06). However, when MAS scores were correlated with each subject's highest physiological scores the correlation was .60 ($p < .01$). If this proves to be a stable finding, the exploration of relationships between physiological indices and personality variables will obviously benefit from this new approach.

MALADJUSTMENT

One would hypothesize that many varieties of psychoneurosis should be characterized by a higher level of manifest anxiety. If Freud's proposals concerning the role of anxiety in symptom-formation are correct, we would expect a high anxiety level to precede the development of symptoms, a low anxiety level to follow the successful development of anxiety-reducing behavior patterns (for example, hysteria), and a high anxiety level to follow any interference with symptoms (for example, the initial stages of psychotherapy). Though research to date with the MAS has not precisely followed the pattern just outlined, there are relevant data available with respect to MAS scores and various aspects of emotional disturbance.

Population Comparisons. Taylor [1953] administered the MAS to 103 neurotic and psychotic patients undergoing psychiatric treatment. Their median score of 34 is considerably higher than the median of 13 obtained by Iowa college students. Half of the patients had scores higher than those of 98 per cent of the students. Figure 10–3 shows a

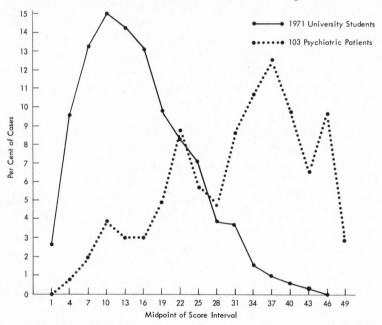

FIG. 10–3. *Comparison of normal and psychiatric populations on the MAS. (Data from Taylor, 1953.)*

comparison of the two groups. Similar findings are reported by Bailey, Berrick, Lachmann, and Ortmyer [1960]. A group of 128 psychiatric outpatients applying for treatment at a VA Mental Hygiene Clinic obtained a mean MAS score of 27.5. Again, the patients are much higher in manifest anxiety than the normative group of college students.

When psychiatric patients are compared with college students, the two groups are different in many respects besides the variable of maladjustment. The students tend to be younger, brighter, and better educated, for example. An investigation comparing MAS scores of 44 psychiatric patients and 29 medical patients matched for age and intelligence was conducted by Matarazzo, Guze, and Matarazzo [1955]. All of the subjects were outpatients. The neuro-psychiatric patients obtained significantly higher MAS scores (mean = 26.20) then the medical patients (mean = 13.31). This finding was cross-validated in a population of VA inpatients, 41 neurotics and 39 medical patients. Again, the means (29.90 vs. 17.61) were significantly different. Another comparison of psychiatric and non-psychiatric groups on the MAS was carried out by Matarazzo, Matarazzo, and Saslow [1961]. Data were obtained for patients at the University of Oregon Medical School. The background variables on which the medical and psychiatric groups differed were in the opposite direction from previous studies in that the psychiatric patients were significantly younger and better educated. Nevertheless, the psychiatric patients obtained significantly higher mean scores than the medical patients on the MAS.

Another type of population comparison involves differences *within* a psychiatric population. Rubin and Townsend [1958] compared the manifest anxiety scores of 82 psychoneurotic patients and 157 schizophrenic patients, all male veterans on the admission ward of a neuro-psychiatric service. The psychoneurotics (mean = 22.4) were significantly more anxious than the schizophrenics (mean = 17.7). Within the psychoneurotic group, no difference in MAS scores existed between the 57 patients with a diagnosis of anxiety reaction and the 25 patients with other psychoneurotic diagnoses. Lack of differentiation among different categories of psychoneurosis was also reported by Matarazzo, Guze, and Matarazzo [1955].

Siegman [1956] compared the MAS scores of 74 patients, divided in terms of clinical diagnosis as anxiety reaction, other neuroses, latent schizophrenia, paranoid schizophrenia, and psychopathic personality. Siegman found that the patients with a diagnosis of anxiety reaction had significantly higher scores than any other group, while those with a diagnosis of psychopathic personality had significantly lower scores than any other group. Similarly, Goodstein and Goldberger [1955] found in a group of 139 hospitalized psychiatric patients that those diagnosed psychoneurotic had higher mean MAS scores (26.5) than any other diagnostic group.

Relationship with Various Measures of Maladjustment. Shatin [1961] developed a Clinical Psychiatric Rating Scale which includes such categories as anxiety and/or tension, depression, suspicion, hostility, and a total pathology score. A group of 40 male psychiatric patients admitted to a general hospital were rated by a psychiatrist on the basis of interview, observation, and discussion with ward personnel. The MAS and the total pathology score correlated .45 ($p < .01$).

In the Matarazzo, *et al.* [1961] investigation of medical and psychiatric patients, the Cornell Medical Index was also administered to the subjects. This index contains questions about both medical and psychiatric symptoms and serves as a standardized medical history. This test correlated .78 with the MAS. The higher the MAS score, the greater is the number of symptoms which are reported.

Utilizing interviews and autobiographical material, an experienced clinical psychologist rank-ordered 20 male college students with respect to repression and optimism-pessimism; six months later the subjects took the MAS. Eriksen and Davids [1955] defined repression as the tendency to forget traumatic experiences or anxiety-arousing events; optimism-pessimism ranges from a happy outlook on life, contentment, and personal satisfaction to a gloomy outlook, dejection, and general dissatisfaction on the other. They found that MAS scores correlated $-.41$ $(p < .05)$ with repression ratings and $-.87$ $(p < .01)$ with optimism-pessimism ratings. Congruent with these findings are those reported by Joy [1963]; the Repression-Sensitization Scale (see Chapter 6) correlated .91 with the MAS in a group of undergraduate students.

Investigations which report correlations between the MAS and other scales of the MMPI raise certain problems. The MAS and the MMPI are taken at the same time as part of the same test, have the same true-false format, and have specific items which appear on both the MAS and some of the other scales. One would expect, then, relationships to be spuriously high. Still, it is of interest to examine the findings. With a sample of 106 male neuropsychiatric patients and 73 normal college males, Brackbill and Little [1954] correlated the MAS with each MMPI scale. As shown in Table 10–2, the relationships tend to be substantial, especially in the patient sample. One conclusion drawn by the authors [Brackbill and Little, 1954, p. 434] was that: ". . . with clinical populations no information would be provided by the scoring of the A scale in the MMPI that is not already present in the current battery of scales."

Table 10–2   CORRELATIONS BETWEEN MAS SCORES
AND SCORES ON OTHER MMPI SCALES

Scale	Patients	Students
F, Validity	.63	.19
K, Defensiveness	−.74	−.56
Hs, Hypochondriasis	.78	.60
D, Depression	.74	.38
Hy, Hysteria	.50	.05
Pd, Psychopathic Deviate	.64	.16
Mf, Masculinity-Femininity	.45	.44
Pa, Paranoia	.59	.15
Pt, Psychasthenia	.92	.81
Sc, Schizophrenia	.83	.56
Ma, Mania	.28	.10

A number of investigators have proposed the use of combinations of MMPI scales as indices of neuroticism and anxiety neurosis. Windle [1955] investigated the relationship between the MAS and four of these measures. With 55 female undergraduates as subjects, a significant positive relationship was found between the MAS and each index. A number of other investigators have also found that the Winne neuroticism scale correlates substantially with the MAS [for example, Kerrick, 1955; Holtzman, Calvin, and Bitterman, 1952].

Thus, with respect to MAS scores and maladjustment, it is well established that the MAS yields higher scores in a psychiatric population than in a normal one, and some evidence exists that patients with anxiety neurosis obtain higher scores than other diagnostic groups. A number of measures of maladjustment are also associated with MAS performance, including ratings of pathology and pessimism, presence of medical and psychiatric symptoms, and scores on most of the MMPI clinical scales and MMPI indices of neuroticism. Those high in manifest anxiety tend to be rated as less repressive and to obtain low scores on an MMPI measure of defensiveness and high scores on an MMPI measure of sensitizing defenses.

INTELLIGENCE AND ACADEMIC PERFORMANCE

In a somewhat general way, a widely accepted belief exists that individuals who become anxious in situations involving intellectual skills will perform less well than individuals whose anxiety level remains relatively low. For example, MAS scores have been found to be negatively correlated with Gough's *Hr* Scale, which is a predictor of scholastic achievement [Bendig, 1959]. Several specific propositions have been made as to the reason for such a relationship to hold:

It may be that persons of lower intelligence are more prone to manifest anxiety. On the other hand, and this seems to be the explanation currently preferred, the presence of manifest anxiety may well serve to depress scores on intelligence or ability. If this latter explanation be true, it may be explained according to the drainage hypothesis of psychoanalytic theory by assuming that energy is dissipated which might otherwise be put into the performance being tested. Or according to Taylor and Spence's interpretation which derives from Hullian theory, competing responses are more difficult to extinguish when drive is high, and therefore more trials are required for learning where competing responses are involved [Kerrick, 1955, p. 75].

The Taylor-Spence propositions will be discussed more fully in a later section of this chapter. Whatever type of explanation ultimately proves more fruitful, it was inevitable that research interest would be directed to the question of the MAS in relation to performance on intelligence tests and achievement tests and with respect to academic grades.

A surprisingly large amount of research time has been spent in attempting to determine this relationship. Intellectual measures have included the WAIS, the A.C.E. college aptitude measures as well as other college entrance examinations, grade-point averages, tests developed in the armed services, and other tests, such as measures of mechanical aptitude, reading comprehension, and clerical aptitude. Subjects have included medical and psychiatric patients, and an incredible number of college students and servicemen. Some of these investigations report significant negative correlations with the MAS [for example, Ate, quoted by Taylor, 1955; Calvin, Koons, Bingham, and Fink, 1955; Grice, 1955; Kerrick, 1955; Matarazzo, et al., 1954; Spielberger and Katzenmeyer, 1959]. A larger number of studies have not yielded significant relationships [for example, Dana, 1957; Klugh and Bendig, 1955; LaMonaca and Berkun, 1959; Matarazzo, Ulett, Guze, and Saslow, 1954; Mayzner, Sersen, and Tresselt, 1955; Sarason, 1956; Schulz and Calvin, 1955; Siegman, 1956; Spielberger, 1958; Voas, 1956].

In those instances in which significant results are reported, there is consistency in that the hypothesized negative relationship between anxiety and the index of intelligence was supported. In the majority of instances, however, the relationship was found to be essentially zero. Why?

Three major possibilities should be considered. First, possibly there is no relationship. If, in fact, no relationship exists between MAS scores and intellectual ability, out of 100 studies in which correlations were computed between the two variables, five would attain statistical significance by chance alone. In addition to the many nonsignificant findings which have been reported, possibly many other investigators have also found zero relationships and have failed to write them up for journal publication or have submitted such articles but had them rejected by journal editors. In terms of actual investigations, then, the few significant findings may have occurred at a chance level. Without actual evidence to this effect, this possibility must remain only a speculation.

Second, differences across investigations may occur as the result of differences in threat:

> Perhaps the determining variable in producing a positive or a negative correlation involves at least two general factors: (a) the amount of threat to the individual aroused by the situation and (b) the differential effects of this threat on high- and low-anxious subjects with the high-anxious subjects showing the greater effect [Maysner, et al., 1955, p. 402].

Again, without data on the threat experienced by subjects in these various studies, this possibility cannot be evaluated without further research specifically designed to test it.

Third, the most frequently suggested reason advanced to account for the diverse findings has to do with differences across studies in the range of intellectual ability represented by the subjects. Compared with the total population, any sample which restricts the range of intelligence scores would be likely to yield a smaller relationship. Given a true relationship of modest magnitude and given many studies with subjects relatively homogeneous with respect to intelligence, the zero correlations are to be expected and would not be generalizable to the total population. Some evidence exists to support this last proposition. In the Calvin, *et al.* [1955] study, the Wechsler Bellevue and the MAS were first compared for a group of 36 students enrolled in an undergraduate psychology course; the correlation was —.21, which is not statistically significant. When, however, the group was made more heterogeneous by adding 15 students who were having scholastic difficulty, the correlation rose to —.31 ($p < .05$). Further evidence is provided by the Spielberger [1958] investigation. He studied different groups of entering male students at Duke for several semesters and found that ACE and MAS correlations ranged from .04 (N.S.) to —.34 ($p < .01$). In seeking an explanation for this variation, he found that as the mean ACE score of a group increased, the magnitude of the negative correlation between MAS and ACE for that group decreased. The rank-order correlation for this relationship was .94. Spielberger [1958, p. 221] suggested: ". . . the obtained correlations were due primarily to the presence of Ss scoring in the lower ranges of the ACE distribution."

A more conclusive answer to the question of the relationship between MAS scores and intellectual performance will have to await future research.

OTHER RELATIONSHIPS

A number of other correlational findings with the MAS have been reported. A few of these relationships will be mentioned briefly.

Several variables which correlate with the MAS may simply constitute other aspects of neuroticism. For example, a positive relationship exists between manifest anxiety and the number of stimuli (for example, noises, other people, dirtiness) felt to be annoying [Martin, 1959], the number of food aversions [Smith, Powell, and Ross, 1955], the number of negatively toned associations given in response to a list of nonsense syllables [Trapp and Kausler, 1959], and a measure of constriction [Wohl and Hyman, 1959]. In addition, the MAS is negatively related to the emotional stability, objectivity, and personal relations scales of the Guilford-Zimmerman Temperament Survey [Linden and Olson, 1959].

Earlier in this chapter we reported that those high on the MAS tend to report more physical symptoms than do low scorers. Consistent with such data are reports that a significant positive correlation exists between the tendency to perceive pain in thematic apperception pictures and MAS scores [Petrovich, 1958] and that individuals with high anxiety scores tend to report a high level of "autonomic feedback" or the tendency to perceive internal stimuli [Mandler, Mandler, and Uviller, 1958]. Some evidence exists that these differences between high- and low-anxious subjects have physiological consequences as well. Davids, DeVault, and Talmadge [1961, p. 76] found in two independent samples of clinic patients that: ". . . women who were later to experience complications in the delivery room or were to give birth to children with abnormalities obtained significantly higher manifest anxiety scores during pregnancy than did women who later had 'normal' delivery room periods." Considerably more research tracing the link between MAS performance and bodily functioning is anticipated.

Dynamics

LEARNING AND PERFORMANCE

As was indicated earlier, the initial reason for constructing the Manifest Anxiety Scale was the need for a measure of individual differences in emotional responsiveness in laboratory conditioning experiments. As Taylor points out:

. . . the interest of the Iowa group has *not* been in investigating anxiety as a phenomenon, but rather in the role of drive in certain learning situations. The assumption has been made that anxiety scores are related in some manner to drive level, but in terms of the major theoretical interests of this group, any other acceptable specification of drive (e.g., hunger) could be used in experimental tests of the hypotheses about the effect of drive level [Taylor, 1956, p. 303].

The influence of drive level (including differences in MAS scores) on behavior depends in part on the complexity of the task. As noted earlier, Hull [1943] proposed that all habits activated in a particular stimulus situation combine in a multiplicative function with total drive state to yield the excitatory potential of a response $E = f (H \times D)$. Using this and certain other constructs from Hull's system, Spence predicted that, i.e., in a simple situation in which one habit is evoked, the higher the drive the greater the response strength. In a complex situation in which several competing responses are evoked along with the correct one, high drive interacts with each habit to increase the strength of a number of different responses. The actual response which occurs in a given instance will be the one with the greatest momentary excitatory potential ($\dot{E}$), the one which most exceeds the threshold (L). In such situations, according to Spence's predictions, if the correct response has less habit strength than the competing responses, a high-drive group would be expected to do less well than a low-drive group. If, however, even in a complex situation the correct response were stronger than the competing responses, the prediction would be like that for a simple one-habit situation; a high-drive group should perform better than a low-drive group.

Given the proposition concerning the effects of differences in manifest anxiety on performance as a function of the number and the relative strengths of the habits evoked in a given situation, a very large number of investigators using a wide variety of situations have attempted to obtain relevant experimental evidence. This body of research has included a number of traditional learning tasks (for example, classical conditioning, maze learning, verbal learning), other familiar laboratory problems (for example, stimulus generalization, reaction time), and many other tasks ranging from anagrams to a chained word-association test. The summary presented here should demonstrate both the fruitfulness of a strong theory in stimulating research and the utility of including a personality variable in research in general experimental psychology.

Classical Conditioning. A relatively simple situation in which a single response is learned is that of classical conditioning. A typical experimental situation [for example, Spence, 1953] is that of eyelid conditioning. Subjects are placed in a fixed position in a dental chair. The unconditioned stimulus is a puff of air which is directed at one eye, eliciting an eyeblink (the unconditioned response). The conditioned stimulus is an increase in brightness of a circular disc made of milk glass. In each conditioning trial, the puff of air is closely followed by the conditioned stimulus. The dependent variable is the number of conditioned responses (eyeblinks in response to the brightness changes) made during a given number of test trials. One would predict that high drive would lead to better performance in this situation, and hence subjects with high scores on the MAS should give more conditioned responses than subjects with low scores on the MAS.

The typical procedure has been to select subjects on the basis of MAS scores. Individuals scoring at the 20th percentile or below are designated as nonanxious and those at the 80th percentile or above as anxious. An illustrative finding is that of Spence and Taylor [1951]. Two levels of air puff intensity (.6 lb. and 2.0 lbs. per square inch) were employed. As shown in Figure 10–4, at each puff intensity, the anxious group gave significantly more conditioned responses than the nonanxious group.

In a number of such investigations, the theoretical predictions have been upheld [for example, Spence and Farber, 1953; Spence, Farber, and Taylor, 1954; Spence and Spence, 1964; Spence and Taylor, 1953; Taylor, 1951]. Spence [1964] reviewed the work conducted on eyelid conditioning and manifest anxiety, both published and unpublished. Out of 25 such investigations, 21 reported differences between anxious and nonanxious subjects in the predicted direction. In examining the studies which did not obtain differences, Spence concluded that factors such as small sample size could be responsible for the nonsignificant results.

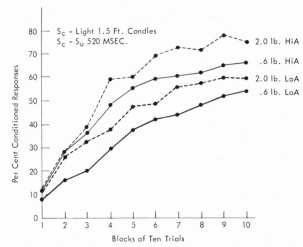

FIG. 10–4. *Performance in eyelid conditioning task as a function of MAS score and intensity of unconditioned stimulus.* (*Adapted from Spence, 1960, p. 132.*)

When subjects with scores in the middle range of the MAS are included in the sample, their conditioning performance tends to fall between the two extreme groups. The correlation between MAS scores and frequency of conditioned responses is about .25 [Taylor, 1956].

Differential Conditioning and Stimulus Generalization. The classical conditioning situation can be made slightly more complex by including a positive conditioned stimulus which is paired with an unconditioned stimulus and a negative conditioned stimulus which is not. One would predict from drive theory that anxious subjects should show greater excitatory strength to both conditioned stimuli. Experimental results do yield significant differences between high and low MAS individuals in responding to the positive conditioned stimulus; for the negative conditioned stimulus, the subjects tend to differentiate in the predicted direction but not to a statistically significant degree [Spence and Beecroft, 1954; Spence and Farber, 1954].

In many respects, experiments which involve stimulus generalization are an extension of the differential conditioning situation. That is, the subjects learn to respond to a particular stimulus (analogous to the positive conditioned stimulus) and later are presented with different stimuli (analogous to negative conditioned stimuli). Response to the latter stimuli is a function of their similarity to the original stimulus. A generalization function may be plotted, often taking a form such as that shown in Figure 10–5. On the basis of drive theory, one would predict that anxious subjects would have a higher generalization gradient (that is, would give more responses to the generalized stimuli) than would nonanxious subjects.

Wenar [1954] trained high- and low-anxious subjects to respond to one of three stimuli, presented at 12-second intervals, by pressing a switch. Fol-

Frequencies Less: 1000   Frequencies Greater:
Cycles
(Training stimulus)

Fig. 10–5. *Hypothetical gradient of generalization.* (*Adapted from Underwood, 1949, p. 252.*)

lowing training, stimuli were presented at intervals longer and shorter than 12 seconds. The generalized stimuli, then, were different from the original stimulus along a temporal dimension. As hypothesized, the generalization gradient was higher for the anxious than for the nonanxious subjects.

In an investigation by Rosenbaum [1956], a rectangular training stimulus was employed, and three other rectangles differing in height served as the generalized stimuli. Subjects were 72 male students from the extreme ends of the MAS distribution of an original group of 574 students. Three levels of experimentally induced anxiety were also included (strong shock, buzzer, weak shock). The high-anxiety subjects had a higher generalization gradient than the low-anxiety subjects, but only in the strong shock condition as shown in Figure 10–6.

Maze Learning. A maze constitutes a relatively complex situation involving a number of competing responses. Here, one would predict that the performance of anxious subjects would be inferior to the performance of nonanxious subjects.

Taylor and Spence [1952] utilized a serial verbal maze. The learning task consisted of 20 stimulus words typed on a continuous tape. In the viewing slot of a memory drum, each word appeared in order for two seconds. After the first trial, the subject's task is to anticipate the word which will appear next. The words were "right" and "left" and appeared in the order: LLRLRRLLRLRRRLRLLRRL. Trials were continued until the subjects could go through the entire list without error for two consecutive trials. Because of interfering response tendencies such as remote associations, anxious subjects were expected to do less well than nonanxious subjects. Both in terms of number of errors and number of trials to criterion, the hypothesis was confirmed.

A stylus maze (shown in Figure 10–7) is used to provide human subjects with a learning task somewhat like that used in animal laboratories. Each subject is blindfolded, given a stylus, and instructed to proceed from the

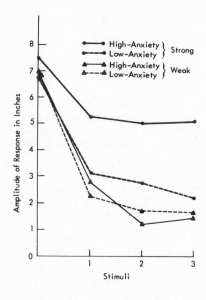

FIG. 10–6. *Generalization gradients as a function of MAS scores and experimentally induced anxiety. The training stimulus is designated as 0, and the generalized stimuli are designated 1, 2, 3, in order of decreasing similarity to the training stimulus. Weak-shock and buzzer conditions have been combined in the curves labeled weak. (Adapted from Rosenbaum, 1956, p. 283.)*

starting circle to the goal. Matarazzo, Ulett, and Saslow [1955] divided a group of 101 seminary students into seven groups on the basis of MAS scores. On the maze, each subject had to continue until he reached a criterion of three perfect runs. The correlation between MAS scores and number of trials required to reach the criterion was .20 ($p < .05$). That is, anxious subjects did not learn the maze as rapidly as nonanxious subjects.

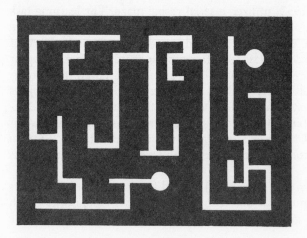

FIG. 10–7. *Stylus maze. Lafayette Instrument Co., Lafayette, Indiana, No. 706-A. (Adapted from Matarazzo, et al., 1955, p. 82.)*

Similarly, Farber and Spence [1953] found that anxious subjects made more errors and required more trials to reach criterion on a stylus maze than did nonanxious subjects.

Serial Learning. One can construct a verbal learning task in such a way as to maximize or minimize the presence of competing responses. The influence of manifest anxiety on learning would be expected to vary as a function of this aspect of the task. Montague [1953] constructed three different lists of serial nonsense syllables differing in amount of intralist interference. On the lists with relatively few competing responses (low similarity and high association value), the anxious subjects performed significantly better than the nonanxious subjects. The groups reversed on the lists with a relatively large number of competing responses (high similarity and low association value).

Lucas [1952] presented subjects with lists of consonants which they were asked to recall. Response competition was manipulated by varying the number of duplicated consonants within a list. The anxious subjects had increasing difficulty in recalling lists as the number of duplicated consonants in a list increased.

Paired-Associates Learning. When subjects are presented with a stimulus word and required to learn the response word associated with it, one can control the variables relating to response strength more precisely than when the task is the learning of a list of words in serial order. Spence, Farber, and McFann describe the use of this technique:

> Paired-associates learning may be conceived as consisting of a set or series of more or less isolated S-R associations or habit tendencies (S_1-R_A, S_2-R_B, S_3-R_C, etc.) that become established as a consequence of the training procedure. Theoretically, if these stimulus-response items were entirely isolated from one another so that the only existent associative tendencies were between each stimulus word and its own paired response word, then Ss with relatively high drive would be expected to perform at a higher level in learning such a series than Ss with a lower drive strength. Essentially, the situation is similar to that of classical conditioning, except that instead of one S-R tendency being conditioned, a number of different S-R tendencies are being established simultaneously. While it may not be possible to obtain complete isolation among the S-R items, it is known how, on the basis of existing experimental knowledge, to approach this limiting condition with its minimal competition among S-Rs. Similarly, it is known how to vary the conditions so as to increase the amount of competition among them [Spence, Farber, and McFann, 1956, p. 298].

Two experiments were reported by Spence, Farber, and McFann [1956]. The two lists of word pairs are shown in Table 10–3. In one, an attempt was made to make the correct S-R tendencies strong and to minimize the presence of competing response tendencies; the stimulus words were very dif-

Table 10–3   NONCOMPETITIVE AND COMPETITIVE LISTS
USED IN PAIRED-ASSOCIATES LEARNING*

	Experiment 1 Noncompetitive		Experiment 2 Competitive and Noncompetitive	
Stimulus	Response		Stimulus	Response
Adept	Skillful		** Barren	Fruitless
Barren	Fruitless		Arid	Grouchy
Complete	Thorough		Desert	Leading
Distant	Remote		** Little	Minute
Empty	Vacant		Petite	Yonder
Frigid	Arctic		Undersized	Wholesome
Insane	Crazy		** Roving	Nomad
Little	Minute		Gypsy	Opaque
Mammoth	Oversized		Migrant	Agile
Pious	Devout		** Tranquil	Placid
Roving	Nomad		Quiet	Double
Stubborn	Headstrong		Serene	Headstrong
Tranquil	Quiet			
Urgent	Pressing			
Wicked	Evil			

* From Spence, Farber, and McFann, 1956, p. 300.
** Pairs with high initial association (noncompetitive).

ferent from each other, and each was strongly associated with its response word. As hypothesized, high-anxious subjects were superior to low-anxious subjects in learning the associations. In the other experiment, an attempt was made to include pairs with high initial association (weak competing response tendencies) and pairs with low association but with high association across stimulus words (strong competing response tendencies). As hypothesized, high-anxious subjects made fewer errors on the four high-association pairs and more errors on the other eight pairs, when compared with low-anxious subjects. Subsequent research with the same general design has tended to confirm these findings [Katahn, 1964; Spence, Taylor, and Ketchel, 1956; Taylor and Chapman, 1955].

Another method for defining relative habit strength for a response was that of Lee [1961]. The author pointed out that most verbal learning studies used normative data in assuming the relative habit strength of correct and incorrect responses. In this experiment, habit strength was manipulated experimentally by giving the subjects preliminary practice on particular sets of stimulus-response pairs that were used in the learning task. After learning a list of 15 adjective pairs, the subjects learned a second list of 15 pairs in which there were five unchanged pairs (from the original list), five neutral pairs (new words), and five changed pairs (stimulus and response words from the initial list but paired differently). The subjects were 30 low- and 30 high-anxious undergraduate males at Ohio University. Analysis of variance indicated that anxious subjects did significantly better than nonanxious subjects when the dominant habit was correct (unchanged pairs) and significantly worse when the dominant habit was incorrect (changed pairs). Similar findings were reported by Standish and Champion [1960].

Performance on Other Simple and Complex Tasks. The effect of drive on response would not be expected to be confined to learning situations. Davids and Eriksen [1955] reasoned that high drive level should lead to a greater number of responses being above threshold in any stimulus situation. Specifically, they hypothesized that anxious individuals would give more associations in response to stimulus words on a chained word association test than would nonanxious individuals. The subjects were 40 male undergraduates. The word-association test consisted of 100 nouns presented by means of a tape recorder, with a 20-second pause between words. The subjects were instructed to write down as many associations as possible to each stimulus word. The 20 subjects with the highest MAS scores gave a mean of 530 associations, while the 20 subjects with the lowest MAS scores gave a mean of 454 associations; a t test indicated a mean difference significant at the .001 level. Using another type of statistical analysis, scores on the MAS were found to correlate .45 ($p < .01$) with number of associations given.

Reaction time to stimuli differing in intensity (strong shock, buzzer, and weak shock) was investigated by Wenar [1954]. With high- and low-anxious subjects, different drive levels were represented by both the stimulus variable and by the personality variable. Reaction time was significantly influenced by both types of variables. High-anxious subjects responded faster than low-anxious subjects, and reaction time was fastest for the most intense stimulus (strong shock) and slowest for the least intense stimulus (weak shock).

Similarly, Reynolds, Blau, and Hurlbut [1961] hypothesized that anxiety should be positively related to speed on simple tasks. One task required subjects to draw lines above the letter X and below the letter O for a group of these letters typed randomly on a sheet of paper; the score was number completed in a two-minute period. The high-anxious subjects completed significantly more lines than the low-anxious subjects.

A more complex task is represented by Bendig's [1959] use of two specially prepared crossword puzzles. Each puzzle was scored for number of puzzle squares correctly filled in within the 10-minute time limit. Scores on the MAS for 73 undergraduates correlated $-.28$ ($p < .05$) with scores on the two puzzles combined.

Still another complex task was used by Taylor and Rechtschaffen [1959].

Subjects had to print the alphabet upside down and backwards as rapidly as possible. Response interference should result from the incompatibility of the highly practiced patterns of normal writing versus the new patterns required by the experimental task. With 32 anxious and 32 nonanxious undergraduates as subjects, the nonanxious subjects completed significantly more letters within the time limits than did those high in manifest anxiety.

Wiggins [1957] utilized the solution of anagrams as a complex task. Examples were ASTK (TASK) and PDESE (SPEED). Subjects consisted of 68 night school students who were given the MAS and a 99-item anagram list. They had only 10 minutes to work on the anagrams. Number of correct anagram solutions correlated $-.26$ ($p < .05$) with MAS scores, as predicted. Wiggins also obtained ACE test scores for 36 of the subjects and found a correlation of $.82$ ($p < .01$) between this measure of intellectual ability and anagram scores. By means of the partial correlation coefficient he was able to determine the relationship between MAS and anagram performance with intelligence held constant; the correlation was found to be $-.82$ ($p < .01$). Wiggins suggested:

Since ability to solve anagrams was found to be related in an important way to both measures of anxiety and intelligence, it may be assumed that productivity on the anagrams is a composite of intellective and affective factors. Thus, productivity in solving anagrams is probably related to effective use of intellectual abilities [Wiggins, 1957, p. 393].

A complex discrimination-reaction-time task was employed by Grice [1955]. Subjects were 60 airmen undergoing basic training at Lackland Air Force base selected on the basis of falling in the upper or lower 10 per cent of a group of 300 trainees on the MAS. One of four lights on a panel came on to inform the subject which of four different problem instructions to follow:

Problem 1 was as follows: Two upper lights, push upper switch; two lower lights, push lower switch; two right lights, push right switch; and two left lights, push left switch. Problem 2 was the reverse of Problem 1. Problem 3 was as follows: Red right of green, push right switch; red left of green, push left switch; red up from green, push upper switch; and red down from green, push lower switch. Problem 4 was the reverse of Problem 3 [Grice, 1955, p. 71].

Subjects were given 80 trials on each problem, and then a series of 80 trials in which the four types of problems were randomly mixed. The non-anxious subjects responded significantly faster than the anxious subjects to this complex task and showed the greatest difference on the last 80 trials. With a different reaction-time situation Rossi [1959] found anxious subjects faster on a simple problem and slower on a more complex problem.

Response to Stress. A number of investigations, including several just described, have included a manipulation of stress as well as a differentiation of subjects on the basis of MAS scores. With a wide variety of different types of stress introduced in different ways in quite different experimental situations, it is perhaps not surprising to find inconsistencies across studies. For example, the magnitude of the difference between anxious and nonanxious subjects has been found to be unaffected by stress and to be increased by stress. A further difficulty is that even "nonstressful" situations may arouse anxiety. As Taylor [1956, p. 312] suggests: ". . . to many college sophomores psychology experiments per se may be seen as somewhat threatening, particularly when the task could be interpreted as reflecting on their personality or intelligence."

Changes in Manifest Anxiety

INCREASED ANXIETY

If scores on the MAS indicate an individual's characteristic emotional state, it would not be surprising to find that the experimental arousal of anxiety failed to bring about changes in test performance. Even though situational changes may not affect MAS performance, the use of hypnotic suggestion could conceivably have such an effect in that subjects could be led to evaluate their characteristic anxiety level differently.

Hypnotic induction of anxiety was attempted by Grosz and Levitt [1959]. A group of 12 medical and nursing students was given the MAS three times: in an ordinary waking state, in an hypnotic trance without special instructions, and in an hypnotic trance with anxiety instructions. The latter group received the following suggestions:

I suggest to you that you will begin to feel in a certain way, that you will have certain definite feelings which I am going to suggest to you. You will begin to feel these feelings and emotions so vividly that your whole person, your whole body, every fiber of yourself, will feel that way—at first slightly, then gradually stronger and stronger. These feelings will last until I suggest to you that they are no longer there. The feelings and emotions which you will begin to experience are those of anxiety—feelings of anxiety, more and more intensely, more and more vividly. You will become more and more anxious. At first, there will just be a feeling of apprehension. Then, gradually you are beginning to feel more and more afraid but you do not know what it is that makes you feel so afraid and so anxious. You just feel that way without knowing why. You feel more and more afraid and anxious all the time, as if something dreadful is going to happen to you. Yet, you do not know what this dreadful thing is. I suggest that you will gradually begin to experience a state in which you feel really panicky, where you are so fearful that you feel an almost unbearable dread, fear, and panic. In fact, you are most likely already feeling this way and you will continue to feel this way more and more strongly [Grosz and Levitt, 1959, p. 282].

In the waking state the mean MAS score was 12.08, in the trance state 12.67, and in the anxiety trance state 25.00. Because of the latter group, analysis of variance yielded an F ratio significant at beyond the .001 level. Clearly one can bring about an increase in anxiety as measured by the MAS.

DECREASED ANXIETY

When situational stress continues over a long period of time, anxiety would be expected to rise and then level off at a relatively high point. Anxiety-reduction should occur when the situation changes sufficiently to remove the stress. For example, anxiety should go up when an individual loses a job, remain high while he is seeking employment, and return to normal after a new job is secured. No one has utilized the MAS in just that way, but data are available which suggest that such a use of the MAS might be promising.

Childbirth. Pregnancy should be sufficiently stressful to arouse anxiety, and the birth of an infant would serve to resolve this particular source of stress. Davids, DeVault, and Talmadge [1961] administered the MAS to pregnant women at about the seventh month of pregnancy. For 20 of these subjects, a retest on the MAS was possible approximately six weeks following childbirth. For this group, the mean MAS score during pregnancy was 18.95; after childbirth the mean was 16.16. In future research one should be able to obtain anxiety measurements before, during, and after the occurrence of a stressful situation.

Psychotherapy. As was discussed in Chapter 7, the evidence with respect to the effectiveness of psychotherapy in bringing about changes in behavior is not impressive. With respect to anxiety, effective psychotherapy should bring about a reduction. Gallagher [1953] investigated the proposition that client-centered therapy influences anxiety, using the MAS as a measure of "anxiety stress." Each of 42 college students was tested before and after receiving therapy at the clinic at Pennsylvania State College. MAS scores were significantly lower after therapy (mean = 13.76) than before (mean = 17.28). Criteria of therapeutic success were a rating by the therapist, a rating by judges who read transcripts of the interviews, a rating by the client, and the ratio of negative to positive feelings expressed in the final therapy session compared to the same ratio in the first interview. Each of these criteria was found to correlate with amount of change in MAS scores. The greater the reduction in anxiety, the greater the success of the psychotherapy.

In a study by Lorr, McNair, Michaux, and Raskin [1962], patients at several VA Mental Hygiene Clinics were given the MAS along with other measures at the beginning of therapy and after 4, 8, and 12 months. Change from pretherapy MAS scores was significant only for the 12-month comparison. The change was from 29.9 to 26.4.

Carbon Dioxide Therapy. One form of somatic therapy which has been used as a treatment of anxiety is the administration of carbon dioxide. At each treatment session, patients breathe a mixture of carbon dioxide and oxygen until a coma is induced. Lebo, Toal, and Brick [1958] selected prisoners at Virginia State Penitentiary who had been diagnosed as having symptoms of manifest anxiety. Half of these were given CO_2 therapy (14 to 22 treatments) while half were untreated. The MAS was administered before and after the treatment period. For the two testings, the control group showed no change (22.0 and 22.5). For the experimental group, a significant reduction in MAS scores (from 28.5 to 19.0) occurred.

Current Status of Manifest Anxiety as a Personality Variable

In the vast body of literature which deals with anxiety, one often finds conclusions to the effect that the very concept of anxiety is a useless one and that the Manifest Anxiety Scale only contributes to the confusion. For example, Sarbin [1964a] traces the current use of the concept of anxiety to certain historical mistakes in interpreting metaphors literally. He concludes: ". . . the mentalistic and multi-referenced term anxiety has outlived its usefulness. Unless a convention is called to decide on more precise existent referents for the term, it would be better to discontinue employing it in scientific discourse" [Sarbin, 1964a, p. 635]. Whether or not Sarbin is correct in suggesting that the concept of "cognitive strain" will be more fruitful than anxiety, the author feels that the research cited in this chapter alone attests to the utility of anxiety as a behavioral variable. With respect to the MAS, it has been criticized for being contaminated by response set, for not measuring whatever it is that the physiological indices measure, for being too general, and even for having ". . . only a tenuous theoretical and empirical coordination to the Hullian construct of drive" [Jessor and Hammond, 1957, p. 169]. What implications do these criticisms have for the meaning of research on anxiety?

SOCIAL DESIRABILITY

As indicated earlier in the chapter, it is not at all clear that it would be reasonable to attempt to control for the effects of social-desirability response set on tests such as the MAS. If, however, anxiety and the tendency to give socially desirable responses are actually different variables with different antecedents, correlates, and consequents, it would be of great value to be able to measure them independently.

One attempt to control for social desirability in measuring anxiety has been that of Heineman [1953] who developed a forced-choice version of the MAS in a pattern much like that of the EPPS. That is, he used judges to establish social-desirability values for anxiety and nonanxiety items and then formed pairs of such items with the same social-desirability value. Thus, when a subject is forced to choose which of the two items best describes him, he cannot choose on the basis of social desirability but only on the basis of anxiety content. Though the Heineman scale has been used to measure anxiety by some experimenters, little interest has yet been aroused in resolving the question of whether anxiety and social-desirability response set are independent dimensions. It would be very helpful to have a series of investigations of the type described in this chapter in which subjects were measured on the MAS, the Heineman scale, and Edwards' Social Desirability Scale. The differential ability or inability of these instruments to predict responses would be most informative.

PHYSIOLOGICAL INDICES

Given the various approaches to the study of anxiety, we would actually not be particularly surprised if physiological responses to stress (such as palmar sweating) were unrelated to individual differences in general anxiety. The Mandler, *et al.*, finding [1961] (in which MAS scores were related to the subject's highest physiological response across a series of measures) suggests that the only reason for negative results in the past has been that the research designs were inappropriate. Research conducted over the next several years should help to resolve this question.

KINDS OF ANXIETY

As with many types of personality measures now in use, the MAS may well be superseded in the future by instruments designed to measure the variable in question more specifically. Thus, there appears to be utility in the concept of a general, multi-situational characteristic in which individuals differ in their level of anxiety. Nevertheless, one of the basic properties of anxiety is the ease with which it can be attached to specific cues. Tests which attempt to measure differences in anxiety evoked by classroom examinations, heterosexual stimulation, competition, or social interaction may turn out to be of greater predictive value than an omnibus measure such as the MAS which attempts to cut across many such situations.

MAS AND DRIVE

The number of situations in which the Hull-Spence system has yielded accurate predictions concerning the effects of drive as measured by the MAS on behavior would seem to be sufficient answer to critics of the test. One can, however, put together a list of studies in which there is seemingly a predictive failure. For example, the lack of relationship between MAS scores and academic success is sometimes cited as a negative instance. A vital point is overlooked by such criticisms, as Taylor explains:

An important consideration that should be noted about making predictions concerning the effect of drive level upon performance in actual experimental situations is that a behavioral analysis of the situation must have been made; only in experimental arrangements in which the results, independent of drive level, permit statements in terms of competing S-R tendencies are deductions from the theory possible [Taylor, 1956, p. 305].

Much of the "negative" evidence with respect to drive as measured by the MAS involves relatively unknown and/or uncontrolled situations in which detailed knowledge of S-R tendencies is lacking.

Summary

Anxiety is often defined as an emotional state in which there is a vague, generalized fear. Anxiety is usually conceptualized as a motive by psychologists. Research on anxiety has been of several kinds. (1) Anxiety is studied in terms of the stimuli which evoke it and the responses (usually physiological) which define it. (2) Through conditioning, fear or anxiety can become associated with previously neutral stimuli. This phenomenon has been of interest both to experimental psychologists and to clinical psychologists and psychiatrists. (3) The motivational properties of fear and anxiety have been of research interest in that instrumental responses are learned as a way of achieving drive-reduction. (4) In the Hull-Spence theoretical system, drive is said to have an energizing effect on behavior, and many experiments have utilized the manipulation of anxiety to test hypotheses derived from that proposition. (5) Individual differences in anxiety have been of interest with respect to each of the other four areas of research.

Theoretical approaches to each aspect of anxiety have been quite varied. Sigmund Freud was a physician who developed the therapeutic technique of psychoanalysis and the large body of observations, constructs, speculations, hypotheses, and analogies which constitutes psychoanalytic theory. Essentially, his approach was one of observation, generalization, further uncontrolled observations, and theory-building. With respect to anxiety, Freud defined it in terms of an unpleasant subjective feeling involving expectation, indefiniteness, and a sense of helplessness. He suggested the origin of anxiety as the emotional state evoked by the process of birth. Anxiety is aroused by various traumatic situations which indicate helplessness and by situations which indicate a threat that a traumatic situation will occur. The presence of anxiety leads to behavior which serves to reduce anxiety, including defense mechanisms and other neurotic behavior. Anxiety was said to be amenable to therapeutic reduction if the patient could be enabled accurately to verbalize the danger cues and thus regain control of his own behavior. A quite different approach to theory-building is represented by the work of Clark Hull and Kenneth Spence though there has been some overlapping of interest with psychoanalytic theory. Hull-Spence theory is built on a base of rigorous laboratory experimentation and the testing of hypotheses deduced from the theory. Among the theoretical constructs is R_A, individual differences in emotional responsiveness. One of Spence's students, Janet Taylor, developed a personality questionnaire designed to measure this dimension.

The first step in constructing the Manifest Anxiety Scale was the presentation of 200 MMPI items to five clinical psychologists who were to judge each item as an indicator of manifest anxiety. On 65 of the items, 80 per cent or better agreement was obtained among the clinicians. An internal consistency item-analysis reduced this number to 50. The reliability of the MAS, in terms of internal consistency and stability over time, is acceptably high. Though the MAS is unaffected by acquiescent response set, it is highly related to a measure of social-desirability response set. At the present time it seems likely that the SD Scale and the MAS are measuring the same dimension of behavior but giving it a different label.

The antecedents of manifest anxiety have been relatively neglected in research to date. One investigation, with adolescent boys and their mothers, found that subjects with low manifest anxiety were satisfied with themselves, met their perception of their mothers' ideal for them, and perceived themselves as being the kind of person their mothers actually wanted them to be.

A number of correlational investigations of the MAS have been of a semivalidational nature. The MAS has been found to be significantly related to a measure of separation anxiety, the number of symptoms an individual reports in response to anxiety-arousing or discouraging situations, anxiety concerning examinations, and Rorschach indicators of anxiety. With few exceptions, scores on the MAS are found to be related to clinical judgments of anxiety level. Many investigations comparing MAS performance and a physiological indicator of anxiety have revealed a lack of relationship; variables include skin conductance, palmar sweating, blink rate, and serum cholesterol. A positive relationship is found, however, between the MAS and muscle action potential and also between manifest anxiety and the specific response index (the subject's highest score on a series of physiological variables regardless of what the variable is). In relating manifest anxiety to maladjustment, psychiatric populations have consistently obtained higher scores than normal groups, and neurotics, especially anxiety neurotics, have been found to score higher than other diagnostic groups. Various measures of maladjustment correlated significantly with the MAS, including a clinical rating yielding a total pathology score, number of reported medical and psychiatric symptoms, ratings of pessimism and tendency not to utilize repressive defenses, various MMPI scales, and MMPI indices of neuroticism and anxiety neurosis. A large number of studies have compared MAS scores with measures of intellectual ability and academic performance. Though most of the reported findings have indicated no relationship, the few significant ones all involved a negative correlation. Possibly manifest anxiety and intellectual performance are unrelated, are related only when the intellectual measure is obtained under threatening circumstances, or are related only when the subjects represent a sufficiently wide range of intellectual ability. Several other findings indicate that those with high scores on the MAS report more stimuli as annoying, dislike more foods, give more negatively toned associations to nonsense syllables, are less emotionally stable and objective, give more pain responses in a thematic test, have a higher level of autonomic feedback, and are more likely to give birth to children with abnormalities.

The initial reason for constructing the MAS was for use in learning experiments—to obtain a measure of individual differences in emotional responsiveness which in turn should be related to drive level. Hull proposed that all habits activated in a particular stimulus situation combine in a multiplicative function with total drive state to yield the excitatory potential of a response. In a simple situation in which one habit is evoked, the higher the drive the greater the response strength. Thus, the performance of high MAS subjects should be superior to that of low MAS subjects in such situations. In a complex situation in which several competing responses are evoked along with the correct one, high drive interacts with each habit to increase the strength of a number of different responses. Thus, the performance of low MAS subjects should be superior to that of high MAS subjects in these situations. These predictions have led to a large number of investigations yielding largely confirmatory findings in situations including classical conditioning, differential conditioning, stimulus generalization, maze learning, serial learning, paired-associates learning, word associations, reaction time, speed on a simple line-drawing task, crossword puzzle performance, printing the alphabet upside down and backwards, and the solving of anagrams.

A few investigations have dealt with altering MAS scores. Increase in anxiety has been achieved by means of hypnotic instructions suggesting anxiety, apprehension, and fear. Decrease in anxiety has been found as a function of childbirth, psychotherapy, and carbon dioxide therapy.

Negative evaluations of the concept of anxiety and of the MAS are frequently given. A sufficiently large body of research has been generated, however, to attest to the fruitfulness of the concept and of this specific measuring instrument. If anxiety and the tendency to give socially desirable responses are actually different variables with different antecedents, correlates, and consequents, it will be of great value if they can be measured independently. Though one would not be very surprised if physiological indicators of anxiety were unrelated to MAS scores, it now appears possible that a relationship does exist. Very likely tests which measure differences in anxiety evoked by specific stimulus situations will be of greater predictive value than multi-situational measures such as the MAS. Finally, a great deal of support exists for the MAS as an indicator of differences in drive, and negative evidence obtained in uncontrolled and/or unknown situations is of little significance for the theory.

CHAPTER 11

Intelligence

The concept of intelligence occupies a peculiar position within the field of psychology. On the one hand, intelligence tests represent perhaps the best-known and most widely influential product of psychological science. In the words of Jenkins and Paterson [1961, p. 81]: ". . . probably no psychological innovation has had more impact on the societies of the Western world than the development of the Binet-Simon scales." At the same time, intelligence often appears to be psychology's unwanted step-child. Neither in terms of theoretical developments nor empirical research has the concept of intelligence been integrated with other work in psychology. It is often not even considered as part of the field of personality. With personality variables defined as dimensions of individual differences, however, intelligence is clearly a personality variable, and it will be examined here from that viewpoint.

In his presidential address to the American Psychological Association, McNemar said:

The Greeks had a word for it, but the Romans had a word with better survival properties. Regardless of the word, what is now called intelligence has been talked about for at least 2,000 years. And as long as 2,000 years before the advent of attempts to measure intelligence, there seems to have been recognition of the fact that individuals differ in intellectual ability.

The earlier attempts at measuring were based on either of two quite distinct conceptions: the Galton-Cattell idea that intellectual ability manifests itself in simple, discrimination functioning, and the Binet notion that cognitive ability reflects itself in more complex functioning. The Binet concept proved to be

385

more fruitful, and by 1925 there was on the market, in addition to various versions of the Binet scale, a flood of group tests of so-called general intelligence [McNemar, 1964, p. 871].

As McNemar indicates, the earliest attempts to measure individual differences in intellectual functioning consisted of the measurement of very simple responses. In the latter half of the nineteenth century, Galton worked with such characteristics as keenness of hearing and ability to form mental images. This type of inquiry was furthered by James McKeen Cattell who studied psychology in Germany and returned to the U.S. in 1890 with a series of simple tests including sensory acuity, strength of grip, and memory. This general approach to measuring intelligence came to a close when Wissler [1901] correlated the scores on a number of such tests with college grades with disappointing results. He found, for example, that grades correlated —.02 with reaction time, —.09 with speed of cancelling letters, and .08 with color naming. Far more fruitful was the approach of Binet, and later of Terman, as will be described in the following section. The major difference lay in an emphasis on complex rather than simple tasks.

Perhaps the most unusual aspect of the work on intelligence is a relative lack of theory. One would reasonably suppose that the items which are included in IQ tests are selected on the basis of their relevance to the test constructor's definition of intelligence. Instead, the general pattern followed has been that of Binet who "learned how to measure something without any very clear idea as to what it was he was measuring" [Hebb, 1958, p. 246]. Binet's approach was to select items primarily on the basis of their ability to discriminate individuals in a way consistent with other such items. The same sort of empiricism has prevailed in attempts to define what it is that these combined items are measuring:

A few words about definition may be in order. First, it might be claimed that no definition is required because all intelligent people know what intelligence is—it is the thing that the other guy lacks. Second, the fact that tests of general intelligence based on differing definitions tend to intercorrelate about as highly as their respective reliabilities permit indicates that, despite the diversity of definitions, the same function or process is being measured—definitions can be more confusing than enlightening [McNemar, 1964, p. 871].

Nevertheless, those working with such instruments have proposed a variety of definitions which stress adaptation to the environment, learning ability, and/or abstract thinking. It is the latter characteristic on which Terman placed the greatest stress.

Only recently [for example, Hebb, 1949; Hunt, 1961; Hayes, 1962] has a reawakening of theoretical interest in intelligence taken place and an attempt been made to build an integrative formulation utilizing the accumulating body of data concerned with genetic influences on behavior and the effects of early experience on later functioning. We will discuss some of these developments later in the chapter.

Background of the Concept of Intelligence

BINET AND THE IDENTIFICATION OF FEEBLE-MINDED CHILDREN

Alfred Binet (1857–1911) was born in Nice, France, in a family of physicians; his father and both grandfathers practiced medicine. At the age of 15, Binet was taken by his mother to Paris to attend the Lycee Louis-le-Grand from 1872 to 1875. He then entered law school, received his license in 1878, and began working on a doctorate.

In this period, an interest in "psychology" developed, and he avidly read the works of John Stuart Mill and the other British associationists. As an armchair psychologist in 1880, Binet published his first paper. In the next 11 years he had four books published, had one in press, and had produced a large number of articles. Like Freud, he was interested in the work of Charcot and others who were exploring hypnosis in both medical treatment and experimental investigations. After a period of stormy arguments and theoretical disputes among those interested in hypnotic phenomena, Binet in 1891 took a position at the Laboratory of Physiological Psychology at the Sorbonne, the first French psychological laboratory.

His specific interest in hypnosis shifted to a more general interest in complex mental processes. Between 1893 and 1911 he worked with and reported the use of numerous types of tests used to explore individual differences in the intellectual ability of children. In 1903, he published *The Experimental Study of Intelligence*. With only a general notion of what kinds of behavior might be appropriate indices of intelligence, Binet tried out such tests as the recall of numbers, moral judgment, mental addition, and tactile discrimination. In working with various children, including his daughters, he found that ability on simple tasks, such as reaction time and discrimination, was unrelated to ability on more complex tasks, such as those involving memory, comprehension, and mathematical manipulation.

At the time this work was in progress, a problem was raised in 1904 by the Paris school system—the identification of "feeble-minded" children so that they could be removed from regular classes and placed in special schools. Teacher ratings could be used for this purpose, but the school administrators were afraid that teachers would make too many mistakes in classifying the children. For example, they might rate a bright trouble-maker as dull to get rid of him and a dull but wealthy child as bright to avoid offending his parents. What was needed was an objective, accurate way of measuring intelligence, and the schools asked Binet if his research might be applicable to the problem.

Putting together the most successful of the various tests which he had been studying, Binet and a colleague, Simon, created the Binet-Simon Scale in 1905; the test was revised in 1908 and again in 1911, the year of Binet's death.

Individual tests in the Binet-Simon instrument were arranged in order of difficulty from easiest to hardest, and the scale was made up of exactly the type of items in use in such tests today. Thus, from the very beginning, the concept of intelligence was of greatest use in solving a practical problem in an applied setting. In addition, there was an empirical and pragmatic rather than a conceptual and theoretical basis for the selection of test items. This measurement technique had a great impact on psychologists and nonpsychologists alike as suggested by such statements as that by Goddard [1912, p. 326] who felt that the Binet-Simon ". . . scale would one day take a place in the history of science beside Darwin's theory of evolution and Mendel's law of heredity." While the evaluation seems somewhat overenthusiastic, nevertheless, much of the history of psychology is intertwined with the history of intelligence testing.

TERMAN AND THE STANFORD-BINET

An American psychologist, Lewis M. Terman (1877–1956) became interested in Binet's work while in graduate school and later adapted the French test for use with American children.

Terman was born on a farm in rural Indiana, the twelfth of 14 children. He has indicated that his family was not a particularly well-educated one and that his early education in a one-room schoolhouse was decidedly inferior by modern standards. He did, however, have an early interest in individual differences:

Whatever the cause, almost as far back as I can remember I seem to have had a little more interest than the average child in the personalities of others and to have been impressed by those who differed in some respect from the common run. Among my schoolmates or acquaintances whose behavior traits especially interested me were a feebleminded boy who was still in the first reader at the age of eighteen, a backward albino boy who was pathetically devoted to his small sister, a spoiled crippled boy given to fits of temper and to stealing, a boy who was almost a "lightning calculator," and a playmate of near my own age who was an imaginative liar and later came into national prominence as an alleged swindler and multi-murderer. I am inclined to think that the associations which I had with such schoolmates were among the most valuable of my childhood experiences [Terman, 1932, pp. 300–301].

Terman did well in school and was promoted from the first to the third grade after being in school six months. Between the ages of 11 and 18, he spent half of each year working on the farm and half in school. As preparation to become a teacher he attended Central Normal College in Danville, Indiana, where he received the B.S. degree in 1896. Interspersing his college work with teaching in rural schools, he later received the "Bachelor of Pedagogy" and A.B. degrees at the Danville school. He married a fellow teacher in 1899, and after two years as a high school principal, he entered Indiana University in 1901 to study psychology. In two years there he received his second A.B. degree and a master's degree. Obtaining a fellowship at Clark University, he moved there in 1903 for two years of graduate work.

At Clark he first learned in detail about Binet's work, from students returning from Europe and from Binet's publications. His dissertation dealt with an experimental study of mental tests. He selected two groups of subjects of the same approximate age, one bright and one dull, and devised tests on which he believed they would perform differently. After receiving the Ph.D. degree at Clark, Terman accepted a job as principal of the high school in San Bernardino. He indicated that he accepted this position rather than his other offers (a Florida normal school and the University of Texas) primarily because of the climate—he had recurring difficulty with tuberculosis. After a year there, he was offered a professorship at the Los Angeles State Normal School where he remained for four years. In 1910, he was offered a position at Stanford University in the School of Education. There, he immediately began an experimental study of the Binet tests. This work culminated in the publication of *The Measurement of Intelligence* in 1916, the first of the Stanford-Binet scales.

Cronbach describes the influence of Terman's test as follows:

> The Stanford-Binet had immediate popularity and became, rightly or wrongly, the yardstick by which other tests were judged. Although there had been various previous mental tests, the outstanding popularity of the Stanford test made its conception of intelligence the standard. The acceptance of the Stanford test was due to the care with which it had been prepared, its success in testing complex mental activities, the easily understood "IQ" it provided, and the important practical results which it quickly produced. Although many criticisms have been made of the test, it was and is an exceptionally useful instrument [Cronbach, 1960, p. 161].

During World War I, Terman served under Yerkes on the committee that devised the first group intelligence tests for the armed forces. His later work at Stanford involved the development of a number of other tests, the study of gifted children, and continued work on the Stanford-Binet and its revisions. He became chairman of the Department of Psychology in 1922 and quickly developed it into an outstanding one, thanks in part to a half-million dollar legacy from Thomas Welton Stanford which was earmarked for psychology.

Construction of the Stanford-Binet Intelligence Scale

Unlike the other measures of individual differences discussed in this text, a great many different intelligence tests have been built, and these instruments tend to correlate highly with one another. For this reason, we can describe research on intelligence in which a variety of different tests have been employed. Among the most widely used of these other instruments are the Wechsler Adult Intelligence Scale or WAIS [Wechsler, 1958] and the Wechsler Intelligence Scale for Children or WISC [Wechsler, 1949]. As an example of the construction of intelligence tests, however, only the Stanford-Binet will be described in any detail.

SELECTION OF TEST ITEMS

In selecting items for the 1916 Stanford-Binet, Terman used 90 tests of the same type that Binet had employed, primarily those involving "the more complex mental processes." Though highly useful, the 1916 test had several inadequacies and was revised in 1937 by Terman and Maud Merrill, a clinical psychologist on the Stanford faculty. The kinds of test items in the 1937 revision were similar to the earlier ones and included such subtests as analogies (Brother is a boy; sister is a ———.); comprehension (What makes a sailboat move?); vocabulary (What is an orange?); similarities and differences (In what way are a baseball and an orange alike, and how are they different?); verbal and pictorial completions (What is gone in this picture? What isn't there?); absurdities (One day we saw several icebergs that had been entirely melted by the warmth of the Gulf Stream. What is foolish about that?); drawing designs; and memory for digits and for verbal material. From a large initial sample of such items, the final test consisted of those items which (1) showed an increase in percentage of children passing it for successive age levels, and (2) were correlated with total score on the test. These items were divided into two equivalent test forms, L and M. Subtests were arranged in age levels, and test scores obtained in terms of Mental Age (MA).

The most recent revision of the Stanford-Binet [Terman and Merrill, 1960] was primarily undertaken in order to bring the test content up to date. Combining Form L and Form M, only one scale was built.

EVALUATION OF TEST ITEMS

Between 1950 and 1954, the 1937 test was administered to 4,498 subjects between the ages of two and one-half and 18 in various communities across the country. In this way, the suitability of the old items could be determined. The evaluation of items was according to the following general procedure. On the basis of the 1937 test, each subject was assigned an MA score. Then, for *each item* the percentage of children passing at successive mental ages was determined, and correlations were computed between score on the item and total test score.

As an example, we will take the vocabulary subtest. It contains a printed list of 45 words at which the subject may look. The examiner says, "I want to find out how many words you know. Listen, and when I say a word, you tell me what it means. What is an orange?" After the subject gives his definition, the next word is asked, and so on. The words are arranged in order of difficulty as determined by the responses of the standardization group. Early in the list are words such as envelope and straw, later are words such as juggler and brunette, and still later words such as regard and disproportionate. The examiner proceeds down the list until the subject misses six consecutive words and then discontinues the vocabulary subtest and goes on to other items. In comparing the 1937 and 1960 tests for order of difficulty, several of the vocabulary words no longer represent the same difficulty level. For example, "Mars" is now apparently a more familiar and hence easier word.

When the vocabulary test was initially built, the task was to determine the mental age score to assign for a given number of correct definitions. For the total test for each age level taking the test, the mean mental age indicated by the test must equal the mean chronological age of the subjects. For any given item, the assignment to a specific age level on the basis of per cent passing curves is an empirical procedure. If, for example, about 50 per cent of the ten-year-olds could define eleven words correctly, a vocabulary score of eleven would give the subject credit at the ten-year MA level. If older children could define a larger number of words, a subject defining more words correctly would get a higher MA score. The actual age levels for varying numbers of correct definitions are shown in Table 11-1.

Table 11-1   NUMBER OF VOCABULARY WORDS CORRECTLY DEFINED
NECESSARY TO OBTAIN MA CREDIT AT VARIOUS
AGE LEVELS IN THE 1937 STANFORD-BINET

Number of Correct Definitions	Age Level
5	6
8	8
11	10
14	12
16	14
20	Average Adult
23	Superior Adult I
26	Superior Adult II
30	Superior Adult III

For the subjects of the 1960 revision, passing scores for a given age level could be determined, and the next step was to plot a per cent passing curve as shown in Figure 11–1. Thus, if 14 correct definitions is still a

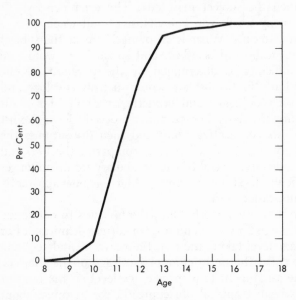

FIG. 11–1. *Distribution of per cent passing the vocabulary subtest at age 12; 14 correct = passing. (Adapted from Terman and Merrill, 1960, p. 30.)*

good measure of intelligence at age 12, about 60 per cent of those with an MA of 12 should perform that well because that was the point at which twelve-year-olds in the 1937 standardization group fell. As may be seen in the figure, a higher percentage of subjects actually did define 14 words correctly. Therefore, the scoring was changed so that 15 correct definitions constitute a passing score at age 12. With this change, a new per cent passing curve could be plotted, as shown in Figure 11–2. From the figure we see that about 60 per cent of those at age 12 receive a passing score, with 15 correct as the criterion of passing. Thus, the scoring for vocabulary at age 12 was changed for the 1960 revision to 15 correct. Similar changes had to be made in vocabulary scoring at some of the other ages.

The curves shown in the two figures are typical of those obtained on the Stanford-Binet items. An item passed by a set percentage of the subjects at any given age is passed by increasingly fewer subjects at younger ages and by increasingly greater numbers of subjects at older ages. The other criterion of item-acceptability is the correlation between performance on a given item and total score on the test. Terman and Merrill [1960] report that vocabulary at age 12 (15 correct) correlates .79 with total score on the test.

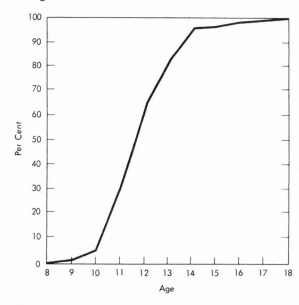

Fig. 11–2. *Distribution of per cent passing the vocabulary subtest at age 12 level; 15 correct = passing.*
(*Adapted from Terman and Merrill, 1960, p. 30.*)

INTELLIGENCE QUOTIENT

In the 1937 Stanford-Binet, the Intelligence Quotient (IQ) consisted of the Mental Age obtained on the test divided by the subject's Chronological Age (CA), with the quotient multiplied by 100. Thus, the average 10-year-old obtains an MA of 10 which is divided by his CA of 10, and the quotient times 100 equals 100 or an average IQ. Scores below 100 indicate test performance below average for an individual's age level, and scores above 100 indicate above average test performance.

The $\frac{MA}{CA} \times 100 = IQ$ approach runs into various difficulties, especially for individuals in late adolescence and beyond. Mental age as measured by the test items does not continue showing yearly increases indefinitely. In the 1937 revision, the IQ formula could not be utilized in its pure form beyond age 13 because MA increases became smaller and smaller. By age 16, no further yearly increases occurred. For this reason, Terman and Merrill [1937] developed a "corrected CA divisor" beginning at age 13 years, 2 months. For example, at CA 16, the divisor was a CA of 15 rather than the actual CA of 16.

To get around this problem, in the 1960 Stanford-Binet IQ is defined in terms of deviations from the average performance of an individual's age group. In order to maintain continuity with the older IQ scores, the test is arranged such that average performance still yields an IQ of 100. The new IQ score is simply a standard score with a mean of 100 and a standard deviation of 16.

One estimate of the internal consistency of the 1960 revision is the average correlation between subtest performance and total score; the average r is .66.

For other types of reliability data, a number of findings with the 1937 revision are probably generalizable to the new test. For example, the average correlation between Form L and Form M was found to be .91 [Terman and Merrill, 1937]. At that time, this correlation constituted a coefficient of equivalence. Since the two forms have been combined in the 1960 revision, this relationship may tentatively be considered as evidence for high internal consistency.

With respect to test-retest reliability, a number of longitudinal studies have been carried out with the Stanford-Binet. Typical of the findings of such investigations are those reported by Sontag, Baker, and Nelson [1958] dealing with stability of IQ over a ten-year period. As might be expected, the longer the interval between testings, the lower the test-retest correlation. Also, the older the child, the higher the correlation between successive testings. For example, IQ at age three correlates .83 with IQ at age four and only .46 with IQ at age 12. In another study, Bradway, Thompson, and Cravens [1958] found that IQ measured in the age range 2–5 correlated .59 with IQ measured in adulthood (26–32). The correlation between IQ in adolescence (11–17) and in adulthood was found to be .85. Clearly, IQ is relatively stable over time, especially from adolescence onward.

Antecedents of Intelligence

A great deal of research interest has arisen over the years concerning the question of the antecedents of individual differences in intellectual ability. In addition, a good portion of this research has involved a controversy between proponents of genetic antecedents and proponents of experiential antecedents—heredity versus environment or nature versus nurture. Some of the flavor of this sort of controversy may be ascertained from the following:

By intelligence, the psychologist understands inborn, all-round, intellectual ability. It is inherited, or at least innate, not due to teaching or training; it is intellectual, not emotional or moral, and remains uninfluenced by industry or zeal; it is general, not specific, i.e., it is not limited to any particular kind of work, but enters into all we do or say or think [Burt, Jones, Miller, and Moodie, 1934, pp. 28–29].

. . . some recent philosophers appear to have given their moral support to the deplorable verdict that the intelligence of an individual is a fixed quantity. . . . We must protest and act against this brutal pessimism. . . . A child's mind is like a field for which an expert farmer has advised a change in the method of cultivating, with the result that in place of desert land, we now have a harvest. It is in this particular sense, the one which is significant, that we say that the intelligence of children may be increased. One increases that which constitutes the intelligence of a school child, namely, the capacity to learn, to improve with instruction [Binet, 1909, pp. 54–55].

In more recent years, there has been a shift away from such either-or questions toward an attempt to investigate all possible antecedents of personality differences, that is, an investigation of multiple determinants. In looking at the findings relevant to IQ differences, we will follow the sort of approach suggested by Anastasi:

Essentially, we are not asking whether a trait depends on heredity or environment. Nor is it a question of arriving at a generalized estimate of the proportional contribution of heredity and environment. Rather, the problem is one of discovering the *modus operandi* of hereditary and environmental factors in the development of behavioral differences. We want to know in what ways different factors contribute and how they combine to yield the observed results [Anastasi, 1958, p. 88, by permission of The Macmillan Co.].

GENETIC DETERMINANTS

Family Resemblances. As was noted in Chapter 4, one of the ways to study genetic determinants of human behavior is to examine behavior similarity as a function of genetic similarity, the latter being defined in terms of closeness of family relationship.

If a group of randomly paired adults and children were given intelligence tests, the correlation between the two members of the various pairings should be .00. If, on the other hand, the adult-child pairs consist of parents and their offspring, the IQ's are found to correlate about .50 [for example, Conrad and Jones, 1940]. The problem with interpreting such findings, of course, is that parents and children are not only more similar than random strangers in hereditary factors, they are also more similar in environmental factors.

Another approach in family resemblance studies is to compare siblings who differ in genetic closeness. Again, random pairs of unrelated children should have IQ correlations of .00. When unrelated children are reared together, their IQ scores are found to correlate .25 [Burt, 1958]. With pairs of siblings, IQ's have been found to correlate about .50 [Conrad and Jones, 1940]. Thus, the greater genetic similarity of siblings than of unrelated children reared together adds to similarity in IQ. Given this same sibling relationship plus *identical* genetic structure, greater IQ similarity in identical twins would further indicate the influence of heredity on intelligence. In the Newman, Freeman, and Holzinger [1937] study discussed in Chapter 4, the identical twins were found to have IQ's that correlated .88, almost as high as these twins correlate in anatomical measures.

Such findings seem clear, but there is a methodological weakness in comparing twin-pair similarity with other sibling-pair similarity. The twins are the same age when tested; the siblings are not. If half of the siblings are four and the other half nine, they do not correlate as highly with each other as pairs of four-year-old twins or pairs of nine-year-old twins. But we know that the four-year-olds are likely to be somewhat different in IQ by the time they are nine and conceivably more similar to their siblings in test score. A way out of this dilemma is to compare fraternal twins with identical twins; here the pairs are the same age in each instance, but different in genetic similarity. Fraternal twins have been found to have IQ correlations ranging from .63 [Newman, et al., 1937] to .70 [Richardson, 1936]. Thus, fraternal twins are similar in IQ, but not as similar as identical twins. Also, apparently the only reason that fraternal twins are more similar than nontwin siblings is the fact that they are the same age. When fraternal twins are tested at different ages, their IQ scores correlate .57 and hence are no more similar than other siblings [Richardson, 1936].

In the Gottesman [1963] twin study described in Chapter 4, the identical and fraternal twins were also given the Otis IQ test. The scores of identical twins correlated .83 while those of fraternal twins correlated .59. The coefficient for identical twins is significantly higher than that for fraternal twins. Gottesman [1963, p. 13] concluded that ". . . 62% of the within-family intelligence variance measured by the Otis is accounted for by hereditary factors in this sample."

Seemingly, then, the twin studies do confirm the proposition that intellectual ability is in part a function of genetic determinants.

   Experiments of Nature. With respect both to twin comparisons and to parent-child comparisons, research has been carried out utilizing "experiments of nature."

We will recall that the Newman, et al. [1937] investigation included as subjects 50 pairs of identical twins reared together and 19 pairs of identical twins[1] who had been separated in infancy or early childhood and reared apart. The correlation between IQ scores for those reared together was .88, while for those identical twins reared apart the coefficient was .77. As indicated in Chapter 4, the homes of the separated pairs were rated in terms of several variables, including educational advantage. When the difference between the educational advantage of their homes was correlated with the difference in IQ for the 19 separated twins, the coefficient was found to be .79. Thus, in spite of the obvious genetic influence toward similarity in

---

[1] McNemar (1938) has presented evidence questioning whether all of these 19 pairs were actually identical twins.

IQ for identical twins, the greater the difference in their environmental opportunities, the greater the difference in their intelligence. As McNemar [1938, p. 249] notes, however, such a conclusion ". . . rests ultimately upon the fact that *four* pairs reared in really different environments were undoubtedly different in intelligence."

The study of adopted children provides the chance to investigate parent-child similarity in IQ with respect to natural parents who do not actually raise the children (genetic influence but no environmental influence) and with respect to foster parents (environmental influence but no genetic influence). Skodak and Skeels [1949] obtained a sample of 100 children (60 boys, 40 girls) who had been placed in their adoptive homes under the age of six months. The children were given the Stanford-Binet test at various times, beginning when they were about two years of age and continuing until they were about 13. As an estimate of parental IQ, educational level was determined for the true parents and for the foster parents. In addition, the Stanford-Binet was given to 63 of the true mothers. The results were somewhat surprising. Beginning when the children were four years of age, their IQ scores correlated significantly with the educational level and with the IQ of their *true mothers*. At age 13, the children's scores correlated .32 with true mothers' educational level and .44 with true mothers' IQ. For the 60 true fathers about whom educational level was known, this estimate of intelligence correlated .44 with child's IQ at age 13 [computed from raw data presented by Skodak and Skeels, 1949]. In contrast, no correlation existed between children's IQ and foster parents' educational level. At age 13, the children's scores correlated .00 with foster fathers' education and .02 with foster mothers' education. The effect of genetic factors is obvious in that the only significant parent-child correlations are with the natural parents and not with the foster parents.

Even the Skodak and Skeels data, however, offer no either-or answer for heredity and environment. The correlations indicate that the *ordering* of the children along a dimension of intelligence is related to the *ordering* of their true mothers and fathers along the same dimension; it says nothing about *level* of intelligence. For the 63 true mothers tested, the mean IQ was 85.7, while the mean IQ of their children at 13 was 106. The children are significantly brighter than their mothers. Since the true mothers were predominantly girls with inferior socioeconomic backgrounds and since the foster homes were relatively good in educational opportunity and socioeconomic level, this last finding could indicate that the foster home environment had a positive effect on the children's IQ. Research such as that of Skodak and Skeels has led to a conceptualization of genetic factors setting some sort of limit or maximum with respect to the development of intellectual ability with environmental factors determining the extent to which development takes place within those limits. Burt says:

In point of fact, with a few rare exceptions, like eye colour or serological differences in the blood, every observable characteristic that geneticists have studied has proved to be the product of the joint action of both heredity and environment. There are, in short, no such things as hereditary characteristics: there are only hereditary tendencies [Burt, 1958, p. 6].

Selective Breeding and Intelligence. The fact that genetic determinants influence individual differences in intelligence could best be shown through research involving selective breeding. Is it possible to develop either brighter or duller offspring on the basis of deliberate parental matching on such characteristics?

Tryon in 1940 used successive generations of rats in an attempt to develop bright and dull subgroups. As a measure of "intelligence," a complicated maze learning task was employed, and each subject's learning ability scored in terms of number of errors. There were wide individual differences in his initial group of over 100 rats with errors ranging from seven to 214. On the basis of these error scores, Tryon selected the brightest and dullest rats and had members of each group mate only with rats similar to themselves in intelligence. This procedure was continued for 18 generations. By the seventh generation, the experimenter had produced two distinct groups, bright rats and dull rats. The dullest member of the bright group was brighter than the majority of the dull group and the brightest member of the dull group was duller than the majority of the bright group.

Even though selective breeding in humans is not a feasible research plan, we might note that at least in our culture selective breeding is actually taking place. That is, marital couples are not randomly paired with respect to IQ. Rather, husband-wife correlations are found to be about .50. This is actually not too surprising, on several grounds. For one thing, similarity in terms of interests and abilities based on intelligence should lead to greater attraction. For another, individuals with similar IQ's are more likely to come in contact with one another and hence have greater probability of meeting, dating, marrying—those who attend college, those who are assigned to technical high schools, those who live in the same neighborhood, those who have similar occupations, and so forth. Whether human beings are directing themselves toward a distant future with bright and dull subpopulations is a matter for speculation.

PRENATAL INFLUENCES

In the course of testing large numbers of mentally retarded children and obtaining case history material on them, Dr. Ruth F. Harrell noticed that bad nutrition in early life was characteristic of a large proportion of these children. Some later research with rats who were either starved or well fed during pregnancy indicated differences in the maze-learning ability of the offspring. Still other animal studies support this general relationship. For example, Maurer and Tsai [1930] found that when young rats are deprived of vitamin B, they require twice as many trials and make twice as many errors in learning a maze as do the normally fed rats in the control group. Work on maternal dietary deficiencies has been of several varieties. One can, for example, significantly increase the number of congenital malformations in the offspring by depriving pregnant rats of such elements as riboflavin and vitamin D [Warkany and Nelson, 1942]. Work with humans has indicated that the incidence of miscarriage, stillbirths, and premature births is higher among women on poor diets during pregnancy than among women on normal diets [Ebbs, Tisdall, and Scott, 1942].

Such observations and findings led to a large-scale experimental investigation of the effects of maternal diet on the intelligence of the offspring by Harrell, Woodyard, and Gates [1955]. The general plan was to supplement the diet of a group of maternity patients, administer placebos to others, and then compare the IQ's of their offspring when the children were old enough to be tested with the Stanford-Binet.

In a large charity maternity clinic in Norfolk, Virginia, 1,200 pregnant women served as subjects. The women were randomly assigned to one of four groups. All were given pills to be taken daily, and the pills were indistinguishable in size and color. Even the nurse who gave them the tablets at each visit did not know which subject was assigned to which group. One-fourth of the women received placebos containing inert material, one-fourth received pills containing ascorbic acid, one-fourth received pills containing thiamine, and one-fourth received pills containing thiamine, riboflavin, niacinamide, and iron (multi-nutrient). The pills were taken during pregnancy and while the mother was nursing the baby. The subjects visited the clinic every two weeks and were given enough pills at each visit to provide one tablet a day until the next visit.

The subjects primarily were residents of slum areas in the city and were 80 per cent Negro, with the remainder consisting of individuals with Mexican, Filipino, German, Lashkar, Italian, Greek, Jewish, French, Irish, and English ancestry. Most of the women worked by the day as laundresses, cooks, or cleaning women.

The second part of the study was carried out a few years later. The offspring of the subjects were contacted on both their third and their fourth birthdays and given Form L of the Stanford-Binet. Because of frequent moves made by the parents and dislocations owing to slum-clearance projects, it was not possible to locate the child of every subject. For the three-year-olds, it was possible to locate and test a total of 518 children, and for four-year-olds the total was 370.

For each age group, the intelligence quotients of the four groups were compared by means of analysis of variance. The mean IQ's are shown in Table 11–2. We see that at each age level, the brightest children were those whose mothers had received the multi-nutrient pills while the least bright children were those whose mothers had not received any dietary supplement. At each age level, analysis of variance indicated: (1) differ-

Table 11–2   INTELLIGENCE OF OFFSPRING AS A FUNCTION
OF MATERNAL DIET DURING PREGNANCY AND LACTATION

	Maternal Diet Supplement			
Offspring	Multi-Nutrient	Thiamine	Ascorbic Acid	Placebo
Three-year-olds	103.3	101.8	101.0	98.3
Four-year-olds	101.6	97.6	97.9	93.7

ences among the four groups significant at the .01 level, (2) differences between the combined vitamin groups significantly higher at the .01 level than the placebo group, and (3) differences among the three vitamin groups which are not significant.

The authors concluded:

. . . this study demonstrates, beyond a reasonable doubt, that vitamin supplementation supplied to pregnant and lactating women under certain circumstances, such as those prevailing in the Norfolk group described in this report, does increase the intelligence of their offspring, at least for the first four years of their lives [Harrell, et al., 1955, p. 62].

In explaining the effects of the vitamin supplements, several possibilities were suggested. Conceivably, the biochemical or structural characteristics of the nervous system were directly affected. Another possibility is that the differences were the result of more general effects on health, bodily vigor, and stamina. In the latter instance:

. . . their gain in intelligence quotient might have been due to greater alertness, more sustained and vigorous activity, feelings of greater security or confidence, or similar factors which might have enabled them to seek and acquire more information, to engage more frequently and steadily in intellectual activities in which skills and techniques of problem solving and the like involved in the Binet test are developed. Indeed it is not impossible that some of the effects were due to greater vitality or to alertness or to vigorous "will to succeed" during the test sessions [Harrell, et al., 1955, p. 64].

A cautionary note is provided by the fact that these same investigators carried out a parallel study in a rural, mountain community in Kentucky and did not find that dietary supplements influenced the IQ of offspring in this setting. There were a great many differences between the samples, including a much better regular diet for the Kentucky group (home-grown vegetables, and the like). Also, the Kentucky mothers visited the clinic less frequently so that supervision of their taking the pills was less controlled, and the Kentucky children were brighter as a group than the Norfolk children. One possibility is that the Norfolk data represent a comparison of a good, balanced diet (containing vitamins) versus a deficient diet (the regular food eaten by the underprivileged members of the placebo group). If so, this would suggest that vitamin supplements during pregnancy would affect the IQ of offspring only in instances of inadequate normal diets. Obviously, this is an area in need of continued research.

SOCIOECONOMIC "INFLUENCES"

Obviously, intelligence is one of the major factors which determine the possibility and probability of obtaining a given educational level and a given occupational level. Individuals below average in intelligence are not likely to become corporation lawyers, and individuals with very high IQ's are not usually employed as unskilled laborers. Large-scale studies in both World War I [Fryer, 1922] and World War II [Stewart, 1947] found a substantial relationship between occupational level and scores on the Army intelligence examinations. Since educational and occupational levels are major criteria in defining socioeconomic status and since parent-child IQ scores correlate about .50, we would expect children from different socioeconomic levels to differ in performance on intelligence tests. A number of investigators have reported findings supporting this proposition.

Occupational Status of Parents. The members of Terman and Merrill's standardization group for the 1937 revision of the Stanford-Binet were divided in terms of occupational classification of their fathers. The IQ variations across groups for two- to five-and-one-half-year-olds are shown in Table 11–3.

Table 11–3 FATHER'S OCCUPATION AND CHILD'S IQ (TWO- TO FIVE-AND-ONE-HALF-YEAR-OLDS)

Father's Occupation	Child's IQ
Professional	116.2
Semiprofessional and Managerial	112.4
Clerical, Skilled Trades, and Retail Business	108.0
Semiskilled, Minor Clerical, Minor Business	104.3
Rural Owners	99.1
Slightly Skilled	95.1
Day Laborers, Urban, and Rural	93.6

Similar findings have been reported with the WISC [Seashore, Wesman, and Doppelt, 1950]. The mean IQ of the children of professional and semiprofessional men was 110.9, while that for the children of urban and rural laborers and farm foremen was 94.6.

Using the Otis Mental Abilities Test in a group of 176 fourth- to twelfth-grade girls, Burchinal [1959] correlated IQ of the subjects with the occupational prestige and educational level of their fathers. Both variables correlated significantly with IQ of the offspring. Intelligence test scores correlated .34 with father's occupational prestige and .25 with father's occupational level.

Socioeconomic Index. A more general measure of socioeconomic level is that developed by W. Lloyd Warner. The index of Status Characteristics [Warner, Meeker, and Eels, 1949] rates individuals with respect to occupation, source of income, house type, and dwelling area; from these ratings a weighted sum is computed. The categories which are then derived from the index are:

Upper-upper: old aristocracy

Lower-upper: newly rich

Upper-middle: business and professional people, the "pillars of society"

Lower-middle: small tradesmen, white collar workers, some skilled laborers

Upper-lower: semiskilled and unskilled workers, "poor but respectable"

Lower-lower: shiftless and disorderly

Warner's index was used by Janke and Havighurst [1945] with a sample consisting of almost all of the 16-year-olds in a Midwestern city. The mean Stanford-Binet scores of the offspring whose parents fall at various levels on the index are shown in Table 11–4.

Table 11–4   SOCIOECONOMIC LEVEL AND IQ OF OFFSPRING*

Social Status	Mean IQ of Offspring
Upper-upper, lower-upper, and upper-middle	128
Lower-middle	112
Upper-lower	104
Lower-lower	98

* Adapted from Janke and Havighurst, 1945, pp. 503–504.

A still different approach is to obtain socioeconomic ratings of an entire community or subcommunity in order to compare these ratings with the IQ scores obtained by the children residing there. Maller [1933] found that the value of home rentals in a neighborhood correlated .50 with the mean IQ of the school children living in that neighborhood. Thorndike and Woodyard [1942] found that per capita income for 30 cities correlated .78 with the mean IQ scores of the sixth graders in those cities.

Social Mobility. Educational attainment is the major way in which individuals in our society are able to raise their socioeconomic status. Schmuck and Schmuck [1961] hypothesized that upwardly mobile families would exert influence on their children to succeed academically and that the children in such families would have higher IQ scores than children in nonupwardly mobile families.

Determination of upward mobility was based on the family's having moved to an area of increased socioeconomic status (for example, Europe to America, Deep South to North, farm to city, city to suburb), the father's occupation being at a higher socioeconomic level than his father's occupation, and the parents having more years of education than their parents. The subjects were 90 fourth-grade children plus their parents. IQ of the children was measured by the Kuhlmann-Finch test.

Of the children in the 25 clearly upwardly mobile families, 19 were high IQ and 6 were low IQ. Of the 27 children in families in which there was negligible upward mobility, 7 were high IQ and 20 were low IQ. This difference is significant at the .001 level.

Interpretation of Socioeconomic Findings. The rather well-established relationship between socioeconomic status of parents and the IQ of their offspring has led to a number of different possible interpretations.

For example, conceivably hereditary factors are operative in that the genetically brighter individuals do better in school, obtain better jobs, select mates similar to themselves in intelligence, are upwardly mobile, and pass on these genes to offspring. Similarly, the genetically less bright individuals do worse in school, obtain lower level jobs, select less bright mates, are not upwardy mobile, and pass on these genes to their offspring.

The other major explanation involves differences across socioeconomic groups in the amount of intellectual stimulation provided for the child in his home environment. As one moves up the socioeconomic hierarchy, the vocabulary of parents becomes larger, the amount of reading material in the home becomes greater, and more opportunity exists for intellectual enrichment (for example, music, art, plays, and the like). Given the same genetic structure, wide differences in environmental opportunities should produce different levels of intelligence.

In all probability, both explanations are partially true. We have exam-

ined some of the evidence concerning genetic influences, and we will
now look more directly at the influence of different types of early experience. In any event, the caution of Terman and Merrill concerning their
occupational findings should be noted with respect to all such findings:

It is hardly necessary to stress the fact that these figures refer to *mean* values
only, and that in view of the variability of the I.Q. within each group the respective distributions greatly overlap one another. Nor should it be necessary to point
out that such data do not, in themselves, offer any conclusive evidence of the
relative contributions of genetic and environmental factors in determining the
mean differences observed [Terman and Merrill, 1937, p. 48].

EXPERIENTIAL INFLUENCES

Intellectual functioning seems to have a long period of development—stretching at least from conception to adolescence. In a relatively "standard" middle-class environment, a regular and steady increase
occurs in mental age from infancy to middle or late adolescence. Given
limits or boundaries set by genetic factors, intellectual functioning should
show a typical growth pattern, and IQ (intellectual functioning in relation to others of the same chronological age) will remain more or less
constant over the years. The fact that all environments are not the same
leads to striking departures from this pattern. Most of the research on
experiential influences on intelligence has dealt with variables which involve either deprivation or enrichment of environmental stimulation over
the period of development.

Environmental Deprivation. One way in which an environmental deficit can be brought about is through the isolation of a group
from the cultural mainstream. For example, Gordon [1923] administered the Stanford-Binet to a group of 76 English canal-boat children.
These youngsters seldom attended school (only when the boats were being
loaded or unloaded), their parents were illiterate, and they had little contact with anyone outside of the family. The mean IQ of these children
was 69.6. More important, however, is the finding that IQ and age correlated —.76. The youngest children (four to six years of age) had a mean
IQ of 90 while the oldest children (12 to 22 years of age) had a mean IQ
of 60. Similarly, Gordon found that age and IQ correlated —.43 in a
group of gypsy children. Findings consistent with these have been reported for children residing in isolated mountain areas in the United
States, in rural communities, in slum areas, and in homes which are
socioeconomically inferior.

Another type of environmental deprivation is represented by the in-
stitutionalization of young children. Goldfarb [1945] has emphasized the
probable importance of parent-child contacts as a source of constant

stimulation. The child's motor and verbal responses evoke parental interest, the parent sings and talks to the child, and there is encouragement to babble, talk, sit, stand, walk, and climb. The child receives toys, is taken to see interesting things, and is encouraged to perform a variety of acts. In contrast, the institutionalized child is one of a large group, and even under the best of circumstances the amount of contact between the child and any adult figure is relatively small. Goldfarb selected a group of 15 children who were placed in an institution in early infancy, had remained there for three years, and were then placed in foster homes. A control group consisted of 15 children who had been placed in foster homes in early infancy rather than in institutions. The two groups were matched for age, sex, age at which they left their real parents, and background characteristics of the true mothers and foster parents. The Stanford-Binet was administered just before the institutional group left the orphanage and again after seven months in the foster homes. The control group was also tested at the same time periods. On the first testing, the control group had a mean IQ of 96 while the institutional group was significantly lower with a mean IQ of 68. Even after seven months in the foster home, there was a 26-point IQ difference between the two groups. Additional research by Goldfarb and others supports the finding that psychological deprivation in infancy produces an IQ decrement, and that subsequent placement in a home does not overcome the deficit even over an extended time period.

One other type of finding that could be a function of deprivation is the negative correlation between intelligence and family size. For example, one investigation found a mean IQ of 113 for only children and steadily lower means as number of siblings increased down to a mean of 91 for children with five siblings [Scottish Council for Research in Education, 1949]. Correlations between IQ and family size in a wide variety of studies tend to run between $-.20$ and $-.30$. Among the several possible explanations of this relationship is the greater deprivation for each individual child in a large family [Anastasi, 1956, p. 204]: "From a psychological viewpoint, another important factor is the degree of adult contact provided in families of different sizes. Available evidence suggests, for example, that such contact may be the most important single factor in linguistic development. . . ." A seemingly more plausible explanation is the greater proportion of large families at lower socioeconomic levels.

Combining the sort of data discussed here with a great many other investigations of the effects of early experience on later behavior, Hunt drew the following conclusions:

It is fairly clear from the evidence . . . that impoverishment of experience during the early months can slow up the development of intelligence. In terms of the traditional measurement of intelligence, this means reducing the IQ. Various bits of the evidence have strongly suggested that such slowed development is permanent, that it may result not only in a permanently reduced IQ but in a failure of the basic criterion capacities of individuals to develop to the degree that they might have developed under other, more varied programs of encounters with the environment which were appropriately matched to the intellectual structures developing within the child. But much remains to be learned about the degree of permanence in such failures to develop and about the conditions under which these failures to develop become permanent [J. McV. Hunt, *Intelligence and Experience,* copyright © 1961, The Ronald Press Company, p. 346].

Environmental Enrichment.   Upward changes in IQ scores are more likely to occur than are downward changes in IQ for children raised in well-educated families, presumably because these families provide greater than average intellectual stimulation [Bayley, 1954]. The primary way in which "enriching" experience has been defined, however, is in terms of schooling. Intellectual stimulation in nursery school, primary and secondary schools, and even in college has generally been found to have a positive effect on IQ scores.

Although a great many investigations have been made of the effect of nursery school attendance on IQ, methodological weaknesses leave the results in doubt. Anastasi [1958] concludes that no effect has been demonstrated. She goes on to add, however, that most of the studies have involved children from relatively superior homes. If enrichment has an effect, this could most reasonably be demonstrated for children from a relatively deprived environment. For example, Kirk [1958] studied several groups of retarded children over a period of years. One group attended a community nursery school, one group an institutional nursery school, a third group lived at home, and a fourth group lived in an institution without attending nursery school. The 43 children in nursery school showed significantly greater increase in IQ than the 38 children who did not have the school experience. Seventy per cent of the nursery school group showed IQ gains of ten points or more. Similarly, Wellman and Pegram [1944] compared below-average orphanage children who were given a preschool experience with a matched orphanage group who were not. Those in the preschool group showed gains in IQ, and the gains were greater for those who attended regularly than for those who did not. McNemar [1945], using the same data, reported that IQ changes correlated as high as .46 with amount and regularity of preschool experience. Part of the impetus for the government's Project Head Start, in which deprived children may attend preschool classes, has been provided by studies such as these.

Quality of the school experience also appears to be crucial. Worbois [1942] compared the effects on IQ of several one-room rural schools with a consolidated central rural school. All of the subjects lived in a farming area in which there was one large consolidated school and 13 small one-room schools. The Stanford-Binet was used to measure IQ. In one comparison, 34 children in the consolidated school and 30 in the one-room schools were tested when they entered first grade and again at the end of the school year. The two groups were not significantly different when they entered school, but those in the consolidated school had significantly higher IQ scores nine months later; there was at that time a five-point difference in mean IQ.

Another comparison involved 16 children in the consolidated school and 14 in the one-room schools who were tested as they entered school and again two years later. As before, there was no difference in IQ at the beginning, but those in the consolidated school were 13 points higher after the two-year period. Worbois found no difference between the parents of the children in the two types of schools (for example, years of education, attitude about schooling), but a number of differences between the schools were found. For example, in the consolidated school the teachers had more years of education and more teaching experience. Consistent with these findings were those reported by De Groot [1951] concerning applicants to an Industrial Training School in Holland. IQ scores showed a significant drop immediately after the war, presumably as a result of inadequate schooling during the German occupation. After five years of post-war recovery, the IQ scores of applicants were back to the prewar levels.

Finally, several studies have reported that college attendance has a positive effect on IQ. For example, Charles and Pritchard [1959] tested 112 students at Iowa State College when they entered and again four years later. A significant increase in IQ scores occurred for both male and female students over the four-year period. Without a control group of nonstudents, this finding is open to question. More convincingly, Lorge [1945] obtained IQ scores of 131 boys who had been tested in the eighth grade and then again 30 years later. Increase in IQ on the second test was a function of the number of years of schooling between the two testings. The more years of school, the higher the adult IQ.

NEGRO-WHITE DIFFERENCES IN IQ

One final question concerning the antecedents of individual differences in intelligence should be noted. Hopefully, it is the kind of question which will seem meaningless to future generations except as an historical curiosity. For reasons which are obvious at the present time, a great deal of research effort and a great deal of emotional writing has centered on the question of differences between Negroes and whites in

IQ and on the explanation for the differences. Having examined the data concerning the variables which influence intellectual development, findings concerning Negro-white differences seem quite consistent with what is known about experiential factors affecting intelligence.

Mean IQ of American Negroes and Mean IQ of American Whites. Investigations stretching over half a century are consistent in reporting IQ differences between these two racial groups; white subjects obtain significantly higher IQ scores than Negro subjects [for example, Bruce, 1940; Garth, 1925; McGurk, 1951; Roen, 1960; Yerkes, 1921]. In surveying a large number of such studies, Klineberg [1944] concluded that the median IQ of Negroes is 86 (versus 100 for whites). Similarly, Shuey [1958] estimated the Negro mean as 85. Before attempting to explain the reason for such racial differences, two points should be made.

First, even with group means differing by 14 or 15 points, a large overlap occurs between groups. Those who like to stress racial differences often speak of there being *only* 20 per cent or *only* 30 per cent overlap between the groups. The overlap, however, refers to the percentage of Negroes falling *above the median* of the white group. Thus, 30 per cent overlap indicates that about one-third of the Negro population is brighter than one-half of all the whites. It also indicates, as Anastasi [1958] points out, that 99 per cent of the Negroes reach or exceed the IQ scores of some whites. Obviously, then, knowledge that a given individual is a Negro or a white does not allow you to estimate his IQ.

Even if racial differences in IQ were greater than they are and even if the median overlap were smaller than it is, there certainly would be no justification for prejudging *every* individual Negro as intellectually inferior and hence not capable of attending certain schools or holding certain jobs. Further, there would be no justification for prejudging *any* individual Negro as unqualified to vote or eat in a particular restaurant or sit in the front of a bus. In Klineberg's [1963, p. 202] words: "The science of psychology can offer no support to those who see in the accident of inherited skin color or other physical characteristics any excuse for denying to individuals the right to full participation in American Democracy."

Negro-White IQ Differences and Experiential Differences. On a number of bases, the most likely explanation for racial differences in IQ is that of different environmental influences for Negroes and whites. The history of the Negro in the United States has been an unenviable one. From the days of slavery to modern ghettoes both North and South, the Negro has been underprivileged educationally, economically, socially, and occupationally. In other words, all of the environmental factors known to affect intelligence have been operative to make the average Negro score lower on IQ tests than the average white. As pro-segregationist writers point out, the existence of negative influences does not demonstrate that the absence of such influences would cancel Negro-white IQ differences. There is, however, more convincing evidence.

First, Negro and white infants are found not to differ in intelligence [Pasamanick, 1946; Gilliland, 1951]. Even among preschool children, racial differences in intelligence are absent [Knobloch and Pasamanick, 1953; Pasamanick and Knobloch, 1955; Anastasi and d'Angelo, 1952]. As children grow older, the Negro and white groups begin to diverge. Osborn [1960] reported a longitudinal study of Negro and white children over a four-year period. There were 815 white and 446 Negro children who were tested in the sixth, eighth, and tenth grades with the California Test of Mental Maturity. The mean IQ's of the white children were about 23 points above those of the Negro children at each testing. On reading and arithmetic achievement tests, the groups were progressively further apart over the four years. Since all of the subjects attended segregated schools in the Deep South and since such Negro schools are demonstrably inferior, the only surprising finding was that even in the tenth grade some Negro children were able to obtain IQ scores which equalled or exceeded the scores of 84 per cent of the whites.

Second, given better schooling, Negro IQ's go up. A study by Klineberg [1935] in New York City and one by Lee [1951] in Philadelphia each showed that the IQ scores of Negro children from the South increase as a function of the number of years of schooling they have had in the North. Lee found the highest IQ's for Negro children born in Philadelphia, next for Negro children born in the South but entering the first grade in Philadelphia, next for Negro children born in the South but entering the second grade in Philadelphia, and so forth. Similarly, after two years of school integration in Louisville, Kentucky, Negro IQ's at every grade level increased [Carmichael, 1959]. Further, Negro-white IQ differences were not found among Los Angeles school children [Clark, 1923]. Even more convincing evidence for the effects of differential schooling is the fact that Negroes from New York, Ohio, and Illinois score higher than whites from Arkansas, Kentucky, and Mississippi [Benedict and Weltfish, 1943; Tyler, 1956].

An additional finding relevant to the question of Negro-white differences is that when Negro families are divided in terms of the types of socioeconomic and parental education variables found to influence IQ's among whites, the same patterns are found in that better-educated, wealthier Negroes with higher status occupations have brighter children [Horton and Crump, 1962].

The genetic versus experiential issue in racial differences in IQ is summed up nicely by Ashley Montagu:

It is possible that . . . "all races are equally endowed with intelligence," but until the great experiment has been performed of allowing the members of all groups called "races" equal opportunities for development we shall never know whether they are or not. No group, "race," or individual is endowed with intelligence. Individuals are endowed with genetic potentials for learning to be intelligent. Intelligence is a socially acquired ability, a complex problem-solving form of behavior which one must learn from other human beings. Not only that, human beings have to learn to learn. The capacity for intelligence becomes an ability only when it has been trained. The capacity itself varies among individuals and, allowing for differences in prenatal influences, these capacities are largely genetically influenced. Allowing for genetic differences, all observers are agreed that what those capacities will become as abilities will largely depend upon the environmental stimulations to which they are exposed. . . . [Montagu, 1964, p. 1415].

A THEORY OF INTELLECTUAL DEVELOPMENT

In attempting to integrate the findings dealing with the antecedents of intelligence, Hayes [1962] has proposed a motivational-experiential theory. First, he suggests that intelligence as measured by IQ tests consists of nothing more than an accumulation of learned facts and skills. Second, genetic influence consists of motivational differences, specifically in tendencies to engage in activities conducive to learning, rather than differences in inherited intellectual capacity. He refers to these genetic tendencies as experience-producing drives. In addition to genetic determinants, experience-producing drives may be altered by a number of factors including early brain damage, the nature and variety of experiences available to the child, and presumably by such factors as adequacy of maternal nutrition during pregnancy and the occurrence of extrinsic as well as intrinsic rewards for engaging in varied activities.

Viewed in this way, no conflict exists in the data provided by genetic studies, prenatal studies, socioeconomic studies, and experiential studies. All of the findings can be conceptualized in terms of variables affecting experience-producing drives. The greater the innate drive, the more the individual will engage in the necessary activities. The more rich and varied are the experiences which are available, the greater the accumulation of learned facts and skills. The greater the accumulation of such facts and skills, the higher the IQ. And, as we shall see in subsequent sections, the higher the IQ, the better the grades in school, the higher the level of possible occupational attainment, the greater the creative ability, and so on and so forth.

This theory of the nature of intelligence provides a way of integrating many other disparate facts in an apparently meaningful way. McNemar [1964, p. 881] suggests that if Hayes' "formulation leads to experimental manipulation of variables, we may eventually make progress in an area that has too long been dominated by ever increasing fractionization . . . with little thought as to how the fractured parts get put together into a functioning whole."

The Place of Intelligence in the Structure of Personality

ACADEMIC PERFORMANCE

Since IQ tests were originally constructed for the purpose of predicting academic performance and since that is the major use to which such instruments are now applied, we would expect to find that scores on intelligence tests are positively correlated with school grades. The two variables generally correlate about .50 [Tyler, 1956].

With fourth, fifth, and sixth graders, Keller and Rowley [1962] found IQ scores on the Otis to correlate substantially with achievement tests covering work knowledge ($r = .47$ to .72), reading ($r = .45$ to .68), language ($r = .34$ to .67), arithmetic problem-solving ($r = .41$ to .67), and science ($r = .47$ to .72).

Frandsen [1950] administered the Wechsler-Bellevue (an earlier version of the WAIS) to 83 senior high school students; IQ was found to correlate .68 with high school grades. Some of the subtests of the Wechsler correlated more highly with grades than others. For example, information (items such as "What does rubber come from?") correlated .56 with grades, while object assembly (similar to jigsaw puzzles) correlated .11. Using only the best subtests, Frandsen obtained a correlation of .76 between test scores and grades.

Spielberger and Katzenmeyer [1959] reported ACE scores to correlate .29 ($p < .01$) with grade-point average over six semesters for 640 students at Duke. Sopchak [1958] found that freshman grades for 356 students at Adelphi College correlated .39 ($p < .01$) with total ACE score, .39 ($p < .01$) with the ACE verbal score, and .23 ($p < .01$) with the ACE quantitative score.

The shorter the time period between testing and grading, the better the prediction. As might be guessed from the fact that IQ is not perfectly stable over time, IQ measured in the first grade has been found to correlate only .21 with college grades [Travers, 1949].

Other studies have investigated the average IQ's obtained by individuals who reach particular educational levels. Embree [1948] and Wrenn [1949] found average IQ to increase at each educational level. The average Stanford-Binet IQ for students entering college was found to be 118, for students graduating from college 123, for those receiving advanced degrees 126, and for those receiving Ph.D. degrees 141.

OCCUPATIONAL LEVEL

As was indicated earlier, a number of investigators have shown a relationship between occupational level and the intelligence of those individuals engaged in the occupations. For example, Ball [1938] obtained IQ scores for two groups of men who had been tested in childhood. These scores were found to correlate with the present occupational level of the subjects, .57 in one group and .71 in the other.

One of the armed services investigations during World War II involved an analysis of civilian occupations and performance on the Army General Classification Test for 18,782 Air Force enlisted men [Harrell and Harrell, 1945]. Again, occupation and intelligence were found to be related. At the upper end of the test scores were accountants, lawyers, and engineers. In the middle range were machinists, foremen, and sales clerks, while at the lower end of the test scores were farmers, miners, and teamsters.

CREATIVITY

The fashion in some quarters is to deplore both the educational emphasis on intelligence tests as selection devices and student performance on objective examinations as the evaluation criterion. The picture is one of a system in which highly creative and original students are bypassed in favor of those with high IQ's whose strongpoint is rote memorization of endless facts. It would be helpful to know the relationship between measures of intelligence and measures of creativity.

Much has been made of the fact that among relatively bright individuals little relationship exists between creativity and general intellectual ability [for example, Getzels and Jackson, 1962; Torrance, 1960]. Ripple and May [1962] rightly point out that the magnitude of the relationship is a function of the variability of the sample. With groups homogeneous in IQ, the absence of a relationship with creativity is not very informative. To explore the question further, they obtained four groups of seventh-grade students who differed in degree of homogeneity with respect to IQ as measured by the Otis Quick Scoring Mental Ability Test. All subjects were given nine tests of creative thinking. In the groups homogeneous in intelligence (either all high or all low), very small and mostly insignificant correlations were found. In the heterogeneous group, however, intelligence and creativity tended to be highly related as shown in Table 11-5. Thus, IQ's are fairly effective in predicting creative behavior in heterogeneous populations. Consistent with these results is the finding by Meer and Stein [1955] of a significant relationship ($r = .40$) between IQ on the Wechsler-Bellevue and creativity ratings of research chemists who were not Ph.D.'s, whereas for Ph.D. chemists the relationship was not a significant one.

In Chapter 5, Barron's [1957] study of original and unoriginal Air Force Officers was described. This group should be more homogeneous than an

Table 11–5 CORRELATIONS BETWEEN IQ SCORES AND MEASURES
OF CREATIVITY IN A HETEROGENEOUS POPULATION

Creativity Measures	r
Expressional Fluency	.73*
Plot Questions	.70*
Object Improvement	.30
Metaphors	.54*
Onomatopoeia	.69*
Object Uses—Fluency	.38**
Object Uses—Flexibility	.60*
Word Uses—Fluency	.11
Word Uses—Flexibility	.73*

$*\ p < .01$
$**\ p < .05$

unselected population but less homogeneous than a group of very bright students. One of the variables he included was intelligence:

It is of course reasonable to expect that intelligence and originality will covary positively. If one defines originality as the ability to respond to stimulus situations in a manner which is both adaptive and unusual, and if one defines intelligence simply as the ability to solve problems, then at the upper levels of problem-solving ability the manifestation of intelligence will be also a manifestation of originality. That is to say, the very difficult problem which is rarely solved requires by definition a solution which is original [Barron, 1957, p. 735].

Using the Concept Mastery Test as a measure of intelligence, Barron found a significant correlation of .33 between IQ and creativity. Thus, in this population the two variables are positively related, as hypothesized. We should also note that the magnitude of the relationship is such that a good many individuals must fall in the "off-quadrants"; that is, some must be bright but not creative, while others are creative but not bright. With a sample of 343 Air Force captains, Barron administered the two types of tests and then selected the two off-quadrant groups. Fifteen individuals were at least one standard deviation above the mean on originality and one standard deviation below the mean on intelligence; 23 individuals had the reverse pattern. Barron summarizes their differences:

Subjects who are relatively original in spite of being relatively unintelligent show a lack of ego-control. They describe themselves as persons whose needs demand immediate gratification and whose aggressive impulses are out in the open. They are willful, obstreperous, and extreme individuals. One would not be inclined to select them as companions for a long trip in a submarine. By contrast, their relatively unoriginal but more intelligent fellows seem very much on the pleasant side, although perhaps a bit *too* bland and unwarlike, all things considered.

When one compares these self-descriptions with the staff descriptions of Ss who are *both* original and intelligent, it appears that intelligence represents the operation of the reality principle in behavior, and is responsible for such characteristics as the appropriate delay of impulse-expression and the effective organization of instinctual energy for the attainment of goals in the world as it is [Barron, 1957, p. 739].

DELAY OF GRATIFICATION

Barron's theorizing concerning intelligence as a requisite for ego-control or the operation of the reality principle leads directly to another series of investigations.

Mischel and Metzner [1962] have conceptualized the capacity for postponing immediate gratification in developmental terms as involving a transition from immediate wish-fulfilling types of behavior to delayable reality testing types. Since learning to delay is bound up with thinking (cognitive reality testing in place of impulsive motor behavior), cognitive ability should be positively related to delaying capacity. In other terms, as intelligence level increases, preference for delayed gratification should increase. A group of elementary school children for whom IQ scores were available served as subjects. As in other investigations by Mischel, the choice behavior was in reference to two candy bars; the children could receive a five-cent Hershey bar now or a ten-cent bar at a later time. The mean IQ of those children choosing the delayed reward (105.7) was significantly higher than the mean IQ of those choosing the immediate reward (99.0). In terms of correlation, the relationship between IQ score and preference for the delayed reward was .29 ($p < .001$).

Another research approach to the same general question has utilized the human movement (M) response on the Rorschach as a measure of the inhibition or ego delay process. Klopfer, Ainsworth, Klopfer, and Holt state:

The implications of inner control are that the person has enough inner resources to enable him to meet emotional impact by delaying action long enough to gain control over outward expression of behavior. The chief sign of inner control is M [Klopfer, Ainsworth, Klopfer, and Holt, 1954, p. 363].

Surveying a number of studies in which IQ and M were investigated, Levine, Spivack, and Wright [1959] indicate that the median correlation between the two variables is .26. They themselves studied the relationship in four different populations: hospitalized schizophrenics, hospitalized nonschizophrenics, psychiatric clinic patients, and adolescents in a residential school. In each group, Rorschach M and IQ as measured by the Wechsler were significantly correlated from .20 to .49.

In still other investigations, additional ego delay measures were used, including the Stroop color-word test (speed at naming colors printed in black versus speed at naming color in which the word is printed when the word and the ink color are incongruent), time estimation (estimate when 30 seconds have passed), cognitive inhibition (after learning paired-associates, subjects must respond to the stimulus words with any word other than the response words), and motor inhibition (write "New Jersey Chamber of Commerce" as slowly as possible without stopping). All of these measures were significantly related to IQ [Levine, Spivack, Fuschillo, and Tavernier, 1959; Spivack, Levine, and Sprigle, 1959].

ADJUSTMENT

Terman's Gifted Children.   In 1921, Lewis Terman obtained a research grant from the Commonwealth Fund of New York City which enabled him to begin an investigation of the characteristics of very bright individuals. His plan was to determine the "physical, mental, and personality traits" of gifted children and to follow the course of their lives into adulthood. The investigation extended over the remainder of Professor Terman's life and is now being continued by Melita Oden. To date, four books have been published describing the findings at various points in the lives of the subjects [Terman, 1925; Burks, Jensen, and Terman, 1930; Terman and Oden, 1947; Terman and Oden, 1959].

On the basis of their performance on the Stanford-Binet, over 1,500 children with IQ's of 140 or more were selected. The parents and teachers of these individuals were urged not to tell the children about the study or about their IQ scores. The mean IQ of the group was 151, and their mean age was 11 years. The amount of data collected over the last half century has been enormous, and only a portion of it will be reported here.

Childhood.   One major research interest was in the physique and health of the gifted children. In both height and weight, these children were above the established norms for unselected children in California. Even their mean birth weight was greater than the norm, by 12 ounces. Compared with normative groups, they walked earlier, talked earlier, and reached puberty at a younger age. Compared with a control group of normal youngsters, they had fewer headaches, fewer hearing defects, and were rated as less nervous. For a subsample of 783 who were given medical examinations, the gifted children were found to have a lower incidence of physical defects and abnormal conditions of almost every kind than the normal population of school children. Terman and Oden note:

The combined results of the medical examinations and the physical measurements provide a striking contrast to the popular stereotype of the child prodigy so commonly depicted as a pathetic creature, overserious and undersized, sickly, hollow-chested, stoop-shouldered, clumsy, nervously tense, and bespectacled. There are gifted children who bear some resemblance to this stereotype, but the truth is that almost every element in the picture, except the last, is less characteristic of the gifted child than of the mentally average [Terman and Oden, 1959, p. 8].

A series of character tests was administered to a random group of 532 of the gifted children and a control group of 533 unselected children. The tests of cheating and emotional stability had previously been shown to discriminate delinquents from nondelinquents. It was found that the gifted group obtained better scores on all of the character tests at every age level, from 10 to 14.

Ratings of 25 traits were made by teachers familiar with each child, and for comparison purposes 523 nongifted children were also rated by the teachers. As may be seen in Table 11–6, the gifted children received

Table 11–6   PERCENTAGES OF GIFTED SUBJECTS
             RATED BY TEACHERS ABOVE THE MEAN
             OF THE CONTROL GROUP*

		Per Cent
1. Intellectual Traits:		
General intelligence	97	
Desire to know	90	
Originality	85	
Common sense	84	
Average of intellectual traits		89
2. Volitional Traits:		
Will power and perseverance	84	
Desire to excell	84	
Self-confidence	81	
Prudence and forethought	81	
Average of volitional traits		82.5
3. Emotional Traits:		
Sense of humor	74	
Cheerfulness and optimism	64	
Permanence of moods	63	
Average of emotional traits		67
4. Aesthetic Traits:		
Musical appreciation	66	
Appreciation of beauty	64	
Average of aesthetic traits		65

Table 11–6 PERCENTAGES OF GIFTED SUBJECTS
RATED BY TEACHERS ABOVE THE MEAN
OF THE CONTROL GROUP* (Cont.)

5. Moral Traits:		
Conscientiousness	72	
Truthfulness	71	
Sympathy and tenderness	58	
Generosity and unselfishness	55	
Average of moral traits		64
6. Physical Traits:		
Health	60	
Physical energy	62	
Average of physical traits		61
7. Social Traits:		
Leadership	70	
Sensitivity to approval	57	
Popularity	56	
Freedom from vanity	52	
Fondness for large groups	52	
Average for social traits		57.4
8. Mechanical ingenuity	47	

* Adapted from Terman and Oden, 1959, p. 14.

higher ratings on most of the traits. Except for leadership, the gifted group tend to be most like the control group on the social traits and slightly below the normals on mechanical ingenuity. Incidentally, the latter rating is probably in error because tests of mechanical ability consistently show gifted children to be better than normals.

Adolescence. The first follow-up investigation was carried out in 1927–1928 when most of the subjects were 16 or 17 and enrolled in high school. Not much change occurred in the composite portrait of the group. In school they were doing well, and they were still superior to nongifted children in such things as size, health, social interests, and leadership.

Adulthood. In 1936, more data were gathered by mail, and records were brought up to date in preparation for a more thorough study of the group in 1939–1940 when their average age was about 29. The subjects were interviewed and given a number of tests. Remarkably, 96 per cent of the original group cooperated actively as subjects in this follow-up. Among the conclusions reached were the following:

That to near mid-life, such a group may be expected to show a normal or below-normal incidence of serious personality maladjustment, insanity, delinquency, alcoholism, and homosexuality. . . .

That in vocational achievement the gifted group rates well above the average of college graduates and, as compared with the general population, is represented in the higher professions by eight or nine times its proportional share. . . .

That marital adjustment of the gifted, as measured by the marital happiness test, is equal or superior to that found in groups less highly selected for intelligence, and that the divorce rate is no higher than that of the generality of comparable age.

That the sexual adjustment of these subjects in marriage is in all respects as normal as that found in a less gifted and less educated group of 792 married couples [Terman and Oden, 1959, pp. 21–22].

Mid-Life.   The most recent follow-ups of these subjects were made in 1950–1952 and in 1955, again with interviews and the administration of a number of tests and questionnaires. By 1955, 104 of the original group were deceased, and 28 could not be located. There were 795 men and 629 women still participating. Among the voluminous findings, a few will be cited.

The mortality rate for these gifted individuals was lower than the expectation for the general population not only with respect to disease, but also with respect to accident-induced mortality. Compared to others of their generation, the gifted men were about one and one-half inches taller and the gifted women about one inch taller. With respect to emotional adjustment, 3.1 per cent of the men and 3.4 per cent of the women had been admitted to a hospital or sanitarium for the mentally ill at least once; these figures do not differ from expectancies for the general population.

Most of the gifted subjects report drinking alcohol moderately or heavily; nevertheless, there was a lower incidence of alcoholism in this group than in the general population. The incidence of crime and delinquency is very low. Three boys spent time in a reform school, and one man served a prison sentence for forgery. Only one woman served a jail sentence. All of these five individuals have since made normal adjustments. The incidence of homosexuality (2 per cent of the men and 1.7 per cent of the women) is considerably below the national figures.

Not surprisingly, the educational record of this gifted group is quite different from the general population. Almost 90 per cent entered college, and about 70 per cent graduated from college. In their generation, the percentage of individuals graduating from college is less than 8 per cent; at the time of the follow-up the figure was about 12 per cent. College grade-point averages of B or better were obtained by 78 per cent of the men and 83 per cent of the women. In addition, 56 per cent of the men and 33 per cent of the women obtained at least one advanced degree. Ph.D.'s or M.D.'s were awarded to 22.3 per cent of the men and 5.4 per cent of the women.

As adults, their occupational level was found to be quite high. A total of 45.6 per cent of the men are in a profession, while 40.7 per cent are in the managerial, official, and semiprofessional group. The most frequent profession is law, followed by university professors, engineers, and physicians. In the managerial group, most are executives or managers in business and industry, followed by banking, finance, and insurance executives, accountants and statisticians, and sales managers. In income, these men are well above average, even when compared to others in the same occupation. Of the women, about half are housewives, while 42 per cent hold full-time jobs with schoolteaching as the most frequent occupation.

Finally, with respect to recognition of achievement, the gifted group is again unusual. In terms of such honors as listing in *American Men of Science*, election to the National Academy of Sciences, listing in the *Directory of American Scholars*, and listing in *Who's Who in America*, the group has done exceptionally well. The men have written 60 books and monographs, 2,000 technical and scientific articles, and have been granted 230 patents. Other writings include 33 novels, 375 short stories, and 265 miscellaneous articles. A great many members of the gifted group are nationally prominent in a variety of fields, while 8 or 10 are internationally known. Included are physical scientists, a biological scientist, social scientists, members of the U.S. State Department, and a motion picture director.

In summing up some of the implications of this large body of findings, Terman has said:

The follow-up of these gifted subjects has proved beyond question that tests of "general intelligence," given as early as six, eight, or ten years, tell a great deal about the ability to achieve either presently or 30 years hence. Such tests do not, however, enable us to predict what direction the achievement will take, and least of all do they tell us what personality factors or what accidents of fortune will affect the fruition of exceptional ability. Granting that both interest patterns and special aptitudes play important roles in the making of a gifted scientist, mathematician, mechanic, artist, poet, or musical composer, I am convinced that to achieve greatly in almost any field, the special talents have to be backed up by a lot of Spearman's g, by which is meant the kind of general intelligence that requires ability to form many sharply defined concepts, to manipulate them, and to perceive subtle relationships between them; in other words, the ability to engage in abstract thinking [Terman, 1954, p. 224].

The Dynamics of Intelligence

In spite of the long history of psychological interest in intelligence and its measurement, the use of this variable in experimental studies has been relatively rare. In view of the research which has been done to date, very probably individual differences in intelligence account for some portion of the variance in responses to a great many stimulus situations.

LEARNING

Since intelligence tests were developed originally in order to predict ability to learn in a school setting and since learning has been one of the major areas of psychological experimentation, one might expect to find a large number of learning experiments in which the IQ of subjects was a matter of research interest. Actually, there are few such investigations.

One of the early studies of this type was carried out by Kenneth Spence and a fellow student as a class project in an experimental psychology course at McGill University [Spence and Townsend, 1930]. Using the Thurstone Intelligence Test, ten high-scoring and ten low-scoring subjects were selected. The learning task was a finger maze made of copper wiring; the subjects were blindfolded. Each trial was timed and the number of errors recorded. Trials continued for each subject until he had finished three perfect consecutive trials. Those subjects with the highest intelligence test scores took fewer trials, made fewer errors, and took less time in learning the maze than those subjects with low IQ scores. Correlations between IQ and the learning variables were also computed; the coefficients were .46 for number of trials, .63 for number of errors, and .60 for time. The authors concluded that the factors which make for a high score on the intelligence test also make for a better performance on the learning task.

Harlow [1951] has proposed that a relationship exists between the evolutionary level of a species and the rate at which members of that species are able to learn a learning set; the higher the point in the evolutionary scale, the greater the ability at "learning to learn" in a situation. A number of investigations have served to support this proposition. Within a species, of course, individual differences in performance occur in learning-set formation. It has been proposed that IQ tests should permit prediction of these differences for human subjects. Koch and Meyer [1959] utilized 33 preschool children as subjects to whom the Stanford-Binet was given. The learning task was very similar to that employed with monkeys in learning-set studies. Each child was individually run, and the experiment was described as a game. A "red penny" (poker chip) was hidden under one of two cards on each trial, and the child was instructed to find as many pennies as possible so that he could buy a toy from the experimenter. On each trial the subject could select only one of the cards. Each card had on it a square of colored paper of various sizes, and the color was the clue to which the subject had to learn to respond. Each day a subject was given 12 different problems, with six trials on each. On the first trial of any problem, the response had necessarily to be a guess, but on subsequent trials the correct response would be the selection of cards with the color under which the penny was located on trial one. Thus, the task was to acquire a set to learn. Each subject was continued until he made 90 per cent correct responses in a day's session. The children varied in the time required to reach the criterion from one to 15 days. This variable was found to correlate $-.59$ ($p < .01$) with mental age on the Stanford-Binet. The higher the intellectual ability of the subject, the fewer days that were required to acquire the learning set. Figure 11–3 shows a comparison of

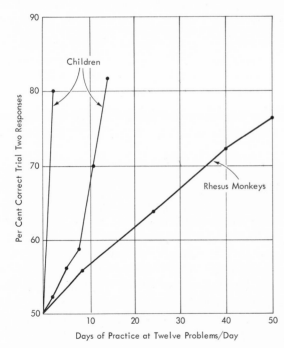

FIG. 11–3. *Comparison of learning-set performance of children at two levels of intelligence, and rhesus monkeys.* (*Adapted from Koch and Meyer, 1959, p. 388.*)

the performance of the seven brightest children, the five least bright children, and a group of 16 Rhesus monkeys who had been given the same problem by Blazek and Harlow [1955].

Another learning-set investigation with mental defectives also found that the set is acquired most quickly by the subjects with the highest mental ages [Ellis, 1958].

Concept formation as a function of IQ was investigated by Osler and Fivel [1961] and replicated by Osler and Weiss [1962]. Subjects consisted of elementary and junior high school students of different age levels who had taken the WISC. Each age level was divided into groups of average intelligence (IQ = 90 to 109) and high intelligence (IQ = 110 and above). Subjects were shown pairs of stimuli as part of a "game" and were told that one was "correct" and one "incorrect." If the subject chose the correct one, he received a marble. In a series of 150 pairs, if enough marbles were collected, the subject would win a toy. One of the concepts used was *bird*. In this instance, the correct choice on each trial would be the picture of a bird. In each experiment IQ level was found to be significantly related to the speed with which the subject grasped the concept, as evidenced by 10 consecutive correct responses. With another group of subjects, the same experiment was repeated but with specific instructions that there was a clue to which picture was correct, that the correct ones had something in common. With this explicit definition of the task, IQ was not related to performance. The authors' interpretation of these findings follows:

If the assumption that specific instructions eliminate the problem-finding component from the task is correct, then the conclusion to be drawn is that high intelligence gave S an advantage in problem definition but not in problem solution in the concept attainment task. It is entirely possible, however, that were the concept task one of greater difficulty, intelligence might also prove to be advantageous in the solution phase of the task [Osler and Weiss, 1962, p. 532].

RESPONSE TO PSYCHOTHERAPY

Another type of stimulus situation in which IQ has some relevance to behavior is that of psychotherapy. The most general form which therapy takes is that of a verbal interchange between therapist and patient. Whatever changes in the patients' behavior take place as a consequence of this interaction are often conceptualized in terms of learning. For example, Dollard and Miller [1950], Dollard, Auld, and White [1953], Mowrer [1953], and Miller [1964] have formulated therapeutic changes in terms of concepts drawn from learning theory. In a recent paper Murray proposed to:

. . . relate psychotherapy to the conceptual framework provided by learning, or behavior, theory. Why learning theory? The principles of learning, to the extent that they are known, constitute an attempt to account for the acquisition, performance, and elimination of all forms of behavior. Since psychotherapy may be viewed as a method of changing behavior, it follows that the principles of learning should apply [Murray, 1964, p. 249].

It also follows that response to psychotherapy should be in part a function of ability to learn, as measured by intelligence tests.

Amount of active participation in group psychotherapy was investigated by McFarland, Nelson, and Rossi [1962]. The subjects were 36 patients in group psychotherapy at the VA Hospital in Palo Alto. Their behavior in therapy was rated on the Finney Interaction Scale; intelligence was measured by three subscales of the Wechsler-Bellevue and by the verbal fluency scale from Thurstone's Primary Mental Abilities Test. Participation in group psychotherapy was found to correlate significantly with estimated IQ on the Wechsler scales ($r = .51$, $p < .01$) and with verbal fluency ($r = .34$, $p < .05$). The highest coefficient ($r = .56$, $p < .01$) was the correlation with an analogies test. Among the extensions of these findings suggested by the authors was the possibility of using IQ tests to select patients who would benefit from psychotherapy. In their sample, a cut-off IQ score of 100 would maximize the chances of excluding from therapy those patients who would not participate and including those who would. They suggest [McFarland, et al., 1962, p. 297]: "Finally, it seems to us that we, as clinical psychologists, are increasingly lost in a concern over dynamics and emotions. This frequently causes us to lose sight of the practical uses of intelligence scores."

A similar therapeutic problem is that of predicting those patients who will continue in psychotherapy versus those who decide to terminate it. Hiler [1958] obtained data for 133 patients at the VA Mental Hygiene Clinic in Detroit for whom Wechsler-Bellevue scores were available. Premature termination of psychotherapy was defined as dropping out within five sessions. Those who remained in psychotherapy were significantly more intelligent (mean IQ = 112.8) than those who terminated prematurely (mean IQ = 102.8). Again, a cut-off score of 100 on the IQ test was found to maximize prediction. Most of those below 100 drop out of therapy, while most of those above 100 remain in therapy. A similar study by Rubinstein and Lorr [1956] with patients from nine different VA mental hygiene clinics reported findings consistent with those of Hiler. Among the best predictors of response to psychotherapy were the vocabulary test from the Stanford-Binet, years of education, and occupational level. Those who remain in therapy are more intelligent, better educated, and have higher-level jobs.

Change in Intelligence

Perhaps more than with most personality dimensions, the distinction between antecedent variables and change variables influencing the dimension of intelligence is a somewhat arbitrary one. As we have seen, intellectual ability shows a relatively steady process of growth from birth through adolescence. We have considered any factors influencing this process as antecedents of individual differences in IQ. We will now consider those variables which influence changes in intelligence in adulthood.

AGING

The first investigations of the effects of aging on intelligence utilized a cross-sectional design. That is, individuals of various ages were tested, and comparisons of different age groups made. The findings were relatively consistent and somewhat discouraging. For example, a World War I study found that Army Alpha scores decreased steadily from young (under 20) groups to older (51–60) groups of officers [Yerkes, 1921]. Jones and Conrad [1933] found the same trend among individuals living in 19 villages in New England. Still other findings were in agreement with these [for example, Jones and Kaplan, 1945; Vincent, 1952]. Wechsler [1958] plotted the standard scores on the Wechsler-Bellevue as a function of chronological age as shown in Figure 11–4. We see in the figure

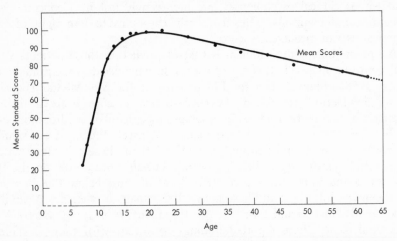

Fig. 11–4. *An age curve of intelligence based on a cross sectional investigation: full scale scores on the* Wechsler-Bellevue, *ages 7 to 65.* (*Adapted from* Wechsler, *1958, p. 31.*)

that intellectual growth seems to reach a peak by late adolescence, remains relatively constant through the 20's, and then begins a sharp decline. Wechsler, for one, concluded:

Every human capacity after attaining a maximum begins an immediate decline. . . . The age at which this maximum is attained varies from ability to ability but seldom occurs beyond 30 and in most cases somewhere in the early 20's [Wechsler, 1944, p. 55].

More recently, data have become available from longitudinal studies of intelligence over the life span. In this approach, *the same individuals* are retested at various ages, and a quite different picture emerges. For example, Owens [1953] compared the test performance of a group of individuals in middle-age with their own test performance 30 years earlier as college freshmen. On every subtest of the Army Alpha their performance was better in middle-age except for the arithmetic items; the test-retest correlation over the 30 years was .77. Others have reported similar findings [for example, Bayley and Oden, 1955; Bentz, 1953; Nisbet, 1957].

One of the important variables in determining the effect of aging on IQ seems to be amount of education. Swanson [1952] retested 55 men on a college entrance test after a 20-year interval. The 22 men who had graduated from college gained a mean of 35 points, the 13 who attended college but did not graduate gained nine points, and the 20 who did not attend college gained seven points. Even with cross-sectional data, tests of higher processes (reasoning, vocabulary, analogies, and the like) given to well-educated people under conditions not involving speed show no downward trend with age between 20 and 65 [Ghiselli, 1957].

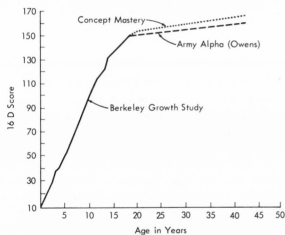

A COMPOSITE AGE CURVE OF INTELLIGENCE

Fig. 11–5. *An age curve of intelligence based on longitudinal investigations: data from the Berkeley Growth Study, the Terman Gifted Study, and Owen's Iowa Study. (Adapted from Bayley, 1955, p. 816.)*

Why does a discrepancy generally occur in the findings when different people are tested at different ages versus when the same people are retested at an older age? Bayley suggests:

The real difference between the conflicting findings seems to lie in the longitudinal as opposed to the cross-sectional method of obtaining scores for successive ages. In the former we have a constant sample whose life experiences, age for age, will have been similar in pervasive environmental conditions, such as wars, technological advances, and methods of education. . . .

Do such tests as the Army Alpha and the Wechsler-Bellevue, for example, measure intelligence in adults? Or do they tend to reflect continued experience in an increasingly enriched environment? Do the younger generations have more opportunity to develop their intellectual capacities than did their parents, or even their older brothers and sisters? Or are we just measuring the effects of increasingly widespread informal education made possible by radio, television, and other modern means of communication? [Bayley, 1955, p. 817]

Based on the data from some of the longitudinal studies, Bayley proposed a new and more encouraging sort of curve describing the relationship between age and intellectual ability, as shown in Figure 11–5.

CHEMICAL ENHANCEMENT OF INTELLIGENCE

From time to time, there has been an interest in the possibility of raising IQ through the use of an appropriate drug. The most notable example is that of glutamic acid. While early reports of the beneficial effects of glutamic acid on the functioning of mental defectives were encouraging, better controlled studies have been uniformly negative [Astin and Ross, 1960].

Similarly, some speculation has arisen that the use of tranquilizing drugs in treating mental illness would result in better performance on intelligence tests. Again, the findings are negative [for example, Ison, 1957].

BRAIN DAMAGE

Obviously any damage to brain tissue from accidents or diseases would have a deleterious effect on intelligence. Strangely enough, however, it seems to be possible to lose substantial quantities of cerebral matter without affecting test scores.

Weinstein and Teuber [1957a] compared two groups of injured men for whom pre-injury test scores on the Army General Classification Test (AGCT) were available. The brain-damaged group consisted of patients who had lost cerebral tissue owing to injury while the control group consisted of patients who had injuries involving peripheral nerves (for example, in the arm). Approximately 10 to 12 years after the injury the AGCT was readministered. The brain-damaged group was significantly different from the control group on this post-injury testing. The difference was, however, not a function of IQ loss owing to brain damage but of *less gain* over the time-span. The control group showed a mean increase of 13 AGCT points while the brain-injured group increased 1.6 points. Similarly, it has been reported that Wechsler-Bellevue scores show no change before and after a prefrontal lobotomy operation [Markwell, Wheeler, and Kitzinger, 1953].

Some investigators have reported a negative effect of brain injury on

IQ [for example, Ross, 1958]. A possible reason for conflicting findings involves the specification of the type of brain damage. Another Weinstein and Teuber [1957b] study dealt with AGCT changes as a function of the area of the brain which had been injured. Again, a group with brain injuries were compared with a control group suffering peripheral nerve injuries. The controls showed a gain in AGCT points as did most of the brain-injured patients. Only those with left parieto-temporal lesions showed a significant decrease in test performance. The patients with lesions in left nonparieto-temporal regions or lesions in the right hemisphere showed gains in test scores almost as high as the control group.

MENTAL ILLNESS

One would not be surprised to find that an individual's ability to function intelligently declines when he becomes mentally ill.

Schwartzman and Douglas [1962] obtained intelligence test scores given by the Canadian Army during World War II and readministered the test to three groups of men. One group consisted of hospitalized schizophrenics, another was a group of schizophrenics who had been discharged from the hospital for at least a year, and the third was a group of normal veterans. The three groups were matched for IQ on the basis of the first testing, age, educational level, occupational status, and ethnic background. The study showed that on the second testing, the schizophrenic patients had lost a mean of 15.2 points on the test, the ex-patients had lost a mean of 5.1 points, and the normal group had gained 11.8 points. These differences between groups were statistically significant. Chronic schizophrenics were also found to have a greater IQ loss than acute schizophrenics. Other investigations of IQ before and after the development of schizophrenia report similar results [for example, Hoyt, Elliott, and Hebb, 1951; Rappaport and Webb, 1950].

Some reports indicate no intellectual loss in schizophrenia [for example, Albee, Lane, Corcoran, and Werneke, 1963]. This finding may be the result of instances of early IQ deterioration long before the schizophrenia became apparent [Lane and Albee, 1963, 1964].

The Schwartzman and Douglas study also suggested that as schizophrenics get better, their IQ scores go up again in that the ex-patients had higher scores than the hospitalized patients. As a more direct test of this proposition, Schwartzman, Douglas, and Muir [1962] followed up as many of the hospitalized patients as could be located eight years after the first study. Again, the Canadian Army examination was given. Of the 23 subjects who were tested, 10 were hospitalized and 13 had been discharged. All but three were diagnosed as chronic schizophrenics. The hospitalized patients showed a steady decline in test scores over the 17

years. As much loss in IQ occurred between the second and third testings as did between the first and second testings. The ex-patients did not
differ from the hospitalized patients in amount of loss between the first
and second tests. The ex-patients did, however, show a significant gain in
IQ between the second and third tests. Their mean score in 1960 was not
significantly different from their original test score obtained in the army.
Apparently, then, intelligence test performance is adversely affected by
schizophrenia but remission of the illness also involves a return of the lost
intellectual ability.

Current Status of Intelligence as a Personality Variable

Perhaps the most important developments with respect to
work on intelligence involve an increasing use of the experimental method
plus a variety of attempts to build a theory of intelligence. There may soon
come a time when psychology's earliest technological success will cease to be
its greatest theoretical embarrassment. Two somewhat special types of development should also be noted: factorial approaches to intelligence and
computer simulation of intelligence.

FACTORS OF INTELLIGENCE

Intelligence as measured by Binet and Terman and many
others is conceptualized as a unitary variable, which Spearman [1927]
designated as g or general intelligence. With the development of factor-
analytic techniques a number of investigators began to speak of a group
of independent intellectual factors or of g plus a series of group factors.
Thurstone, for example, found seven "primary mental abilities" which he
called spatial, perceptual, number, verbal, word fluency, memory, and
reasoning, and a test was built to measure each [Thurstone, 1938; Thurstone
and Thurstone, 1941].

Among the many factorial studies of intelligence, the work of Guilford
[1959] provides the most detailed structural framework in which intellect
consists of five different abilities (cognition, memory, covergent thinking,
divergent thinking, and evaluation), each of which may involve different
kinds of content (figural, symbolic, semantic, and behavioral). With each
ability applied to each kind of content, there are six possible kinds of
products (units, classes, relations, systems, transformations, and implications). Thus, Guilford proposes a three-dimensional model with five
abilities, four contents, and six products. This means that the measurement
of intelligence will be best accomplished by the use of 120 independent
tests. Guilford concludes:

The structure of intellect as I have presented it to you may or may not stand
the test of time. Even if the general form persists, there are likely to be some

modifications. Possibly some different kind of model will be invented. Be that as it may, the fact of a multiplicity of intellectual abilities seems well established [Guilford, 1959, p. 479].

As convincing as the factor-analytic argument may appear, there is reason to question the notion that the future approach to intelligence will be via the measurement of multiple factors [McNemar, 1964]. One problem is that when tests are constructed to measure the independent intellectual factors, they are found *not* to be independent. Significant correlations between these supposedly different dimensions suggest a general factor such as Spearman's *g* underlying the scales. Secondly, the predictive ability of the factor tests with respect to such criteria as school grades is no better than that of the measures of general intelligence such as the Stanford-Binet. Unless they yield more accurate prediction, little justification exists for conceptualizing factorially pure tests as something new and different and better. While these considerations do not necessarily mean that future developments in factor approaches to IQ will have the same outcome, the empirical evidence is not supportive of the superiority of this way of measuring intelligence.

COMPUTER SIMULATION OF INTELLIGENCE

One of the newest and most unusual developments in the study of intellectual functioning has been the use of digital computers to simulate intelligent behavior. Presumably, if we can design a computer to behave as human beings do, we will be able to extend our understanding of the functions involved. Computers are remarkable devices and, with suitable instructions, can perform such acts as solving equations, keeping books, and playing chess [Green, 1963]. Further, computer programs can be written which are so complex that the person who wrote the program is unable to predict precisely what the computer will do with a given problem [for example, Newell, Shaw, and Simon, 1958].

With respect to the kinds of tasks that are included in intelligence tests, programs have been constructed which enable a computer to deal with such problems as verbal comprehension ("How many games did the Red Sox win by one run in 1959?") [Green, Wolf, Chomsky, and Laughery, 1961], verbal fluency (making original sentences out of words stored in the machine's memory bank) [Klein, 1964], perception and reasoning (solving problems such as geometric analogies) [Evans, 1964], numerical skills ("The distance from New York to Los Angeles is 3000 miles. If the average speed of a jet plane is 600 miles per hour, find the time it takes to travel from New York to Los Angeles by jet.") [Bobrow, 1964], learning and memory (rote learning of nonsense syllables and paired-associates learning) [Feigenbaum, 1961], and reasoning (proving theorems in plane geometry and solving problems in integral calculus) [Green, 1964]. Thus, a computer can be provided with the same general abilities that are involved in human intelligence.

Since computers can demonstrate these basic skills, computer specialists [for example, Green, 1964] argue that our best approach to understanding what is involved in intelligent functioning is to develop a computer model of the processes required to answer test items and then to discover what internal changes in the model lead to individual differences in performance. Green proposes:

> With a hierarchy of such programs we would have a machine capable of getting high scores on any battery of intelligence tests. The same machine could get low scores or any particular pattern of scores depending on the settings of its parameters. When we produce such a machine, we will understand a very great deal more about intelligence than we do now [Green, 1964, p. 62].

Summary

Intelligence tests represent the best-known and most widely influential product of psychological science. At the same time, little integration of the concept of intelligence with the remainder of work in psychology has occurred. The earliest attempts to measure individual differences in intellectual functioning consisted of the measurement of very simple responses, but scores on such tasks were found to be unrelated to criteria such as school grades. The use of complex tasks by investigators such as Binet and Terman proved considerably more fruitful. Perhaps the most unusual aspect of the work on intelligence is the relative lack of theory. Definitions of intelligence tend to stress adaptation to the environment, learning ability, and/or abstract thinking.

Alfred Binet, a French psychologist, was interested in the measurement of intellectual differences among children, and in 1905 developed the first intelligence test in response to a request from the Paris school system. An American psychologist, Lewis M. Terman, became interested in Binet's work and in 1916 published the Stanford-Binet Intelligence Scale which set the pattern for all subsequent measures of intelligence.

The 1916 Stanford-Binet was revised in 1937 and again in 1960 by Terman and Merrill. The test items primarily involve the more complex mental processes and include such things as analogies, comprehension, vocabulary, similarities and differences, completions, absurdities, drawing designs, and memory for digits and verbal material. From a large pool of possible items, the final test items were selected on the basis of (1) showing an increase in percentage of children passing them at successive age levels, and (2) correlating with the total score on the test. In the 1937 Stanford-Binet, the IQ was defined as the Mental Age obtained on the test divided by the subject's Chronological Age and multiplied by 100. Because MA does not continue to show large yearly increases indefinitely, after age 13 it was necessary to substitute a corrected CA divisor in the IQ formula. In order to avoid such difficulties, on the 1960 test IQ is defined in terms of deviation from the average performance of an individual's age group. Now, IQ is simply a standard score with a mean of 100 and a standard deviation of 16. The test has high internal consistency, is stable over time, and correlates highly with other IQ tests.

A great deal of the research on the antecedents of individual differences in intelligence has involved a controversy between proponents of genetic antecedents and proponents of experiential antecedents. Such controversy has been eliminated by the present-day concern with determining the ways in which all factors contribute to a given behavior. Genetic determinants have been investigated by a number of means including the study of family resemblances. While the IQ's of random pairs of adults and children correlate .00, parent-child correlations are .50. Similarly, random pairs of unrelated children show correlations of .00, unrelated children reared together correlate .25, sibling IQ's correlate .50, fraternal twins correlate .63 to .70, and identical twins have correlations of .88. A comparison of such relationships indicates rather clearly the joint contribution of genetic and experiential variables to IQ differences. Experiments of nature include instances in which identical twins have been separated in infancy and reared apart; their IQ's correlate less highly ($r = .77$) than do the scores of identical twins reared together but higher than the scores of ordinary siblings reared together. Another such natural experiment involves adopted children. The IQ of children is found to correlate significantly with that of their natural parents but not with their adoptive parents. In the selective breeding of rats, investigators have been able to develop subgroups of maze-bright and maze-dull subjects. Prenatal influences on IQ have been found in that the addition of vitamin supplements to the diets of pregnant women was found to have a significantly positive effect on the IQ of their offspring as measured at ages three and four. Apparently, this effect is achieved only when the mother's ordinary diet is an inadequate one.

Considerable evidence also exists that the higher the occupational level of fathers, the higher the IQ of their offspring. Positive relationships are also found between IQ and socioeconomic class of parents, upward social mobility of parents, value of home rentals in the child's neighborhood, and per capita income in the city in which he lives. When children are isolated from normal environmental stimulation in infancy and childhood, a negative influence on IQ occurs. This deprivation effect has been found for canal-boat children, gypsy children, and others in isolated or inferior home settings. Also, IQ is lower for children raised in an institution rather than in a regular home and for children with a large number of siblings. Environmental enrichment has the opposite effect; a positive influence on IQ has been found with respect to well-educated parents, and attendance of nursery school, high quality elementary schools, and college. Many of the studies of IQ antecedents have dealt with Negro-white differences. Studies have shown that whites obtain a higher mean score on IQ tests than Negroes (though large group overlaps occur), that Negro and white infants and preschoolers do not differ, that in good schools Negro IQ's go up (to a level higher than whites in bad schools), and that when Negro parents are well educated and reach a higher socioeconomic level their children are brighter than the children of less fortunate parents. In attempting to integrate the findings dealing with the antecedents of intelligence, Hayes has proposed a motivational-experiential theory. He suggests that intelligence consists of nothing more than an accumulation of learned facts and skills. Genetic influence consists of motivational differences in the tendency to engage in activities conducive to learning. In addition to genetic determinants, experience-producing drives may be modified by a number of factors.

As would be expected, scores on intelligence tests show a positive relationship with grades in school, with an average correlation of about .50. Prediction is better as the time between testing and grading is shortened. Scores on intelligence tests are also found to correlate positively with occupational level, creativity, and ability to delay gratification. The largest-scale study of overall adjustment as a function of IQ has been carried out by Terman and his associates. Beginning in 1921, over 1,500 gifted children (IQ of 140 and above) were selected, and they have been studied at regular intervals ever since. Terman found that gifted children were taller, heavier, and healthier than normal children and were above average on a large number of characteristics. As adults, they were below average in the incidence of serious personality disturbances, insanity, delinquency, alcoholism, homosexuality, and in mortality rate. Their educational and vocational attainments are remarkable in terms of grades, degrees, income, accomplishments, and honors. Both achievement and adjustment appear to be facilitated by high intelligence.

The use of intellectual measures in experimental studies has been relatively rare. Scores on IQ tests have been found to be related to performance in learning a maze, in acquiring a learning set, and in the problem-finding phase of concept formation tasks. Response to psychotherapy also appears to be a function of IQ in terms of amount of active participation in group psychotherapy and of positive response to individual psychotherapy.

When cross-sectional investigations of different age groups were carried out, intellectual growth was consistently found to reach a peak by late adolescence, remain relatively constant through the 20's, and then begin a sharp decline. When longitudinal investigations are conducted, however, intellectual ability is found to *increase* over the total age span, and this trend is especially true for well-educated individuals. Presumably, the discrepancy in findings is caused by differences across generations in educational opportunities and other factors. Attempts to raise intelligence by means of drugs, such as glutamic acid or tranquilizers, have not been successful. Damage to brain tissue has much less effect on IQ than might be expected; brain-damaged patients, however, tend to show *less gain* over time than nondamaged control subjects, for example. Also, the location of the injury within the brain appears to be a crucial factor, with damage to the left parieto-temporal region having the most negative effect on IQ. Finally, evidence exists that intellectual impairment is brought about by schizophrenia, and that IQ returns to normal when the patient improves.

Perhaps the most important developments with respect to work on intelligence involve an increasing use of the experimental method plus a variety of attempts to build a theory of intelligence. Intelligence is most often conceptualized as a unitary variable, designated as *g* or general intelligence. With the development of factor-analytic techniques a number of investigators began to conceptualize a group of independent intellectual factors. Among the difficulties with this approach is that the scales measuring the independent factors are found to be correlated with one another, and such tests yield no better predictions than the measures of general intelligence. One of the newest developments has been the use of digital computers to simulate intelligent behavior. Computers have been programmed in such a way as to demonstrate the same kinds of abilities that are involved in human intelligence. Proposals have been made that the building of computer models which yield individual differences in performance will lead to an increased understanding of intellectual functioning.

CHAPTER 12

Self-Concept

Many individuals who have been concerned with the study of personality have expressed the conviction that the most fruitful approach is to deal with man as an organized whole rather than in terms of atomistic units such as authoritarianism and achievement need. In attempting to conceptualize behavior in terms of a single, unified process, many theorists have utilized the notion of self-concept. Hall and Lindzey [1957] suggest that the term *self* has come to have two distinct meanings to psychologists: self-as-object and self-as-process. Self-as-object may be defined simply as the total aggregate of attitudes, judgments, and values which an individual holds with respect to his behavior, his ability, his body, his worth as a person—in short, how he perceives and evaluates himself. Self-as-process is defined in terms of activities such as thinking and perceiving and coping with the environment; *ego* is another term used to describe this same construct.

In the following section, the point of view is presented that the self-concept defined in terms of self-as-object is an important aspect of personality and that individual differences along this dimension are as meaningful as differences in attitudes, motives, and abilities, but no more so. Some reservations exist, however, about the utility of self-as-process. To conceptualize perceptual behavior, defensive behavior, expressive behavior, motivations, and cognitions, for example, as manifestations of the self-concept does not add anything to our description or explanation of the behavior in question. That is, to say that a given behavior is a manifestation of the self does not seem to lead to any different or more accurate prediction of behavior. Similarly, the self-as-process definition often leads toward reification, and one finds that "the self" (or "the ego") is responsible for behavior (as when the ego defends itself against anxiety) and has thing-like qualities (as when the ego is described as strong or weak). No modern theorist proposes "a psychic agent or 'inner manikin' which regulates man's actions" [Hall and Lindzey, 1957, p. 48], but descriptions of the self-as-process appear at least to lean in that direction.

In any event, self-theorists are concerned with extremely important variables, and this theoretical orientation has generated a great deal of research. Among the proponents of self-theory have been Mead [1934], Angyal [1941], Hilgard [1949], Snygg and Combs [1949], Symonds [1951], Sarbin [1952], Sullivan [1953], and Carl R. Rogers, whose work will serve as a base for our presentation of research dealing with the concept of self. We will see that Rogers' approach involves observation, generalization, experimental verification of hypotheses, and theory-building. Therefore, the question may arise as to whether any differences exist between the theoretical approach of stimulus-response psychologists as represented by the Hull-Spence tradition and that of self-theorists such as Rogers. At least part of the difference seems to be emotional and aesthetic and linguistic rather than a basic quarrel about how to build a science of behavior. In contrasting his point of view with that of stimulus-response psychologists, Rogers says:

. . . I have been asked to cast our theoretical thinking in the terminology of the independent-intervening-dependent variable, in so far as this is feasible. I regret that I find this terminology somehow uncongenial. I cannot justify my negative reaction very adequately, and perhaps it is an irrational one, for the logic behind these terms seems unassailable. But to me the terms seem static —they seem to deny the restless, dynamic, searching, changing aspects of scientific movement. There is a tendency to suppose that a variable thus labeled, remains so, which is certainly not true. The terms also seem to me to smack too much of the laboratory, where one undertakes an experiment *de novo*, with everything under control, rather than of a science which is endeavoring to wrest from the phenomena of experience the inherent order which they contain. Such terms seem to be more applicable to the advanced stages of scientific endeavor than to the beginning stages. . . .

It should be quite clear from the foregoing that the model of science which I find most helpful is not taken from the advanced stages of theoretical physics. In a field such as psychotherapy or personality the model which seems more congenial to me would be taken from the much earlier stages of the physical sciences [Rogers, 1959, pp. 189–190].

However, a few aspects of self-theory are quite different from modern stimulus-response psychology, and these aspects will be discussed in the following section. Included are an emphasis on the total individual rather than on bits and pieces of behavior and an emphasis on the importance of the phenomenal field. The latter term refers to the individual's total subjective perception of experience; his behavior is based on this perception rather than on an externally defined environment. The influence or lack of influence of these conceptions on research growing out of Rogers' formulations will be discussed.

Theoretical Background

ROGERS AND CLIENT-CENTERED THERAPY

Carl Rogers (1902–   ) has described his own background in terms of the influence of his early family experiences on his work. Born in Oak Park, Illinois, he moved with his family to a farm at the age of 12. His was a large, hard-working, conservative, Protestant family whose religious beliefs he describes as almost fundamentalist. Rogers was originally interested in scientific agriculture, and this interest carried over to some degree in his undergraduate work at the University of Wisconsin. Religion remained an important concern, however, and he spent two years at the Union Theological Seminary. His philosophical position eventually moved him away from the church, and he entered Teachers College, Columbia University. After a clinical internship at the Institute for Child Guidance, he received the Ph.D. degree in educational and clinical psychology in 1931. He then spent 12 years at a community guidance clinic in Rochester, New York. His efforts to conceptualize the work of psychotherapists and to understand the behavior of their clients involved a continuing quest for a theoretical model to account for psychotherapy and, more generally, personality.

Rogers' move into the academic world in 1940 (Ohio State University) came at a time when his ideas concerning client-centered psychotherapy were crystallizing. He moved from Ohio State in 1944 to spend an extremely productive 12 years at the University of Chicago. His therapeutic work at the Counseling Center there, his research, his development of theory, and his influence on graduate students and colleagues brought Rogers a major role in the field of psychology. In 1957, he became Professor of Psychology and Psychiatry at the University of Wisconsin. Here, his interest was directed toward the problem of more serious behavior disorders, and a large-scale project was undertaken to investigate the effects of psychotherapy with schizophrenics. Since 1963, he has been at the Western Behavioral Sciences Institute at La Jolla, California.

The personality theory which Rogers formulated grew out of his work in psychotherapy, just as did the theory of Freud. As Rogers developed his own particular approach to psychotherapy, he concurrently proposed theoretical formulations to account for the apparent success of the nondirective or client-centered method and for the changes observed in clients. Rogers describes his theorizing:

There is no need for theory until and unless there are phenomena to explain. Limiting our consideration to psychotherapy, there is no reason for a theory of therapy until there are observable changes which call for explanation. Then a unifying theory is of help in explaining what has happened, and in providing testable hypotheses about future experiences. Thus, in the field of therapy the first requisite is a skill which produces an effective result. Through observation of the process and the result a parsimonious theory may be developed which is projected into new experiences in order to be tested as to its adequacy. The theory is revised and modified with the purpose—never fully attained—of providing a complete conceptual framework which can adequately contain all the observed phenomena. It is the phenomena which are basic, not the theory [Rogers, 1951, pp. 15–16].

The therapeutic methods developed by Rogers and his co-workers represented a departure from the traditional procedures such as psychoanalysis. The therapist is not seen in an interpretive, evaluative role, and the process of therapy is not viewed as an intellectual enterprise in which insightful interpretations facilitate the bringing of unconscious material into consciousness. Rather, the therapist is one who simply facilitates the natural growth processes of the client by offering acceptance, understanding, and empathy. Rogers proposes:

In the emotional warmth of the relationship with the therapist, the client begins to experience a feeling of safety as he finds that whatever attitude he expresses is understood in almost the same way that he perceives it, and is accepted. He then is able to explore, for example, a vague feeling of guiltiness which he has experienced. In this safe relationship he can perceive for the first time the hostile meaning and purpose of certain aspects of his behavior, and can understand why he has felt guilty about it, and why it has been necessary to deny to awareness the meaning of this behavior. But this clearer perception is in itself disrupting and anxiety-creating, not therapeutic. It is evidence to the client that there are disturbing inconsistencies in himself, that he is not what he thinks he is. But as he voices his new perceptions and their attendant anxieties, he finds that this acceptant alter ego, the therapist, this other person who is only partly another person, perceives these experiences too, but with a new quality. The therapist perceives the client's self as the client has known it, and accepts it; he perceives the contradictory aspects which have been denied to awareness and accepts those too as being a part of the client; and both of these acceptances have in them the same warmth and respect. Thus it is that the client, experiencing in another an acceptance of both these aspects of himself, can take toward himself the same attitude. He finds that he too can accept himself even with the additions and alterations that are necessitated by these new perceptions of himself as hostile. He can experience himself as a person having hostile as well as other types of feelings, and can experience himself in this way without guilt. He has been enabled to do this (if our theory is correct) because another person has been able to adopt his frame of reference, to perceive with him, yet to perceive with acceptance and respect [Rogers, 1951, p. 41].

Over the years such formulations were extended into a theory of personality and even more broadly into theoretical implications accounting for behavior in a variety of situations, including education, interpersonal relationships, and family life.

SELF-CONCEPT

Several general points of Rogers' theoretical approach should be noted. It attempts to deal with the total individual as an organized whole. Behavior is believed to be a function of the individual's perception of events, and the frame of reference of the scientist must be internal rather than external. Thus, the manipulation of external stimuli defined in the experimenter's terms would tend to overlook the fact that the subjects are responding in terms of their own individual perceptions, and their structuring of the environment (their phenomenal fields) may well be different from one another and from that of the experimenter. Related to this concern is the tendency to emphasize internally directed behavior as opposed to externally directed behavior. Behavior is not seen as a response to stimuli but ". . . *is basically the goal-directed attempt of the organism to satisfy its needs as experienced, in the field as perceived*" [Rogers, 1951, p. 491].

The most important aspect of an individual's phenomenal field is that portion which consists of the perceptions of "I" or "me"—the self. The one basic motive of the organism is the actualizing tendency, an inherent tendency to develop all its capacities in ways which serve to maintain or enhance the organism.

Either on the basis of inheritance or learning, a need for positive regard develops universally. The satisfaction of this need is dependent on other human beings, specifically on the individual's perception of the way in which others regard him. This need is sufficiently important that the person will be more influenced by it than by his actual organic experience. A child can learn that his feces are disgusting, that he does not hate his baby sister, or that sexual thoughts are sinful and hence a source of fear even though his own original felt experiences in each instance might have yielded quite different perceptions.

Developing out of the need for positive regard from others is the need for positive self-regard. The child's self-concept is formed by means of interactions with others, and the child adopts for himself or internalizes this need to be thought worthwhile. Each person becomes "his own significant social other." Rogers describes the process:

The infant learns to need love. Love is very satisfying, but to know whether he is receiving it or not he must observe his mother's face, gestures, and other ambiguous signs. He develops a total gestalt as to the way he is regarded by his mother and each new experience of love or rejection tends to alter the whole gestalt. Consequently each behavior on his mother's part such as a specific disapproval of a specific behavior tends to be experienced as disapproval in general. So important is this to the infant that he comes to be guided in his behavior not by the degree to which an experience maintains or enhances the organism, but by the likelihood of receiving maternal love.

Soon he learns to view himself in much the same way, liking or disliking himself as a total configuration. He tends, quite independently of his mother or others, to view himself and his behavior in the same way they have. This means that some behaviors are regarded positively which are not actually experienced organismically as satisfying. Other behaviors are regarded negatively which are not actually experienced as unsatisfying. It is when he behaves in accordance with these introjected values that he may be said to have acquired conditions of worth. He cannot regard himself positively, as having worth, unless he lives in terms of these conditions. He now reacts with adience or avoidance toward certain behaviors solely because of these introjected conditions of self-regard, quite without reference to the organismic consequences of these behaviors. That is what is meant by living in terms of introjected values (the phrase formerly used) or conditions of worth [Rogers, 1959, p. 225].

Almost inevitably, then, some lack of congruence occurs between the conditions of worth as defined by the self-concept and the person's experiences with respect to both internal and external events. Some experiences are in accord with his self-concept and are accurately perceived and symbolized in consciousness. He goes several hours without food, notices that he feels hungry, and decides to eat some potato chips. Some experiences are contrary to his self-concept and are perceived selectively, distorted, and denied to awareness either in whole or in part. He sees his sister in the bathtub, is unable to accept his subsequent reactions as having anything to do with sexual attraction, and is aware only of feeling disgust and anger concerning her appearance. Such defensive processes lead to rigidity of perception, inaccurate perception of reality, and the tendency to conceptualize experience in overgeneralized and abstract terms.

Whenever an incongruency exists between self and experience, by definition psychological maladjustment occurs and hence vulnerability to anxiety, threat, and disorganization is present. For example, if feelings of dependency are inconsistent with an individual's self-concept, any situation which suggests the need for someone else's help is necessarily threatening though the person is not able to verbalize the reason why. Similarly, the person's own behavior may be consistent with his self-concept and accurately perceived, or it may be inconsistent with the self-concept and thus subject to distorted perception and lack of awareness. In the latter instance the individual may disavow the behavior itself or its meaning: "I was not myself." "I pointed out your weaknesses for your own good, not to hurt you." "I don't know why I do such things."

If a sufficient degree of incongruence exists between self and experience, the occurrence of such experiences may lead to a breakdown of the defenses, an extreme arousal of anxiety, a disorganization of the self-structure. There may be a severe attack of anxiety, the occurrence of behavior which is quite inconsistent with the person's previous behavior, or an acute psychotic breakdown. An individual can find himself overwhelmed, without direction, and unable to function adequately as anxiety mounts. It is hardly unusual to read in the newspaper of the model high school boy, described by all who knew him as nice and polite, who suddenly rapes a small neighbor girl after choir practice. Similarly, a meek and submissive man comes home from work one day and shoots his wife and children.

One of the major ways in which these various negative processes (inaccurate perception, defensiveness, and breakdown) may be reversed is by receiving unconditional positive regard from a significant other. This may occur in psychotherapy, in marriage, through a close friendship, and so forth. This experience leads to an increase in the person's own unconditional positive self-regard. With this reduction of threat, there is less need for defense and more possibility for accurate perception and symbolization of experience. With self and experience more congruent, psychological adjustment is increased. The individual functions on the basis of his own felt experience and not on the basis of his distorted perceptions. He can thus become a fully functioning person open to experience, free of defensive distortion, and able to have a high positive regard for both self and others.

This brief summary suggests that Rogers has proposed a theory of personality development, personality functioning, and personality change with the concept of self as its central focus. We will now look at the self-concept as a dimension of personality and examine some of the research which has grown out of Rogers' theoretical framework.

Measuring the Self-Concept

"REALITY AS PERCEIVED"

When theorists adopt the phenomenological position and insist that psychologists should approach behavior from within a subject's frame of reference rather than from without, this general idea strikes a responsive chord in many individuals. Different people do perceive the same event differently, and one may logically suggest that each person responds on the basis of reality as he perceives it rather than on the basis of reality as defined by someone else. The objective facts that the "oasis" is a mirage, that the "best of all possible girls" is stupid and shallow, that the "sinister plot against his life" is only a delusion are irrelevant in terms of the perceptual field of the individual in question. And, in terms of predicting behavior, quite different predictions might be made on the basis of an external definition of reality versus reality as perceived by the individual.

As reasonable as the phenomenological approach may seem, the transition from the abstract level of speculation to the concrete level of research presents an apparently insolvable dilemma. That is, how do you operationalize the "internal frame of reference"? How do you go about determining the subject's perception of reality? There is simply no way of avoiding the fact that the operations utilized by the experimenter must by definition involve observable stimuli and responses. Thus, in actual research the definition of self-concept or self-regard or any other characteristic of the self has in almost all instances involved the presentation of verbal stimulus material to the subject and the elicitation of verbal responses from him. Such responses may or may not accurately reflect the phenomenal field.

Stephenson [1953], in developing operations for the measurement of the self-concept, proposed that the study of self-psychology must begin from the standpoint of what a person says about himself and his beliefs about what he is like. Defined in that way, variables dealing with the self may easily be reduced to operations. Stephenson [1953, pp. 243–244] further points out that he cannot logically accept a phenomenological viewpoint in the way that self-theorists such as Rogers have done.

Thus Snygg and Combs [1949] in a recent formulation of the principles upon which they suggest self-psychology should be based, posit the usual phenomenal field, which can never have an existence independent of the person experiencing it, which is never open to direct observation, and yet which is the cause of behavior. These fields are supposedly experienced at instants of action, and the psychologist's job is to reconstruct them by inference. There is a one-to-one relationship between the person's phenomenal field and his outward behavior, the latter, of course, being public. All such postulates, we believe, are quite unnecessary. What is at issue, it seems to us, is the fact that each of us can reflect and make reference to himself: life has in it many occasions when we think about ourselves. We wonder about *our* unworthiness at church, *our* grip of things at business, *our* hopes and aspirations. These matters can be studied without phenomenological speculations [Stephenson, 1953, pp. 243–244].

Research on self-theory, then, is not different in kind from other types of personality research. Variables must be operationalized, measurement problems such as reliability and response sets must be met, and investigations must deal with the establishment of orderly relationships between stimuli and responses and between responses and other responses. As with any other aspect of personality, the study of individual differences in self-concept requires research dealing with measurement, antecedents, structure, dynamics, and change with respect to this dimension.

As an example of one approach to measuring the self-concept, the most widely used technique will be described: the Q-sort.

THE Q-SORT

The Q-technique was developed by Stephenson [1953] as a way of getting at various aspects of the self. The rationale of the Q-sort has been described by Butler and Haigh [1954]. First, the assumption is made that many specific self-perceptions exist for each individual. These perceptions can be ordered along a continuum from "unlike me" to "like me." For example, one might feel that the characteristic "loyal to friends" is very much a part of himself, while the characteristic "artistically gifted" is not at all descriptive of his qualities. Further, he might indicate that "high intelligence" is even more "like me" than is "loyal to friends." Such an ordering of self-descriptions does not, however, indicate the subject's value judgments about the characteristics. For example, he might be very happy about his high intelligence but feel that being loyal to his friends is a weakness that should be overcome. To get at this aspect of the self-concept, a second assumption is that self-perceptions can be ordered along another continuum—from "like my ideal" to "unlike my ideal." This second ordering yields an ideal self-concept or that organization of self-perceptions which the individual holds as desirable and undesirable for himself. When the same set of characteristics has been ordered along both dimensions, one can determine the discrepancy between the two. This measure, called self-ideal discrepancy, has been frequently used in research on self-theory as an indication of self-esteem or self-value. One way to obtain a discrepancy score is to correlate *for each person* his self-statements with his ideal-self-statements.

Unlike many of the personality measures which have been discussed, the Q-sort has not been standardized into an agreed-upon set of statements or a single set of instructions given to subjects or even into a specific number of categories into which the statements are sorted. One can, however, give examples of typical instructions, typical statements, and typical sorting procedures, which constitute the "Chicago Q-sort."

Butler and Haigh gave the following instructions to subjects:

1. *Self-sort.* Sort these cards to describe yourself as you see yourself today, from those that are least like you to those that are most like you.

2. *Ideal sort.* Now sort these cards to describe your ideal person—the person you would most like within yourself to be [Butler and Haigh, 1954, p. 57].

Many who have utilized Q-sort measuring devices have required subjects to sort the group of statements in such a way as to form a normal distribution in order to facilitate statistical handling of the data. For example, Dymond [1954, p. 77] asked subjects to sort 100 statements into nine piles, putting a prescribed number of cards into each pile as shown in Table 12–1.

Table 12–1   NORMAL DISTRIBUTION OF Q-SORT CARDS

	"Least Like Me"					"Most Like Me"			
Pile Number	0	1	2	3	4	5	6	7	8
Number of cards	1	4	11	21	26	21	11	4	1

A typical set of self-statements is that developed by Butler and Haigh [1954]. A group of 100 statements was taken at random from therapy protocols and reworded to make them more clear, and then each statement was placed on a card suitable for Q-sorting. In a subsequent investigation, Dymond [1954] obtained judgments from two clinical psychologists about each statement with respect to whether a well-adjusted person should indicate that it was like him or unlike him. The psychologists agreed that 26 of the items were irrelevant with respect to adjustment, and the remaining 74 statements were given to four new judges. Again, very good agreement occurred among the judges concerning the items and what they indicated about adjustment as shown in Figure 12–1.

FIG. 12–1.   *Q-sort statements.*

Positive Items: Indicates Good Adjustment if Subject Says It Is "Like Me" (Pile No. 5, 6, 7, or 8)

I make strong demands on myself.
I often kick myself for the things I do.
I have a warm emotional relationship with others.
I am responsible for my troubles.
I am a responsible person.
I can accept most social values and standards.
Self-control is no problem to me.
I usually like people.
I express my emotions freely.
I can usually live comfortably with the people around me.
My hardest battles are with myself.

I am optimistic.

I am liked by most people who know me.

I am sexually attractive.

I can usually make up my mind and stick to it.

I am contented.

I am poised.

I am impulsive.

I am a rational person.

I am tolerant.

I have an attractive personality.

I am ambitious.

I have initiative.

I take a positive attitude toward myself.

I am assertive.

I am satisfied with myself.

I am likable.

My personality is attractive to the opposite sex.

I am relaxed, and nothing really bothers me.

I am a hard worker.

I feel emotionally mature.

I am intelligent.

I am self-reliant.

I am different from others.

I understand myself.

I am a good mixer.

I feel adequate.

Negative Items: Indicates Good Adjustment if Subject Says It Is "Unlike Me"
(Pile No. 0, 1, 2, or 3)

I put on a false front.

I often feel humiliated.

I doubt my sexual powers.

I have a feeling of hopelessness.

I have few values and standards of my own.

It is difficult to control my aggression.

I want to give up trying to cope with the world.

I tend to be on my guard with people who are somewhat more friendly than
I had expected.

I usually feel driven.

I feel helpless.

My decisions are not my own.

I am a hostile person.

I am disorganized.

I feel apathetic.

I don't trust my emotions.

It's pretty tough to be me.

I have the feeling that I am just not facing things.

I try not to think about my problems.

I am shy.

I am no one. Nothing seems to be me.

I despise myself.

I shrink from facing a crisis or difficulty.

I just don't respect myself.

I am afraid of a full-fledged disagreement with a person.

I can't seem to make up my mind one way or another.

I am confused.

I am a failure.

I am afraid of sex.

I have a horror of failing in anything I want to accomplish.

I really am disturbed.

All you have to do is just insist with me, and I give in.

I feel insecure within myself.

I have to protect myself with excuses, with rationalizing.

I feel hopeless.

I am unreliable.

I am worthless.

I dislike my own sexuality.

In addition to the Q-sort, a number of related instruments are used in research on the self-concept. For example, Worchel [1957] developed the Self Activity Inventory (SAI) which consists of 54 items of the type shown in Figure 12–1. Subjects are asked to indicate on a five-point scale how much of the time the activity described is like him, from "never" to "very often." With the same items, the subjects indicate on another five-point scale how the activity relates to him as he would like to be. The difference between the two ratings yields a self-ideal discrepancy score. A group of 76 college students was given the test on two occasions eight weeks apart. Test-retest reliability coefficients of .79 and .72 were found for the self-ratings and ideal self-ratings respectively.

The interrelationships of several such measures of self-concept were investigated by Crowne, Stephens, and Kelly [1961]. The tests consisted of a modification of the Chicago Q-sort, Bills' Index of Adjustment and Values, which contains 49 adjectives for self-ratings, Buss' scale, which is also made up of adjectives to be rated for self and ideal, and Gough's Adjective Checklist which has 300 adjectives that can be scored for self-acceptance and self-criticality. The subjects were undergraduates at Ohio State. The investigators found that these measures tend to be interrelated, with higher correlations the more similar the tests. With similar tests, the average correlation among the self-acceptance scores was .60 for males and .68 for females. With less similar tests, the mean intercorrelations were .50 and .45. This and other investigations suggest that various self-concept tests are measuring something in common, but the relatively moderate size of the intercorrelations does not indicate that these are interchangeable instruments.

SOCIAL DESIRABILITY

As might be expected on the basis of the findings with the Manifest Anxiety Scale, Edwards' Social Desirability Scale has been found to be related to measures of self-concept. In the Crowne, *et al.* [1961] investigation just described, all of the self-acceptance measures were correlated with the SD scale ($r = -.45$ to $-.58$). That is, the greater the tendency to give socially desirable responses, the less the reported discrepancy between self and ideal self.

A more direct method of determining the relationship between self-concept measures and social desirability is to obtain social-desirability ratings of the self-items themselves by a group of judges and then to determine whether response to the items is related to the scale value of the items. Kenny [1956] followed this procedure by having a group of 25 self-statements scaled for social desirability. Then, the statements were administered to three different samples of university students in three different forms: as a questionnaire, as a rating scale, and as a Q-sort. Social-desirability ratings were found to correlate from .59 to .82 with the probability of subjects endorsing a trait. Even higher relationships ($r = .91$ and $.96$) were reported by Cowen and Tongas [1959] between social-desirability ratings and self-scores obtained from Bills' Index of Adjustment and Values. Kenny suggests that the social-desirability variable should be controlled:

. . . social desirability could be partially controlled by utilizing traits which are ambiguous in terms of social desirability. Ambiguity could be defined in terms of the standard deviations of the social-desirability ratings. Another procedure for controlling social desirability in unstructured samples would be to use only neutral trait items, that is, those items near the median of judged social desirability [Kenny, 1956, p. 318].

The position taken by Cowen and Tongas [1959] is more like that taken earlier in this text with respect to the MAS and social desirability. They suggest that whether the self-measures have any meaning independent of the social-desirability variable is questionable. The only problem is what is the best name to be given to the variable in question and hence the most reasonable interpretation of the findings. A time will come when sufficient research will clarify whether these are in fact highly correlated but different variables or simply one variable being measured in different ways with different labels.

Antecedents of the Self-Concept

THEORETICAL BACKGROUND

As discussed earlier, Rogers has proposed that an individual's self-concept and his values which specify the conditions of worth are acquired on the basis of early interactions with a significant other person, usually the mother. Two contrasting parent-child interactions are described by Rogers [1951] as having quite different consequences in terms of development of the self.

For all infants, the first dawning of awareness is assumed to involve likes and dislikes, pleasure and pain. Being cold is disliked, being cuddled is liked. In addition to physical stimuli, evaluations by others come to be perceived as pleasant or unpleasant. "You're a good child," is pleasurable to hear while "You're a naughty boy" is not.

Since the evaluative statements by parents often come to have greater influence than the physical stimuli, inconsistency between them can lead to the types of distortions in perception and symbolization previously discussed. For example, a child may enjoy hitting his baby brother but is told by his parents that he feels only love for him:

. . . parental attitudes are not only introjected, but what is much more important, are experienced not as the attitude of another, but in distorted fashion, *as if* based on the evidence of one's own sensory and visceral equipment. . . . "I like baby brother" remains as the pattern belonging in the concept of self, because it is the concept of the relationship which is introjected from others through the distortion of symbolization, even when the primary experience contains many gradations of value in the relationship, from "I like baby brother" to "I hate him!" In this way the values which the infant attaches to experience become divorced from his own organismic functioning, and experience is valued in terms of the attitudes held by his parents, or by others who are in intimate contact with him [Rogers, 1951, p. 500].

The consequence of such a pattern of development is maladjustment, as we have seen. Rogers suggests that different types of interaction between parent and child should have quite different consequents with respect to the child's self-structure. It should be possible for early experience to form the basis for a psychologically well-adjusted self. The beginning would be the same, with the infant coming to experience likes and dislikes. Again, he enjoys various activities, including hitting his baby brother.

At this point, a difference in parental behavior is possible. The parent may (1) accept the child's feeling of satisfaction in hurting his sibling, (2) at the same time accept and love the child himself, and (3) nevertheless point out clearly that this particular behavior cannot be accepted in the family. Rogers proposes:

The child in this relationship experiences no threat to his concept of himself as a loved person. He can experience fully and accept within himself and as a part of himself his aggressive feelings toward his baby brother. He can experience fully the perception that his hitting behavior is not liked by the person who loves him. . . . Because the budding structure of the self is not threatened by loss of love, because feelings are accepted by his parent, the child in this instance does not need to deny to awareness the satisfactions which he is experiencing, nor does he need to distort his experience of the parental reaction and regard it as his own. He retains instead a secure self which can serve to guide his behavior by freely admitting to awareness, in accurately symbolized form, all the relevant evidence of his experience in terms of his organismic satisfactions, both immediate and longer range [Rogers, 1951, p. 502].

Given this general picture of the possible child-rearing antecedents of differential development of the self-structure, what are the relevant research findings?

PERCEIVED PARENTAL ATTITUDES AND THE SELF-CONCEPT

If the child strives to maintain parental love by introjecting their values, it follows that self-regard would depend on the degree to which the child felt he was successful in maintaining the positive evaluation of his parents. Jourard and Remy [1955] obtained attitudes about self and the subject's perception of father's and mother's attitudes toward him on a 40-item self-cathexis scale. In addition, the Maslow Test of Psychological Security-Insecurity [Maslow, Hirsh, Stein, and Honigmann, 1945] was given. The subjects were 99 undergraduates at Emory University.

For both males and females, significant correlations were found between the self-cathexis score and the perceived attitudes of parents toward self, as shown in Table 12–2.

Table 12–2   CORRELATIONS BETWEEN SELF-CONCEPT
AND PERCEIVED ATTITUDES OF PARENTS TOWARD SELF

	Perceived Ratings by Mother	Perceived Ratings by Father
Female Subjects	.77*	.66*
Male Subjects	.70*	.65*

* $p < .01$

Similarly, security as measured by the Maslow scale was significantly related to attitudes toward self and perceived attitudes of parents toward self. Those who evaluated themselves negatively and who believed that their parents evaluated them negatively were more insecure.

The authors correctly point out that the actual attitudes of the parents may or may not correspond to the perceptions of the offspring. Nevertheless, "If it is indeed true that self-evaluations are determined by parental evaluations of one's self, then it follows that if a person believes that his parents approve of his traits, even though this belief be false, he will tend to approve of his traits as well" [Jourard and Remy, 1955, p. 366].

PARENTAL INFLUENCES ON THE SELF-CONCEPT

Parental Ideals for Child. In his doctoral research at the University of Illinois, Helper [1955] tested a number of hypotheses concerning familial influences on the development of children's self-concepts. The subjects were 50 freshmen and subfreshmen students at a small high school and their parents. The students were given a list of 42 pairs of adjectives that were polar opposites and asked to indicate for each pair which was more descriptive of themselves. They also were asked to describe themselves as they would most like to be and as they would least like to be, and to describe their mothers. A week later, this procedure was repeated except that they were asked to describe their fathers rather than their mothers. Each parent also filled out the checklist, describing self, spouse, child, and ideal child.

Helper reasoned that if a parent saw his or her spouse as actually being like the ideal for the child, the child would be rewarded for behaving like the spouse. If a mother thought her husband represented the ideal male model for her son, she would be expected to reward the son each time his behavior resembled that of his father. A mother who wanted her son to be different from her husband would not be expected to reward father-imitating behavior. As predicted, the more the mother's concept of her spouse was like her ideal-child concept, the more her son was actually like her husband. The analogous relationship for daughters was not significant. Helper suggested that this finding is consonant with the belief that mothers influence the psychological development of the children more than fathers do.

Another type of data obtained was that of the sociometric status of each child among his peers. Each student was asked to select three other children as partners for a class project. The number of choices received was taken as an index of how well an individual was liked by his group. It was found that, for boys, the more an individual was like his father, the more he was liked. For girls, similarity to mother was not related to sociometric status.

Still another question was the effect of parental differences in their concepts of an ideal child on the child's self-concept. One hypothesis was that if parents differ in their ideal-child concepts, the child's own ideal-self-concept would be unstable. Instability was defined as shifts in the child's ideal-self between the two testing sessions. Helper found that the greater the discrepancy between husband and wife in describing the ideal child, the more unstable was the child's ideal-self.

Among other things, this investigation raises questions concerning possible differences in the way in which males and females develop self-concepts. For boys, whether the mother rewards behavior which is like the father's behavior seems to influence father-son similarity and also the son's popularity among his peers. For girls, this sort of relationship is not found. Helper proposed that a different source of reward for self-descriptions must occur for girls, perhaps her peers rather than her parents.

Acceptance of Self and Parent. On a number of grounds, one might hypothesize that acceptance of self would be greatest for those who feel most positively toward their parents. In an investigation using 82 male high school seniors, Suinn [1961] administered Q-sort measures of self-concept, ideal-self, the subject's perception of his father, and his perception of an ideal father. Self-acceptance was defined as the magnitude of the correlation between self and ideal. Father-acceptance was defined as the magnitude of the correlation between perceived father and ideal father. Another variable, self-father similarity, was defined as the magnitude of the correlation between self-concept and perception of father.

A significant positive correlation of .32 ($p < .005$) was found between self-acceptance and father-acceptance. Suinn further hypothesized that the greater the self-father similarity, the less the discrepancy between self-acceptance and father-acceptance. This hypothesis was confirmed at the .05 level.

A possible interpretation of this finding is in terms of reinforcement for identifying with father. The Helper [1955] study found that the more the husband was seen by the wife as an ideal for their son, the more the son's ideal was like his father's ideal for him and the more the son was like the father. Helper suggested that the mother who perceived her husband as a good model would reward the son's behavior the more it was like the father's behavior, while the mother who rejected the father as a model would not reward father-like behavior in the son. Suinn's data are consistent with this formulation. That is, sons who are rewarded for being like their father would be expected to accept both father and self and to see themselves as like their father.

As is obvious, research to date dealing with the antecedents of the self-concept is only in the beginning stages. Many of the more intriguing formulations proposed by Rogers have yet to be tested.

The Place of the Self-Concept in the
Structure of Personality

SELF-IDEAL DISCREPANCY AS AN INDEX OF MALADJUSTMENT

In part because of its origin in observations of therapist-client interactions, Rogers' self-theory deals extensively with the problem of maladjustment. In the theory, maladjustment is defined in terms of the magnitude of the discrepancy between self and experience. Increasing discrepancy leads to anxiety, disorganization of the self-structure, and (with maximum discrepancy) psychological breakdown. Presumably, these progressive changes would be reflected in the magnitude of the discrepancy between self and ideal self.

Population Comparisons. Once again, as with investigations discussed in earlier chapters, one index of maladjustment which has been utilized in studies of self-concept is membership in a group defined as less well adjusted than the norm. Two groups of boys, aged 9 to 12, were compared by Davids and Lawton [1961]. The normal group consisted of 30 boys at a YMCA camp. The maladjusted group was made up of 25 emotionally disturbed youngsters undergoing psychiatric treatment. With self-concept measured by means of an adjective checklist, the normal group was found to have a significantly more positive self-concept.

In his dissertation research at the University of Colorado, Chase [1957] selected an adjusted and a maladjusted group of male, hospitalized veterans. The adjusted group consisted of 50 medical and surgical patients who had given no evidence of psychiatric difficulty. The maladjusted group was made up of 19 psychotics, 20 neurotics, and 17 patients with character disorders. All subjects were given a 50-item Q-sort dealing with self and ideal self. Self-ideal correlations were computed for each subject, and mean correlations for each group determined. The mean for the adjusted subjects ($r = .64$) was significantly higher than for the maladjusted subjects ($r = .36$). An additional finding was that all subjects tended to have similar conceptions of the ideal self; differences occurred with respect to the self-concept.

Other Measures of Adjustment. A number of investigators have utilized measures of adjustment other than membership in a group so defined. Turner and Vanderlippe [1958] used the Chicago Q-sort items to measure self-concept and ideal self in a group of 175 undergraduates. From this sample, the 25 with the greatest and the 25 with least self-ideal discrepancy were selected for comparison. The congruent group had a mean self-ideal correlation of .79, while the discrepant group had a mean correlation of .11. Using Dymond's [1954] adjustment scoring system described earlier, the congruent group was found to have a significantly higher adjustment score than the discrepant group. Other data relevant to adjustment were also available. Compared to the high-discrepancy group, members of the congruent group were found to participate more in extra-curricular activities, have higher sociometric status in their living groups, and to have a higher grade-point average even though they were not different in terms of ACE college aptitude scores. Still another measure used was the Guilford-Zimmerman [1949] Temperament Survey. The degree of self-ideal congruence was found to be positively related to the scales measuring general activity, ascendance, sociability, emotional stability, and thoughtfulness. "In each instance, the scores for those high in self-ideal congruence are indicative of better adjustment than are those for Ss low in self-ideal correspondence" [Turner and Vanderlippe, 1958, p. 205].

A group of 78 male juniors in a Catholic high school were used as subjects by Hanlon, Hofstaetter, and O'Connor [1954]. A modified Q-sort technique was the measure of self and ideal self while the California Test of Personality [Tiegs, Clark, and Thorpe, 1941] served as the adjustment measure. Each subject's self-ideal correlation was correlated with scores on the California test. A wide range of self-ideal congruence was found with individual correlations from $-.34$ to $+.79$. This variable was significantly related to the test measure of self-adjustment ($r = .70, p < .001$) and social adjustment ($r = .59, p < .001$) and unrelated to IQ. The authors concluded that the congruence between self-concept and ideal self-concept can be used as a measure of adjustment with considerable confidence. Other investigators, utilizing various measures of self-concept and adjustment have reported similar findings [for example, Calvin and Holtzman, 1953; Davids and Lawton, 1961; Smith, 1958].

DEFENSIVENESS AND THE CURVILINEARITY HYPOTHESIS

The studies just discussed have each dealt with a linear relationship between self-ideal discrepancy and maladjustment. As discrepancy between self and ideal increases, maladjustment increases. A number of investigators have raised questions concerning this relationship centering on the problem of accepting as accurate the subject's statements concerning his self-concept. In part, this problem brings us back to the difficulties which arise in adopting a phenomenological approach. If self-statements are taken as accurate representations of an individual's internal world, then maladjustment should be directly related to discrepancy. If, however, self-statements are viewed simply as verbal responses to be studied, one would not be surprised to find that positive self-appraisals were a function of a number of variables including deliberate lying, unconsciously motivated mechanisms of repression, and lack of contact with reality. Given such possibilities, maladjustment could conceivably be reflected in a large discrepancy between self and ideal or in an unrealistically low discrepancy between self and ideal. In other words, a curvilinear relationship between self-satisfaction and adjustment would seem to be a likely possibility.

Repression-Sensitization. In Chapter 6, the repression-sensitization dimension was described in terms of individual differences in response to threat. At one extreme are avoidance behaviors such as denial and repression while at the other extreme are approach behaviors such as intellectualization and sensitization. Presumably, those individuals at either end of this dimension are less well adjusted than individuals falling in the middle range. Using the Repression-Sensitization (R-S) Scale as a measure of defenses, a number of investigators have reported that subjects with repressive defenses tend to present themselves positively on self-concept measures while subjects with sensitizing defenses present themselves negatively. This general finding has been reported in investigations using such self-measures as Worchel's SAI [Byrne, 1961b; Byrne, Barry, and Nelson, 1963], Leary's Interpersonal Checklist [Altrocchi, Parsons, and Dickoff, 1960], Bills' Index of Adjustment and Values [Hanson, 1963], and Gough's Adjective Checklist [Byrne, 1961b; Lucky and Grigg, 1964].

Other approaches to the measurement of defense mechanisms have yielded results consistent with these. Kamano [1961] obtained self, ideal-self, and least-liked-self scores with a measure involving bipolar adjectives with a group of 44 institutionalized female schizophrenics. The subjects were then divided into the 17 most self-satisfied and the 27 least self-satisfied. As a measure of defensiveness, a paragraph containing statements favorable and unfavorable to each subject was read, and then the subject was asked to recall as much of the paragraph as possible. The self-satisfied subjects (those who had low self-ideal discrepancy) recalled significantly fewer unfavorable statements in the passage than did the self-dissatisfied subjects. The two groups did not differ in their recall of favorable items. This finding was interpreted in terms of the use of denial mechanisms by the high self-esteem individuals. As Kamano [1961, p. 496] suggests: "Such schizophrenic subjects have an unusually high self-concept which, of course, represents an unrealistic self-appraisal."

Population Comparisons. Depending on the degree and type of defense mechanisms developed in response to threat, maladjusted individuals could be expected to show either greater self-ideal discrepancy than normals or a magnitude of discrepancy equal to that of normals [Hillson and Worchel, 1957]. Using the SAI as the measure of self-concept, groups of normal (students), anxious (neurotic patients in treatment), and defensive (hospitalized schizophrenic patients) individuals were compared. The neurotics were found to have significantly higher self-ideal discrepancy scores than the normals. Similarly, the neurotics had significantly higher discrepancy scores than the psychotics. The normals and psychotics did not differ in self-satisfaction. A subsequent investigation by Worchel and Hillson [1958] involved a comparison on the SAI of a normal group of males with male prisoners in a penitentiary. The criminal group had a significantly more positive self-concept and a significantly smaller self-ideal discrepancy than the normal subjects.

Friedman [1955] compared normals, neurotics, and paranoid schizophrenics on a Q-sort measure and reported findings consistent with those of Hillson and Worchel. He suggested that the positive self-concepts of the normals and negative self-concepts of the neurotics were based on realistic self-appraisal, whereas the positive self-concepts of the schizophrenics were based on unrealistic self-appraisal and self-enhancing defenses.

Other Measures of Adjustment. One of the early investigations in which a curvilinear relationship between self-satisfaction and adjustment was hypothesized was that of Block and Thomas [1955]. A group of 56 undergraduates was given a Q-sort using adjectives in which self and ideal self were assessed. Scores on MMPI scales served as the independent measure of adjustment. For each subject, the correlation between his self-sort and ideal sort was obtained and used as the self-satisfaction index. This coefficient was then correlated with scores on the MMPI scales. High self-ideal discrepancy was found to be indicative of maladjustment in that self-dissatisfied individuals tend to score higher on hypochondriasis, depression, psychopathic personality, psychasthenia, and schizophrenia. At the same time, evidence showed that extremely low self-ideal discrepancy was also indicative of maladjustment, though of a different kind. Self-satisfied individuals tended to score higher on scales measuring overcontrol, denial, constriction, and lack of candor. On the basis of these findings plus a subsequent item-analysis of the Q-sort material, the authors concluded that the best-adjusted individuals were those with a medium degree of self-ideal discrepancy. Block and Thomas describe such individuals as:

. . . reasonable and accepting in their self-appraisals. They would like more of what they value and less of what makes them uncomfortable. They accept the ambiguity of emotions and are comfortable in their relations with others. They have their problems, certainly, but they neither despair nor deny [Block and Thomas, 1955, p. 258].

A similar comparison of self-concept measures and MMPI performance was made by Zuckerman and Monashkin [1957] with 43 psychiatric patients. Essentially the same relationships were found in this population as those reported by Block and Thomas [1955] with the college students.

One general finding which seems clear on the basis of research dealing with maladjustment and self-perception is that self-ratings alone cannot be used as a straightforward index of adjustment. Self-satisfaction may result from a realistic appraisal of psychological well-being or from a defensive denial of realistic concerns.

SOCIAL COMPETENCE

The concept of social competence proposed by Zigler and Phillips [1960, 1961a, 1961b, 1962] involves the idea of a developmental process in which intellectual and social functioning pass through various levels of maturity. Progress along this continuum is characterized by increasing differentiation, hierarchical structuring, and independence of psychological functioning. It has been found, for example, that mental patients high in social competence prior to hospitalization have a better prognosis than those low in social competence [Zigler and Phillips, 1961b]. What is the relationship between this variable and self-concept?

With respect to self-ideal discrepancy, Achenbach and Zigler [1963] hypothesized that for both normal and psychiatric patients, level of competence would be positively related to amount of discrepancy. They reasoned that at higher levels of social competence, a greater number of social demands, mores, and values have been incorporated, and hence there is a greater potential for guilt. Their subjects were 20 psychiatric and 20 nonpsychiatric patients at Worcester State Hospital. Social-competence level was determined on the basis of case history material according to the scheme shown in Table 12–3. Mean social-competence scores were determined, and a high- and a low-competence group were identified within each group of patients. Self and ideal self were measured by means of a questionnaire and a checklist of traits. As predicted, in both patient groups, high-competence subjects manifested higher self-ideal discrepancy scores than low-competence subjects. In discussing these findings, Achenbach and Zigler suggested:

Contrary to the Rogerian position, self-image disparity is not a simple function of maladjustment or self-dissatisfaction, nor is it invariably a correlate of maladjustment in individuals employing particular defensive patterns. Indeed, the present study indicates that high self-image disparity is concomitant with the demonstrated capacity to achieve in areas most valued in our society. Rather than being ominous in nature, high self-image disparity would invariably appear to accompany the attainment of higher levels of development since the greater cognitive differentiation found at such levels invariably leads to a greater capacity for self-derogation, guilt, and anxiety. . . . What is being suggested here is that the attainment of higher developmental levels is not an unmitigated blessing. While such attainment guarantees the individual a greater ability to deal with whatever problems confront him, his greater cognitive differentiation also gives him the capacity to construct more problems for himself [Achenbach and Zigler, 1963, p. 204].

Table 12–3   SOCIAL COMPETENCE CRITERIA

	Social Competence Level		
Variable	Low = 0	Medium = 1	High = 2
Psychiatrist's Rating of IQ	Low	Average	Superior
Education	None or some grade school	Finished grade school, some high school, or finished high school	Some college or more
Occupation	Unskilled or semi-skilled	Skilled or service	Clerical, sales, professional, or managerial
Employment History	Usually unemployed	Seasonal, fluctuating, frequent shifts, or part-time employment	Regularly employed
Marital Status	Single	Separated, divorced, remarried, or widowed	Single continuous marriage

Given the findings reported earlier in the studies of maladjustment, it appears somewhat contradictory to find that high self-ideal discrepancy is more characteristic of those at high levels of social competence than of those at lower levels. The question still remains, however, about the relationship between self-concept and effective behavior at a *given level of social competence*. While the possibilities for social demands and hence a feeling of inadequacy may increase as one proceeds up this developmental scale, possibly also the least competent individuals at a particular level may have the greatest discrepancy between self-concept and ideal self-concept. Some relevant data are provided by Hatfield [1961] who obtained supervisor's ratings of all of the students entering the student teacher program at Northern State Teachers College in 1958–1959. The 19 students receiving the lowest ratings were matched with 19 of the highest rated students on the basis of age, sex, amount of teaching experience, grade level in college, IQ, and socioeconomic background. These two groups can be assumed to be equal in social-competence level. The 38 high- and low-rated subjects were given a Chicago Q-sort; self-sort and ideal-sort correlations were computed for each individual. The mean self-ideal coefficient of the superior student teachers was .86, while that of the inferior student teachers was .63. The difference between the groups was found to be significant at the .01 level. Further analysis revealed that the ideal self-concept of the two groups did not differ; it was with respect to self-ratings that the poor student teachers gave negative self-evaluative responses. Thus, self-ideal congruence appears to be characteristic of those individuals performing most adequately at a particular developmental level.

Dynamics of the Self-Concept

RESPONSE TO STIMULI NOT CONSISTENT WITH THE SELF-CONCEPT

Perceptual Defense. In describing Rogers' self-theory, one of the major propositions discussed was the response to experiences contrary to the self-concept. It was proposed that such experiences would not be perceived or would be perceived in a distorted form. This sort of response to threat has been labeled *perceptual defense;* by defending oneself against inconsistent stimuli, the stability of the self-concept is presumably protected. The greater the discrepancy between self and experience, the greater the potential threat from the environment and hence the more perceptual defense.

Chodorkoff's [1954] doctoral dissertation at Wisconsin reported a clever method for assessing discrepancy between self and experience. Self-concept was measured in the familiar way by means of a Q-sort given to 30 male undergraduates. Then, an independent assessment of each subject was made by clinical psychologists who made a Q-sort for each subject using the same group of items. The clinicians' judgments were based on the subject's responses to a biographical inventory, the Rorschach, a word-association test, and the Thematic Apperception Test. The correlation between each subject's self-sort and the judges' sort constituted the measure of discrepancy, an index of the accuracy of the individual's self-perception.

The perceptual defense task was specially prepared for each subject. On the basis of his reaction times for the word-association items, the 10 words yielding the longest reaction times (that is, most threatening) and the 10 words yielding the shortest reaction times (that is, least threatening) were used. Presumably, the stimuli for each subject represented personally relevant threatening and neutral words. These 20 words were presented randomly by means of a tachistoscope, first at .01 second exposure time and then at increasingly slower speeds until the subject perceived it correctly on two consecutive trials. The more trials necessary for correct perception of a word, the greater the perceptual defense. For each subject, the perceptual defense score equalled his mean recognition threshold for the threatening words minus his mean recognition threshold for the neutral words.

The correlation between the accuracy of self-perception score and the perceptual defense score was −.53 ($p < .01$). In other words, the more the self-sort was like the judges' sort, the less perceptual defense against threatening stimuli. Further, the judges' estimate of each subject's adjustment correlated significantly with the perceptual defense measure; the better the adjustment, the less the perceptual defense ($r = −.62; p < .01$). In addition to supporting Rogers' formulations concerning defenses, these findings also suggest other possibilities:

> The better adjusted individual attempts to obtain mastery over threatening situations by getting to know, as quickly as possible, what it is that is threatening. He may be alerted to the possibility of threat and may be influenced by a set which leads him to try to differentiate and symbolize aspects of himself and his environment which are potentially threatening. The less adequately adjusted individual, in contrast, may be thought of as influenced by a set to keep threat inadequately differentiated and inadequately symbolized.
>
> Furthermore, it can be argued that adequate behavior depends upon adequate perception. If an individual cannot differentiate and symbolize aspects of himself and his environment, his behavior in turn will not be adequate. He will also be unable to resolve threatening situations when they confront him, for if he does not recognize threat, how can he be expected to deal with it effectively? [Chodorkoff, 1954, p. 511]

Difficulty in Recall.   Proceeding from the same aspect of self-theory as did Chodorkoff, Cartwright [1956] tested the proposition that differential recall of stimuli would take place as a function of the consistency of those stimuli with respect to the self-concept. He further suggested that differential recall of consistent and inconsistent stimuli should be greater for maladjusted than for adjusted individuals.

A total of 80 subjects was used; 25 who had applied for psychotherapy but not yet begun and 10 for whom psychotherapy was judged to be unsuccessful constituted the maladjusted group. The adjusted group was made up of 20 individuals for whom psychotherapy had been successful and 25 who had not had nor planned to have psychotherapy. Each subject sorted 56 statements into seven piles from "most like me" to "most unlike me."

For each of the 56 statements, another card had been prepared containing an adjective comparable to the statement. For example, for the statement "I have an attractive personality," another card was prepared with the word "attractive." While the subjects performed an unrelated task, the experimenter prepared the adjective cards corresponding to the Q-sort cards which the subject had placed in the two most extreme piles on each end of the continuum. Among other learning tasks, the subjects were asked to learn these self-consistent and self-inconsistent adjectives in serial order in groups of eight; trials were repeated until all eight adjectives were recalled in correct order, and then the next list was begun. For each subject, recall scores were obtained for the consistent and inconsistent words.

For the group as a whole, recall for the consistent adjectives was significantly better than recall for the inconsistent adjectives ($p < .005$). Also, as predicted, in the maladjusted group there was a significantly greater difference between recall for the two types of adjectives than in the adjusted group. This suggested that inconsistent stimuli constituted a greater source of threat for the maladjusted subjects.

A further finding was evidence supporting Rogers' proposal that experiences inconsistent with the self may be admitted into awareness in distorted form. Cartwright notes:

> There was considerable evidence of distortion in immediate recall for inconsistent adjectives. Typical examples, all from different Ss are: "satisfied" was misrecalled as "dissatisfied" for one trial; "hopeless" was misrecalled as "hopeful" for two trials; "hostile" was misrecalled as "hospitable" for three trials; "tolerant" was misrecalled as "intolerant" for five trials. Since Ss had sorted their cards to say they were *not* satisfied, hopeless, etc., it is clear that misrecall resulted in making the stimulus word consistent with their self-structure [Cartwright, 1956, p. 217].

RESPONSE TO FRUSTRATION

For the individual who is well adjusted in terms of congruence between experience and his self-concept, frustrating conditions should lead to the arousal of hostile impulses which are accurately conceptualized. Further, these impulses should be directed toward the appropriate target, the frustrating agent. In contrast, the individual whose self-concept is such that aggressive impulses are not admitted into awareness should respond quite differently in a frustrating situation. They should not be able to verbalize feelings of hostility toward the frustrating agent, but they conceivably would express aggression in some more disguised form such as self-blame or displacement onto an inappropriate target.

Self-Depreciation. Given a frustrating task in which one cannot attain a high degree of success, we would predict that individuals with high self-ideal discrepancy would direct any feelings of hostility inwardly. Moses and Duvall [1960] administered the SAI to 250 undergraduates and selected extreme groups of the 24 highest and the 24 lowest in terms of self-ideal discrepancy scores. The experimental task was a Humphries board in which there were three lights and three keys. The subject was instructed to predict which light would go on for each of 210 trials by pressing the corresponding key. Actually, one light went on randomly

66 per cent of the time, one light went on randomly 33 per cent of the time, and one light never went on.

After the last trial, each subject was asked to estimate the total number of correct guesses he had made on the 210 trials. The high and low discrepancy groups did not differ in the actual number of correct guesses they had made (108.25 for the high-discrepancy and 109.04 for the low-discrepancy subjects). There was a significant difference, however, in the estimates of their performance. The low-discrepancy group guessed that they had responded correctly on 95.58 trials, while the high-discrepancy group guessed 76.88 trials. One possible interpretation of this finding is that any hostility aroused by the task was directed inwardly in the form of self-depreciation by those whose self-concepts and ideal self-concepts were least congruent.

       Aggression Toward an Actual Frustrating Agent. A more direct test of the proposition that the appropriate expression of aggression is dependent on self-ideal congruence is provided by Worchel [1958]. A frustrating situation was created by administering an "intelligence test" to several classes of undergraduates. Worchel describes the procedure:

The intelligence test was then administered with the instruction that each subtest was timed but that sufficient time had been allowed for most of the students to complete the tests. As the students worked, *E* walked around noting the students' progress, urging faster work, belittling their efforts, and unfavorably comparing their poor performance to that of other classes. He interrupted frequently by urging them to skip over the ones they could not do and to try the easier ones first [Worchel, 1958, p. 356].

Immediately after this experience, the subjects filled out a rating scale in which their attitudes about the test administration were determined. A hostility score was obtained on the basis of attitudes expressed toward the test-administrator, the one who instigated the aggression. Each subject was also given the SAI. An analysis of variance of the hostility scores was carried out for 64 subjects drawn to fit the categories of high versus low self-ideal discrepancy and male versus female.

The self-ideal discrepancy variable yielded an F ratio significant at the .05 level. Those with high discrepancy between self and ideal expressed significantly less hostile feelings toward the test administrator than those with low discrepancy scores. Males and females did not differ in this respect.

A somewhat different type of investigation, which was reported in Chapter 6, yielded results consistent with these. Worchel and McCormick [1963] presented high- and low-discrepancy subjects with agreeing and disagreeing strangers. The greatest hostility toward the disagreeing stranger was expressed by the individuals with the least discrepancy between self and ideal.

Aggression Toward an Imaginary Frustrating Agent. The investigations reported thus far have shown that frustration evokes greater hostility from low-discrepancy subjects and greater self-depreciation from high-discrepancy subjects. What evidence is there that the latter individuals ever express aggression outwardly?

In an experiment primarily concerned with the effects of arbitrary versus nonarbitrary frustration, Rothaus and Worchel [1960] presented high- and low-discrepancy subjects with imaginary situations about which they were asked to give their probable response. For example, "Your date phones at the last minute and breaks the appointment without an adequate explanation" [Rothaus and Worchel, 1960, p. 110]. The hostility of the subjects' responses was determined by two judges. The subjects were 160 undergraduates who had also taken the SAI.

In this situation, with a hypothetical response to an imaginary situation, subjects with high self-ideal discrepancy responded with significantly more hostility than did subjects with low self-ideal discrepancy. In other words, the subjects responded exactly the opposite way to a hypothetical frustration as to an actual frustration. We might hypothesize from this that those individuals with high self-ideal discrepancy were not threatened by the imaginary situation and thus could express hostile impulses, at least at the verbal level.

Rational Aggression and Displaced Aggression. A final study in this series was conducted by Veldman and Worchel [1961] using a relatively elaborate design. Not only were subjects divided in terms of differences in self-ideal discrepancy as measured by the SAI but an attempt was also made to separate subjects in terms of defensiveness by means of the K scale of the MMPI. The four types of subjects (20 students of each type) were:

1. Low K and low self-ideal discrepancy: well adjusted.
2. High K and low self-ideal discrepancy: repressive.
3. Low K and high self-ideal discrepancy: anxious.
4. High K and high self-ideal discrepancy: distorting.

Another variable of interest was the time between the frustrating event and the measurement of hostility. All groups were given the frustrating intelligence test procedure described earlier with frequent interruptions and distractions by the examiner; in addition, the time limits were inadequate. The test administrator left the room immediately afterward, and the experimenter assessed hostility. For half of the subjects, hostility was measured immediately after the frustration. For the other half, a 20-minute delay was interpolated between frustration and assessment of hostility. The hostility ratings included a measure of rational aggression or blaming the test administrator for difficulties in their performance. The test included items such as: "The examiner was to blame for some of the errors I made." Displaced hostility was measured by means of responses to a sentence completion test.

With respect to rational aggression, analysis of variance yielded a significant triple interaction of self-ideal discrepancy, defensiveness, and time at which hostility was assessed. The well-adjusted subjects expressed the greatest amount of rational aggression immediately after frustration and then dropped more than any other group after the 20-minute delay. The repressive group expressed the least amount of rational aggression immediately after frustration, but after delay there was actually a slight increase in aggression. "Even where the frustrating agent is clearly responsible for interfering with performance, the repressive subjects show far less rational aggression than the adjusted subjects" [Veldman and Worchel, 1961, p. 323].

Both of the high self-ideal discrepancy groups responded with more displaced hostility than the low-discrepancy groups. Thus, these individuals when frustrated are expressing hostility not toward the agent of frustration but toward other persons. The authors suggested that high-discrepancy individuals would be more prejudiced than low-discrepancy individuals, prejudice being conceptualized as another form of displaced hostility. Actually, support for this proposition has been provided by Tabachnick [1962] who found that fifth-grade children who were self-satisfied tended to be less prejudiced than those who were dissatisfied with themselves.

These various experimental investigations of personality dynamics give evidence that individual differences in the self-concept substantially affect behavior in a variety of situations. We will next turn to research dealing with efforts to bring about changes in the self-concept.

Changes in the Self-Concept

EVALUATION BY OTHERS

Self-theory proposes that one's self-concept is developed on the basis of evaluations by others communicated during interpersonal interactions. While the earliest and presumably most general aspects of the self-concept develop in interactions between the child and parental figures, continuing changes in the self-concept should take place as a consequence of later interactions. Thus, the reactions of siblings, peers, teachers, colleagues, spouse, offspring, and/or therapist would be expected to have various degrees of influence on changes made in the self-concept.

Videbeck [1960] hypothesized that one could bring about changes in the self-concept through experimental manipulation of the type of evaluation of an individual given by others. He suggested that evaluations by others should be influential as a function of the number of times a particular evaluation is made, the appropriateness or qualifications of the other person to make an evaluation, the strength of the motivation of the subject with respect to the evaluated attribute, and the intensity with which the approval or disapproval is expressed.

The subjects were 30 students who had been rated by their speech instructors as superior in speaking ability. They were asked to participate in an experiment to "determine whether men or women were better in certain forms of oral communication." In the experiment, each subject read six poems. After each poem, an individual described as a visiting speech expert evaluated the subject's performance. On a random basis, the subjects were assigned to one of two conditions: approval or disapproval. Irrespective of the quality of the performance, the "expert" gave either all positive or all negative evaluations. Before and after the poem-reading sessions, the students gave self-ratings and ideal self-ratings of adequacy with reference to speaking skills and ability to communicate effectively in various social situations.

The self-ratings of the two groups prior to the experimental treatment did not differ. After the evaluation session, the self-concepts of those in the approval group became more positive while the self-concepts of subjects in the disapproval group became more negative. Self-ideal discrepancy became smaller in the approval group and larger in the disapproval group.

Determining the extent to which such effects are lasting or transitory and the specific conditions under which relatively enduring changes take place would be of further value.

MOOD FLUCTUATION

Human beings are commonly observed to be subject to periodic variations in mood, often for reasons not at all clear to the individual himself. Research dealing with this phenomenon has tended to involve repeated measurement of mood over a period of time by means of self-ratings of mood and thereby has attempted to determine the correlates and antecedents of these mood swings. The data to date are relatively meager. For example, those who have the greatest mood changes have been found to be less happy than those with minor variations [Flugel, 1925]. Another finding is that depression is characterized by less energy, less friendliness, more indecisiveness and diffidence, and a tendency to withdraw from social interaction [Johnson, 1937].

Whatever the antecedents of mood fluctuation, one would expect that changes in mood would bring about changes in the self-concept. Wessman, Ricks, and Tyl [1960] formulated a series of hypotheses concerning mood changes including several propositions dealing with concomitant changes in self-ideal discrepancy. Their subjects were 14 female students at Radcliffe College. Over a six-week period, the girls were asked to record their feelings each night. The Mood Scale consisted of 10 phrases ranging from "complete elation, rapturous joy, and soaring ecstasy" to "utter depression and gloom. Completely down. All is black and leaden. Wish it were over." The subjects were to rate themselves just before retiring each evening. In addition, a 45-item Q-sort for self and ideal self was given during the six-week period—once when mood reached an extreme high and once when it was at an extreme low.

As hypothesized, self-ideal congruence was significantly lower when the subject was depressed than when she was elated. The median self-ideal correlation during an elated mood was .55. During depression, the median correlation was .07. Also found was that most of the difference resulted from changes in the self-concept rather than from changes in the ideal self. One of the additional findings was that mood tended to be lower (and hence self-ideal discrepancy greater) on the two days prior to menstruation.

These findings suggest, among other things, that attempts to assess more or less enduring changes in the self-concept would do well to take into account the regular and temporary fluctuations in self-esteem. Otherwise, mood changes might overshadow changes resulting from the independent variable under investigation.

AGE

Research dealing with personality change as a function of the age of the individual suggests that the many inevitable physical and social alterations which occur over time are accompanied by changes in various personality dimensions. For example, Kuhlen [1964] has summarized the evidence dealing with changes in motivation, in goals and interests, in drive level and degree of involvement in life, in anxiety and maladjustment, and in conservatism-liberalism. Changes in the self-concept accompanying the various other changes which take place during the developmental cycle would not be surprising.

In an investigation of 172 eighth and tenth graders over a two-year period, Engel [1959] found a significant increase in self-acceptance between the two testing periods. Conceivably, a steadily more positive self-concept is characteristic as individuals pass through adolescence and into young adulthood.

The fact that a curvilinear relationship has been found between age and degree of personal happiness [Kuhlen, 1956] led Bloom [1961] to hypothesize that self-acceptance or self-esteem would also be related to age in a curvilinear fashion. The subjects were 83 male surgical patients at a VA hospital in New York. The group consisted primarily of clerical workers, craftsmen, and those engaged in skilled trades. Ages ranged from the early twenties to the late sixties. An adjective checklist served as the measure of the self-concept.

The relationship between self-acceptance and age was found to be a curvilinear one as hypothesized; the correlation ratio was .35. Self-acceptance showed a steady increase from age 20, reached a peak during the age period 50–59, and then began a steady decline. Bloom proposed the following description of the aging process:

During the 20–29 year period, most individuals are confronted by personal problems in a number of areas for which they seek solution. Some of these problems are: the need to make a satisfactory vocational adjustment; increased responsibilities; anxiety over interpersonal, social, and sexual problems; and so forth. These adjustment problems lead to doubts concerning the individual's self worth or self esteem, hence self acceptance is at a low ebb. As the individual finds solutions for these problems, self acceptance increases, until in the 40's, most individuals have achieved some measure of stability. During the 50–59 year period, possibly as a result of stereotypes of aging along with concrete evidence of slow down in functioning, there comes the realization of getting old. The individual is again confronted by doubts and anxieties and thus self acceptance declines [Bloom, 1961, p. 537].

PSYCHOTHERAPY

In an investigation by Ewing [1954], the subjects consisted of 39 college students who received counselling concerning some type of personal problem. Self and ideal-self measures were obtained soon after counselling was begun by means of ratings of 100 trait names (for example, fearful, sociable, anxious, clever). After the completion of the therapeutic interviews, the self-ratings were repeated. Because of differential time required for therapy, the time between the two self-ratings ranged from two months to 15 months, and the number of therapy sessions varied from four to 58. At the conclusion of therapy, each client was judged by his counsellor as to amount of improvement.

The extent of change in the self-concept varied considerably across subjects. The greatest change is represented by one individual whose pre-therapy self-sort correlated $-.45$ with his post-therapy self-sort. The individual with the least change had a correlation of .83 between his two self-sorts. The amount of change in the self-concept was found to be directly related to amount of improvement as judged by the counsellor ($r = .38$). Also, the greater the increased similarity between self and ideal self, the greater the improvement rating ($r = .48$).

As with any experimental manipulation, assessing the effects of psychotherapy without utilizing a control group for comparison has many weaknesses. Is the change the result of the therapy, of other events occurring over the time period, of the assessment procedures, or what? The kinds of problems raised by omitting a control group are shown by investigations such as that of Taylor [1955]. He had a group of 26 students who were not in therapy make repeated Q-sorts over a period of several days. The same general trends were found as in studies of patients in therapy. That is, the self-concepts became more positive and self-ideal discrepancy became smaller. One possibility raised was that the introspection about self, which was necessitated by going through the Q-sort items over and over, actually served to bring about improved adjustment.

CLIENT-CENTERED THERAPY VERSUS A CONTROL GROUP

In 1954, Rogers and Dymond edited a book reporting a series of investigations dealing primarily with research on psychotherapy and its effect on the self-concept. The general plan [Grummon, 1954] of the study was to obtain behavioral measures before, during, and after psychotherapy for clients at the University of Chicago Counseling Center. All of the interactions between client and therapist were recorded. There were 29 clients in the *experimental group*, of whom 16 were university students while the remainder were nonstudents. Two types of control groups were established. The *own-control group* was formed by asking half of the clients in the experimental group to defer their therapy for 60 days. The *equivalent-control group* was made up of individuals who volunteered to serve as subjects for a project involving "research on personality." They were matched with the experimental group on the basis of sex, student versus nonstudent status, age, and socioeconomic class. The own-control group served to control for effects such as the degree of disturbance, personality characteristics, and motivation for psychotherapy. The equivalent-control group served to control any effects dependent on simply the passage of time. Environmental influences in the everyday lives of the subjects were, of course, not controlled, but these effects should have been randomly distributed across all groups.

A number of different therapists participated in the project, and each handled approximately equal numbers of clients. After subjects had agreed to participate, the first testing session took place. The battery included the Thematic Apperception Test and the Chicago Q-sort. A short personal history form was also filled out. The schedule of testing is shown in Figure 12–2. We see that the two "no-wait" groups were tested three times while the other two groups were tested four times. Other measures obtained included therapist ratings of the outcome of therapy.

Self-Ideal Changes. Butler and Haigh [1954] reported that the self-ideal correlations of the client groups before therapy averaged

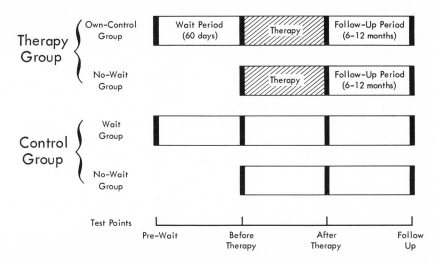

Fig. 12–2. *General design of the Chicago Psychotherapy Research Project.* (*Adapted from Rogers and Dymond, 1954, p. 38.*)

—.01. The mean self-ideal correlation after therapy was .34, and at the time of the later follow-up it was .31. Thus, a change in self-ideal congruence (significant at the .01 level) occurred between the pretherapy period and the post-therapy period. One test of whether therapy-motivated individuals change simply with the passage of time is provided by the own-control group. When first tested, these 15 clients had a self-ideal correlation of —.01; after the 60-day waiting period, the correlation was still —.01. In contrast to the client groups, the equivalent control group had a mean self-ideal correlation of .58 at the beginning and .59 at the follow-up period. These subjects had less self-ideal discrepancy than the client group both before and after the clients had undergone therapy, but the control subjects showed no change over time.

Within the therapy group, clients differed in terms of the effects of psychotherapy. On the basis of therapist ratings of success at the end of therapy and on the basis of independent judgments of TAT protocols, 17 clients were identified as definitely improved. For this subgroup of individuals, the self-ideal correlation was .02 before therapy and .44 at the follow-up period. The improved group could not be distinguished from the eight unimproved clients at the beginning of therapy, but the group showed significantly more self-ideal congruence after therapy.

Changes in Adjustment. As described earlier, Dymond [1954] developed a scoring system for the Q-sort items which yielded an adjustment score for the self-sort. Adjustment scores were obtained for the various groups in the research project.

One comparison was between the client group that had the 60-day wait and their matched controls. The therapy group described themselves as significantly poorer in adjustment than did the control subjects. Neither group changed in adjustment over the waiting period, and they were still significantly different from each other 60 days later.

Table 12–4 shows the comparison of the total experimental group and the total equivalent-control group. Analysis of the data revealed that the experimental group significantly increased in adjustment over the therapy period, while the control group showed no change. The difference between the two groups is significant at the pretherapy period but not after therapy.

Table 12–4   Q-SORT ADJUSTMENT SCORES OF EXPERIMENTAL
             (THERAPY) GROUP AND CONTROL GROUP

Time	Experimental Group	Control Group
Pretherapy	28.80	44.96
Post-therapy	39.80	45.12
Follow-up	38.36	44.52

Improvement During the Waiting Period. Among the clients assigned to the own-control group, there were eight individuals who were tested at the beginning, tested again after the 60-day waiting period, then had one or two therapy sessions but failed to return after that. This group of "attriters" were found to be different from the group of own-control subjects who went on to complete psychotherapy. While the latter group showed no improvement in adjustment scores over the 60 days, the attriters revealed a significant improvement by the time therapy was to begin. Dymond [1955] reported that the therapy group had Q-sort adjustment scores of 28.6 and 30.2 in the two testings; the attrition group had scores of 32.0 and 42.9. The two groups were not different at the first testing, but the attriters had a significantly higher adjustment score at the second testing.

Since the Q-sort depends on what the individual is able or willing to say about himself, Dymond investigated the adjustment scores obtained on the TAT. On this measure, *neither* the therapy group nor the attrition group gave evidence of improvement over the 60-day waiting period. The Q-sort adjustment score and the TAT adjustment score are usually found to be positively correlated. For the therapy group, the two measures correlated .47 at the first testing and .30 at the pretherapy period. For the attrition group, the correlations were .39 and —.20. Thus, at the pretherapy testing, for the attrition group the two measures are negatively correlated.

This finding led Dymond to propose that the Q-sort improvement was not genuine improvement but the result of defensiveness on the part of the attriters. She carried out an item-analysis of the Q-sort to explore the possibility of differences between the self-descriptive Q-sorts of attriters at the pretherapy point and of those who successfully completed the psychotherapy at the post-therapy point. In other words, both groups were describing themselves as well adjusted, one after a waiting period and the other after successful psythotherapy. Dymond sums up the differences between the two groups:

The attriters appear to be a group of "rugged individualists" who are hanging on tight to the idea, "I *am* someone, I *am* superior, I *do* want to cope and will do it *myself*." They seem to have difficulty accepting the idea of help from others (I am an aloof, reserved person; I make strong demands on myself; I am self-reliant, competitive; I have to protect myself with excuses, with rationalizing). It does not seem surprising in the light of this pattern that they have made a strong effort during the waiting period to pull themselves up by their own bootstraps; they have decided that therapy is not for them and do not follow it through; and their TAT's do not show any deep personality change.

What are the characteristics of the successful psychotherapy subjects in contradistinction to the attriters who "go it alone"? Some answer is given by the items: I express my emotions freely, I am liked by most people who know me, I trust my emotions, I respect myself, I understand myself. All of these were more characteristic of the self-descriptions of the successes than of the attriters [Dymond, 1955, pp. 105–106].

Rogers sums up his conclusions based on the findings of this project:

It appears reasonable to conclude that the psychotherapy is the effective agent of change, since changes of comparable magnitude do not occur in a control group or in our clients during a control period. In our judgment the research sets forth for the first time objective evidence that one defined approach to psychotherapy produces certain measurable and significant changes in the individual coming for help . . . [Rogers, 1954, p. 433].

PSYCHOTHERAPY WITH PSYCHOTIC PATIENTS

Almost all of the early work of Rogers and his co-workers concentrated on the relatively mild forms of emotional disturbances. The typical clients seen in psychotherapy were bright, well-educated, verbal, somewhat neurotic college students. Rogers' self-theory was developed primarily on the basis of observations of such individuals. At Wisconsin, a large-scale six-year-research project was undertaken by Carl Rogers, Eugene Gendlin, Charles Truax, and others involving the application of client-centered therapy to schizophrenics. Among the early reports of this work [Truax, 1963] are indications that psychotherapists high in "accurate empathy" are able to bring about changes in the self-concepts of schizophrenic patients. The important therapist attitudes include an effort to share the client's perceptions and feelings, being on the client's side and having a warm regard for him, and an attempt by the therapist to be himself [Gendlin, 1962]. When schizophrenics were treated by therapists low in empathy, however, they not only failed to improve but actually got worse. As Rogers [1963, p. 14] noted: "Clinically, this is a very sobering finding; scientifically, it is of great importance." When this problem is better understood, we may know more about therapy and about schizophrenia.

In an independent research effort dealing with schizophrenics in psychotherapy, Satz and Baraff [1962] reported an investigation involving the comparison of eight patients in therapy with a matched control group of eight patients. Half of the experimental group received 13 hours of intensive occupational therapy and two hours of group psychotherapy a week for 10 weeks. The other half received the same amount of occupational therapy without the group psychotherapy. The control group received neither type of therapy and were not even allowed to attend their regular occupational therapy sessions. All subjects were given the Chicago Q-sort for self and ideal self before the experimental period, in the middle of the period, and at the end of the 10 weeks.

Table 12–5 shows the comparison of the three groups over the three testing periods in terms of mean self-sort ideal-sort correlations. The findings are somewhat difficult to explain. The patients receiving treatment gave little evidence of change in self-ideal discrepancy, and the change

Table 12–5   SELF-IDEAL CORRELATIONS OF TREATED
AND UNTREATED SCHIZOPHRENIC PATIENTS

Groups	Pretherapy	In-therapy	Post-therapy
Occupational therapy plus group psychotherapy	.01	.06	—.03
Occupational therapy only	.29	.33	.16
Control group	.08	.23	.33

which did take place was for the worse. The only improvement indicated was for the control group who received no therapy for 10 weeks. These findings are, however, consistent with those of Rogers' group in that schizophrenic patients may actually be made worse by inadequate therapy.

Current Status of the Self-Concept as a Personality Variable

ANTECEDENTS OF THE SELF-CONCEPT

As suggested earlier in the chapter, Rogers has built an elaborate and detailed picture of the antecedents of both healthy and unhealthy self-structures. The effects of conditional versus unconditional acceptance of the child and the effects of teaching accurate versus inaccurate labels for experience, for example, have been specified. Nevertheless, surprisingly little research has been directed to the task of verifying and extending such propositions.

Seemingly research and application in this area would gain as much or more from concentration on the developmental aspects of self as from concentration on attempts to bring about alterations in the self-concepts of adults. Historically, Rogers' theory has grown out of psychotherapy, but its implications for developmental psychology have barely begun to be explored.

EFFECTS OF CLIENT-CENTERED PSYCHOTHERAPY ON BEHAVIOR

One of the major accomplishments of Rogers and his co-workers has been that of exposing all aspects of psychotherapeutic interaction and outcome to the critical eye of research methodology. More than with any other group, the adherents of client-centered psychotherapy have been amenable to the presence of tape recorders and movie cameras in therapy sessions, to behavior measurement before and after therapy, to detailed analysis of client-therapist interactions, and to the use of control groups in the evaluation of the effectiveness of psychotherapy. Further, such research efforts have yielded the most consistent body of data now available to support the notion that psychotherapy does, in fact, bring about behavior change.

In spite of all this, there is a nagging problem concerning what it is that client-centered therapists have demonstrated. Content analyses of the therapy sessions reveal significant changes in what clients talk about during the course of psychotherapy, such as decreased mention of symptoms and increased evidence of self-satisfaction from beginning to end of psychotherapy. Ratings are also obtained from therapists as to the client's adjustment or improvement, but in the final analysis these judgments are based primarily on the verbal behavior of the clients. The behavior measures which have been used to compare patients' pre- and post-therapy or to compare therapy groups with control groups have depended almost entirely on the verbalizations of the subjects. Thus, whether the measuring instrument is a Q-sort, an adjective checklist, or a self-rating scale, the patient is essentially asked to state the degree to which he is anxious, depressed, self-satisfied, and so forth.

While all of this evidence may well mean that significant behavioral changes are involved, equally possible is that the changes all represent simple changes in verbal response patterns. Therapists reinforce certain types of verbalizations, while other types are either punished or allowed to extinguish. With relatively bright, relatively verbal, not very maladjusted clients, the rapid learning of a new style of verbalizing about themselves is not terribly surprising. Numerous experimental investigations have shown the ease with which the verbal responses of subjects can be altered by means of selective reinforcement administered by the experimenter. Reinforcement has included murmurs of "mmm-hmm" and "huh-uh" for certain classes of words [Greenspoon, 1955] and agreement or paraphrasing of the subject's statements [Verplanck, 1955]. If psychotherapy is simply an extended series of verbal learning sessions, the reason for the relative ineffectiveness of therapy with relatively dull, relatively nonverbal, severely maladjusted clients is readily apparent.

What would be of considerably greater importance than the demonstration of verbal learning by clients is the determination of whether these changed verbalizations are accompanied by, or are reflective of, or result in other types of behavior change. Since the evidence to date is convincing with respect to changes in self-concept (as traditionally measured) during psychotherapy, future research on the effect of psychotherapy could go on to a somewhat different proposition. If psychotherapy brings about changes in the self-concept, all behavior related to self-structure should be different after therapy compared to that same behavior before therapy. Based on some of the research findings reported in this chapter, for example, after therapy the client's perception of parental attitudes should be more positive, participation in extracurricular school activities should increase, grade-point average should rise, sociometric status among peers should improve, effectiveness in situations such as student teaching should increase, perceptual defense against threatening stimuli should decrease, greater hostility should be expressed toward an actual frustrating agent, less hostility should be expressed toward an imaginary frustrating agent, hostility following frustration should dissipate more quickly, and less displacement of hostility should occur. A body of evidence of this sort would be relatively convincing with respect to the effects of psychotherapy on the self-concept. Negative findings, on the other hand, would suggest that the verbal changes which take place in therapy patients are severely limited in generality.

CONGRUENCY BETWEEN SELF-CONCEPT AND EXPERIENCE

One of the major formulations within self-theory has to do with the effects of varying degrees of congruency between an individual's self-concept (or his "conditions of worth") and his actual experience. Thus, all forms of maladjustment are simply the result of this incongruency. Feelings of anxiety, perceptual distortions, self-deceptions, and even psychoses are all traceable to having developed a self-concept which is inconsistent with the stimuli impinging on the organism. In the research which deals with the self, however, we find that most investigators have relied on a different variable—congruency between self-concept and ideal self-concept. While self-descriptive measures such as the Q-sort have proven to be of considerable research usefulness, they would not seem to be an adequate substitute for an index of congruency between self and experience.

The reason for side-stepping this problem in most investigations is an obvious one—how do you operationalize the theoretical constructs? The primary solution so far attempted has been a somewhat indirect one; self-reports are contrasted with judgments by experts. For example, Chodorkoff [1954] compared self-concept as measured by the Q-sort with descriptions of the person by clinical psychologists; presumably the greater the discrepancy between the two measures the greater the incongruency between self and experience. Though this approach seems closer to the theory than does a self-ideal discrepancy measure, it still appears that a more appropriate set of operations could be devised.

One possibility might be to establish a set of stimulus situations which, normatively at least, evoke certain internal experiences. Examples would be stimuli which evoke hostility, sexual excitement, and feelings of dependency. Those individuals who fail to respond in the normal way, who misperceive the stimuli, and who become anxious and disorganized should be the ones whose conditions of worth were incompatible with their experience in the situation. In any event, this sort of approach to the identification of individuals with incongruency between self and experience seems to approximate what is specified in the theory.

The more general problem involved here is the one of dealing scientifically with variables which are internal and unobservable. While we can ignore such variables and hope to build a science around them, we can also seek operations to define them. For example, we know that threatening stimuli evoke tension, but many therapists suggest that when clients are induced to think about that which threatens them, this is actually a step toward reducing the tension. How could such a proposition be investigated? Gendlin and Berlin [1961] gave subjects tape-recorded instructions to do various things followed by a period of silence in which they could carry out the instructions. When the subjects were instructed to focus inwardly on the felt meanings of an unpleasant personal problem, there was a *decrease* in tension as measured by galvanic skin response, skin temperature, and heart rate. Thus, the observable consequences of internal events were utilized by the investigators.

Operationalizing the kinds of variables long stressed by self-theorists is a major challenge for future research.

Summary

In attempting to conceptualize behavior in terms of a single, unified process, many theorists have utilized the notion of self-concept. The term *self* has come to have two distinct meanings to psychologists: self-as-object and self-as-person. Individual differences in the self-concept (self-as-object) constitute a dimension which may be studied in the same way as any other personality dimension. On the other hand, the self-as-process definition seems to involve a simple relabeling of certain behavior and leads toward reification of "the self" or "the ego." The approach of self-theorists, such as Rogers, is often contrasted with the approach of stimulus-response psychologists, especially with respect to emphasis on the total individual and on the importance of the phenomenal field.

Carl Rogers developed an approach to psychological treatment known as client-centered psychotherapy. The therapist is seen as one who facilitates the natural growth processes of the client by offering acceptance, understanding, and empathy. The personality theory which Rogers formulated grew out of his work in psychotherapy. Self-theory attempts to deal with the total individual as an organized whole rather than with stimulus-response units. Behavior is believed to be a function of the individual's perceptions, and thus the behavioral scientist should attempt to achieve an internal rather than an external frame of reference. Behavior is the goal-directed attempt of the organism to satisfy its needs as experienced, in the field as perceived. The most important part of the phenomenal field is the self. The satisfaction of the need for positive regard depends on other human beings, and the individual can be more influenced by this need than by his actual organic experience. Growing out of this need is the need for positive self-regard. Almost inevitably some lack of congruence occurs between the conditions of worth as defined by the self-concept and the person's experiences with respect to both internal and external events. Experiences contrary to the self-concept are perceived selectively, distorted, and denied to awareness. Such incongruency is defined as maladjustment and leaves the person vulnerable to anxiety, threat, and disorganization. A large enough degree of incongruence between self and experience can lead to a breakdown of defenses, an extreme arousal of anxiety, and a disorganization of the self-structure. Such negative processes may be reversed by receiving unconditional positive regard from a significant other. An increase occurs in the person's own unconditional positive self-regard. With threat reduced, there is less need for defense and more possibility for accurate perception and symbolization of experience.

As reasonable as the phenomenological approach may seem, the experimenter cannot avoid the fact that the operations utilized must involve observable stimuli and responses. As a measure of the self-concept and ideal self-concept, Stephenson developed the Q-sort technique. The discrepancy between self and ideal is often used as a measure of self-esteem. In the Chicago Q-sort, 100 statements are sorted by the subject in a forced normal distribution once to describe self and once to describe ideal self. A number of other measuring devices are also used for the self-concept including the Self Activity Inventory, adjective checklists, and various questionnaires. Self-description measures are usually found to correlate substantially with measures of social desirability. The greater the tendency to give socially desirable responses, the less the reported discrepancy between self and ideal self.

Typically, children are raised in such a way as to learn to respond on the basis of the introjected values of parents rather than on the basis of their own subjective experience. The parent should be able, however, to respond to unacceptable behavior by (1) accepting the child's feelings concerning the behavior, (2) accepting and loving the child himself, but (3) showing clearly that the behavior cannot be allowed to continue. Research on the antecedents of differences in self-concept has indicated that positiveness of self-concept is related to perceiving one's parents as feeling positively toward oneself. And, the more the mother's concept of her spouse is like her ideal-child concept, the more her son is actually like her husband. The more different the parents are in their ideal-child concepts, the more unstable is the child's ideal-self concept. Also, acceptance of self is greater for those who feel positively toward their parents.

In self-theory, maladjustment is defined in terms of the magnitude of the discrepancy between self and experience. Various groups of maladjusted individuals have been found to have more negative self-concepts and hence greater self-ideal discrepancy than normals. In addition, self-ideal discrepancy has been found to be related to several measures of adjustment including Dymond's adjustment scoring system for Q-sorts, scales of the Guilford-Zimmermann Temperament Survey, and the California Test of Personality. Still other findings suggest that a curvilinear relationship exists between self-ideal discrepancy and adjustment. Either a very large discrepancy or an unrealistically low discrepancy may indicate maladjustment. Very low discrepancy has been found to be characteristic of individuals who utilize repressive defense mechanisms, hospitalized schizophrenics, and prisoners, and to be related to such variables as overcontrol, denial, constriction, and lack of candor. As social competence increases, self-ideal discrepancy also increases; at a given level of social competence, however, more effective behavior is related to relatively low self-ideal discrepancy.

Inaccuracy in self-perception is related to perceptual defense against threatening stimuli. Similarly, recall of stimuli consistent with the self-concept is better than recall of inconsistent stimuli. For the individual whose self-concept is congruent with his experience, the hostility aroused by frustration is accurately conceptualized and directed appropriately toward the frustrating agent. When aggressive impulses are not admitted into awareness, individuals tend not to verbalize hostility toward the agent of frustration but rather toward themselves or onto inappropriate targets through displacement.

While the earliest and most general aspects of the self-concept develop in interaction between the child and parental figures, changes can be brought about as a consequence of later interactions. Self-concepts can be made more positive or more negative as a function of the type of evaluation received from others. Fluctuations in mood also bring about changes in the self-concept. Age is another variable related to self-concept; self-concept is progressively more positive through adolescence and up to the 50–59 age period, and then it begins a steady decline. Psychotherapy brings about a more positive self-concept and less discrepancy between self and ideal. When compared to individuals in various types of control groups, those receiving psychotherapy show greater changes and an increase in adjustment. Some individuals who plan to undergo therapy and then decide not to do so also show positive changes in the self-concept; on the basis of other measures of adjustment, however, the improvement of these individuals appears not to be genuine but rather the result of defensiveness. Finally, the evidence is growing that psychotherapy with severely disturbed psychotics has less effect on the self-concept and may even make the patient worse.

Historically, Rogers' theory has grown out of psychotherapy, but its implications for developmental psychology have barely begun to be explored. Research by client-centered therapists has yielded the most consistent body of data now available to support the notion that psychotherapy brings about behavior change. The evidence, however, is almost entirely based on the verbal responses of clients and may represent simple changes in verbal response patterns. What is now needed is evidence that these changed verbalizations are accompanied by other types of change in behavior. A major construct of self-theory involves the degree of congruency between an individual's self-concept and his actual experience. Research operations, however, have used only self-ideal discrepancy or discrepancy between self-ratings and ratings by an expert judge. An approach is needed which more closely approximates the theoretical description of self-experience incongruency. Operationalizing the kinds of unobservable variables stressed by self-theorists is a major challenge for future research.

Part Four

INTEGRATION
OF PERSONALITY
VARIABLES

CHAPTER 13

Describing the Individual

Throughout this text, the term "personality" has primarily been used to denote specific kinds of behavioral variables: dimensions of individual differences. In other contexts, a more familiar usage has to do with the overall combination of an individual's various characteristics. Most definitions of personality, in fact, include some aspect of a unified description of a "whole person." For example, McClelland [1951, p. 69] defines personality as ". . . the most adequate conceptualization of a person's behavior in all its detail that the scientist can give at a moment in time." He goes on to add: *"Personality is a theoretical interpretation derived from all a person's behavior."*

What becomes of this holistic conception when personality research is pursued in the atomistic, variable-by-variable manner described in the preceding 12 chapters? One possibility has been raised by Allport [1961, p. 27] who rejects the operational approach of "extreme positivistic behaviorism." He suggests that with such an approach, "only outer, visible, manipulable operations are tolerated. Personality as such evaporates in a mist of method."

Can one refute Allport's charge? Can one take such bits and pieces of behavior as authoritarianism, achievement need, anxiety, intelligence, and self-concept and reassemble them in order to present a coherent picture of a specific and perhaps unique individual? In the first chapter, the field of personality was defined as that branch of psychology which deals with dimensions of individual differences. It follows that an individual's personality consists of his standing on all such dimensions or in Guilford's [1959,

p. 5] terms: *"An individual's personality, then, is his unique pattern of traits."* This definition suggests that one can reconstruct the individual by combining the separate bits of information about him.

Before discussing such a process in any detail, a somewhat better perspective may be gained by turning to the more general problem of what is meant by personality description. The descriptions written by novelists, psychiatrists, and clinical psychologists will be sampled.

Personality Description

NOVELISTS

We live in a culture grown accustomed to the presentation of fictional beings whose behavior, motives, abilities, needs, and other characteristics are displayed in varying depths of detail. By means of plays, movies, and television programs, we are familiar with legions of imaginary individuals, some more real and better known to us through the artistry of their creators than our real acquaintances. Like the multi-wall television of Ray Bradbury's [1953] future world in which the imaginary TV "family" makes the viewer one of them, existing media allow us to know countless different personalities.

Of course, to create such beings with words alone as the writer of novels or short stories must do is even more difficult. The attempt verbally to present either real or imaginary personalities has a relatively short history considering the probable length of time man has existed. And, once the attempt was first made, individual artists took still more time to progress from two-dimensional characters with stylized attributes to complex, highly differentiated personalities.

What is the technique by which words bring life and individuality to a fictional character? Briefly, we will take a look at two creations: one of Dickens' near caricatures and one of Tolstoy's minor portraits. Each character, of course, is represented by only a few paragraphs rather than the total space taken by the authors in developing them more completely.

Among a multitude of individuals created by Dickens is our annual Christmas visitor, Ebenezer Scrooge:

Oh! but he was a tight-fisted hand at the grindstone. Scrooge! a squeezing, wrenching, grasping, scraping, clutching, covetous, old sinner! Hard and sharp as flint, from which no steel had ever struck out generous fire; secret, and self-contained, and solitary as an oyster. The cold within him froze his old features, nipped his pointed nose, shrivelled his cheek, stiffened his gait; made his eyes red, his thin lips blue; and spoke out shrewdly in his grating voice. A frosty rime was on his head, and on his eyebrows, and his wiry chin. He carried his own low temperature always about with him; he iced his office in the dog-days, and didn't thaw it one degree at Christmas.

External heat and cold had little influence on Scrooge. No warmth could warm, no wintry weather chill him. No wind that blew was bitterer than he, no falling snow was more intent upon its purpose, no pelting rain less open to entreaty [Dickens, 1843, p. 18].

Though Scrooge may not seem quite "real," characters like Prince Stepan Arkadyevich Oblonsky are as differentiated and believable personalities as are one's neighbors even though Prince Oblonsky "lived" a century in the past in the Russia of the Czars:

Stepan Arkadyevich had learned easily at school, thanks to his excellent abilities, but he had been idle and mischievous, and therefore was one of the lowest in his class. But in spite of his habitually dissipated mode of life, his inferior grade in the service, and his comparative youth, he occupied the honorable and lucrative position of president of one of the government boards at Moscow. This post he had received through his sister Anna's husband, Alexei Alexandrovich Karenin, who held one of the most important positions in the ministry to which the Moscow office belonged. But if Karenin had not got his brother-in-law this berth, then through a hundred other personages—brothers, sisters, cousins, uncles and aunts—Stiva Oblonsky would have received this post or some other like it, together with the salary of six thousand absolutely needful for him, as his affairs, in spite of his wife's considerable property, were in a poor state. . . .

Stepan Arkadyevich was not merely liked by all who knew him for his good humor, his bright disposition, and his unquestionable honesty; in him, in his handsome, radiant figure, his sparkling eyes, black hair and eyebrows, and his white and pink complexion, there was something which produced a physical effect of kindliness and good humor on the people who met him [Tolstoy, 1875, pp. 16–17].

What, then, do authors do? In order to describe individuals to us, authors tend to present a description of the physical attributes of the individual, often a sketch of the parents and the childhood and the early experiences of the person, and a great deal about the character's personality. That is, by presenting something of the specific behavior and general traits of the person, he is assembled as a variegated individual.

PSYCHIATRISTS

The traditional medical history or case report bears little relation to the novel. It provides instead relevant background information (for example, age and sex of patient), medical history if available, and those symptoms and signs which indicate a particular diagnosis. Ideally, the latter information conveys a great deal in that a given disease entity is brought about by a specific cause, the disease runs a typical course, and it can be cured by a specific treatment procedure.

As psychiatry and psychoanalysis developed, a different approach was required. Behavioral problems required that much be described and brought together in the report with respect to observations not reducible to labels or summary background data. Even after diagnostic categories became available, they conveyed little information about cause, course, or treatment. What came to be accepted as more important was a detailed, insightful description of personality. In a curious way, the attempts by physicians interested in behavioral disorders to describe their patients involve the use of techniques similar to those of novelists.

To provide the student with the flavor of psychiatric descriptions, two brief examples will be presented. Boatman and Szurek [1960] have presented a number of cases based on their work with schizophrenic children at the Langley Porter Neuropsychiatric Institute in San Francisco. Included was the following description of an entire family:

One boy, seen by us first at age 6, had worried his educated, successful parents since age 2½ because he did not speak. As an infant they had considered him "model" because he did not fuss although left alone a good deal, even to the extent of mother's propping his bottle for "efficient" nursing. He had been diagnosed as aphasic at 5 when 2 years of speech-therapy exercises had not helped. Although sure-footed to the point of dangerous daring and, like his father, unusual in mechanical skills, he had been slow in early motor development and difficult in toilet training (holding feces as well as soiling). He had not learned to dress himself. He alternately ignored and made whining demands on his parents. Between 5 and 6 he had developed severe temper tantrums and vicious cruelty to his pets. He was put out of a special school because he couldn't learn and didn't play with others. He insisted on bathing each time he was made to use the toilet. When admitted to our Children's Ward he was a silent, handsome, poker-faced 6-year-old, who often screamed loudly but tonelessly. He refused all psychological tests except performance items, on which he scored in the superior range. In the subsequent 4 years of psychotherapy (1 inpatient and 3 outpatient) he became a bright, responsive youngster, who sometimes chattered animatedly with his parents and who spoke appropriately with everyone but his therapist, with whom he remained mute.

During the parents' early therapy, we slowly learned how inaccurate had been their first insistence that they had no troubles but the son. His elder sister was shy and fearful, and his younger sister suffered from enuresis, stuttering, and severe thumb-sucking. The father, a self-driving son of an ambitious mother, was a success in a service career and also in several hobbies and extra money-making ventures. His assignments to overseas posts had necessitated several family moves and one lengthy separation prior to and during most of his son's first 4 years of life. Even when home he had often worked long hours 7 days a week. Despite his successes, he actually felt very unsure of his capabilities. He disliked and ignored all children who were not old enough to *talk*. The mother, a pretty, unusually youthful-appearing woman, felt little closeness to her own "helpless" mother (whom she looked like) and had been "dominated" all her life by her stern father (whom her son looked like). She felt disfigured when pregnant, was repulsed by the thought of breast feeding or cuddling her babies, and felt fearful of and seldom talked to the children as infants. During a visit with her parents prior to her son's birth, she and they had been shocked at the expression of unexpectedly violent feelings by one of her sisters. When the sister's outburst culminated in an overt psychotic episode, her already pervasive fear of how dangerous it was to express strong feelings of any kind had been strengthened. In therapy, this fear was first expressed around her anger at her therapist's expectation that she come for interviews until close to term with her fourth pregnancy. As this was resolved, she also expressed her smoldering rage about her husband's long hours and her son's silences and demands [Boatman and Szurek, 1960, pp. 436–437].

With psychoanalytic descriptions of personality, the major addition to the ordinary psychiatric approach is a tendency to interpret behavior in Freudian terms. An example is Savitt's description of a heroin addict who was in analysis:

A precocious young musician had had his promising career disrupted by his morbid cravings. From birth the mother left his care to others, and not until the age of four was he somewhat integrated into the family group. When he entered treatment he was in one of his periodic states of exile from his family, living occasionally with his grandparents. Usually, however, he wandered around in the demoralizing atmosphere of the various "pads" occupied by fellow addicts.

One of his earliest statements was, "Once I get something into my body I feel safe." He spoke of himself as a milk addict and lover of sweets. An injection of heroin proved to be unconsciously equated with the incorporation of mother-breast-food. He had previously gone through the gamut of oral substitutive gratifications: alcohol, marijuana, and opiates by mouth; also several periods of abnormal craving for food during which he became moderately obese. From sixteen to eighteen he passed through a stage of sexual promiscuity and hypersexuality from which he had regressed into occasional homosexuality.

For this patient the incorporation of heroin also meant being swallowed and engulfed by mother. Thus, in one intravenous injection a mutual incorporation of mother and child was achieved [Savitt, 1963, pp. 45–46].

CLINICAL PSYCHOLOGISTS

In many respects, clinical psychologists have had an unenviable goal in their approach to personality description. Like psychiatrists, they have attempted to combine the descriptive power of novelists with the physician's emphasis on symptoms and diagnosis. In addition, the psychologist brings to the task a background of research training and a scientific concern with evidence and prediction.

Thus, the typical descriptive productions of clinicians include specific data such as test responses, test scores, and comparison with normative groups plus a tendency to predict future behavioral probabilities and recommendations for intervention to bring about change. Again, two examples will serve to illustrate these points.

The first case is a clinical report about a 25-year-old male:

This patient is of bright normal intelligence (IQ 114) and still in good contact with his environment. He seems to have felt insecure most of his life because of conflicts in his feelings toward his mother (his birth was illegitimate) as well as towards his own sexual problems. Abnormally low affect and the fact that he has cut himself off from all former associations seem to indicate a schizophrenic reaction, paranoid type, but this reaction has apparently not progressed to the point of his experiencing delusions. He has, however, experienced auditory hallucinations of a mildly persecutory nature. He shows some insight into his problems, and the prognosis is favorable provided his present good contact with reality can be maintained. For this reason, group therapy seems indicated, whether or not insulin treatment is effected. . . .

Personality Factors:

The primary personality factor seems to be a homosexual conflict in which feelings of hostility towards his mother are involved. These latter feelings are probably related to the illegitimacy of his birth.

The primary homosexual conflict is most clearly indicated in the Rorschach responses. A punitive attitude towards women was noted in several responses (mutilated female figures); also there was considerable vacillation in deciding the sex of human figures identified. A strong fear of overpowering male figures was noted, especially in response to Card IV: "Helluva looking thing—some kind of giant after you."

The interview material confirms the above interpretation. . . . One encouraging fact is that he apparenty has some (though incomplete) insight into his problems. "Maybe if I could really get straightened out about men, women . . . that sort of thing. . . ."

This homosexual conflict mentioned above thus seems to be the central problem. The patient's way of handling it seems to involve a degree of compulsivity: for example, the drawings on the Bender-Gestalt showed an exaggerated degree of neatness and precision. However, this handling of the problem has not been wholly successful, as evidenced by the somewhat impaired intellectual functioning in conceptual areas, and by the feelings of unworthiness and the severance of relationships with other people, mentioned during interviews.

The most extreme result from a symptomatic point of view, of the patient's unsuccessful handling of his problem is the occurrence of auditory hallucinations. These are of a mildly persecutory nature: scolding, ridiculing, hostile voices, which "constantly belittled" him for his "unworthiness." These hallucinations were apparently unaccompanied by any delusions, and the patient reports that he has experienced no hallucinations since entering the hospital.

The TAT stories were brief and of relatively little plot. This latter fact may have resulted primarily from the patient's feelings of defensiveness towards this test. The examiner noted some hostility at this point, in contrast to little affect displayed during other phases of testing and interviewing.

Prognosis and Recommendations:

. . . Group therapy . . . seems indicated. The patient's relatively good intellectual functioning should enable him to perform to advantage in the group-situation, and this, together with the consequent opportunities for him to assume some leadership in group activities should have the effect of arresting and reversing his present trend towards continually increasing withdrawal. Increased insight into the real nature of his problem should be promoted, but perhaps this should not be attempted until insulin therapy and group therapy have been initiated [Hammond and Allen, 1953, pp. 184–187].

A second example is that of a college student at a large Midwestern university who applied to the university counselling center for assistance. Holtzman, Thorpe, Swartz, and Herron present the following background material:

A slightly effeminate, physically unattractive white male, Jack first came to the counsellor in the middle of his freshman year for help in deciding upon his major field of study. Although he had originally planned to major in geology, he was now considering a change to psychology and wanted to learn more about himself in relation to an occupational choice. During the initial interview it soon became apparent that Jack was worried about much more than choosing a field of study. He expressed little self-confidence, remarked that he had few friends, and vaguely mentioned difficulties in getting along with his parents. He said that he had been forced to argue for a long time to get their approval for majoring in geology, and he thought he would have even more difficulty in getting them to agree to his proposed change to psychology. Moreover, he was not certain that he possessed the right personality characteristics for success as a psychologist.

Jack expressed considerable concern about the security of highly personal information revealed to the counsellor. Toward the end of the first interview he hesitantly confided that he thought he had strong homosexual tendencies, hastening to add that he had never really had an overt homosexual experience. However, he mentioned that he did spend a good deal of time reading magazines dealing with male physical culture or sex and hanging around with several boys who were actively homosexual. He stated that he lacked the nerve to plunge into active homosexual relations and wondered whether homosexuality would prevent him from becoming a successful psychologist.

Jack's scholastic aptitude, though not outstanding, was above average for freshmen. He had ranked in the second quarter of his graduating class in a large high school and scored at the seventy-sixth percentile on the university's admission test. His grades during the first semester of college work were mediocre but not quite low enough to place him on probation. Jack agreed to take a battery of psychological tests, and arrangements were made for a series of interviews with an experienced counselling psychologist [Holtzman, Thorpe, Swartz, and Herron, 1961, pp. 222–223].

Psychological testing in this instance included the Strong Vocational Interest Blank and the Edwards Personal Preference Schedule, but the major emphasis in the report was the client's performance on the Holtzman Inkblot Technique. The summary of what was learned from the ink-blot responses was as follows:

In summary, it can be said with some confidence that Jack has a severe personality disorder bordering on overt schizophrenia and characterized by excessive preoccupation with homosexual fantasies. Although he may be able to maintain sufficient control of his autistic thought processes to cope with a daily routine and appear superficially normal, the sexual confusion, hostility, bizarre associations, and complete lack of conventionality characteristic of his inkblot responses suggest that he is a seriously disturbed individual. In spite of this generally disturbed picture, some hopeful signs are present. In side remarks and subtle verbal qualifications, Jack indicates some awareness of the bizarre, confused nature of his fantasies. On a number of inkblot variables related to developmental level, and possibly, degree of ego differentiation, he scores rather well, indicating that he may have sufficient inner resources to improve in an intensive course of psychotherapy [Holtzman, et al., 1961, pp. 226, 247].

With respect to this student, we might note that the background information, the information from the series of counselling interviews, and the information from another testing session some months later revealed no evidence of overt homosexual behavior. More intensive psychotherapy was recommended, and "Jack" left the university.

Having briefly examined three different, though related, general approaches to personality description, what is the possible contribution of the field of personality to this task? What could the methods and the goals of science contribute?

Prediction as the Goal of Description

PREDICTION VERSUS UNDERSTANDING

As in Chapter 1 when the goals of science were discussed, we must consider the purpose of the activity being undertaken. For the novelist, it is sufficient to entertain and to provide something of interest to the reader. If he succeeds further in creating an emotional bond of recognition and empathy and identification between reader and fictional creation, the real artistic goal is achieved. For the psychiatrist, as an applied medical scientist, presumably the diagnostic goal is paramount. With an adequate nosological system, a sufficient body of knowledge, and well-developed techniques for accurate diagnosis, the determination of the proper label would provide a considerable amount of useful information about an individual. The problem unfortunately is that the actual situation is quite different from that. Quite possibly the basic idea of a medical model for behavioral problems represents an inadequate and inaccurate approach because maladjusted behavior is not a disease caused by some biological agent. At best, however, the present state of knowledge renders the diagnostic goal less useful in psychiatry than in other fields of medicine. At the present time, diagnostic labels serve primarily a descriptive function rather than a predictive one.

In the role of applied behavioral scientists, the clinical psychologist brings to the problem the potential of a quite different framework. The goal of personality description need not be entertainment, interest value, emotional involvement of the reader, or diagnostic label. Most important, there is no reason to attempt to provide understanding or to help anyone "get the feel" of the person being described. Rather, the task is to say something meaningful, to provide predictive accuracy.

Continuing Holt's contrast of the goals of art and science:

There is a legitimate art of personality, literary biography. An artist like Andre Maurois is not hindered by not being a scientist of any kind. We should recognize that an artist's quest for "truth" differs from a scientist's in being a striving not for strict verisimilitude but for allusive illumination; its criterion is the effect on some audience—something to which science must remain indifferent.

Since some personologists (notably Freud, Murphy, Allport, and Murray) have had much of the artist in them as well as the scientist and have been masters of prose writing, it is no wonder that at times the artistic side of their identities has come uppermost. If Allport had been less aesthetically sensitive, he might not have failed to distinguish between artistic and scientific goals. Often, too, poor scientists are at the same time poor writers, and an inferior case study may be poor either because its facts are wrong and its interpretations undiscerning, or because it is poorly put together and lacks the literary touch that can put the breath of life into even a routine case report. The more art a scientist possesses—so long as he does not let it run away with him—the more effective a scientist he can be, because he can use his aesthetic sense in constructing theory as well as in communicating his findings and ideas to others [Holt, 1962, p. 390].

The importance of prediction versus understanding is more than just a scientific bias. In the pragmatic world of the clinic, the industrial concern, or the courtroom, a great need exists for accurate predictions about specific behaviors. Word pictures which provide a vague feeling of understanding by way of untestable propositions are of questionable utility. In an article criticizing the assertions of some psychologists giving expert testimony in courts of law, Jeffery presented excerpts from court transcripts of insanity cases in which psychologists testified concerning test findings:

Q. What does this drawing that Kent [the defendant] made for another psychologist indicate to you?

A. The transparency of the picture—that is, seeing through the figure to something beneath—suggests pathology.

Q. Do you usually use an extensive battery of tests before reaching a diagnosis?

A. Yes.

Q. Do you usually arrive at the diagnosis on the basis of one Rorschach administered twice within an hour?

A. Frequently.

Q. What else in the drawing is significant psychologically?

A. The irregularity or sketchiness of the lines may suggest tension and anxiety. The attention paid to details—to the belt-bow-tie, and pockets—indicate a little-boy-like quality about the defendant.

Q. Is it significant that the figure is running to the left, and not to the right?

A. To some people, yes. I don't place any significance on it.

Q. What about this drawing, made by Kent for another psychologist? What is significant about it?

A. The minimization of the breasts and the three lines across the genital area indicate tension in the sexual area. Breasts are symbolic of motherhood and early infant experiences. By minimizing the breasts the defendant indicates he has not received the satisfaction from women he had hoped to.

Q. Now, I will show you the picture Kent drew for you on September 9, 1961. What is significant about it?

A. The overemphasis of the breasts indicates how upset the defendant was because his father had been announced [Jeffery, 1964, p. 841].

The type of questions asked suggest to some degree the negative light in which such descriptive statements about personality may be cast. Jeffery quotes a more direct negative response from the judge trying a similar case:

(On questioning concerning the Szondi Test, the witness testified that a psychologist could diagnose illness by the pictures a subject selected as those he liked or disliked. At this point the judge threw the cards down. At a Bench conference the defense attorney asked: "May the record reflect that after the last question the Court slammed the cards down?")

Court. The record may reflect it but the record may show I am throwing it all out. That will take care of that session [Jeffery, 1964, p. 843].

THE CONTRIBUTION OF CASE HISTORY MATERIAL

What is the role of background data or the subject's case history if our only goal is that of prediction? Consider for a moment the following individual.

Charles is a 28 year old unmarried clerk whose education was terminated after he graduated from high school. He was the third of five children, and his family regularly attended the Lutheran church in their small rural community.

He describes both his father and mother as affectionate. His father has been a semi-invalid for some years, and his early home conditions were perceived as constituting near-poverty. Charles expressed some feelings of dislike toward school, had a relatively poor record of deportment, but earned fairly good grades.

After leaving high school, he obtained a position as a clerk in a small store, expresses his enjoyment of his occupation, and has done well at it. His approach to religion is on a shallow and intellectualized level, and his participation is little more than a formal ritual acquired from his parents.

Charles has had an average number of dates, but his hetero-sexual adjustment is described as relatively poor. He does not have an adequate sexual outlet. Otherwise, his social adjustment is relatively good, and he seems to be adept in social skills and poise. His recreational interests include a mixture of solitary and social pursuits. His interests are broad, his level of aspiration high, and he has a clear life plan. With respect to stability, Charles is described as moderately variable.

Now, what do we know about Charles that we did not know before—with respect to being able to make predictive statements about him? Very little. In fact, all that we can assert with greater than chance accuracy is that Charles is more likely to be characterized as normal than as schizophrenic. This statement is based on the fact that Charles is a hypothetical individual drawn from an excellent, but rare, investigation of the meaning of case history data.

Schofield and Balian [1959] obtained comprehensive personal history statistics of a sample of 178 schizophrenics at the University of Minnesota Hospitals. For comparison purposes, a group of 150 normals were investigated. These subjects consisted of hospital patients, hospital employees, students, employees of a large industrial firm, and office workers. By "normal" is meant that each of the subjects was free of psychiatric disturbance and had no history of a previous mental disorder. Further, the normals were matched with the schizophrenics with respect to age, sex, and marital status. Each subject was given a comprehensive clinical interview lasting 45 to 90 minutes. In our "case history" of Charles, the first paragraph simply describes the modal normal subject. All of the other "facts" are simply items which were significantly more true of the normal sample than of the schizophrenic sample. Schofield and Balian say:

The single most impressive feature of the data . . . is the sizable overlap of the normal Ss and schizophrenic patients in the distributions of the various personal history variables. Of the 35 separate tests which were run, 13 (or 37%) failed to reveal a reliable difference between the two samples. Further, on 5 of the remaining 22 variables, the distributions showed a reliably greater presence in the normals of negative or undesirable conditions. In those instances where the statistical tests did indicate a reliable characterization of the schizophrenics by prevalence of a pathogenic variable, the normals generally also showed a closely approximating degree of the same factor [Schofield and Balian, 1959, p. 222].

They go on to suggest:

It seems necessary that we turn some of our research energies toward a discovery of those circumstances or experiences of life which either contribute directly to mental health and emotional stability or which serve to delimit or erase the effects of pathogenic events. For this purpose, we will need to make extensive psychological study of the biographies of normal persons as well as of patients, with such biographies recorded so that their coverage and uniformity facilitate analysis [Schofield and Balian, 1959, p. 224].

Until or unless a vast body of such data becomes available, little or nothing will be gained by including case history material in our descriptions of personality. Other than a dubious literary exercise or the possible titilation of vicarious keyhole peeking, case history material would seem to belong on data sheets in research projects rather than providing an aura of facts which actually serve no function.

In another sense case history material could be useful as a research tool. At the observational stage of scientific inquiry, perhaps a large body of such material could be studied for the purpose of yielding generalizations about human behavior. Holt suggests:

Writing case studies (on the genesis and structure of individual personalities) turns out not to be a particularly fruitful method, except for the generation of hypotheses. This is a very important exception, but the point is that personology does not proceed mainly by adding one exhaustive scientific biography to another, looking for generalization afterwards [Holt, 1962, p. 399].

CONTRIBUTION OF GENERAL TRUTHS

          Another class of material appears in personality descriptions. Before discussing them, let us examine another brief personality sketch.

Mr. Syme is a personnel manager in a large firm. He has a great need to be liked and admired by others. He tends to be self-critical and, perhaps in part because of this, has a great deal of unused capacity which he has not turned to his advantage. It has generally been possible for him to compensate for his few personality weaknesses in the pursuit of one of his major life goals: security.

To some degree, sexual adjustment has presented him with problems. He is disciplined and self-controlled outwardly, but he is inwardly worrisome and insecure. At times, he has serious doubts as to whether he has made the right decision or done the right thing. Some of his aspirations tend to be pretty unrealistic.

Mr. Syme prefers a certain amount of change and variety; he becomes dissatisfied when hemmed in by restrictions and limitations. He prides himself as an independent thinker and does not accept others' statements without satisfactory proof.

He has found it unwise to be too frank in revealing himself to others. At times, he is extroverted, affable, and sociable while at other times he is introverted, wary, and reserved.

What has been said about Mr. Syme? The statements in the above description were gathered by Forer [1949] from dream books and astrology charts. Stagner [1958] utilized them in a demonstration with a group of 168 personnel managers attending a conference at the University of Illinois. They were given a personality inventory and told that each would be given a personality analysis based on his responses. Actually, each man received the same "personality analysis" in the form of statements such as those used above. Before the subjects were told of the deception, they filled out a questionnaire indicating their evaluation of the report's validity in describing themselves. Half of the subjects marked the description as "amazingly accurate." The remainder divided between "rather good" (40 per cent) and "about half and half" (10 per cent). In similar studies, 62 per cent of a group of college students and 81 per cent of a class of industrial supervisors considered that the characterization of themselves was amazingly accurate or rather good. As Stagner indicates, the propositions are so general that they can apply to anyone. They consist of glittering generalizations which apply to almost everybody and hence are distinctive for no one. In terms of prediction, they obviously supply no differential information.

In a similar vein, Schaefer [1948] defines interpretation in psychological reports as predictions about the subject. He cautions against what he calls "free rides" which are vague general statements that pass as meaningful interpretations, such as "adjustment problems in difficult situations," "primitive impulses are active," and "occasionally becomes evasive."

The "general truths" of the type described here say no more about a given individual than would a statement indicating that he is a human being raised in the contemporary American culture. Of course, general truths which involve established behavioral laws applicable to all individuals would be *extremely* useful for predictive purposes. Still no reason would exist to include them in the personality description of a *specific individual*. To do so would be like describing the qualities of a specific automobile by stating Newton's laws of motion.

CONTRIBUTION OF KNOWLEDGE CONCERNING
PERSONALITY DIMENSIONS

Though they do not produce an exciting flow of descriptive prose, an individual's scores on a variety of personality dimensions do provide a considerable amount of information relevant for behavior prediction. Given a body of data concerning a particular dimension, the fact that an individual obtains a specific score on an instrument designed to measure that dimension permits a large number of greater than chance predictions to be made about him.

As an example, let us take authoritarianism as measured by the California F Scale. With just the research findings presented in Chapter 8, what could you say about a person who obtains a given score? Normative data with respect to the scale permits one to state where he stands in relation to other people on this particular dimension and with respect to the ideology represented by the individual items. More importantly, perhaps, quite specific predictions could be made about his attitudes concerning family structure along an autocratic-democratic continuum, the type of disciplinary techniques he prefers to use with children, his perception of the punitiveness of his parents, his relative restrictiveness or permissiveness in child-rearing attitudes, the authoritarianism of his parents, and the authoritarianism of his spouse. Still other predictions could be made concerning his attitudes toward Jews, his degree of ethnocentrism, his attitudes toward Negroes, the type of hostility expressed in his dreams and on a measure of manifest hostility, his response to a war game situation, his political and economic conservatism, his response to the idea of socialized medicine, his voting behavior in any given election, his reaction when faced by a requirement to sign a noncommunist loyalty oath, his acceptance of the ideology of the armed services, his response to some MMPI scales, the probability of his offspring being maladjusted, his relative tolerance or intolerance of certain types of ambiguity, his intelligence and scores on several aptitude tests, his grade-point average, his religious preferences, and the regularity of his church attendance. In specified situations, one could predict his ability to perceive ambiguous sexual and aggressive stimuli, his response to fictional characters portraying sexual roles, his evaluation of the artistic depiction of nudes as pornographic, his tendency to conform to group pressure, his behavior and effectiveness as a leader in a group situation, the likelihood of his being nominated as a leader by his peers, his rigidity, and his resistance to changing his opinion on the basis of new data. Finally, one could specify certain conditions under which his authoritarianism would be expected to increase or decrease.

At this point in the development of the field, the above statements are somewhat grandiose, even though they are conservative when compared with statements made in many personality descriptions. Some of the behavior predicted above could be ascertained much more easily and accurately with a direct approach (for example, religious preference). If anything of importance depended on the decision made, further research data would be essential with respect to many of the predictions. Finally, some of the predictions, even though of greater-than-chance accuracy, account for only a small proportion of the variance of the behavior to be predicted. For example, while choice of a particular political candidate is related to authoritarianism, voting behavior is a function of many other variables in addition to that measured by the F Scale. Such limitations obviously are not unique to predictions based on personality dimensions.

Ideally, one could know more about an individual than simply his score on one personality measure. What could be predicted on the basis of knowing an individual's score on several dimensions? As an exercise, the student should list the predictions that could be made about an individual's behavior if he had taken the California F Scale, a series of n Ach pictures, the Manifest Anxiety Scale, the Wechsler Adult Intelligence Scale, and a self-ideal Q-sort.

We can envision a time at which a large number of well-designed and highly reliable personality tests are available along with a large body of research findings dealing with the antecedents, correlates, and consequents of each. With such a battery of measuring devices (10 tests?, 20 tests?, 100 tests?), the scores made by an individual would yield a profile describing his standing on each dimension. A further step (probably carried out by a computer in which all relevant data were stored) would be the determination of *all* other behaviors which would be predicted on the basis of the person's scores on the various tests and combinations of tests. The end result might be a profile sheet plus a long list of predictive statements and the relative accuracy or range of confidence of each.

The way of arriving at such a set of dimensions is a matter of controversy. One major approach is the piecemeal, one-variable-at-a-time research described throughout this text. The other major approach involves the use of many variables at a time and the clarification of the underlying dimensions involved by means of factor analysis. Tests emerging from this multivariate, factor-analytic methodology should constitute internally homogeneous dimensions relatively independent of one another. Proponents of the multivariate approach include H. J. Eysenck at the University of London, J. P. Guilford at the University of Southern California, and Raymond B. Cattell at the University of Illinois. Psychologists in both camps could agree on the goal, but they differ in their estimate of the best strategy. One could argue, for example, that the clarification of personality dimensions via factor analysis would be more meaningful after a period of time spent in isolating and operationalizing and conducting research with individual variables. Cattell argues that the dimensions should be determined as a preliminary step in personality research:

> . . . at this primitive stage of personality research especially, the multivariate method offers a swifter and surer approach to the significant variables for controlled experimentation. In personality, as in psychology and the life sciences as a whole, the investigator has an *infinite* array of variables from which to choose. It is not surprising—and is perhaps a comment on our ways of striving for originality—that one and the same empirical (not conceptual) variable rarely gets confirmatory investigation by as many as two psychologists. Apparently, there are at least as many variables claimed to be of outstanding significance as there are psychologists [Cattell, 1959, p. 263].

However the dimensions are determined, agreement exists that a finite set will ultimately be specified. If personality description were defined in terms of an individual's profile of scores on the dimensions, the product would be quite different from that of the novelist, the psychiatrist, or the present clinical psychologist. Personality description as an art form would have given way to personality description as a series of predictions about the probable behavior of a given person. A number of psychologists, including Cattell, believe that this is precisely what the field of personality is all about:

> *Personality is that which permits a prediction of what a person will do in a given situation.* The goal of psychological research in personality is thus to establish laws about what different people will do in all kinds of social and general environmental situations [Cattell, 1950, pp. 2–3].

Cattell's emphasis on prediction *in a given situation* brings us back to the point made in Chapter 1. When psychologists conceptualize a predictive science of behavior, this is done in terms of the prediction of responses made to particular stimuli. Thus, general laws of behavior take the form: $R = f(S)$. The contribution of knowledge about personality is the refinement or further specification of those laws in order to permit the differential prediction of the behavior of individuals.

HAS PERSONALITY "EVAPORATED IN A MIST OF METHOD"?

Returning to Allport's criticism of the operational approach and positivistic behaviorism, can we now say that his criticisms have been answered? When we assemble a personality profile based on scores obtained from a large battery of measures and make a series of predictions with greater-than-chance accuracy, have we reconstructed in scientific form the sort of personality which Allport and others are talking about?

In one sense, the answer must be no. Allport [1961, pp. xi–xii] says: "My own view is that, taken in the large, the evidence before us does not depict man as a reactive robot." However, as the knowledge of biological functioning, cellular chemistry, the molecular secrets of heredity, and even of responses evoked by stimuli grows more complete each day, the conception of man inexorably changes. Those who conceive of man as something uniquely different in the universe, operating with some degree of independence from natural laws, and having special qualities placing him forever beyond the realm of science are increasingly hard-pressed by contrary evidence. The special qualities of man are suggested by Allport: "He is more than a bundle of habits, more than a point of intersection of abstract dimensions. He is more than a representative of his species, more than a citizen of the state, more than an incident in the movements of mankind. He transcends them all" [Allport, 1961, p. 573]. There is a tinge of nostalgia in contrasting the poetic figure of man as historically pictured with the mechanistic picture which has been emerging over the past century or two. But, man has had to adjust to a universe in which his planet is not the hub and to a classification of himself as one of the species of primates in an evolutionary chain; surely the idea of man's behavior being lawfully determined by antecedents presents a threat of no greater magnitude.

In another sense, the emerging conception of human personality in quantified, predictable terms does, in fact, encompass the sort of phenomena described by the nonbehavioristic theorists. This is not as if knowledge about man's behavior and the ability to predict and control it will destroy the human qualities which we value. When we know the relationship between pressure applied to the keys of a piano and the nature of the subsequent vibrations of air molecules, the music is no less beautiful. Knowledge of antecedent-consequent relationships in behavior will not somehow prevent the occurrence of a Shakespeare or a Brahms or a Lincoln or an Einstein. On the contrary, future developments may enable us to increase the incidence of such personalities and to decrease the incidence of less desirable personalities. It might be said that behavioral science allows us to eat our cake and have it, too.

The General Utility of Personality Description

NEED FOR PERSONALITY DESCRIPTION

At that distant date when all basic personality dimensions have been identified and an enormous body of data has been assembled, the task of producing a complete personality description of just one subject will be a formidable one. Testing time alone might well consume days or even weeks. The task of scoring the test instruments and assembling the data could presumably be adapted to mechanical and electronic procedures. The outcome (profile plus predictive statements) which describes one individual could quite conceivably constitute a good-sized book. Is it sufficiently worthwhile to obtain a complete personality description to warrant the required lavish expenditure of time, effort, and money?

Though we may only guess about a situation to arise in the future, the author's opinion is that the need for personality descriptions would be relatively limited. Only one major type of situation would seem to be clearly appropriate. When a key individual is being selected for a position in which his behavior in response to a variety of situations has widespread consequences for others, it would seem well worth the investment to be able to predict his behavior as accurately and as completely as possible. Examples are candidates for the presidency, astronauts to be sent on a long and arduous exploratory mission, and potential board chairmen of large corporations. Knowledge of every strength and weakness of such individuals in responding to many different stimulus situations could obviously be of crucial importance.

If these possibilities arouse fears of a regimented future world, the points made in Chapter 1 concerning the application of scientific knowledge should be noted again. Decisions must be made about presidential candidates, astronauts, and board chairmen. The only question is on what basis they are made and the relationship between the decision and the ensuing consequences.

AN ALTERNATIVE USE FOR PERSONALITY VARIABLES

When examined closely, most predictions now made by psychologists in applied settings are in relation to one or at most to a very limited number of questions. Thus, we find questions involving academic potential, ability to sell life insurance, likelihood of committing suicide, marital compatibility of two individuals, ability to benefit from psychotherapy, ability to drive an automobile safely, and so on and so forth. Answers to specific questions of this type are not likely to require exhaustive knowledge of each individual's total personality. For the most part, personality descriptions would represent a waste of time on irrelevancies.

With a specific criterion behavior to be predicted, the task would be to determine which combination of personality variables (appropriately weighted) yield the best predictive statement. This approach is, of course, already utilized in a great many decision-making situations. What is needed is more and better knowledge of personality variables and their relevance to the behavior which we wish to predict.

We must consider one final and more futuristic possibility. Conceivably the time will come when the task is not that of making decisions about individuals on the basis of appropriate personality factors. Rather, we will be able to alter the personality structure of the individual to insure maximal performance in the situation. For example, instead of allowing only safe drivers to obtain licences, the aim would be to bring about the necessary changes in the unsafe drivers.

One criticism which is sometimes raised against the idea of changing behavior in the manner suggested here is that we would be moving toward a homogeneous, colorless, bland society. The specter arises of mindless masses marching in lock-step. Certainly such an outcome is not a necessary result of instituting personality changes. An analogy is provided by the application of medical science. Compared to the previous century, we now have greater homogeneity in that, for example, people need no longer be disfigured by smallpox, be crippled by poliomyelitis, or be labeled as lepers to roam the countryside with a warning bell hanging from their necks. Even in the social sphere, sufficient changes have been brought about to remove some of the color and interest of previous times. We can no longer see galley slaves rowing great ships, attend public executions as a family outing, or visit the auction block to buy one's servants and laborers. Equally great changes in personality would deprive us of the human variety represented by schizophrenics, juvenile delinquents, sadists, mentally retarded individuals, or neurotics. Rather than bland human robots, the individuals of the future can be creative, bright, happy, democratic, kind, and so on within the limits of our applied skills and the values of our society.

Man has refused to accept the limitations imposed by his physical and biological world. Transportation, communication, temperature, physical health, and conception, for example, are increasingly under man's control. We have no reason to believe that behavior should be or will be left out of man's technological progress.

Summary

Most definitions of personality include some aspect of a unified description of an individual. If personality is defined in terms of a collection of traits or a series of dimensions, the problem of combining separate bits of information to describe a person is sometimes seen as a difficult one.

Personality description began with novelists who over the centuries developed techniques which infused life and individuality into fictional characters. Authors tend to present a description of the physical attributes of the individual, often something about the parents and the childhood and the early experiences of the person, and a great deal about the character's specific behavior and general traits. Psychiatrists have the traditional medical interest in symptoms and diagnoses which (at least eventually) should convey information about the cause, course, and treatment for specific behavioral problems. In addition, an attempt is made to describe personality in much the way that novelists do. Clinical psychologists have tended to follow the pattern of psychiatrists with respect to such descriptions except that they add a scientific concern with evidence and with prediction.

The goals of those engaged in personality description are varied. The novelist hopes to entertain and engage the emotions of the reader. The psychiatrist strives for diagnostic accuracy. The primary goals of the clinical psychologist include accurate prediction. The reason for describing the personality of an individual is to make possible the prediction of behavior rather than to elicit a feeling of understanding in those who read the description. From this viewpoint, items of case history information serve no purpose in personality description unless evidence shows that particular background data lead to a specific prediction. General truths which hold for almost everyone serve no purpose in descriptions of personality. In contrast, knowledge of an individual's score on a measure of a personality dimension provides a considerable amount of predictive information to the extent that research has been done with that dimension. If an individual's standing on each of several personality dimensions were known, a very large number of behavior predictions could be made. A battery of measuring devices would yield an individual's personality profile. This in turn could yield a long list of predictive statements (based on existing research) concerning that individual. The most appropriate strategy for arriving at the best possible set of dimensions is a matter of some controversy. Approaches vary from univariate research in which one variable at a time is isolated and investigated to multivariate research in which many variables are investigated simultaneously in order to clarify the underlying dimensions by means of factor analysis. The conception of personality in antecedent-consequent terms does not satisfy some theorists, but the lawfulness of man as a biological organism becomes more and more difficult to refute.

In the future, when all basic personality dimensions have been identified and an enormous body of data has been assembled, the task of producing a complete personality description of just one subject will be a formidable one. Very likely the need for such a description will be limited. Possibly the only justifiable use will be when a key individual is being selected for a position in which his behavior in response to a variety of situations has wide-spread consequences for others. Much more frequently, the problem of behavior prediction arises in relation to one or at most to a very limited number of questions. With a specific criterion behavior in a specific situation to be predicted, the task would be to determine which combination of personality variables (appropriately weighted) yields the best predictive statement. A more distant possibility is the development of psychological technology which will enable man to alter the personality structure of an individual in order to insure maximal performance in the situation.

References

Abelson, P. H. Prestige. *Science*, 1964, **145**, 771.

Abrams, L. Aggressive behavior in the authoritarian personality. Unpublished doctoral dissertation, University of Texas, 1964.

Achenbach, T., and Zigler, E. Social competence and self-image disparity in psychiatric and nonpsychiatric patients. *J. abnorm. soc. Psychol.*, 1963, **67**, 197–205.

Adams, H. B., Cooper, G. D., and Carrera, R. N. The Rorschach and the MMPI: A concurrent validity study. *J. proj. Tech.*, 1963, **27**, 23–34.

Ader, R., and Belfer, M. L. Prenatal maternal anxiety and offspring emotionality in the rat. *Psychol. Rep.*, 1962, **10**, 711–718.

————, and Conklin, P. M. Handling of pregnant rats: Effects on emotionality of their offspring. *Science*, 1963, **142**, 411–412.

Adorno, T. W., Frenkel-Brunswik, Else, Levinson, D. J., and Sanford, R. N. *The authoritarian personality*. New York: Harper, 1950.

Albee, G. W., Lane, Ellen A., Corcoran, Clare, and Werneke, Ann. Childhood and intercurrent intellectual performance of adult schizophrenics. *J. consult. Psychol.*, 1963, **27**, 364–366.

Allport, G. W. *Pattern and growth in personality*. New York: Holt, Rinehart and Winston, 1961.

Alpert, R., and Haber, R. N. Anxiety in academic achievement situations. *J. abnorm. soc. Psychol.*, 1960, **61**, 207–215.

Altrocchi, J., Parsons, O. A., and Dickoff, Hilda. Changes in self-ideal discrepancy in repressors and sensitizers. *J. abnorm. soc. Psychol.*, 1960, **61**, 67–72.

American Psychological Association, Committee on Psychological Tests. *Technical standards for psychological and educational tests*. Washington, D.C.: APA, in press.

Anastasi, Anne. Intelligence and family size. *Psychol. Bull.*, 1956, **53**, 187–209.

———. *Differential psychology*. 3rd Ed. New York: Macmillan, 1958.

———, and d'Angelo, R. Y. A comparison of Negro and white preschool children in language development and Goodenough Draw-a-Man IQ. *J. genet. Psychol.*, 1952, **81**, 147–165.

Angyal, A. *Foundations for a science of personality*. New York: Commonwealth Fund, 1941.

Aronson, E. The need for achievement as measured by graphic expression. In J. W. Atkinson (Ed.), *Motives in fantasy, action, and society*. Princeton: Van Nostrand, 1958. Pp. 249–265.

———, and Carlsmith, J. M. The effect of the severity of threat on the devaluation of forbidden behavior. *J. abnorm. soc. Psychol.*, 1963, **66**, 584–588.

Asch, S. E. Studies of independence and submission to group pressure: 1. A minority of one against a unanimous majority. *Psychol. Monogr.*, 1956, **70** (Whole No. 416).

Astin, A. W., and Ross, S. Glutamic acid and human intelligence. *Psychol. Bull.*, 1960, **57**, 429–434.

Atkinson, J. W. The achievement motive and recall of interrupted and completed tasks. *J. exp. Psychol.*, 1953, **46**, 381–390.

———. Explorations using imaginative thought to assess the strength of human motives. In M. R. Jones (Ed.), *Nebraska symposium on motivation 1954*. Lincoln: University of Nebraska Press, 1954. Pp. 56–112.

———. Motivational determinants of risk-taking behavior. *Psychol. Rev.*, 1957, **64**, 359–372.

———. *An introduction to motivation*. Princeton: Van Nostrand, 1964.

———, Heyns, R. W., and Veroff, J. The effect of experimental arousal of the affiliation motive on thematic apperception. *J. abnorm. soc. Psychol.*, 1954, **49**, 405–410.

———, and Litwin, G. H. Achievement motive and test anxiety conceived as motive to approach success and motive to avoid failure. *J. abnorm. soc. Psychol.*, 1960, **60**, 52–63.

———, and McClelland, D. C. The projective expression of needs. II. The effect of different intensities of the hunger drive on thematic apperception. *J. exp. Psychol.*, 1948, **38**, 643–658.

———, and Reitman, W. R. Performance as a function of motive strength and expectancy of goal-attainment. *J. abnorm. soc. Psychol.*, 1956, **53**, 361–366.

———, and Walker, E. L. The affiliation motive and perceptual sensitivity to faces. *J. abnorm. soc. Psychol.*, 1956, **53**, 38–41.

Aumack, L. Effects of imprisonment upon authoritarian attitudes. *Psychol. Rep.*, 1956, **2**, 39–42.

Ax, A. F. The physiological differentiation between fear and anger in humans. *Psychosom. Med.*, 1953, **15**, 433–442.

Bailey, M. A., Berrick, M. E., Lachmann, F. M., and Ortmyer, D. H. Manifest anxiety in psychiatric outpatients. *J. clin. Psychol.*, 1960, **16**, 209–210.

Ball, R. S. The predictability of occupational level from intelligence. *J. consult. Psychol.*, 1938, **2**, 184–186.

Bandura, A., Ross, Dorothea, and Ross, Sheila A. Imitation of film-mediated aggressive models. *J. abnorm. soc. Psychol.*, 1963, **66**, 3–11.

Banta, T. J., and Hetherington, Mavis. Relations between needs of friends and finances. *J. abnorm. soc. Psychol.*, 1963, **66**, 401–404.

Barron, F. Some personality correlates of independence of judgment. *J. Pers.*, 1953, **21**, 287–297.

———. Threshold for the perception of human movement in inkblots. *J. consult. Psychol.*, 1955, **19**, 33–38.

———. Originality in relation to personality and intellect. *J. Pers.*, 1957, **25**, 730–742.

———, and Leary, T. F. Changes in psychoneurotic patients with and without psychotherapy. *J. consult. Psychol.*, 1955, **19**, 239–245.

Bass, B. M. Authoritarianism or acquiescence? *J. abnorm. soc. Psychol.*, 1955, **51**, 616–623.

Bayley, Nancy. Some increasing parent-child similarities during the growth of children. *J. educ. Psychol.*, 1954, **45**, 1–21.

———. On the growth of intelligence. *Amer. Psychologist*, 1955, **10**, 805–818.

———, and Oden, Melita H. The maintenance of intellectual ability in gifted adults. *J. Gerontology*, 1955, **10**, 91–107.

———, and Schaefer, E. S. Relationships between socio-economic variables and the behavior of mothers toward young children. *J. genet. Psychol.*, 1960, **96**, 61–77.

Bechtoldt, H. P. Response defined anxiety and MMPI variables. *Iowa Acad. Sci.*, 1953, **60**, 495–499.

———. Construct validity: A critique. *Amer. Psychologist*, 1959, **14**, 619–629.

Bendig, A. W. Predictive and postdictive validity of need achievement measures. *J. educ. Res.*, 1958, **52**, 119–120.

———. Personality variables related to individual performance on a cognitive task. *J. gen. Psychol.*, 1959, **60**, 265–268. (a)

———. An inter-item factor analysis of the California F (Authoritarianism) Scale. *J. psychol. Stud.*, 1959, **11**, 22–26. (b)

———. A further factor analysis of the California F (Authoritarianism) Scale. *J. psychol. Stud.*, 1960, **11**, 248–252.

Benedict, R., and Weltfish, G. *Races of mankind.* New York: Public Affairs Comm., 1943.

Bentz, V. J. A test-retest experiment in the relationship between age and mental ability. *Amer. Psychologist*, 1953, **8**, 319–320. (abstract)

Bergmann, G., and Spence, K. W. The logic of psychophysical measurement. *Psychol. Rev.*, 1944, **51**, 1–24.

————. Theoretical psychology. In C. P. Stone and D. W. Taylor (Eds.), *Annual review of psychology*. Vol. 4. Stanford, California: Annual Reviews, 1953.

Berlew, D. The achievement motive and the growth of Greek civilization. Unpublished bachelor's thesis, Wesleyan University, 1956.

Binet, A. *L'étude expérimentale de l'intelligence*. (1903) Paris: Alfred Costes, 1922.

————. *Les idées modernes sur les enfants*. Paris: Ernest Flamarion, 1909. Cited in Stoddard, G. D. The IQ: Its ups and downs. *Educ. Rec.*, 1939, **20**, 44–57.

Birney, R. C. The reliability of the achievement motive. *J. abnorm. soc. Psychol.*, 1959, **58**, 266–267.

Blazek, N. C., and Harlow, H. F. Persistence of performance differences on discriminations of varying difficulty. *J. comp. physiol. Psychol.*, 1955, **48**, 86–89.

Block, J. Personality characteristics associated with fathers' attitudes toward child-rearing. *Child Develpm.*, 1955, **26**, 41–48.

————, and Thomas, H. Is satisfaction with self a measure of adjustment? *J. abnorm. soc. Psychol.*, 1955, **51**, 254–259.

Bloom, K. L. Age and the self concept. *Amer. J. Psychiat.*, 1961, **118**, 534–538.

Boatman, Maleta J., and Szurek, S. A. A clinical study of childhood schizophrenia. In D. D. Jackson (Ed.), *The etiology of schizophrenia*. New York: Basic Books, 1960. Pp. 389–440.

Bobrow, D. G. *Natural language input for a computer problem solving system.* Cambridge: MAC-TR-1, Project MAC, M.I.T., 1964.

Bonney, M. E. A sociometric study of the relationship of some factors to mutual friendships on the elementary, secondary, and college levels. *Sociometry*, 1946, **9**, 21–47.

Book, J. A. Genetical aspects of schizophrenic psychoses. In D. D. Jackson (Ed.), *The etiology of schizophrenia*. New York: Basic Books, 1960. Pp. 23–36.

Boring, E. G. *A history of experimental psychology*. (2nd ed.) New York: Appleton, 1950.

————. Cognitive dissonance: Its use in science. *Science*, 1964, **145**, 680–685.

Boswell, J. *The life of Samuel Johnson L.L.D.* (1791) Vol. 2. New York: Heritage, 1963.

Bounds, C. E. Authoritarianism and authoritarian aggression. Unpublished doctoral dissertation, University of Texas, 1964.

Brackbill, G., and Little, K. B. MMPI correlates of the Taylor scale of Manifest Anxiety. *J. consult. Psychol.*, 1954, **18**, 433–436.

Brackbill, Yvonne. Extinction of the smiling response in infants as a function of reinforcement schedule. *Child Develpm.*, 1958, **29**, 115–124.

Bradburn, N. M. N Achievement and father dominance in Turkey. *J. abnorm. soc. Psychol.*, 1963, **67**, 464–468.

Bradbury, R. *Fahrenheit 451*. New York: Ballantine, 1953.

Bradway, K. P., Thompson, C. W., and Cravens, R. B. Preschool IQs after twenty-five years. *J. educ. Psychol.*, 1958, **49**, 278–281.

Brophy, I. N. The luxury of anti-Negro prejudice. *Publ. opin. Quart.*, 1956, **9**, 456–466.

Brown, J. S. *The motivation of behavior*. New York: McGraw-Hill, 1961.

Brown, R. W. A determinant of the relationship between rigidity and authoritarianism. *J. abnorm. soc. Psychol.*, 1953, **48**, 469–476.

Bruce, M. Factors affecting intelligence test performance of whites and Negroes in the rural South. *Arch. Psychol.*, 1940, No. 252.

Budner, S. Intolerance of ambiguity as a personality variable. *J. Pers.*, 1962, **30**, 29–50.

Bugental, J. F. T. Humanistic psychology: A new break-through. *Amer. Psychologist*, 1963, **18**, 563–567.

Burchinal, L. G. Social status, measured intelligence, achievement, and personality adjustment of rural Iowa girls. *Sociometry*, 1959, **22**, 75–80.

Burks, Barbara S., Jensen, Dortha W., and Terman, L. M. *The promise of youth: Follow-up studies of a thousand gifted children*. Vol. III of *Genetic studies of genius*, Terman, L. M. (Ed.). Stanford: Stanford University Press, 1930.

Burris, R. W. The effect of counseling on achievement motivation. Unpublished doctoral dissertation, University of Indiana, 1958.

Burt, C. The inheritance of mental ability. *Amer. Psychologist*, 1958, **13**, 1–15.

————, Jones, E., Miller, E., and Moodie, W. *How the mind works*. New York: Appleton-Century-Crofts, 1934.

Buss, A. H. A follow-up item analysis of the Taylor Anxiety Scale. *J. clin. Psychol.*, 1955, **11**, 409–410.

————, Wiener, M., Durkee, A., and Baer, M. The measurement of anxiety in clinical situations. *J. consult. Psychol.*, 1955, **19**, 125–129.

Butler, J. M., and Haigh, G. V. Changes in the relation between self-concepts and ideal concepts consequent upon client-centered counseling. In C. R. Rogers and Rosalind F. Dymond (Eds.), *Psychotherapy and personality change*. Chicago: University of Chicago Press, 1954. Pp. 55–75.

Byrne, D. Drive level, response to humor, and the cartoon sequence effect. *Psychol. Rep.*, 1958, **4**, 439–442.

————. Interpersonal attraction and attitude similarity. *J. abnorm. soc. Psychol.*, 1961, **62**, 713–715. (a)

————. The Repression-Sensitization Scale: Rationale, reliability, and validity. *J. Pers.*, 1961, **29**, 334–349. (b)

——. Some inconsistencies in the effect of motivation arousal on humor preferences. *J. abnorm. soc. Psychol.*, 1961, **62**, 158–160. (c)

——. Response to attitude similarity-dissimilarity as a function of affiliation need. *J. Pers.*, 1962, **30**, 164–177.

——. Assessing personality variables and their alteration. In P. Worchel and D. Byrne (Eds.), *Personality change.* New York: Wiley, 1964. Pp. 38–68. (a)

——. Repression-sensitization as a dimension of personality. In B. A. Maher (Ed.), *Progress in experimental personality research.* New York: Academic Press, 1964. Pp. 169–220. (b)

——. Parental antecedents of authoritarianism. *J. pers. soc. Psychol.*, 1965, **1**, 369–373.

——, Barry, J., and Nelson, D. Relation of the revised Repression-Sensitization Scale to measures of self-description. *Psychol. Rep.*, 1963, **13**, 323–334.

——, and Blaylock, Barbara. Similarity and assumed similarity of attitudes between husbands and wives. *J. abnorm. soc. Psychol.*, 1963, **67**, 636–640.

——, and Bounds, C. The reversal of F Scale items. *Psychol. Rep.*, 1964, **14**, 216.

——, and Clore, G. The arousal of the competence motive. Unpublished manuscript, 1965.

——, Golightly, Carole, and Capaldi, E. J. Construction and validation of the Food Attitude Scale. *J. consult. Psychol.*, 1963, **27**, 215–222.

——, McDonald, R. D., and Mikawa, J. Approach and avoidance affiliation motives. *J. Pers.*, 1963, **31**, 21–37.

——, and Nelson, D. Attraction as a linear function of proportion of positive reinforcements. *J. pers. soc. Psychol.*, 1965, **1**, 659–663.

——, and Sheffield, J. Response to sexually arousing stimuli as a function of repressing and sensitizing defenses. *J. abnorm. Psychol.*, 1965, **70**, 114–118.

——, and Wong, T. J. Racial prejudice, interpersonal attraction, and assumed dissimilarity of attitudes. *J. abnorm. soc. Psychol.*, 1962, **65**, 246–253.

Calvin, A. D., and Holtzman, W. H. Adjustment and the discrepancy between self concept and inferred self. *J. consult. Psychol.*, 1953, **17**, 39–44.

——, Koons, P. B., Jr., Bingham, J. L., and Fink, H. H. A further investigation of the relationship between manifest anxiety and intelligence. *J. consult. Psychol.*, 1955, **19**, 280–282.

Cameron, N. *The psychology of behavior disorders: A bio-social interpretation.* Boston: Houghton Mifflin, 1947.

Camilleri, S. F. A factor analysis of the F-Scale. *Soc. Forces*, 1959, **37**, 316–323.

Carmichael, O. Television Program of Sept. 13, 1959. Report, Dec. 15, 1959, Southern Regional Council, Atlanta.

Cartwright, D. S. Self-consistency as a factor affecting immediate recall. *J. abnorm. soc. Psychol.*, 1956, **52**, 212–218.

Cattell, R. B. *Personality: A systematic, theoretical, and factual study.* New York: McGraw-Hill, 1950.

―――. Personality theory growing from multivariate quantitative research. In S. Koch (Ed.), *Psychology: A study of a science.* New York: McGraw-Hill, 1959. Pp. 257–327.

―――, Beloff, H., and Coan, R. W. *Handbook for the IPAT High School Personality Questionnaire.* Champaign, Ill.: Institute of Personality Ability Testing, 1958.

Chapman, L. J., and Campbell, D. T. Response set in the F Scale. *J. abnorm. soc. Psychol.*, 1957, **54**, 129–132.

―――, ―――. Absence of acquiescence response set in the Taylor Manifest Anxiety Scale. *J. consult. Psychol.*, 1959, **23**, 465–466.

Charles, D. C., and Pritchard, Sally A. Differential development of intelligence in the college years. *J. genet. Psychol.*, 1959, **95**, 41–44.

Chase, P. H. Self concepts in adjusted and maladjusted hospital patients. *J. consult. Psychol.*, 1957, **21**, 495–497.

Chodorkoff, B. Self-perception, perceptual defense, and adjustment. *J. abnorm. soc. Psychol.*, 1954, **49**, 508–512.

Christie, R. Changes in authoritarianism as related to situational factors. *Amer. Psychologist*, 1952, **7**, 307–308. (abstract)

―――, Havel, Joan, and Seidenberg, B. Is the F Scale irreversible? *J. abnorm. soc. Psychol.*, 1958, **56**, 143–159.

Clark, R. A., Teevan, R., and Ricciuti, H. N. Hope of success and fear of failure as aspects of need for achievement. *J. abnorm. soc. Psychol.*, 1956, **53**, 182–186.

Clark, W. W. Los Angeles Negro children. *Educ. Res. Bull., Los Angeles,* 1923, **3** (2), 1–2.

Cole, D., Jacobs, S., Zubok, Bea, Fagot, Beverly, and Hunter, I. The relation of achievement imagery scores to academic performance. *J. abnorm. soc. Psychol.*, 1962, **65**, 208–211.

Cole, Nyla J., Shaw, Orla M., Steneck, J., and Taboroff, L. H. A survey assessment of current parental attitudes and practices in child rearing. *Amer. J. Orthopsychiat.*, 1957, **27**, 815–822.

Conant, J. B. *On understanding science.* New York: New American Library, 1947.

Conrad, H. S., and Jones, H. E. A second study of familial resemblance in intelligence: environmental and genetic implications of parent-child and sibling correlations in the total sample. *39th Yearb., Nat. Soc. Stud. Educ.*, 1940, Part II, 97–141.

Cooper, J. F. *The deerslayer* (1841). New York: Heritage, 1961.

Cortes, J. B. The achievement motive in the Spanish economy between the 13th and 18th centuries. *Econ. Develpm. cult. change*, 1960, **9**, 144–163.

Cottle, W. C. Card versus booklet forms of the MMPI. *J. appl. Psychol.*, 1950, **34**, 255–259.

Couch, A., and Keniston, K. Yeasayers and naysayers: agreeing response set as a personality variable. *J. abnorm. soc. Psychol.*, 1960, **60**, 151–174.

Cowen, E. L., and Tongas, P. N. The social desirability of trait descriptive terms: applications to a self-concept inventory. *J. consult. Psychol.*, 1959, **23**, 361–365.

Cox, Catherine C. *The early mental traits of three hundred geniuses.* Vol. II of *Genetic studies of genius*, Terman, L. M. (Ed.). Stanford: Stanford University Press, 1926.

Cox, F. N. An assessment of the achievement behavior system in children. *Child Develpm.*, 1962, **33**, 907–916.

Cronbach, L. J. The two disciplines of scientific psychology. *Amer. Psychologist*, 1957, **12**, 671–684.

———. *Essentials of psychological testing.* (2nd ed.) New York: Harper, 1960.

Crowne, D. P., Stephens, M. W., and Kelly, R. The validity and equivalence of tests of self-acceptance. *J. Psychol.*, 1961, **51**, 101–112.

Crutchfield, R. S. Conformity and character. *Amer. Psychologist*, 1955, **10**, 191–198.

Dana, R. H. Manifest anxiety, intelligence, and psychopathology. *J. consult. Psychol.*, 1957, **21**, 38–40.

Darwin, C. *On the origin of species by means of natural selection.* (1859) New York: The Heritage Press, 1963.

———. *The expression of the emotions in man and animals.* New York: Appleton, 1897.

Davids, A. Some personality and intellectual correlates of intolerance of ambiguity. *J. abnorm. soc. Psychol.*, 1955, **51**, 415–420.

———. The influence of ego-involvement on relations between authoritarianism and intolerance of ambiguity. *J. consult. Psychol.*, 1956, **20**, 179–184.

———, DeVault, S., and Talmadge, M. Anxiety, pregnancy, and childbirth abnormalities. *J. consult. Psychol.*, 1961, **25**, 74–77.

———, and Eriksen, C. W. The relation of manifest anxiety to association productivity and intellectual attainment. *J. consult. Psychol.*, 1955, **19**, 219–222.

———, ———. Some social and cultural factors determining relations between authoritarianism and measures of neuroticism. *J. consult. Psychol.*, 1957, **21**, 155–159.

———, and Lawton, Marcia J. Self-concept, mother concept, and food aversions in emotionally disturbed and normal children. *J. abnorm. soc. Psychol.*, 1961, **62**, 309–314.

Davis, H. *The works of Plato.* Vol. II. London: Bohn, 1849.

Davidson, L. A. Adaptation to a threatening stimulus. Unpublished doctoral dissertation, University of California, Berkeley, 1963.

de Charms, R., and Moeller, G. H. Values expressed in American children's readers: 1800–1950. *J. abnorm. soc. Psychol.*, 1962, **64**, 135–142.

DeGroot, A. D. War and the intelligence of youth. *J. abnorm. soc. Psychol.*, 1951, **46**, 596–597.

Deutsch, M., and Collins, Mary E. *Interracial housing*. Minneapolis: University of Minnesota Press, 1951.

Dickens, C. A Christmas carol. (1843) In C. Dickens, *Five Christmas novels*. New York: Heritage Press, 1939. Pp. 17–88.

Dollard, J., Auld, F., and White, M. A. *Steps in psychotherapy*. New York: Macmillan, 1953.

———, Doob, L. W., Miller, N. E., and Sears, R. R. *Frustration and aggression*. New Haven: Yale University Press, 1939.

———, and Miller, N. E. *Personality and psychotherapy*. New York: McGraw-Hill, 1950.

Doob, L. W. The behavior of attitudes. *Psychol. Rev.*, 1947, **54**, 135–156.

Doris, J., and Fierman, Ella. Humor and anxiety. *J. abnorm. soc. Psychol.*, 1956, **53**, 59–62.

Drake, L. E. A Social I. E. Scale for the Minnesota Multiphasic Personality Inventory. *J. appl. Psychol.*, 1946, **30**, 51–54.

———, and Thiede, W. B. Further validation of the Social I. E. Scale for the Minnesota Multiphasic Personality Inventory. *J. educ. Res.*, 1948, **41**, 551–556.

Dunnette, M. D., Kirchner, W. K., and DeGidio, JoAnne. Relations among scores on Edwards Personal Preference Schedule, California Psychological Inventory, and Strong Vocational Interest Blank for an industrial sample. *J. appl. Psychol.*, 1958, **42**, 178–181.

Dworin, J., and Wyant, O. Authoritarian patterns in the mothers of schizophrenics. *J. clin. Psychol.*, 1957, **13**, 332–338.

Dymond, Rosalind F. Adjustment changes over therapy from self-sorts. In C. R. Rogers and Rosalind F. Dymond (Eds.), *Psychotherapy and personality change*. Chicago: University of Chicago Press, 1954. Pp. 76–84.

———. Adjustment changes in the absence of psychotherapy. *J. consult. Psychol.*, 1955, **19**, 103–107.

Dynes, R. R., Clarke, A. C., and Dinitz, S. Levels of occupational aspiration: some aspects of family experience as a variable. *Amer. Sociol. Rev.*, 1956, **21**, 212–215.

Ebbs, J. H., Tisdall, F. F., and Scott, W. A. The influence of prenatal diet on the mother and child. *Milbank Memorial Fund Quarterly*, 1942, **20**, 35–45.

Edwards, A. L. The relationship between the judged desirability of a trait and the probability that the trait will be endorsed. *J. appl. Psychol.*, 1953, **37**, 90–93.

———. *The social desirability variable in personality assessment and research*. New York: Dryden, 1957.

————. *Edwards Personal Preference Schedule manual.* New York: Psychological Corporation, 1959.

Eliasberg, W. G., and Stuart, I. R. Authoritarian personality and the obscenity threshold. *J. soc. Psychol.*, 1961, **55**, 143–151.

Elizur, A. Content analysis of the Rorschach with regard to anxiety and hostility. *Rorschach Res. Exch. and J. proj. Tech.*, 1949, **13**, 247–284.

Ellis, N. R. Object-quality discrimination learning sets in mental defectives. *J. comp. physiol. Psychol.*, 1958, **51**, 79–81.

Embree, R. B. The status of college students in terms of IQ's determined during childhood. *Amer. Psychologist*, 1948, **3**, 259.

Engel, Mary. The stability of the self-concept in adolescence. *J. abnorm. soc. Psychol.*, 1959, **58**, 211–215.

Eriksen, C. W., and Davids, A. The meaning and clinical validity of the Taylor Anxiety Scale and the hysteria-psychasthenia scales from the MMPI. *J. abnorm. soc. Psychol.*, 1955, **50**, 135–137.

Estabrook, A. H. *The Jukes in 1915.* Washington, D.C.: Carnegie Institution, 1916.

Evans, T. G. A heuristic program to solve geometric analogies problems. *AFIPS Conf. Proc.*, 1964, **25**, 327–338.

Ewing, T. N. Changes in attitude during counseling. *J. counsel. Psychol.*, 1954, **1**, 232–239.

Eysenck, H. J. The effects of psychotherapy: an evaluation. *J. consult. Psychol.*, 1952, **16**, 319–324.

Farber, I. E. A framework for the study of personality as a behavioral science. In P. Worchel and D. Byrne (Eds.), *Personality change.* New York: Wiley, 1964. Pp. 3–37.

————, and Spence, K. W. Complex learning and conditioning as a function of anxiety. *J. exp. Psychol.*, 1953, **45**, 120–125.

Feather, N. T. The relationship of persistence at a task to expectation of success and achievement-related motives. *J. abnorm. soc. Psychol.*, 1961, **63**, 552–561.

————. The relationship of expectation of success to need achievement and test anxiety. *J. pers. soc. Psychol.*, 1965, **1**, 118–126.

Feigenbaum, E. A. The simulation of verbal learning behavior. *AFIPS Conf. Proc.*, 1961, **19**, 121–132.

Feigl, H. Principles and problems of theory construction in psychology. In *Current trends in psychological theory.* Pittsburgh: University of Pittsburgh Press, 1951. Pp. 179–213.

Festinger, L. Informal social communication. *Psychol. Rev.*, 1950, **57**, 271–282.

————. Informal social communication. In L. Festinger, K. Back, S. Schachter, H. H. Kelley, and J. Thibaut (Eds.), *Theory and experiment in social communication.* Ann Arbor, Michigan: Edwards Brothers, 1952. Pp. 3–17.

————. A theory of social comparison processes. *Hum. Relat.*, 1954, **7**, 117–140.

————. A *theory of cognitive dissonance*. Stanford, California: Stanford University Press, 1957.

————. The psychological effects of insufficient rewards. *Amer. Psychologist*, 1961, **16**, 1–11.

————, and Freedman, J. L. Dissonance reduction and moral values. In P. Worchel and D. Byrne (Eds.), *Personality change*. New York: Wiley, 1964. Pp. 220–243.

Field, W. F. The effects on thematic apperception of certain experimentally aroused needs. Unpublished doctoral dissertation, University of Maryland, 1951.

Flugel, J. C. A quantitative study of feeling and emotion in everyday life. *Brit. J. Psychol.*, 1925, **15**, 318–355.

Forer, B. R. The fallacy of personal validations: a classroom demonstration of gullibility. *J. abnorm. soc. Psychol.*, 1949, **44**, 118–123.

Frandsen, A. N. The Wechsler-Bellevue Intelligence Scale and high school achievement. *J. appl. Psychol.*, 1950, **34**, 406–411.

Freedman, M., Webster, H., and Sanford, N. A study of authoritarianism and psychopathology. *J. Psychol.*, 1956, **41**, 315–322.

French, Elizabeth. Interrelation among some measures of rigidity under stress and non-stress conditions. *J. abnorm. soc. Psychol.*, 1955, **51**, 114–118.

————. Development of a measure of complex motivation. In J. W. Atkinson (Ed.), *Motives in fantasy, action, and society*. Princeton: Van Nostrand, 1958. Pp. 242–248.

————, and Ernest, R. R. The relation between authoritarianism and acceptance of military ideology. *J. Pers.*, 1955, **24**, 181–191.

Frenkel-Brunswik, Else. Intolerance of ambiguity as an emotional and perceptual personality variable. *J. Pers.*, 1949, **18**, 108–143.

————. Dynamic and cognitive personality organization as seen through the interviews. In T. W. Adorno, Else Frenkel-Brunswik, D. J. Levinson, and R. N. Sanford (Eds.), *The authoritarian personality*. New York: Harper, 1950. Pp. 442–467.

Freud, S. On the grounds for detaching a particular syndrome from neurasthenia under the description "anxiety neurosis." (1895) In J. Strachey (Ed.), *The standard edition of the complete psychological works*. Vol. 3. London: Hogarth and Institute of Psycho-analysis, 1959.

————. Wit and its relation to the unconscious (1905). In *The basic writings of Sigmund Freud*. New York: Random House, 1938.

————. Lines of advance in psychoanalytic therapy (1919). *Standard edition*. London: Hogarth and Institute for Psychoanalysis, 1955.

————. Jenseits des Lustprinzips. In *Gesammelte Werke*, 1920, Vol. XIII. London: Imago Publishing Co., 1940.

————. Inhibitions, symptoms and anxiety (1926). In J. Strachey (Ed.), *The standard edition of the complete psychological works.* Vol. 20. London: Hogarth and Institute of Psycho-analysis, 1959. Pp. 77–175.

Friedman, I. Phenomenal, ideal, and projected conceptions of self. *J. abnorm. soc. Psychol.*, 1955, **51**, 611–615.

Fruchter, B., Rokeach, M., and Novak, E. G. A factorial study of dogmatism, opinionation, and related scales. *Psychol. Rep.*, 1958, **4**, 19–22.

Fryer, D. Occupational intelligence standards. *Sch. and Soc.*, 1922, **16**, 273–277.

Funkenstein, D. H., King, S. H., and Drolette, M. E. *The mastery of stress.* Cambridge: Harvard University Press, 1957.

Gallagher, J. J. Manifest anxiety changes concomitant with client-centered therapy. *J. consult. Psychol.*, 1953, **17**, 443–446.

Galton, F. The history of twins as a criterion of the relative powers of nature and nurture. *Fraser's Mag.*, 1875, **12**, 566–576.

Garth, T. R. A review of racial psychology. *Psychol. Bull.*, 1925, **22**, 343–364.

Gendlin, E. T. Client-centered developments and work with schizophrenics. *J. counsel. Psychol.*, 1962, **9**, 205–211.

————, and Berlin, J. I. Galvanic skin response correlates of different modes of experiencing. *J. clin. Psychol.*, 1961, **17**, 73–77.

Getzels, J. W., and Jackson, P. W. *Creativity and intelligence: explorations with gifted students.* New York: Wiley, 1962.

Ghiselli, E. E. The relationship between intelligence and age among superior adults. *J. genet. Psychol.*, 1957, **90**, 131–142.

Gibbon, E. *The decline and fall of the Roman Empire.* (1776) Vol. 1. New York: Heritage, 1946.

Gilliland, A. R. Socioeconomic status and race as factors in infant intelligence test scores. *Child Develpm.*, 1951, **22**, 271–273.

Gleser, G., and Ulett, G. The Saslow Screening Test as a measure of anxiety-proneness. *J. clin. Psychol.*, 1952, **8**, 279–283.

Goddard, H. H. *The Kallikak family.* New York: The Macmillan Company, 1912.

————. Echelle metrique de l'intelligence de Binet-Simon. *Annee Psychol.*, 1912, **18**, 288–326.

Goldfarb, W. Effects of psychological deprivation in infancy and subsequent stimulation. *Amer. J. Psychiat.*, 1945, **102**, 18–33.

Golding, L. A., and Harvey, Virginia. Relationship between anxiety and serum cholesterol. *Psychon. Sci.*, 1964, **1**, 149–150.

Golightly, Carole C. The reinforcement properties of attitude similarity-dissimilarity. Unpublished doctoral dissertation, University of Texas, 1965.

————, and Byrne, D. Attitude statements as positive and negative reinforcements. *Science*, 1964, **146**, 798–799.

Goodstein, L. Interrelationships among several measures of anxiety and hostility. *J. consult. Psychol.*, 1954, **18**, 35–39.

————, and Goldberger, L. Manifest anxiety and Rorschach performance in a chronic patient population. *J. consult. Psychol.*, 1955, **19**, 339–344.

Gordon, H. *Mental and scholastic tests among retarded children.* Education Pamphlet No. 44. London: Board of Education, 1923.

Gorfein, D. Conformity behavior and the "authoritarian personality." *J. soc. Psychol.*, 1961, **53**, 121–125.

Gottesman, I. I. Heritability of personality: a demonstration. *Psychol. Monogr.*, 1963, **77**, No. 9 (Whole No. 572).

Gough, H. G. *Manual for the California Psychological Inventory.* Palo Alto, California: Consulting Psychologists Press, 1957. (a)

————. Imagination—undeveloped resource. *Proc. first conf. res. develop. personnel management.* Los Angeles: University of California Institute of Industrial Relations, 1957. Pp. 4–10. (b)

————. Researchers' summary data for the differential Reaction Schedule. Unpublished manuscript, 1957. (c)

Green, B. F. *Digital computers in research.* New York: McGraw-Hill, 1963.

————. Intelligence and computer simulation. *Trans. N.Y. Acad. Sci.*, 1964, **27** (No. 1), 55–63.

————, Wolf, Alice K., Chomsky, Carol, and Laughery, K. Baseball: an automatic question answerer. *AFIPS Conf. Proc.*, 1961, **19**, 219–224.

Greenspoon, J. The reinforcing effect of two spoken sounds on the frequency of two responses. *Amer. J. Psychol.*, 1955, **68**, 409–416.

Grice, G. R. Discrimination reaction time as a function of anxiety and intelligence. *J. abnorm. soc. Psychol.*, 1955, **50**, 71–74.

Grosz, H. J., and Levitt, E. E. The effects of hypnotically induced anxiety on the Manifest Anxiety Scale and the Barron Ego-Strength Scale. *J. abnorm. soc. Psychol.*, 1959, **59**, 281–283.

Grummon, D. L. Design, procedures, and subjects for the first block. In C. R. Rogers and Rosalind F. Dymond (Eds.), *Psychotherapy and personality change.* Chicago: University of Chicago Press, 1954. Pp. 35–52.

Guilford, J. P. *Personality.* New York: McGraw-Hill, 1959. (a)

————. Three faces of intellect. *Amer. Psychologist*, 1959, **14**, 469–479. (b)

————. Factorial angles to psychology. *Psychol. Rev.*, 1961, **68**, 1–20.

————, Wilson, R. C., and Christensen, P. R. *A factor-analytic study of creative thinking: II. Administration of tests and analysis of results.* Los Angeles: University of Southern California, Psychol. Lab., No. 8, 1952.

————, and Zimmerman, W. S. *The Guilford-Zimmerman temperament survey: manual of instructions and interpretations.* Beverly Hills, California: Sheridan Supply Co., 1949.

Gundlach, R. H. Effects of on-the-job experiences with Negroes upon racial attitudes of white workers in Union shops. *Psychol. Rep.*, 1956, **2**, 67–77.

Guthrie, E. R. *The psychology of learning.* New York: Harper, 1935.

————. Conditioning: A theory of learning in terms of stimulus, response, and association. *Natl. Soc. Stud. Educ.*, 1942, 41st Yearbook, Part II, 17–60.

———, and Horton, G. P. *Cats in a puzzle box*. New York: Holt, Rinehart and Winston, 1946.

Haber, R. N., and Alpert, R. The role of situation and picture cues in projective measurement of the achievement motive. In J. W. Atkinson (Ed.), *Motives in fantasy, action, and society*. Princeton: Van Nostrand, 1958. Pp. 644–663.

Hall, C. S. The inheritance of emotionality. *Sigma Xi Quart.*, 1938, **26**, No. 1, 17–27.

———. The genetics of behavior. In S. S. Stevens (Ed.), *Handbook of experimental psychology*. New York: Wiley, 1951. Pp. 304–329.

———, and Lindzey, G. *Theories of personality*. New York: Wiley, 1957.

Hammond, K. R., and Allen, J. M., Jr. *Writing clinical reports*. Englewood Cliffs, N.J.: Prentice-Hall, 1953.

Handlon, B. J., and Squier, L. H. Attitudes toward special loyalty oaths at the University of California. *Amer. Psychologist*, 1955, **10**, 121–127.

Hanlon, T. E., Hofstaetter, P. R., and O'Conner, J. P. Congruence of self and ideal self in relation to personality adjustment. *J. consult. Psychol.*, 1954, **18**, 215–218.

Hanson, Judith E. Personal communication, 1963. Quoted in Byrne, 1964.(b)

Harlow, H. F. Primate learning. In C. P. Stone (Ed.), *Comparative psychology*. Englewood Cliffs, N.J.: Prentice-Hall, 1951. Pp. 183–238.

———. The heterosexual affectional system in monkeys. *Amer. Psychologist*, 1962, **17**, 1–9.

Harrell, Ruth F., Woodyard, Ella, and Gates, A. I. *The effect of mothers' diets on the intelligence of offspring*. New York: Bureau of Publications, Teachers College, Columbia University, 1955.

Harrell, T. W., and Harrell, M. S. Army General Classification Test scores for civilian occupations. *Educ. psychol. Measmt.*, 1945, **5**, 229–239.

Hart, I. Maternal child-rearing practices and authoritarian ideology. *J. abnorm. soc. Psychol.*, 1957, **55**, 232–237.

Hatfield, A. B. An experimental study of the self-concept of student teachers. *J. educ. Res.*, 1961, **55**, 87–89.

Hathaway, S. R., and McKinley, J. C. A multiphasic personality schedule (Minnesota): I. Construction of the schedule. *J. Psychol.*, 1940, **10**, 249–254.

———, ———. *Minnesota Multiphasic Personality Inventory manual*. Rev. Ed. New York: Psychological Corporation, 1951.

Hayes, K. J. Genes, drives, and intellect. *Psychol. Rep.*, 1962, **10**, 299–342.

Haythorn, W., Couch, A., Haefner, D., Langham, P., and Carter, L. F. The behavior of authoritarian and equalitarian personalities in groups. *Hum. Relat.*, 1956, **9**, 57–74.

———, Haefner, D., Langham, P., Couch, A., and Carter, L. The effects of varying combinations of authoritarian and equalitarian leaders and followers. *J. abnorm. soc. Psychol.*, 1956, **53**, 210–219.

Hayward, S. C. Modification of sexual behavior of the male albino rat. *J. comp. physiol. Psychol.*, 1957, **50**, 70–73.

Hebb, D. O. *The organization of behavior*. New York: Wiley, 1949.

———. *A textbook of psychology*. Philadelphia: Saunders, 1958.

Heider, F. *The psychology of interpersonal relations*. New York: Wiley, 1958.

Heineman, C. E. A forced-choice form of the Taylor anxiety scale. *J. consult. Psychol.*, 1953, **17**, 447–454.

Helper, M. M. Learning theory and the self concept. *J. abnorm. soc. Psychol.*, 1955, **51**, 184–194.

Henry, Edith M., and Rotter, J. B. Situational influences on Rorschach responses. *J. consult. Psychol.*, 1956, **20**, 457–462.

Heyns, R. W., Veroff, J., and Atkinson, J. W. A scoring manual for the affiliation motive. In J. W. Atkinson (Ed.), *Motives in fantasy, action, and society*. Princeton: Van Nostrand, 1958. Pp. 205–218.

Hiler, E. W. Wechsler-Bellevue intelligence as a predictor of continuation in psychotherapy. *J. clin. Psychol.*, 1958, **14**, 192–194.

Hilgard, E. R. Human motives and the concept of the self. *Amer. Psychologist*, 1949, **4**, 374–382.

———, Jones, L. V., and Kaplan, S. J. Conditioned discrimination as related to anxiety. *J. exp. Psychol.*, 1951, **42**, 94–99.

Hillson, J. S., and Worchel, P. Self concept and defensive behavior in the maladjusted. *J. consult. Psychol.*, 1957, **21**, 83–88.

Himelstein, P., Eschenbach, A. E., and Carp, A. Interrelationships among three measures of need achievement. *J. consult. Psychol.*, 1958, **22**, 451–452.

Hites, R. W., and Kellogg, E. P. The F and Social Maturity Scales in relation to racial attitudes in a Deep South sample. *J. soc. Psychol.*, 1964, **62**, 189–195.

Hollander, E. P. Authoritarianism and leadership choice in a military setting. *J. abnorm. soc. Psychol.*, 1954, **49**, 365–370.

Holmberg, A. R. The Siriono. Unpublished doctoral dissertation, Yale University, 1946.

Holt, R. R. Individuality and generalization in the psychology of personality. *J. Pers.*, 1962, **30**, 377–404.

———. Forcible indoctrination and personality change. In P. Worchel and D. Byrne (Eds.), *Personality change*. New York: Wiley, 1964. Pp. 289–318.

Holtzman, W. H., Calvin, A. D., and Bitterman, M. E. New evidence for the validity of Taylor's Manifest Anxiety Scale. *J. abnorm. soc. Psychol.*, 1952, **47**, 853–854.

———, Thorpe, J. S., Swartz, J. D., and Heron, E. W. *Inkblot perception and personality*. Austin: University of Texas Press, 1961.

Horney, Karen. *Our inner conflicts*. New York: Norton, 1945.

Horton, C. P., and Crump, E. P. Growth and development: XI. Descriptive analysis of the backgrounds of 76 Negro children whose scores are above or below average on the Merrill-Palmer scale of mental tests at three years of age. *J. genet. Psychol.*, 1962, **100**, 255–265.

Houston, J. P., and Mednick, S. A. Creativity and the need for novelty. *J. abnorm. soc. Psychol.*, 1963, **66**, 137–141.

Hoyt, D. P., and Magoon, T. M. A validation study of the Taylor Manifest Anxiety Scale. *J. clin. Psychol.*, 1954, **10**, 357–361.

Hoyt, Ruth, Elliott, H., and Hebb, D. O. The intelligence of schizophrenic patients following lobotomy. *D.V. A. Treatm. Serv. Bull.*, 1951, **6**, 553–557.

Hull, C. L. Mind, mechanism, and adaptive behavior. *Psychol. Rev.*, 1937, **44**, 1–32.

———. *Principles of behavior*. New York: Appleton, 1943.

———. Clark L. Hull. In E. G. Boring, H. S. Langfeld, H. Werner, and R. M. Yerkes (Eds.), *A history of psychology in autobiography*. Vol. IV. Worcester, Massachusetts: Clark University Press, 1952. Pp. 143–162.

———, Hovland, C. I., Ross, R. T., Hall, M., Perkins, D. T., and Fitch, F. B. *Mathematico-deductive theory of rote learning*. New Haven: Yale University Press, 1940.

Hunt, J. McV. *Intelligence and experience*. New York: Ronald, 1961.

Hyman, H. H., and Sheatsley, P. B. Attitudes toward desegregation. *Scientific Amer.*, 1964, **211**, 16–23.

Immergluck, L. Determinism-freedom in contemporary psychology: an ancient problem revisited. *Amer. Psychologist*, 1964, **19**, 270–281.

Ison, M. Gail. The effect of "thorazine" on Wechsler scores. *Amer. J. ment. Def.*, 1957, **62**, 543–547.

Jackson, D. D. A critique of the literature on the genetics of schizophrenia. In D. D. Jackson (Ed.), *The etiology of schizophrenia*. New York: Basic Books, 1960. Pp. 37–87.

Jackson, D. N., and Bloomberg, R. Anxiety: unitas or multiplex? *J. consult. Psychol.*, 1958, **22**, 225–227.

———, and Messick, S. J. Content and style in personality assessment. *Psychol. Bull.*, 1958, **55**, 243–252.

———, ———, and Solley, C. M. How "rigid" is the "authoritarian"? *J. abnorm. soc. Psychol.*, 1957, **54**, 137–140.

———, and Pacine, L. Response styles and academic achievement. *Educ. Psychol. Measmt.*, 1961, **21**, 1015–1028.

Jacobson, F. N., and Rettig, S. Authoritarianism and intelligence. *J. soc. Psychol.*, 1959, **50**, 213–219.

Janis, I. L., and Feshbach, S. Effects of fear-arousing communications. *J. abnorm. soc. Psychol.*, 1953, **48**, 78–92.

———, and King, B. T. The influence of role playing on opinion change. *J. abnorm. soc. Psychol.*, 1954, **49**, 211–218.

Janke, L. L., and Havighurst, R. J. Relations between ability and social status in a midwestern community: II. sixteen-year-old boys and girls. *J. educ. Psychol.*, 1945, **36**, 499–509.

Jeffery, R. The psychologist as an expert witness on the issue of insanity. *Amer. Psychologist*, 1964, **19**, 838–843.

Jenkins, J. J., and Paterson, D. G. (Eds.), *Studies in individual differences.* New York: Appleton, 1961.

Jenness, A. Personality dynamics. In P. R. Farnsworth, Olga McNemar, and Q. McNemar (Eds.), *Annual review of psychology.* Vol. 13. Palo Alto, California: Annual Reviews, Inc., 1962. Pp. 479–514.

Jessor, R., and Hammond, K. R. Construct validity and the Taylor anxiety scale. *Psychol. Bull.*, 1957, **54**, 161–170.

Johnson, Winifred B. Euphoric and depressed moods in normal subjects. *Character & Pers.*, 1937, **6**, 79–98, 188–202.

Jones, H. E., and Bayley, Nancy. The Berkeley growth study. *Child Develpm.*, 1941, **12**, 167–173.

———, and Conrad, H. S. The growth and decline of intelligence. *Genet. Psychol. Monogr.*, 1933, **13**, 223–298.

———, and Kaplan, O. J. Psychological aspects of mental disorders in later life. In O. J. Kaplan (Ed.), *Mental disorders in later life.* Stanford: Stanford University Press, 1945.

Jones, M. B. Religious values and authoritarian tendency. *J. soc. Psychol.*, 1958, **48**, 83–89.

Jourard, S. M., and Remy, R. M. Perceived parental attitudes, the self, and security. *J. consult. Psychol.*, 1955, **19**, 364–366.

Joy, V. L. Repression-sensitization and interpersonal behavior. Paper read at Amer. Psychol. Ass., Philadelphia, August, 1963.

Jung, C. G. *Two essays on analytical psychology.* Balliere, Tindall, and Cox, 1928.

Kagan, J. Socialization of aggression and the perception of parents in fantasy. *Child Develpm.*, 1958, **29**, 311–320.

Kahn, R. L., Pollack, M., and Fink, M. Social attitude (California F Scale) and convulsive therapy. *J. nerv. ment. Dis.*, 1960, **130**, 187–192.

Kallmann, F. J. Genetic theory: analysis of 691 twin index families. *Amer. J. Psychiat.*, 1946, **103**, 309.

Kamano, D. K. Self-satisfaction and psychological adjustment in schizophrenics. *J. consult. Psychol.*, 1961, **25**, 492–496.

Katahn, M. Effect of anxiety (drive) on the acquisition and avoidance of a dominant intratask response. *J. Pers.*, 1964, **32**, 642–650.

Kates, S. L., and Diab, D. N. Authoritarian ideology and attitudes on parent-child relationships. *J. abnorm. soc. Psychol.*, 1955, **51**, 13–16.

Katz, D., and Braly, K. W. Racial stereotypes of one hundred college students. *J. abnorm. soc. Psychol.*, 1933, **28**, 280–290.

Keller, E. D., and Rowley, V. N. Anxiety, intelligence, and scholastic achievement in elementary school children. *Psychol. Rep.*, 1962, **11**, 19–22.

Keller, F. S., and Schoenfeld, W. N. *Principles of psychology.* New York: Appleton, 1950.

Kelley, T. L. The selection of upper and lower groups for the validation of test items. *J. educ. Psychol.*, 1939, **30**, 17–24.

Kelly, J. G., Ferson, Jean E., and Holtzman, W. H. The measurement of attitudes toward the Negro in the South. *J. soc. Psychol.*, 1958, **48**, 305–317.

Kelman, H. C., and Barclay, Janet. The F Scale as a measure of breadth of perspective. *J. abnorm. soc. Psychol.*, 1963, **67**, 608–615.

Kendler, H. H., and Kendler, Tracy S. Vertical and horizontal processes in problem solving. *Psychol. Rev.*, 1962, **69**, 1–16.

Kenny, D. T. The influence of social desirability on discrepancy measures between real self and ideal self. *J. consult. Psychol.*, 1956, **20** 315–318.

———, and Ginsberg, Rose. The specificity of intolerance of ambiguity measures. *J. abnorm. soc. Psychol.*, 1958, **56**, 300–304.

Kerrick, Jean S. Some correlates of the Taylor Manifest Anxiety Scale. *J. abnorm. soc. Psychol.*, 1955, **50**, 75–77.

Kimble, G. A. Social influence on Rorschach records. *J. abnorm. soc. Psychol.*, 1945, **40**, 89–93.

Kirk, S. A. *Early education of the mentally retarded.* Urbana: University of Illinois Press, 1958.

Klein, E. B. Stylistic components of response as related to attitude change. *J. Pers.*, 1963, **31**, 38–51.

Klein, S. *Control of style with a generative grammar.* Santa Monica, California: SP 1633 System Development Corporation, 1964.

Klineberg, O. *Negro intelligence and selective migration.* New York: Columbia University Press, 1935.

———, (Ed.). *Characteristics of the American Negro.* New York: Harper, 1944.

———. Negro-white differences in intelligence test performance: a new look at an old problem. *Amer. Psychologist*, 1963, **18**, 198–203.

Klopfer, B., Ainsworth, Mary D., Klopfer, W. G., and Holt, R. R. *Developments in the Rorschach technique.* Vol. I. *Technique and theory.* Yonkers-on-Hudson, New York: World Book, 1954.

Klugh, H. E., and Bendig, A. W. The Manifest Anxiety and ACE Scales and college achievement. *J. consult. Psychol.*, 1955, **19**, 487.

Knapp, R. H. *n* Achievement and aesthetic preference. In J. W. Atkinson (Ed.), *Motives in fantasy, action, and society.* Princeton: Van Nostrand, 1958. Pp. 367–372.

———, and Garbutt, J. T. Time imagery and the achievement motive. *J. Pers.*, 1958, **26**, 426–434.

Knobloch, H., and Pasamanick, B. Further observations on the behavioral development of Negro children. *J. genet. Psychol.*, 1953, **83**, 137–157.

Koch, Margaret B., and Meyer, D. R. A relationship of mental age to learning-set formation in the pre-school child. *J. comp. physiol. Psychol.*, 1959, **52**, 387–389.

Kogan, N. Authoritarianism and repression, *J. abnorm. soc. Psychol.*, 1956, **53**, 34–37.

Krebs, A. M. Two determinants of conformity: age of independence training and *n* Achievement. *J. abnorm. soc. Psychol.*, 1958, **56**, 130–131.

Krug, R. E. An analysis of the F Scale: I. Item factor analysis. *J. soc. Psychol.*, 1961, **53**, 285–291.

———, and Moyer, K. E. An analysis of the F Scale: II. Relationship to standardized personality inventories. *J. soc. Psychol.*, 1961, **53**, 293–301.

Krumboltz, J. D., and Farquhar, W. W. Reliability and validity of the *n* Achievement Test. *J. consult. Psychol.*, 1957, **21**, 226–228.

Kuhlen, R. G. Changing personal adjustment during the adult years. In J. E. Anderson (Ed.), *Psychological aspects of aging.* Washington, D. C.: American Psychological Association, 1956. Pp. 21–29.

———. Personality change with age. In P. Worchel and D. Byrne (Eds.), *Personality change.* New York: Wiley, 1964. Pp. 524–555.

Lacey, J. I., and Lacey, Beatrice C. Verification and extension of the principle of autonomic response-stereotypy. *Amer. J. Psychol.*, 1958, **71**, 50–73.

Laffal, J. Response faults in word association as a function of response entropy. *J. abnorm. soc. Psychol.*, 1955, **50**, 265–270.

LaMonaca, H. L., and Berkun, M. M. Army data on Taylor MAS, intelligence, and ego strength. *Educ. Psychol. Measmt.*, 1959, **19**, 577–578.

Lane, Ellen A., and Albee, G. W. Childhood intellectual development of adult schizophrenics. *J. abnorm. soc. Psychol.*, 1963, **67**, 186–189.

———, ———. Early childhood intellectual differences between schizophrenic adults and their siblings. *J. abnorm. soc. Psychol.*, 1964, **68**, 193–195.

Lansing, J. B., and Heyns, R. W. Need affiliation and frequency of four types of communication. *J. abnorm. soc. Psychol.*, 1959, **58**, 365–372.

Lauterbach, C. G. The Taylor A Scale and clinical measures of anxiety. *J. consult. Psychol.*, 1958, **22**, 314.

Lazarus, R. S., and Alfert, Elizabeth. The short circuiting of threat by experimentally altering cognitive appraisal. *J. abnorm. soc. Psychol.*, 1964, **69**, 195–205.

———, Speisman, J. C., Mordkoff, A. M., and Davison, L. A. A laboratory study of psychological stress produced by a motion picture film. *Psychol. Monogr.*, 1962, **76**, No. 34 (Whole No. 553).

Leavitt, H. J., Hax, H., and Roche, J. H. "Authoritarianism" and agreement with things authoritative. *J. Psychol.*, 1955, **40**, 215–221.

Lebo, D., Toal, R. A., and Brick, H. Manifest anxiety in prisoners before and after CO_2. *J. consult. Psychol.*, 1958, **22**, 51–55.

Lee, E. S. Negro intelligence and selective migration: a Philadelphia test of Klineberg's hypothesis. *Amer. sociol. Rev.*, 1951, **61**, 227–233.

Lee, Lee C. The effects of anxiety level and shock on a paired-associate verbal task. *J. exp. Psychol.*, 1961, **61**, 213–217.

Lesser, G. S., Krawitz, Rhoda N., and Packard, Rita. Experimental arousal of achievement motivation in adolescent girls. *J. abnorm. soc. Psychol.*, 1963, **66**, 59–66.

Leventhal, H., Jacobs, R. L., and Kudirka, N. Z. Authoritarianism ideology and political candidate choice. *J. abnorm. soc. Psychol.*, 1964, **69**, 539–549.

Levine, M., Spivack, G., Fuschillo, Jean, and Tavernier, Ann. Intelligence, and measures of inhibition and time sense. *J. clin. Psychol.*, 1959, **15**, 224–226.

————, ————, and Wright, B. The inhibition process, Rorschach human movement responses, and intelligence: some further data. *J. consult. Psychol.*, 1959, **23**, 306–312.

Levinson, D. J., and Huffman, Phyllis E. Traditional family ideology and its relation to personality. *J. Pers.*, 1955, **23**, 251–273.

Levitt, E. E. The effect of a "causal" teacher training program on authoritarianism and responsibility in grade school children. *Psychol. Rep.*, 1955, **1**, 449–458.

Linden, J. D., and Olson, R. W. A comparative analysis of selected Guilford-Zimmerman Temperament Survey scales with the Taylor Manifest Anxiety Scale. *J. clin. Psychol.*, 1959, **15**, 295–298.

Lindgren, H. C. Authoritarianism, independence, and child-centered practices in education: A study of attitudes. *Psychol. Rep.*, 1962, **10**, 747–750.

Lindsley, D. B. Emotion. In S. S. Stevens (Ed.), *Handbook of experimental psychology*. New York: Wiley, 1951. Pp. 473–516.

Lindzey, G., Lykken, D. T., and Winston, H. D. Infantile trauma, genetic factors, and adult temperament. *J. abnorm. soc. Psychol.*, 1960, **61**, 7–14.

Littig, L. W., and Yeracaris, C. A. Academic achievement correlates of achievement and affiliation motivations. *J. Psychol.*, 1963, **55**, 115–119.

————, ————. Achievement motivation and intergenerational occupational mobility. *J. pers. soc. Psychol.*, 1965, **1**, 386–389.

Lorge, I. Schooling makes a difference. *Teach. Coll. Rec.*, 1945, **46**, 483–492.

Lorr, M., McNair, D. M., Michaux, W. W., and Raskin, A. Frequency of treatment and change in psychotherapy. *J. abnorm. soc. Psychol.*, 1962, **64**, 281–292.

Lowell, E. L. A methodological study of projectively measured achievement motivation. Unpublished master's thesis, Wesleyan University, 1950.

————. The effect of need for achievement on learning and performance. *J. Psychol.*, 1952, **33**, 31–40.

Luborsky, L., and Schimek, J. Psychoanalytic theories of therapeutic and developmental change: implications for assessment. In P. Worchel and D. Byrne (Eds.), *Personality change*. New York: Wiley, 1964. Pp. 73–99.

Lucas, J. D. The interactive effects of anxiety, failure, and interserial duplication. *Amer. J. Psychol.*, 1952, **65**, 59–66.

Lucky, A. W., and Grigg, A. E. Repression-sensitization as a variable in deviant responding. *J. clin. Psychol.*, 1964, **20**, 92–93.

Lyle, W. H., and Levitt, E. E. Punitiveness, authoritarianism, and parental discipline of grade school children. *J. abnorm. soc. Psychol.*, 1955, **51**, 42–46.

MacKinnon, D. W. The nature and nurture of creative talent. *Amer. Psychologist*, 1962, **17**, 484–495.

Mahler, I. Attitudes toward socialized medicine. *J. soc. Psychol.*, 1953, **38**, 273–282.

Maller, J. B. Mental ability and its relation to physical health and social economic status. *Psychol. Clinic*, 1933, **22**, 101–107.

Mandler, G., and Cowen, Judith E. Test anxiety questionnaires. *J. consult. Psychol.*, 1958, **22**, 228–229.

———, Mandler, Jean M., Kremen, I., and Sholitan, R. D. The response to threat: relations among verbal and physiological indices. *Psychol. Monogr.*, 1961, **75** (Whole No. 513).

———, ———, and Uviller, Ellen. Autonomic feedback: the perception of autonomic activity. *J. abnorm. soc. Psychol.*, 1958, **56**, 367–373.

———, and Sarason, S. B. A study of anxiety and learning. *J. abnorm. soc. Psychol.*, 1952, **47**, 166–173.

Mann, G. V., and White, H. S. The influence of stress on plasma cholesterol levels. *Metabolism*, 1953, **2**, 47.

Mann, J. H. The effect of inter-racial contact on sociometric choices and perceptions, *J. soc. Psychol.*, 1959, **50**, 143–152.

Markwell, E. D., Jr., Wheeler, W. M., and Kitzinger, Helen. Changes in Wechsler-Bellevue test performance following prefrontal lobotomy. *J. consult. Psychol.*, 1953, **17**, 229–231.

Marlowe, D. Relationships among direct and indirect measures of the achievement motive and overt behavior. *J. consult. Psychol.*, 1959, **23**, 329–332.

Martin, B. The measurement of anxiety. *J. gen. Psychol.*, 1959, **61**, 189–203.

———, and McGowan, B. Some evidence on the validity of the Sarason Test Anxiety Scale. *J. consult. Psychol.*, 1955, **19**, 468.

Marx, M. H. The general nature of theory construction. In M. H. Marx (Ed.), *Psychological theory*. New York: Macmillan, 1951. Pp. 4–19.

Masling, J. M. How neurotic is the authoritarian? *J. abnorm, soc. Psychol.*, 1954, **49**, 316–318.

Maslow, A. H., Hirsh, E., Stein, M., and Honigmann, I. A clinically derived test for measuring psychological security-insecurity. *J. gen. Psychol.*, 1945, **33**, 21–42.

———, and Mintz, N. L. Effects of esthetic surroundings: I. Initial effects of three esthetic conditions upon perceiving "energy" and "well-being" in faces. *J. Psychol.*, 1956, **41**, 247–254.

Matarazzo, J. D., Guze, S. B., and Matarazzo, Ruth G. An approach to the validity of the Taylor Anxiety Scale: scores of medical and psychiatric patients. *J. abnorm. soc. Psychol.*, 1955, **51**, 276–280.

———, Ulett, G. A., Guze, S. B., and Saslow, G. The relationship between anxiety level and several measures of intelligence. *J. consult. Psychol.*, 1954, **18**, 201–205.

———, ———, and Saslow, G. Human maze performance as a function of increasing levels of anxiety. *J. gen. Psychol.*, 1955, **53**, 79–96.

Matarazzo, Ruth G., Matarazzo, J. D., and Saslow, G. The relationship between medical and psychiatric symptoms. *J. abnorm. soc. Psychol.*, 1961, **62**, 55–61.

Maurer, S., and Tsai, L. S. Vitamin B deficiency and learning ability. *J. comp. Psychol.*, 1930, **11**, 51–62.

Mausner, B. Entrepreneurial behavior. *Contemporary Psychol.*, 1963, **8**, 291–292.

Mayzner, M. S., Sersen, E., and Tresselt, M. E. The Taylor Manifest Anxiety Scale and intelligence. *J. consult. Psychol.*, 1955, **19**, 401–404.

McClearn, G. E. The inheritance of behavior. In L. Postman (Ed.), *Psychology in the making*. New York: Knopf, 1962.

McClelland, D. C. *Personality*. New York: Holt, Rinehart and Winston, 1951.

———. Some social consequences of achievement motivation. In M. R. Jones (Ed.), *Nebraska symposium on motivation 1955*. Lincoln: University of Nebraska Press, 1955.

———. Methods of measuring human motivation. In J. W. Atkinson (Ed.), *Motives in fantasy, action, and society*. Princeton: Van Nostrand, 1958. Pp. 7–42. (a)

———. Risk-taking in children with high and low need for achievement. In J. W. Atkinson (Ed.), *Motives in fantasy, action, and society*. Princeton: Van Nostrand, 1958. Pp. 306–321. (b)

———. *The achieving society*. Princeton: Van Nostrand, 1961.

———. n Achievement and entrepreneurship: a longitudinal study. *J. pers. soc. Psychol.*, 1965, **1**, 389–392. (a)

———. Toward a theory of motive acquisition. *Amer. Psychologist*, 1965, **20**, 321–333. (b)

———, Atkinson, J. W., Clark, R. A., and Lowell, E. L. *The achievement motive*. New York: Appleton, 1953.

———, Clark, R. A., Roby, T. B., and Atkinson, J. W. The effect of the need for achievement on thematic apperception. *J. exp. Psychol.*, 1949, **37**, 242–255.

———, and Liberman, A. M. The effect of need for achievement on recognition of need-related words. *J. Pers.*, 1949, **18**, 236–251.

———, Rindlisbacher, A., and de Charms, R. C. Religious and other sources of parental attitudes toward independence training. In D. C. McClelland (Ed.), *Studies in motivation*. New York: Appleton, 1955.

McDonald, R. D. The effect of reward-punishment and affiliation need on interpersonal attraction. Unpublished doctoral dissertation, University of Texas, 1962.

McFarland, R. L., Nelson, C. L., and Rossi, A. M. Prediction of participation in group psychotherapy from measures of intelligence and verbal behavior. *Psychol. Rep.*, 1962, **11**, 291–298.

McGurk, F. C. J. *Comparison of the performance of Negro and white high school seniors on cultural and noncultural psychological test questions.* Washington, D.C.: Catholic University of America Press, 1951.

McKinley, J. C., and Hathaway, S. R. The Minnesota Multiphasic Personality Inventory. V. Hysteria, hypomania and psychopathic deviate. *J. appl. Psychol.*, 1944, **28**, 153–174.

McNemar, Q. Newman, Freeman, and Holzinger's twins: a study of heredity and environment. *Psychol. Bull.*, 1938, **35**, 237–249.

———. Note on Wellman's re-analysis of IQ changes of orphanage preschool children. *J. genet. Psychol.*, 1945, **67**, 215–219.

———. Lost: our intelligence? Why? *Amer. Psychologist*, 1964, **19**, 871–882.

Mead, G. H. *Mind, self, and society.* Chicago: University of Chicago Press, 1934.

Meer, B., and Stein, M. I. Measures of intelligence and creativity. *J. Psychol.*, 1955, **39**, 117–126.

Meer, S. J. Authoritarian attitudes and dreams. *J. abnorm. soc. Psychol.*, 1955, **51**, 74–78.

Melikian, L. H. The relationship between Edwards' and McClelland's measures of achievement motivation. *J. consult. Psychol.*, 1958, **22**, 296–298.

Mendel, G. J. Versuche über Pflanzen-Hybriden. *Verh. Naturf. Ver. in Brunn*, 1865, **4**, 3–47.

Meyer, D. R. On the interaction of simultaneous responses. *Psychol. Bull.*, 1953, **50**, 204–220.

Meyer, H. H., Walker, W. B., and Litwin, G. H. Motive patterns and risk preferences associated with entrepreneurship. *J. abnorm. soc. Psychol*, 1961, **63**, 570–574.

Miller, N. E. Studies of fear as an acquirable drive: I. Fear as motivation and fear-reduction as reinforcement in the learning of new responses. *J. exp. Psychol*, 1948, **38**, 89–101. (a)

———. Theory and experiment relating psychoanalytic displacement to stimulus-response generalization. *J. abnorm. soc. Psychol*, 1948, **43**, 155–178. (b)

———. Liberalization of basic S-R concepts: Extensions to conflict behavior, motivation, and social learning. In S. Koch (Ed.), *Psychology: A study of a science.* Vol. 2. New York: McGraw-Hill, 1959. Pp. 196–292.

———. Some implications of modern behavior theory for personality change and psychotherapy. In P. Worchel and D. Byrne (Eds.), *Personality change.* New York: Wiley, 1964. Pp. 149–175.

————, and Dollard, J. *Social learning and imitation.* New Haven: Yale University Press, 1941.

Millon, T. Authoritarianism, intolerance of ambiguity, and rigidity under ego- and task-involving conditions. *J. abnorm. soc. Psychol.,* 1957, **55,** 29–33.

Mills, J. Changes in moral attitudes following temptation. *J. Pers.,* 1958, **26,** 517–531.

Milton, O., and Waite, B. Presidential preference and traditional family values. *Amer. Psychologist,* 1964, **19,** 844–845.

Minor, C. A., and Neel, R. G. The relationship between achievement motive and occupational preference. *J. counsel. Psychol.,* 1958, **5,** 39–43.

Mischel, W. Preference for delayed reinforcement: an experimental study of a cultural observation. *J. abnorm. soc. Psychol.,* 1958, **56,** 57–61.

————. Delay of gratification, need for achievement, and acquiescence in another culture. *J. abnorm. soc. Psychol.,* 1961, **62,** 543–552.

————, and Gilligan, Carol. Delay of gratification, motivation for the prohibited gratification, and responses to temptation. *J. abnorm. soc. Psychol.,* 1964, **69,** 411–417.

————, and Metzner, R. Preference for delayed reward as a function of age, intelligence, and length of delay interval. *J. abnorm. soc. Psychol.,* 1962, **64,** 425–431.

————, and Schopler, J. Authoritarianism and reactions to "sputniks." *J. abnorm. soc. Psychol.,* 1959, **59,** 142–145.

Montagu, A. *Human heredity.* New York: New American Library, 1959.

————. Problems of our own making. *Science,* 1964, **146,** 1415–1416.

Montague, E. K. The role of anxiety in serial rote learning. *J. exp. Psychol.,* 1953, **45,** 91–96.

Moran, L. J., Kimble, J. P., Jr., and Mefferd, R. B., Jr. Repetitive psychometric measures: Memory-for-Faces. *Psychol. Rep.,* 1960, **7,** 407–413.

————, Mefferd, R. B., Jr., and Kimble, J. P., Jr. Idiodynamic sets in word association. *Psychol. Monogr.,* 1964, **78,** No. 2 (Whole No. 579).

Morgan, Christiana D., and Murray, H. A. A method for investigating fantasies. *Arch. Neur. Psychiat.,* 1935, **34,** 289–306.

————, ————. Thematic apperception test. In H. A. Murray (Ed.), *Explorations in personality.* (1938) New York: Science Editions, 1962. Pp. 530–545.

Morgan, H. H. Measuring achievement motivation with "picture interpretations." *J. consult. Psychol.,* 1953, **17,** 289–292.

Morgan, J. N. Entrepreneurial behavior. *Contemporary Psychol.,* 1963, **8,** 289–291.

Moses, M., and Duvall, R. Depreciation and the self concept. *J. clin. Psychol.,* 1960, **16,** 387–388.

Mowrer, O. H. Neurosis, psychotherapy, and two-factor learning theory. In O. H. Mowrer (Ed.), *Psychotherapy: theory and research.* New York: Ronald, 1953. (a)

————. *Psychotherapy: theory and research.* New York: Ronald, 1953. (b)

————, Light, B. H., Luria, Z., and Zeleny, M. P. Tension changes in psychotherapy with special reference to resistance. In O. H. Mowrer (Ed.), *Psychotherapy: theory and research.* New York: Ronald, 1953. Pp. 546–640.

Murray, H. A. *Explorations in personality.* (1938) New York: Science Editions, 1962.

————. What should psychologists do about psychoanalysis? *J. abnorm. soc. Psychol.,* 1940, **35**, 150–175.

————. Preparations for the scaffold of a comprehensive system. In S. Koch (Ed.), *Psychology: a study of a science.* Vol. 3. New York: McGraw-Hill, 1959. Pp. 7–54.

Murray, E. J. Direct analysis from the viewpoint of learning theory. *J. consult. Pychol.,* 1962, **26**, 226–231.

————. Sociotropic-learning approach to psychotherapy. In P. Worchel and D. Byrne (Eds.), *Personality change.* New York: Wiley, 1964. Pp. 249–288.

Mussen, P. H., and Scodel, A. The effects of sexual stimulation under varying conditions on TAT sexual responsiveness. *J. consult. Psychol.,* 1955, **19**, 90.

Nadler, E. B. Yielding, authoritarianism, and authoritarian ideology regarding groups. *J. abnorm. soc. Psychol.,* 1959, **58**, 408–410.

Newcomb, T. M. An approach to the study of communicative acts. *Psychol. Rev.,* 1953, **60**, 393–404.

————. The prediction of interpersonal attraction. *Amer. Psychologist,* 1956, **11**, 575–586.

————, and Svehla, G. Intra-family relationships in attitude. *Sociometry,* 1937, **1**, 180–205.

Newell, A., Shaw, J. C., and Simon, H. A. Chess-playing programs and the problem of complexity. *IBM J. res. Develpm.,* 1958, **2**, 320–335.

Newman, H. H., Freeman, F. N., and Holzinger, K. J. *Twins: a study of heredity and environment.* Chicago: University of Chicago Press, 1937.

Nisbet, J. D. Symposium: contributions to intelligence testing and the theory of intelligence: IV. Intelligence and age: retesting with twenty-four years' interval. *Brit. J. educ. Psychol.,* 1957, **27**, 190–198.

Nowlis, V., and Nowlis, Helen H. The description and analysis of mood. *Ann. N.Y. Acad. Sci.,* 1956, **65**, 345–355.

O'Connell, W. E. The adaptive functions of wit and humor. *J. abnorm. soc. Psychol.,* 1960, **61**, 263–270.

O'Connor, Patricia. Ethnocentrism, "intolerance of ambiguity," and abstract reasoning ability. *J. abnorm. soc. Psychol.,* 1952, **47**, 526–530.

O'Neil, W. M., and Levinson, D. J. A factorial exploration of authoritarianism and some of its ideological concomitants. *J. Pers.,* 1954, **22**, 449–463.

Orlansky, H. Infant care and personality. *Psychol. Bull.,* 1949, **46**, 1–48.

Osborne, R. T. Racial differences in mental growth and school achievement: a longitudinal study. *Psychol. Rep.*, 1960, **7**, 233–239.

Osler, Sonia F., and Fivel, M. W. Concept attainment: I. The role of age and intelligence in concept attainment by induction. *J. exp. Psychol*, 1961, **62**, 1–8.

————, and Weiss, Sandra R. Studies in concept attainment: III. Effect of instructions at two levels of intelligence. *J. exp. Psychol*, 1962, **63**, 528–533.

Owens, W. A., Jr. Age and mental abilities: a longitudinal study. *Genet. Psychol. Monogr.*, 1953, **48**, 3–54.

Palmore, E. B. The introduction of Negroes into white departments. *Hum. Organization*, 1955, **14**, 27–28.

Parrish, J., and Rethlingshafer, Dorothy. A study of the need to achieve in college achievers and nonachievers. *J. gen. Psychol.*, 1954, **50**, 209–226.

Pasamanick, B. A comparative study of the educational development of Negro infants. *J. genet. Psychol.*, 1946, **69**, 3–44.

————, and Knobloch, H. Early language behavior in Negro children and the testing of intelligence. *J. abnorm. soc. Psychol.*, 1955, **50**, 401–402.

Petrovich, D. V. The Pain Apperception Test: psychological correlates of pain perception. *J. clin. Psychol.*, 1958, **14**, 367–374.

Precker, J. A. Similarity of valuings as a factor in selection. *J. abnorm. soc. Psychol.*, 1952, **47**, 406–414.

Rankin, R. E., and Campbell, D. T. The galvanic skin response to Negro and white experimenters. *J. abnorm. soc. Psychol.*, 1955, **51**, 30–33.

Raphelson, A. C. The relationships among imaginative, direct verbal, and physiological measures of anxiety in an achievement situation. *J. abnorm. soc. Psychol.*, 1957, **54**, 13–18.

Rappaport, S. R., and Webb, W. B. An attempt to study intellectual deterioration by premorbid and psychotic testing. *J. consult. Psychol.*, 1950, **14**, 95–98.

Reissman, L. Level of aspiration and social class. *Amer. Sociol. Rev.*, 1953, **18**, 233–242.

Reynolds, W. F., Blau, B. I., and Hurlbut, Barbara. Speed in simple tasks as a function of MAS score. *Psychol. Rep.*, 1961, **8**, 341–344.

Richardson, S. K. The correlation of intelligence quotients of siblings of the same chronological age levels. *J. juv. Res.*, 1936, **20**, 186–198.

Ricks, D., and Epley, D. Foresight and hindsight in the TAT. Paper read at Eastern Psychological Association, New York, April, 1960.

Ripple, R. E., and May, F. B. Caution in comparing creativity and I.Q. *Psychol. Rep.*, 1962, **10**, 229–230.

Robbins, Lillian C. The accuracy of parental recall of aspects of child development and of child rearing practices. *J. abnorm. soc. Psychol.*, 1963, **66**, 261–270.

Robinson, P. The measurement of achievement motivation. Unpublished doctoral dissertation, Oxford University, 1961.

Rodgers, D. A. In favor of separation of academic and professional training. *Amer. Psychologist*, 1964, **19**, 675–680.

Roen, S. R. Personality and Negro-white intelligence. *J. abnorm. soc. Psychol.*, 1960, **61**, 148–150.

Rogers, C. R. *Client-centered therapy*. Boston: Houghton Mifflin, 1951.

————. An overview of the research and some questions for the future. In C. R. Rogers and Rosalind F. Dymond (Eds.), *Psychotherapy and personality change*. Chicago: University of Chicago Press, 1954. Pp. 413–434.

————. A theory of therapy, personality, and interpersonal relationships, as developed in the client-centered framework. In S. Koch (Ed.), *Psychology: a study of a science*. Vol. 3. *Formulations of the person and the social context*. New York: McGraw-Hill, 1959. Pp. 184–256.

————. The actualizing tendency in relation to "motives" and to consciousness. In M. R. Jones (Ed.), *Nebraska symposium on motivation*. Lincoln, Nebraska: University of Nebraska Press, 1963. Pp. 1–24.

————, and Dymond, Rosalind F. (Eds.). *Psychotherapy and personality change*. Chicago: University of Chicago Press, 1954.

Rokeach, M. *The open and closed mind*. New York: Basic Books, 1960.

Rorer, L. G. The great response-style myth. *Psychol. Bull.*, 1965, **63**, 129–156.

Rorschach, H. *Psychodiagnostics*. Berne: Hans Huber, 1921.

Rosen, B. C. The achievement syndrome: a psychocultural dimension of social stratification. *Amer. sociol. Rev.*, 1956, **21**, 203–211.

————, and D'Andrade, R. The psychosocial origins of achievement motivation. *Sociometry*, 1959, **22**, 185–218.

Rosenbaum, G. Stimulus generalization as a function of clinical anxiety. *J. abnorm. soc. Psychol.*, 1956, **53**, 281–285.

Rosenzweig, S. A transvaluation of psychotherapy—a reply to Hans Eysenck. *J. abnorm. soc. Psychol*, 1954, **49**, 298–304.

Ross, A. O. Brain injury and intellectual performance. *J. consult. Psychol.*, 1958, **22**, 151–152.

Rossi, A. M. An evaluation of the Manifest Anxiety Scale by the use of electromyography. *J. exp. Psychol.*, 1959, **58**, 64–69.

Rothaus, P., and Worchel, P. The inhibition of aggression under nonarbitrary frustration. *J. Pers.*, 1960, **28**, 108–117.

Rothstein, R. Authoritarianism and men's reactions to sexuality and affection in women. *J. abnorm. soc. Psychol.*, 1960, **61**, 329–334.

Rubin, H., and Townsend, A. H. The Taylor Manifest Anxiety Scale in differential diagnosis. *J. clin. Psychol.*, 1958, **14**, 81–83.

Rubinstein, E. A., and Lorr, M. A comparison of terminators and remainers in outpatient psychotherapy. *J. clin. Psychol.*, 1956, **12**, 345–349.

Sanders, R., and Cleveland, S. E. The relationship between certain examiner personality variables and subjects' Rorschach scores. *J. proj. Tech.*, 1953, **17**, 34–50.

Sarason, I. G. The relationship of anxiety and "lack of defensiveness" to intellectual performance. *J. consult. Psychol.*, 1956, **20**, 220–222.

———. Interrelationships among individual difference variables, behavior in psychotherapy, and verbal conditioning. *J. abnorm. soc. Psychol.*, 1958, **56**, 339–344.

———. Empirical findings and theoretical problems in the use of anxiety scales. *Psychol. Bull.*, 1960, **57**, 403–415.

———. Characteristics of three measures of anxiety. *J. clin. Psychol.*, 1961, **17**, 196–197.

Sarason, S. B., Davidson, K. S., Lighthall, F. F., Waite, R. R., and Ruebush, B. K. *Anxiety in elementary school children.* New York: Wiley, 1960.

Sarbin, T. R. A preface to a psychological analysis of the self. *Psychol. Rev.*, 1952, **59**, 11–22.

———. Anxiety: reification of a metaphor. *Arch. gen. Psychiat.*, 1964, **10**, 630–638. (a)

———. Role theoretical interpretation of psychological change. In P. Worchel and D. Byrne (Eds.), *Personality change.* New York: Wiley, 1964. Pp. 176–219. (b)

Satz, P., and Baraff, A. S. Changes in the relation between self-concepts and ideal concepts of psychotics consequent upon therapy. *J. gen. Psychol.*, 1962, **67**, 291–298.

Savitt, R. A. Psychoanalytic studies on addiction: ego structure in narcotic addiction. *Psychoanalytic Quart.*, 1963, **32**, 43–57.

Schaefer, E. S., and Bell, R. Q. Development of a parental attitude research instrument. *Child Develpm.*, 1958, **29**, 339–361.

Schaefer, R. *The clinical application of psychological tests.* New York: International Universities Press, 1948.

Schaie, K. W. Rigidity-flexibility and intelligence: A cross-sectional study of the adult life span from 20–70 years. *Psychol. Monogr.*, 1958, **72** (Whole No. 462).

Scheier, I. H., and Cattell, R. B. *Temporary handbook for the IPAT 8-Parallel-Form Anxiety Battery.* Champaign, Ill.: Institute for Personality and Ability Testing, 1960.

Schmuck, R. A., and Schmuck, R. W. Upward mobility and I. Q. performance. *J. educ. Res.*, 1961, **55**, 123–127.

Schofield, W., and Balian, Lucy. A comparative study of the personal histories of schizophrenic and nonpsychiatric patients. *J. abnorm. soc. Psychol.*, 1959, **59**, 216–225.

Schooley, Mary. Personality resemblances among married couples. *J. abnorm. soc. Psychol.*, 1936, **31**, 340–347.

Schulz, R. E., and Calvin, A. D. A failure to replicate the finding of a negative correlation between manifest anxiety and ACE scores. *J. consult. Psychol.*, 1955, **19**, 223–224.

Schwartzman, A. E., and Douglas, Virginia I. Intellectual loss in schizophrenia: Part I. *Canad. J. Psychol.*, 1962, **16**, 1–10.

———, ———, and Muir, W. R. Intellectual loss in schizophrenia: Part II. *Canad. J. Psychol.*, 1962, **16**, 161–168.

Scott, W. A. Attitude change through reward of verbal behavior. *J. abnorm. soc. Psychol.*, 1957, **55**, 72–75.

Scottish Council for Research in Education. *The trend of Scottish intelligence.* London: University of London Press, 1949.

Sears, R. R. Experimental analysis of psychoanalytic phenomena. In J. McV. Hunt (Ed.), *Personality and the behavior disorders.* New York: Ronald, 1944. Pp. 306–332.

———, Hovland, C. I., and Miller, N. E. Minor studies of aggression: 1. Measurement of aggressive behavior. *J. Psychol.*, 1940, **9**, 275–295.

———, Maccoby, Eleanor E., and Levin, H. *Patterns of child rearing.* Evanston, Illinois: Row, Peterson, 1957.

Seashore, H., Wesman, A., and Doppelt, J. The standardization of the Wechsler Intelligence Scale for Children. *J. consult. Psychol.*, 1950, **14**, 99–110.

Seashore, S. H., and Seashore, R. H. Individual differences in simple auditory reaction times of hands, feet, and jaws. *J. exp. Psychol.*, 1941, **29**, 342–345.

Shatin, L. A clinical correlative study of the Manifest Anxiety Scale. *J. clin. Psychol.*, 1961, **17**, 198.

Shipley, T. W., and Veroff, J. A projective measure of need for affiliation. *J. exp. Psychol.*, 1952, **43**, 349–356.

Shuey, A. M. *The testing of Negro intelligence.* Lynchburg, Virginia: J. P. Bell, 1958.

Siegel, S. M. The relationship of hostility to authoritarianism. *J. abnorm. soc. Psychol.*, 1956, **52**, 368–372.

Siegman, A. W. Cognitive, affective, and psychopathological correlates of the Taylor Manifest Anxiety Scale. *J. consult. Psychol.*, 1956, **20**, 137–141.

Silverman, R. E. The Manifest Anxiety Scale as a measure of drive. *J. abnorm. soc. Psychol.*, 1957, **55**, 94–97.

Simpson, G. G. *This view of life.* New York: Harcourt, Brace and World, 1964.

Simpson, W. J. A preliminary report on cigarette smoking and the incidence of prematurity. *Amer. J. Obstet. Gynecol.*, 1957, **73**, 805–815.

Singer, R. D. The effects of verbal reinforcement of pro-democratic responses upon subsequent expression of authoritarian opinions and social prejudice. Unpublished doctoral dissertation, University of Pennsylvania, 1960.

———, and Feshbach, S. Some relationships between manifest anxiety, authoritarian tendencies, and modes of reaction to frustration. *J. abnorm. soc. Psychol.*, 1959, **59**, 404–408.

Sinick, D. Two anxiety scales correlated and examined for sex differences. *J. clin. Psychol.*, 1956, **12**, 394–395.

Skinner, B. F. *The behavior of organisms.* New York: Appleton, 1938.

――――. *Science and human behavior.* New York: Macmillan, 1953.

Skodak, Marie, and Skeels, H. M. A final follow-up of one hundred adopted children. *J. genet. Psychol.*, 1949, **75**, 85–125.

Smith, F. T. An experiment in modifying attitudes toward the Negro. *Teach. Coll. Contr. Educ.*, 1943, No. 887.

Smith, G. M. Six measures of self-concept discrepancy and instability: their interrelations, reliability, and relations to other personality measures. *J. consult. Psychol.*, 1958, **22**, 101–112.

Smith, W., Powell, Elizabeth K., and Ross, S. Manifest anxiety and food aversions. *J. abnorm. soc. Psychol.*, 1955, **50**, 101–104.

Snygg, D., and Combs, A. W. *Individual behavior.* New York: Harper, 1949.

Solomon, R. L., and Postman, L. Frequency of usage as a determinant of recognition thresholds for words. *J. exp. Psychol.*, 1952, **43**, 195–202.

Sontag, L. W., Baker, C. T., and Nelson, V. L. Mental growth and personality development: a longitudinal study. *Monogr. Soc. Res. in Child Developm.*, 1958, **23**, No. 2.

Sopchak, A. L. Prediction of college performance by commonly used tests. *J. clin. Psychol.*, 1958, **14**, 194–197.

Spearman, C. *The abilities of man.* New York: Macmillan, 1927.

Spence, K. W. The nature of theory construction in contemporary psychology. *Psychol. Rev.*, 1944, **51**, 47–68.

――――. Learning and performance in eyelid conditioning as a function of the intensity of the UCS. *J. exp. Psychol.*, 1953, **45**, 57–63.

――――. A theory of emotionally based drive (D) and its relation to performance in simple learning situations. *Amer. Psychologist*, 1958, **13**, 131–141.

――――. The postulates and methods of behaviorism. *Psychol. Rev.*, 1948, **55**, 67–78.

――――. The empirical basis and theoretical structure of psychology. In K. W. Spence, *Behavior theory and learning.* Englewood Cliffs, N.J.: Prentice-Hall, 1960. Pp. 71–88.

――――. Anxiety (drive) level and performance in eyelid conditioning. *Psychol. Bull.*, 1964, **61**, 129–139.

――――, and Beecroft, R. S. Differential conditioning and level of anxiety. *J. exp. Psychol.*, 1954, **48**, 399–403.

――――, and Farber, I. E. Conditioning and extinction as a function of anxiety. *J. exp. Psychol.*, 1953, **45**, 116–119.

――――, ――――. The relation of anxiety to differential eyelid conditioning. *J. exp. Psychol.*, 1954, **47**, 127–134.

————, ————, and McFann, H. H. The relation of anxiety (drive) level to performance in competitional and noncompetitional paired-associates learning. *J. exp. Psychol.*, 1956, **52**, 296–305.

————, ————, and Taylor, Elaine. The relation of electric shock and anxiety to level of performance in eyelid conditioning. *J. exp. Psychol.*, 1954, **48**, 404–408.

————, and Spence, Janet T. Relation of eyelid conditioning to manifest anxiety, extraversion, and rigidity. *J. abnorm. soc. Psychol.*, 1964, **68**, 144–149.

————, and Taylor, Janet A. Anxiety and strength of the UCS as determiners of the amount of eyelid conditioning. *J. exp. Psychol.*, 1951, **42**, 183–188.

————, ————. The relation of conditioned response strength to anxiety in normal, neurotic and psychotic subjects. *J. exp. Psychol.*, 1953, **45**, 265–272.

————, ————, and Ketchel, Rhoda. Anxiety (drive) level and degree of competition in paired-associates learning. *J. exp. Psychol.*, 1956, **52**, 306–310.

————, and Townsend, S. A comparative study of groups of high and low intelligence in learning a maze. *J. gen. Psychol.*, 1930, **3**, 113–130.

Spielberger, C. D. On the relationship between manifest anxiety and intelligence. *J. consult. Psychol.*, 1958, **22**, 220–224.

————, and Katzenmeyer, W. G. Manifest anxiety, intelligence, and college grades. *J. consult. Psychol.*, 1959, **23**, 278.

Spivack, G., Levine, M., and Sprigle, H. Intelligence test performance and the delay function of the ego. *J. consult. Psychol.*, 1959, **23**, 428–431.

Stagner, R. The gullibility of personnel managers. *Personnel Psychol.*, 1958, **11**, 347–352.

Standish, R. R., and Champion, R. A. Task difficulty and drive in verbal learning. *J. exp. Psychol.*, 1960, **59**, 361–365.

Steiner, I. D., and Johnson, H. H. Authoritarianism and "tolerance of trait inconsistency." *J. abnorm. soc. Psychol.*, 1963, **67**, 388–391.

Stephenson, W. *The study of behavior. Q-technique and its methodology.* Chicago: University of Chicago Press, 1953.

Stevens, S. S. Psychology and the science of science. *Psychol. Bull.*, 1939, **36**, 221–263.

Stewart, L. H. Manifest anxiety and mother-son identification. *J. clin. Psychol.*, 1958, **14**, 382–384.

Stewart, Naomi. A.G.C.T. scores of army personnel grouped by occupation. *Occupations*, 1947, **26**, 5–41.

Strickland, J. F. The effect of motivation arousal on humor preferences. *J. abnorm. soc. Psychol.*, 1959, **59**, 278–281.

Suinn, R. M. The relationship between self-acceptance and acceptance of others: a learning theory analysis. *J. abnorm. soc. Psychol.*, 1961, **63**, 37–42.

Sullivan, H. S. *The interpersonal theory of psychiatry.* New York: Norton, 1953.

Swanson, E. O. The relation of vocabulary test-retest gains to amount of college attendance after a 24-year period. *Amer. Psychologist,* 1952, **7**, 368. (abstract)

Swift, J. *Gulliver's travels.* (1726) New York: Heritage, 1940.

Symonds, P. M. *The ego and the self.* New York: Appleton, 1951.

Tabachnick, B. R. Some correlates of prejudice towards Negroes in elementary age children. *J. genet. Psychol.,* 1962, **100**, 193–203.

Taylor, D. M. Changes in the self concept without psychotherapy. *J. consult. Psychol.,* 1955, **19**, 205–209.

Taylor, Janet A. The relationship of anxiety to the conditioned eyelid response. *J. exp. Psychol.,* 1951, **41**, 81–92.

————. A personality scale of manifest anxiety. *J. abnorm. soc. Psychol.,* 1953, **48**, 285–290.

————. The Taylor Manifest Anxiety Scale and intelligence. *J. abnorm. soc. Psychol.,* 1955, **51**, 347.

————. Drive theory and manifest anxiety. *Psychol. Bull.,* 1956, **53**, 303–320.

————, and Chapman, J. P. Paired-associate learning as related to anxiety. *Amer. J. Psychol.,* 1955, **68**, 671.

————, and Rechtschaffen, A. Manifest anxiety and reversed alphabet printing. *J. abnorm. soc. Psychol.,* 1959, **58**, 221–224.

————, and Spence, K. W. The relationship of anxiety level to performance in serial learning. *J. exp. Psychol.,* 1952, **44**, 61–64.

Terman, L. M. *The measurement of intelligence.* Boston: Houghton Mifflin, 1916.

———— (Ed.), *et al. Mental and physical traits of a thousand gifted children.* L. M. Terman (Ed.), *Genetic studies of genius.* Vol. I. Stanford: Stanford University Press, 1925.

————. Trials to psychology. In C. Murchison (Ed.), *A history of psychology in autobiography.* Vol. II. Worcester, Massachusetts: Clark University Press, 1932. Pp. 297–331.

————. The discovery and encouragement of exceptional talent. *Amer. Psychologist,* 1954, **9**, 221–230.

————, and Merrill, Maud A. *Measuring intelligence.* Boston: Houghton Mifflin, 1937.

————, ————. *Stanford-Binet intelligence scale.* Boston: Houghton Mifflin, 1960.

————, and Miles, Catharine C. *Sex and personality: studies in masculinity and femininity.* New York: McGraw-Hill, 1936.

————, and Oden, Melita H. *The gifted child grows up.* L. M. Terman (Ed.), *Genetic studies of genius.* Vol. IV. Stanford: Stanford University Press, 1947.

————, ————. *The gifted group at mid-life: thirty-five years' follow-up of the superior child*. L. M. Terman (Ed.), *Genetic studies of genius*. Vol. V. Stanford: Stanford University Press, 1959.

Thorndike, E. L. *The psychology of learning*. New York: Teachers College, 1913.

————, and Lorge, I. *The teachers word book of 30,000 words*. New York: Teachers College, Columbia University, Bureau of Publications, 1944.

————, and Woodyard, Ella. Differences within and between communities in the intelligence of children. *J. educ. Psychol.*, 1942, **33**, 641–656.

Thorndike, R. L. *Personnel selection*. New York: Wiley, 1949.

Thurstone, L. L. *Primary mental abilities*. Chicago: University of Chicago Press, 1938.

————, and Chave, E. J. *The measurement of attitudes*. Chicago: University of Chicago Press, 1929.

————, and Thurstone, T. G. *Factorial studies of intelligence*. Chicago: University of Chicago Press, 1941.

Tiegs, E. W., Clark, W. W., and Thorpe, L. P. The California test of personality. *J. educ. Res.*, 1941, **35**, 102–108.

Tolman, E. C. *Drives toward war*. New York: D. Appleton-Century, 1942.

Tolstoy, L. *Anna Karenina*. (1875) New York: Heritage Press, 1952.

Torrance, E. P. Explorations in creative thinking. *Educ.*, 1960, **81**, 216–220.

Trapp, E. P., and Kausler, D. H. Association tendencies of groups differentiated on the Taylor Manifest Anxiety Scale. *J. consult. Psychol.*, 1959, **23**, 387–389.

Travers, R. M. W. Significant research on the prediction of academic success. In W. T. Donahue, C. H. Coombs, and R. M. W. Travers, *The measurement of student adjustment and achievement*. Ann Arbor: University of Michigan Press, 1949. Pp. 147–190.

Truax, C. B. Effective ingredients in psychotherapy: an approach to unraveling the patient-therapist interaction. *J. counsel. Psychol.*, 1963, **10**, 256–263.

Tryon, R. C. Genetic differences in maze-learning ability in rats. *Thirty-ninth Yearb. Nat. Soc. Stud. Educ.*, 1940, Part I. Pp. 111–119.

————. Psychology in flux: the academic-professional bipolarity. *Amer. Psychologist*, 1963, **18**, 134–143.

Turner, R. H., and Vanderlippe, R. H. Self-ideal congruence as an index of adjustment. *J. abnorm. soc. Psychol.*, 1958, **57**, 202–206.

Tyler, Leona E. *The psychology of human differences*. New York: Appleton, 1956.

Ullman, A. D. Sociocultural backgrounds of alcoholism. *Ann. Amer. Acad. Pol. Soc. Sci.*, 1958, **315**, 48–54.

Underwood, B. J. *Experimental psychology*. New York: Appleton, 1949.

Vance, F. L., and MacPhail, Sharon L. APA membership trends and fields of specialization of psychologists earning doctoral degrees between 1959 and 1962. *Amer. Psychologist*, 1964, **19**, 654–658.

Veldman, D. J., and Worchel, P. Defensiveness and self-acceptance in the management of hostility. *J. abnorm. soc. Psychol.*, 1961, **63**, 319–325.

Veroff, J. A projective measure of the achievement motivation of adolescent males and females. Unpublished honors thesis, Wesleyan University, 1950.

———, Wilcox, S., and Atkinson, J. W. The achievement motive in high school and college age women. *J. abnorm. soc. Psychol.*, 1953, **48**, 108–119.

Verplanck, W. The control of the content of conversation: reinforcement of statements of opinion. *J. abnorm. soc. Psychol.*, 1955, **51**, 668–676.

Videbeck, R. Self-conception and the reactions of others. *Sociometry*, 1960, **23**, 351–359.

Vincent, D. F. The linear relationship between age and score of adults in intelligence tests. *Occup. Psychol.*, London, 1952, **26**, 243–249.

Voas, R. B. Intelligence and the distortion of responses on the Taylor Anxiety Scale. *Psychol. Rep.*, 1956, **2**, 87–89.

Warkany, J., and Nelson, R. C. Congenital malformations induced in rats by maternal nutritional deficiency. *J. Nutrition*, 1942, **23**, 321–333.

Warner, W. L., Meeker, Marchia, and Eells, K. *Social class in America: a manual of procedure for the measurement of social status.* Chicago: Science Research Associates, 1949.

Watson, J. B., and Raynor, R. Conditioned emotional responses. *J. exp. Psychol.*, 1920, **3**, 1–14.

Weatherley, D. Maternal response to childhood aggression and subsequent anti-Semitism. *J. abnorm. soc. Psychol.*, 1963, **66**, 183–185.

Weber, M. *The Protestant ethic and the spirit of capitalism.* New York: Scribner's, 1930.

Wechsler, D. *The measurement of adult intelligence.* 3rd. Ed. Baltimore: Williams and Wilkins, 1944.

———. *Wechsler intelligence scale for children.* New York: Psychological Corporation, 1949.

———. *The measurement and appraisal of adult intelligence.* 4th Ed. Baltimore: Williams and Wilkins, 1958.

Weiner, B. Need achievement and the resumption of incompleted tasks. *J. pers. soc. Psychol.*, 1965, **1**, 165–168.

Weinstein, S., and Teuber, H. L. The role of preinjury education and intelligence level in intellectual loss after brain injury. *J. comp. physiol. Psychol.*, 1957, **50**, 535–539. (a)

———, ———. Effects of penetrating brain injury on intelligence test scores. *Science*, 1957, **125**, 1036–1037. (b)

Wellman, Beth L., and Pegram, E. L. Binet IQ changes of orphanage pre-school children. *J. genet. Psychol.*, 1944, **65**, 239–263.

Wells, W. D., Weinert, G., and Rubel, Marilyn. Conformity pressure and authoritarian personality. *J. Psychol.*, 1956, **42**, 133–136.

Wenar, C. Reaction time as a function of manifest anxiety and stimulus intensity. *J. abnorm. soc. Psychol.*, 1954, **49**, 335–340.

Wessman, A. E., Ricks, D. F., and Tyl, Mary McI. Characteristics and concomitants of mood fluctuation in college women. *J. abnorm. soc. Psychol.*, 1960, **60**, 117–126.

Whiting, Beatrice B. Paiute sorcery. *Viking Fund Publ. Anthrop.*, 1950, no. 15.

Whiting, J. W. M., and Child, I. L. *Child training and personality: a cross-cultural study.* New Haven: Yale University Press, 1953.

Wiggins, J. G. Multiple solution anagram solving as an index of anxiety. *J. clin. Psychol.*, 1957, **13**, 391–393.

Wilner, D. M., Walkley, Rosabelle P., and Cook, S. W. Residential proximity and intergroup relations in public housing projects. *J. soc. Issues*, 1952, **8**, 45–69.

Winder, C. L., and Rau, Lucy. Parental attitudes associated with social deviance in preadolescent boys. *J. abnorm. soc. Psychol.*, 1962, **64**, 418–424.

Windle, C. The relationship among five MMPI "anxiety" indices. *J. consult. Psychol.*, 1955, **19**, 61–63.

Winterbottom, Marian R. The relation of need for achievement to learning experiences in independence and mastery. In J. W. Atkinson (Ed.), *Motives in fantasy, action, and society.* Princeton: Van Nostrand, 1958. Pp. 453–478.

Wissler, C. *The correlation of mental and physical tests.* New York: Columbia University Press, 1901.

Wohl, J., and Hyman, M. Relationship between measures of anxiety and constriction. *J. clin. Psychol.*, 1959, **15**, 54–55.

Wong, T. J. The effect of attitude similarity and prejudice on interpersonal evaluation and attraction. Unpublished master's thesis, University of Texas, 1961.

Worbois, G. M. Changes in Stanford-Binet IQ for rural consolidated and rural one-room school children. *J. exp. Educ.*, 1942, **11**, 210–214.

Worchel, P. *Adaptability screening of flying personnel: development of a self-concept inventory for predicting maladjustment.* Randolph AFB, Texas: SAM, USAF, 1957. (No. 56–62)

———. Personality factors in the readiness to express aggression. *J. clin. Psychol.*, 1958, **14**, 355–359.

———, and Hillson, J. S. The self-concept in the criminal. *J. indiv. Psychol.*, 1958, **14**, 173–181.

———, and McCormick, Betty L. Self-concept and dissonance reduction. *J. Pers.*, 1963, **31**, 588–599.

Wrenn, C. G. Potential research talent in the sciences based on intelligence quotients of Ph.D.'s. *Educ. Rec.*, 1949, **30**, 5–22.

Wright, J. M., and Harvey, O. J. Attitude change as a function of authoritarianism and punitiveness. *J. pers. soc. Psychol.*, 1965, **1**, 177–181.

Wrightsman, L. S., Jr., Radloff, R. W., Horton, D. L., and Mecherikoff, M. Authoritarian attitudes and presidential voting preferences. *Psychol. Rep.*, 1961, **8**, 43–46.

Yarrow, Marian R. Problems of methods in parent-child research. *Child Develpm.*, 1963, **34**, 215–226.

Yerkes, R. M. Psychological examining in the U.S. Army. *Memoirs: Nat. Acad. Sci.*, 1921, **15**, 1–890.

Young, R. K., Benson, W. M., and Holtzman, W. H. Change in attitudes toward the Negro in a southern university. *J. abnorm. soc. Psychol.*, 1960, **60**, 131–133.

———, Clore, G., and Holtzman, W. H. Further change in attitude toward the Negro in a southern university. In D. Byrne and M. L. Hamilton (Eds.), *Personality research: a book of readings*. Englewood Cliffs, N.J.: Prentice-Hall, 1966.

Zatzkins, J. The effect of the need for achievement on linguistic behavior. Unpublished master's thesis, Wesleyan University, 1949.

Zigler, E., and Phillips, L. Social effectiveness and symptomatic behaviors. *J. abnorm. soc. Psychol.*, 1960, **61**, 231–238.

———, ———. Case history data and psychiatric diagnosis. *J. consult. Psychol.*, 1961, **25**, 458. (a)

———, ———. Social competence and outcome in psychiatric disorder. *J. abnorm. soc. Psychol.*, 1961, **63**, 264–271. (b)

———, ———. Social competence and the process-reactive distinction in psychopathology. *J. abnorm. soc. Psychol.*, 1962, **65**, 215–222.

Zubin, J. Psychopathology and the social sciences. In O. Klineberg and R. Christie (Eds.), *Perspectives in social psychology*. New York: Holt, Rinehart, & Winston, 1965.

———, and Katz, M. M. Psychopharmacology and personality. In P. Worchel and D. Byrne (Eds.), *Personality change*. New York: Wiley, 1964. Pp. 367–395.

Zuckerman, M., Barrett-Ribback, Beatrice, and Monashkin, I. Normative data and factor analysis on the parental attitude research instrument. *J. consult. Psychol.*, 1958, **22**, 165–171.

———, and Monashkin, I. Self-acceptance and psychopathology. *J. consult. Psychol.*, 1957, **21**, 145–148.

———, and Oltean, Mary. Some relationships between maternal attitude factors and authoritarianism, personality needs, psychopathology, and self-acceptance. *Child Develpm.*, 1959, **30**, 27–36.

Author Index

Subject Index